ROUTLEDGE HANDBOOK OF SOCIAL, ECONOMIC, AND CRIMINAL JUSTICE

This authoritative volume explores different perspectives on economic and social justice and the challenges presented by and within the criminal justice system. It critically discusses key concerns involved in realizing economic and social justice, including systemic issues in economic and social justice, issues related to organizations and social institutions, special issues regarding specific populations, and a review of national and international organizations that promote economic justice. Addressing more than just the ideology and theory underlying economic and social justice, the book presents chapters with practical examples and research on how economic and social justice might be achieved within the criminal justice systems of the world. With contributions from leading scholars around the globe, this book is an essential reference for scholars with an interest in economic and social justice from a wide range of disciplines, including criminal justice and criminology as well as sociology, social work, public policy, and law.

Cliff Roberson, LLM, PhD, is Emeritus Professor of Criminal Justice at Washburn University, Topeka, Kansas, and retired Professor of Criminology at California State University, Fresno, California. He has authored or co-authored over 60 books and texts on legal subjects. His previous academic experiences include Associate Vice President for Academic Affairs, Arkansas Tech University; Dean of Arts and Sciences, University of Houston, Victoria; Director of Programs, National College of District Attorneys; Professor of Criminology and Director of Justice Center, California State University, Fresno; and Assistant Professor of Criminal Justice, St. Edwards University. His nonacademic experience includes U.S. Marine Corps service as an infantry officer, trial and defense counsel and military judge as a marine judge advocate, and Director of the Military Law Branch, U.S. Marine Corps. Other legal employment experiences include Trial Supervisor, Office of State Counsel for Offenders, Texas Board of Criminal Justice, and judge pro tem in the California courts.

Roberson is admitted to practice before the U.S. Supreme Court, U.S. Court of Military Appeals, U.S. Tax Court, Federal Courts in California and Texas, Supreme Court of Texas, and Supreme Court of California. He holds a PhD in Human Behavior from U.S. International University; an LLM in Criminal Law, Criminology, and Psychiatry from George Washington University; a JD from American University; a BA in Political Science from the University of Missouri; and one year of post-graduate study at the University of Virginia School of Law.

ROUTLEDGE HANDBOOK OF SOCIAL, ECONOMIC, AND CRIMINAL JUSTICE

Edited by Cliff Roberson

Routledge
Taylor & Francis Group

LONDON AND NEW YORK

First published 2018 by Routledge

2 Park Square, Milton Park, Abingdon, Oxfordshire OX14 4RN

52 Vanderbilt Avenue, New York, NY 10017

Routledge is an imprint of the Taylor & Francis Group, an informa business

First issued in paperback 2019

Library of Congress Cataloging-in-Publication Data
Names: Roberson, Cliff, 1937– editor.
Title: Routledge handbook of social, economic, and criminal justice / edited by Cliff Roberson.
Description: 1 Edition. | New York : Routledge, [2018] | Includes bibliographical references and index.
Identifiers: LCCN 2017060145 (print) | LCCN 2018004153 (ebook) | ISBN 9781351002707 (master) | ISBN 9781138545649 (hardback) | ISBN 9781351002707 (ebk)
Subjects: LCSH: Social justice. | Economics—Moral and ethical aspects. | Distributive justice. | Criminal justice, Administration of.
Classification: LCC HM671 (ebook) | LCC HM671 .R683 2018 (print) | DDC 303.3/72—dc23
LC record available at https://lccn.loc.gov/2017060145

ISBN: 978-1-138-54564-9 (hbk)
ISBN: 978-0-367-81911-8 (pbk)

Typeset in Bembo
by Apex CoVantage, LLC

CONTENTS

Contents

PREFACE

The Routledge Handbook of Social, Economic, and Criminal Justice is an edited handbook that discusses the issues involved in obtaining equality and social justice for all. As noted in Jeffrey H. Reiman and Paul Leighton's text, *The Rich Get Richer and the Poor Get Prison*, each year the inequities grow between the wealthy and the rest of the population. For example, it is estimated that three individuals in the United States possess one-half of the U.S.'s wealth and the remaining 325 million plus U.S. citizens possess the remaining half of the country's wealth. It is this issue of disparity that concerns many researchers regarding the criminal justice system.

The handbook consists of 31 chapters involving social justice and economic issues contributed by leading researchers and professors from seven different countries. The authors were given wide latitude in developing their contributions; accordingly, there are some overlaps in the material. The chapters are divided into five major parts. In some cases, it was difficult to put a chapter in one part rather than another. But that is to be expected on the broad issues of economic and social injustice.

Part I of the handbook provides a general introduction to the issues. Part II reviews specific situations in which there is disparity in our justice. Part III concerns transnational and international issues and establishes that economic disparity and social justice are worldwide issues. In Part IV, the disparity issues involved in criminal justice and society are discussed. The concluding part, Part V, examines the government's role in social justice. Included at the end of Chapter 31 are the bios of the editor and contributors.

Comments, corrections, etc., may be submitted to the editor and will be welcomed: Cliff Roberson at cliff.roberson@washburn.edu

Cliff Roberson, LLM, PhD
Professor Emeritus, Washburn University

PART I

Introduction to Criminal and Economic Justice

1

VIOLENCE AGAINST WOMEN AS A SOCIAL JUSTICE ISSUE

Nicole Wilkes

Introduction

The United Nations described violence against women as "perhaps the most shameful human rights violation."[1] Additionally, many scholars have labeled violence against women as a public health issue.[2] Over the years, many officials, agencies, and scholars have considered violence against women as both issues of public health and human rights. However, the idea of violence against women as a social justice issue has had minimal attention. Despite the lack of discussion on issues of violence against women being labeled as a social justice issue, these issues have fallen under the umbrella of social justice. Violence against women is an issue of social justice; in addition, the response to crimes of violence against women also have ties to social justice.

It has been argued that violence against women is the most pervasive and the least recognized human rights violation in the world.[3] Individuals who experience acts of violence face disproportionate burdens and hardships as a result of the violence itself, gaps in the response to violence, and lack of liberties related to restoration after the crime. The following discussion will explore the principles of social justice explored by scholars and how they relate to violence against women, mainly drawing from scholars Rawls's and Miller's writings on social justice.

Definitions and Prevalence of Violence Against Women

Over the past three decades, research has suggested violence against women is highly prevalent and negatively affects the health and quality of life of survivors. Multiple deleterious health issues have found to be associated with being a victim of these types of violence. Violence against women can take many forms; however, there is no universally agreed upon definition of violence against women.[4] This discussion on violence against women will focus on violence within the United States and will address intimate partner violence, sexual assault, stalking, and sex trafficking. Violence against women impacts individuals and communities globally, but there are variations in the types of violence by region and the responses to violence related to social justice principles vary by communities, states, and countries. For the scope of this discussion it is necessary to focus on one nation.

While there is no clear cause of violence against women in the empirical literature, the causal roots are often believed to be tied to issues of gender equity. Many scholars and activists have argued the cause of violence against women is connected to gender inequality, which is believed to be perpetuated by social norms and structures.[5] Traditionally, feminists consider violence against women to be an issue of power, which is linked to domination, intimidation, and victimization of one person by another.[6] It is believed that women experience these crimes, often inflicted by men, because of their gender.

Intimate Partner Violence

The most prevalent form of violence against women is intimate partner violence (IPV).[7] IPV is defined as "any behavior within an intimate relationship that causes physical, psychological or sexual harm to those in the relationship" (p. 89).[8] Specific acts that could be classified as IPV include physical aggression, psychological abuse, forced intercourse, sexual coercion, and controlling behaviors.[9] Survey research has revealed relatively high rates of IPV incidence and prevalence in the United States. The Centers for Disease Control and Prevention (CDC) estimated more than 35% of women or 42.4 million women in the United States experience violence from an intimate partner in their lifetimes.[10] IPV is also connected to cases of femicide; over 41% of female homicides in the United States, between 1980 and 2008, were committed by a spouse, ex-spouse, or boyfriend/girlfriend.[11]

Sexual Assault

Research conducted by the Centers for Disease Control and Prevention looked at the prevalence of sexual violence and found 18.3% of women and 1.4% of males experienced rape in their lifetime.[12] Multiracial and American Indian or Alaska Native women have the highest prevalence of sexual assault, and females 11–24 years of age are disproportionally impacted by sexual assault.[13] While there are multiple forms of sexual violence, the focus for this discussion is on sexual assault, which is also commonly known as rape. Rape is generally defined as forced penetrative sex, including vaginal, anal, or oral penetration without consent.[14]

Stalking

Stalking is generally defined as a course of conduct directed at a specific person or group of people that would cause a reasonable person to feel fear. Stalking itself is a complex phenomenon, particularly since some of the individual acts are normal and innocuous behaviors outside of a stalking relationship (e.g., gifts, e-mails, phone calls). Additionally, stalking differs from other criminal acts in that it is a pattern of behavior over time and not a single event. The CDC estimated that more than 16% of women or 19.3 million women in the United States experienced stalking in their lifetime.[15] Stalking is often perpetrated by intimate partners; the aforementioned CDC study found more than two-thirds of female stalking victims reported being stalked by a current or former intimate partner.[16]

Sex Trafficking

Human trafficking has been labeled as a form of modern-day slavery and falls under two categories: labor trafficking and sex trafficking. Given sex trafficking predominately victimizes females, the following discussion will focus on sex trafficking. The Department of State defines sex trafficking of adults as "when an adult engages in a commercial sex act, such as prostitution, as the result of force, threats of force, fraud, coercion or any combination of such means" (p. 17).[17] The definition of child sex trafficking varies from that of adults. Child sex trafficking is defined by the Department of State as "when a child (under 18 years of age) is recruited, enticed, harbored, transported, provided, obtained, patronized, solicited, or maintained to perform a commercial sex act" (p. 17).[18] Victims of sex trafficking in the United States can be citizens of the United States or foreign nationals. Vulnerable populations often targeted as trafficking victims include runaway and homeless youth and victims of domestic violence, sexual assault, war, or social discrimination.[19] There are no accurate estimates available on the incidence or prevalence of sex trafficking in the United States.

Social Justice Framework for Violence Against Women

While there is no consistent definition of social justice within the literature, most definitions include ties to equality or equal opportunity within a society. The first book on social justice was published in 1900 and raised questions of social and economic institutions treating people justly.[20] David Miller, in *Principles of Social Justice*, and John Rawls, in *Justice as Fairness*, have been two of the most well-known scholars on social justice principles. Their prominent writings on the subject include overlaps in the main ideas.[21] Rawls's approach looked at justice as fairness and the idea of citizens of a society being free and equal.[22] Miller's theory addressed the distribution of good and bad in a society and how they should be distributed.[23] The following discussion will further explore Rawls's and Miller's theories as they relate to violence against women, focusing on distribution of disadvantage, needs and safety, and basic liberties.

Distribution of Disadvantage

Miller wrote about the distribution of good and bad in society and explained,

> when we attack some policy or some state of affairs as socially unjust, we are claiming that a person, or more usually a category of persons, enjoys fewer advantages than the person or group of persons ought to enjoy (or bears more of the burdens than they ought to bear) given how other members of the society in question are faring.[24]

For individuals who experience crimes that are classified as one of the forms of violence against women, they face a disproportionate amount of disadvantage. A host of disadvantages come with experiencing violence: the violence in itself is harmful to physical and emotional health, and a number of additional burdens often follow the victimization for many survivors. Susan Herman explained that victimization is different from other types of loss; being a victim causes trauma and harm that causes the individual to suffer as a result of intentional acts of cruelty.[25] As a result of the intentionality in cases of violence against women, processing and recovering from the trauma can take more time and it can be emotionally more difficult to address than other negative life events.

The forms of violence against women are believed to be associated with a number of physical and emotional health issues. Some of the health effects are unique to the type of victimization, while others spread across many forms of violence against women. Some of the health effects of violence against women found in research include depression, heavy alcohol use, sexually transmitted infections, increased sexual health risk-taking behaviors, chronic disease, injuries, increased stress, post-traumatic stress disorder, physical disability, substance abuse, and anxiety.[26,27,28,29,30]

Other consequences of violence against women cross into other areas of life. Unfortunately, there has been less research conducted on non-health-related effects of violence against women. Nonetheless, the available research indicates those who experience forms of violence against women also experience other disadvantages. For example, a research study on IPV found that experiencing IPV can have negative effects on women's job stability and economic well-being, and the effects can last up to three years after the IPV ends.[31] Additionally, a study on the impact of IPV experiences during adolescence found exposure to IPV diminished women's educational attainment.[32]

Needs and Safety

The idea of need was also central to Miller's theory on social justice. Scherlen and Robinson summarized Miller's approach of need through explaining, "need is a claim that one is lacking in basic necessities and is being harmed or is in danger of being harmed and/or that one's capacity to function is being impeded" (p. 66).[33] When an individual experiences an act of violence, including forms of violence against women, their basic necessities of safety and security are violated. For example, in situations of IPV the victims are often physically abused and their individual safety and security, as well as basic needs, are violated by their intimate partners.

Both Miller and Rawls also explore the idea of social justice issues being human rights issues as well. Neither Miller nor Rawls specifically addresses safety under the umbrella of human rights; however, in exploring Miller's and Rawls's ideas, Scherlen and Robinson explain that human rights include freedom, dignity, and security—all of which can be infringed upon in acts of IPV, sexual assault, stalking, and sex trafficking. Safety and security are universally agreed upon principles and are included in the Universal Declaration of Human Rights, a document which is often linked to approaches of social justice.[34]

Violence against women first began to be considered a social problem in the United States during the 1970s, with the emergence of the Women's Movement.[35] Over the past four decades, there have been significant changes in the perception of violence against women, as well as how the criminal justice system, medical systems, and victim service organizations respond to and provide services to victims. Over this same period, advocacy groups have brought attention to issues of violence against women and progress has been made to improve the response from healthcare providers and the criminal justice system; however, despite their efforts, many gaps remain to meet the needs of survivors and in the accountability of perpetrators.

The improvements to the response to violence against women and increases in available services have assisted in addressing some of the safety needs of victims; however, many gaps remain. In addition to experiencing the crime itself, there are many gaps in services that result in failures to address the victims' safety and security following the violence. The following discussion will explore four gaps in services related to safety and security following victimization, including inadequate housing for victims of IPV, criminal justice response to cases of stalking, few prosecutions in cases of sexual assault, and jurisdictional issues in responding to cases of sexual assault of Native American and Alaska Native women on tribal lands.

Domestic violence shelters were first initiated as a safe place for women and their children to go when fleeing IPV in the 1970s and became institutionalized in the 1980s.[36] In 2015, the number of shelters in the United States for victims of IPV was estimated to be 1,894.[37] Despite the growth of the shelter movement, the amount of shelters available to victims of IPV is insufficient. In 2014, it was estimated that there were 196,467 unmet needs for shelter of IPV victims, which was a 13% increase over 2010.[38] The availability of shelters has not been meeting the needs of IPV victims seeking shelter for several years. In recent years, the organizations running the shelters have seen cuts in funding and reductions in staff.[39] The funding cuts are presumed to limit their abilities to fill the gaps in the availability of shelter space and the general the needs of victims in search of shelter. When women and children are turned away from shelters as a result of inadequate space, their safety and security needs are further exacerbated, as they may return to their abusive partners or end up in other circumstances that leave them vulnerable to other abuse or unsafe circumstances.

Stalking first became a crime in 1990 in California and has since become a crime in every state. Unfortunately, the criminal justice response to stalking has faced less attention than IPV and sexual assault, and the criminal justice system's response to stalking has been understudied as well.[40] A recent studied by Brady and Nobles found few reports of stalking and even fewer police incident reports and arrests for stalking in one jurisdiction. The study took place in Houston, the fourth largest city in the United States; given the prevalence estimates of stalking from prior studies, Houston should experience tens of thousands of stalking cases annually.[41] Over eight years, between 2005 and 2013, there were 3,756 stalking calls for service, 66 stalking-related incident reports, and 12 arrests for stalking. The findings of the study indicate most stalking calls were not generating an incident report and arrests rarely occurred. While this study occurred in one city, findings are not generalizable to other locations. Despite the limitations of this study and the need for additional research, the findings raise questions of a potential problem in the criminal justice system's response to stalking in one city and the effectiveness of other jurisdictions' response to cases of stalking and the usefulness of current laws on stalking for offender accountability. In response to stalking, it is important that the criminal justice system takes steps to prevent further victimization, holds offenders accountable, and assists victims in receiving support to improve their safety and well-being.[42]

Given the high prevalence of sexual violence, the number of perpetrators convicted of sexual assault is disproportionately low. Among sexual assault cases reported to law enforcement, estimates indicate 0.4–5.4% are prosecuted, 0.2–5.2% result in a conviction, and 0.02–2.8% of offenders are incarcerated.[43] Data from the National Crime Victim Survey indicated 86% of sexual assaults reported to the police involved the officer taking a report, 48% of officers questioned witnesses and/or searched, and 31% resulted in an arrest.[44] Low numbers for reporting, prosecution, and conviction of sexual assaults indicate most perpetrators of sexual assault are not being held accountable for their crimes. Given the low prosecution rates in sexual assault rates, it is worth exploring the reasons why and the role police actions play in prosecutorial decisions. Shaw and colleagues offer three explanations on the low prosecution rates: (1) prosecutors decide not to prosecute following a police referral, (2) police decide not to refer the case to the prosecutors, and (3) the decision not to move the case from investigation to prosecution is made jointly by police and prosecution.[45] The police and prosecutorial responses are key to increasing offender accountability in cases of sexual assault and providing justice to victims who report their cases to police.

Violence against Native American and Alaska Native women has been labeled as an epidemic as a result of high rates of violence perpetrated against Native women.[46] Jurisdictional issues of law enforcement agencies and courts have resulted in complexities that are leading to added difficulties for authorities to respond to and address these cases. The most recent reauthorization of the Violence Against Women Act in 2013 attempted to close these gaps in cases of sexual assault; however, the bill that was passed did not include those provisions for sexual assault. Currently, in cases of sexual assault, if the victim and offender do not have an intimate relationship and the offender is non-Indian, the tribal criminal authority does not have jurisdiction over the case. As a result, tribes do not have jurisdictional authority over most acquaintance rapes and all stranger rapes.[47] The issues of jurisdiction can be complex in these communities and can lead to no systematic response, accountability, or legal protection for victims—particularly when the offender is non-Native and the crime occurred on tribal land.[48]

Basic Liberties

Rawls argued, "each person has the same indefeasible claim to a fully adequate scheme of basic liberties, which scheme is compatible with the same scheme of liberties for all."[49] While victim services play an important role for individuals who experience violence against women in the United States, the system is not designed to provide them with the same life and liberties as individuals who have not experienced these types of events. More specifically, there are generally no systems in place to assist victims in rebuilding their lives and obtaining the same liberties as others.

In general, victim services are limited and not intended to meet victims' long-term needs in recovering from the effects of experiencing a crime. The majority of victim services are either focused on the initial needs of victims, when many are in a crisis phase, or their needs as they navigate the criminal justice system. For example, many communities have victim services available to assist with initial needs—such as crisis lines, emergency shelters, filing a protective order, and safety planning, while other victim services provide information on dates of court hearings and writing a victim impact statement. If the victim's case goes to prosecution, they are mostly there to serve as a witness and testify for the prosecution. It is uncommon for victim services to extend beyond these two phases.

In addition to the disadvantages of experiencing forms of violence against women, victims of crime face additional challenges in the United States with the criminal justice system's response. Much of the criminal justice system is focused on justice for the offenders and not the victim. While there is need to address offenders in the system, there is also need to consider the victims and their needs. In many cases, victims can be seen merely as pawns in the criminal case. As Susan Herman explained, "there is no societal commitment to achieve justice for victims" (p. 1).[50]

Crime victims' rights are an important piece of the criminal justice systems' response to victimization, including the forms of violence against women. Victims' rights can be categorized as the following rights: right to information, right to be present at criminal hearings, right to notice of and opportunity to be heard at proceedings, right to financial recompense, right to protection, and right to privacy. Every state has adopted its own victims' rights, and they also exist within the federal system.

Despite their importance, there are major flaws with implementation of these rights and accountability in providing the rights to victims. Training on victims' rights is often infrequent or not available for criminal justice professionals and victim service providers. Effective training and implementation is needed so that these officials can provide the victims their due rights. It is also important that the officials fully understand the scope of the rights and how they can be accessed, as the rights and how they operate in a state can be complicated.

Also, there are minimal efforts to enforce compliance with victims' rights and few options to remedy situations if the rights are not granted and the victim wanted to access them. To date, Arizona is the only state with compliance efforts on victim rights. In other states, issues of victims' rights receive little attention if they are not provided, and states generally have little authority if a part of the criminal justice system is not granting victims the rights available to them under law. Victims' rights can be seen as an attempt to restore basic liberties after a victimization has occurred; however, successfully granting the victim their rights is a needed step in the process of basic liberties in cases of violence against women that go through the court system.

Summary

Violence against women is a public health issue, a human rights issue, as well as a social justice issue. Victims of violence against women face a multitude of physical and psychological health consequences as a result of the victimization. In addition to the acts of violence against women being social justice issues in themselves, society's response to these issues also alludes to additional social justice issues that are also related to violence against women. The writings of Miller and Rawls provided the framework to analyze violence against women as a social justice issue. While violence against women has not be discussed in the literature as a social justice issue, the principles discussed here that aligned with the work of Miller and Rawls indicated that it is possible to classify violence against women as a social justice issue.

Discussion Questions

1. Based on your knowledge of victim services and the criminal justice system, what other gaps exist in addressing victims' needs and safety related to violence against women?
2. Did you find it surprising that violence against women had not been labeled as a social justice issue in previous literature?

3. Does it change the dialogue or perception around violence against women to classify it as a social justice issue?
4. How would the societal issues pertaining to the response to violence against women and social justice vary in international contexts?
5. Do you believe the criminal justice system's focus on offenders, while not addressing victim needs, is a good approach?

Notes

1. Annan, K. (1999, March 8). *Remarks on international women's day*. Interagency videoconference for a World Free of Violence against Women, New York. Retrieved from www.un.org/News/Press/docs/1999/19990308.sgsm6919.html
2. Ellsberg, M., & Heise, L. (2005). *Researching violence against women: A practical guide for researchers and activists*. Washington, DC: World Health Organization, PATH.
3. Heise, L., Ellsberg, M., & Gottmoeller, M. (2002). A global overview of gender-based violence. *International Journal of Gynecology and Obstetrics, 1*, S5–S14.
4. Ellsberg, & Heise, 2005.
5. Samarasekera, U., & Horton, R. (2015). Prevention of violence against women and girls: A new chapter. *The Lancet, 385*(9977), 1480–1482. http://dx.doi.org.proxy.libraries.uc.edu/10.1016/S0140-6736(14)61775-X
6. Chrisler, J. C., & Ferguson, S. (2006). Violence against women as a public health issue. *Annals of the New York Academy of Sciences, 1087*, 235–249.
7. Heise, Ellsberg, & Gottmoeller, 2002.
8. Heise, L., & Garcia-Moreno, C. (2002). Violence by intimate partners. In E. G. Krug, L. L. Dahlberg, J. A. Mercy, A. B. Zwi, & R. Lozano (Eds.), *World health report on violence and health* (pp. 149–181). Geneva, Switzerland: World Health Organization.
9. *Ibid.*
10. Black, M. C., Basile, K. C., Breiding, M. J., Smith, S. G., Walters, M. L., Merrick, M. T., & Stevens, M. R. (2011). *National intimate partner and sexual violence survey*. Atlanta, GA: Centers for Disease Control and Prevention.
11. Bureau of Justice Statistics. (2011). *Homicide trends in the United States, 1980–2008*. Washington, DC: U.S. Department of Justice. Retrieved from www.bjs.gov/content/pub/pdf/htus8008.pdf
12. Black, Basile, Breiding, Smith, Walters, Merrick, & Stevens, 2011.
13. *Ibid.*
14. Tjaden, P., & Thoennes, N. (2000). *Full report of prevalence, incidence, and consequences of violence against women: Findings from the national violence against women survey* (NCJ 183781). Washington, DC: U.S. Department of Justice, National Institute of Justice.
15. Black, Basile, Breiding, Smith, Walters, Merrick, & Stevens, 2011.
16. *Ibid.*
17. Department of State. (2017). *Trafficking in persons report: June 2017*. Washington, DC: U.S. Government Printing Office.
18. *Ibid.*
19. Polaris Project. (2017). *Sex trafficking*. Retrieved from https://polarisproject.org/sex-trafficking
20. Miller, D. (2003). *Principles of social justice*. Cambridge, MA: Harvard University Press.
21. Robinson, M. (2010). Assessing criminal justice practice using social justice theory. *Social Justice Research, 23*, 77–97.
22. Rawls, J. (2001). *Justice as fairness: A restatement*. Cambridge, MA: The Belknap Press of Harvard University Press.
23. Miller, 2003.
24. *Ibid.*, p. 1.
25. Herman, S. (2010). *Parallel justice for victims of crime*. Washington, DC: National Center for Victims of Crime.
26. Coker, A. L., Davis, K. E., Arias, I., Desai, S., Sanderson, M., Brandt, H. M., & Smith, P. H. (2002). Physical and mental health effects of intimate partner violence for men and women. *American Journal of Preventive Medicine, 23*, 260–268.
27. Woods, S. J., Hall, R. J., Campbell, J. C., & Angott, D. M. (2008). Physical health and posttraumatic stress disorder symptoms in women experiencing intimate partner violence. *Journal of Midewifery & Women's Health, 53*(6), 538–546.

28. Carbone-Lopez, K., Kruttscnitt, C., & Macmillian, R. (2006). Patterns of intimate partner violence and their associations with physical health, psychological distress, and substance use. *Public Health Reports, 121,* 382–392.
29. Campbell, R., Sefl, T., & Ahrens, C. E. (2004). The impact of rape on women's sexual health risk behaviors. *Health Psychology, 23,* 67–74.
30. Ottisova, L., Hemmings, S., Howard, L. M., Zimmerman, C., & Oram, S. (2016). Prevalence and risk of violence and the mental, physical and sexual health problems associated with human trafficking: An updated systematic review. *Epidemiology and Psychiatric Sciences, 25,* 317–341.
31. Adams, A. E., Tolman, R. M., Bybee, D., Sullivan, C. M., & Kennedy, A. C. (2013). The impact of intimate partner violence on low-income women's economic well-being: The mediating role of job stability. *Violence against Women, 18*(12), 1345–1367.
32. Adams, A. E., Greeson, M. R., Kennedy, A. C., & Tolman, R. M. (2013). The effects of adolescent intimate partner violence on women's educational attainment and earnings. *Journal of Intimate Partner Violence, 28*(17), 3283–3300.
33. Scherlen, A., & Robinson, M. (2008). Open access to criminal justice scholarship: A matter of social justice. *Journal of Criminal Justice Education, 19*(1), 54–74.
34. Wronka, J. (2017). *Human rights and social justice: Social action and services for the helping and health professions.* Thousand Oaks, CA: Sage.
35. Schechter, S. (1982). *Women and male violence: The visions and struggles of the battered women's movement.* Cambridge, MA: South End Press.
36. Botein, H., & Hetling, A. (2016). *Home safe home: Housing solutions for survivors of intimate partner violence.* New Brunswick, NJ: Rutgers University Press.
37. National Network to End Domestic Violence. (2016). *Domestic violence counts 2015: A 24 hour census of domestic violence shelters and services.* Washington, DC: National Network to End Domestic Violence. Retrieved from https://nnedv.org/mdocs-posts/census_2015_handout_report/
38. *Ibid.*
39. *Ibid.*
40. Brady, P. Q., & Nobles, M. R. (2017). The dark figure of stalking: Examining law enforcement response. *Journal of Intimate Personal Violence, 32*(20), 3149–3173.
41. *Ibid.*
42. *Ibid.*
43. Lonsway, K. A., & Archambault, J. (2012). The "justice gap" for sexual assault cases future directions for research and reform. *Violence against Women, 18*(2), 145–168.
44. Planty, M., Langton, L., Krebs, C., Berzofsky, M., & Smiley-McDonald, H. (2013). *Female victims of sexual violence, 1994–2010.* Bureau of Justice Statistics.
45. Shaw, J., Campbell, R., Cain, D., & Feeney, H. (2016). Beyond surveys and scales: How rape myths manifest in sexual assault police records. *Psychology of Violence, 7*(4), 602–614.
46. Deer, S. (2015). *The beginning and end of rape: Confronting sexual violence in native America.* Minneapolis: University of Minnesota Press.
47. *Ibid.*
48. Amnesty International. (2007). *Maze of injustice: The failure to protect indigenous women from sexual violence in the USA.* New York: Amnesty International USA. Retrieved from www.amnestyusa.org/pdfs/mazeofinjustice.pdf
49. Rawls, 2001, p. 42.
50. Herman, 2010, p. 1.

2
DECRIMINALIZING POVERTY

Erin Grant

In a sense, social and economic conditions "cause" crime. Crime flourishes, and always has flourished, in city slums, those neighborhoods where overcrowding, economic deprivation, and racial discrimination are endemic.[1]

Introduction

What constitutes an acceptable cause of crime has varied over time; prior to the era of enlightenment, witchcraft, demons, and other supernatural occurrences were blamed for criminal behavior. Those who committed crimes were deemed unsuitable and often put to death. Criminologists later provided biology as an explanation for crime. Policy implications of these theories included eugenics and sterilization. Later came theories of crime that provided for less draconian policy.

Theories with less severe policy implications are among those that can be used to elaborate upon the relationship between poverty and crime. Their focus is on micro-level factors, such as parenting and education, as well as those at the macro level, including economic structure and neighborhood organization. In the United States, violence and crime are higher in low-income/high-poverty areas.[2] This chapter begins with an explanation of how poverty can be defined, as well as insight into the issues with the measurement of crime and its relationship to poverty. Risk factors will then be elaborated upon, followed by the theories of crime in which they play a role. Policy implications to reduce crime per each theory will be provided, many of which address the issues surrounding poverty itself. The chapter will conclude with a summary of these implications that may aid in the decriminalization of poverty.

Poverty and Crime

Poverty can be examined in several ways. In the most general sense, it is the shortage of necessary goods, including clean water, food, and safe housing.[3] Often, poverty is viewed through a lens of deprivation. Absolute deprivation exists when individuals are unable to afford essential needs. These individuals are among the most socially marginalized and isolated.[4] They experience blocked opportunities and a lack of social control due to eroding trust among peers, and they may participate in deviant subcultures.[5] The result of such experiences is a sense of frustration, which is hypothesized to increase participation in criminal behavior, including violent and aggressive acts.[6]

11

In addition to absolute deprivation, relative deprivation may help explain the poverty-crime relationship in an area. When those with little access to the bare necessities compare themselves to other who have more than they need, it can lead to a sense of dissatisfaction and a lack of self-respect.[7] This comparison to others may corrupt how individuals interact with those others in society, with the potential for criminal behavior to occur.[8] When measuring the relationship between crime and any variable, the potential weaknesses of the data must be noted.

When studying the underlying causes of crime, the data used often comes from what is reported by citizens to local agencies and eventually to the FBI. This data has been consistently plagued with rampant underreporting; first by victims themselves, and later by the police.[9] With the exceptions of murder and auto theft, all categories of offenses have this issue. Regardless of the history of underreporting, there is little difficulty finding a relationship between crime and poverty. As a note, the relationship between poverty and crime is exacerbated by race; minority members have a greater chance of arrest and processing than do their nonminority counterparts. However, the poverty-crime relationship remains strong, regardless of race or ethnic status.

Risk Factors

Many risk factors moderate the relationship between poverty and crime. These can affect people in early childhood; the number one indicator of propensity to delinquency is living in poverty.[10] Children born into families of low socioeconomic status (SES) have rates of crime over three times that of those born into high SES families; this remains true even later in life. The relationship between being born into low SES families and criminal behavior has been found in both self-reported and official data.[11]

In many low-income families, children receive inadequate parenting. Parents at higher income levels can spend more time with their children, providing for necessary supervision. Those at a lower income bracket work longer hours and at multiple jobs to provide for their families, decreasing the amount of child-parent interaction.[12] These children receive less maternal care and experience a lack of parental attachment. The interaction that does occur includes harsher punishment than for their wealthier counterparts.

Neglect, high rates of punishment, and child abuse are more common in impoverished families. This parental rejection creates strain, as it can seriously threaten many of the child's identities and thus goals, values, needs, and activities. Such treatment can be explained as a projection of the inequality the parent experiences in the workplace. Those in lower-status employment receive inconsistent control, which leads to negative attitudes. Without the social support those at higher income brackets receive, there are no outlets for these individuals to blow off steam. This pent-up frustration can lead to an unsuitable environment for children. Considering this social isolation, and with less access to resources often available to families, children are mistreated and are thus more likely to commit crime.[13]

As early as 1835, neighborhood factors have been used to understand the relationship between poverty and crime. Individuals who live in impoverished, disadvantaged settings are forced to navigate through public spaces, adjusting their routines to avoid the threat of victimization.[14] The threat of violence plaguing these areas limits the ability to engage with others in communities and schools. Resources and activities available in local schools and community centers may not be used due to the threat of victimization.[15] Due to this limited exposure to environmental stimulation, those who grow up in poverty are more likely to have adjustment problems, are at risk to have lower verbal abilities,[16] and perform poorly in an academic setting.[17]

The ability to perform well in an academic setting is of utmost importance. Lack of educational attainment is another risk factor in the relationship between poverty and crime. When youth are kept busy and off the street, school attendance may be beneficial, not only in finding gainful employment, but also for having a future negative effect on criminal participation. Completion of higher levels of education increases one's wage rates. Incarceration means time away from the labor market. The stigma of a criminal conviction is more damaging to those in the middle class than in the lower working class.[18] The opportunity costs of crime are increased, which alone may be enough to prevent many in higher income brackets from committing crime. These explanations suggest that an increase in an individual's schooling attainment will decrease the probability that the individual will engage in crime.[19] The U.S. educational system is set up in such a way that poor families receive access to an inferior education to that of their counterparts. This lack of adequate education, with limited ability to use the resources available due to the potential for danger, sets children up for failure.

In addition to living in poverty, income inequality has a significant and positive effect on crime.[20] When those at an economic disadvantage commit crime, they tend to commit violent crimes. When economic growth takes place, violent crime decreases. As such, violent crime is determined not just by income, but also the way in which it is distributed.

Each of the variables presented here play a role in the crime theories presented below. These theories are useful in making the connection between poverty and crime clearer. Perhaps more important are the policy implications provided by each; it is through understanding these relationships that crime may be deterred and poverty can be effectively decriminalized.

Theories of Crime and Poverty

Crime theory can be used to explain the relationship between poverty and crime. For this chapter, several of these theories will be presented, at both the micro and macro levels. Policy implications suggested by these theories will be provided as well. These policies are meant to reduce the strength of the relationship between poverty and crime through a variety of tactics. None of these alone can fully address crime, but each will provide insight into methods that can move in a direction of reduction.

Strain Theory

Strain theory is one of the most influential theories in the relationship between poverty and crime. Durkheim is responsible for early strain theory, with the proposal of anomie (i.e., a state of normlessness). Anomie, which is a word for the normlessness that is present when there is a lack of social structure, was determined to be a major determinant of criminal behavior. This concept was later use by Merton to propose strain theory.

Merton's theory argued that the overemphasis on monetary aspirations that one finds in places like the United States is a leading cause of criminal behavior. While many may have high aspirations of wealth, access to this type of success is not equally distributed. The disconnect between aspirations and opportunity causes strain and leads individuals to turn toward innovative, potentially illegal, means of achievement. Those who are impoverished turn to crime because they lack the resources required to pursue culturally defined legitimate mechanisms of success. This discrepancy may manifest as a sense of powerlessness, anxiety, or anger, which can lead to greater levels of violence when conflict arises.[21] In this early strain theory, links were made specifically between social structure and crime.[22] Agnew later built off Merton's work to include more potential sources of stress.

In addition to strain caused by lack of achievement, Agnew pointed out that the perceptions of whether the access to opportunity or lack thereof is distributed fairly may cause strain. When distribution is perceived as unjust, the likelihood for criminal response increases. Agnew's general strain theory focuses on what individuals use as coping strategies for strain and includes the importance of macro-level factors that affect the probability of delinquency. The level of importance placed on monetary goals changes based on social environment. One's social environment can also influence sensitivity to certain types of strain by altering how they can address it. Strains most often result in crime when they are high in magnitude and associated with low social control (to be discussed later).[23]

Strain theory also seeks to explain how the micro-level social aspects of those who are impover-ished are not conducive to law-abiding behavior. Within impoverished homes, adequate parenting is a commodity not all experience. Poor families are plagued with harsh discipline that reduces parental attachment, thus instilling within a child that strain should be solved with violence. This lesson that violence is the answer can lead to individuals acting out as youth and potentially for the rest of their lives.[24] A lack of education received by those in lower income areas is yet another source of strain. Receiving poor grades due to inadequate teachers can exacerbate the issue, leading to dropping out or delinquency. Without a good education, it is more difficult for those in poverty to gain lucrative employment and overcome their status in legitimate ways.

Two major policy recommendations flow from general and other strain theories. The first of these is to reduce exposure to strain and therefore the likelihood that individuals will cope with it through crime. The ways in which negative behaviors are dealt with may also be addressed; harsher treatment may cause less strain which in turn may lead to less offending. Currently, parents, teachers, and crimi-nal justice officials sanction individuals in ways that are disliked. Altering the ways in which sanc-tions are administered can reduce the likelihood that they will appear unfair or extreme, reduce social control, or otherwise create incentive to engage in crime. Restorative justice and related movements seek to improve these conditions.[25]

Strain theory does not exist in a vacuum; the relationship between poverty and crime is affected by social variables. Theories that explain the way social aspects affect the relationship between poverty and crime include differential association, social learning, and social control. These theories propose that increased rates of crime among individuals from poor and disadvantaged backgrounds is due to greater exposure to criminal peers and environments.

Differential Association

Where strain theories explain the link between crime and socioeconomic disadvantage as being due to stress, differential association theory lays greater emphasis on processes that relate to peer influence and motivation towards criminal activity.[26] Sutherland's theory suggests that as individuals are exposed to more pro-criminal behavior and attitudes, the greater their own likelihood to offend. Low SES can increase the exposure to pro-criminal individuals. The very nature of impoverished neighborhoods exposes individuals to attitudes that are either pro-crime or avoidance.

The policy implications for this theory are simple—remove individuals from situations in which they will be surrounded by those who are pro-crime. This may include the removal of families from impoverished neighborhoods where crime tends to thrive. If this is not feasible, as often it is not by the very nature of being impoverished, the creation of programs in which children are provided more prosocial role models and mentors may also be beneficial to reduce crime.

Social Learning Theory

While differential association focuses more on the relationships one has with delinquent associates, a social learning model argues that variations in crime rates are predominately due to early learning experiences that predispose young people to offending. Per this theory, crime and pro-crime values are taught in the same way that one is taught any other skill or value. This model would suggest that it is through family interaction that one first learns; thus, poor child-rearing and inadequate supervi-sion encourage the development of crime. One might surmise that differences in rates of crime across social status may be due to variations in the child-rearing practices within.[27]

Policy implications of this theory would include providing for additional, and adequate, parental supervision. Programs that would provide more time for parents to spend with their children in a positive environment would include those that supplement a family's income, such as CHIP, WIC, and food stamps. Parenting courses teaching best practices in care and discipline would also benefit the low-income family.

Social Control Theory

Often related to social learning is social control. It is by the very instrument of social learning that one may be controlled. Social control theory proposes that motivation towards deviance is constant across individuals, and social bonds constrain these impulses. Attachment to parents and school and family stability are examples of social bonds. When these bonds break down, an individual is more prone to engage in deviant behavior.

People living in poverty are more prone to have weakened networks of social control.[28] The policy implications one might glean from social control theory are like those of the previously mentioned social theories. Programs that permit parents to spend more time at home with their children would provide for more family stability, which may lead to attachment between children and parents. Access to good schools with good teachers would provide an opportunity to invest in one's education and to be around others who value an education.

Social Disorganization

Social networks are revisited in social disorganization theory. This macro-level theory seeks to explain the relationship between poverty and crime by way of these networks. Shaw and McKay presented this theory after completing research that demonstrated rates of delinquency decreased as one moved farther away from the inner city. Their findings also suggested that certain characteristics were common in areas of concentrated crime and delinquency; many of these characteristics have already been examined in this chapter (e.g., family, social networks, and economic inequality).[29]

Revisions of the theory continue to explain the relationship between concentrated disadvantage and negative outcomes that put individuals at a higher risk of crime. The ties that individuals in an area have with one another continue to be a major emphasis, including shared values and goals.[30] Neighborhoods of concentrated poverty are most vulnerable to crime and disorder due to an inability to come up with these shared goals. This in turn keeps the neighborhood unstable; people choose not to reside in such areas for long periods, transitioning instead into areas in which there is a sense of community. With this population turnover, there is no chance to create norms, perpetuating the crime cycle.[31]

It has been suggested that the relationships between people in areas of poverty are the best way to predict crime. Little is done to intervene within these communities and attempt to create a culture that citizens will buy into.[32] Thus, policy implications suggested by this theory would be ways in which to create a sense of community or shared culture in an area.

Conflict Theory

The final theory presented in this chapter to explain the relationship between poverty and crime is the conflict perspective. There are many versions of this theory; what each has in common is its reliance on social structure and economic status. Those with the most money have the most power; those with the most power determine what is and is not deviant. Those in power also influence public institutions (e.g., schools and churches), which aid in shaping the views of members of society. These institutions include criminal justice and legal systems, which are used as tools to encourage buy-in of those at a lower economic standing while serving to protect the power and interests of the wealthy.[33]

Laws are created by those in power to protect their own interests. By outlawing certain behaviors, lower status groups are prevented from gaining power; at the same time, attention is diverted from the criminal behavior of the wealthy. The powerful may break their own laws with little consequence, while others are arrested and labeled for breaking laws they may not accept.

Social stratification plays a role in whether individuals buy into the laws of the land. Some critical theorists make this their focus, examining the social reality of crime. Crime is a social construct, created by society's authority figures. Different groups of people have different patterns of behavior learned in their own social setting. Some of this learned behavior may be normal at their group level, but deemed delinquent at a larger level. Whether an individual offends is based on their place in life, determined by how well their group is organized and the power that it holds. This power is based on an emphasis on materialism, with capitalism being a major culprit.[34]

Much of the blame is placed on capitalism itself; some theorists suggest that juveniles are at the most disadvantage in a capitalistic system.[35] As mentioned throughout this chapter, there are several risk factors that have a greater effect on juveniles. In low SES homes, family violence is more common. The stresses of poverty, poor housing, and poor education lead to family violence at a greater rate than in those homes without such barriers. Often, the low SES homes are also at the low end of the power spectrum within patriarchal society—including mostly women-headed families.[36] Juveniles, inferior by their very nature, have a greater likelihood of breaking norms than do adults, as they are not always aware of the consequences of their behaviors. The support network of their peers is often not fully aware of laws and the consequences of breaking them and their parents are less present due to long working hours.

The policy implied by conflict theory reflects that implied by the previously mentioned theories. Those in lower income brackets should be given access to better educational opportunities, parents should have access to parenting courses and aid with their food, insurance, and other bills. What is added in this theory is the suggestion that the system itself needs to change. Capitalism is to blame for the criminalization of poverty and thus a new model should be adopted. This, however, is a seemingly impossible feat, and the focus of the final section will emphasize other ways in which poverty may be decriminalized.

Decriminalizing Poverty

Decriminalizing poverty can occur in one of three ways. The first of these is addressing the underlying risk factors experienced by those living in poverty that may lead to delinquency. Changes in crime policy may also help to address the poverty-crime relationship. Finally, a change in the way leaders are elected and laws are passed can bring broad changes to the ways in which those in poverty are treated.[37] The last of these requires organizing and activism beyond the scope of this chapter, thus the first two will be addressed.

Risk factors that lead to delinquency which are common among those in poverty have been discussed in the previous pages: strain, family, neighborhood, education, etc. Efforts to address these have been made in the past. These include efforts made at reducing the exposure of children to high-poverty neighborhoods. Programs have been implemented to subsidize the movement of families from low-income to wealthier neighborhoods. The changes in neighbors, it is believed, will increase quality of life, decreasing one's propensity to crime.[38]

An example of this type of program is the U.S. Department of Housing and Urban Development: Moving to Opportunity, which is currently located in five cities.[39] Nearly all the families that are moved using this program are single, African American mothers escaping the gangs and drugs of lower income areas. Studies have demonstrated that this move may decrease violent juvenile behavior by up to 50%.[40],[41] These results may be due to several factors. It might be that the move itself has led to decreased criminal behavior. The school system may be of a higher caliber in the new environment. It may also be that parents with this opportunity spend less time at work and more time with their children, reducing their opportunities to interact with delinquent peers and act out.

Other programs that put less stress on parents working long hours include Medicare, Medicaid, CHIP, food stamps, job opportunity, and basic skills training programs with incentives and mandates for moving from welfare to work. Effectively implemented, these programs may lead to less stress to make ends meet and more consistent discipline. Used seldom in the United States, income transfer programs, in which impoverished individuals are provided with money to use as they deem fit, are another option. Studies have demonstrated that these programs moderately reduce criminal behavior and arrests. Other antipoverty programs include those that are structured to provide incentives for work, with benefits decreasing as income increases.[42]

Changes in policy can also aid in decriminalizing poverty. Restorative justice movements are at the forefront of changes in the way the criminal justice system goes about business. Programs that are restorative in nature are meant to increase perceived justice or fairness of sanctions received, reduce the magnitude of sanctions, provide sanctions that do not add pressure to commit additional crime, and increase social control. Under this model, offenders are treated with respect, are made aware of the harm caused, are provided a voice when sanctions are determined, and are reintegrated into society in a positive way. Parenting and school-based programs may also be structured in this way. By doing so, the likelihood that strain via discipline will occur leading to criminal coping will be minimized.[43]

Summary

This chapter provided a brief outline of the relationship between poverty and crime. Factors, such as family, education, and delinquent peers, can exacerbate the status of being impoverished, which may increase crime. Several crime theories have addressed these, providing a sure direction in which to go about decriminalizing poverty. The most extreme of these, conflict theory, suggests that there be a major system change in the methods by which laws are enacted. While this may be idealistic, it is also something that takes place in a long-term process. In the meantime, addressing underlying risk factors via a variety of methods will aid in reducing the strength of the relationship between poverty and crime.

Discussion Questions

1. What is the difference between absolute and relative poverty? Which theories do well to explain relative poverty?
2. What are some variables that affect the relationship between poverty and crime? What are some others you can think of that may not have been presented in this chapter?
3. Strain theory suggests that experiencing a disjoint between goals and ability to achieve them can lead to increased criminal behavior. What are some economic strains that you have experienced that may have led to criminal behavior?
4. Explain differential association, social learning, and social control theories. How do these differ? How are they similar? Can you think of a program or policy that may reduce crime based on the implications of these theories?
5. How does social disorganization relate to other theories of crime?
6. Does conflict theory have any realistic policy implications? Why or why not?
7. What ways can you come up with to decriminalize poverty based on the risk factors provided in this text?

Notes

1. Flango, V. E., & Sherbenou, E. L. (1976). Poverty, urbanization, and crime. *Criminology, 14*(3), 331. (p. 332).
2. Heller, S. B., Jacob, B. A., & Ludwig, J. (2011). Family income, neighborhood poverty, and crime. In P. J. Cook, J. Ludwig, & J. McCary (Eds.), *Controlling crime: Strategies and tradeoffs* (pp. 419–459). Chicago, IL: University of Chicago Press.

3. Sileika, A., & Bekeryte, J. (2013). Theoretical issues of relationship between unemployment, poverty, and crime in sustainable development. *Journal of Security and Sustainability Issues, 2*(3), 59–70.

4. Patterson, E. B. (1991). Poverty, income inequality, and community crime rates. *Criminology, 29*(4), 755–776.

5. Santos, M. R., Testa, A., & Weiss, D. B. (2017). Where poverty matters: Examining the cross-national relationship between economic deprivation and homicide. *British Journal of Criminology azx013.*

6. Hsief, C., & Pugh, M. D. (1993). Poverty, income inequality, and violent crime: A meta-analysis of recent aggregate data studies. *Criminal Justice Review, 18*(2), 182.

7. Patterson, 1991.

8. Santos, Testa, & Weiss, 2017.

9. Flango, & Sherbenou, 1976.

10. Patterson, 1991.

11. Fergusson, D. M., Swain-Campbell, N. R., & Horwood, L. J. (2004). How does childhood economic disadvantage lead to crime? *Journal of Child Psychology & Psychiatry, 45*(5), 956–966.

12. Heller, Jacob, & Ludwig, 2011.

13. Berti, C., & Pivetti, M. (2017). Childhood economic disadvantage and antisocial behavior: Intervening factors and pathways. *Child and Youth Services Review.* https://doi.org/10.1016/j.childyouth.2017.06.007

14. Sharkey, P., Besbris, M., & Friedson, M. (2016). Poverty and crime. In D. Brady & L. M. Burton (Eds.), *The Oxford hand book of the social science of poverty.* Oxford: Oxford University Press.

15. *Ibid.*

16. Sileika, & Bekeryte, 2013.

17. Berti, & Pivetti, 2017.

18. Lochner, L., & Moretti, E. (2004). The effect of education on crime: Evidence from prison inmates, arrests, and self-reports. *The American Economic Review, 94*(1), 155–189.

19. Burnstein, J. (2017). *Examining the relationship between crime, economic, and government policy and crime and recidivism rates* (Unpublished honors thesis). Duke University, Durham.

20. Fajnzylber, P., Lederman, D., & Loayza, N. (2002). Inequality and violent crime. *The Journal of Law and Economics, 45*(1), 1–39.

21. Santos, Testa, & Weiss, 2017.

22. Fergusson, Swain-Campbell, & Horwood, 2004.

23. Agnew, R. (2001). Building on the foundation of general strain theory: Specifying the types of strain most likely to lead to crime and delinquency. *Journal of Research in Crime and Delinquency, 38*(4), 319–361.

24. Fergusson, Swain-Campbell, & Horwood, 2004.

25. Burnstein, 2017.

26. Fergusson, Swain-Campbell, & Horwood, 2004.

27. *Ibid.*

28. *Ibid.*

29. Burnstein, 2017.

30. *Ibid.*

31. Hipp, J. R., & Yates, D. K. (2011). Ghettos, thresholds, and crime: Does concentrated poverty really have an accelerating increasing effect on crime? *Criminology, 49*(4), 955–990.

32. Boggess, L. N., & Hipp, J. R. (2010). Violent crime, residential instability and mobility: Does the relationship differ in minority neighborhoods? *Journal of Quantitative Criminology, 26*(3), 351–370.

33. Grant, E. G. (2017). Conflict theory. In C. J. Schreck, M. Leiber, H. Ventura-Miller, & K. Welch (Eds.), *The encyclopedia of juvenile delinquency and justice.* Hoboken, NJ: Wiley-Blackwell.

34. Quinney, R. (1980). *Class, state, and crime,* 2nd ed. New York: Longman.

35. Grant, 2017, pp. 1–4.

36. *Ibid.*

37. Burnstein, 2017.

38. Jacob, B. A., & Ludwig, J. (2009). Improving educational outcomes for poor children. In M. Cancian & S. Danzinger (Eds.), *Changing poverty, changing policies.* New York: Russell Sage Foundation.

39. Ludwig, J., Duncan, G. J., & Hirschfield, P. (2001). Urban poverty and juvenile crime: Evidence from a randomized housing mobility experiment. *The Quarterly Journal of Economics, 116*(2), 655–679.

40. *Ibid.*

41. Haveman, R., Blank, R., Moffitt, R., Smeeding, T., & Wallace, G. (2015). The war on poverty: Measurement, trends, and policy. *Journal of Policy Analysis and Management, 34*(3), 593–638.

42. Ludwig, Duncan, & Hirschfield, 2001.

43. Fergusson, Swain-Campbell, & Horwood, 2004.

3

KEY THEORIES OF JUSTICE

Melissa Thorne and Robert D. Hanser

Introduction

Though people may not be familiar with the term, the concept of social justice is something that is almost intuitively understood by most. Indeed, understanding fundamental fairness in the treatment of other human beings is an inherent characteristic of any civilized society. Throughout history, as civilizations have evolved, nearly every generation has witnessed the fight for some type of social injustice; women's rights, African Americans' rights, and LGBTQ rights are three of the most prominent examples from the last century, when social justice began to emerge within American political and legal philosophy. The term "social justice" was first coined around 1840 and was first used among Catholic clergy who sought to provide aid to the poor. During the mid-1800s, this term was used in secular writings as well.

Social justice in its early days focused on poverty and equal distribution of resources.[1] In discussing the emergence of social justice, it may be best to first provide some type of synopsis of what we mean when we use the term social justice. In doing so, we will rely on the work of Harvey,[2] who proposes that there are four competing theories of justice, each of which ranks in importance along a defined hierarchy. These four theories of justice serve as a fundamental basis to the development of social justice. They include the positive law perspective, the utilitarian perspective, the social contract perspective, and the natural rights perspective.

Harvey's view of positive law contends that justice is simply when we continue to uphold the law that currently exists. These laws are those that have been generated by governments through law-making bodies or persons and that take the shape and form of that which suits the ruling class and/or those with social power. The utilitarian perspective is one wherein justice is seen as that which results in the greatest good for the greatest number and, based on this rationale, distinguishes between good laws and bad laws. Harvey's social contract perspective can be historically connected to the work of Rousseau and John Rawls, who contended that justice is based on a non-codified but implicit contract between citizens of a given society. While more will be mentioned later in this chapter regarding Rawls's work, it is sufficient to say that the incentive for this contract involved the mutual benefit for all persons included and served to protect their rights, which were considered universal, permanent, and unchanging, even when and/or if these rights ran counter to the utilitarian notion of the "greatest good" of society. Lastly, the natural law or natural rights perspective holds that rights are not dependent on the laws or customs of a given government and that, despite what those with power might contend, supersede power created through force by existing regimes. An example of natural rights might be those listed in the Declaration of Independence as the right to life, liberty, and the pursuit of happiness.[3] In contemporary times, many people equate human rights with social justice.

Today, the term social justice refers broadly to more concentrated approaches to the moral treatment of citizens, as well as reciprocal relationships within a community. Social justice implies that members of a community have roles and responsibilities to each other to create an equal distribution of advantages and disadvantages among members of the community. The key theories of social justice include utilitarianism, libertarianism, egalitarianism, and virtue-based approaches. In this chapter, we will first provide an overview of each theory; we will discuss them in depth later in this chapter, showing interconnections between each of these theories with social facets and areas of study to include criminology, government operations, and social change in the modern world.

A Theoretical Breakdown and Overview

The utilitarian approach to social justice is the idea that the benefit of a great number of people is more important than the benefit of an individual. Jeremy Bentham, one of the first theorists of utilitarianism, designed a calculation for determining the value of pleasure versus pain; he posited that pleasure minus pain equals utility. Bentham also noted the importance of the number of people who benefit from an act versus those who consequently suffer. John Stuart Mill continued to develop the work of Jeremy Bentham; he faced much criticism for stating that happiness was the only desire of most people. Mill believed there should be less of a division among owners and workers. He believed that all people have the right to basic needs as well as social welfare. Critics of utilitarianism point out that it conflicts with common-sense approaches to morality. The common-sense approach to morality maintains that the suffering of all individuals is equally important, regardless of how many people may benefit from the sacrifice of one. Karl Marx criticized Bentham's version of utilitarianism by pointing out that different people desire different things from life. Theorists of utilitarianism continue to develop the work of Bentham and Mills, but the results are accused of being too simplistic to explain complex human behavior.[4]

The egalitarian approach to social justice holds that all people are equal and, therefore, deserve the same opportunities. Egalitarianism is the idea that no group of people is dominant or treated differently in ability or opportunity. Evidence hints that prehistoric societies were egalitarian; each person in a society had a specific role and was treated equally. Egalitarianism encompasses the causes of all specific groups who have fought for social justice; a true egalitarian will be supportive of equal rights for all rather than for some. One potential issue with this approach to social justice is that the focus is too dispersed, with the lack of focus leading to no progress toward equality. Criticisms of classic egalitarianism have branched off and relabeled themselves as more specific forms. New egalitarianism is an emerging view that raises the question of how different groups of people will be able to live together in the same community. Luck egalitarianism points out that luck cannot be eliminated from the equation of behavior versus consequence.[5]

The libertarian approach to social justice concentrates on greater individual freedom and less governmental power. Libertarians believe that people should be able to regulate their own lives and behavior so long as another person is not gravely injured. Robert Nozick favored a libertarian view that protected property rights. Nozick believed that humans have no ethical obligation to help others. This approach ignores the necessity of altruism to the survival of humans. The libertarian approach to social justice also leads to those who have wealth and property having access to more resources, more power, and more education than the poor do. One problem with a libertarian approach is that some individuals may knowingly oppress other individuals to foster their own wealth or success; less governmental power means fewer policies to regulate this type of behavior.[6]

John Rawls was an influential American philosopher who published *A Theory of Justice* in 1971. His book addressed freedom and equality, which he saw as competing forces. Rawls's goal was to showcase freedom and equality as one cause, and he coined the term "justice as fairness" to explain his position. In his book, Rawls discusses two principles of justice. The liberty principle states that all citizens should have equal basic liberties, such as the freedom of expression. Like Nozick, Rawls addresses the right to personal property, but his description includes moral capacity rather than simply focusing on a given right to own something. Rawls's second principle, fair equality of opportunity, addresses opportunity for a meaningful life. Rawls believed that people have a right to have a chance to live a meaningful life, therefore affording them the right to equal opportunities as those with similar abilities and qualifications. Rawls suggested that his principles of justice were applicable to societal institutions as a basic structure model for the distribution of social justice. Critics of Rawls's work claimed that his theory, which he contrasted with utilitarianism, lacked utility; critics pointed out that Rawls's principles of justice favored the least advantaged rather than the greater number of citizens.[7]

Virtue-based approaches to social justice rely on an individual's virtues and character traits to predict their actions toward others; this approach says that character traits are stable and consistent. Society recognizes the virtue of kindness and associates it with certain behaviors. A virtue-based approach would assume that if a person possesses the virtue of kindness, he or she would behave in a certain way toward others. A virtue-based approach to social justice expects that a person deemed kind by society would behave in the expected manner toward *all* other people. One criticism of this theory is that many people said to possess the virtue of kindness by their peers do not in fact behave kindly toward groups of people who are different from themselves. Another criticism of a virtue-based approach is that virtues and traits are fluid, developing over time and circumstance. Virtue is also relative to the culture in question.[8]

Morality is another principle relative to culture and era. A moral system includes rules about acceptable behavior that are decided upon by a majority of a society. Social cooperation is necessary for a society to function as a collective entity in enforcing decided rules. Morality is somewhat fluid, changing as society changes, giving way for constant reevaluation of systems.[9] Opotow explored the concept of moral exclusion as related to perhaps the most famous instance of social injustice, the Holocaust.[10] Most of the world experienced shock and disbelief that such heinous acts could be imposed upon another human. The Jewish people were stripped of their rights over time and deemed inferior by leaders. This progression led to much of the general public adjusting to the idea that Jewish people were inferior and therefore not deserving of the same moral treatment as other citizens.

Opotow defines moral exclusion as acts that occur against those who are considered outside the bounds of moral values. Moral exclusion ranges from discrimination to genocide. A person or group may be considered outside the bounds of social justice in one region but not another. She also discusses the Holocaust in terms of moral exclusion as a process that built over time within the social climate of the era. She points out that since the end of the Holocaust, rules and regulations that were more morally inclusive have been established but continue to be challenged.[11]

A more modern-day version of moral exclusion would be that encountered with the War on Terror. Opotow identified problems with the use of torture against suspects of terrorism, such as that which occurred in Abu Ghraib (U.S. POW prison in Iraq) and Guantanamo Bay, Cuba (where Al Qaeda detainees were kept by the U.S. government). While the labeling of this as moral exclusion may be correct, these were single albeit important occasions. However, we would like to assert that the larger social justice problem was the way that the War on Terror was insidiously equated to a war on Islam. While the assertion that there was a war on Islam was most strongly suggested and supported in the Islamic states themselves, there were many people in the United States who, not truly educated on international politics, mistakenly considered the War on Terror to be a war against Islam itself.[12] During this time, informal pejoratives against Muslims and Middle Easterners were common, as were various forms of racial profiling.[13] Further, this profiling and public anger sometimes manifested itself against persons who appeared to be Middle Eastern but were, in fact, Latino, Sikh, or Indian in descent. This was so true that U.S. media eventually were compelled to provide messages to dispel this idea.

However, it was not until the Obama administration inherited the presidency that this line of thought was truly eradicated, though even his countering of these negative public sentiments fell under the scrutiny of public concern.

One last more-or-less modern example would be the moral exclusion of the same-sex population in the United States. Traditionally, up until the last decade or so, the lesbian, gay, bisexual, and transgender (LGBT) population was systematically discriminated against throughout the United States. Indeed, laws that targeted this population were prevalent, and the LGBT population was excluded from basic fundamental freedoms (such as the ability to publicly and officially marry) as well as opportunities (the ability to join the military), where questionable laws and policies, such as "don't ask, don't tell," gave contradictory and ambiguous messages. Ultimately, due to social pressure and changing public sentiments, states have repealed discriminatory laws and the federal government has officially granted rights to the LGBT population that have traditionally only been afforded to the heterosexual population, such as the right to marry, which was established in the landslide Supreme Court case of *Obergefell v. Hodges* (2015).[14]

Robinson addresses ideals of social justice in relation to the criminal justice system. He asserts that most citizens would not agree with many practices of criminal justice if educated about them; he discusses the "veil of ignorance" that is present in society, despite claims of the importance of social justice.[15] Robinson calls for a reform of the criminal justice system to better align it with the ideals of social justice.[16] This mirrors many of the tenets presented by Jeffrey Reiman and Paul Leighton in their book titled *The Rich Get Richer and the Poor Get Prison*, where they show disparities in treatment against the poor and/or politically weak that exist at every stage of the criminal justice system.[17] The final outcome of these disparities are that prison consists largely of individuals who are poor, lack education, and tend to be minorities.

Prosocial behavior promotes survival and plays a role in social justice. Altruism is the concern for or willingness to help others; altruistic societies tend to be more successful. Reciprocal altruism involves helping others with the hope that the behavior will be reciprocated in the future. Perhaps humans only fight for social justice in order to promote their own agenda, survival through cooperation. Altruism is also an important survival mechanism for humans. Cooperation with other humans is often the means to the end, survival.[18]

Another biological aspect of human behavior that promotes prosocial behavior and influences social justice is empathy. Cognitive empathy is the ability to imagine another person's perspective, while affective empathy is the ability to show appropriate emotion and affect in reaction to the pain of another person.[19] Decety and Yoder suggest that cognitive empathy is a motivating force in seeking social justice. That is, if a person has the capacity to see things from a perspective other than their own, they are likely more inclined to fight for social justice.[20] Naturally, the opposite is true as well. Those who are self-centered and calloused will not feel any motivation to counter an unjust circumstance for others and will, more likely, become roused for activity only when an issue impacts them, specifically.

This last point is one of concern and also one that social justice advocates will find ripe for work within today's society. Indeed, research during the early to mid-2000s and beyond has found that people in general, and youth in particular, throughout the United States have higher rates of narcissism,[21] lower rates of empathy,[22] and are more socially isolated than they were 20 or 30 years ago.[23] These findings are important as they may explain social circumstances that are more frequently caught on media recordings. For instance, shootings of unarmed citizens by police officers have been in the news media during the past four or five years much more frequently. In turn, the ambushing and shooting of police officers around the nation has also generated substantial concern. These occurrences get widespread public attention and have an impact on citizen perceptions of police, crime, and justice.

Whether the lack of empathy, narcissism, or social isolation is a cause to these incidents is not necessarily clear. However, such characteristics clearly are consistent with the mindset. Also, when considering offenders who are in prison, there has been very clear and consistent research showing that those with antisocial personality characteristics tend to also suffer from empathy deficits. These are also among the most chronic offenders, being recidivists with long-term longitudinal criminal careers.[24] According to Postick,[25] the following three key points regarding the importance of empathy can be made about criminal behavior, citizen views on punishment of criminals, and police-community relations:

1. Empathetic people are less likely to engage in delinquency or crime. But those who have trouble perceiving how others feel, and have difficulty sharing those feelings, are more likely to engage in wrongful acts—everything from minor juvenile delinquency to the most serious of violent crimes.
2. Empathy affects how people think about crime and punishment in complex ways. People capable of empathy tend to support tough punishments for crime, but at the same time they are less likely to call for the harshest punishments, such as the death penalty.
3. Empathy and perceptions of empathy help to shape the interactions of police and members of the communities they are assigned to protect. Research on citizen interactions with the police has consistently indicated that the way officers behave determines how they are evaluated by people with whom they interact.

From the comments above and from findings by a wide array of researchers and writers,[26] it is clear that offenders are in need of empathy-building exercises and treatment programs rather than simply being given harsh punishments. Likewise, it is also clear that society is receptive to the notions of offender rehabilitation, if done correctly.[27] Lastly, police-community relations are greatly enhanced when police employ standard community policing approaches in a manner that is sincere and consistent.[28] Thus, it would appear that as social justice is a mechanism to assist those who are in a one-down position by convincing those in a one-up position of the benefit of facilitating such social elevation, those in power and those who are politically active will need to be empathetic to their plight. Such would be the case regardless of the particular group who is aggrieved, victimized, or discriminated against. Thus, social empathy should be viewed as a complimentary characteristic to any social justice initiative. We now turn our attention to social justice and its relationship with critical criminology. In each example that will be provided by Arrigo[29] and other researchers, we ask that the basic tenets and theoretical perspectives of social justice be kept in mind. In all of the following examples, the need for societal levels of empathy should be self-evident to the reader.

Social Justice and Critical Criminology

Without any doubt, there is an intuitive connection between social justice and critical criminology. Perhaps part of the reason for this is that, at the base of it, both social justice and critical criminology have some of their origins in the socialistic thinking of Karl Marx.[30] It is our contention that this common link in origin makes social justice and critical criminology naturally complementary to one another. As such, many authors associated with critical criminological perspectives proposed a model of social justice that was integrated with critical criminology perspectives.

Arrigo notes that in the case of critical criminologists, a perceived struggle persists between the citizen and society and, in the process, an "emancipatory conflict" ensues, displaying that people are not simply the result of structural social forces around them (i.e., the economy, the media, the educational system) but they are also partners in the shaping of their identity.[31] Therefore, for critical criminologists, the real expression of social justice is the struggle to be human. For critical criminologists, the sense of autonomy is precisely what leads to social justice for all. Thus, social justice transcends simple redistribution of economic resources. It includes one's ability to establish a social identity. This is important because some researchers contend that social justice is centered primarily on economic equality. Though this is, of course, an important aspect of equality, the concept of equality entails a number of other facets and dimensions to existence, as well. This then is precisely the point that critical criminologists make, extending the thoughts and tenets beyond mere economic equality.

Radical criminologists, on the other hand, base their perspectives on crime and law in the belief that capitalist societies define crime through a process whereby the wealthy use their power and influence to have laws enacted that will serve their own desires and will keep the working class under control. In order that social justice may be achieved, it would be necessary to overthrow capitalist forms of government and to replace them with social systems of government. In social systems, class and economic disparities are eliminated so as to maintain a sense of egalitarian balance.[32]

Similarly, social conflict theories share the radical criminologists' view that crime is defined by laws enacted by powerful groups who engage in social control of the population so as to prevent challenges to their values and interests.[33] However, social conflict criminologists contend that these types of powerful groups exist in all large and modernized societies and that they all tend to utilize the lawmaking process to further their own social interests while thwarting the goals of other competitive groups. Thus, numerous groups work in tandem and independently to further their own vested interests, sometimes in league with one another through processes of shifting alliances and allegiances until mutual interests are disbanded. In such cases, perceptions of social justice may be quite varied, depending on the particular power group considered.

Another interesting group within the critical criminology arena that has a definite vested interest in social justice are the socialist feminists. For socialist feminists, the economic conditions help to reinforce a position of servitude among women. At the heart of their angst is the gendered nature of money acquisition and opportunities in the world of work. In the process, the interests of women are given secondary thought and consideration. Further still, these criminologists point toward the patriarchal aspects of modern society as well as the historic patriarchy of past society, wherein women were considered the property of men. For this group, social justice consists of removing the glass ceiling that limits women and ensuring equality of economic and political power between men and women.

The last group of critical criminologists that we will consider are the peacemaking criminologists. Peacemaking examines global acts of violence and victimization and advocates for providing awareness of more peaceful and productive processes. Indeed, this is likely to be considered the primary activity of peacemaking criminologists. According to Arrigo, educating for peace is an affirmative effort to restore and reinvigorate humane, dignified, and meaningful relationships between offenders and victims, between countries at war, and so forth.[34]

Each of the prior groups of critical criminology have, as and underlying theme, a party who is either in a one-down position or has been aggrieved. As we noted in our opening introduction, social justice seeks to address some type of injustice. In most cases, these injustices have been economic. However, the injustices that fall under the umbrella of social justice concerns now include victimization through economic exploitation, political maneuverings, lawmaking, physical force, and other forms of coercion, entrapment, or harm done to people who are, in most cases, at a disadvantage and struggle to gain relief from their mistreatment. It is for this reason that critical criminology has been showcased in this chapter—to connect the various aspects of social justice with a variety of potential hindrances to developing equity and equality in a variety of spheres of human existence, all within the perspective of a criminal justice or criminology orientation.

The Big Lesson: Should We Reprioritize Our Wealth?

During the late 1990s, military spending from the prior Cold War era had reached an all-time high. During this same period, much less emphasis was placed on help for the poverty stricken. One author, Dorothy Van Soest, conducted an analysis from a social justice perspective of the dichotomy between military spending and public aid assistance.[35] Van Soest noted that, in most respects, the meaning of social justice is in the eye of the beholder. Nevertheless, some citizens may perceive that military defense is for the common good and is the function of government due to the rights of citizens to be protected. On the other hand, others view the lack of funding for those persons who are in most need to be an injustice. They seek to balance this allocation of resources so as to relieve misery and suffering. Van Soest provided an analysis of three conceptions of justice that support providing enhanced funding to persons in need within the United States. These three perspectives are the libertarian perspective, the utilitarian perspective, and the egalitarian perspective.[36]

The libertarian perspective, according to Van Soest, "strongly opposes welfare rights, any coercive mechanism by the state to get some citizens to aid others, and all attempts to impose any" intended pattern of economic distribution throughout society.[37] Within the libertarian perspective are three primary human rights that the government is obligated to protect. These are paraphrased from Van Soest's work, as follows:

1. Every person has a right to life. Any attempt to take away that life and/or to injure that person is a violation of the potential victim's human rights.
2. Every person has the right to liberty, meaning that every person has the right to live their life as a personal choice, so long as it is not at the expense of another person's human rights.
3. Everyone has the right to property, presuming that the property is legally acquired, and the right to dispose of it as he or she pleases, so long as the disposal of property does not present a risk to the welfare of the public.

Naturally, as one has likely guessed, these rights are reflected in the United States Constitution. Thus, libertarians would disapprove of state-run programs to assist disadvantaged youth and families, programs for the homeless, and most other forms of social aid for the needy. At the same time, libertarians are staunch supporters of the notion that everyone has the right to life, liberty, and property, so long as they are self-reliant and independent in these pursuits.

For classic utilitarians, the main idea is that "society is rightly ordered and just when its major institutions are arranged in such a way as to achieve the greatest net balance of satisfaction summed over all the individuals belonging to it."[38] Because of this underlying tenet, utilitarianism has been used as a basis to reallocate wealth and it has even served as a basis for unequal wealth distribution, benefits, and opportunities; in both cases being touted for the good of the whole.[39]

While the utilitarian approach seems to have a certain quantitative appeal, it still ignores that the determination of the "common good" is very subjective and quite open to interpretation. We will provide more discussion on this later, but for the moment, it is sufficient to simply note that the common good would seem to be a matter of perspective, with the definition of the common good depending on your own particular position within a given society. If you work on Wall Street, your version of the common good is likely to be much different from those working in Harlem. The two locations in New York are substantially different from one another.

Likewise, the common good is subjective in terms of worldviews of military and crime-fighting priorities. Indeed, if the common good becomes an emphasis on military campaigns (the Cold War, the War on Terror) or crime campaigns (the War on Drugs, the War on Crime) that emphasize staunch responses, then the common good becomes what is achieved using the barrel of a gun and becomes a reality of "us against them." However, if we redefine the common good as a healthy, educated, and productive population, the utilitarian approach is expressed more in terms of access to medicine, access to education, and adequate access to employment. The two worldviews are substantially different from one another.

The last perspective of justice that we will discuss in this section is the egalitarian perspective. This theoretical approach counters the idea that society can be correctly ordered whenever it is based on social and/or economic inequalities. This goes back to our earlier discussion of John Rawls, who argued against the utilitarian notion that hardships experienced by a few could, somehow, be justified or offset by the greater common good experienced by the majority. However, Rawls believed that the distribution of income and wealth did not need to be equal, so long as it was to the advantage of everyone. This is a bit off-center from a pure egalitarian perspective, in which the main idea is that the only inequalities that are morally presentable are those that work to the utmost and absolute advantage of those who are the worst-off and most poor in our society.[40]

To make it clear, egalitarian theory provides the most clear and direct argument for social justice by simply staging that the redistribution of wealth and opportunities in society is a moral obligation. As Van Soest states, "egalitarians would propose that the unmet needs that should be redressed first are those of the least well off people, beginning with restoration of the programs for poor people that have been disproportionately cut."[41] This is an important distinction, because it claims that those with the least should come first and those with the most should come last. Not only does this have an almost biblical ring to it, there is an inherent condemnation of capitalism as well, mirroring more a Marxist view wherein the poor (the proletariat) will eventually overcome the rich (the bourgeoisie).

Conclusion: The Underlying Message

Throughout this chapter, several perspectives of social justice have been presented and have demonstrated a variety of means by which social justice is important for the welfare of a society, in general, and how it applies to the fields of criminology, law enforcement, and penology, specifically. Going further, it is clear that the definition of social justice varies among cultures and regions. It goes without saying that cultural norms can influence the definition of social justice in a specific region of the world. For every new social justice theory, criticisms emerge. Even within the United States, the definition of social justice differs slightly among various groups of people. Approaches to social justice may also be relative to an individual's motives or to current social problems.

Justice itself is important; social justice is important because it allows for equality in property, power, opportunity, health, and education. While no single approach to social justice may be the shining example, each theoretical approach has some value in determining societal structure. What should be clear to the reader is that, in one way or another, social justice is about seeking fundamental fairness in a society so that all participants of that society share in and benefit from the protections and opportunities of that society. The specific definition of fairness, however, serves as a major challenge to being assured that justice is achieved.

In addition, the membership of a given community or society must have an adequate level of care or concern so as to translate into action. This is, to a large extent, required for the "social contract" between members of a society to be successful. Otherwise, there could be no mutual trust among members that other members will follow through on their own commitments in kind. A society without basic empathy becomes a group of self-absorbed individuals who shirk such responsibilities, thereby causing the implicitly understood social contract to unravel and fall apart.

Further, when addressing criminal justice issues, critical criminologists have made it clear that there are disparities in offender treatment. The means by which crime occurs are considered important, as are the means by which punishment is meted out. The importance is not just for the offender, but it is also important for the welfare of society. A heavy-handed and reactionary approach is, ironically, simply likely to make the crime problem worse. Thus, social justice approaches to all aspects of the criminal justice system (the police, the courts, and corrections) should be a theme that is not driven by economics but is instead driven by long-term strategies to eliminate the benefit of criminal behavior and provide prosocial opportunities for communities at risk.

Lastly, as we noted before, social justice is perhaps most appropriately expressed through better access to healthcare, education, and work opportunities in the United States, not additional squad cars, tough-on-crime legislation, or bigger prison facilities. The first approach is the mark of a successful civilization; the second is the approach of one that is failing. Thus, preventative agendas to crime are part and parcel to social justice. The more affluent, the more educated, and the better treated a population is, the less that criminal activity appears as a viable option in society.

To be clear, we do understand that regardless of what is done, some crime will likely exist no matter how "just" society becomes. Random crime that is irrational, impulsive, or due to mental illness will not be completely eradicated, but we assert that in a peace-oriented society where compassion, empathy, and social connection are emphasized, honored, and rewarded, even this type of crime can be reduced. There are examples of these types of society around the world, so this is not "pie-in-the-sky" thinking, as many critics would naturally claim. Rather, nations like Australia, Canada, Germany, Japan, and Sweden all have much lower crime rates than the United States and, at the same time, have higher life expectancy rates, are rated in the top 20 for educational systems, and have Human Development Index (HDI) scores that are either superior to or very close to the HDI of the United States; all are in the top 20 compared to the global community.[42] Thus, it can be done.

Discussion Questions

1. Identify and discuss the main tenets of the libertarian approach.
2. Explain how decisions are made from a utilitarian perspective.
3. Who was John Rawls and why was he important?
4. What common bond do both social justice and critical criminology share?
5. Should social justice focus primarily on equal economic distribution or should it be more encompassing, as the authors seem to imply? Explain your answer.

Notes

1. Adams, P. (2013). Practicing social justice: A virtue-based approach. *Social Work & Christianity*, *40*(3), 287–307.
2. Harvey, D. (1992). Social justice, postmodernism and the city. *International Journal of Urban and Regional Research*, *16*(1), 588–601.
3. *Ibid.*
4. Sheskin, M., & Baumard, N. (2016). Switching away from utilitarianism: The limited role of utility calculations in moral judgment. *PLoS One*, *11*(8), 1–14.
5. Otteson, J. R. (2017). The misuse of egalitarianism in society. *Independent Review*, *22*(1), 37–47.
6. Harris, J. W. (2002). Rights and resources-libertarians and the right to life. *Ratio Juris*, *15*(2), 109.
7. Bankston, I. L. (2010). Social justice: Cultural origins of a perspective and a theory. *Independent Review*, *15*(2), 165–178.
8. Adams, 2013.
9. Luco, A. (2014). The definition of morality: Threading the needle. *Social Theory & Practice*, *40*(3), 361–387.
10. Opotow, S. (2011). How this was possible: Interpreting the holocaust. *Journal of Social Issues*, *67*(1), 205–224.
11. *Ibid.*
12. Hanser, R. D., & Gomila, M. N. (2014). *Multiculturalism in the criminal justice system*. Upper Saddle River, NJ: Pearson Prentice Hall.
13. *Ibid.*
14. *Obergefell v. Hodges*, 135 S. Ct. 2584 (2015).
15. Robinson, M. (2010). Assessing criminal justice practice using social justice theory. *Social Justice Research*, *23*(1), 77–97.
16. *Ibid.*
17. Reiman, J., & Leighton, P. (2017). *The rich get richer and the poor get prison: Ideology, class, & criminal justice*, 11th ed. New York: Routledge, Taylor & Francis.
18. Greenberg, M. S., Block, M. W., & Silverman, M. A. (1971). Determinants of helping behavior: Person's rewards versus other's costs. *Journal of Personality*, *39*(1), 79–93.
19. Decety, J., & Yoder, K. J. (2016). Empathy and motivation for justice: Cognitive empathy and concern, but not emotional empathy, predict sensitivity to injustice for others. *Social Neuroscience*, *11*(1), 1–14.
20. *Ibid.*

21. Twenge, J. M. (2008). Generation me: The origins of birth cohort differences in personality traits, and cross-temporal meta-analysis. *Social and Personality Psychology Compass*, *2–3*, 1440–1454.

   Twenge, J. M., Konrath, S., Foster, J. D., Campbell, K. W., & Bushman, B. J. (2008). Further evidence of an increase in narcissism among college students. *Journal of Personality*, *76*(4), 919–927.

22. Konrath, S., O'Brien, E., & Hsing, C. (2010). Changes in dispositional empathy in American college students over time: A meta-analysis. *Personality and Social Psychology Review*, *15*(2), 180–198.

23. Zaki, J. (2011, January 1). What, me care? Young are less empathetic. *Scientific American Mind*. Retrieved from www.scientificamerican.com/article/what-me-care/

24. Postick, C. (2013). *The role of empathy in crime, policing, and justice*. Scholars Strategy Network. Retrieved September 19, 2017, from www.scholarsstrategynetwork.org/brief/role-empathy-crime-policing-and-justice

25. *Ibid.*, p. 1.

26. Arrigo, B. A. (2000). Social justice and critical criminology: On integrating knowledge. *Contemporary Justice Review*, *3*(1), 7–37.

   Postick, C., Rocque, M., & Rafter, N. (2012). More than a feeling: Integrating empathy into the study of lawmaking, lawbreaking, and reactions to lawbreaking. *International Journal of Offender Therapy and Comparative Criminology*, *58*(1), 5–26.

   Hanser, R. D., Gallagher, C. S., & Kuanliang, A. (2016). Citizen satisfaction with police: The effects of income level and prior victimization experiences on citizen perceptions of police. In J. Eterno & A. Verma (Eds.), *Global issues in contemporary policing* (pp. 177–202). New York: Taylor & Francis Group.

27. Hanser, R. D., & Mire, S. M. (2011). *Correctional counseling*. Upper Saddle River, NJ: Pearson Prentice Hall; Postick, Rocque, & Rafter, 2012.

28. Hanser, Gallagher, & Kuanliang, 2016; Postick, Rocque, & Rafter, 2012; Hanser, & Gomila, 2014.

29. Arrigo, 2000.

30. Arrigo, 2000; Van de Veer, D. (1973). Marx's view of justice. *Philosophy and Phenomenological Research*, *33*(3), 366–386. Retrieved from www.jstor.org/stable/2106949?seq=1#page_scan_tab_contents

31. Arrigo, 2000.

32. *Ibid.*

33. Bernard, T. J. (1981). Distinction between conflict and radical criminology. *Journal of Criminal Law and Criminology*, *72*(1), 362–379.

34. Arrigo, 2000.

35. Van Soest, D. (1994). Strange bedfellows: A call for reordering national priorities from three social justice perspectives. *Social Work*, *39*(6), 710–717.

36. *Ibid.*

37. *Ibid.*, p. 713.

38. *Ibid.*, p. 715

39. *Ibid.*

40. Van Soest, 1994; Dworkin, R. (1992). Hypothetical contracts and rights. In J. P. Sterba (Ed.), *Justice: Alternative political perspectives* (pp. 145–157). Belmont, CA: Wadsworth.

41. Van Soest, 1994, p. 715.

42. United Nations. (2017). *Human development report, 2016*. Vienna, Austria. Retrieved September 17, 2017, from http://hdr.undp.org/en/2016-report

4

CAN JUSTICE REINVESTMENT DELIVER SOCIAL JUSTICE?

Kevin Wong

Introduction: What Is Justice Reinvestment?

Since its origins in the seminal paper by Susan Tucker and Eric Cadora in 2003,[1] justice reinvestment (JR) has been advocated as a response to mass incarceration. It has become both an ideal and an approach to the delivery of a more socially just criminal justice system. Underpinning it is an explicit *economic argument*, centered on using data and evidence to make changes that will provide a better return for society than does the existing criminal justice system.

The term first appeared in Tucker and Cadora's article for *Open Society* in 2003.[2] It captured the imagination of prison reform advocates with a simple but compelling argument—it was better to redirect funds spent on prisons to rebuilding the human, social, and physical resources of neighborhoods affected by high levels of incarceration.

Tucker and Cadora's concept of JR was based on research by Cadora and others, which gave rise to the phrase that best captures the essence of JR, that of "million dollar blocks"; city blocks in Brooklyn where a million dollars was being spent on incarcerating residents.[3] As a response to mass incarceration and to those communities most affected by incarceration, by default, it offered a way of addressing the disproportionate representation within prison of people from "low income neighborhoods of color."[4]

Since then, as noted by some commentators, JR has come to mean different things to different people.[5] Therefore, it is worth considering Tucker and Cadora's original vision of JR in some detail. This will be covered in the next section. The rest of this chapter will examine the following:

- the extent to which this vision (for the purposes of this chapter), held up as the *social justice ideal*, has been achieved in three countries with relatively high levels of incarceration: the United States (U.S.), the United Kingdom (UK) and Australia;[6]
- how social justice generated through JR can be measured, drawing on learning primarily from the U.S. and UK; and finally
- the future of JR.

Justice Reinvestment and Social Justice

Tucker and Cadora's socially inclusive vision is projected through three key themes. First, an explicit call is made for prison funding to be redirected for non-criminal justice spending, specifically, to rebuild "the human resources and physical infrastructure—the schools, healthcare facilities, parks and public spaces—of neighbourhoods devastated by high levels of incarceration."[7] Second, emphasis is given to devolving accountability and responsibility to a local level, "seeking community level solutions to community level problems."[8] The third theme is a preventative approach to public safety that "targets money for programs in education, health, job creation, and job training in low income communities."[9] It also involves looking for preventative solutions outside the criminal justice system.

Looking beyond the U.S., the emphasis on community-focused, place-based initiatives has been championed enthusiastically by JR proponents in other countries. In the UK, Rob Allen, an early proponent of JR, argued that JR should "improve the prospects not just of individual cases but of particular places."[10] The argument for what in the UK is termed localism was further reinforced by the Commission on English Prisons Today[11] and the UK House of Commons Justice Committee.[12] In Australia, arguments have also been made for trialing JR in high-crime communities[13] and earlier by Brown, Schwartz, and Boseley as a mechanism for addressing the overimprisonment of indigenous people.[14]

As a mechanism for effecting prison reform, JR was intended to "depoliticise the issue of mass incarceration," which was acknowledged by Susan Tucker in an interview over a decade after the publication of the original paper.[15] It was acknowledged as an attractive feature by commentators such as Ross Homel, who described JR as intertwining the themes of "a rational social policy, the intelligent use of data on the geography and sociology of crime, the futility (and, implicitly the savagery) of imprisonment as a cure all for crime and safety problems."[16] Fox, Albertson, and Wong had also identified the potential for the economic underpinning of JR to transcend populist punitivism.[17] Thus, providing politicians and policymakers with a publicly acceptable justification for reducing prison populations, particularly in the wake of the economic crises of 2007 and 2008. This was noted by Brown, Schwartz, and Boseley as JR being "compatible with various tenets of neo-liberalism" in using economic incentives to change public policy.[18]

What has emerged in the last decade since Tucker and Cadora's social justice vision of JR is an approach to JR primarily, described as criminal justice system redesign[19] based on delivering efficiencies within the criminal justice system rather than alternatives outside the system.[20]

Justice Reinvestment in Practice

This section examines the differing trajectories of JR implementation in the U.S., UK, and Australia. It will assess, in broad terms, the extent to which implementation has followed a social justice or criminal justice system redesign model. These are not necessarily mutually exclusive and instead can be conceived of as two ends of a continuum, along which individual initiatives may be located.[21]

Justice Reinvestment in the U.S.

The implementation of JR in the U.S. has been both advanced and limited by the Justice Reinvestment Initiative (JRI), a federal program that has supported the development of JR in the U.S. It can be considered to be advanced, because the most extensive implementation of JR has occurred in the U.S. (compared to the UK and Australia), as a consequence of the funding provided by the Bureau of Justice Assistance to states and localities.[22] However, it can also be viewed as limited in relation to upholding the social justice principles of Tucker and Cadora,[23] because it has largely followed a criminal justice system redesign model. In their review of the JRI, Austin, Cadora, Clear, Dansky, Greene, Gupta, Mauer, Porter, Tucker, and Young commented that the JRI had abandoned the basic tenets of JR, specifically the commitment to place-based strategies and reinvestment of savings in communities with high incarceration rates.[24] This is not to say that what has been achieved by the JRI is not laudable. In a wry comment, Mark Mauer, interviewed by Brown and colleagues for their comprehensive review of JR for the book, observed that the article (referenced immediately above) that he contributed to should have been retitled "What you are doing is good . . . but don't call it Justice Reinvestment."[25]

In the U.S., JR has operated at both state and local levels.[26] At a state level, through preinvestment, funding has been provided for programs based on anticipated savings; postinvestment, actual savings have been reinvested and spending has been averted.[27] At a local level, pre- and postinvestment has been more limited.[28]

In their detailed analysis of JR implementation in the United States, Brown and colleagues discerned two parallel developments based on administrative and jurisdictional boundaries, with the "shape" of JR determined by whether this occurred at a state or local level.[29]

At a state level, they concluded that the model operated as a "political and legislative process to address over-incarceration in state controlled (and funded) prisons and is largely driven by the work of the CSG [Council for States Government]."[30]

This was based on the four-step "justice mapping" blueprint advocated by the Council for States Government. This requires (1) analyzing the prison population and public spending in the communities that prisoners return to, (2) examining the provision of options for generating savings and increases in public safety, (3) the quantification of savings and reinvestment in high-stakes communities, and finally (4) the measurement of impacts and evaluation of program effectiveness.[31]

However, as noted by some commentators by 2011, the four steps had narrowed to three.[32] The third step, the place-based strategy of reinvesting savings in communities with high rates of incarceration, had been removed; alongside an absence of analyzing public spending in the communities which prisoners returned to.[33]

As noted by Brown and colleagues, "What remains is a reform program centred on consensus-driven passage of legislation aimed at a reduction in corrections expenditure without jeopardising public safety."[34] The focus on the legislative component may have helped to make reform more durable and reduce the likelihood of punitive relapses;[35] however, arguably it has lost the key social justice component of reinvestment in high-incarceration communities.

This has not been lost on those at the forefront of promoting JR in the U.S. Marshall Clement, the director of CSG's Justice Center (interviewed for the book by Brown and colleagues), suggested that the structural challenges inherent in the criminal justice system made it difficult to move beyond these to consider a more community-based focus, added to which there was a lack of community development expertise.[36]

At a local level, the focus has been on individuals incarcerated in county jails, identified as being a generally low-risk, high-churn population that frequently recycled back into the criminal justice system.[37] Legislative action has not dominated these local initiatives; instead, more focus has been placed on working with stakeholders on the ground, at sites with a history of progressive criminal justice reform.[38] The opportunity for a more place-based, social justice oriented approach to JR may have been more possible. In practice, the potential for focusing on high-incarceration neighborhoods has not been realized, with attention given instead to countywide prison populations.[39]

It is worth noting three distinctive features about the development of JR in the U.S. compared to the UK and Australia. First, political bipartisanship and support are necessary to receive federal financial support.[40] Second, a shift in the political narrative about crime solutions from being "tough on crime" to being "smart on crime" was embraced across the political spectrum.[41] Third, the role of faith-based organizations, such as the Prison Fellowship, promote JR through a restorative approach to justice, articulated through a redemptive agenda—giving prisoners a "second chance" and being "smart on crime."[42]

Justice Reinvestment in the UK

By contrast, in the United Kingdom, despite the interest in JR by politicians and policymakers immediately after the financial crisis, there has been no overarching guiding force behind JR development, such as the JRI in the U.S.[43] Consequently, implementation has been fragmented and limited to a set of largely uncoordinated schemes, originating in different government departments—the Ministry of Justice (MoJ), Department of Health, and Department of Communities and Local Government.[44] In the main, JR in the UK has largely been diverted along a payment by results (PbR) route. Two explicit JR programs commissioned by the Ministry of Justice were the Youth Justice Custody Reinvestment Pathfinder and the Local Justice Reinvestment Pilot, both PbR pilots.[45]

However, taking a broader view of what constitutes JR, i.e., beyond the two pilot programs explicitly labeled as JR, Wong and Christmann identified other JR schemes in the UK.[46] These operated at different levels of administration—national, regional, and local, working to targets ranging from specified fiscal savings and reduction in reoffending to a basket of measures spanning the disparate spheres of employment, crime, child welfare, and mental and physical health.[47] This unplanned, mixed economy of development has arguably allowed for the testing of JR solutions both inside and outside of the criminal justice system. The most significant of these outside the justice system was and (at time of writing) remains the Troubled Families Programme that operated in 143 English local authorities.[48] However, this implicit JR initiative has been tainted by controversy.[49]

In the UK, while the disproportionality of black and minority ethnic individuals within prison and the criminal justice system (more generally) exists,[50] it has not been a significant feature of the discourse around JR in the UK.

While the capacity and capability to implement JR has been addressed in the U.S. through the funding of technical assistance as part of the JRI, in the UK, the issue of capacity and capability has been largely unconsidered.[51]

The redemptive agenda, a key feature of JR in the U.S., has so far played little role in the development of JR in the UK. It was given prominence in the announcements around prison reform by UK Prime Minister David Cameron in February 2016.[52] However, both the political interest in offering prisoners a "second chance" and the prison reforms have proved to be short-lived, kicked into the long grass by the political earthquake of the "Brexit" vote and subsequent and lasting diversion of political attention and effort to securing an exit from the European Union.[53]

Justice Reinvestment in Australia

In Australia, there was support for the Commonwealth adopting a leadership role in facilitating the implementation of JR across the country.[54] However, this did not materialize first because of political opposition to the leadership role and then a change of government.[55] Instead, developments have been driven at a community level.[56] In broad terms, of the three countries considered in this chapter, Australia has adhered most closely to the social justice principles outlined in Tucker and Cadora's original 2003 paper—in particular, the focus on place-based initiatives and explicit commitment to addressing the disproportionate representation of indigenous people in the criminal justice system.[57]

The actual implementation of JR has been less extensive in Australia than either the U.S. or UK, as noted by Brown and colleagues in their comprehensive examination of JR in the U.S., UK, and Australia.[58] Nevertheless, their review of JR implementation in Australia identified four themes which have marked out its development.

The first of these is the community involvement aspect of the Australian pilots. The most advanced of these in Bourke, New South Wales (NSW), is community led and seeks to address the overrepresentation of Aboriginal young people in custody.[59]

The second is the involvement of a number of nongovernmental organizations in individual states that have consistently advocated for JR and have been actively involved in developing pilots such as Just Reinvest in the Bourke pilot in NSW;[60] the Australian Red Cross involved in a community project in Wooribinda, Queensland;[61] and Smart Justice, campaigning for a youth justice reinvestment approach in the state of Victoria.[62]

The third is at a state level, with government and political support for JR, such as an election commitment from the New South Wales Labor party to invest $4 million in three JR pilots[63] and the Australian Capital Territory (ACT) government setting out a four-year justice reinvestment strategy from 2014 to 2018.[64]

The fourth and final theme are the academic projects that have developed to advocate for and inform community, state, and national developments around justice reinvestment. The most prominent of these projects are that of Brown and his colleagues—the Australian Justice Reinvestment Project—and a project to examine reinvestment options in Cowra NSW led by Dr. Gill Guthrie from the National Centre for Indigenous Studies at the Australia National University.[65]

Measuring the Impact of Justice Reinvestment on Social Justice

The extent to which social justice has been achieved through justice reinvestment has been examined by assessing the approaches adopted in the United States, United Kingdom, and Australia against the originating principles set out by Tucker and Cadora.[66] Inevitably, the development of JR across these three countries has been shaped by funding, capability, and political will. Arguably, adhering to the original social justice principles is not altogether simple. If anything, the experience thus far suggests that to achieve this requires a wider range of capabilities than is required to achieve a criminal justice redesign JR solution.[67]

As acknowledged by governmental bodies across all three countries[68] and JR commentators,[69] JR is "avowedly data-driven and evidence-based."[70] Therefore, the impact of JR in delivering social justice should be measurable. With some notable exceptions, however, Brown and colleagues concluded that "there has been limited critical analysis of what counts as evidence, the measures used and to whom they are applied."[71]

While this framework draws together the best of JR measurement available at the time, it is nevertheless limited by what has been developed and implemented thus far. In particular, given that to date JR implementation has done little to encompass and address the social determinants of crime,[72] the framework provides a starting point for measurement and would benefit from further refinement as JR itself develops.

Conclusion: The Future of Justice Reinvestment

JR implementation has the potential to develop in a way that approaches the social justice ideal set out by Tucker and Cadora.[73] The development of JR to date can be viewed as a journey moving from criminal justice system redesign models to a more social justice oriented iteration of JR. Reviewing what has been implemented thus far in the U.S., UK, and Australia, examples of place-based initiatives, solutions outside of the criminal justice system, and a focus on addressing racial disproportionality within the incarcerated populations specifically and within the criminal justice system more broadly can be found. Perhaps more encouragingly, the discourse and debate around shifting JR to that social justice ideal has not abated; if anything, it is being kept alive by policymakers, commentators, and researchers in the field.[74]

JR has the potential to develop as a specific response to vulnerable groups within the criminal justice system, such as women and girls, young people, young adults, and those with mental health problems.[75]

In the U.S., the JRI has taken JR implementation along the direction of efficiencies within the justice system, focused on back-end measures such as parole processing, post-release support, and dealing with probation and parole violations.[76] However, JR development at a local level (in the U.S.) demonstrates the potential of front-end options: addressing the characteristics of "frequent flyers", diverting offenders and improving case processing, and engaging agencies outside of the criminal justice system in identifying solutions.[77]

In the UK, formal devolution to the English regions and police and crime commissioners with responsibility for countywide areas, making good on the "and crime" part of their remit, may provide an opportunity for the development of a more localized JR response in the UK.[78]

In Australia, the community-led nature of JR development offers a template for bottom-up approaches in other jurisdictions and may be instructive in helping to shape the way in the which the social determinants of crime may be factored into a more sophisticated conceptualization and measurement of JR.[79]

Summary

The phrase justice reinvestment (JR) was used by Susan Tucker and Eric Cadora in a seminal paper published in 2003, which argued for tackling mass incarceration by diverting prison funds to rebuilding the human, social, and physical resources of neighborhoods affected by high levels of incarceration. This place-based approach was founded on the principles of using data and evidence to inform changes intended to create a more socially just criminal justice system. Since 2003, there has been support for this approach from prison reformers, politicians, policymakers, and academics in the United States, United Kingdom, and Australia.

The trajectory of JR implementation in these three countries has varied considerably. In the U.S., supported by the Bureau of Justice Assistance, JR has been driven by the Justice Reinvestment Initiative (JRI), which has led it down a criminal justice redesign approach, focusing on efficiencies within the criminal justice system. States have generally adopted a legislative route for JR based on preinvestment and postinvestment of resources. Localities have seen a wider engagement of stakeholders, including those outside the justice system, but JR has tended to focus on whole prison populations rather than high-incarceration neighborhoods.

In the UK, a mixed economy of JR implementation has been characterized by being commissioned through a payment by results process. Some JR initiatives have operated within a criminal justice system redesign approach, and others have aimed for solutions outside the justice system and reflected a social justice approach.

In Australia, implementation has been less extensive than in the U.S. and U.K.; however, the JR pilots and policy discourse here have adhered most closely to Tucker and Cadora's vision, with place-based initiatives targeting indigenous communities, which are overrepresented in the prison population.

The measurement of the impact of JR on social justice is nascent, with the approach proposed here based on the best practice to date but subject to refinement as JR implementation itself develops.

JR has the potential to contribute to creating a more socially just criminal justice system and by default a more socially just society. The future development of JR in the U.S., UK, and Australia offers the promise that this may be possible.

Discussion Questions

1. How did the original conception of justice reinvestment intend to deliver social justice?
2. How has justice reinvestment developed in different jurisdictions?
3. What have been the facilitators and barriers to justice reinvestment and why?
4. Has justice reinvestment achieved the goal of social justice?
5. How might justice reinvestment develop in the future?

Notes

1. Tucker, S., & Cadora, E. (2003). *Justice reinvestment: To invest in public safety by reallocating justice dollars to refinance education, housing, healthcare, and jobs [Monograph] Ideas for an Open Society*, 3. Retrieved March 2, 2016, from www.soros.org/publications/ideas-open-society-justice-reinvestment

2. *Ibid.*
3. *Ibid.*
4 Tucker & Cadora, 2003, p. 1.
5. Wong, K., Fox, C., & Albertson, K. (2014). Justice reinvestment in the United Kingdom in an age of auster-ity. *Victims and Offenders, 9*, 76–99, 201Copyright © Taylor & Francis Group, LLC; Fox, C., Albertson, K., & Wong, K. (2013). *Justice reinvestment: Can the criminal justice system deliver more for less?* London: Routledge; Brown, D., Schwartz, M., & Boseley, L. (2012). The promise of justice reinvestment. *Alternative Law Journal, 37*, 2.
6. Brown, D., Cunneen, C., Schwartz, M., Stubbs, J., & Young, C. (2016). *Justice reinvestment: Winding back imprisonment.* Basingstoke: Palgrave MacMillan.
7. Tucker & Cadora, 2003, p. 1.
8. *Ibid.*
9. *Ibid.*, p. 4.
10. Allen, R. (2007). From restorative prisons to justice reinvestment. In R. Allen & V. Stern (Eds.), *Justice reinvest-ment: A new approach to crime and justice* (p. 5). London: International Centre for Prison Studies.
11. Commission on English Prisons Today. (2009). *Do better, do less: The report of the commission on English prisons today.* London: Howard League for Penal Reform.
12. House of Commons Justice Committee. (2010). *Cutting crime: The case for justice reinvestment.* London: The Stationary Office Limited; House of Commons Justice Committee. (2014). *Crime reduction policies: A co-ordinated approach?* London: The Stationary Office Limited.
13. Australian Red Cross. (2016). *Re-thinking justice: Vulnerability report 2016.* Carlton: Australian Red Cross.
14. Brown, Schwartz, & Boseley, 2012.
15. In Brown, Cunneen, Schwartz, Stubbs, & Young, 2016, p. 19.
16. Homel, R. (2014). Justice reinvestment as a global phenomenon. *Victim and Offenders, 9*, 6. Taylor and Francis Group.
17. Fox, Albertson, & Wong, 2013.
18. Brown, Schwartz, & Boseley, 2012, p. 97.
19. Fox, Albertson, & Wong, 2013.
20. La Vigne, N. G., Neusteter, R. S., Lachman, P., Dwyer, A., & Nadeau, C. A. (2010). *Justice reinvestment at the local level, planning and implementation guide.* Washington: Urban Institute, Justice Policy Center; Lanning, T., Loader, I., & Muir, R. (2011). *Redesigning justice: Reducing crime through justice reinvestment.* London: Institute for Public Policy Research.
21. Wong, Fox, & Albertson, 2014; Fox, Albertson, & Wong, 2013.
22. Brown, Cunneen, Schwartz, Stubbs, & Young, 2016; Wong, K., & Christmann, K. (2016). *Justice reinvestment: "Motherhood and apple pie?": Matching ambition to capacity and capability,* Federal Sentencing Report Vol. 29. No 1, pp. 58–67.
23. Tucker & Cadora, 2003.
24. Austin, J., Cadora, E., Clear, T. R., Dansky, K., Greene, J., Gupta, V., Mauer, M., Potter, N., Tucker, S., & Young, M. C. (2013). *Ending mass incarceration: Charting a new justice reinvestment.* Sentencing Project.
25. Brown, Cunneen, Schwartz, Stubbs, & Young, 2016, p. 73.
26. La Vigne, N., Bieler, S., Cramer, L., Ho, H., Kotonias, C., Mayer, D., . . . Samuels, J. (2014). *Justice reinvestment initiative state assessment report.* Washington: Urban Institute, Justice Policy Center; Cramer, L., Harvell, S., McClure, D., Sankar-Bergmann, A., & Parks, E. (2014). *The justice reinvestment initiative: Experiences from the local sites.* Washington: Urban Institute, Justice Policy Center.
27. La Vigne et al., 2014.
28. Cramer et al., 2014.
29. Brown, Cunneen, Schwartz, Stubbs, & Young, 2016, p. 58.
30. *Ibid.*
31. Council of State Governments. (2010). *Justice reinvestment overview.* Retrieved November 2, 2012, from www.justicereinvestment.org/files/JR_overview_2010_rev.pdf
32. Brown, Cunneen, Schwartz, Stubbs, & Young, 2016; Austin et al., 2013.
33. Council of State Governments. (2011). *Justice reinvestment: About the project.* Retrieved from http://justice reinvestment.org/about
34. Brown, Cunneen, Schwartz, Stubbs, & Young, 2016, p. 74.
35. *Ibid.*
36. *Ibid.*, p. 74.
37. *Ibid.*
38. *Ibid.*
39. *Ibid.*

40. Bureau of Justice Assistance. (2015). Retrieved from www.bja.gov/programs/justicereinvestment/how_do_i_participate.html
41. Brown, Cunneen, Schwartz, Stubbs, & Young, 2016.
42. Greene, E. (2017). *Justice reform: Unlocking second chances and more.* Prison Fellowship. Retrieved August 28, 2017, from www.prisonfellowship.org/2017/03/justice-reform-unlocking-second-chances/
43. Allen, R. (2014). *Justice reinvestment: Empty slogan or sustainable future for penal policy?* London: Transform Justice; Allen, R. (2015). *Rehabilitation devolution: How localising justice can reduce crime and imprisonment.* London: Transform Justice Wong, & Christmann, 2016.
44. Wong, & Christmann, 2016.
45. Wong, Fox, & Albertson, 2014.
46. Wong, & Christmann, 2016.
47. *Ibid.*
48. This aimed to "turn around" the lives of "troubled families" characterized by worklessness, children not being in school, adult and children involved in crime and anti-social behavior, and poor mental and physical health. Department of Communities and Local Government. (2015). *The benefits of the troubled families programme to the taxpayer.* London: Department for Communities and Local Government.
49. As noted by Wong, & Christmann, 2016, while some UK JR initiatives have been explicitly labeled as JR interventions, others have had non-JR aims but in intent have had a JR focus.
50. Lammy, D. (2016). *Review of Racial Bias and BAME representation in the Criminal Justice System: A review to consider the treatment of, and outcomes for Black, Asian and Minority Ethnic (BAME) Individuals within the criminal justice system (CJS) in England and Wales.* Open letter to the UK Prime Minister.
51. Wong, & Christmann, 2016.
52. Cameron, D. (2016). *Speech on prison reform given at policy exchange.* Westminster, London. Retrieved May 30, 2016, from www.gov.uk/government/speeches/prison-reform-prime-ministers-speech
53. The Prison Reform Bill announced in the Queen's speech (which sets out the legislative agenda for the UK) in 2016 was omitted in the Queen's speech following the General Election in June 2017, with 8 of the 27 pieces of legislation related to Brexit (BBC 2017).
54. Senate Legal and Constitutional Affairs Committee. (2013). *Value of a justice reinvestment approach to criminal justice in Australia, Commonwealth of Australia.*
55. Brown, Cunneen, Schwartz, Stubbs, & Young, 2016.
56. *Ibid.*
57. Brown, Schwartz, & Boseley, 2012; Brown, Cunneen, Schwartz, Stubbs, & Young, 2016; Australian Red Cross, 2016.
58. Brown, Cunneen, Schwartz, Stubbs, & Young, 2016.
59. Just Reinvest. (2017). *Justice reinvestment in Bourke.* Retrieved August 31, 2017, from www.justreinvest.org.au/justice-reinvestment-in-bourke/
60. *Ibid.*
61. Australian Red Cross, 2016.
62. Smart Justice. *What is the justice reinvestment project?* Retrieved August 28, 2017, from www.smartjustice.org.au/cb_pages/justicereinvestment_sjfyp.php
63. The Guardian. (2015). Indigenous issues largely ignored in NSW election campaign, say community. Retrieved August 27, 2017, from www.theguardian.com/australia-news/2015/mar/25/indigenous-issues-largely-ignored-in-nsw-election-campaign-say-community
64. Australian Capital Territory Justice Reinvestment Strategy. Retrieved August 27, 2017, from www.justice.act.gov.au/page/view/3829/title/justice-reinvestment-strategy
65. Brown, Cunneen, Schwartz, Stubbs, & Young, 2016.
66. Tucker & Cadora, 2003.
67. Brown, Cunneen, Schwartz, Stubbs, & Young, 2016; Wong, & Christmann, 2016; Wong, Fox, & Albertson, 2014.
68. Council of States Government, 2010; House of Commons Justice Committee, 2010; Senate Legal and Constitutional Committee, 2013.
69. Allen, 2014; Fox, Albertson, & Wong, 2013; Clear, T. (2010). Policy and evidence: The challenge to the American society of criminology: 2009 presidential address to the American society of criminology. *Criminology, 48*(1), 1–25.
70. Brown, Cunneen, Schwartz, Stubbs, & Young, 2016, p. 141.
71. *Ibid.*, p. 143.
72. Fox, Albertson, & Wong, 2013, Brown, Cunneen, Schwartz, Stubbs, & Young, 2016.
73. Tucker & Cadora, 2003.

74. Brown, Cunneen, Schwartz, Stubbs, & Young, 2016; Austin et al., 2013; Cadora, E. (2014). Civic lessons: How certain schemes to end mass incarceration can fail. *The Annals of the American Academy of Political and Social Science, 651*(6), 277–285.
75. Brown, Cunneen, Schwartz, Stubbs, & Young, 2016; Allen, 2014, 2015; Wong, & Christmann, 2016; Wong, Fox, & Albertson, 2014.
76. Austin, J. (2011). Making imprisonment Unprofitable. *Criminology and Public Policy, 10*(3), 629–635.
77. Lachman, P., & Neusteter, S. R. (2012). *Tracking costs and savings through Justice Reinvestment at the Local Level Brief 1*. Washington, DC: Urban Institute.
78. Fox, C. (2017). *Justice devolution: An opportunity for Greater Manchester*. Metropolis: Manchester Metropolitan University; Wong, & Christmann, 2016; Allen 2015 Supra note 43.
79. Brown, Cunneen, Schwartz, Stubbs, & Young, 2016.

PART II

Justice in Specific Situations

5

EQUAL PAY, THE WAGE GAP, AND SEXUAL HARASSMENT

Shelly Clevenger and Brittany Acquaviva

Introduction

The difference in pay between individuals based on gender and/or race or ethnicity, with Caucasian men making the most money, is commonly referred to as the wage gap. Many factors relating to one's gender and race influence the wage gap in the United States. To address this issue, there have been initiatives in the form of legislation, with the intent to create more equal opportunities in terms of employment and better pay for women and minorities. But these pieces of legislation, while creating chances for individuals to be successful and work in fields and positions that previously they may not have the ability to, has also increased problems for women and minorities in the form of harassment, including sexual harassment. So while more opportunities and protections are in place for advancement, there is also the danger for women to experience harassment in the workplace.

This chapter will provide an overview of the wage gap, including some of the potential causal factors that lead to why this is occurring. This chapter will also address legislation that has been passed to assist women and minorities in gaining more equal opportunities and protections in education and the workplace. Finally, an overview of sexual harassment will be offered, with specific focus on the criminal justice system.

The Existence of the Wage Gap

Employee discrimination occurs when an individual is denied employment and/or access to higher-paying jobs due to demographic characteristics. Legislation has been implemented to protect specific groups of individuals who have historically been discriminated against. The existence of the wage gap is contingent on the presence of discrimination over a multitude of occupations. Even with multiple laws prohibiting discrimination and promoting equality with employment, a gap in pay is still seen between men and women, as well as between races. In 2015, the median full-time income for women was $40,742 compared to men's median full-time income reported at $51,212, representing women earning 79 cents for every dollar that a man earns.[1]

In 2016, the U.S. Department of Labor reported that between ages 16–65, men earned more than women across all age groups.[2] The closest equal weekly full-time median income between men and women was during the ages of 16–24 and then again during the ages 25–34.[3] The biggest wage gap between men and women was present during the ages 55–64, where women's weekly median full-time income was 26% less than men's.[4]

Women, in general, receive less than their male counterparts do. However, women with children receive even lower wages than women who do not have children.[5] Although the United States has made strides with legislation focusing on promoting equality among employment opportunities, they lack internationally compared to other industrialized countries in regards to addressing problems that are present with employees, specifically women involving children.[6] Women with children earned less than women who did not, with a 10–15% difference in their wages.[7] Examining and taking into account situational factors that may influence earning potential, such as career choice, work experience, and education, the wage gap still prevailed. Men with children also experience wage differences. Married men who have children earn more than men without children.[8]

The wage gap is a problem between genders; however, a large gap also exists in wages based on race. In 2017, the U.S. Bureau of Labor statistics published the quarterly earnings for all individuals who were employed. It was reported that all women fell victim to the wage gap regardless of race or ethnicity. However, when comparing gender to each race and ethnic background, the wage gap between men and women continued to exist within races and ethnicities. White women earn 15.9% less than white men, African American women earned 3.7% less than African American men, Asian women earned 25.8% less than Asian men, and Hispanic women earned 10.8% less than Hispanic men in the second quarter of 2017.[9] Men who identified their race as Asian earned $512 per week in the second quarter of 2017, making them the highest median weekly full-time paid race.[10] Hispanics were the lowest paid race, with women making $250 per week and their male counterparts making $280. Hispanic men and women earned less than did both genders of Asian and Caucasian ethnicity and less than African American men. African American men and women came in as the second lowest earning full-time median income. According to the U.S. Bureau of Labor Statistics, African American men made $287 a week and women made $276.[11] Although the gender wage gap within the African American race is the smallest compared to all the other races, they still earn less than Caucasians and Asians within the workforce.

Legislature Protecting Equality for Women

The fight for gender pay equality was particularly strong in the 1980s due to the increasing number of women receiving higher education and entering the labor force.[12] In particular, the increase was seen specifically among mothers who once had to stay at home with children but now were entering the workforce. The high number of women working had never been seen in the nation's history, which influenced legislation being passed to protect women in the workplace. This decade of legislature laid the foundation for women in the labor force as the beginnings of protecting women's right for equality. Executive Order 11246, Title VII of the Civil Rights Act of 1964, Title IX of the Education Amendments of 1972, the Pregnancy Discrimination Act of 1978, and the Family Medical Leave Act of 1993 all contributed to better working conditions and expanded the number of opportunities for higher earnings for women. With amendments protecting women and creating opportunities for women, more mothers were seen to be entering the workforce.[13]

Executive Order 11246

Executive Order 11246, signed by President Lyndon B. Johnson on September 24, 1965, mandates federal contractors and subcontractors who perform $10,000 in government-issued business to follow regulations regarding discrimination. Specifically, this order prohibits any form of discrimination against its employees involving race, color, religion, sex, national origin, and ethnicity. Executive Order 11246 also ensures positive employment opportunities for all who are qualified. Later amendments to this order prohibited discrimination against an individual's sexual orientation and/or gender identity as well.[14] Executive Order 11246 also permits employees to freely discuss and share information pertaining to their pay or the pay of coworkers,[15] which allows women and men to discuss their salaries or weekly wages if they wish to. This amendment was particularly important as it made it permissible for a topic that was once not talked about in the workplace to be freely communicated among employees. This led to women's realization that they were being paid significantly less than their male counterparts were.

Title VII of the Civil Rights Act of 1964

According to the U.S. Department of Labor, Title VII prohibits any discrimination during the firing, promotion, discharge, pay, infringement on benefits, job training, classification, and/or referral process across all national companies.[16] This also prohibits an individual's race, ethnicity, color, religion, sex, and/or national origin to infringe on any possible employment opportunities in the future. Title VII of the Civil Rights Act of 1964 was part of the women's rights movement that placed a heavy emphasis on equal employment opportunities, as well as equal pay for the same jobs shared by men and women. Title VII was also the first and most comprehensive legislation to aid disadvantaged minorities.[17] In order to oversee compliance, the Equal Employment Opportunity Commission was established with five members comprising the agency.[18]

Title IX of the Education Amendment of 1972

Although Title IX mainly applies to equal opportunities for education, the amendment also applies to financial assistance offered to students. Title IX requires the disbursement of federal financial assistance to be a neutral process, in which decisions are not based on a student's race, color, sex, and/or national origin.[19] This is important, as an individual's educational status plays a role in the amount they are able to earn weekly or annually. Title IX of the education amendment of 1972 allows for all individuals, no matter their sex or race, to be able to apply for financial assistance, giving the opportunity to achieve post-secondary education. With Title IX, more females and minorities are able to obtain an education, which makes them able to acquire higher-paying employment and professional jobs. Title IX of the Education Amendment of 1972 also prohibits any educational facilities, as well as any activities or programs held at these institutions that receive federal financial assistance, from denying job opportunities to individuals based on their sex.[20] In other words, jobs that men already occupied were opened up to women within the educational field or at educational facilities. As more women entered the workforce in the 1980s, Title IX of the Education Amendment of 1972 allowed for the demand for jobs suitable for women to be met without worry of hiring discrimination.

The Pregnancy Discrimination Act of 1978

The Pregnancy Discrimination Act of 1978 is an amendment to Title VII of the Civil Rights Act of 1964.[21] This was added to the Title VII Act under the prohibition of discrimination based on a person's sex. The amendment created a subsection under the Title VII of the Civil Rights Act that clarified sexual discrimination, declaring that the denial of employment based on a women's pregnancy status was prohibited. It also made it unlawful for employers to ask about a woman's plans to have children in the future. The Pregnancy Discrimination Act of 1978 allowed women to demand equal employment opportunities as well as mutual treatment in the workforce and the ability to bear children without being fired from their job.[22] This amendment allowed women the same opportunities to gain access to a career even though they were pregnant or may become pregnant in the future. This was a legislative attempt to keep women employed no matter their pregnancy status or their plans to conceive, which have both been seen to be factors that contribute to the wage gap in America.

Although this act protects pregnant women, the stress and responsibilities of having a child are still seen as tertiary reasons contributing to the wage gap. Women are at a greater likelihood of accepting a pay reduction or leaving paid work to care for their children, which then sequentially adds to the existing wage gap between men and women.[23]

Family Medical Leave Act of 1993

Although the Pregnancy Discrimination Act of 1978 was a initially created to protect women, it was not until 1993 that the Family Medical Leave Act (FMLA) was passed to protect individuals from being fired from their jobs when the following occurs: the birth of a child, giving a child up for adoption, caring for a close family member (spouse, son, daughter, or parent) who has a serious health condition, and if the employees own health deems the employee unable to perform the essential functions of their job.[24] Much research has shown that women are more likely than men to attend to a range of sick family members, which can push women out of the workforce to fulfill their caregiver duty.[25] There is also research showing that African Americans are more likely than Caucasians to highly value their family ties, and therefore within their culture they are expected to take care of their elderly family members, which pushes them out of the workforce as well.[26]

Women and minorities are underrepresented in the workforce, and additional cultural roles place them at a disadvantage in achieving and maintaining high-wage occupations, even with the assistance of the Family Medical Leave Act of 1993. A factor that directly plays into the wage gap among women and minorities within this specific legislation are the requirements that grant an employee eligibility for FMLA. In order for an employee to receive benefits granted by FMLA, they need to be employed for at least 12 months and during this time have worked at least 1,250 hours, and work in a location where the employer has at least 50 employees within 75.[27] Individuals, specifically women and minorities, who may have just started a job and do not meet these requirements, would not be able to take a leave for one of the approved events by the U.S. Department of Labor without the risk of being let go by their employer.

Factors Contributing to the Wage Gap

While protections have been put in place under the law, there still remains a wage gap today. Factors such as an individual's educational attainment, the jobs that certain genders and races perform, and gender negotiation differences were found to play a significant role in what individuals earned and contribute to the current wage gap.

Educational Attainment

According to the U.S. Bureau of Labor Statistics, an individual's earning potential depends heavily on their education, regardless of gender.[28] With limited education comes a block in occupational opportunities. In 2015, women who receive their bachelor's degree earned 2.5 times more than women who had not completed high school.[29] Women are more likely to obtain educational qualifications such as diplomas and certificates at every level of education then men are.[30] However, in 2015 it was reported that women who had achieved their associate degree or had some college education still earned less than men who only had graduated from high school.[31] While higher educational attainment is associated with an increase in earning potential for women, it does not significantly alter the earning differences between races. African American and Hispanic women had the lowest weekly full-time median wages and earned the lowest at each educational success level (graduating high school, bachelor's degree, master's degree, or doctoral degree) compared to Asian and Caucasian women.[32]

Occupation

To explain the reasons for the wage gap, the Department of Labor examined occupations that men and women commonly possess. In almost every occupation examined, men's weekly median full-time income was higher than women's. More specifically, in 29 out of the 30 "women-dominated" occupations, men still reported earning more than women. For example, in 2015, two common occupations for women were financial manager and office clerk.[33] Women earned 34.8% less than their male counterparts did in the financial manager occupation, and for the office clerk occupation women were paid 2.1% more than men. The reasoning given for this was that both genders were underpaid for the position.[34] The median weekly income for full-time work in 2015 was listed at $809; in the office clerk occupation women earned $622 and men earned $609 per week.

In 2015, the two highest paying "women-dominated" occupations were chief executives and pharmacists, where women made up over half of all full-time pharmacists and about 30% of full-time chief executives.[35] Three out of the ten occupations that women earned the most in, however, were considered "nontraditional" jobs for women, meaning women made up less than 25% of all workers in that specific occupation. Asian women were more likely to obtain post-secondary education than women of any other race, as well as use their higher education to work in jobs such as STEM and managerial occupations.[36] Both STEM and managerial occupations fall under the list of highest paying "nontraditional occupations" for women. Asian women earn more than women of any other race because they not only obtain more education, but also as work in mathematical and engineering-based jobs.

Gender Negotiation Differences

The last factor that has been linked to gender wage differences is salary negotiation behaviors. Research suggests that the differences found between men and women in the negotiation of starting salary as well as salary growth have crucial effects on the gender wage gap.[37] Women are less likely than men to try to negotiate for a higher salary. When women do try to negotiate their salaries aggressively, they are often viewed negatively by their management, whereas men do not receive the same stigma.[38]

Recent State Responses to the Wage Gap

The year 2016 was groundbreaking for changes in equal pay laws.[39] Although federal and state statutes already existed to prohibit gender pay discrimination amendments, four states, California, New York, Massachusetts, and Maryland, enacted laws to try to narrow the gap.

California was able to restructure their standards for equal pay with the addition of their Fair Pay Act, which expanded their pay equality laws in three ways. The Fair Pat Act added to the already existing labor laws while cracking down and ensuring quality in three major areas. First, California added the ability for employees to compare their pay, no matter their location.[40] This allows employees the ability to talk and compare pay regardless of whether they are located at the same establishment. Second, employees can now be compared based on responsibility. The expanded law allows for comparing employee wages, even if they do not hold the same job title, as long as they show "substantially similar work, are composed of skill, efforts, responsibility, and work under similar working conditions."[41] Finally, the last amendment to California's Fair Pay Act requires employers to justify and explain wage differences. Reasons that are seen as acceptable for wage differences includes a seniority system and/or a merit system, quantity and/or quality of production of an individual, and factors such as skills, education, training, experience, shift time, and geography.[42]

Much like California's amendments on equal pay, New York made similar requirements to their equal pay laws. California employees are able to compare salaries with employees of other establishments, and New York adopted this as well. New York's law requires employees to be located within the same geographical region and limits employees to being within the same county.[43] This opens up a large area for employees to discuss wages and be able to obtain equality within pay. Another amendment New York added was the requirement for employers to justify differential pay among their employees, similar to California.

In 2016, Massachusetts became the first state to prohibit employers' requests for applicants' compensation history during the hiring process, unless it is voluntarily disclosed by the applicant.[44] This law requires the revision of many occupations' hiring processes, as well as recruitment processes, to allow every applicant an equal opportunity regardless of past compensation. This legislation also prohibits the employer's discouragement of employee disclosure and/or discussion involving their wages, allowing for wage differences between men and women as well as minorities to be discussed openly among employees.

Maryland's Equal Work Act strengthened the protection of equal pay among all individuals as well as specifically prohibiting employers from giving favorable employment opportunities to individuals based on their sex or gender identity.[45] This law prohibits employers from placing employees in less favored career tracks or positions, failing to provide information on promotions/advancements, and limiting employment opportunities.[46] Maryland's amendments can be seen as a movement to protect the LGBTQ community in regards to prohibiting individual discrimination based on gender identity.

Sexual Harassment

Introduction

The inequality of pay in the workforce can lead to women feeling less valued and inadequate at work. However, this is not the only obstacle or struggle that women face. Women also are more prone to suffer from sexual harassment in the workplace than men are. Sexual harassment relates to stereotypes regarding gender and the overall historical oppression of women. In most occurrences of sexual harassment, men are the individuals perpetrating the crime and women are at the receiving end as the victims.[47,48] Sexual harassment is also a worldwide problem, affecting women all over the globe.[49,50] Sexual harassment, while often thought of as happening to women in the streets or other public open spaces,[51] also occurs in schools, universities,[52] workplaces,[53] public transportation,[54] shopping malls,[55] and restaurants.[56] It is a problem that does not have a specific location, but rather is a challenge that women face everywhere in their daily existence.

Sexual harassment is a particular issue for women working in the criminal justice system. Women working in male-dominated areas, such as the criminal justice system, often experience sexual harassment from colleagues and superiors, as well as subordinates.[57] Women working in academia as faculty and instructors within the discipline of criminal justice also may experience sexual harassment from male colleagues.[58] Sexual harassment is an issue for women in all areas of work and life, but often presents more of a challenge for women in criminal justice, as they are working in a system that is masculine in nature and they regularly find themselves the gender minority.

Defining Sexual Harassment

Sexual harassment was first defined by the U.S. Equal Employment Opportunity Commission (EEOC) in 1980 as follows:

> Unwelcome sexual advances, requests for sexual favors, and other verbal or physical conduct of a sexual nature constitute sexual harassment when this conduct explicitly or implicitly affects an individual's employment, unreasonably interferes with an individual's work performance, or creates an intimidating, hostile, or offensive work environment.
>
> *(EEOC, 1980, p. 74677)*

More recently, in 2017, the EEOC defined harassment as "unwelcome conduct that is based on race, color, religion, sex (including pregnancy), national origin, age (40 or older), disability or genetic information." The EEOC denotes that sexual harassment includes unwelcome sexual advances, verbal or physical harassment that is sexual in nature, requests for sex favors, and making offensive comments about a person's sex. Harassment is illegal and considered a form of employment discrimination under Title VII of the Civil Rights Act of 1964, the Age Discrimination in Employment Act of 1967 and the Americans with Disabilities Act of 1990. In order for acts of harassment to be considered illegal, the acts must be serious and frequent enough to create a hostile and/or offensive work environment and/or resulting in issues with the person's employment, such as being fired or receiving a demotion in their position.

Scholars have also worked to define sexual harassment. Till provides one of the earlier examinations of what constitutes sexual harassment by outlining five forms that it can take.[59] First, Till argues that there is gender harassment, which is belittling someone based on their sex. Second, sexual seduction is unwanted sexual attention by an aggressor.[60] Sexual bribery, as well as sexual coercion, involves quid pro quo, in which the perpetrator may be threatening the victim or offering benefits in exchange for sexual favors. Finally, sexual imposition involves assault and other acts that would be criminal and punished by law. The Sexual Experiences Questionnaire (SEQ) found that behaviors from others, such as unwanted sexual attention, sexually suggestive comments made to or about an individual, and/or inappropriate touching were considered sexual harassment.[61] Fitzgerald, Swan, and Magley define sexual harassment in terms of unwanted behavior in the workplace that is sexual in nature and is interpreted by the recipient as offensive and threatening.[62]

Prevalence

The EEOC and Fair Employment Practice Agency (FEPA) report that there were 11,364 reports of sexual harassment for 2011 (the most current year listed on the site), with 16% coming from men and 84% coming from women.

Most incidents of sexual harassment go unreported. A reason for this may be that individuals who experience sexual harassment do not label their experience as this, with research estimates that fewer than 20% of individuals who experience sexual harassment actually label it as such.[63] However, those that do label it as sexual harassment may not file an official claim reporting the offense. Research estimates that less than 25% of women file a formal complaint.[64,65,66,67] This has been found to be the case even in situations in which a crime was committed. Research that examined workplace rape found that of women who experienced an attempted or completed rape, only 21% filed an official report and only 19% quit their job afterwards.[68] Individuals who are victims of sexual harassment may not report because they believe that nothing will be done to the individual to improve the situation and that reporting it actually may make things worse.[69]

Impact of Sexual Harassment

Sexual harassment can have a devastating effect on its victims, especially women, who may not feel valued in a job because they make less pay than their male counterparts do. Sexual harassment can impact overall job satisfaction,[70] as well the commitment that an employee has to the organization and their overall job performance and productivity.[71] It can also have an impact on the psychological functioning and mental health of an individual, with effects such as low self-esteem, self-blame, alcohol use, eating disorders, increased prescription drug use, depression, anger, and chronic health issues.[72] The longer and more severe the harassment, the greater influence the harassment has on the individual.[73]

Sexual Harassment Within the Criminal Justice System

Sexual harassment is an issue for women in many occupations; however, those working within the criminal justice system often face unique challenges due to the nature of the work and the fact that most of the agencies within the system, particularly law enforcement and corrections, are male dominated. Research that has examined the sexual harassment of women working in law enforcement has revealed different ranges of prevalence and experiences. One study found that 24% of policewomen reported that they constantly experience offensive remarks,[74] and 100% of policewomen in another study reported that they have experienced at least one incident of sexual harassment within their career.[75] Other research has indicated that there is a range that falls between 53% and 77% of policewomen experiencing sexual harassment on the job.[76] Research that surveyed 1,269 policewomen found that 61% had experienced at least one form of sexual harassment within the last six months, but that only 23% formally complained to someone in their agency and 15% formally complained outside the agency. Women working in law enforcement, which is a nontraditional field for women, most often face gender harassment, without the intent and purpose of extorting sexual activity or experiencing sexual behaviors from the offender, such as quid pro quo harassment experienced by women in other professions, and were also more likely to experience harassment by a coworker.[77]

Similar experiences have been reported for women who work in the correctional field. Women working in corrections often face sexual harassment and issues with negative perceptions by coworkers and supervisors.[78,79] Women who experienced sexual harassment in corrections did not typically report it. In one study, women interviewed who worked in correctional institutions indicated that if they had reported or said something to their male colleague, they do not think that they would have been promoted. In order to keep their jobs and work towards advancing their careers, they said nothing.[80]

Summary

The legislation that has been passed regarding employment equality has provided opportunities for women to attain better paying and higher status positions. However, America has remained rather stagnant in ensuring equality among employees. Women and minorities still do not earn the same as Caucasian men. While states have recently begun to implement their own regulations for equality, such as California, New York, Massachusetts, and Maryland in 2016, there is still a wage gap. Educational attainment is a major determinant of how financially successful an individual can become. However, even with equal educational attainment between the genders or among the races, different negotiating tactics often put women and minorities at a disadvantage when negotiating for a higher salary. Women and minorities often have different family obligations and roles that may put them at a disadvantage to be able to excel in their occupation, and working in "women-dominated" positions makes it harder to bridge the wage gap. Arguably, the movement for federal legislation that mandates all states to follow the same requirements involving equal paying positions and opportunities for all individuals will be the only solution to eliminate the wage gap. Currently, this has been a push from many special interest organizations, as well as communities across the United States. Many are fighting for a piece of federal legislation that would ratify equal pay under the law regardless of gender. The recent initiatives of the states to ensure more equality under the law is a start.

Sexual harassment that women face in their daily lives, particularly at the workplace, can be seen as proof that even as women work to achieve equality in terms of positions in employment, they are not seen as equal by their male coworkers. Harassment based on gender stereotypes that are often used to belittle or undermine the work and status of women is not acceptable and does not assist women in feeling valued at work. Also, the fact that some instances of sexual harassment involve males trying to extort sex or sexual favors in return for preferential treatment or perks at work also demeans women.

Since more women have entered the workforce, they have had to fight to be seen as competent, intelligent, and good as a man at work. This is particularly an issue for women who work in male-dominated fields, such as the criminal justice system. The presence of sexual harassment makes this goal even harder, and coupled with the fact that women earn less per dollar than men do sends the message to women that they are not as valuable as the men who occupy the same roles. The passing of a federal-level Equal Pay Amendment, establishing that all persons, regardless of sex, race, and/or ethnicity make the same wage is needed to assist women in feeling valued and could potentially curb sexual harassment of females at work.

Discussion Questions

1. What is your opinion about the legislation that has been passed to help ensure equality? Do you think that they will create more equal opportunities? Please explain.
2. Which piece of legislation do you think has been the most successful? Why?
3. Do you think that a federal equal pay amendment will ever be passed? Why or why not?
4. What are some ways that we could work to reduce or prevent sexual harassment?

Notes

1. U.S. Department of Labor: Women's Bureau. *Women's earnings and the wage gap.* Issue Brief. Retrieved August 28, 2017, from www.dol.gov/wb/resources/Womens_Earnings_and_the_Wage_Gap_17.pdf
2. Bureau of Labor Statistics, U.S. Department of Labor. *Economics daily, women's and men's earnings by age in 2016.* Retrieved August 28, 2017 from www.bls.gov/opub/ted/2017/womens-and-mens-earnings-by-age-in-2016.htm
3. *Ibid.*
4. *Ibid.*
5. Waldfogel, J. (1998). Understanding the "family gap" in pay for women with children. *The Journal of Economic Perspectives, 12*(1), 137–156.
6. *Ibid.*
7. *Ibid.*
8. *Ibid.*
9. U.S. Bureau of Labor Statistics. *Usual weekly earnings of wage and salary wages second quarter 2017.* Retrieved August 30, 2017 from www.bls.gov/news.release/pdf/wkyeng.pdf
10. *Ibid.*
11. *Ibid.*
12. U.S. Department of Labor: Women's Bureau. *Women's earnings and the wage gap.*
13. *Ibid.*
14. U.S. Department of Labor. *Federal employment compliance programs (OFCCP).* Executive Order 11246. Retrieved August 29, 2017, from www.dol.gov/ofccp/regs/compliance/ca_11246.htm
15. *Ibid.*
16. U.S. Department of Labor. *Equal employment opportunity.* Ethnic/National Origin. Retrieved August 29, 2017, from www.dol.gov/general/topic/discrimination/ethnicdisc
17. Miller, Jr., R., S. (1966). Sex discrimination and title VII of the Civil Rights Act of 1964. *Minnesota Law Review, 51*(5), 877–898.
18. *Ibid.*
19. U.S. Department of Labor. *Equal employment opportunity.* Ethnic/National Origin.
20. U.S. Department of Labor. *Equal employment opportunity.* Federal Financial Assistance Programs. Retrieved August 29, 2017, from www.dol.gov/general/topic/discrimination/fedfinanassdisc
21. Siegel, R. B. (1985). Employment equality under the Pregnancy Discrimination Act of 1978. *The Yale Law Journal, 94*(4), 929–956.
22. *Ibid.*
23. U.S. Department of Labor: Women's Bureau. *Women's earnings and the wage gap.*
24. U.S. Department of Labor. (2012). *Wage and hour division.* The Family and Medical Leave Act. Retrieved August 29, 2017, from www.dol.gov/whd/regs/compliance/whdfs28.htm
25. Brody, E. M. (1990). *Women in the middle: Their parent care years.* New York: Springer.

26. Collins, P. H. (1994). Shifting the center: Race, class, and feminist theorizing about motherhood. In E. N. Glenn, G. Chang, & L. R. Forcey (Eds.), *Mothering: Ideology, experience and agency*. New York: Routledge.

27. U.S. Department of Labor. (2012). *Wage and hour division*.

28. Bureau of Labor Statistics. *U.S. Department of Labor, The Economics Daily, Median weekly earnings by educational attainment in 2014*. Retrieved August 31, 2017, from www.bls.gov/opub/ted/2015/median-weekly-earnings-by-education-gender-race-and-ethnicity-in-2014.htm

29. U.S. Department of Labor: Women's Bureau. *Women's earnings and the wage gap*.

30. *Ibid.*

31. *Ibid.*

32. *Ibid.*

33. U.S. Bureau of Labor Statistics. *Usual weekly earnings of wage and salary wages second quarter 2017*.

34. U.S. Department of Labor: Women's Bureau. *Women's earnings and the wage gap*.

35. U.S. Bureau of Labor Statistics. (2015). *U.S. Bureau of Labor Statistics, current population survey, 2015 annual averages*. Retrieved September 1, 2017, from https://www.bls.gov/opub/reports/womens-earnings/2015/pdf/home.pdf

36. *Ibid.*

37. Leibbrandt, A., & List, J. A. (2014). Do women avoid salary negotiations? Evidence from a large-scale natural field experiment. *Management Science, 61*(9), 2016–2024.

38. Bowles, H. R., Babcock, L., & Lai, L. (2007). Social incentives for gender differences in the propensity to initiate negotiations: Sometimes it does hurt to ask. *Organizational Behavior and Human Decision Processes, 103*(1), 84–103.

39. Seyfarth Shaw Pay Equity Group. (2016). *The new U.S. pay equality laws: Answering the biggest questions*. Retrieved September 1, 2017, from www.seyfarth.com/dir_docs/publications/PayEquityBrochure.pdf

40. *Ibid.*

41. *Ibid.*

42. *Ibid.*

43. *Ibid.*

44. *Ibid.*

45. *Ibid.*

46. *Ibid.*

47. Herzog, S. (2007). Public perceptions of sexual harassment: An empirical analysis in Israel from consensus and feminist theoretical perspectives. *Sex Roles, 57*, 579–592.

48. Macmillan, R., Nierobisz, A., & Welsh, S. (2000). Experiencing the streets: Harassment and perceptions of safety among women. *Journal of Research in Crime and Delinquency, 37*, 306–322.

49. Lahsaeizadeh, A., & Yousefinejad, E. (2012). Social aspects of women's experiences of sexual harassment in public places in Iran. *Sexuality and Culture, 16*, 17–37.

50. Lenton, R. L., Smith, M. D., Fox, J., & Morra, N. (1999). Sexual harassment in public places: Experiences of Canadian women. *The Canadian Review of Sociology and Anthropology, 36*, 517–540.

51. Madan, M., & Manesh, K. (2016). Sexual harassment in public spaces: Examining gender differences in perceived seriousness and victimization. *International Criminal Justice Review, 26*(2), 80–97.

52. Chuang, L.-M., & Kleiner, B. H. (1999). Sexual harassment in public schools. *Equal Opportunities International, 18*, 13–17.

53. Mushtaq, M., Sultana, S., & Imtiaz, I. (2015). The trauma of sexual harassment and its mental health consequences among nurses. *Journal of the College of Physicians and Surgeons Pakistan, 25*, 675–679.

54. Gekoski, A., Gray, J. M., Horvath, M. A. H., Edwards, S., Emirali, A., & Adler, J. R. (2015). *What works in reducing sexual harassment and sexual offences on public transport nationally and internationally: A rapid evidence assessment*. London, England: British Transport Police and Department for Transport.

55. Lenton, R. L., Smith, M. D., Fox, J., & Morra, N. (1999). Sexual harassment in public places: Experiences of Canadian women. *The Canadian Review of Sociology and Anthropology, 36*, 517–540.

56. Macmillan, Nierobisz, & Welsh, 2000.

57. Lonsway, K., Moore, M., Harrington, P., Smeal, E., & Spillar, K. (2003). *Hiring and retaining more women: The advantages to law enforcement agencies*. Beverly Hills, CA: National Center for Women & Policing [Electronic version].

58. Champion, D. R. (2006). Sexual harassment: Criminal justice and academia. *Criminal Justice Studies, 19*(2), 101–109.

59. Till, F. (1980). *Sexual harassment: A report on the sexual harassment of students*. Washington, DC: National Advisory Council on Women's Educational Programs.

60. *Ibid.*

61. Cortina, L. M., & Berdahl, J. L. (2008). Sexual harassment in organizations: A decade of research in review. In C. Cooper & J. Barling (Eds.), *Handbook of organizational behavior* (pp. 469–497). Thousand Oaks, CA: Sage.
62. Fitzgerald, L. F., Swan, S., & Magley, V. J. (1997). But was it really sexual harassment? Legal, behavioral, and psychological definitions of the workplace victimization of women. In W. O'Donohue (Ed.), *Sexual harassment: Theory, research, and treatment* (pp. 5–28). Needham Heights, MA: Allyn & Bacon.
63. Magley, V., Zickar, M., Salisbury, J., Drasgow, F., & Fitzgerald, L. (1997). *Evaluating the effectiveness of sexual harassment training.* Paper presented at the Annual Meeting of the Society for Industrial and Organizational Psychology, St. Louis, MO.
64. Cochran, C., Frazier, P., & Olson, A. (1997). Predictors of responses to unwanted sexual attention. *Psychology of Women Quarterly, 21*(1), 201–226.
65. Cortina, L. (2004). Hispanic perspectives on sexual harassment and social support. *Personality and Social Psychology Bulletin, 30*(5), 570–584.
66. Culberlson, A., & Rosenfeld, P. (1994). Assessment of sexual harassment in the active-duty Navy. *Military Psychology, 6*(2), 69–93.
67. Schneider, K., Swan, S., & Fitzgerald, L. (1997). Job-related and psychological effects of sexual harassment in the workplace: Empirical evidence from two organizations. *Journal of Applied Psychology, 82*(4), 401–415.
68. Schneider, B. E. (1991). Put up and shut up: Workplace sexual assaults. *Gender & Society, 5*, 533–548.
69. Cortina, L. (2004). Hispanic perspectives on sexual harassment and social support. *Personality and Social Psychology Bulletin, 30*(5), 570–584.
70. Lapierre, L. M., Spector, P. E., & Leck, J. D. (2005). Sexual versus nonsexual workplace aggression and victims' overall job satisfaction: A meta-analysis. *Journal of Occupational Health Psychology, 10*(3), 155–169.
71. Parker, S., & Griffin, M. (2002). What is so bad about a little name-calling? Negative consequences of gender harassment for over performance demands and distress. *Journal of Occupational Health Psychology, 7*(3), 195–210.
72. Cortina, & Berdahl, 2008.
73. Langhout, R., Bergman, M., Cortina, L., Fitzgerald, L., Drasgow, F., & Williams, J. H. (2005). Sexual harassment severity: Assessing situational and personal determinants and outcomes. *Journal of Applied Social Psychology, 35*, 975–1007.
74. Timmins, W. M., & Hainsworth, B. E. (1989). Attracting and retaining females in law enforcement: Sex-based problems of women cops in 1988. *International Journal of Offender Therapy and Comparative Criminology, 33*, 197–205.
75. Haar, R. N. (1997). Patterns of interaction in a police patrol bureau: Race and gender barriers to integration. *Justice Quarterly, 14*(1), 54–83.
76. Bartol, C. R., Bergen, G. T., Volckens, J. S., & Knoras, K. M. (1992). Women in small-town policing: Job performance and stress. *Criminal Justice and Behavior, 19*, 240–259.
77. Leskinen, E. A., Cortina, L. M., & Kabat, D. B. (2011). Gender harassment: Broadening our understanding of sex-based harassment at work. *Law & Human Behavior, 35*(1), 25–39.
78. Cassirer, N., & Reskin, B. (2000). High hopes: Organizational position, employment experiences, and women's and men's promotion aspirations. *Work and Occupations, 27*, 438–453.
79. Griffin, M. L., Armstrong, G. S., & Hepburn, J. R. (2005). Correctional officer's perceptions of equitable treatment in the masculinized prison environment. *Criminal Justice Review, 30*, 189–206.
80. Matthews, C., Monk-Turner, E., & Sumter, M. (2010). Promotional opportunities: How women in corrections perceive their chances for advancement at work. *Gender Issues, 27*, 53–66. doi: 10.1007/s12147-010-9089-5

6

DEATH PENALTY AND THE POOR

Amanda K. Cox

Introduction

In its 1984 opinion in the case of *United States v. Cronic*,[1] the United States Supreme Court stressed the importance of defendants' Sixth Amendment rights with the words of Walter Vincent Schaefer, "Of all the rights an accused person has, the right to be represented by counsel is by far the most pervasive, for it affects his ability to assert any other rights he may have." Indeed, a person who finds him- or herself within the purview of the criminal justice system is best equipped to exercise their due process rights when they enjoy the assistance of a skilled, experienced, and zealous attorney. There is, perhaps, no group so in need of such assistance than those who face the punishment of death. Ironically, these individuals are among the least able to acquire effective assistance of counsel, as virtually all capital defendants are poor, rendering them less able to pay for a team of skilled attorneys.[2] The result is a sentence given not as a consequence of the circumstances or severity of the crime in question, but due to the financial and social status of the defendant.

This chapter begins with a brief description of death row inmates with focus on their socioeconomic status and social background, before moving on to a discussion of the reasons that the poor are more likely to be sentenced to death. Implications of the relationship between poverty and death sentencing for social justice are discussed at the close of the chapter.

The Poor on Death Row

As of September 2017, 2,843 men and women sit on death rows in 31 states across the United States of America.[3] While these inmates are separated from one another by walls, bars, and state lines, research indicates that they have commonalities. The majority of death row inmates are male and disproportionately minority,[4] but this is only part of the story. Capital defendants overwhelmingly come from the low end of the socioeconomic spectrum, and the majority of those executed between 1977 and 1999 were poorly educated and worked in low-paying, menial jobs at the time the capital crime was committed. Overall, research indicates that capital defendants and, by extension, death row inmates are invariably poor and disadvantaged. Further, a study of United States clemency petitions from Texas and Virginia gives insight into the reasons that the poor may be more likely to find themselves charged with capital crimes. Themes drawn from these clemency documents reveal that those sentenced to death, and subsequently executed, lived lives of poverty, abuse, and neglect. The story of Joe Wise provides particular insight into the lives led by death row inmates prior to their condemnation. Joe's clemency petition describes a life of wretched poverty. He never consistently lived in housing with indoor plumbing, and he was brutally beaten by his cruel parents. Such stories are not uncommon among the condemned,[5] but often are left out of the penalty phase of capital trials by incompetent or inexperienced defense attorneys.

As condemned inmates, these individuals face the possibility of one day losing their most basic right as human beings—the right to life. Because "death is different," specifically in terms of its severity and finality, it is essential that the death penalty be imposed in a fair and consistent manner. While post-*Gregg*[6] death penalty statutes introduced bifurcated trials, guided discretion statutes, and automatic appellate review into existing death penalty legislation with the intention of eliminating capriciousness in death sentencing, research indicates that fairness remains out of reach for defendants of low socioeconomic status, who ultimately end up making their homes on death rows across the country.

The Road to Death Row

While it is true that death row inmates are poor, this is not to say that prosecutors, judges, and juries practice outright discrimination against them. Theoretically, every capital defendant has the same constitutional rights, which should ensure a fair trial for each defendant, regardless of their social standing. However, full access to one's constitutional rights is not a guarantee for poor capital defendants.[7] Such defendants are typically indigent, meaning that they cannot afford to hire private counsel. Approximately 90% of capital defendants are unable to afford private counsel and are, therefore, indigent.[8] Research shows that prosecutors may be more likely to charge defendants with a capital crime when they are represented by court-appointed counsel, as they may see these cases as being more "winnable." Further, studies show that indigent capital defendants are more than two times as likely to receive a sentence of death than those who hire private attorneys.

Court-Appointed Attorneys

Indigent defendants must rely on legal assistance from one of two sources: a public defender or court-appointed attorney.[9] The best-case scenario for an indigent capital defendant is that they have access to a well-funded and experienced team of public defenders via a state or local public defender's office. Research indicates that public defender offices have better performance records than do appointed counsel. However, experienced public defenders may be difficult to come by for some capital defendants. Typically, public defender offices are located only in large cities, and many states have no public defender offices.[10] For example, Harris County, Texas, has no public defender office, despite it having the second largest death row population in the country.[11]

Indigent capital defendants in jurisdictions that do not have public defender offices must rely on court-appointed attorneys to prepare their defense. Court-appointed attorneys typically work in private practice but take on the cases of indigents when assigned by judges. Horror stories abound with the experiences of poor capital defendants who found themselves being represented by inexperienced court-appointed attorneys. Cases in which court-appointed attorneys have come to court drunk, slept through trial proceedings, and neglected to bring up crucial mitigating evidence in the penalty phase are not uncommon and are a capital defendant's worst nightmare, often leading to a conviction and sentence of death. Research indicates that there are many problems with court appointment, which may lead to such outcomes. First, standards by which attorneys are appointed to capital cases are not always rigorous. In Alabama, for example, a state that does not have public defender offices, court-appointed attorneys are required only to be a member of the Alabama Bar Association and have five years of criminal defense experience prior to taking on a capital case.[12] Lack of experience in litigating capital trials is problematic, as these cases tend to be the most complex, expensive, and time-consuming.[13] Capital trials, for instance, involve a penalty phase, which is not standard in other criminal trials. This process involves the presentation of aggravating and mitigating circumstances, and having a competent attorney during this phase can mean the difference between life and death for poor capital defendants. By presenting mitigating evidence (such as that described above in the case of Joe Wise), the defense attorney may be able to show that the defendant is less deserving of a capital sentence and save them from death. Research, however, shows that court-appointed attorneys rarely present sufficient evidence of mitigation during the penalty phase.[14] An effective mitigation investigation involves interviewing dozens or hundreds of witnesses; locating school, work, and health records; and consulting with potential expert witnesses. This does not appear to happen for many poor capital defendants. For instance, a 2016 report released by the *Fair Punishment Project* showed that court-appointed attorneys in the most active death penalty counties across the United States often put on less than one day of mitigating evidence and, in some cases, successfully encouraged their clients to waive their right to present mitigating evidence during the penalty phase of the trial, effectively quashing any chance the defendant might have had to preserve his or her life.

The second shortcoming of relying on court-appointed attorneys lies within the system itself. The appointment method may create conflicting economic incentives for the defense team. Judges appoint defense attorneys in capital cases, so a defense attorney who advocates well for his or her client, filing many pretrial motions and making numerous requests of the judge, may find him- or herself in a position of discontent with the judge. A displeased judge may not be inclined to appoint such attorneys in future cases. Likewise, court-appointed attorneys are often underpaid and overworked. Low pay does not provide a great deal of incentive for court-appointed attorneys to strive for perfection, or even efficiency, in capital cases. Further, well-meaning attorneys may be unable to perform to the best of their ability if they are plagued by high caseloads.

It is also noteworthy that court-appointed attorneys are dependent on judges for the resources necessary to put on an adequate defense for their clients, since judges are responsible for allocating the financial resources necessary to prepare a zealous defense. A Harris County, Texas, study examined the outcome of legal counsel on prosecutors' decisions to seek the death penalty by comparing defendants with privately hired counsel to those with court-appointed counsel. Results indicated that judges in that jurisdiction commonly provide court-appointed attorneys only with enough money to hire local experts, who may or may not be the most qualified to testify on behalf of a capital defendant. Additionally, a court-appointed attorney cannot possibly prepare a defense equal to the case prepared by the prosecution, which enjoys better pay and the assistance of local police to handle the pretrial investigative work that court-appointed defense attorneys must do themselves. Even if the defense is sufficiently experienced and motivated to prepare an adequate defense, a lack of sufficient funding impairs their ability to locate and interview witnesses, gather evidence, and question scientific evidence offered by the state.

Post-Conviction Legal Counsel

As described above, it is rarely disputed in research that poor defendants are more likely to receive ineffective assistance of counsel than their wealthy counterparts are.[15] It is also true, however, that capital defendants enjoy the right to a lengthier appeals process than do typical criminal defendants. With the reinstatement of the death penalty following the *Gregg v. Georgia* decision, automatic and extensive appellate review was introduced into death penalty statutes across the country, theoretically allowing the condemned to have their cases reexamined for mistakes and rights violations, including those occurring as a result of ineffective assistance of counsel. However, the ability to exercise the right to such appeals is, once again, limited for the poor.

While capital defendants have the right to counsel during their trial and the automatic review of their death sentence, the majority of states do not provide counsel for further appeals. This means that the condemned, if they wish to continue the appeals process in hopes of correcting any errors made in their case, must file appeals for themselves or rely upon the charity of a few private lawyers and organizations (for example, the Southern Prisoners Defense Committee) that take on post-conviction capital inmates. Such organizations often have few resources and, therefore, must limit the number of clients they can represent.

Condemned inmates who must represent themselves during the appeals process face an uphill battle, to be sure. As has been established, those who find themselves on death row are typically undereducated and lack the ability to adequately represent themselves. This means that they are at a distinct disadvantage when it comes to understanding the complex legal process involved in filing an appeal and having the skills needed to prepare a convincing legal document. Further, the ability to win an appeal is difficult even for skilled attorneys, given that an appeal based on ineffective assistance of counsel is subject to the Strickland standard. The Strickland standard is used to determine whether a defense attorney in a criminal trial was ineffective. The two-prong test requires that (1) the defendant demonstrate that his or her attorney was deficient; and (2) the error(s) made by the attorney were prejudicial, meaning that the defendant did not receive a fair trial and may have been acquitted but for the errors of his or her defense attorney.[16] Historically, proving that the jury would have come to a different verdict had the defense not made errors has been difficult for appeals attorneys. Obviously, this task is even more difficult for a poor, uneducated death row inmate. As a result, poor death row inmates are unlikely to have the ability to fully exercise their post-conviction appeals.

Implications for Social Justice

As a result of many capital defendants' low rank on the social ladder, they have an increased likelihood of being sentenced to death and executed. Those who can afford a private, competent defense are least likely to be sentenced to death, while capital defendants represented by court-appointed attorneys are more than two times as likely to receive a death sentence. Further, the inability to afford post-conviction counsel decreases the likelihood that the condemned will be able to correct the errors and injustices that characterize their cases.

In addition to poor, guilty defendants being more likely to land on death row and be executed due to their inability to afford a competent defense attorney, the poor also are more likely to be found guilty of a capital crime of which they are factually innocent. This is, perhaps, the worst-case scenario. A study of 23 years of death penalty appeals conducted at Columbia University indicated that ineffective defense attorneys were the most significant contributor to wrongful convictions of criminal defendants in capital cases.[17] One can scarcely imagine a more unjust outcome than the capital conviction of an innocent person simply because that person could not afford to fully assert their due process rights at trial. Since 1973, 159 people have been exonerated and freed from death row, indicating that wrongful conviction is a significant problem.[18] Even more concerning is the possibility that innocent people have already been executed, in part, because they were unable to afford counsel who could zealously represent them in court. The case of Cameron Todd Willingham is, perhaps, the most well-known. Willingham was executed in 2004 for the burning death of his three daughters in spite of new scientific evidence indicating that the fire was accidental. At trial, Willingham's court-appointed attorney failed to challenge the state's evidence and expert witness and neglected to investigate Willingham's background, which showed no history of violence toward his children.

Conclusion

Capital defendants most frequently come from the low end of the socioeconomic spectrum and often bring with them backgrounds filled with poverty, abuse, and neglect. A lack of financial means and social status means that these disadvantaged individuals are much more likely than wealthy people to rely upon representation by court-appointed defense counsel at trial. This, paired with the inability of the poor to acquire adequate post-conviction counsel, results in death rows and execution chambers occupied solely by the United States' poorest citizens. This has serious implications for the ability of our criminal justice system to achieve justice. A system cannot be just if it punishes on the basis of socioeconomic status and allows miscarriages of justice to go uncorrected simply because those who suffer the injustice do not have the means to correct it themselves.

Summary

Capital trials, death rows, and execution chambers are reserved solely for the underclass of American society. Although everyone is "guaranteed" the right to a fair trial by the United States Constitution, the poor often find this right to be out of their grasp. Because the poor are less able to afford private counsel when facing capital charges, they are at an increased likelihood of being sentenced to death and executed.

Poor capital defendants' reliance on court-appointed attorneys means that their defense is wrought with inexperience, errors, and injustices. Court-appointed attorneys also may lack the incentive to provide an enthusiastic defense for their clients because they are overworked, are underpaid, and must rely upon good relationships with judges to ensure appointments in the future.

At the post-conviction stage, condemned inmates again find themselves at the mercy of a system that values wealth. Post-conviction inmates who cannot afford counsel to handle their appeals are not always provided with defense attorneys to assist them and, therefore, may end up attempting to file complex legal documents on their own without the benefit of education. Likewise, the two-prong Strickland standard sets the bar high for proving ineffective assistance of counsel. Together, these factors make it very difficult for condemned inmates to have legal errors in their cases corrected at the post-conviction stage.

Because the United States criminal justice system is best maneuvered by those who have money, poor capital defendants find themselves in a situation in which they are condemned not because their crimes were the most heinous, but because they lacked the capital necessary to provide themselves with a rigorous defense. Likewise, a lack of resources has been shown to contribute to the likelihood that an innocent person will be sentenced to death and possibly even executed. A criminal justice system that punishes and condemns based on socioeconomic status is not one that can promise any degree of social justice to its clients.

Discussion Questions

1. Why is the right to effective assistance of counsel so important in capital cases?
2. Why are the poor more likely to be sentenced to death than those with greater financial means?
3. What are the problems with court-appointed attorney systems? How might these problems be addressed?
4. Why is the presentation of mitigating evidence important during the penalty phase of capital trials?
5. Why are poor capital defendants disadvantaged when it comes to exercising their right to post-conviction appeals? What could be done about this?
6. What are the injustices that result from poor capital defendants' inability to hire private legal counsel in their trials?

Notes

1. *United States v. Cronic*, 466 U.S. 648, 654, (1984).
2. Phillips, S. (2009). Legal disparities in the capital of capital punishment. *The Journal of Criminal Law and Criminology, 99*, 717–755. doi: 009-4169/09/9903-0717

3. Death Penalty Information Center. (2017). *Death row.* Retrieved April 1, 2017, from https://deathpenaltyinfo.org/death-row

4. Death Penalty Information Center. (2017). *Race of death row inmates executed since 1976.* Retrieved August 20, 2017, from https://deathpenaltyinfo.org/race-death-row-inmates-executed-1976

5. Sarat, A. (2008). Memorializing miscarriages of justice: Clemency petitions in the killing state. *Law and Society Review, 42,* 183–224.

6. *Gregg v. Georgia,* 428 U.S. 153, (1976).

7. Costanzo, M. (1997). *Just revenge: Costs and consequences of the death penalty.* New York: St. Martin's Press.

8. Cawley, W. (2007). Raising the bar: How *Rompilla v. Beard* represents the Court's increasing efforts to impose stricter standards for defense lawyering in capital cases. *Pepperdine Law Review, 34,* 1–15.

9. Culver, J. H. (1999). Twenty years after Gilmore: Who is being executed? *American Journal of Criminal Justice, 24,* 1–14.

10. Miller-Potter, K. (2005). Capital punishment: The myth of murder as effective crime control. In V. E. Kappeler & G. W. Potter (Eds.), *The mythology of crime and criminal justice* (pp. 329–355). Long Grove, IL: Waveland Press, Inc.

11. Death Penalty Information Center. (2013). *Death row inmates by county.* Retrieved August 9, 2017, from https://deathpenaltyinfo.org/death-row-inmates-county-sentencing

12. Breglio, A. (2011). Let him be heard: The right to effective assistance of counsel on post-conviction appeal in capital cases. *Georgetown Journal on Poverty and Law Policy, 18,* 247–262.

13. American Civil Liberties Union. (2010). *Slamming the courthouse doors: Denial of justice and remedy in America.* New York: American Civil Liberties Union.

14. Fair Punishment Project. (2016). *Too broken to fix part I: An in-depth look at America's outlier death penalty counties.* Chapel Hill, NC: Fair Punishment Project.

15. Reiman, J. (2010). *The rich get richer and the poor get prison,* 9th ed. Boston: Pearson.

16. *Strickland v. Washington* (1984). 466 U.S. 668.

17. Gould, J., Carrano, J., Leo, R., & Young, J. (2012). *Predicting erroneous convictions: A social science approach to miscarriages of justice.* National Institute of Justice. Retrieved from www.ncjrs.gov/pdffiles1/nij/grants/241389.pdf

18. Death Penalty Information Center. (2017). *Innocence and the death penalty.* Retrieved September 28, 2017, from https://deathpenaltyinfo.org/innocence-and-death-penalty

7

EDUCATION INEQUALITY IN AMERICA

Dwayne Roberson

Introduction

America has been known as a "melting pot" for immigrants since the landing of Columbus and the later waves of immigrants to its shores. The Statue of Liberty and Ellis Island are reminders from our past that provide numerous contexts for the basis of our society in America. Unlike countries with a homogenous population, America's population consists of many different ethnicities from various countries that came to the United States in numerous waves. American culture is represented by the assimilation and acculturation of people from various ethnic enclaves within the United States. The contributions of the immigrants to American society has been the trademark of our culture.

America also has a dark past with the introduction of the transatlantic slave trade, which was the forcible movement of Africans to the Western Hemisphere to harvest sugar cane and other raw materials for export. Africans were denied basic legal rights human rights, including that of access to education. Since the beginning of the slave trade to current times, African Americans have made great strides towards equality despite social and institutional unfairness to former slaves and their subsequent generations. This legacy continues with the structures of slavery replaced over time with other structures of racism meant to further disenfranchise African American citizenship rights (Wahab, 2011). Educational inequality in America can be viewed in current research, different periods, and major landmark education cases. Through the lenses of these viewpoints, historical educational inequality in America can be seen through the evolution of cases that argued for basic rights. Different periods and court cases illustrate the effort of African Americans to obtain basic rights and the government's refusal to protect the rights of all Americans.

Our Modern Education System

The American education system today is complex, with a variety of ethnic and minority groups represented in classrooms throughout the country. Compulsory education requiring all school-age children to attend some type of public or private education is mandated by local and state laws. However, it is important to note that education is not a right to school-age children in America under the Constitution. As a constitutional right, education is considered a right in 176 countries, but it is not expressly written in the Constitution of the United States (Lurie, 2013). The individuals who drafted the Constitution wanted more self-control and less government. The result was a declaration to the British Empire that gave political power to a federal system, as well as local political power to the original colonies. The drafters of the Constitution resented the British monarchy and therefore demanded political rights outside of the British empire, establishing an independent federal and local system of government. The drafting of the Tenth Amendment of the Constitution in 1791, "The powers not delegated to the United States by the Constitution, nor prohibited by it to the States, are reserved to the States respectively, or to the people" (United States Constitution 10th Amendment, 1791), resulted in state and local control of school districts, whereas other industrialized countries of the world have national education systems. The evolution of the American education system came later with the introduction of many different pieces of legislation giving control to local school boards via state laws. Our education system today offers learning and growth outcomes to students from different minority and ethnic groups.

Educational inequality in America has its origins in the suppression of minority groups through legal and social control. To understand how inequality began in America, you must first understand the plight and struggle endured by African slaves brought to the Western Hemisphere during the transatlantic slave trade and their continued struggle for basic rights while being denied the right of citizens of their own country. African Americans have always had a history of inequality in America due to societal and institutional unfairness. This societal inequality was fueled by racism and beliefs of superiority that were exacerbated by theories developed about "inferior races."

Current Research

The bases of social structure for which inequality exist are racism and classicism (Caliendo, 2014). Caliendo's dissection of inequality within American society gives the cause of poverty in the understanding of poverty itself.

> We are taught to believe that those who are financially successful (as well as those who have access to excellent institutions) are fully deserving of that privilege while those who are not must have acted badly at some point and, therefore, deserve their poverty.
>
> *(Caliendo, 2014)*

His view of social structure is rooted in how the elite view their privilege. Systematic inequality exists in politics, wealth, housing, education, crime, employment, health and affirmative action (Caliendo, 2014).

Developmental Theories

In *Inequality in the Promised Land: Race, Resources, and Suburban Schooling* (McCoy, 2014), a theory of development that describes two ways of raising adolescent children is explained by two educational researchers. Lareau and Ogbu speculate about "natural growth" and "concerned cultivation." "Natural growth" households were typically low income and use services of the local and state governments in the raising of children. The differences in outcomes were based on observations of Caucasian and African American households. There were noticeable differences between the two types of development. "Concerned cultivation" generally led to positive relationships with others and institutions of learning. "Concerned cultivation" centers around direct involvement of the parent in aspects of the child's life. The support of the child is a way of maintaining the current middle class standing of the parents. These parents believe that this will help continue their position within the middle class. "Natural growth" is described as a method of raising adolescents with less formal structure. These adolescents are raised with less structure and fewer opportunities. Governmental and active social structures (school, community centers, and church or other places of worship) are used to help with the raising of adolescent children. The study by McCoy (2014), illustrated not inequality but the need by parents to maintain the level of the child's social standing either through direct intervention or the use of social services. Both outcomes replicate parents' social standings (McCoy, 2014).

Inequality Perpetuated by Racial and Genetic Perceptions

Inequality is further perpetuated by linking genetic racial perceptions with low school performance (Berg, 2010). This inequality is perpetuated by the belief that certain racial groups are inferior. Numerous studies in the early 19th century also noted this inequality in society. Darwin's *Evolution of Species* led to the development of subsequent theories that furthered notions of racial superiority. The development of ideas like eugenics, which perpetuated racial difference and superiority between groups, became commonplace subjugating African Americans.

Periods of Education Inequality in America

Colonial America

Historical accounts of the first slaves in the Americas date back to the 17th century, where they were used as forced labor. The transatlantic slave trade brought Africans to the Americas in a forced migration. During this period, educational inequality was at its absolute highest. The education of slaves was considered illegal and the teaching of reading was only used for religious purposes (Levine & Levine, 2014). Some slaves were educated in various trades and skills to assist the slave owner on the plantation. In *Somerset v. Stewart*, a British officer in Boston brought his slave back to England. Somerset, who was a slave sold to Stewart, argued that the British colonies had laws against slavery, and Parliament had made laws that recognized slavery as unlawful.

Scott v. Sandford

Scott v. Sandford (1857) held that no slaves could be citizens of the United States regardless of birth status. It further held that "Negroes" had no standing in federal court. Scott was a slave whose owner had moved to the Wisconsin Territory, where the Missouri Compromise had prohibited slavery under the law. In 1837, Scott's owner moved to Missouri and left Scott to sell his labor in Wisconsin Territory. The selling of Scott's slave labor constituted slavery in a free state. Later, when his owner moved to Louisiana, he sent for the Scotts, who had a baby while they traveled. The Scotts' baby was born in a free state, constituting a person being free and not a slave. The Scott decision challenged the legality of slavery. The ruling of the Supreme Court (7–2) against Scott held that living in places where slaves were free did not constitute slaves being free. To allow slaves who travel to free states to become free would be a detriment to slave owners' property rights. Additionally, territories established could not be regulated by the federal government (Bracey, Finkelman, & Konig, 2010). This decision ultimately upheld the rights of slave owners. Other challenges to basic civil rights and educational equality would follow with greater success.

Civil War and Emancipation

On January 31, 1865, the Thirteenth Amendment to the United States Constitution abolished slavery, after many years of civil war in the United States that culminated in the Emancipation Proclamation and the freeing of all slaves. The Thirteenth Amendment of the constitution abolished slavery and ended involuntary servitude.

> Section 1. Neither slavery nor involuntary servitude, except as a punishment for crime whereof the party shall have been duly convicted, shall exist within the United States, or any place subject to their jurisdiction. Section 2. Congress shall have power to enforce this article by appropriate legislation.
>
> *(Thirteenth Amendment United States Constitution, 1865)*

The passage of the Thirteenth Amendment legally abolished slavery and reversed a previous decision by the Supreme Court in *Dred Scott v. Sandford* (also known as the Dred Scott case).

At the end of the Civil War, states that wished to join the Union were required to draft a new state constitution to be considered for entry to the Union. Newly emancipated African Americans participated in the redrafting of their states' constitutions. Many of the newly free African Americans and others argued for mandatory public schooling for all children. The redrafting of these constitutions led to the formation of our public schools today, but they failed to integrate students. The failure of the Reconstruction period was the inability of the federal government to provide equal access after emancipation. The political power of the time projected an idea of "equal citizenship" as a means providing separate and unequal education to former slaves. Local governments legislated measures to further disenfranchise African Americans. The failure of government to enact national policies to protect African Americans led to further segregation at the hands of state legislatures, whose goal is to provide unequal segregated education (Anderson, 2015).

Resistance to Equality

Following the end of the American Civil War, state and local governments engaged in a practice of legislating laws with the intent of creating barriers to equal access of citizenship. The "Jim Crow" era demonstrated this idea of legislating unequal access to education. The description below describes how the term "Jim Crow" likely got its start:

> Come listen all you galls and boys,
> I'm going to sing a little song,
> My name is Jim Crow.
> Weel about and turn about and do jis so,
> Eb'ry time I weel about I jump Jim Crow.
> (*Who Was Jim Crow?* Jim Crow
> Museum, Ferris State University)

The origin of Jim Crow is thought to have come from this song in the early part of the 1830s. The White performer would dress in mocking fashion of African American slaves and perform songs. This term "Jim Crow" was symbolic of the type of legislation towards the disenfranchisement of African Americans. This trend in legislation became popular especially in the South after the Civil War. Challenges to the legal system during the 1800s largely resulted in a failure of courts to legislate reasonable responses to law that disenfranchised African Americans. Future challenges to legislation will provide better access, but early challenges failed in the light of common sense against any form of equality.

Cummings v. School Board of Richmond County

In 1899, Cummings sued the Board of Education in Richmond County because a tax levied within the county was used for funding a White-only school. In 1879, Georgia established one of the first public schools. Ware High School was operating until 1897, when the money was set aside for a private school for African Americans and parents of Ware High School filed suit under the Equal Protection Clause of the Fourteenth Amendment of the Constitution. Cummings argued that the tax was illegal because it did not set aside any funding for public school for African Americans. Cummings was not trying to get the African American school integrated into the school district or complaining about the separation of the ethnicities. He was attempting through litigation to withhold tax payments to the White school until the school for African Americans was funded. The case was appealed all the way to the Supreme Court. The court decided that the school district could not afford to educate all students within the Richmond school district. The school board determined that:

Four hundred or more negro children were being turned away from the primary grades unable to be provided with seats or teachers; because the same means and the same building which were used to teach sixty high school pupils would accommodate two hundred pupils in the rudiments of education; because the board at this time was not financially able to erect buildings and employ additional teachers for the large number of colored children who were in need of primary education and because there were in the City of Augusta at this time three public high schools—the Haines Industrial School, the Walker Baptists Institute and the Paine Institute—each of which were public to colored people and were charging fees no larger than the board charged for pupilage in the Ware High School.

(Connally, 2000)

Cummings argued under the Equal Protection Clause of the Fourteenth Amendment that African Americans were denied equal protection because of unequal funding. *Cummings v. School Board of Richmond County* was one of the first cases that argued against the "separate but equal" clause of the Constitution.

First, That the statute of the State of Georgia, as construed by the Supreme Court of Georgia, giving a discretion to the said county board of education to establish and maintain high schools for white persons and to discontinue and refuse to maintain high schools for persons of the negro race, was, and is, contrary to the Constitution of the United States, and especially to the Fourteenth Amendment thereof. Second, That the said court decided and held that the Constitution of the United States was not violated by the action of the said board in establishing and maintaining public high schools for the education of white persons exclusively, and in refusing to establish and maintain high school for the education of persons similarly situated of the negro race. Third, in deciding and holding that persons of the negro race could, consistently with the Constitution of the United States, be by the laws or authorities of Georgia, taxed, and the money derived from their taxation be appropriated to the establishment and maintenance of high schools for white persons, while pursuant to the same law the said board, at the same time, refused to establish and maintain high schools for the education of persons of the negro race. Fourth, That the said Superior Court erred in dismissing the complaint of the plaintiff in error.

(Connally, 2000)

Although Cumming's challenge was unsuccessful, future challenges would bring about more equal access to education.

Civil Rights Movement

Brown v. Board of Education *(1954)*

In the time since *Brown v. Board of Education*, the achievement of African Americans has improved, although with much difficulty due to legislative barriers to equality. As the lot of African Americans improve, the greatest impediment to equality is economic segregation (Johnson, 2014). Brown filed suit against the Topeka Board of Education because her daughter had to walk to the bus stop to take a bus to her segregated school. Her walk to the bus stop took her past a White school in her own neighborhood. At the beginning of the school year, the law that was determined under *Plessy v. Ferguson* maintained segregation. The opinion of the Supreme Court was to end school segregation and integrate the schools, and historic accounts show White opposition to the integration of African Americans to the public school system (Klarman, 2007).

Funding as a Means of Segregation

For most school districts in the United States, property tax is relied upon as a means of funding most expenditures. This local funding of schools through property taxes and state-level spending produces varying levels of disproportionate funding. Local control of education has affected the quality of education by basing the quality of education on realty prices (Ingram, 2014).

San Antonio Independent School District v. Rodriguez *(1973)*

The financing of public schools in Texas involves the taxation of property along with other sources of revenue to fund school districts. Rodriguez and other parents sued the school district because of unequal opportunity offered to students within the San Antonio school district and other surrounding districts. The suit was brought by parents against the San Antonio Independent School District and neighboring school districts. The Supreme Court found that:

> In *San Antonio Independent School District v. Rodriguez* (1973), the court held that the Constitution does not protect a right to education. This decision foreclosed a federal judicial remedy for disparities in funding that had relegated Mexican American children in the predominantly low-income Edgewood Independent School District of San Antonio, Texas, to an education that was inferior to that of students in the city's affluent, mostly white Alamo Heights district.
>
> *(Ogletree & Robinson, 2017)*

This argument held that school funding through property tax violated the Equal Protection Clause of the Fourteenth Amendment. School funding as a source of revenue for local school districts can provide funding based on local areas' revenue take. The result of this is more funding for affluent areas and less funding for economically disadvantaged areas (Lewis, 2015). The courts held that the reasonable administration of public education did not violate the Equal Protection Clause, although unequal access existed in the public school system. The unequal access to public facilities did not violate students' rights, because the court held that the school district was reasonable in distribution of resources to student learning. Areas of unequal access can now exist under the decision of *San Antonio Independent School District v. Rodriguez*.

Integration of Public School Via Busing

After the Supreme Court ruling in *Brown v. Board of Education*, African Americans had been segregated in neighborhoods away from Whites. One of the major ways that schools brought in students was the use of busing. Many states used busing to quickly integrate students into White schools. Through many decades of busing, the movement of "Whites" to the suburbs left many schools with populations of African Americans students bused all the way across town to a formerly White school (Kelley, 1974). The lack of diversity in these new schools was attributed to the way in which racial demographic settlement patterns were drawn. The busing addressed the immediate need to integrate schools but could not address the scourge of racism.

State of Educational Inequality

Since the Emancipation Proclamation and later legal challenges, African Americans have struggled to overcome institutional and social barriers. More than 150 years after Lincoln's most popular speech liberated former slaves, what is the current state of inequality? Although there is some uncertainty as to whether inequality can be accurately measured, what is the state of inequality in the United States?

The National Center for Education Statistics reports that the dropout rate for African Americans has dropped:

> In each year from 2000 to 2015, the status dropout rate was lower for White youth than for Black youth, and the rates for both groups were lower than the rate for Hispanic youth. During this period, the status dropout rate declined from 6.9 to 4.6 percent for White youth; from 13.1 to 6.5 percent for Black youth; and from 27.8 to 9.2 percent for Hispanic youth. As a result, the gap between White and Black youth narrowed from 6.2 percentage points in 2000 to 1.9 percentage points in 2015. The gap between White and Hispanic youth narrowed from 20.9 percentage points in 2000 to 4.6 percentage points in 2015.
>
> *(National Center for Education Statistics)*

As illustrated in the passage, the rates of African Americans and other ethnicities dropping out of school has shrunk dramatically. *U.S. News and World Report* published a surprising study about African Americans and rates of college completion. "But those improvements aren't equal among subgroups of students, and the overall improvement masks an especially disturbing trend: the widening of the graduation gap between black and white students" (Camera, 2016). The study looked at 272 universities and their graduation rates and found a large difference between the graduation rates of Whites and African Americans. "The University of Missouri–Kansas City, for example, increased its graduation rate by approximately 10 percentage points over roughly the last decade, but its graduation gap between black and white students grew by 22.7 percentage points over the same time" (Camera, 2016). Although these portray a picture of difficulty, future generations will be able to overcome the great barriers to equality set before them.

Summary

America has been known as a country of immigrants since the landing of Christopher Columbus and later waves of immigrants. Our country also has a dark past from our history of the transatlantic slave trade. The forcible movement of Africans to the Western Hemisphere introduced servitude and slavery. Africans who came to the Western Hemisphere faced many challenges, including death. Harsh treatment by slave owners and others led to a later abolitionist movement. Through many legal challenges, African Americans gained equality with the rest of society. The African American story is one of numerous social and institutional barriers to success, including educational inequality.

Our education system today is based on local control, with most of the funding for public schools financed by property taxes within the local area. Because of this system, students within the United States are faced with varying levels of educational equity and equality, meaning that not everyone in America has an equal and equitable right to the same education. Unlike most countries of the world, the United States does not have education as a right expressly written in its constitution. The Tenth Amendment of the U.S. Constitution expressly gives powers to the state that aren't directly expressed in the Constitution, resulting in local control for school districts. The education system today has varying levels of equality and equity for different groups and ethnicities throughout our country, because the United States does not have an expressed national system of education within its own basic founding documents.

This elitist view of society is systemic and perpetuates inequality throughout our society, including politics, wealth, housing, education, crime, employment, health, and affirmative action. In the early part of the 20th century, racial inequality was linked to perceptions of genetic inferiority.

In the earliest periods of American history, educational inequality was at its highest. The introduction of the transatlantic slave trade to the Western Hemisphere brought forcible slavery and servitude. Early legal challenges to slavery failed to emancipate African slaves and make them equal citizens. Numerous legal challenges to educational inequality, such as *Scott v. Sandford*, *Cummings v. School Board of Richmond*

County, and *Brown v. Board of Education of Topeka* (Kansas), resulted in greater equity for minority students. The overcoming of barriers such as Jim Crow laws and other unconstitutional laws towards African Americans is a story of success. However, as we look at the state of educational inequality, we can see that even though they have overcome numerous institutional and social barriers, there is still a lot more work to be done to bring about equality and equity in the system for African Americans.

Discussion Questions

1. Is education a fundamental right in the United States?
2. Does every child in America deserve to have an education?
3. Does America have a system of equal education?
4. What factors caused a system of inequality to exist?

References

Anderson, J. D. (2015). Eleventh annual "Brown" lecture in education research a long shadow: The American pursuit of political justice and education equality. *Educational Researcher, 44*(6), 319–335.

Berg, G. A. (2010). *Low-income students and the perpetuation of inequality: Higher education in America.* Farnham, Surrey, England: Routledge.

Bracey, C. A., Finkelman, P., & Konig, D. T. (2010). *The Dred Scott case: Historical and contemporary perspectives on race and law.* Athens, OH: Ohio University Press.

Caliendo, S. M. (2014). *Inequality in America: Race, poverty, and fulfilling democracy's.* New York: Westview Press.

Camera, L. (2016). "The college graduation gap is still growing." *U.S. News & World Report.* Retrieved March 23, 2016, from www.usnews.com/news/blogs/data-mine/2016/03/23/study-college-graduation-gap-between-blacks-whites-still-growing

Connally, C. E. (2000). Justice Harlan's "Great Betrayal"? A reconsideration of Cumming v. Richmond county board of education. *Journal of Supreme Court History, 25*(1), 72.

"Constitution of the United States." *U.S. Senate: Constitution of the United States.* Retrieved February 15, 2017, from www.senate.gov/civics/constitution_item/constitution.htm#amdt_13_(1865)

Ingram, G. K. (2014). *Education, land, and location.* Cambridge, MA: Lincoln Institute of Land Policy.

Johnson, O. (2014). Still separate, still unequal: The relation of segregation in neighborhoods and schools to education inequality. *The Journal of Negro Education,* (3), 199. doi: 10.7709/jnegroeducation.83.3.0199

Kelley, J. (1974). The politics of school busing. *Public Opinion Quarterly, 38*(1), 23–39.

Klarman, M. J. (2007). *Brown v. board of education and the civil rights movement.* Oxford: Oxford University Press.

Levine, M., & Levine, A. G. (2014). Coming from behind: A historical perspective on Black education and attainment. *American Journal of Orthopsychiatry, 84*(5), 447–454. doi: 10.1037/h0099861

Lewis, T. T. (1973). San Antonio Independent School District v. Rodriguez. In *Salem Press Encyclopedia.* Ipswich, MA: Salem Press.

Lewis-McCoy, R. L'Heureux (2014). *Inequality in the promised land: Race, resources, and suburban schooling.* Stanford, CA: Stanford University Press.

Lurie, S. (2013, October 16). *Why doesn't the Constitution guarantee the right to education?* Retrieved September 4, 2017, from www.theatlantic.com/education/archive/2013/10/why-doesnt-the-constitution-guarantee-the-right-to-education/280583/

The NCES fast facts tool provides quick answers to many education questions (National Center for Education Statistics). National Center for Education Statistics (NCES) Home Page, a Part of the U.S. Department of Education. Retrieved from http://nces.ed.gov/fastfacts/display.asp?id=16

Ogletree, C., & Robinson, K. (2017). Inequitable schools demand a federal remedy. *Education Next, 17*(2).

U.S. Constitution. Amendment. X.

Wahab, A., & Jones, C. (2011). *Free at last? Reflections on freedom and the abolition of the British transatlantic slave trade.* Newcastle upon Tyne: Cambridge Scholars Publishing.

Who Was Jim Crow?—Jim Crow Museum—Ferris State University. Retrieved from http://ferris.edu/HTMLS/news/jimcrow/who/index.htm

8

POLICE POWER AND HUMAN RIGHTS

Jason Jolicoeur

Introduction

Human rights have become an increasingly relevant social issue over the last several decades as a result of the many economic, political, social, and cultural shifts that have taken place across an increasingly global society. Shifts of this nature have necessitated a substantive reevaluation of not only the underlying meaning and purpose of human rights in contemporary culture, but also of the processes and practices that facilitate the continuation and refinement of these rights. Many recent controversies surrounding the provision and protection of human rights have centered on the criminal justice and legal fields. Controversies of this nature in the law enforcement field have been especially important in shaping public attitudes towards the significance and place of human and civil rights in society. This makes a great deal of intuitive sense given that law enforcement officers act as the most visceral representation of the underlying power and authority of the state. Police officers exercise an immense amount of authority during the course of their professional duties, and the discretionary exercise of this power can serve to either sustain or negate the existing human rights protections enjoyed in a given society. In this chapter, a substantive overview of the significance of the law enforcement function as it relates to both individual and collective human rights will be undertaken. More specifically, this chapter will examine the coercive powers exercised by contemporary law enforcement officers in an attempt to determine how these powers influence the provision, application, and maintenance of human rights in contemporary society.

Background

Human rights have a long and somewhat convoluted history, especially insofar as they apply to formalized systems of social control, like those that are so aptly represented by the contemporary law enforcement profession. This involved process of historical development might best be described as slow and uneven, rather than rapid and linear. Some of the earliest documented references to formally recognized human rights protections are contained in historical artifacts such as the Cyrus Cylinder and the Code of Hammurabi. The Cyrus Cylinder was originally created at the bequest of the Persian King Cyrus the Great (600–550 BC). On its face, this artifact appears to advocate for the establishment of both individual liberties and collective religious freedoms. Although there is some disagreement regarding the extent to which these freedoms were practiced in actuality in Persian society, the statements contained in the cylinder were significant in their own right.[1] Language referring to freedoms of this nature was rather groundbreaking during a time when such freedoms were widely unknown. Additionally, such artifacts were symbolically significant, in a tangential manner, to the formalized systems of social control that would later develop and to the human rights standards that would come to be associated with their development. Rather than establishing practices and provisions that were directly applicable to contemporary social control systems, these early artifacts established many of the underlying ideals upon which more formalized and nuanced conceptions of human rights would later be based.

An even earlier example that served as a more direct predecessor of codified criminal codes and human rights legislation, in a form that would be relevant to the contemporary policing profession, can be found in the Code of Hammurabi (1810–1750 BC). The Code of Hammurabi is a legal code propagated during the reign of Hammurabi, a Babylonian king. While Hammurabi's code did not usher in the universally accepted lofty human rights standards that many continue to hope for today, it was still significant because it identified a number of specific societal rights, duties, and responsibilities incumbent on Babylonian citizens.[2] A number of these rights, duties, and responsibilities are largely reflective of larger contemporary human rights standards.[3] For instance, the Code of Hammurabi contained specific provisions related to fairness and protection before the law that would almost certainly be viewed as being directly related to the contemporary civil and human rights protections granted in many societies today. Collectively, the ideas contained within these and other early codes and artifacts (Ten Commandments, Justinian's Code, Law of the Twelve Tables, etc.) established ideals concerning the rights and protections that were due individuals simply because of their inherent humanity.

The specifically proscribed and prohibited behaviors that were included in the Code of Hammurabi, along with the related sanctions for violation of each of these provisions, shared a number of similarities with contemporary criminal codes. Legislation of this nature would roughly equate to a rudimentary version of the contemporary codes police officers deal with on a regular basis during the course of their duties today. The relevance of this early legislation to contemporary policing is perhaps not surprising given that such legislation ultimately necessitates the development and continuation of some form of societally recognized enforcement mechanism if it is to be effective at controlling human behavior. In other words, once laws are created, they demand enforcement or their legitimacy may be questioned by the public. By extrapolation, we can reason that such a mechanism is also required if society is to prevent individuals from violating human rights standards and protections with impunity. In contemporary society, the police act as a necessary enforcement mechanism and have been granted the powers necessary to compel or coerce individual compliance with their directives during the course of carrying out their professional duties. As the following sections will illustrate, this enforcement capacity places the police in a unique position, where they have the ability to act as either a facilitating or an undermining force in relation to the protection of individual and collective human rights in modern society.

The Police as a Facilitating Force

In contemporary democracies, like the United States, many of the commonly recognized and frequently touted human rights protections that are said to be granted to the population are rooted in foundational documents and legislative enactments thought to represent the broader collective conscience. Documents such as the United States Constitution and the Bill of Rights depict protections, such as equitable treatment, freedom of speech and expression, and freedom of religious belief and practice, that are associated with broader ideals regarding the nature and substance of human rights.[4] While many of the philosophical, spiritual, and theoretical elements of human rights ideology transcend their written representation, codified depictions remain important to any discussion of the facilitating or negating role played by the police. This is especially true of the written law, given the substantive influence that it has on police practice and behavior. It is important to note that the police do not exercise this power in a vacuum, because a number of relevant factors constrain and limit the exercise of police power and authority. The police are only one branch of a much larger system intended to propagate and protect basic rights, privileges, and protections. In practice, this means that police influence can be offset by the actions and behaviors of external branches of the broader system in which law enforcement operates. Further, police behavior is constrained by a number of policies and procedures emanating from within the profession that exert a direct influence and robust control over officer actions and behaviors. Perhaps most importantly, the police have little real influence or control over the transcendental aspects of human rights ideology that drive societal ideas and public sentiment.

However, given their fundamental role as formal social control agents, law enforcement officers have significant control and influence over the regulation of the more visceral and codified representations of human rights ideology. In spite of the constraining forces on their behavior (policy manuals, supervisory oversight, etc.), law enforcement officers exercise a great deal of discretion in the manner in which they carry out their duties and the actions they take when interacting with members of the public. While other branches of the justice system (legislative, judicial, etc.) are responsible for producing codified civil and criminal codes, the police are ultimately responsible for the manner in which the enforcement of those codes is undertaken. If the protections and privileges encompassed in the codified law reflects the human rights protections that are important to a given society, then the police can rightly be viewed in many ways as the guardians of these broader protections. Many have argued that the written law is more strongly associated with civil rights than it is with human rights. There is some merit to this assertion, as human rights oftentimes carry a larger and more substantive connotation than do civil rights, which may, or may not, qualify as human rights according to most definitions.[5] However, with this in mind, it is still important to recognize that in spite of distinctions of this nature, the law still tends to act as an imperfect personification of the ideals, privileges, and protections that are the quintessential tenets of broader human rights protections.[6]

The official relationship between the police and the law is a clear one in many regards. Violations of the law necessitate a formal response of some type, which is carried out by the police officers who act as the enforcement arm of the state. If officers find sufficient cause, they have the legal authority to take action against those responsible and to introduce those individuals into the larger legal and justice systems for further processing. Since the commission of criminal offenses by one individual can undermine the rights and safety of others in society, the police enforcement response has the capacity to preserve human rights protections in two primary ways. First, an immediate and direct individual benefit is associated with police enforcement efforts. The arrest of offenders who demonstrate a willingness to undermine the human rights of others through victimization stops violations from occurring and provides immediate protections for those who would have otherwise been harmed. Second, the enforcement actions undertaken by officers can have an indirect influence on the protection of human rights. The arrest, prosecution, and punishment of those individuals intent on victimizing others, and in the process undermining their human rights, may have a deterrent effect on victimizations across society. Whether this effect is specific in directly deterring an individual offender or general in having a broader deterrent effect, many believe that it may help reduce the likelihood of future criminal actions that would undermine human rights protections. In fact, some have argued that one of the primary purposes for the existence of the police is to protect human rights.[7] While the official enforcement role is certainly an important consideration, it alone does not fully define the police role as a facilitating factor in relation to the protection of contemporary human rights.

Perhaps more importantly, the actions of the police largely determine what human rights mean in actual practice, rather than merely reflecting what we might ideally desire them to be in the form of our collective social conscience. Scholars in the field have referred to the distinction between the law as written and the law as practiced as law in action, as opposed to black letter law (the law as it is formally written in criminal statutes).[8] Given the discretion that they exercise when carrying out their duties, the police have the ability to pragmatically define many of the parameters related to contemporary human rights standards. For instance, the law may very well call for freedom of speech, expression, and assembly, but if officers fail to protect individuals when others threaten the practice of these rights, the protections cease to have any applied meaning. When officers actively defend the civil rights of others through their professional actions, they ultimately help facilitate the human rights that underscore them and make them a pragmatic reality. The professional role that the police occupy in this regard is shaped by a number of factors, including the discretion that officers exercise, the manner in which they interpret the law, their perspective regarding their professional role and function, and the organizational factors that constrain and influence their behaviors. Collectively, these factors help to define the law from a procedural standpoint, and in the process contribute to the degree to which the rights and protections provided by the law conform to the broader societal aspirations that drove their creation. Since the law serves as a reasonable approximation for societal ideals regarding human rights, police officers are largely responsible through their actions for determining whether form follows function regarding the provision and facilitation of human rights.

The police can certainly serve as an important means by which human rights, at least insofar as they are represented by the codified law, can be preserved and safeguarded. However, this safeguarding role is tentative and contextual, as it is based upon the police acting in a manner that aligns and supports implicit societal expectations regarding what human rights should be and how they can best be preserved and nourished. When professional actions and behaviors of police officers are thought to be proper or legitimate from a societal standpoint, the police are more likely to be acting in a manner conducive to their role as human rights advocates. However, as a variety of recent controversial events in society involving law enforcement have illustrated, the public does not always universally agree on what legitimate police behavior is or that the police are behaving in a manner that is universally agreed upon as being legitimate police behavior. Many believe that the police fail to live up to their expectations under the social contract by acting in a manner that fails to follow the spirit of the law or to enhance the overall public good.[9] When this occurs, police actions come into conflict with broader public expectations, and the police may start to be seen as a threat to human rights protections rather than a protector.

Police as an Undermining Force

Conversely, the very factors (enforcement capacity, coercive power, discretionary abilities, etc.) that allow the police to safeguard human rights can also allow them to act in a caustic capacity by restraining or undermining the free practice of these very same rights. At best, this can result in the police inhibiting human rights and at worst nullifying their protections altogether. The dualistic nature of the policing function as it applies to human rights can have both theoretical and pragmatic implications for modern democratic societies. On the one hand, the police can act to protect and further human rights, but on the other, they can become one of the most direct, common, and substantive threats to the continuation and practice of these rights.[10] The potential threat posed by organized policing systems is associated with their foundational role as the enforcement arm of organized government. In this role, the police have an inherent professional responsibility for ensuring public compliance with the mandates that government bodies create vis-à-vis enforcement of the written law. During the course of these enforcement duties, the police have frequent occasions to engage and interact with the public. On these occasions, police actions can significantly affect many of the important individual civil liberties that collectively embody the broader category commonly recognized as human rights.

While we typically associate human rights abuses with individuals who commit deviant or criminal acts against others, it is important to recognize that this traditional view of the criminal offender and their propensity to victimize others may be unnecessarily narrow. Other institutions and individuals within society who are not commonly labeled criminal (government agencies, elected officials, public employees, and community leaders) are also capable of threatening the substance and purpose of human rights protections. Given their professional status and the role they play in society, police officers are a critical member of this secondary threat group. Police officers can contribute to human rights violations through both acts of commission and acts of omission.

Acts of commission are the more recognized form of police human rights violation because they tend to generate the greatest amount of public attention and to invoke a more visceral societal reaction. These types of violations involve officers actively engaging in behaviors that violate the protections that represent the collective conscience regarding the basic human rights protections endowed to all people. While they tend to get less public attention, police acts of omission are no less significant in terms of the detrimental influence that they have on human rights. These types of violations involve officers passively allowing human rights violations to occur without intervening to ameliorate the resultant harm that they cause. For instance, during the course of their duties officers may become aware of misconduct occurring within their department that directly undermines the human rights of local residents. Officers who refuse to take some form of action (formal or informal) to remedy these violations are tacitly allowing the behavior to continue. In doing so, officers are by omission failing to uphold their oath of office, undermining public faith in their profession, and contributing to the ongoing violation of both civil and human rights.

All acts of police misconduct are substantive societal concerns that should be seriously considered to determine both their cause and best means of amelioration. However, the severity of police misconduct actions can also be placed along a threat continuum that allows them to be characterized as being more or less serious in relation to the harm they pose to contemporary human rights standards. Violations that pose a minor potential threat to human rights, even if they are not universally believed to constitute police misconduct, can be placed at one end of the threat continuum. The passive acceptance of gratuities provides one example of this type of behavior. While many would not view gratuities, in the form of free meals or drinks, as an example of police misconduct, it is possible that the passive acceptance of these items could influence the discretionary exercise of police authority. Officers accepting minor gratuities could decide that they will no longer fully enforce the law against the individuals providing these benefits in order to ensure their continuation. The inequity of treatment that would result from this differential enforcement could constitute a violation of the human rights principle of equality of treatment before the law, even if the violation itself did not cause serious harm. On the other end of the threat spectrum are serious acts of misconduct that are universally condemned because of the significant harm that they cause, the severe impact they have on human rights protections, and the manner in which they are indicative of failed policing efforts.[11] The purposeful use of excessive force to denigrate and degrade others would be an example of this type of behavior. Not only are acts of this nature more serious because of the direct harm that they cause the individual, they also fully undermine the foundational human rights standards associated with inherent human value and individual self-worth that form the foundation for many other important safeties and protections. Acts of this nature are particularly destructive when they target the most vulnerable in society, who may lack the capacity to fully understand the nature of their victimization.[12,13]

In spite of the dangers the policing function can pose to human rights, the police have assumed an important role in the broader social control framework in contemporary society. Given the significance of this position and the degree to which the public has increasingly come to rely on formalized social controls in the form of police services, there is little doubt that there will be an ongoing societal need for the police function in the future. This ongoing need does not necessarily equate with a broader social consensus regarding the police function. To the contrary, disagreement regarding the proper role, mission, and purpose of the policing function remains. However, in spite of the differences in opinion that exist, few would argue for the abolition of the police function in its entirety. One of the key future challenges pertaining to the police–human rights relationship that will have to be effectively addressed in the future concerns what is commonly referred to as the great dilemma.[14]

In essence, the great dilemma is a concept that refers to the challenge that is invariably associated with the necessary delegation of power to individuals and organizations, such as the police, within a given society. While power may be necessary if the police are to effectively enforce the law and mandate compliance with evolving civil and human rights standards, it also creates the potential for exploitation and abuse in the hands of the officers who command it. This creates a significant challenge concerning the best means by which the benefits commonly associated with a powerful state can be maintained, while at the same time ensuring that the exercise of power does not act against the best interest of the individual or the collective welfare. Finding a proper balance between individual rights and the need for a strong state is an imposing task that oftentimes eludes public consensus and ultimately offers few simple policy solutions. This likely explains both the fluid nature of public sentiment and the vacillating appearance of governmental action regarding intractable issues of this nature.

Reflecting Societal Values and Driving Social Change

The police ability to either facilitate or undermine human rights is an important consideration for contemporary society, but it is not the only significant role that the police play in this regard. In many ways, the relationship that exists between the police and the public regarding human rights is a symbiotic one that is rooted in mutual interdependence. This is perhaps most directly observable in the manner in which relevant police behaviors reflect or contradict broader public sentiment regarding the evolving status of human rights protections. In this role, the police act as a barometer capable of gauging societal attitudes pertaining to what human rights protections the public should or should not enjoy and how these rights should be implemented in practice. This is an especially cogent issue when the public experiences greater feelings of collective dread stemming from an increased fear of victimization or an enhanced threat to community safety. During these times, general public attitudes towards crime and criminals harden as the public seeks relief from the enhanced anxiety they are experiencing. Efforts of this nature are oftentimes associated with a general public sentiment that is less supportive of individual protections and more supportive of measures intended to ensure collective safety. As a result, the public becomes more likely to capitulate to government requests for enhanced power, even if those requests are associated with reduced civil liberties and restricted personal freedoms.

Attitudes of this nature ultimately create a social and legal climate less conducive to the protection of both civil liberties and human rights. The public may become more willing to grant the government additional powers, thereby expanding government influence and restricting personal protections. At the same time, the public may become more accepting of the aggressive policing tactics that are commonly associated with bolder enforcement initiatives. As a result, the societal significance of human rights diminishes as they are relegated to a lower level of importance in relation to growing public safety concerns. Legislative and judicial processes respond to public concerns with policy efforts that often serve only to further constrain freedoms. While public attitudes of this nature may have an adverse influence on the application of human rights, public sentiment is contextual in nature and subject to frequent fluctuations. When public attitudes are more positive and a heightened sense of optimism and satisfaction underscores societal sentiment, feelings of insecurity decline. A more positive public outlook is frequently accompanied by greater feelings of community security, which in turn drives communal desires for broader individual freedoms and fewer restrictions on civil liberties. Public attitudes become less tolerant towards police policies and practices viewed as being abusive or invasive. Police actions thought to be too aggressive result in amplified calls for police restraint, increased demands for organizational transparency, and intensified requests for more meaningful community oversight. Calls of this nature are oftentimes accompanied by public appeals for expanded civil liberties, which serve as a symbolic expression of deeper community desires to place human rights at the center of the policing function.[15]

As previously noted, public attitudes towards human rights tend to be largely contextual and fluid. As a result, the actions or behaviors of the police can serve as a social mirror that reflects broader community attitudes towards the necessity and desirability of human rights protections. At the same time, the police can also act as a catalyst for facilitating changes in societal expectations regarding the nature, substance, and extent of these same rights. While attitudinal changes can be driven by a variety of different factors, police actions often serve as a catalyst for change that is both rapid and significant. Changes in public sentiment related to the police typically pertain to public dissatisfaction with law enforcement behaviors that are viewed as being abusive, excessive, or a violation of community expectations. The public resentment that arises from police behaviors of this nature need not necessarily involve a direct violation of an established human rights standard, but they oftentimes do so either directly or collaterally. Rising public anger at this type of police behavior often fuels calls for greater public oversight of law enforcement agencies, increased transparency related to police practices, enhanced sanctions for rogue officers, and broader restrictions on police practice. At the same time, these calls are often accompanied by public demands for enhanced individual freedoms and expanded protections from the direct application of state power. Ultimately, change of this nature can not only constrain and restrict police practice, but also drive broader social change that can lead to expanded human rights protections in an attempt to reduce the likelihood of future violations occurring.

Summary

There is little doubt that a symbiotic relationship exists between the contemporary policing function and the individual and collective human rights granted to the public. Since the earliest origins of organized systems of law enforcement, the police have influenced the development and practice of human rights in a number of important ways. Two major perspectives permeate contemporary thought regarding the nature of the police–human rights relationship. As a result, the police have vicariously been viewed as either a substantive threat or important ally of existing human rights protections. Further complicating this somewhat convoluted relationship is the fluid and evolving role that the police have occupied in relation to social justice and human rights across time, contexts, and populations. The police may be viewed as facilitating human rights by one community but undermining them by another. Similarly, the police may be seen as strengthening human rights at certain times, while weakening them at others. Fluctuations of this nature underscore the importance of context in determining whether the police are viewed as enemies or champions of individual and collective human rights. Ultimately, it may be best to view the police as a calculated risk and a necessary evil in this regard. They are needed to help secure human rights, but the power that they exercise also provides them with opportunities to undermine the core values associated with these same rights. In spite of the potential harm that they pose, the police have historically occupied an important position in contributing to the substance and practice of human rights and they will likely continue to do so well into the foreseeable future.

Discussion Questions

1. Describe the significance of the Cyrus Cylinder and Code of Hammurabi in relation to contemporary ideas regarding individual and collective human rights.
2. Does the law act as a perfect representation of human rights? Why or why not? If not, why is the law still an important consideration when evaluating the police and their relationship to human rights?
3. Describe two different ways in which enforcement efforts can help the police protect human rights in society.

4. Describe the difference between police acts of commission and police acts of omission as they relate to contemporary human rights standards.
5. What is the "great dilemma" facing contemporary democratic societies and how is this concept important in relation to the police use of coercive power?
6. Describe how police behaviors can influence the pragmatic meaning of human rights in actual practice.
7. Compare and contrast the law in action and black letter law. How is each type of law related to broader societal ideals regarding the substantive nature of human rights?
8. How do the police act as a barometer in relation to public sentiment towards the need for human rights protections in contemporary society?
9. Discuss how the police can act as a catalyst for change in human rights standards and expectations in contemporary society.
10. Describe how the police can act to both undermine and safeguard individual and collective human rights.

Notes

1. Finkel, I. (2013). The Cyrus Cylinder: The Babylonian perspective. In I. Finkel (Ed.), *The King of Persia's proclamation from ancient Babylon: The Cyrus Cylinder* (pp. 4–34) New York: I.B. Tarius and Company Limited.
2. Ishay, M. R. (2008). *The history of human rights: From ancient times to the globalization era.* Berkeley, CA: University of California Press.
3. Cook, S. A. (2010). *The law of Moses and the Code of Hammurabi.* New York: Cosimo Classics.
4. Neuman, G. L. (2003). Human rights and constitutional rights: Harmony and dissonance. *Stanford Law Review, 55*(5), 1863–1900.
5. Greene, J. R. (2010). *Ideas in American policing: Policing through human rights.* Washington, DC: Police Foundation.
6. Maher, G. (1986). Human rights and the criminal process. In T. Campbell, D. Golderg, S. McLean, & T. Mullen (Eds.), *Human rights: From rhetoric to reality* (pp. 197–222) New York: Basil Blackwell, Inc.
7. Padmakumar, K. (2011). Human rights and policing in a plural democracy. In P. S. Nair (Ed.), *Human rights in a changing world* (pp. 328–331). New Delhi, India: Kalpaz Publications.
8. Greene, 2010.
9. Manning, P. K. (2010). *Democratic policing in a changing world.* New York: Paradigm Publishers.
10. Maher, G. (1986). Human rights and the criminal process. In T. Campbell, D. Goldberg, S. McLean, & T. Mullen (Eds.), *Human rights: From rhetoric to reality* (pp. 197–222). New York: Basil Blackwell, Inc.
11. Crawshaw, R. (2009). *Police and human rights: A manual for teachers and resource persons and for participants in human rights programmes,* 2nd ed. Boston, MA: Kluwer Law International.
12. Ungar, M. (2013). Crime, society, and the challenge to human rights protection. In K. Hite & M. Ungar (Eds.), *Sustaining human rights in the twenty-first century: Strategies in Latin America* (pp. 195–217). Baltimore, MD: John Hopkins University Press.
13. Greene, 2010.
14. Dunmah, R. G., & Alpert, G. P. (2015). The foundation of the police role in society. In R. G. Dunham & G. P. Alpert (Eds.), *Critical issues in policing: Contemporary readings* (7th ed., pp. 3–10). Long Grove, IL: Waveland Press.
15. Neyroud, P., & Beckley, A. (2012). *Policing, ethics, and human rights.* New York: Routledge.

9

BIAS-BASED POLICING AND RACIAL PROFILING

Ralph E. Ioimo

Introduction

Bias-based policing takes on many forms and has many components. Racial profiling is a form of bias-based policing that uses race as a determining factor associated with crime. Often the terms "racial profiling" and "bias-based policing" are used interchangeably. Bias-based policing is not easily defined and is confusing to most police officers as well as to the average citizen.[1,2,3] Defining bias-based policing practices is a difficult task, primarily because there is no single accepted definition of the term. To date, the author has been unable to identify a standard definition of bias-based policing or racial profiling. Certainly, if a police officer openly admits to stopping a Black person for no other reason than he was a Black man walking in an all-White neighborhood, this is a form of racial profiling. But what if the situation were reversed, and an officer stopped a White person walking in a Black neighborhood known to be a high drug trafficking area—is that racial profiling or good police work? Because there is no universally accepted definition of bias-based policing or racial profiling, the operational definition used within this chapter is *bias-based policing includes practices by individual officers, supervisors, managerial practices, and departmental programs, both intentional and non-intentional, that incorporate prejudicial judgments based on sex, race, ethnicity, gender, sexual orientation, economic status, religious beliefs, or age that are inappropriately applied.*

Bias has many factors, some that are valid and many that are not. As an example, if police officers believe that minorities commit most drug offenses even though this is untrue, it becomes a self-fulfilling prophecy.[4,5,6] Because police look for drugs primarily among Blacks and Latinos, they find a disproportionate number of these individuals with contraband.[7] This perception creates the profile that results in more stops of minority drivers.[8,9] Harris (1999) reports that Blacks constitute 13% of the country's drug users; 37% of those arrested on drug charges; 55% of those convicted; and 74% of all drug offenders sentenced to prison.[10,11] This type of bias contributes significantly to prison overcrowding and a disproportionate number of minorities that make up prison populations.

Implicit Versus Explicit Bias

Bias exists throughout our society; it is not limited to police. The science of bias shows that there are two forms of bias, implicit, which is difficult to identify because it is often unconscious but lurks under our outward behaviors, and explicit bias that shows clear and deliberate bias. If you asked someone if they were biased toward Mexicans, they would tell you that they were not. An example of unconscious bias is if a carful of Mexican men is seen in an affluent White neighborhood, and the White officer becomes concerned that these men are up to no good and stops the vehicle, but a carful of Caucasian males seen in the same area never arouses suspicion on the part of the officers. With implicit bias, people do not know that they have a prejudice.[12]

Explicit bias is more overt and is often identified through a deliberate police action. Explicit bias requires strong management processes to control. Typically, explicit biases are actions taken that clearly demonstrate a bias. Explicit bias cannot be tolerated in the criminal justice system, just as it cannot be tolerated in other parts of our society. Distinct police policies and procedures that control explicit bias are necessary to ensure explicit biases are not tolerated. Fortunately, explicit bias has decreased over the years, primarily because of the policies and procedure designed to control such behaviors.

As indicated, implicit bias is more difficult to identify. Police officers' actions that might be perceived as biased to others, do not appear biased to someone who holds an implicit bias. Training is the key to dealing with implicit bias. Unfortunately, this type of training often meets with resistance. This type of introspective training causes students to examine areas of their thinking that they do not associate with bias-based policing. The training needs to permeate the entire department, from top-level executives to patrol officers, and needs to occur on a regular basis.

A History of Bias

While it is unnecessary to once again recite the long and sordid legacy of bigotry and injustice throughout American history, perhaps a few reminders would suffice to set the tone surrounding minority concerns, especially those of Black Americans. The history of bias-based policing is founded in these early events. American society had passed discriminatory laws (Jim Crow laws) and the police vigorously enforced them. It is hard to accept the racial situation and hatred that existed in the 1950s and 1960s in the United States. Murder, beatings, Ku Klux Klan (KKK) activities, separate facilities for Whites and "Colored," police brutality toward minorities, separate schools, and government bodies spying on those involved in civil rights efforts were commonplace. Who can forget those incidents etched on the public memory, such as the efforts of Rosa Parks and the Montgomery bus boycott (1955); the fire hoses and police dogs during the Birmingham civil rights riots (1963); Governor George C. Wallace at the doors of the University of Alabama (1963); the Sixteenth Street Baptist Church bombing (1963); the assassination of Dr. Martin Luther King Jr. in Memphis (1968); Robert Russa Moton High School, Virginia (1951); and the "Bloody Sunday" Selma to Montgomery march (1965)? Many older Blacks and Whites today have vivid memories of such incidents and lived through those difficult times. Younger citizens have learned these lessons through their school history classes, documentaries, and parents and friends. Each person, to one degree or another, has a historical reference by which he/she evaluates present actions of the government and its agents of social control.

We have seen recent news media accounts of police abuse of power. Such incidents are daily reminders of police actions, such as the use of force against Black citizens by White police officers in the Cincinnati, Ohio, case of Timothy Thomas (2001), the beating of Rodney King in Los Angeles (1991), the Riverside, California, shooting of 19-year-old Tyisha Miller (1998), and the New York City shootings of Amadou Diallo (1999) and Andre Dorismond (2002). More recently, Ferguson, Missouri (2014), Baltimore, Maryland (2015), and Cincinnati, Ohio (2015) have brought bias-based policing issues to the forefront. Further, only rarely are officers involved in the use of force incidents found at fault. To some, this documents the fact that officers acted correctly, but to others it is a further sign of racial prejudice and bias-based policing at its worst. The perception that officers escape justice when they use force against Blacks is nothing more than further proof of collusion to many

Blacks of the White elites and a White criminal justice system protecting White officers. We have seen many major city departments come under investigation for police abuse of authority related to bias-based policing. Pattern and practice federal investigations have been undertaken in such departments as Miami, Washington, and Los Angeles due to concerns of police brutality and bias-based policing against Blacks and other minorities.

Identifying Bias-Based Policing

Black males represent 45% of the inmate population in the United States, while 34% of the male inmate population is White and 18% Hispanic.[13] In addition, while Blacks represent approximately 12% of the population, they account for 40% of the country's current death row prisoners, and one in three executed individuals since 1977.[14] However, a cautionary note must be interjected at this point. This data, in and of itself, cannot be taken at face value as an indication of bias, which is a recurring topic throughout this chapter. The issue is far more involved. As Engel[15] and her associates have stated,

> The problem with interpreting these findings is that the mere presence of disparity in the aggregate rate of stops does not, in itself, demonstrate racial prejudice, any more than racial disparity in prison populations demonstrates racial prejudice by sentencing judges.
>
> *(p. 250)*

Again, this does not mean that bias is nonexistent, only that disparity alone does not necessarily make for bias. Without appropriate methodological intervention to bring scientific analysis to the issue, certainty in the conclusions drawn cannot be determined.

We have also seen civil rights leaders calling for a White House summit (1999) to address the issue of police brutality on minorities, and any number of newspaper articles, studies, and television news programs on police brutality, bias, and the misuse of force against Blacks and other minorities. Perhaps the President's Advisory Board[16] said it best when they stated,

> Our Nation still struggles with the impact of its past policies, practices, and attitudes based on racial differences. Race and ethnicity still have profound impacts on the extent to which a person is fully included in American society and provided the equal opportunity and equal protection promised to all Americans.
>
> *(p. 2)*

This issue is not a Black issue alone; it is very much a White issue as well. Our history of Black subjugation and slavery has had a tremendous impact on both the Black and White psyche. Do not think for a moment that Whites have not been and are still not affected by this history, what it represents, and its belief system. While emphasis is traditionally placed on the obvious victims of such repressive systems, they do not stand alone as victims. Creating thought processes that allow for and support the subjugation of humans is damaging for all humans. Further, this mental process requires an outward process of developing a myriad of requisite psychological and physical control mechanisms, which are also psychologically destructive. The process of psychological and/or physical violence needed to support slavery and subjugation, from a human perspective, is a highly damaging human endeavor. This aspect of social violence coupled with the physical and psychological suffering of the minority victims presents deep-seated, often unspoken, misunderstood, and unrealized emotions and biases that must be worked through if we are to achieve a higher level of equality and fairness. Not to acknowledge these deep-seated fears and injuries for each race is to overlook an important aspect in resolving police bias, and bias in general.

Bias Is a Two-Way Street

Minorities also demonstrate bias towards police. The author was part of a large bias-based policing study of the Commonwealth of Virginia, and in one of the cities in the study, minority citizens complained of a specific officer who they said was biased. This officer was White, and to prove his bias they told us to look at the number of traffic citations that he wrote and assess the number of Black citizens versus the number of White citizens to whom he wrote tickets. We did as we were asked and looked into this issue, and we learned that this officer did write more citations to Black citizens than he did White; however, the area he was responsible for was an all-Black community, thus he came into contact with more Black drivers than he did White. We presented these facts to these citizens, but they insisted the officer was biased against Blacks and that was the reason he wrote more tickets to Black drivers. When pressed as to why they felt this way, they responded because the officer was White.[17] The officer had been aware of the complaints against him and developed his own policy that he referred to as his "Open Door Policy." When questioned about the policy, he stated, "it means if I open the door of my vehicle you are getting a ticket." This was regardless of race. This eliminated discretion on his part and insured his traffic enforcement had no bias.

In another Virginia community focus group meeting, an older Black man told a story of when he was given a speeding ticket and was adamantly convinced that the only reason he was given the ticket was because he was Black. In relaying the story, he stated that one evening he passed two police cars that had a car pulled over to the side of the road. One police car then began to follow him and proceeded to stop him. When he asked the officer why he was being stopped, the officer answered because he was speeding. When we asked if he was speeding, he responded, "I was only doing 10 miles over the speed limit and that the only reason the officer stopped me was because I was Black, not because I was speeding." This had occurred 10 years earlier, but his anger over the incident was as if it had occurred that day. He did not see that the officer had every right to give him the citation. He just saw a White officer stopping him and giving him a ticket as a form of bias-based policing/racial profiling.

During this study, we also ran into another story told by a Black officer, which speaks to the bias that Black people hold against police. He stated that he arrested an older Black man for drunk driving, and as he was walking him to the booking area the man stated to the officer, "the only reason you arrested me was because I am Black." The young Black officer turned toward the elderly man and, while looking at his own arm, said, "excuse me." After telling this story, the officer stated that when he is in uniform other Black people do not see him as being Black. He also stated that because he is a police officer, members of his own family won't even talk to him anymore. This also demonstrates the bias minorities have toward the police.

What Does the Research Show?

Many researchers believe that the war on drugs fosters negative encounters with minorities. The basis of racial profiling is the premise that minorities commit most drug offenses.[18] The premise is factually untrue, but it has nonetheless become a self-fulfilling prophecy. Because police look for drugs primarily among Blacks and Latinos, they find a disproportionate number of these individuals with contraband. This perception creates the profile that results in more stops of minority drivers.[19,20,21]

Weitzer and Tuch[22] found a common belief that a Black person is more likely to be stopped by police than a White person, but corroborating information on such stops is limited. The 1999 police-public contact survey by the Bureau of Justice Statistics[23] found that Blacks were somewhat more likely than were Whites and Hispanics (12.3%, 10.4%, and 8.8% respectively) to report being stopped by police. Stops by police officers can have lasting, adverse effects on citizens, especially when the stop appears to be racially motivated or as described above, even when the traffic stop is legitimate.[24] Based upon the citizen group meetings held throughout Virginia, the author found this to be true. Citizens raised complaints that dated back many years, but when the citizen relayed the incident, it generated intense anger and frustration that was visible to everyone in the room. We also learned that other citizens, who perhaps did not directly have a negative contact with police, presented cases or incidents they believed were examples of bias-based policing practices, which they learned from relatives and friends who might have directly experienced such a negative contact. There are obvious issues with taking an individual's word that their treatment by the police occurred in a biased manner. It lacks an opposing view and the issues can rarely be sufficiently examined.

The Officer's Approach

The officer's approach to the citizen further exacerbates these adverse effects. In Virginia, we learned while talking to the officers from each department that the Commonwealth-run academy teaches recruits to ask for the driver's license and vehicle registration before they tell the person why they were stopped. They are taught to take control of the situation by being firm without any form of pleasantries. Most of the time, the officers do not tell the citizen the reason for the stop. Obviously, some officers' personalities are such that they conduct business in a brusque manner. The citizens that the researchers spoke with indicated that the officer's approach tends to set the tone. Other research has shown that citizens, and Blacks especially, are much more likely to cooperate with officers when given a reason for the stop, and that people put a premium on officers reacting politely, listening to citizens, and explaining their actions.[25],[26],[27],[28] Weitzer and Tuch[29] point out that when officers maintain a proper demeanor and explain the basis for stops, citizens are less likely to conclude that the stop was racially motivated. When officers do not take the time to explain why they stopped the person that is when both White and Black citizens have a problem with the stop and the officer. White citizens explain that officers are just rude, while minority citizens point to bias-based policing as the reason for the perceived rudeness.

Police Force Diversity

Recent encounters with police and Black communities in Ferguson, Baltimore, Cleveland, etc. suggest that the solution to bias-based policing problems is a more racially heterogeneous police force, one that reflects the makeup of the community being served. You often hear of a need for racial proportionality in police force staffing. During the study of the Commonwealth of Virginia, it became questionable if even this would help solve some of these problems. During focus group meetings held in several communities across the Commonwealth, interesting discussions transpired between Black and White citizens conducted by the research staff. The intensity of Black citizens' distrust of and dissatisfaction with the police on various levels came out clearly. Unexpectedly, Black citizens were as concerned about Black officers as they were White officers. Departments throughout the country have enhanced their recruiting and hiring practices to ensure, to one degree or another, racial diversity throughout the department. Certainly, this is less true as you ascend the ranks, but overall significant strides have been made. Black citizens were, on the one hand, quick to applaud the inclusion of minorities in the ranks of the police, but unexpectedly they would later make such statements as "They do what their White masters tell them." When asked, "If it was wrong, why would Black officers do those things?" The response was, "If they didn't, they would get fired."[30]

One of the perceived advantages of ensuring a racial distribution among officers that represents the racial distribution of the population being policed is the assumption that the department will become more sensitive to the community. We discovered, however, that this assumption might not be completely accurate. In fact, officers, White and Black, admitted to the researchers that some Black officers are harder on members of their own race than are White officers. There seems to be an effort on those Black officers' part to prove themselves to their colleagues. It represents a form of overcompensation, and/or could be a reaction to a form of embarrassment they perceive toward members of their racial class that are posing a problem for the police.[31] Police departments also are having difficulties recruiting minorities for a variety of reasons. Part of the recruitment problem is rejection by family and peers, as discussed earlier.

Police and Community Cooperation: How Do We Get There

Police and community involvement, cooperation, and communication on bias-based policing issues are imperative. The structure that such forums take can and should differ between and among communities over time. The overriding goal is that regardless of how these forums are structured, they should serve to meet the needs of the community. Such efforts to enhance community involvement is inherent in community-based policing and is not a new idea for police departments. In fact, many departments across the country have already made inroads with their communities. The key is to further improve the viability of these forums in order to enhance results. These forums should include the beat officer as a full participant. This should be considered a part of his/her community policing responsibilities. Simply to have the department head or one of his/her designees attend these forums, while important, is not sufficient. The entire department needs to be involved. The better a department meets this recommendation, the better all aspects of policing will be for everyone in the community. Further, a department should consider the use of professional facilitators to help initiate the communication or to reinitiate the communication process if success is slow or an impasse is reached.

The use of qualified facilitators cannot be overemphasized as a means for a department and its community to address such a vital, volatile, and important issue as bias-based policing. A neutral, trained facilitator can help to organize, overcome problems, direct, and develop recommendations and plans of action. A facilitator can help direct participants to address underlying issues and come to workable solutions. Department heads should not think that they have to address these issues alone or without qualified professional assistance. The lack of true communication, commitment, and the ability of communities to address underlying issues will greatly impact the overall success of their efforts. Trained neutral facilitators can be very useful in achieving positive results in a timely fashion. Moreover, it is not a one-time, single-issue effort, but a continuous undertaking.

An essential key to thwarting improper police behavior is good management. In fact, without good management, no effort, policy, or threat will be successful. Good management means clear bias-based policing policies, procedures, oversight, and management and officer bias-based policing training, supervision, and commitment. This would include such management aids as early warning systems, sniffer software, in-car videotaping, body cameras, evaluation of various productivity measures, and the encouragement of a culture in the department that supports fairness.

The leadership in the department must be clear in their support of bias-based policing policies and procedures for addressing possible and found bias-based policing. Any failure on the part of management, such as the exclusion of a policy, lack of appropriate training, and/or appropriate procedures for enforcement of their policy, will have a deleterious impact on the department and the community. There can be no misunderstanding among department personnel that bias-based policing is neither "officially" nor "unofficially" supported in the department. Further, it must be crystal clear among department personnel that there is an expectation that bias-based policing policies will be enforced.

Police agencies should discontinue the use of soft profiling. A soft profile is something like, "looking for a Black male, 5'11", 180 pounds." This is too broad of a description and allows officers to stop just about any Black male on the street. It has no value but serves to irritate Black males that meet that description. Hard profiling provides specific information such as, "a Black male 5'10" to 6', with a gold earring in his left ear and a tattoo on the upper right arm that says 'Mom' driving a 1999 blue Ford Mustang." Hard profiling can provide the police with usable information to increase their chances for success and reduce public perceptions of lawlessness among their police. Unless a profiling process is subjected to strict scientific methods and continually evaluated, it does not have any place in the profession. Soft profiling is simply "dumb policing."

Improper profiling not only has the potential to impede upon the civil rights of innocent citizens, but it also causes consternation toward the police and provides cause for innocent citizens to question the officer's reasoning for subjecting them to such practices. Further, inaccurate profiling allows the guilty to subvert detection by avoiding known profiles used by the police. Profiling has its place in policing, but only if properly developed and maintained. Profiles change, and the police must use scientific methods to develop and evaluate the profiles they use.

Another police tactic frequently viewed as a form of bias-based policing are random roadblocks. If police use random roadblocks for drunken driving checks, seatbelt enforcement, or other similar checks, the roadblocks should truly be random. Police set up these types of roadblocks more frequently in less rather than more affluent areas of the community. During the Virginia study, police also openly stated that if they tried to set up such roadblocks in the more affluent areas of town, they would immediately meet resistance that would likely have political ramifications. While police will also tell you that these checks yield significant results in minority communities, they would likely produce similar results in the affluent neighborhoods, if allowed. This, once again, is a form of bias-based policing that can be resolved by conducting these roadblocks in all areas of the city.

In an effort to assess bias-based policing tactics associated with traffic stops, a number of agencies force the collection of specific data about each stop that goes beyond that which is collected on the citation. While this is taking place, there is no consistency and the information is hard to obtain because of a patchwork of laws and regulations across the country. Connecticut has been very active in this area and developed a computerized way of tracking traffic stop data to help identify bias-based policing tactics. California's Governor Jerry Brown signed a similar law into effect.[32]

Summary

The issue of bias-based policing in today's society has become critical. Over the past several years, we have seen relations between the police and the citizens they serve deteriorate significantly. Police community relations is not a new topic; it has been an issue for many years. Recently, however, we have seen relations deteriorate to the point of danger, with officers and citizens alike being killed. The worst incident was the killing of five Dallas Police officers in July 2016. These killings were in retaliation for police killings in Minnesota and Louisiana. The tension between police and the Black community continue to escalate. The killing of Trayvon Martin and the acquittal of his killer gave rise to Black Lives Matter. Street demonstrations erupted after Michael Brown's death in Ferguson, Missouri, Eric Garner's in New York City, and Freddie Gray's in Baltimore.

In the cases of Michael Brown, Eric Gardner, and Freddie Gray, the officers were all acquitted. In the case of Trayvon Martin, he was killed by George Zimmerman, who was not a police officer but a vigilante who claimed self-defense under Florida's "Stand Your Ground Law"; similar laws have become popular across the United States. Unfortunately, Zimmerman has been identified or associated with police. These events have contributed significantly to the eroding of police community relations and the insistence that these were all examples of bias-based policing.

The intent of this chapter was to highlight the issue of bias-based policing and to stimulate thought surrounding bias-based policing practices and policies so we can all gain an understanding of bias-based policing and how we can overcome its challenges.

Discussion Questions

The following are questions designed to stimulate thought and conversation pertaining to bias-based policing.

1. Bias-based policing and racism are often viewed as the same. Discuss the difference, as you see it, between bias-based policing and racism.
2. Describe implicit and explicit bias and how as a police administrator you would deal with both.
3. Recently, a number of Black citizens have been killed by police officers. While the officers doing the shooting were arrested and charged with murder, none has been convicted. Discuss this issue. Provide your opinion as to why none of these officers has been convicted. Support your opinion with facts.
4. For most citizens, the only contact they have with police is a traffic citation. In Virginia, officers are taught to approach citizens at a level 5 on a scale of 1–10, whereas the California Highway Patrol (CHP) encourages officers to begin at a level 1. Virginia believes starting at a 5 allows officers to take control and avoids confrontations, whereas the CHP believes starting out low key is best. Provide your opinion. Which do you believe is the better approach?
5. Discuss the two forms of profiling. Which is legitimate and which should never be used in policing? Discuss why.

Notes

1. Malti-Douglas, F. (2002). Review essay / the "p" word: Profiling. *Criminal Justice Ethics*, 21(2), 66–73.
2. Coker, D. (2003). Foreword: Addressing the real world of racial injustice in the criminal justice system. *Journal of Criminal Law & Criminology*, 93(4), 827–852.
3. Mac Donald, H. (2001, Spring). The myth of racial profiling. *City Journal*, 11(2). Retrieved August 9, 2004, from www.papillonsartpalace.com/mythof.htm
4. Coker, 2003.
5. Dateline NBC. (2004, April 10). *What is a consent search?* Retrieved May 17, 2004, from http://msnbc.msn.com/id/4703573
6. Mac Donald, 2001, Spring.
7. Coker, 2003.
8. Coker, 2003.
9. Harris, D. A. (1999). *Driving while Black racial profiling on our nation's highways.* New York: American Civil Liberties Union.
10. Ioimo, R., Tears, R., Meadow, L., Becton, B., & Charles, M. (2007, September 1). The police view of bias-based policing. *Police Quarterly*, 10(3), 227–287. Sage Publication.
11. Harris, 1999.
12. Means, Randy; Thompson, Paul; (July 2016). Implicit Bias in Policing: Part 1: Explicit versus Implicit. Law and Order; Willmette 64.7 10–11.
13. Bureau of Justice Statistics. (2003, August 27). *Bulletin: Prisoners in 2002.* Washington, DC: U.S. Department of Justice, Office of Justice.
14. Amnesty International. (2003, April 24). *United States of America death by discrimination: The continuing role of race in capital cases.* Retrieved April 30, 2004, from http://web.amnesty.org/library/Index/ENGAMR510462003
15. Engel, R. S., Calnon, J. M., & Bernard, T. J. (2002). Theory and racial profiling shortcomings and future directions in research. *Justice Quarterly*, 19(2), 249–272.
16. President's Advisory Board on Race. (1998). *One America in the 21st century: Forging a new future.* Retrieved March 19, 2004, from http://clinton2.nara.gov/Initiatives/OneAmerica/PIR.pdf
17. Ioimo, R., Tears, R., Meadow, L., Becton, B., & Charles, M. (2005). *Biased based policing: A study for the commonwealth of Virginia.* (Tech Report). Montgomery, AL: Auburn University at Montgomery, Center for Government.
18. Coker, 2003.
19. *Ibid.*

20. Harris, 1999.
21. Harris, D. A. (2002). *Profiles in injustice: Why racial profiling cannot work.* New York: The New Press.
22. Weitzer, R., & Tuch, S. A. (2002). Perceptions of racial profiling: Race, class, and personal experience. *Criminology, 40*(2), 435–457.
23. Bureau of Justice Statistics. (2001, February). *Contacts between police and the public: Findings from the 1999 national survey.* Washington, DC: U.S. Department of Justice.
24. Weitzer, & Tuch, 2002.
25. Skogan, W., & Hartnett, S. (1997). *Community policing, Chicago style.* New York: Oxford University Press.
26. Stone, V., & Pettigrew, N. (2000). *The views of the public on stops and searches.* London: Home Office.
27. Weitzer, & Tuch, 2002.
28. Wiley, M. G., & Hudik, T. (1974). Police-citizen encounters: A field test of exchange theory. *Social Problems, 22,* 119–127.
29. Weitzer, & Tuch, 2002.
30. Ioimo, R., Tears, R., Meadow, L., Becton, B., & Charles, M. (2005). *Biased based policing: A study for the commonwealth of Virginia.* Montgomery, AL: Auburn University at Montgomery, Center for Government.
31. *Ibid.*
32. Ramachandran, V., & Kramon, K. (2016, August). *Are Traffic Stops Prone to Racial Bias? The Marshall Project Report.* Retrieved February 4, 2018, from www.themarshallproject.org/2016/06/21/are-traffic-stops-prone-to-racial-bias

10

POLICE PERFORMANCE MANAGEMENT AND SOCIAL JUSTICE

John A. Eterno and Eli B. Silverman

Background

Police performance management began in 1994 in New York City. It was called Compstat (compare statistics). In that year, Police Commissioner William Bratton, assisted by others, especially Deputy Commissioner Jack Maple, developed an innovative way of managing police. It focused on crime control—especially index crime. Index crimes are those used to determine the crime rate. The Federal Bureau of Investigation collects data from approximately 95% of police departments in the United States. Agencies voluntarily inform the FBI of the number of crimes that occurred in their jurisdictions based on reports taken by their officers. Murder/non-negligent manslaughter, robbery, burglary, aggravated assault, forcible rape, larceny-theft, and motor vehicle theft are the crimes are used to determine the crime rate. This method of counting crimes is called the uniform crime reporting system. Police are well aware of the index crimes and know that agencies often compare themselves to one another through these numbers. The FBI conducts exceedingly minimal inspection of these police reports and their reporting mechanisms. There are many reasons for this, including political and economic explanations, but the lack of oversight can also be attributed to the voluntary nature of the system itself with little or no funding.

Compstat compels commanders to compare current index crime numbers within their areas of responsibility (usually a precinct or similar area at the lower level, but higher levels will examine an entire region or agency) to the previous year. No mayor, police chief, or commander wants the numbers to increase in their jurisdictions. For some local commanders, fear is often the main motivator. Compstat meetings are held regularly at headquarters. Commanders of precincts (mid-level managers) are brought up before the higher echelon of the department and are especially grilled about their crime numbers. Over time, other numbers also became important, such as the number of summonses, arrests, and stop and frisk reports (forcible stops of suspects by police officers—sometimes called *Terry* stops from the court case *Terry v. Ohio* [1068]). Commanders are questioned if the numbers are going in the "right" direction (i.e., crime is decreasing). If so, then there is little issue. However, if the numbers do not look good (crime is increasing), commanders will often be targeted for interrogation by high-ranking inquisitors running the meetings. Local commanders are made to feel responsible for any increases in crime, and ultimately the police are blamed for the illegal acts committed by criminals. The high-ranking questioning officials (inquisitors) will, at times, bully, berate, and even embarrass commanders, so that when the commanders return to their precinct, they know what is expected of them—make the numbers look good or else. The unspoken message is, "if your numbers look good, you will have a great career and be promoted. However, if the numbers do not look good, you will have a terrible career and never be promoted." It should be noted that politics also plays a role. Those who know the right person will often be treated more delicately at these meetings. Additionally, as crime dropped precipitously, commanders had more difficulty keeping the numbers going in the right direction. In New York City, for example, by 2002 crime was down 60%. Keeping the numbers going down became a real chore for commanders. One commander that we interviewed stated, "As crime goes down, the pressure to maintain it got great . . . it was a numbers game."

Initially, Compstat had a positive effect. Officers of all ranks were brought together to problem solve about real crime reports. Over time, however, much of Compstat morphed into a bean counting exercise that nearly everyone knew was a game that had to be played in order to get their ticket punched for promotion.

This is not to say that Compstat was a failure. Indeed, we think just the opposite. It is an excellent tool for leadership—if used properly. We now explain some of the well-known positive aspects of Compstat. Finally, we will point out the lesser-known negative aspects and focus on those aspects that affect social justice.

Positive Aspects of Compstat

There are some very effective aspects of Compstat. Its four-part mantra when used properly is truly innovative. The mantra begins with accurate and timely intelligence. Securing information from complaint reports, informants, other community contacts, other agencies, and other sources form the foundation of Compstat. Accurate intelligence is the substance of police work. For example, obtaining and deciphering intelligence helps develop patterns to identify criminals, provides information to detectives for follow-up, helps crime analysts reveal trends, and is ultimately critical to police operations and decision-making. One way intelligence might be used is if several rape complaints are filed with the same modus operandi (way of doing the crime), a pattern could emerge. That is, the crime is probably conducted by the same perpetrator. In New York City, Compstat led to the formation of pattern identification modules to help identify patterns quickly and prevent future crimes. This was innovate and effective. Such innovation is a key aspect of Compstat.

The second element in the mantra is to develop effective tactics to deal with the intelligence information. New ideas such as civil enforcement by the Legal Bureau (attorneys who work for the department) was a brilliant innovation. This involved using civil law (lawsuits) rather than criminal law to address problem establishments. Using this strategy could close down drug dens, areas where shooting is rampant, and other crime-ridden businesses.

Such innovative strategies were promoted citywide through the Compstat meetings. In this way, everyone in the NYPD would be informed about an innovate technique and adopt it quickly. For example, the use of high school yearbooks became commonplace after one suspect was identified that way and it was mentioned at Compstat.

Another key aspect to these meetings is that many officers of all ranks and units are brought together in one forum. This helps prevent what is commonly known as the silo effect. Silo effect occurs when units, divisions, and bureaus work on their own, in isolation of other units. There is no cross-communication among personnel, so each bureaucracy must solve problems without knowing what others are doing. Sometimes this leads to impeding another entity's efforts or developing a tactic that never sees the light of day in the entire organization. This is inefficient and, at times, detrimental to the mission of police. Compstat provides a way for many different arms of the agency to interact, problem solve, and develop and/or simply borrow strategies. If one precinct develops a useful strategy, the entire department will become aware of it through Compstat. Also, if one precinct has a particular problem, say drugs, the entire department's resources will now be aimed at solving the issue. Narcotics Units (who work in another bureau and generally do not interact with precinct personnel) may, for example, be able to provide personnel and resources on an issue that they may previously have been unaware of until the Compstat meeting.

The third part of the four-part mantra is rapid deployment. Resources based on the tactical plan developed in the previous mantra must be deployed quickly and efficiently. If an establishment was to be closed due to drug dealing and civil enforcement was to be used, then a plan would be quickly developed. Rather than wait, languishing in a huge bureaucracy, plans are quickly put into place so that the operation can be assessed at the next Compstat meeting. Ultimately, if the plan failed to achieve the desired results, the final part of the mantra—relentless follow-up and assessment—would close the loop. New intelligence would let officers know whether the tactic worked. If there were continued drug dealing, a new strategy would have to be developed based on new intelligence. In this way, Compstat is very effective.

To demonstrate Compstat's effectiveness, NYPD has boasted about its reduction in crime for many years. Based on NYPD's statistics, crime is now down over 80% in the city. Mayors have been bragging for years that it is the "safest big city in America." While the extent of this drop is questionable, some decrease is clearly taking place. How much of this is due to police behavior is another question. However, at least some of the drop in crime is likely due to the police being more effective due to Compstat. NYPD widely publicizes the decrease in crime and its Compstat system; however, it rarely admits any weaknesses.

Compstat has some very important aspects. The promotion of innovative strategies, four-part mantra, prevention of the silo effect, development of patterns, and sharing of innovative ideas to all are just some of the positive aspects of performance management.[1] However, over time, these positive qualities devolved into a bean counting, emotionless bureaucracy that ultimately failed in its mission to protect basic rights.

Negative Aspects of Compstat Related to Social Justice

The negative aspects of police performance management are far less publicized. The constant boasting about lower crime in New York City has become part of the mainstream rhetoric from the police department and politicians. Based on specific research conducted by the authors of this chapter, we can confidently state that over time Compstat morphed into a numbers-crunching bureaucracy in New York City. Its lack of connection to its own members and the public (especially minorities) became the new cornerstone of performance management. As a result, the system went amok. While we believe that this does not have to be the case, the New York City system has been and continues to be emulated throughout the democratic world. As international policing scholar David Bayley suggests, NYPD is a flagship department that other agencies emulate.[2] As they copy the NYPD, these other agencies fall into the same traps. Consent decrees, court-ordered oversight, and other remedies are omnipresent throughout the democratic world as problems with bullying by bosses, racist and undemocratic policing as well as crime report manipulation are rapidly being uncovered in many jurisdictions, which include Baltimore, New Orleans, Los Angeles, Pittsburgh, Chicago, Boca Raton, and Milwaukee nationally, and Australia, Sweden, the United Kingdom, and France, another other nations, internationally. The performance management system needs to be carefully monitored by watchful and caring leaders lest the following negative behaviors rear their ugly head.

Bullying Behaviors by Supervisors

One negative aspect of Compstat is bullying behavior by higher-ranking officers. Most police departments have a rank structure similar to the military. This demonstrates to all who is in charge and a system of rigid discipline. In New York City, the ranks (from lowest to highest) are police officer/ detective, sergeant, lieutenant, captain, deputy inspector, inspector, deputy chief, assistant chief, and chief. At the highest levels, there are also deputy commissioners and the police commissioner who are civilians (not sworn, uniformed members). Other civilian ranks are mixed in, but they have very specific roles, such as staff analyst, administrative assistant, and so forth. Our research indicates that bullying behaviors by high-ranking managers echo throughout the organization and even influence how police interact with communities.

At Compstat meetings, the inquisitors are very high-ranking officials. In New York City, this usually includes the chief of department, the deputy commissioner of operations, and sometimes even the police commissioner. Such officials already have enormous authority. The tone of the entire Compstat meeting is set by the inquisitors, so if they are screaming and yelling, then everyone tends to follow their lead. Unfortunately, from what our surveys and interviews suggest, the inquisitors will often lord their authority over underlings.

While Compstat meetings can be professional, commanders of precincts can be berated by inquisitors. Say, for example, crime numbers are going up in the command. The commander may be told he/she is doing an ineffective job. Indeed, meetings have been known to deteriorate into outright berating and scolding of commanders. Examples of statements about such activities are revealed in our interviews. One advised,

> People [commanders] were embarrassed in front of peers, often condescending . . . A lot of people cannot present themselves . . . It's all about numbers. . . . If you missed it, then you are dead. Compstat created a lot of pressure . . . Most of the pressure is with crime numbers . . . a lot of pressure on how things looked.

Another example:

> Compstat was the best thing that ever happened to the NYPD, when done right . . . Some beatings were warranted but they went too far. . . . You are out of your mind if you want to be a Captain.

And another,

> People's careers were made at the podium. . . . Numerous hardworking [commanders] got screwed because they could not speak . . . This destroyed morale in the detective bureau. . . . I observed one commander get bullied. They publicly embarrassed him. He was good with the community but could not get his point across at the podium.

This chapter is not sufficiently long to include all comments about NYPD behaviors. The research can be summarized as follows—the key managerial style is fear based on a top-down approach. Indeed, three key themes emerge: (1) top-down management style; (2) hierarchical pressure; and (3) commander morale, abuse, and embarrassment.

Is this an accurate portrayal of Compstat at other agencies? Many police departments simply emulate what NYPD does.[3] John Timoney, former first deputy commissioner of NYPD, former police commissioner of Philadelphia, and former Miami police chief, notes, "Unfortunately, early on, I think many departments looked at Compstat, went back to their cities and said, 'I know how to do this. You just bring somebody up and yell at them.' But that is not necessarily going to work in other cities."[4]

In terms of social justice, the inequality of ranks should never lead to bullying behaviors. If we expect street-level officers to treat citizens with respect and dignity, they need to receive the same from their supervisors. Furthermore, if officers are treated poorly by their supervisors, such behaviors may be emulated by officers in the field. That is, the bullying and pressures of high-ranking officials will have a ripple effect throughout the agency. Lower-ranking supervisors will treat officers poorly and, in turn, police officers will treat citizens poorly. Indeed, increased levels of pressure from supervisors have led to increased civilian complaints, lawsuits, and other negative behaviors by officers, as seen in the next section. As we have stated, these behaviors have been observed in many of the departments that have adopted the NYPD model of policing, such as Newark, Baltimore, Chicago, New Orleans, Los Angeles, and others in the U.S., as well as internationally in the United Kingdom, Australia, France, and other countries that have simply copied the NYPD model. While bullying behaviors are a major concern, they also are a springboard for other negative aspects of performance management that influence social justice throughout the United States and the world.

Racism, Unconstitutional Policing, and Disrespecting Basic Rights

Current events show that police and minority relations are at a low point. Michael Brown in Ferguson, Missouri; Eric Garner in New York City; Tamir Rice in Cleveland; demonstrations in St. Louis due to the acquittal of former officer Jason Stockley for killing Anthony Lamar Smith; demonstrations in Baltimore over the death of Freddie Gray in the rear of a police transport vehicle; the ambush and assassinations of New York City police officers Rafael Ramos and Wenjian Liu are just some examples of the tense relations between police and minorities in the United States. Well-known police behaviors are associated with unprofessional and even illegal activity by police, such as "driving while Black," testifying, and racial profiling. These are common sayings reflecting some of the public's attitude toward police. Recent opinion polls show a wide gap between minorities and Whites regarding police. From 2014 through 2016, a Gallup poll shows a 29% gap between Whites and Blacks with respect to confidence in the police. Of Blacks surveyed, 29% indicated that they had a great deal or quite a lot of confidence in the police. However, 58% of Whites showed high confidence in the police.[5] While the racial divide among citizens is clear, it is equally important to note that police are feeling the issue as well. Another recent survey shows that police feel their job is harder due to racial difficulties.[6] So whether we view the issue from the viewpoint of the citizens or law enforcement, it is clear that tensions are high.

Additionally, with the election of Donald Trump as president of the United States, race relations appear to be near a boiling point. For example, White supremacists demonstrated in Charlottesville, Virginia, causing a ruckus with little or no police intervention. President Trump chimed in on the issue, blaming both sides equally.[7] Placing White supremacists on equal footing with other protesters is questionable and morally reprehensible—to say the least. Such a message from the top does not appear to bode well for race relations between police and minority communities—at least in the foreseeable future.

The police performance management system exacerbates these racial tensions. Pressures emanating from the upper echelon, who use the meeting as a podium and magnifier of their power, has severely aggravated the already tense relationship between minorities and police. The pressures from the top, including the bullying behaviors we noted, are aimed at making the measured numbers look better. This especially includes pressures to write summonses, make arrests, reduce recorded crimes, and, importantly, increase stop and frisk. Commanders are constantly compared to last year's figures. Crime numbers are the most important. However, commanders are grilled on these other areas as well. Rarely are the pressures extended to accurately count crimes or ensure basic rights. Indeed, our 2012 survey of New York City Police indicates that the pressure on officers to write summonses, make arrests, and conduct forcible stops were at a high point (due to Compstat) in the first decade of the 21st century. Further, the pressures to protect constitutional rights were eroding.[8]

Unfortunately, the performance management system, when not properly utilized, can have a deleterious influence on police respect for constitutional rights and can even lead to racist behavior by police. The aforementioned bullying behaviors, which emanate from the top, ultimately lead police officers on the streets to practice racist policing, use unnecessary force, and have a disrespect for human rights.

The preeminent NYPD Compstat system provides a key example. Under the auspices of stopping crime, the NYPD engaged in racist policing practices. In New York City, for example, there were two critical court cases in this area, *Floyd v. City of New York* and *Stinson v. City of New York*. The city lost the first case at trial, and in the second, the plaintiffs settled for approximately $75 million.[9]

The *Floyd* case is a landmark case for the NYPD. The police department claimed that the super-aggressive use of stop and frisk was necessary to keep crime down and take guns off the streets. Yet, nothing could be further from the truth.

What is stop and frisk? In New York City, it is a policy based on the United States Supreme Court case *Terry v. Ohio* (1968). In this case, the United States Supreme Court allows police officers to forcibly stop criminal suspects based on a lower level of proof, termed reasonable suspicion. In nontechnical language, this means that officers must be about 20% to 25% sure that a person committed, is about to commit, or is in the process of committing a crime. Officers can forcibly stop the person for a short period to determine if the person is a perpetrator. If the officers develop probable cause (more evidence is gained so that the officer is about 50% sure a crime is committed), then the officer may arrest the individual. However, if probable cause is not developed, the officer must let the suspect leave. It is short term—the officer cannot hold the person indefinitely while the investigation is being done. The officer can ask pertinent questions, such as the reason for a behavior. For example, officers can ask the reason why the person is in the area and so forth. Sometimes the officer can frisk the criminal suspect as well (a frisk is a patting of the outer garments). The frisk is only for weapons and not illegal drugs or other contraband. The officer must have reasonable suspicion that the person stopped has a weapon before conducting the frisk. Some crimes, such as robbery, allow an automatic frisk due to the nature of the crime. If an object that feels like a suspected weapon is felt, the officer can then search—go inside the suspect's clothing to determine if the object felt is indeed a weapon.

This is the essence of the stop and frisk policy. However, the New York City police department took this to new levels. Until about 2002, the NYPD would conduct about 1,000,000 stops per year. Then in 2002, corresponding to the election of Michael Bloomberg and the appointment of Police Commissioner Raymond W. Kelly, the department changed its policy and the defense of the policy. Based on our research, we found that officers were placed under tremendous pressure to get a certain number of stops, summonses, and arrests. It was a strict quota, so that the numbers could be reflected at Compstat.[10] To make matters worse, the department tried to defend itself, stating that the aggressive increase was needed to keep crime down and keep guns off the streets. Even the most cursory review of the department's own figures showed these justifications to be a complete fantasy—as we see in the *Floyd* decision.

For example, crime was down 60% by 2001. This was achieved without the aggressive policy of stop and frisk. Thus, crime was already down 60% *before* the aggressive increase in forcible stops. By 2011, the department was conducting nearly 700,000 stops without the concurrent enormous decrease in crime. The department claimed that if they discontinued stop and frisk, the streets would be chaos and guns would pour down upon residents. In 2011, many began to question the wisdom of this policy. Of course, the NYPD placed itself in an untenable position. Namely, if crime is down so much in the city, how is it possible that there are nearly one million criminal suspects to forcibly stop? Additionally, how were they able to drive crime down so much without the aggressive tactic through 2001? The department also claimed that stop and frisk was very effective at getting guns off the streets. However, less than 0.2% of stops led to the retrieval of guns. Additionally, other tactics such as gun buy-back programs, interrogation of suspects, and working with federal agencies to stop gun running and other illegal practices that bring guns into the city were far more fruitful. A final claim was that murder was being controlled by the aggressive tactic. However, in 2001—before the aggressive tactic began—there were 586 murders, which was down from 2,245 murders in 1990. Further, in 2011—at the height of aggressive stop and frisk—there were 515 murders, a small drop compared to the 600% increase in stops. More recently, with stops at a low due to the *Floyd* decision and a federal monitor on the police, fewer than 50,000 stops are being recorded and murders are now below 400.

Our research also indicated that the Compstat pressures on officers to conduct forcible stops, write summonses, and make arrests markedly increased. The research cited in the *Floyd* case shows clear trends of increasing pressures on officers to create activity reflected in the Compstat numbers. At the same time, the pressures to uphold the Constitution markedly *decreased*. Our published research, cited in the *Floyd* case, indicates that before 1995, only 9.1% of officers felt high pressures to write stop and frisk reports. After 2001, however, over 35% felt high pressure to write stop and frisk reports. This is from a survey of nearly 2,000 New York City officers of all ranks. Similar increases in pressure are seen for summonses and arrests. Simultaneously, officers surveyed perceived less pressure from the department to obey constitutional rights—from 47% in the period 1995 to 2001 to 36% in 2002 and after.[11] This combination—enormous increases in pressure to create activity and decreases in pressures to obey the law—is clearly problematic and likely a major cause of the egregious racist behavior we see in the *Floyd* opinion.

Minorities were alienated by these practices. Grassroots groups organized themselves against the tactic. The Police Reform Organizing Project and Communities United for Police Reform are two examples of these groups. Some critics of these organizations argue that this is simply aggressive policing. However, the facts speak for themselves. By any measure, the department's practices were ineffective, illegal, and racist. Approximately 90% of the forcible stops occurred in minority neighborhoods. The vast majority of these stops were of completely innocent people. Making matters worse, the NYPD Compstat performance management system is based on getting accurate and timely intelligence. Alienating minorities is certainly not a way to get more information. Indeed, the National Crime Victimization Survey (NCVS) indicates that citizens in New York City are among the least likely to make an official report about a crime, compared the rest of the United States.[12]

Alienation of minorities by the NYPD is also seen in their Demographics Unit. Recently disbanded, the unit was spying on Muslims in and around New York City. The department had no evidence on any of these groups and merely acted out of religious stereotyping. Spying was conducted at New York City's John Jay College of Criminal Justice, in New Jersey, and in many other locations. The NYPD did not notify local authorities or the college president of any of its work. In court, the former commanding officer of the unit testified under oath that not one incident of terror was uncovered by these efforts. The level of protest and alienation was considerable. Even the Federal Bureau of Investigation was publicly outraged that the NYPD may have compromised its operations in New Jersey. The FBI had developed a policy of working closely with the Muslim communities so that they could voluntarily get information on possible radicalized youth. The FBI publicly berated the NYPD for hurting this intelligence-gathering operation.[13]

Faced with clear facts, why the department remained so stubborn in its position we may never know. As a side note, the department today makes less than 50,000 stops and crime continues to decrease. While this would seem to be a step in the right direction, the damage is already done and lessons must be learned.

New York City is exporting this management system throughout the nation and the world. Yet little is understood about its racist and unconstitutional side effects. Similar practices have been observed in other cities such as Newark, Baltimore, and New Orleans—among other cities now under consent decrees or court monitoring due to their unconstitutional practices. The theory behind these very aggressive policing policies is generally termed broken windows, zero tolerance, or similar words. Essentially, the police take this to mean that they will enforce every law in the books to the maximum—even the most minor of violations. Officers scour the streets looking for any legal violations, such as drinking a beer in the streets, loitering, smoking a marijuana cigarette, playing chess in a park without a child under the care of the chess player, eating doughnuts in a park without a minor present, writing graffiti, washing windows of cars stopped at red lights, and putting feet up on subway seats late at night. The officers do not enforce these laws with warnings but write summonses or make arrests, later reflected in the Compstat numbers. Such activity can then be used by the commander to cover him- or herself at the Compstat meeting. For example, if a robbery took place in the precinct, the commander can talk about how many forcible stops were done, how many summonses were written, and so forth, demonstrating a clear police presence in the area—regardless of the quality of the policing that is being done. As demonstrated, such activity is far more damaging than helpful and even illegal.

Corruption of Crime Numbers

The bedrock of policing is securing accurate and timely intelligence. Information and reports can then be analyzed to fight crime and maintain (or at least work toward) democratic principles. With crime reports so critical to policing, it is unfortunate that another debilitating side effect of the Compstat performance management system is corruption of crime reports. More specifically, the corruption of the crime reporting system is exacerbated under the pressures of Compstat.

In two separate surveys we conducted, we not only demonstrated the aforementioned bullying by supervisors and racist and unconstitutional policing, but we also revealed that crime reports were manipulated by mid- and lower-ranking officers.[14] Our first survey was distributed in 2008 to retired captains and higher ranks.

One important question of the survey is, "With respect to the following criteria and based on your personal experience, on a scale of 1 to 10 (with 1 being the least and 10 the most), how much pressure was there from management/supervisors to decrease index crime?" This question shows the largest single difference in responses between those who retired before Compstat and those who retired after in the entire study. The average response from commanders who worked pre-Compstat was 5.66. The average response from those commanders who worked post-Compstat was 8.26. This is a large mean difference of 2.6. For those with statistical knowledge, this is a large size effect ($r = .557$), and the probability of a result of this size occurring by chance is slim ($p < .001$). Essentially, what this means is that those commanders who worked in the Compstat era felt much more pressure from management/supervisors to reduce the level of index crime. This confirms Compstat's enormous pressures to reduce index crime.

The next comparison is based on another question, which reads, "To what extent did management demand integrity in crime statistics?" This question is also on a scale of 1 to 10, with 1 being slight demand and 10 being high demand. We expect that demand for integrity in statistics would be about the same, or perhaps even more during the Compstat era, because of the new focus on crime statistics. The results from the survey, however, indicate that demand for integrity in crime statistics was significantly greater in the pre-Compstat era. The average response was 7.18 for pre-Compstat commanders and 6.52 for Compstat commanders. The mean difference is .66, which is statistically significant ($p < .01$). In addition, of the 82 respondents who stated there was slight demand for integrity in the crime statistics, nearly 80% were working in the Compstat era. This reveals that Compstat-era commanders felt much *less* demand from management for integrity in the statistics compared to their counterparts who did not work during the Compstat era.

We also asked a question regarding managerial pressure to downgrade index crime to non-index crime. This is different from pressure to decrease index crime. Pressure to decrease index crime is something we might normally expect of a police department. That is, crime should be low and such pressures might be considered normal. However, pressure to downgrade index crime to non-index crime is a specific practice requiring commanders to find ways to move crime from one category (index) to another category (non-index). An example of this activity is a commander feeling pressure to move grand larceny to lost property. We expect this pressure to be low because, by its nature, downgrading is suspect (unethical) activity.

This is a very important distinction. When we see pressure to downgrade index crimes to non-index crimes, it means that commanders are not considering actual criminal activity but rather the numbers of reports in each category. They are experiencing pressure to make sure that the numbers are not too high in the index crime category, which means they feel pressure to play the numbers game.

Importantly, pressures to downgrade index crime were significantly higher in the Compstat era. The average response of commanders in the Compstat era was 3.88 and the average response of commanders in the non-Compstat era was 2.51. The difference is 1.37. This was a statistically significant difference ($p < .001$) and a small size effect ($r = .077$). What this means is that once again the pressures are higher for Compstat-era commanders, in this case, to downgrade index crime to non-index crime.

We also asked directly whether captains were aware of crime report manipulation. Of the 309 commanders who worked in the Compstat era, roughly half (160) indicated they were aware of any changes to reports whatsoever. Since changes to reports occur every day, we removed those who are aware of no changes at all. This is because these commanders likely did not have assignments with complaint reports being taken (e.g., police academy, headquarters, and other such units). Of the 160 respondents who were aware of any changes, over half (53.8%) indicated that the changes observed were highly unethical. An additional 23.8% indicated the changes were moderately unethical. The remainder indicated the changes were ethical. With over half of those aware of changes indicating that those changes were highly unethical, there can be no doubt that unethical manipulation was taking place at a high rate.

This survey shows clear evidence of extensive crime report manipulation. However, we took this even further. We wanted to be sure that our results accurately reflected what was occurring at the police department, so we conducted a second survey with a different sample. This sample included all ranks. The results of this second survey conducted four years later in 2012 replicated the previous one. For this second survey, we used sophisticated statistical tests to demonstrate that misuse of the performance management system and pressures from Compstat are key explanations for crime report manipulation.[15] One analysis, for example, shows that 55.5% of those who retired after 2001 (in the aggressive Compstat era) were aware of crime reports being manipulated to make the crime numbers look better; however, only 30.3% were aware of such manipulation before Compstat began. The result was fairly strong and statistically significant ($\gamma = .337; p < .001$).[16]

The manipulation of crime reports has serious repercussions for victims of crime. They are being heard incorrectly or not being heard at all, as report wording is manipulated to make it appear that crimes are not as serious as they actually are. This makes the department look better but fails to help victims properly and catch perpetrators efficiently. A good example of this is Detective Harold Hernandez of the NYPD. He was interrogating a recently arrested rapist who admitted to other rapes in the precinct. When the detective went to close out the other complaints, he found all of the reports were listed as minor crimes, such as criminal trespass. The reports had no mention of the rapes. They were all downgraded by not recording the sexual aspects of the incidents. Such reporting is unconscionable. A rape pattern could have been uncovered and rapes prevented had the reports been taken as they should have been. Indeed, sex crimes victims groups approached the police commissioner and informed him of the problem. Such was the extent of the manipulation.

Manipulation of crime reports continues and is fairly well known in other jurisdictions as well. An exposé by *Chicago* magazine is particularly striking. Even murders are being hidden.[17] The impact on social justice can only be surmised, as the extent of the problem largely remains hidden.

Social Justice and Policing

We have revealed three key areas of concern regarding police and social justice: bullying behaviors by supervisors that may be emulated by street officers in the field, racist and unconstitutional policing, and crime report manipulation by officers. Countless lives have been impacted by these police behaviors. Police brutality, racist policing, and failure to help victims of crime are only some of the issues that are touched upon by these police behaviors. The abuse of the police performance management system is a catalyst increasing the levels of these disturbing behaviors by police. What can be done?

Essentially, our suggested reforms fall into three broad categories: external review, transparency, and community partnerships. External review should be in the form of a permanent committee or group that oversees the police. This arm of government should be free from the executive branch such that the police are effectively checked and balanced. We suggest a committee set up by the legislative branches of local, state, and federal authorities. The chair in charge must have some police experience and knowledge. The positions should be paid and permanent. The body needs to have the power to subpoena witnesses and other evidence, as well as the power to grant immunity (while working with district and United States attorneys). Today, we have seen such bodies work (albeit on a temporary basis) as a result of consent decrees or court orders. Another example includes temporary commissions such as Knapp, Mollen, Kerner, and others. These bodies have been very successful at achieving change in very stagnant departments such as Los Angeles, New York City, Pittsburgh, Maryland State Troopers, and New Jersey State Troopers (to name a few).

To the extent possible, police departments need to be more transparent. Information and data that was collected with taxpayer money should be widely available. Police must think of themselves as public servants. Information such as stop and frisk reports and misdemeanor crime reports (with proper and lawful redactions) should be widely available without having to sue a department. NYPD had to be sued on both counts.[18]

Last, meaningful community partnerships need to be developed. In this way, communities will work closely with the police and be willing to share information on terrorists and drug dealers. Recently, one of us was in the United Kingdom. The message that was broadcasted by authorities about suspicious activity on the trains was, "if you see it, say it and *we will sort it*." By contrast, in the United States the typical announcement is, "if you see something, say something." While the same message is intended, the one in the United States suggests that those who say something will now be involved. In other words, the police will not handle it (sort it). While this is seemingly a trivial difference, it demarks a very different attitude by authority. It does not show a service mentality. Rather, the suggestion is that the police will not take care of the situation; the public may have to get very involved and may no longer go on their business. The nuance is important. Working with a helpful public will reveal information. However, if the public feels they will be intruded upon, they will stay quiet. Police need to gain public support, not the other way around. Police need to educate and work with communities rather than browbeat citizens into submission like an army of occupation. This is the essence of the social contract that police must abide by in democratic society. This is not easy, nor is it meant to be. Policing can be difficult and dangerous, and officers are expected to be the utmost professionals. Because it is such a high calling and officers risk their lives, they should also be well paid and well trained. This is all easier said than done but necessary to attain a higher level of social justice.

Summary

The police performance management system known as Compstat is ubiquitous. It has both positive and negative aspects. On the positive side, it makes a department more efficient and helps to bring down crime. However, the negative side is far less studied and understood. We bring our powerful research to bear to explain these weaknesses. We show how police performance management can have devastating effects on social justice if not carefully monitored. We point out three key areas of concern, including bullying behaviors by supervisors, racist and unconstitutional policing, and crime report manipulation. Overall, pressures from Compstat meetings can translate into quota-driven policing, illegal forcible stops especially in minority communities, a failure to assist victims, and much more. We recommend greater transparency, community partnerships, and a permanent outside body to check and balance poor police behaviors.

Discussion Questions

1. Explain what police performance management is.
2. What are index crimes? Explain their importance.
3. What are some positive aspects of police performance management?
4. How does police performance management influence social justice?
5. How are the pressures of Compstat translated by officers at the street level? Give some specific examples.
6. Are victims of crime influenced by Compstat?
7. Using studies from this chapter, explain how research can help inform policy.
8. List and explain some of the solutions recommended by the authors of the chapter.
9. Can you come up with any other solutions to these concerns?

Notes

1. See Silverman, E. B. (2001). *NYPD battles crime*. Boston, MA: Northeastern University Press for more information on the positive aspects of Compstat.
2. Bayley, D. (1994). *Police for the future*. Oxford: Oxford University Press.
3. *Ibid.*
4. John Timoney cited in Police Leaders . . ., 2011, p. 2.
5. Gallup. *Public opinion context: Americans, race and police*. Retrieved from www.gallup.com/opinion/polling-matters/193586/public-opinion-context-americans-race-police.aspx
6. *Poll finds stark disconnect between police and public*. Reported by CNN. Retrieved from www.cnn.com/2017/01/11/us/pew-police-poll-trnd/index.html
7. CNBC. *Trump again blames both sides for Charlottesville violence*. Retrieved from www.cnbc.com/2017/09/14/trump-again-blames-both-sides-for-charlottesville-violence.html
8. Eterno, J. A., Barrow, C. S., & Silverman, E. B. (2017). Forcible stops: Police and citizens speak out. *Public Administration Review*, 77(2), 181–192. doi: 10.1111/puar.12684
9. *New York Times*. *New York to pay up to &75 million over dismissed summonses*. Retrieved from www.nytimes.com/2017/01/23/nyregion/new-york-city-agrees-to-settlement-over-summonses-that-were-dismissed.html?mcubz=0
10. Eterno, J. A., & Silverman, E. B. (2012). *The crime numbers game: Management by manipulation*. Boca Raton, FL: CRC Press, Taylor and Francis.
11. *Ibid.*, note 8.
12. Karmen, A. (2015). *Evaluating how the NYPD handles crime victims: Judgments based on statistical performance measures*. Cited in Eterno, J. (2015). *The New York City police department: The impact of its policies and practices* (pp. 47–59). Boca Raton, FL: CRC Press, Taylor and Francis.
13. A good history of NYPD and its alienation of many law enforcement policies can be found at the website NYPD Confidential, written by Leonard Levitt. Retrieved from http://nypdconfidential.com/columns/2017/170102.html
14. Eterno, & Silverman, 2012.; Eterno, J. A., & Silverman, E. B. (2010). The NYPD's Compstat: Compare or compose statistics. *International Journal of Police Science and Management*, 12(3), 426–449; Eterno, J. A., Verma, A., & Silverman, E. B. (2016). Police manipulations of crime reporting: Insider's revelations. *Justice Quarterly Justice Quarterly*, 33(5), 811–835. doi: 10.1080/07418825.2014.980838
15. *Ibid.*, note 8.
16. Eterno, Verma, & Silverman, 2016.
17. Bernstein, D., & Jackson, N. The truth about Chicago's crime rates. *Chicago Magazine*. Retrieved from www.chicagomag.com/Chicago-Magazine/May-2014/Chicago-crime-rates/
18. *Ibid.*, note 8.

11

SEXUAL ASSAULT AT THE MARGINS

Recognizing the Experiences of Male Survivors

Jordana N. Navarro

Introduction

Sexual assault[1] as a serious social problem began to be recognized in the 1970s in the early days of the burgeoning victimology field, but male sexual assault was not recognized until later and was initially understood as an issue that arose within correctional facilities.[2] During this time, concern surrounding sexual assault was largely limited to the female survivor, as evidenced by the pivotal work of two important scholars within the field: Susan Brownmiller[3] and Mary Koss.[4,5] Additional evidence of this focus is also seen in the Federal Bureau of Investigation's (FBI's)[6] historical definition of rape that required the "carnal knowledge of a *female* forcibly and against her will" (emphasis added). Because of that focus, male sexual assault survivors could not access the criminal justice system post-victimization nor could any female survivor whose experience did not align with that definition. The change in the FBI's[7] definition, which became effective in 2013, to "penetration, no matter how slight, of the vagina or anus with any body part or object, or oral penetration by a sex organ of another person, without the consent of the person" (p. 1) reflects the unfortunate reality that men are also sexually victimized.

To be clear, substantial progress has occurred since the 1970s. Laypersons recognize that sexual assault is a serious social problem—particularly in institutions of higher education. It also continues to be clear, through the vast amount of research on this topic, that females are more at risk of experiencing sexual assault than are males.[8,9] This chapter is not intended to detract from or diminish that grim reality. Yet, what is also clear is that certain areas of the sexual assault field remain underresearched, such as the sexual victimization of men, which inadvertently marginalizes those survivors.[10,11] In this chapter, a brief overview of the topic is presented with the hope that it leads to greater recognition of these survivors in the fight to stop sexual violence.

Prevalence of Male Sexual Assault

General Population

Regardless of demographic background, sexual assault remains extremely underreported, especially among men, for reasons discussed later.[12] As a result, the sparse existing research likely presents an incomplete picture of the extent of the problem. In terms of understanding the scope of the problem, findings from the nationally representative National Intimate Partner and Sexual Violence Survey (NISVS) indicated that the lifetime prevalence of experiencing a sexual assault other than rape among men was over 20%, regardless of sexual orientation (bisexual men = 47.4%; gay men = 40.2%; heterosexual men = 20.8%).[13] Though these results indicate that all men are at risk, the risk posed to men who identify as bisexual or gay is significantly greater.[14] To put those percentages into perspective, a substantial number of men have likely been sexually assaulted in their lifetimes (bisexual men = 903,000; gay men = nearly 1.1 million; heterosexual men = approximately 21.6 million).[15] Finally, approximately 1% of heterosexual men, or 770,000 individuals, have likely experienced a rape in their lifetimes.[16]

Findings from the NISVS align with earlier nationally representative research, such as the National Violence Against Women Survey (NVAS), that also underscored the prevalence of the problem. In the NVAS, Tjaden and Thoennes found that 3% of men experienced an attempted and/or completed rape in their lifetimes, which equated to approximately 2.8 million men.[17] Similarly, in another national study completed by Elliott and colleagues, nearly 4% of men reported experiencing an unwanted sexual experience in adulthood.[18] Finally, this pattern of criminal activity is not isolated to the United States. For instance, in a nationally representative study of Australian adults, de Visser and colleagues found that sexual assault had affected the lives of 5% of male respondents.[19] Aside from these nationally representative studies, scholars continue to highlight the importance of this problem through studies focused on particular subgroups of men—such as men who identify as a sexual minority.

Bisexual, Gay, and Queer Men

Throughout the years, research focused on understanding the unwanted sexual experiences of bisexual and gay men has steadily grown. In one review of the literature that comprised 75 scholarly papers, researchers found the lifetime prevalence rate for experiencing a sexual assault among bisexual and gay men ranged from approximately 12% to 54%.[20] In another review of the literature consisting of 87 studies, similar prevalence rates were noted: 2% to 57%.[21] Findings since those reviews have continued to align with that range as well. For example, in a study completed by Semple and colleagues, while approximately 60% of male respondents had *not* experienced a sexual assault within the prior year, a substantial percentage (39%) were victimized.[22] Though the study did not focus exclusively on bisexual and gay men, a majority of respondents involved in that study identified as non-heterosexual (96.5%).[23]

In the analysis of male sexual assault among sexual minorities, scholars have also examined how this group compares to heterosexual men, which has produced alarming results. Several studies comparing the prevalence of sexual assault among heterosexual men and men identifying as a sexual minority have found that the latter group is more at risk of experiencing violence.[24,25,26] For example, in a study including these groups (i.e., gay, bisexual, and queer men) and heterosexual men, Richardson and colleagues found that college men who identified as a sexual minority were more likely to experience sexual victimizations, as well as suffer injuries from sexual victimizations, compared to heterosexual college men.[27] These results align with similar research on college men conducted by Edwards and colleagues, in which a significantly greater proportion of males who identified as a sexual minority experienced a sexual victimization (nearly 16%) compared to heterosexual men (nearly 7%).[28] Although the research is limited, several studies have identified notable risk factors that can be utilized to inform prevention programming.

Research focused on this area of male sexual assault has uncovered several risk factors that impact the odds of experiencing a sexual assault. In one study, for example, findings indicated that younger bisexual and gay men might be at more risk compared to older individuals.[29] In other studies, scholars have also found that childhood exposure to abuse and substance use also increases the risk of experiencing a sexual assault.[30,31,32]Additionally, depression and internalized homophobia were also identified as important factors in the consideration of risk of experiencing a sexual assault.[33,34] In terms of perpetrator characteristics, scholars have found that men who identify as a sexual minority are often assaulted by other men in most cases.[35,36,37] Finally, research indicates that stranger-perpetrated assaults typically include force and occur in public locations, whereas acquaintance-perpetrated violence typically involves the utilization of alcohol and occurs in a known location (e.g., offender/victim residence).[38]

Heterosexual Men

A dearth of information remains about the sexual assault of heterosexual men—especially compared to men who identify as a sexual minority. However, as previously mentioned, national studies have shown—and *continue* to show—that the problem exists. For example, in a 2016 study involving more than 8,000 respondents, Cook and colleagues found that nearly 6% of men had been sexually assaulted by a female perpetrator.[39] In another study, men with disabilities were identified as particularly vulnerable to sexual violence compared to men without disabilities.[40] Indeed, in a study by Mitra and colleagues, a significantly greater proportion of men with disabilities (nearly 9%) were sexually assaulted compared to men without disabilities (6%).[41] Although male-on-male sexual assault is not uncommon, studies have highlighted the importance of recognizing that females perpetrate sexual violence as well—especially when investigating the experiences of heterosexual survivors.[42,43,44] Unfortunately, the lack of information known about heterosexual male sexual assault illustrates one of the most significant challenges in researching this area of victimization: men, especially heterosexual men, do not disclose victimization out of fear and shame stemming from how laypersons will perceive their victimization in light of wider cultural conceptions of masculinity.

Challenges to Researching Male Sexual Assault

Sexual Assault Myths

Despite that awareness of sexual assault has grown throughout the years, several barriers remain to researching and understanding the full scope of the problem—particularly among men. One of the most significant barriers facing male sexual assault survivors specifically is laypersons' general misunderstanding of the crime, which likely stems from the continued endorsement of several harmful myths.[45,46,47,48,49] These myths comprise several inaccurate beliefs about male rape, which have been condensed and summarized into the following statement: sexual assault primarily affects homosexual men, females, or incarcerated men, because "real" men cannot be overpowered unless they secretly desired the assault to happen or deserved to be assaulted given their lifestyle choices.[50,51,52] One additional harmful myth also purports that homosexuality is linked to experiencing male sexual assault.[53,54,55] Although research on male sexual assault has consistently challenged these myths, evidence suggests that belief in these harmful statements persists among men and women.[56] Regrettably, these false beliefs can arise during disclosure to family and friends as well as to social service personnel[57] during a survivor's help-seeking post-victimization, as the story of David illustrates.[58]

In a poignantly written manuscript, Willis recaps the revictimization of a male sexual assault survivor named David (pseudonym) by social service personnel following his drug-facilitated rape by two men.[59] After his assault, the perpetrators left David bleeding on the lawn of a stranger's house until he awoke and called a friend for help.[60] Noticing that David was bleeding badly, his friend insisted on calling first responders whom, upon arriving, were reluctant to transport the survivor to the hospital.[61] Then, after arriving at the hospital, the revictimization continued as David's attending physician advised him against involving the police, because the drugs placed within his drink to facilitate the incapacitation were likely still in his system.[62] In the weeks following the assault, the revictimization of David persisted among medical personnel as he sought surgery to repair the damage inflicted by the perpetrators that night.[63] As he notes to Willis, the whole experience left him feeling abandoned and ashamed.[64] Willis concludes the manuscript by calling for greater assistance and recognition of male sexual assault survivors, particularly among the psychiatric community.[65]

David's experiences represent how harmful and pervasive myths about male sexual assault can lead to the revictimization of survivors during their help-seeking activities[66] or deter them from disclosing altogether.[67] Evidence of this fear is apparent in scholarly research that has found male sexual assault survivors fail to disclose out of fear of experiencing victim blaming and/or fear that they will be met with these harmful beliefs.[68,69] For example, in Navarro and Clevenger's study of sexual assault among college-aged men, nearly 8% of male survivors did not disclose due to the belief that they would be blamed for the victimization or out of fear that others would not understand.[70] Moreover, almost 12% of survivors noted that they did not disclose their victimization, because they were concerned about "not being taken seriously."[71] While the rationale for not disclosing varied among survivors in Navarro and Clevenger's study, their results indicate that the perpetuation of harmful myths acts as a serious barrier for both sexual assault survivors post-victimization as well as the research community endeavoring to raise awareness of this problem.

One step towards eradicating these myths is to recognize and address their origin. As numerous scholars have noted, these myths ultimately originate from a strong adherence to gender norms that dictate ideal feminine and masculine traits, which children are socialized into from infancy.[72,73,74,75] For men, these ideal traits include aggressiveness, sexual prowess, and strength among others.[76,77,78,79] Taking into account that "manliness" is often equated with those traits within the dominant culture, the palpable fear experienced by male sexual assault survivors about whether to disclose is a reality that warrants social change. Indeed, these myths not only impact disclosure and help-seeking activities post-victimization, but are also related to the psychological consequences suffered by survivors.[80]

In a comprehensive review of the male sexual assault literature, Peterson and colleagues directly challenge the myth that men do not suffer negative consequences following a sexual assault.[81] Indeed, according to their findings, male sexual assault survivors experience a range of consequences: identity crises, psychological damage, and the questioning of their sexual orientation.[82] In terms of the questioning of one's sexual orientation, Peterson and colleagues note this impact is especially documented among heterosexual survivors and, again, ultimately stems from harmful myths perpetrated in the wider culture.[83] The scholars explicitly draw this connection in the following quote (p. 20):

> sexual assault perpetrated by a female may result in fewer negative psychological sequelae than sexual assault perpetrated by a male because sexual activity—even coerced sexual activity—with a woman fits the stereotypical male sex role; whereas sexual activity—especially coerced sexual activity—with a man does not fit the stereotypical male sex role.[84]

Lack of Resources

Aside from the barriers presented by the endorsement of harmful myths, male sexual assault survivors also encounter several unique additional challenges in their help seeking, which then impacts the ability of researchers to learn about the extent of this problem. One of the most apparent challenges is the sheer lack of resources dedicated to assisting male sexual assault survivors.[85] Indeed, although community resources exist to address domestic abuse and sexual violence, services tend to emphasize aiding the female survivor in the aftermath of male-perpetrated violence.[86] As a result, the assistance provided to male sexual assault survivors may be limited or nonexistent.[87] This gap in services is underscored by research that noted several countries had no services dedicated to assisting male abuse survivors (e.g., China, India, and Japan) and several countries had limited resources.[88]

Methodological Variations

A final important barrier to researching male sexual assault concerns the wide variation of methodological study utilized by scholars within the field.[89] As Peterson and colleagues note, sexual assault is defined in various ways across disciplines, which can dramatically affect results.[90] For example, studies that include broad definitions of sexual assault often result in higher prevalence rates compared to research that utilizes narrowed definitions.[91] While the former likely presents a more expansive picture of the extent of male sexual assault, utilizing too broad of a definition can also result in losing important contextual information among offense types.[92] In contrast, though, utilizing too narrow of a definition can result in an incomplete picture of the types of male sexual assault that are actually occurring.[93] Ultimately, Peterson and colleagues note that there are advantages and disadvantages to both approaches, and it is important for scholars in the field to be cognizant of these when conducting research on male sexual assault.[94]

In addition to the definitions utilized in studies, researching male sexual assault is hindered by the lack of a standardized measurement tool.[95] Although scholars have utilized existing reliable and valid measurement tools to assess the extent of this problem (e.g., the sexual experiences survey),[96] typically these instruments must be reworked to apply to male sexual assault.[97] Related to the lack of a standardized measurement tool, scholars also utilize different approaches when querying respondents on their sexual experiences, which can impact findings.[98] For example, some scholars utilize behavior-driven questions and categorize responses after data collection, while others allow respondents to self-identify as survivors.[99] While each approach is valuable, both also have their drawbacks. For example, not utilizing behavior-driven questions can result in an underreporting of the extent of male sexual assault—particularly among heterosexual survivors.[100]

Summary

The preceding discussion provided a broad overview of what is known about two types of male sexual assault: the sexual assault of heterosexual men and the sexual assault of men who identify as a sexual minority. However, there are other areas of male sexual assault that also warrant further attention: the sexual assault of male inmates, the sexual assault of male sex workers, and a wider intersectional approach to the topic overall (e.g., sexual minority men who also identify as race/ethnic minority). In addition to providing a broad overview on these two areas of male sexual assault, this chapter also presented some of the challenges and barriers to researching this type of sexual violence. Although these barriers and challenges present substantial obstacles to learning about male sexual abuse, they are not insurmountable and can start being addressed merely by challenging wider cultural conceptions of masculinity. Ultimately, the information in this chapter challenges the notion that male sexual assault is nonexistent within the general population. While it is true that research continues to indicate that females are more likely to experience a sexual assault compared to men, society as a whole (academics and laypersons) must endeavor to call greater recognition to male sexual assault as well.

Discussion Questions

1. When you think about male sexual assault, what are some survivor characteristics that you imagine? How do these characteristics relate (or not) to wider cultural conceptions of manliness?
2. When you think about male sexual assault, what are some perpetrator characteristics that you imagine? How do these characteristics relate (or not) to wider gender norms?
3. Look up two recent cases of male sexual assault, but with one event involving a female perpetrator and one event involving a male perpetrator. In your research, attempt to find cases that are fairly similar situationally (e.g., involving a school official). As you read about these cases, discuss whether the female-perpetrated incident is reported on differently than the male-perpetrated incident.

4. Using your location as a reference point, investigate whether there are any services available to male sexual assault survivors within a 200-mile radius. If so, ensure you document the agency name, the agency mission, and the services provided to male survivors. Discuss whether gaps in service exist for male sexual assault survivors.

5. Taking into account everything you've learned in this chapter, discuss how you would address male sexual assault beyond the interpersonal level. In other words, what needs to happen at the societal level to help bring attention to male sexual assault?

Notes

1. Instead of focusing on any one type of sexual crime in particular, the term sexual assault is used throughout this chapter to broadly discuss all sexual offenses, including rape.
2. Javaid, A. (2015). Male rape myths: Understanding and explaining social attitudes surrounding male rape. *Masculinities and Social Change, 4*(3), 270–294.
3. Brownmiller, S. (2013). *Against our will: Men, women and rape.* New York: Open Road Media.
4. Koss, M. P., & Oros, C. J. (1982). Sexual experiences survey: A research instrument investigating sexual aggression and victimization. *Journal of Consulting and Clinical Psychology, 50*(3), 455–457.
5. Turchik, J. A., Hebenstreit, C. L., & Judson, S. S. (2016). An examination of the gender inclusiveness of current theories of sexual violence in adulthood: Recognizing male victims, female perpetrators, and same-sex violence. *Trauma, Violence, & Abuse, 17*(2), 133–148.
6. Federal Bureau of Investigation. (2014). *Frequently asked questions about the change in the UCR definition of rape.* Washington, DC: N.A.
7. *Ibid.*
8. Abrahams, N., Devries, K., Watts, C., Pallitto, C., Petzold, M., Shamu, S., & García-Moreno, C. (2014). Worldwide prevalence of non-partner sexual violence: A systematic review. *The Lancet, 383*(9929), 1648–1654.
9. Walters, M. L., Chen, J., & Breiding, M. J. (2013). The National Intimate Partner and Sexual Violence Survey (NISVS): 2010 findings on victimization by sexual orientation. *Atlanta, GA: National Center for Injury Prevention and Control, Centers for Disease Control and Prevention, 648*(73), 6.
10. Turchik, Hebenstreit, & Judson, 2016.
11. Andersen, T. H. (2013). Against the wind: Male victimization and the ideal of manliness. *Journal of Social Work, 13*(3), 231–247.
12. Navarro, J. N., & Clevenger, S. (2017). Calling attention to the importance of assisting male survivors of sexual victimization. *Journal of School Violence, 16*(2), 222–235.
13. Walters, Chen, & Breiding, 2013.
14. *Ibid.*
15. *Ibid.*
16. Walters, Chen, & Breiding, 2013.
17. Tjaden, P., & Thoennes, N. (1998). *Prevalence, incidence, and consequences of violence against women: Findings from the National Violence against Women Survey.* Research in Brief.
18. Elliott, D. M., Mok, D. S., & Briere, J. (2004). Adult sexual assault: Prevalence, symptomatology, and sex differences in the general population. *Journal of Traumatic Stress, 17*(3), 203–211.
19. de Visser, R. O., Smith, A. M. A., Rissel, C. E., Richters, J., & Grulich, A. E. (2003). Experiences of sexual coercion among a representative sample of adults. *Australian and New Zealand Journal of Public Health, 27*(2), 198–203.
20. Rothman, E. F., Exner, D., & Baughman, A. L. (2011). The prevalence of sexual assault against people who identify as gay, lesbian, or bisexual in the United States: A systematic review. *Trauma, Violence, & Abuse, 12*(2), 55–66.
21. Peterson, Z. D., Voller, E. K., Polusny, M. A., & Murdoch, M. (2011). Prevalence and consequences of adult sexual assault of men: Review of empirical findings and state of the literature. *Clinical Psychology Review, 31*(1), 1–24.
22. Semple, S. J., Stockman, J. K., Goodman-Meza, D., Pitpitan, E. V., Strathdee, S. A., Chavarin, C. V., . . . Patterson, T. L. (2017). Correlates of sexual violence among men who have sex with men in Tijuana, Mexico. *Archives of Sexual Behavior, 46*(4), 1011–1023.
23. *Ibid.*
24. Edwards, K. M., Sylaska, K. M., Barry, J. E., Moynihan, M. M., Banyard, V. L., Cohn, E. S., . . . Ward, S. K. (2015). Physical dating violence, sexual violence, and unwanted pursuit victimization: A comparison of incidence rates among sexual-minority and heterosexual college students. *Journal of Interpersonal Violence, 30*(4), 580–600.

25. Richardson, H. B., Armstrong, J. L., Hines, D. A., & Palm Reed, K. M. (2015). Sexual violence and help-seeking among LGBQ and heterosexual college students. *Partner Abuse, 6*(1), 29–46.
26. Balsam, K. F., Rothblum, E. D., & Beauchaine, T. P. (2005). Victimization over the life span: A comparison of lesbian, gay, bisexual, and heterosexual siblings. *Journal of Consulting and Clinical Psychology, 73*(3), 477–487.
27. Richardson, Armstrong, Hines, & Palm Reed, 2015.
28. Edwards et al., 2015.
29. Hequembourg, A. L., Parks, K. A., Collins, R. L., & Hughes, T. L. (2015). Sexual assault risks among gay and bisexual men. *The Journal of Sex Research, 52*(3), 282–295.
30. *Ibid.*
31. Semple et al., 2017.
32. Stermac, L., Del Bove, G., & Addison, M. (2004). Stranger and acquaintance sexual assault of adult males. *Journal of Interpersonal Violence, 19*(8), 901–915.
33. Hequembourg, Parks, Collins, & Hughes, 2015.
34. Semple et al., 2017.
35. Walters, Chen, & Breiding, 2013.
36. Richardson, Armstrong, Hines, & Palm Reed, 2015.
37. Stermac, Del Bove, & Addison, 2004.
38. Turchik, Hebenstreit, & Judson, 2016.
39. Cook, M. C., Morisky, D. E., Williams, J. K., Ford, C. L., & Gee, G. C. (2016). Sexual risk behaviors and substance use among men sexually victimized by women. *American Journal of Public Health, 106*(7), 1263–1269.
40. Mitra, M., Mouradian, V. E., Fox, M. H., & Pratt, C. (2016). Prevalence and characteristics of sexual violence against men with disabilities. *American Journal of Preventive Medicine, 50*(3), 311–317.
41. *Ibid.*
42. Richardson, Armstrong, Hines, & Palm Reed, 2015.
43. Walters, Chen, & Breiding, 2013.
44. Weiss, K. G. (2010). Male sexual victimization: Examining men's experiences of rape and sexual assault. *Men and Masculinities, 12*(3), 275–298.
45. Turchik, Hebenstreit, & Judson, 2016.
46. Fuchs, S. F. (2004). Male sexual assault: Issues of arousal and consent. *Cleveland State Law Review, 51*, 93–121.
47. Javaid, 2015
48. Javaid, A. (2016). Feminism, masculinity, and male rape: Bringing male rape "out of the closet". *Journal of Gender Studies, 25*(3), 283–293.
49. Turchik, J. A., & Edwards, K. M. (2012). Myths about male rape: A literature review. *Psychology of Men & Masculinity, 13*(2), 211–226.
50. *Ibid.*
51. Javaid, 2015.
52. Javaid, 2016.
53. Turchik, & Edwards, 2012.
54. Javaid, 2015.
55. Javaid, 2016.
56. Turchik, & Edwards, 2012.
57. *Ibid.*
58. Willis, D. G. (2009). Male-on-male rape of an adult man: A case review and implications for interventions. *Journal of the American Psychiatric Nurses Association, 14*(6), 454–461.
59. *Ibid.*
60. *Ibid.*
61. *Ibid.*
62. *Ibid.*
63. *Ibid.*
64. *Ibid.*
65. *Ibid.*
66. *Ibid.*
67. Navarro, & Clevenger, 2017.
68. *Ibid.*
69. Braun, V., Schmidt, J., Gavey, N., & Fenaughty, J. (2009). Sexual coercion among gay and bisexual men in Aotearoa/New Zealand. *Journal of Homosexuality, 53*(3), 336–360.
70. Navarro, & Clevenger, 2017.
71. *Ibid.*

72. Cheung, M., Leung, P., & Tsui, V. (2009). Asian male domestic violence victims: Services exclusive for men. *Journal of Family Violence, 24,* 447–462.
73. Navarro, & Clevenger, 2017.
74. Javaid, 2015.
75. Javaid, 2016.
76. Cheung, Leung, & Tsui, 2009.
77. Navarro, & Clevenger, 2017.
78. Javaid, 2015.
79. Javaid, 2016.
80. Peterson, Voller, Polusny, & Murdoch, 2011.
81. *Ibid.*
82. *Ibid.*
83. *Ibid.*
84. *Ibid.*
85. Cheung, Leung, & Tsui, 2009.
86. *Ibid.*
87. *Ibid.*
88. *Ibid.*
89. Peterson, Voller, Polusny, & Murdoch, 2011.
90. *Ibid.*
91. *Ibid.*
92. *Ibid.*
93. *Ibid.*
94. *Ibid.*
95. *Ibid.*
96. Koss, & Oros, 1982.
97. *Ibid.*
98. *Ibid.*
99. *Ibid.*
100. *Ibid.*

12

IMPORTANCE OF LANGUAGE AND COMMUNICATION FOR SOCIAL JUSTICE

Tamara L. Wilkins

The purpose of this chapter is to offer communication techniques and tips when working with or simply talking with others. Understanding who we are, as individuals and as social participants, helps us to better comprehend and communicate with others. Similarities or differences among us should not matter if fairness or social justice is desired, but our social world plays upon our differences. Of importance is acknowledging that the material in this chapter is aimed at improving individual language skills, not the group(s) within which the person belongs. The target audience for this chapter is anyone who wants to learn, seasoned experts, staunch advocates and devoted activists, or the novice who has just started to think about all the injustices in our social world and wants to play a role in trying to help change the status quo.

The first section of this chapter is rather brief, but establishes two main goals for interpersonal interactions when we want to impart social justice. We need to understand, as individuals: (1) what we can do to improve our social relationships, as well as (2) what we should avoid when interacting with others. Developing ourselves helps us provide meaning to others. Others may hold very different ideas, beliefs, and practices than an individual does; however, understanding what that person can do so as not to inflame or aggravate the other is crucial for peaceful dialogue. "What one hears is not always what is intended."[1]

The second section of this chapter outlines who we are with regards to our roles and positions in our social world. Racial and/or ethnic identity, social class, age, occupation, ability, sex and gender, and religious and/or political affiliation all provide each of us with our own way of looking at others, social standing, and level of power (or powerlessness). One may hold a superior social position (privileged), while another person is deemed inferior (oppressed). A few of us hold significant power and have the ability to influence the lives of countless people, whereas others of us have virtually no power or influence, other than perhaps at home, at school, or in our workplace. Power and privilege versus oppression and subjugation are at the heart of social injustice.

Managing ourselves is the gist of the third section of this chapter. Attitudes, emotions, and demeanor all play a role when we interact with others. The ability to convey a message, both verbally and nonverbally, determines if others are put at ease or not, or if a situation is inflamed or calmed. In addition, it is likely that most, if not all, of us hold prejudices. But, how deep we bury our prejudicial ideas, beliefs, and thoughts matters if we want to truly listen to others and eliminate discriminatory treatment of others. Gender-inclusive language, "people-first language," tips for communicating with others when English is a second language, as well as cross-cultural language barriers are offered as practical guides to communication. When these language tips are instilled and practiced in everyday life, we share with others their importance in the facilitation of social justice. We raise awareness in ourselves as well as others. It is the responsibility of those of us who want social justice to be cognizant of the positions we hold and how we express ourselves. The language we use is crucial to fairness and a moral obligation in the promise of justice.

The fourth and final section of this chapter is a summary. Knowledge of appropriate language and communication strategies are key to building social relationships. Individuals can make a difference by learning more about who they are, who the others are, and what we can do to bring about change. Teaching others the same things learned here and elsewhere will only advance our quest for social justice.

Interpersonal Relationships

"Inter" is a prefix meaning between or among. "Between" means two and "among" means three or more people are involved. Relationship is a concept widely understood; however, simply a connection, of any type, is all that is necessary for this personal association. The connection may be nothing more than someone speaking and another responding. When we think about social justice, we must realize how crucial what we say and how we say it can be to someone who is listening. If we want to get a positive response from someone, we must use language and communication tactics that generate or prompt the listener to become active, in order to form a relationship. Relationships may build slowly (and may end quickly), and often depend on trust to evolve and grow. Being aware of the terminology we use and knowing about the language and communication styles of others are just as important as knowing what *not* to say and do in order to cause no harm when creating or growing relationships.

What Can We Do to Improve Our Social Relationships?

As social "justicians" and proponents of change, we frequently seek to form relationships with others, regardless of who they are or what they are doing or saying. We want to find amicable ways to gain the ability to speak and be heard. We initially approach another, usually knowing if that person is either inside or outside our social circle. Regardless, to make the contact positive, following what is known as the "Golden Rule" may help. The idea of the Golden Rule is to treat others the way that we wish to be treated. Our responsibility is to know who we are and what we want. If we truly understand ourselves, then we can easily identify how we should go about approaching others. We would approach others the same way we would like to be approached. The Golden Rule is the epitome of fairmindedness. If social justice is our goal, we need to treat all others with impartiality, objectivity, equality, and/or fairness. In order to achieve this "justice," we must understand who we are as individuals before we attempt to know about others. For example, how much personal space do we want? Do all people of all cultures want the same amount of personal space? Do some people require significantly less space than we do? The more we learn about ourselves helps to determine similarities or differences with whom we are engaging. The better we understand others, the easier it is to treat them with fairness and equality. Knowing how one wishes to be treated means we can utilize the Golden Rule and treat them in the way that is right for them without sacrificing who we are or what we represent.

What Should We Avoid When Interacting With Others?

Adopting the goal to "do no harm" to others has its benefits. One benefit is that people can learn to speak a common language with those folks who are both inside and outside their own social groups. Another benefit is that a careful consideration of resources can aid in balancing the allocation of future resources. Implementing a fair way to distribute future resources is a significant challenge.[2]

If social justice is the goal, does this mean an egalitarian method for distributing money and other valued resources is possible? Who gets to determine what is truly balanced or equal? For example, is making a shirt more challenging than brain surgery? Who gets to decide how much a shirtmaker is compensated, compared to the wages received by a brain surgeon? Who will monitor and oversee the decision maker? To do no harm involves knowing virtually everything about the labor involved as well as how much labor is extended by the individuals working in a particular occupation. Determining what is fair compensation for these skilled workers is far beyond the scope and capability of many, if not most, of us. Further, what amount of pay should the decision maker receive? Deciding what is fair and just is a complex mess that might be impossible to untangle.

Another predicament to doing no harm involves language. For example, for years, members of the United States Congress often spoke to television audiences about our soldiers during times of war. Many of these members would talk about the sacrifices "our boys" were making by being at war in a foreign nation. Rarely did one hear a member of Congress say something about our "men and women" serving in the military. In other words, the failure to include women was common. So when a mother, sister, daughter, or girlfriend was serving during a time of conflict, "she" was not thought of by these members of Congress. Failing to include all the females serving in a foreign nation during wartime was not noticed by most people; thus, no harm was done to them. But, for the family or friends of a female, harm was felt because their female loved one was not acknowledged by the speaker, a member of Congress! We must notice gender-laden terminology, recognize its bias, and learn to use gender-inclusive (e.g., military personnel) rather than gender-exclusive language (e.g., "our boys"). If we fail to do so, we risk harming those who were ignored as well as those who noticed the neglect. More information about gender-neutral or -inclusive language will be found in a later part of this chapter (see "Managing Ourselves and the Language We Use").

Our Social Identity and Standing

Our social identity is at root in the complex process of communicating to others. Individual and group identities are a reality in our social world.[3] Identities are the answers to two questions: (1) "Who am I?" and (2) "Who am I in relation to others?"[4] Our social identity is noteworthy at both the individual and group level. "The ways in which individuals and collectivities are distinguished is in their social relations with other individuals and collectivities."[5] Our personal identity is grounded in "one's sense of self in terms of variables such as personality traits."[6] Instead of depicting how identities are classified at a personal level, let's turn our attention back to social identities. In this chapter, the focus is on both ascribed and achieved statuses. Ascribed statuses are "statuses assigned to individuals without reference to their abilities or personal efforts, such as age, sex, race, ethnicity and family background."[7] In other words, these are traits a person was born with or assigned at birth. Achieved statuses are "secured through effort and ability."[8] Examples of achieved status include an occupational title such as teacher, professor, dentist, etc. Church member, spouse, elder, juvenile delinquent, etc. are other achieved statuses. In other words, "achieved statuses are gained by experience, education, or training."[9]

Our statuses play a significant role in the power we hold. For our purposes, power is simply the ability to achieve an objective or to be heard. In part, power is the probability of a person or group to carry out their will even when opposed by others.[10] Suffice it to say, each of the eight statuses or social identities below (race and/or ethnicity, social class, age, occupation, ability, sex and gender, sexuality, and religious and/or political affiliation) are assigned various levels of power or authority, and they are often distinguishable as being a dominant group or powerful trait or a subordinate or minority status, which typically equates to less powerful. Each social identity may also be classified by a ranking or stratification system, and/or based upon an element of prestige. Prestige is a measure of respect and admiration. In our society, individuals belong to numerous social identity groups. A person may hold power or prestige for one or more statuses, but little to no power or influence based upon another status or statuses. We learn how to answer the two questions above by interacting with others. Interactions with others about ourselves or others and how to identify ourselves and others is based on the ability to communicate and/or on language.[11]

Race and/or Ethnicity

When people in our society think about race, often times they think in terms of White, Black or other. Usually there is some unique physical trait, most often the color of one's skin, that teaches us White from Black. The third catch-all group, "others," is assigned to people who do not appear to be Black, but who look "different" from Americans of European backgrounds. Mann and Zatz, in the article "The Power of Images," offer us not only the previous statement, but provide us the social perspective that race is socially constructed.

> Race changes as social conditions change. Race isn't a fixed identity. It is socially, not biologically determined. There's a historical context to what is meant by "race" in specific social relations. Racial dynamics are flexible, fluid, and always political. There's a process in which we attach meaning and importance to racial categories. The same process is at work when we formulate our individual identities. But, at the societal level, it is structural and based on social relations between groups.[12]

Ethnicity, like race, is normally a minority or subordinate group identity that is distinguishable from the dominant group (i.e., White American), because of a cultural characteristic like nationality, language, geographic location, religion, etc. Examples of such groups are Irish Americans, Jewish Americans, Somalian Americans, etc. A hierarchy of sorts exists in which those groups that can easily assimilate or make their way into the larger society without dramatic difficulty often hold a higher rank than do those groups that cannot easily blend in or assimilate. Assimilation is a process by which formerly distinct and separate groups merge and become one group. If the group formed resembles, in some way, the dominant group in society (e.g., by physical appearances or language), a higher rank is usually assigned.[13] It is important to know if another's racial or ethnic identify is trivial and unimportant (to you or to them) or if there is significance to them that requires particular attention. Are we in competition for power? Do we speak the same language? Do we have regular social contact with members of a particular different group? Are we able to easily understand each other and each other's cultural ways? Should we make eye contact or avert our eyes to show respect? The divisions between and among various racial and/or ethnic group members and dominant group members are deeply embedded in virtually every aspect of our society, particularly in our economy. The distribution of wealth and power are vastly unequal and play a vital role in our individual identities.

Social Class

Social class is a location or position in society that is based on socioeconomic status (which is largely comprised of income, education, and occupational prestige). There are numerous ways to categorize social class, but for our purposes, let's say there are four social classes: upper class, middle class, working class, and lower class. If one is in the upper class, he or she is extremely affluent or exuberantly wealthy or "rich." He or she is "elite" and sometimes considered a member of the "ruling class." That person holds a level of power, control, prestige, and influence that is very different from that available to someone who lives in poverty (i.e., lower class). While the lives of the very rich are sometimes depicted on television, the lives of those who are "impoverished" are frequently noticed, and often threatened, as a means to motivate others from falling down the economic chain. If one doesn't get a degree or work hard, they won't be able to "get ahead."

> Poor people do our society's dirty work . . . they work for low wages, making life easier for the affluent . . . they serve as guinea pigs . . . buy goods no one else wants like "day-old bread and second-hand clothes.
>
> *(p. 278)*[14]

"One's economic position influences not only our behaviors, but even our ideas and attitudes. Less privileged means less power, less influence."[15] In the United States, social classes are not clearly defined and most of us seek to classify ourselves somewhere in the middle. We are not willing to express a high level of prestige or wealth (e.g., when confronted by someone wanting money, we often say, "Sorry. I don't have any change/cash."), nor are we willing to admit to living in extreme poverty (e.g., no money, no home, no car, no job, going hungry, appearing "dirty" or consistently wearing dirty clothing, etc.).

We live in a very materialistic society, so our social class is a vital part of who we are and who we correspond with on a daily basis. How often do we have contact with people from a different social class? Does social class influence the degree to which one is concerned about social justice? Does social class influence one's decision to learn more about the issues of social justice? Do we speak "down" or "up" to people in a different socioeconomic position?

Age

Everyone's life experiences shape who they are—whether man or woman, and across all races, ethnicities, and religions. It is no surprise, therefore, that people who grew up in different time periods would have different world views, expectations and values, resulting in preferred methods of communicating and interacting with one another.[16]

It may not have always been the case, but our current communication styles are unique based on our age. Experience, literally time on earth, plays a role in whether we handwrite letters or write a check to pay our bills or to purchase groceries. Many older Americans do not know how to use a "smartphone" or send an e-mail. Their normal communication method is face to face.

Younger Americans prefer text messaging or instant messaging.[17] Face-to-face communication is not the desired communication standard. Many wear "ear buds" when walking somewhere and listening to whatever music, noise, voices, etc. is playing into their ears; therefore, others receive no response when they speak to them. Face-to-face interaction is significantly less frequent among younger generations.

> They grew up with (electronic) technologies in abundance, and new ones being developed regularly. Unlike older generations, they are unafraid of new technologies and are often what marketers would call "first adapters"—the first to try, buy, and spread the word about cool new gadgets/technologies.
>
> *(p. 101)*[18]

The age of a person also plays a role in how they feel about and perceive social justice. The Cone Institute offered survey data that shows "younger Americans (born between 1979 and 2001) see themselves as accountable for making a difference in the world."[19] Are they truly different from the Baby Boomers, who were born between 1945 and 1965? Did they not see themselves as actually making a difference (e.g., civil rights movement, women's liberation, Victims of Crime Act, etc.)? The point is we must determine the most effective way to communicate respect and understanding of both our similarities and differences with regards to age. We must not fail to recognize the long history of social injustice that older generations lived. Nor should we forget the myriad technological advancements, made over more recent times. Younger generations are able to learn about virtually anything in a moment's time by being online. Older generations may not be as quick to access information and may not understand the language used by people who are technologically savvy.

Occupation

As mentioned above, one element of social class involves occupational prestige. This is the idea that some occupations are more highly valued, financially rewarded, respected, and admired than others. Essentially, jobs that "require extensive formal education and provide much authority and autonomy rank highest, whereas manual labor jobs, which require little training and have virtually no authority, rank lowest" (p. 214).[20] Physicians, college professors, judges, attorneys, and engineers are ranked near the top of the occupation prestige rankings scale, whereas janitors, waiters, cashiers, and truck drivers rank near the bottom. Another example is that teachers receive a higher ranking than do teacher's aides. In addition, "white collar jobs" like accountant or office manager are assigned a higher status than are truck drivers or automobile mechanics, which are considered "blue collar jobs."[21]

The occupation of those with whom we are trying to connect, regarding issues of social justice, might be a personal attribute to consider. Is the person with whom you're speaking someone who is a medical doctor or a farmer? Is the person a local judge who has a history of mandating severe punishments for women but less lengthy ones for men, even though the charges were the same? Whether or not we want to consider the occupation and/or formal education of someone when conversing with them is really no question. If we know the occupational status of a person, we may speak differently to him/her based on our perceptions. On the other hand, learning what someone "does" may instead be something that unites or connects us (i.e., a commonality or a shared ingredient). Do people speak differently to physicians than they do their local convenience store clerk? Do some people talk down or "dumb down" their language? We need to rethink what we are sometimes taught: "Higher income, a bigger house, and more wealth are valued as if people who have these things are better than those who have less."[22] To ensure fairness, we must not perpetuate this bias, and instead find ways to eliminate this prejudicial way of thinking.

Ability

When thinking about ability, we often think of disability as being its opposite. Ableism is normal and disability is presumed to be negative, a bad thing, and if possible, should be eliminated or cured. "Disability is not determined by a specific condition but by how the specific condition (impairment) affects an individual" (p. 152).[23] Based on the Americans with Disabilities Act, being unable to engage in a major life activity is the result of the impairment. We know people often perpetuate the impression that a person without an impairment is "better" than an individual with an impairment. Able-bodied persons are perceived as being normal, whereas anyone with a disability is deviant or abnormal.[24]

How we go about curbing the privilege of "ableism" is to first recognize its reality. Social advantages are assigned to individuals who have no disability or impairment. There are numerous ways to see the many aspects of a person, without having to categorize primarily one's physical and/or mental ability. We must stop seeing ability as "good" or "superior" and disability as "bad" or "inferior" (p. 217).[25] "Individuals need to examine their own stereotypes, biases, and assumptions in relation to disability/impairment and to critically examine their validity and purpose" (p. 306).[26]

> Individuals with impairment/disability are whole people who have multiple identities, talents, and unique characteristics and their impairment/disability is only one dimension of

one identity among multiple identities. Individuals need to not only advocate for individuals with impairment/disability but also work together to promote equal access at the institutional and government levels. We must demand social inclusion between people with and without impairment/disability. We must learn from each other and connect because of our numerous human qualities.[27]

Sex and Gender

Sex is biologically determined, typically male or female. Gender is socially created as a dichotomy or range from masculine to feminine. Most people use the terms interchangeably or as meaning the same thing. Even though they're different, they are very much related or connected. Gender is an acquired identity and an important role we learn very early in childhood. Our gender (and sex) is emphasized throughout our lives. We learn to identify ourselves first as boys or girls, and as we grow, we identify as men and women. Boys gain respect and independence as they grow into "manhood." Girls grow into "womanhood," becoming helpers and dependent on males for both safety and security. Subordination becomes expected of women and dominance is justified in men. Men are taught to become leaders, women are not. Even though gender roles are changing and our roles are becoming more similar as time goes by, our society remains plagued with sexism.

Sexism, which is discrimination based on gender, runs rampant. When thinking about power, women still fall short in every social institution. Women are the nurses and secretaries, and men are the doctors and managers. Men are the protectors of helpless women and children. Even the English language is male dominated. An example of how our language is masculine is by "the use of generic masculine pronouns to refer to individuals who might be female or male (e.g., referring to a police officer as "he"). Some people do not notice that terms like "he," him," or "his" are neglectful of women. There are numerous ways we can change the everyday language we use to be more inclusive of women. Several suggestions, like gender-free or gender-neutral terms, will be offered in the next section.

Some barriers women face in the workplace challenge us to break down some of them by ending pay inequity and breaking the glass ceiling.[28] The glass ceiling is that invisible barrier that prevents women from reaching top positions in the workplace. Shared, equal relationships must take place at work and at home, and we must end sexual harassment and gender stereotyping, which will also be discussed shortly.

On a personal level, we need to communicate by using "I" instead of "you." We often blame the other when we use "you." Saying "you" is telling someone what he or she thinks or feels, or what he or she should or shouldn't do or say. We must convey to others our own feelings, thoughts, and behaviors by using "I."[29]

Sexuality

Sexuality is a complex, multidimensional term. The identity we develop regarding our sexuality is related to social expressions of relationships, whether they be real or imagined. There are differences among sexual behaviors, desires, and orientation or "personhood."[30] A seven-point continuum of sexuality was offered as ranging from "exclusively heterosexual" to "exclusively homosexual."

The social discourse regarding sexuality has become more public; it is far more common, frank, and direct today than just a decade or so ago. Gay, lesbian, bisexual, transgender, and queer (GLBTQ) communities have become more vocal, and a number of support organizations and allies are at work to gain fair treatment in society. We have dialogues about sexuality both in the political arena and based on religious beliefs and affiliation. Several states now legally recognize same-sex marriage. However, homosexuality or fitting under the GLBTQ umbrella is still less common and perceived as "deviant" when compared to heterosexuality. Heterosexuality remains the superior classification of sexuality (i.e., heterosexism). Homophobia corresponds to heterosexuality. Homophobia is the "fear and/or hatred of those who love and sexually desire those of the same sex, and includes prejudice, harassment, and acts of violence brought on by that fear and hatred" (p. 268).[31]

The federal and state governments, mass media, educational systems, family, and the church have exerted a powerful influence on our perceptions and beliefs about various aspects of sexuality. What can heterosexuals do to be more inclusive and gain equal treatment for non-heterosexuals? What is your sexual identity? Are you willing to speak in public about your identity? If you are willing, is it because you know you belong to the privileged category (i.e., heterosexual)? While many of us understand the need to stand up to the oppression of non-heterosexuals and seek changes that promote equality, there is still great resistance in that many still think of sexuality as a "private" issue. Heterosexuals may be oblivious to the fact their sexuality is publicly demonstrated when they become part of a couple.

Religious and/or Political Affiliation

Bias and discrimination based on religion or political affiliation have a very long history. Probably the best-documented evidence of discrimination based on religion took place in Germany in the early to mid-1900s. Jews were not considered as having complete citizenship and experienced genocide at the hands of the German government. Genocide is the deliberate, systematic, intentional destruction of a particular political or cultural group.

Most recently, in the United States, people who are of Middle Eastern descent have been targeted as potential terrorists. "Muslims" are people who "practice or identify with Islam. "Islamic" does not mean "Arabic," nor does it mean "Middle Eastern." Islamic is merely an adjective referring to the religion of Islam. The majority of Muslims in the United States are African American, not Arab or Middle Eastern.[32]

The most recent figures for hate crime occurrences (2015) indicate that of the more than 5,800 hate crime incidents, 21.4% were motivated by religious bias (even though religious affiliation may be identified as ethnicity). Of the 1,402 victims of anti-religious hate crimes, 52.1% were victims because of the offender's anti-Jewish sentiment. Anti-Islamic (Muslim) bias accounted for 21.9% of religious-based hate crimes.[33] It is important to note that these figures represent only those crimes reported to the police. We know a significant number of victims never report the crime to police due to a number of reasons (e.g., don't believe police can or will help, fear of retaliation, not sure how to go about reporting, fear that law enforcement is corrupt, etc.).

The social identity of someone may or may not include one's political affiliation. For one thing, many Americans don't participate politically or admit to having a political affiliation. In many states, talking about or campaigning for a particular candidate or political party is not covered under antidiscrimination laws and being terminated is legal. Thus, there are likely people who have political preferences but are not willing to publicly disclose their position. Understanding their public silence should be recognized on a personal level, but not necessarily supported or condoned at the societal level.

Managing Ourselves and the Language We Use

Before we influence others to accept our ideas about what constitutes social justice, we must determine our own social identities. We need to know which of our ascribed and achieved statuses are dominant or subordinate, and what these features mean for us to be able to voice our ideas and beliefs, as well as influence others. Also vital to being heard is our ability to communicate in a way that accounts for another's background and identities, as well as our use of appropriate language. While we may share cultural traits (or even all the attributes listed above), we are not the same. Effective communication is not a one-way process. It requires a message, and a sender and a receiver who conjointly come to a shared understanding. Effective communication is difficult and problematic oftentimes because "although the words may be the same, the meaning can be very different. The same expression can have a different connotation or emotional emphasis."[34]

Verbal and Nonverbal Communication

Arguments abound concerning how much communication is nonverbal or uses body language and how much is vocal or verbal. This debate will not be settled, as it is highly situational and involves not just the message, the sender, and the receiver but the mutual understanding. Verbal communication involves speaking clearly and confidently, being concise, and varying tone or knowing when to emphasize certain points. It is crucial to remember that in order to be a good speaker, one should be a good listener and able to read the involvement or attentiveness of the audience or person with whom one is speaking. Nonverbal cues also provide ways for people to interpret what is being said.

Eye contact is one of those nonverbal cues that may be very different depending upon one's cultural background. For example, eye contact is often expected by teachers. However, some groups, such as many Asian Americans, are raised to not hold eye contact with an authority figure as a sign of respect. Failing to avert one's eyes would be considered by the student as rude or impolite. Likewise, this same student may not question the teacher, because it is wrong to challenge the authority figure and is believed to show arrogance. The way we pause in our speech, how and where we hold our arms, leaning back or forward, facial expressions, using gestures, and the personal space we require are other nonverbal features of communication.

Prejudice and Discrimination

The terms prejudice and discrimination have been used throughout the preceding pages of this chapter; however, it is important to recognize the difference. Prejudice is a culturally learned thought, belief, or connotation. Discrimination is an action, behavior, or arrangement that results in the unfair or preferential treatment of an individual or group. Discriminatory treatment takes place at the individual, group, and institutional levels.

Going back to prejudice, we must recognize both the positive and negative biases we hold. We must recognize not only how we prejudge others, but also diagnose the privileges we hold. Prejudice intensifies in development when (1) a society is homogenous (meaning very similar or the same), (2) upward mobility is valued, (3) aggression is favored over bigotry, (4) a minority group is large and increasing, and (5) communication barriers and ignorance between groups are common.[35] This list is not inclusive of all possibilities. What are some other social occasions that may increase prejudicial development? How might social privilege be related to prejudice and discrimination? The most famous work on privilege was a paper presented at a conference in 1986, and later published in 1988, by Peggy McIntosh. She says, "I think whites are carefully taught not to recognize white privilege, as males are taught not to recognize male privilege."[36] Perhaps the greatest privilege is not being aware or conscious of one's privilege. She offers 46 conditions or ways in which privilege shows itself. Some conditions are:

> I can go shopping alone most of the time, pretty well assured that I will not be followed or harassed. When I am told about our national heritage or about "civilization," I am shown that people of my color made it what it is. I can do well in a challenging situation without being called a credit to my race. I can talk with my mouth full and not have people put this down to my color. I am never asked to speak for all the people of my racial group. I can be pretty sure that if I ask to talk to the "person in charge", I will be facing a person of my race. If I have low credibility as a leader, I can be sure that my race is not the problem.[37]

McIntosh also states, "I have come to see white privilege as an invisible package of unearned assets which I can count on cashing in each day, but about which I was meant to remain anonymous."[38] What can be done to decrease or end White (and male) privilege?

Explicit and Implicit Bias

Explicit bias is overt or obvious prejudice that encompasses the beliefs and attitudes we have about a person or group on a conscious level. These biases are usually grounded in the perception of a threat. If we think a threat is real, we are more likely to justify harm to another (i.e., discriminate or violate).

Implicit bias is more arduous and covert. It is imbedded and unintentionally buried in our subconscious. We gain this type of bias over our lifetimes, starting in childhood. These biases provide us with both good and bad impressions of people based on age, appearance, race, ethnicity, etc. They are not chosen, but are involuntarily learned from both direct and indirect messaging. We all have these biases. Some researchers argue implicit bias can be unlearned, while others aren't so sure we aren't at least somewhat aware of these biases.[39] To learn about your own implicit biases, go online (https://implicit.harvard.edu/implicit/) and take the Implicit Association Test (IAT).

Gender-Inclusive Language

Virtually all research indicates women and men communicate differently. Men understand their position as being at the top of the gender hierarchy. Women know they are often held to a higher or different standard than men. Rather than focus on the numerous distinctions, the point here is to give everyone some tools to rid themselves of sexist language.

- Avoid sexist jokes or comments. Someone is bound to be offended. The same goes for racist jokes.
- Avoid using terms or words that are patronizing or diminish a woman's professional status (e.g., "chick," "babe," honey," etc.).
- Use terms that are inclusive, rather than exclusive, of everyone's gender (e.g., firefighter instead of fireman or chair rather than chairman or chairwoman).[40]

The terms listed in Table 12.1 are male and gender specific. When an individual uses one of these terms, that person is using an "exclusive" term and typically visualizes a male when using such concepts. Try the exercise below.[41] Provide a term that is inclusive of both males and females. Convert the following compound words with the suffixes "-boy, -man, or –men" into gender-neutral, inclusive terms that do not specify gender.

Table 12.1 Exclusive and Inclusive Language Terms

EXCLUSIVE LANGUAGE TERM	INCLUSIVE LANGUAGE TERM
Airmen	Pilots
Policeman	Police officer
Sportsman	
Fisherman	
Repairman	
Craftsman	
Mailman	
Layman	
Freshman	
Busboy	
Salesman	
Crewmen	
Congressman	

Initially, many people are not comfortable attempting to change common phrases, but with practice it becomes easier and not so challenging. Another way we can see gender is through the same type of words (nouns) that are not commonly gendered (e.g., teachman or runman or artmen). Pay attention to the language used by others as well as yourself. When you say something that is not gender-free or gender inclusive, correct yourself. Another way gender is played through words is difficult to put into words, but can be found in long-standing traditions.

Recently, a wedding was performed and the preacher said, "I now pronounce you 'man' and 'wife'." Notice how he is still a man? She has somehow adopted a new role. Likewise, in the traditional marriage ceremony, there is a custom in which the father (and sometimes the mother too now) is asked "who gives this woman away in marriage?" He says, "I/We do." Is this not demonstrating informal ownership of the bride being transferred to her husband? She is also traditionally escorted down the aisle by her father or another man. Her future husband stands independently, on his own, up front. She is unable to walk by herself and needs accompaniment.

Can you think of other ways, both formally and informally, gender is rooted in tradition? Can you practice using gender-inclusive language? It can be difficult at first, but it gets easier with frequency and time.

People-First Language

People-first language emphasizes the person first, rather than the disability. We use people-first language as a way of speaking respectfully about an individual who has a disability. It acknowledges what a person *has* and not that the person *is* the disability.

The U.S. Department of Health and Human Services offers suggestions on how to communicate with and about people with disabilities. These suggestions can be found in Table 12.2.[42]

Table 12.2 People-First Language

People-First Language	Language to Avoid
Person with a disability	The disabled, handicapped
Person without a disability	Normal person, healthy person
Person with an intellectual, cognitive, or developmental disability	Retarded, slow, simple, moronic, defective or afflicted, special person
Person with a mental health issue or emotional, behavioral, or a psychiatric disability	Insane, crazy, psycho, nuts, maniac
Person who is hard of hearing	Hearing impaired, suffers a hearing loss
Person who is Deaf	Deaf and dumb, mute
Person who is blind or has a visual impairment	The blind
Person who has a communication disorder, is unable to speak, or uses a device to speak	Mute, dumb
Person who uses a wheelchair	Confined or restricted to a wheelchair, wheelchair bound
Person with a physical disability	Crippled, lame, deformed, invalid, spastic
Person with epilepsy or seizure disorder	Epileptic
Person with multiple sclerosis	Afflicted with MS
Accessible parking or bathrooms	Handicapped parking or bathrooms
Person who is successful, productive	Has overcome his/her disability or he/she is courageous

There are numerous publications and guides available to learn more about people with disabilities. For example, here are a few helpful communication tips that are beneficial to a person who has a hearing impairment or is Deaf: (1) when standing in front of a light source (like a window), lip-reading and reading your expressions is virtually impossible; (2) don't cover your mouth when speaking or turn away when speaking to an individual with hearing difficulties; (3) learning the 26 letters of the American Sign Language alphabet could be crucial to communication when a pen and paper are not available. Likewise, there are a number of helpful communication tips to know when communicating with people who have a different disability (e.g., blindness, uses a wheelchair, etc.). Go to the U.S. Department of Labor's website (at www.dol.gov/odep/pubs/fact/communicating.htm) for tools to better assist and communicate with people who have specific types of disabilities or limitations.[43]

We all deserve respect and we are all people first. Some of us do not yet have impairments that impede our abilities to function, while others of us already have a disability. Keep in mind, always, that a person with a disability, just like everyone who doesn't have a disability, wants to be treated kindly, fairly, and equally.

Cross-Cultural Language and Communication Tips and Barriers

Regardless of the cultural background of someone we encounter, we need to possess the skills and knowledge necessary to communicate effectively. Our society is made up of people from a multitude of unique cultures and nations. Many of our urban areas are host to citizens and visitors from all over the world. Chances are, even in a very small town, people from various ethnic backgrounds make up the community.

With communication as our goal, recognizing racial and ethnic identities is necessary in order to know, generally speaking, what might be anticipated in the dialogue. We need to "be self-aware about our early life experiences that helped to shape our perceptions and assumptions about people, and how we feel toward someone who is 'different.' We need to refrain from denying that differences exist, or imitate 'them' in order to feel more comfortable."[44] "Learn to be sensitive to cultural differences as well as open-minded about cultural differences. Understand power structures may vary by cultural background. Think critically about power and oppression, and appropriate actions that apply in context to others."[45] Be mindful of possible biases and stereotypes you and they may hold.

When conversing with someone who is not fluent in English (but you are), know that a listener can easily misunderstand the spoken words. Find a variety of ways to interpret terms you don't understand.[46] Don't use acronyms or abbreviations unless you are certain the other person is aware of the correct meaning. The following are some additional tips for communicating with others for whom English is a second language.[47]

1. Speak slowly and enunciate clearly.
2. Face the person and speak directly (even if using a third party as a translator).
3. Avoid concentrated eye contact if the other speaker is not making direct eye contact.
4. Do not use jargon, slang, idioms, or reduced forms of speech (e.g., "gonna," "gotta," "wanna," "couldja").
5. Repeat key issues and questions in different ways.
6. Avoid asking questions that can be answered by yes or no; rather, ask questions so that the answer can show understanding.
7. Use short, simple sentences.
8. Pause between sentences.
9. Use only one idea per sentence.
10. Respect the silence that non-native English speakers need to formulate their sentences and translate them in their minds.
11. Check comprehension by having the other speaker repeat what was said.

12. Encourage and provide positive feedback regarding the person's ability to communicate.
13. Be patient.
14. Do not speak louder. It will not help.

Summary

In our quest for social justice, we must learn language and communication skills to be better at treating others in the same manner that we would like to be treated, as well as how to avoid doing harm. Our social identities depict us to others as privileged or oppressed, and play a role in the level of power we hold. For social justice to occur, we must start with ourselves and work to ensure fairness and find ways to eliminate both explicit and implicit bias. To do so requires that we be effective communicators. According to Brian Fitch, if we want to be competent communicators, we must (1) assess our current abilities, (2) practice being better communicators by understanding how others perceive our verbal and nonverbal behaviors, adjusting our tone and style to suit the person and the situation, and (3) gain feedback that is both timely and specific.[48]

Many of us want to make a difference in our social world. We are civic-minded and feel the responsibility to help curb social injustices. We must learn from one another. We must be open and honest with each other. The "What Can We Do" chapter written by Allan G. Johnson in his book entitled *Privilege, Power, and Difference* offers numerous suggestions.[49]

1. Acknowledge that our "divisive" problems exist.
2. Do something.

   a. Make noise, be seen. Volunteer, speak out, write letters, sign petitions, and/or just show up.

   b. Find little ways to withdraw support from paths of least resistance and people's choices to follow them, starting with yourself. This may be as simple as not laughing at a racist or heterosexist joke or saying you don't think it's funny.

   c. Dare to make people uncomfortable, beginning with yourself. For example, if your location isn't the exception, ask why principles and other school administrators are usually White and male, yet the teachers they supervise are female and people of color.

   d. Openly choose and model alternative paths. This is the idea that we must be the change we want to see or using the language we believe is inclusive and fair.

   e. Actively promote change in how systems are organized around privilege. Speak out for equality, and against violence and harassment wherever they occur, whether at home, at work, or on the street.

   f. Support the right of women and men to love whomever they choose.

   g. Pay attention to how different forms of oppression interact with one another.

   h. Work with other people. Being in the company of people who support what you're doing can make all the difference in the world. Share a book like this one!

   i. Don't keep it to yourself. Privilege and oppression are not a personal problem that can be solved through personal solutions. It makes sense to start with yourself, but it's equally important not to end with yourself.

   j. Don't let other people set the standard for you. Start where you are and work from there.

Johnson's final paragraph is very much worth sharing, by suggesting how we can avoid becoming so frustrated wanting and working for change, yet wanting to give up when things don't happen the way we think they should, when another injustice is witnessed. He says:

> The human capacity to choose how to participate in the world empowers all of us to pass along something different from what's been passed to us. With each strand of the knot of

privilege that we help to work loose and unravel, we don't act simply for ourselves, we join a process of creative resistance to oppression that's been unfolding for thousands of years. We become part of the long tradition of people who have dared to make a difference.[50]

In closing, social justice starts with dialogue that is effective. There are volumes upon volumes of written works that attempt to help our plight to become better communicators in our quest for social justice. Building relationships, building trust and rapport, and building bridges take knowledge, skill, motivation, and time. Have perseverance, be true to yourself, keep your faith, and peace to all.

Discussion Questions

1. What are some of the ways offered to improve our social relationships?
2. When interacting with others, what should we avoid?
3. Why is social standing so important?
4. What are some of the ways offered to calm down a situation?
5. What is meant by "gender-inclusive language?" Do you practice "gender-inclusive language?"
6. What is meant by "people-first language?" Do you practice "people-first language?"
7. Offer some cross-cultural language tips and barriers.

Notes

1. Shusta, R. M., Levine, D. R., Wong, H. Z., Olson, A. T., & Harris, P. R. (2015). *Multicultural law enforcement: Peacekeeping in a diverse society*. Boston: Pearson, p. 111.
2. Engelstad, S., Otieno, M., & Owino, D. (2008). *Do no harm in Somalia*. Cambridge, MA: CDA.
3. Berger, P., & Luckmann, T. (1966). *The social construction of reality: A treatise in the sociology of knowledge*. New York: Doubleday.
4. Howard, J. A., & Alamilla, R. M. (2001). Gender and identity. In D. Vannoy (Ed.), *Gender mosaics: Social perspectives* (pp. 54–64). Los Angeles: Roxbury.
5. Jenkins, R. (1996). *Social identity*. London, New York: Routledge, pp. 3–4.
6. Allen, B. J. (2011). *Difference matters: Communicating social identity*, 2nd ed. Long Grove, IL: Waveland Press, Inc.
7. Thompson, W. E., & Hickey, J. V. (1994). *Society in focus: An introduction to sociology*. New York: HarperCollins College Publishers, p. 93.
8. *Ibid.*, p. 94.
9. Spradley, J. P., & McCurdy, D. W. (1980). *Anthropology: The cultural perspective*, 2nd ed. New York: Wiley Press, p. 68.
10. Marshall, G. (Ed.). (1994). *The concise Oxford dictionary of sociology*. Oxford, New York: Oxford University Press, pp. 411–412.
11. Burr, V. (1995). *An introduction to social constructionism*. London: Routledge, p. 51.
12. Mann, C. R., Zatz, M. S., & Rodriguez, N. (2006). *Images of color, images of crime*, 3rd ed. Los Angeles: Roxbury, pp. 1–13.
13. Healey, J. F. (2009). *Race, ethnicity, gender, and class: The sociology of group conflict and change*, 5th ed. Los Angeles: Pine Forge Press, pp. 49–50.
14. Gans, H. J. (1972). The positive functions of poverty. *American Journal of Sociology*, 78(2), 275–289.
15. Henslin, J. M. (2003). *Sociology: A down-to-earth approach*, 6th ed. Boston: Allyn & Bacon, p. 281.
16. Glass, A. (2007). Understanding generational differences for competitive success. *Industrial and Commercial Training*, 39(2), pp. 98–99. Retrieved August 31, 2017, from https://doi.org/10.1108/00197850710732424
17. *Ibid.*, pp. 98–103.
18. *Ibid.*, p. 101.
19. Cone, Inc. (2006). *Cone Millennial Cause Study*. The Millennial Generation: Pro-Social and Empowered to Change the World. In Collaboration with AMP Agency. Retrieved August 31, 2017, from www.centerforgiving.org/Portals/0/2006%20Cone%20Millennial%20Cause%20Study.pdf
20. Treiman, D. J. (1977). *Occupational prestige in comparative perspective*. New York: Academic Press.
21. Thompson, & Hickey, 1994, p. 214.

22. Jun, H. (2010). *Social justice, multicultural counseling, and practice: Beyond a conventional approach.* Los Angeles: Sage, p. 192.
23. Campbell, F. A. K. (2008). Exploring internalized ableism using critical race theory. *Disability and Society, 23*(2), pp. 151–162.
24. *Ibid.,* p. 154.
25. Jun, 2010, p. 217.
26. Smith, L., Foley, P. F., & Chaney, M. P. (2008). Addressing classism, ableism, and heterosexism in counselor education. *Journal of Counseling and Development, 86,* pp. 303-309, p. 306.
27. Jun, 2010, pp. 218–219.
28. Carr-Ruffino, N. (2009). *Managing diversity: People skills for a multicultural workplace,* 8th ed. New York: Pearson Custom Publishing, pp. 212–213.
29. Jun, 2010, p. 147.
30. Allen, 2011, p. 125.
31. Blumenfeld, W. J. (2000). Heterosexism. In M. Adams, W. J. Blumenfeld, R. Castaneda, H. W. Hackman, M. L. Peters, & X. Zuniga (Eds.), *Readings for diversity and social justice* (pp. 267–275). New York: Routledge.
32. Shusta et al., 2015, p. 211.
33. *Ibid.,* p. 343.
34. *Ibid.,* p. 116.
35. Ponterotto, J. G., & Pederson, P. B. (1993). *Preventing prejudice.* Thousand Oaks, CA: Sage.
36. McIntosh, P. (1988). *White privilege and male privilege: A personal account of coming to see correspondence through work in women's studies.* Working Paper No. 189. Wellesley, MA: Center for Research on Women, p. 1.
37. *Ibid.,* pp. 2–5.
38. *Ibid.,* p. 1.
39. Kirwan Institute for the Study of Race and Ethnicity at The Ohio State University. (2015). *Understanding implicit bias.* Retrieved August 31, 2017, from http://kirwaninstitute.osu.edu/research/understanding-implicit-bias/
40. Shusta et al., 2015, p. 131.
41. Author unknown.
42. Center for Disease Control (date unknown). U.S. Department of Health and Human Services. Retrieved August 31, 2017, from www.cdc.gov/ncbddd/disabilityandhealth/pdf/disabilityposter_photos.pdf
43. U.S. Department of Labor. Office of Disability Employment Policy. Retrieved August 31, 2017 from www.dol.gov/odep/pubs/fact/communicating.htm.
44. Shusta et al., 2015, 121.
45. Allen, 2011, p. 75.
46. Shusta et al., 2015, p. 111.
47. *Ibid.,* p. 113.
48. Fitch, B. D. (2016). *Law enforcement interpersonal communication and conflict management.* Los Angeles: Sage, pp. 113–115.
49. Johnson, A. G. (2001). *Privilege, power, and difference.* Mountain View, CA: Mayfield Publishing, pp. 137–171.
50. *Ibid.,* p. 171.

References

Allen, B. J. (2011). *Difference matters: Communicating social identity,* 2nd ed. Long Grove, IL: Waveland Press, Inc.

Berger, P., & Luckmann, T. (1966). *The social construction of reality: A treatise in the sociology of knowledge.* New York: Doubleday.

Blumenfeld, W. J. (2000). Heterosexism. In M. Adams, W. J. Blumenfeld, R. Castaneda, H. W. Hackman, M. L. Peters, & X. Zuniga (Eds.), *Readings for diversity and social justice* (pp. 267–275). New York: Routledge.

Burr, V. (1995). *An introduction to social constructionism.* London: Routledge, p. 51.

Campbell, F. A. K. (2008). Exploring internalized ableism using critical race theory. *Disability and Society, 23*(2), 151–162.

Carr-Ruffino, N. (2009). *Managing diversity: People skills for a multicultural workplace,* 8th ed. New York: Pearson Custom Publishing.

Center for Disease Control (date unknown). U.S. Department of Health and Human Services. Retrieved August 31, 2017, from www.cdc.gov/ncbddd/disabilityandhealth/pdf/disabilityposter_photos.pdf

Cone Inc. (2006). *Cone millennial cause study.* The Millennial Generation: Pro-Social and Empowered to Change the World. In Collaboration with AMP Agency. Retrieved August 31, 2017, from www.centerforgiving.org/Portals/0/2006%20Cone%20Millennial%20Cause%20Study.pdf

Engelstad, S., Otieno, M., & Owino, D. (2008). *Do no harm in Somalia.* Cambridge, MA: CDA.

Federal Bureau of Investigation. (2015). *Hate crime statistics, 2015.* Retrieved August 31, 2017, from https://ucr.fbi.gov/hate-crime/2015

Fitch, B. D. (2016). *Law enforcement interpersonal communication and conflict management.* Los Angeles: Sage.

Gans, H. J. (1972). The positive functions of poverty. *American Journal of Sociology, 78*(2), 275–289.

Glass, A. (2007). Understanding generational differences for competitive success. *Industrial and Commercial Training, 39*(2), 98–103. https://doi.org/10.1108/00197850710732424

Healey, J. F. (2009). *Race, ethnicity, gender, and class: The sociology of group conflict and change,* 5th ed. Los Angeles: Pine Forge Press.

Henslin, J. M. (2003). *Sociology: A down-to-earth approach,* 6th ed. Boston: Allyn & Bacon.

Howard, J. A., & Alamilla, R. M. (2001). Gender and identity. In D. Vannoy (Ed.), *Gender mosaics: Social perspectives* (pp. 54–64). Los Angeles: Roxbury.

Jenkins, R. (1996). *Social identity.* London, New York: Routledge, pp. 3–4.

Johnson, A. G. (2001). *Privilege, power, and difference.* Mountain View, CA: Mayfield Publishing.

Jun, H. (2010). *Social justice, multicultural counseling, and practice: Beyond a conventional approach.* Los Angeles: Sage.

Kirwan Institute for the Study of Race and Ethnicity at The Ohio State University. (2015). *Understanding implicit bias.* Retrieved August 31, 2017, from http://kirwaninstitute.osu.edu/research/understanding-implicit-bias/

Mann, C. R., Zatz, M. S., & Rodriguez, N. (2006). *Images of color, images of crime,* 3rd ed. Los Angeles: Roxbury.

Marshall, G. (Ed.). (1994). *The concise Oxford dictionary of sociology.* Oxford, New York: Oxford University Press.

McIntosh, P. (1988). *White privilege and male privilege: A personal account of coming to see correspondence through work in women's studies.* Working Paper No. 189. Wellesley, MA: Center for Research on Women.

Ponterotto, J. G., & Pederson, P. B. (1993). *Preventing prejudice.* Thousand Oaks, CA: Sage.

Shusta, R. M., Levine, D. R., Wong, H. Z., Olson, A. T., & Harris, P. R. (2015). *Multicultural law enforcement: Peacekeeping in a diverse society.* Boston: Pearson.

Smith, L., Foley, P. F., & Chaney, M. P. (2008). Addressing classism, ableism, and heterosexism in counselor education. *Journal of Counseling and Development, 86,* 303–309.

Spradley, J. P., & McCurdy, D. W. (1980). *Anthropology: The cultural perspective,* 2nd ed. New York: Wiley Press.

C:\Users\smitchell\Desktop\My Titles\Roberson 15031-1633\02 Roberson CE files\15031-1633-Ref Mismatch Report.docx - LStERROR_35Thompson, W. E., & Hickey, J. V. (1994). *Society in focus: An introduction to sociology.* New York: HarperCollins College Publishers.

Treiman, D. J. (1977). *Occupational prestige in comparative perspective.* New York: Academic Press, In William E. Thompson and Joseph V. Hickey, Society in Focus: An Introduction to Sociology. New York: HarperCollins, 1994:214.

PART III

International and Transnational Issues

13

NATIONAL STATUS/IMMIGRATION AND SOCIAL JUSTICE

Robert D. Hanser

Introduction

For the past decade or so, concern over immigration issues has been at the forefront of debate among politicians. While, for some, the issue centers on whether tighter controls should be placed on immigration, especially immigration from Mexico across the southwestern border of the United States, others counter with arguments that most of these initiatives are poorly implemented and ineffective, and that there is an inherent and fundamental contradiction with such policies and the very philosophical foundation of the United States.

At the present time, there is a serious backlog in processing work visas, which causes challenges for many businesses in regions where documented immigrant workers are employed. Further, many undocumented immigrant workers are, in order to keep their jobs, willing to work in environments that are dangerous and/or not in compliance with many of the health and safety standards usually expected in work environments. Last, the emphasis on deportation tends to ignore the reality that families in the southwestern region often consist of both legal and illegal migrants, thereby separating familial members in a manner that is detrimental to the social welfare of the family and the community around them. These and other issues are all of importance when attempting to develop a pragmatic approach to immigration, especially when involving the southwestern United States.

These issues serve as the substantive components of a system in which justice for U.S. immigrants is flawed. Immigrants caught in the removal system, which includes arrest, a hearing, and deportation, are the victims of procedural injustice. These removal processes run counter to the ideas of due process and fundamental fairness. Compounding the problem is the fact that a system that has traditionally been considered civil law has been enhanced with a long list of new crimes that can qualify an immigrant for deportation, as well as the more accepted practice of having local police involved in immigration enforcement in some states.

This chapter proposes that such developments in immigrant processes and treatment actually conflict with the overarching identity of the United States and that, in reality, such attempts are counterproductive. While this will be discussed later in more detail, the practical realities of the illegal migrant issue preclude reactionary measures from being effective to addressing it. For both practical and philosophical reasons, it is unwise for the United States to adopt the stance that has currently been taken, one that consists of murky and contradictory policy and social outcomes that are detrimental to the citizen and the undocumented immigrant alike.

121

The Blurring of Criminal Law and Civil Law

While the problems of injustice and immigration issues may seem inconsequential to some, the deportation process does not have safeguards for individual protections that are provided in our criminal system, ostensibly because it is considered a civil process. Yet, our very Supreme Court, in *Padilla v. Kentucky*,[1] acknowledged that "deportation is a particularly severe penalty," adding that "deportation is . . . intimately related to the criminal process." The court, in acknowledging both the increased blurring of distinctions between the civil proceedings of the immigration system and criminal sanctions that sometimes result, determined that noncitizen immigrants should be afforded a criminal defense attorney to provide advice prior to entering into any type of plea agreement.[2]

The blurring of criminal and civil law issues have also been showcased through prior lawsuits and case law from other researchers.[3] Indeed, consider that, in 2012, the United States Supreme Court handed down a ruling that upheld the practice of requiring immigration status checks during routine police stops in a 5–3 majority vote.[4] However, this ruling was accompanied by cautionary commentary against detaining individuals for prolonged periods of time if they do not have their immigration documents and also warned against the potential for racial profiling to occur. As a result, legislation limited the use of racial factors in arrests, holding that police may not consider race, color, or national origin beyond what is currently permissible by prior case law. Thus, as with this prior case law, race (and the appearance of having Mexican ancestry) may be considered a relevant factor in enforcing immigration law, but it cannot be the sole basis for making a stop and/or an arrest.[5]

This is an important point that can be complicated, at best, and quite confusing, at worst. While racial characteristics can be used as part of a composite rationale for a stop, it has to be articulated with other observed facts. Again, however, this creates a conundrum from a legal perspective because, unless the officer observes some other type of criminal activity, there are no grounds for questioning via a reasonable suspicion (other than the appearance of the individual) to determine that an immigration violation exists. This also means that there would be no probable cause for criminal activity. Thus, one must ask, why then would the officer have grounds to inquire in the first place? In most cases, he or she would not have any reasonable grounds for questioning, particularly if the encounter was not very near to the United States and Mexico border.[6]

Failure to Uphold Legal Requirements

Even more recently, in 2017, a class action lawsuit was filed that challenged the practice of turning away asylum seekers who request United States protection at ports of entry along the border between the United States and Mexico.[7] Plaintiffs in this case allege that agents of the Customs and Border Protection use a variety of tactics—including misrepresentation, threats and intimidation, verbal abuse and physical force, and coercion—to deny bona fide asylum seekers the opportunity to pursue their claims. Complainants in this case note that when the U.S. government refuses to allow asylum seekers to pursue their claims, it is a violation of the Immigration and Nationality Act, the Administrative Procedure Act, the Due Process Clause of the Fifth Amendment, as well as the doctrine of *non-refoulement* under international law.

The issue of *refoulement*, in particular, warrants additional attention. Refoulement refers to the expulsion of individuals who have the right to be recognized as refugees. This legal principle was first established by the United Nations Convention of 1954 which, in Article 33(1), holds the following:

> No Contracting State shall expel or return ('refouler') a refugee in any manner whatsoever to the frontiers of territories where his life or freedom would be threatened on account of his race, religion, nationality, membership of a particular social group or political opinion.[8]

Further, it is important to clarify that this principle does not only restrict countries from sending refugees back to their nation of origin, it also prohibits the return of those refugees to any other country wherein it would be likely that they would be persecuted or subject to widespread victimization due to their national status, culture, race, or other demographic feature. The only exception to this is when the individual is a potential threat to national security.

While the non-refoulement policy has been accepted around the globe, there have been problems with its adoption in some cases, usually because immigrants under this stipulation are required to have official refugee status. Further, not all nations around the globe are members of the United Nations Convention on the Status of Refugees and/or have established official processes to determine who does or does not have refugee status within their borders. This leads to ambiguity and a lack of consistency in these cases.

Issues with turning refugees back and failing to afford protection have been leveled at the United States and rose to a crescendo during the immigration crisis the occurred in 2014. During this time, there was a noticeable increase of children from several Central American nations who sought entry into the United States. In 2014, this influx of unprotected and unchaperoned youth numbered in the tens of thousands from El Salvador, Guatemala, and Honduras. To be fair, some of these youth did have adult women who were either mothers or guardians but, for the most part, these youth migrated in droves, of their own accord.

The reason for this spike in undocumented immigration has to do with the extreme violence that erupted throughout Central America. These youth fled poverty and excessive violence from gangs, extremist groups, and drug organizations alike.[9] The murder rates in these countries also increased and were among the highest in the international community, with Honduras having the highest murder rate in the world.[10] While it was true that these youth fled their home countries due to danger, many also fled to reunite with other family members in the United States who had not been deported. The perception among many Central Americans was that the United States was, as a general policy, allowing immigrant children to remain in the United States.

These perceptions developed because these youth were seldom quickly deported and, even though immigration proceedings were promptly started, overall they took a long time, during which these youth would be allowed to stay with a family member or sponsor in the United States. The grounds for this were related to anti-trafficking laws that prohibited the immediate deportation of youth from Central America until a court hearing was provided. In the meantime, the Department of Health and Human Services provided health screenings and immunization shots, while assigning an average shelter stay of 35 days or more, when necessary.

The key point to all of this is that the United States, due to its own statutory requirements regarding safeguards against the potential victimization and trafficking of immigrant youth (known as the Trafficking Victims Protection Reauthorization Act or the TVPRA)[11] and due to the obvious dangers that exist to these youth who are returned to their own countries (especially Honduras), has a legal obligation under international non-refoulement policies to treat these youth as refugees. Despite this, the current Trump administration has proposed to draft policy that will deport over 150,000 of these youth who came without adult supervision, once they turn 18 years of age. Such a process would essentially dump thousands of youth into a dangerous region without the benefit of protection, essentially making the United States a culpable and contributory party to their future victimization, regardless of whether they are classified as adults.[12] Further, such policy is considered while there is clear evidence from Senate-level investigations that many of these youth are at risk of being trafficked in the labor market in the United States and abroad.[13]

When considering immigration against the backdrop of social justice, it is clear that it is unjust to send these youth to known areas of danger. This is particularly true when one considers that in 2015, 1.38 million foreign-born immigrants moved to the United States, with India, China, and Mexico accounting for nearly 500,000 of these immigrants.[14] Currently, out of the total population of 321 million in the United States, immigrants account for 43 million, which is less than 14% of the entire U.S. population.[15] This means that the absorption of the total youth currently in the United States could occur quite easily, particularly since many will, by the time they turn 18 years of age, be educated and acculturated into our national landscape. Indeed, by that point, the U.S. will have already paid for the education, housing, upbringing, and other aspects of getting these youth to the age of majority. It seems silly and illogical to simply send these youth back to a dangerous and unstable environment after they have reached the age of majority and can contribute to the economy; it stands to benefit the U.S. none at all. Therefore, current thinking on this issue seems to be both reactive and irrational—a calloused approach that lacks any true pragmatic grounding.

Civil Rights Violations in Immigration Detention Facilities

In late 2015, the U.S. Commission on Civil Rights, established by Congress in 1957, conducted an investigation into the actual types of response and conditions of confinement that existed within federal detention facilities holding immigrants. They examined a variety of facilities administered through the Office of Refugee Resettlement (ORR), which is required to maintain certain standards of care and custody of immigrant children. These standards of care include medical and mental health, education, family reunification efforts, and the provision of recreational activities.

This investigation resulted in the generation of a corrective action plan outlining the needs for providing better medical and mental health services. Further, this plan recommended that programs provide youth care workers with additional communications training when working with unac-companied immigrant children and foster nurturing and positive interactions.[16] Keep in mind that these are youth who are held without parents, legal guardians, or other adult figures. They are also detained under civil law, not criminal law, themselves not being suspected of criminal activity and, in the United States legal system, being considered juveniles, not adults, which implies that they should be provided with added protections due to their age.

Children's detention centers are required to provide classroom education taught by teachers with a minimum four-year college degree. Upon investigation, the U.S. Commission on Civil Rights found that numerous educational workers did not meet minimal standards for hire. The Commission, in its report, pointed out that educational programming is vital to a child's development and that education for unac-companied immigrant children gives them better odds of integrating into American society, as a whole, and into the American job sector, specifically, should they remain in the United States. A failure to provide this essentially ensures that these youth remain in an unstable and disadvantaged status and increases the likelihood that they will not be productive within mainstream American society. This again is counter-productive both to the welfare of these youths and to the United States economy and social dignity.

Detention Facility Housing Conditions

During the past two to three years, there has been growing concern that the U.S. Customs and Border Protection (CBP) agency has maintained facilities that are no different from prison facilities designed for common criminals. This includes facilities that house entire families (men, women, and children) who are being detained civilly, not for criminal offenses committed in the United States. It should be emphasized that these concerns are not simply liberal or anti-establishment rhetoric. Indeed, even members of Congress have voiced concerns about the punitive nature of immigration detention facil-ities. In fact, 136 members of Congress signed and endorsed a letter to the Department of Homeland Security's chief administrator, indicating that:

> We are disturbed by the fact that many mothers and children remain in family detention despite serious medical needs. In the past year, we have learned of the detention of children

with intellectual disabilities, a child with brain cancer, a mother with a congenital heart disorder, a 14-day-old baby, and a 12-year-old child who has not eaten solid food for two months, among many others. Recently, we learned of a three-year-old child at the Berks County Residential Center who was throwing up for three days and was apparently offered water as a form of medical treatment. It was only after the child began throwing up blood on the fourth day that the facility finally transferred her to a hospital. This is simply unacceptable.[17]

Naturally, the U.S. Sentencing Commission supported these congressional concerns, adding that additional concerns included not just family detention centers, but reports of unsuitable conditions in border patrol facilities and adult-only detention facilities.

In particular, the Commission found conditions of extreme cold, overcrowding, and inadequate food to be a common problem throughout numerous CBP facilities.[18] Again, this should not be interpreted as isolated incidents but instead the norm throughout these facilities. Some facilities resembled the conditions of a prison rather than detention. Naturally, while some locations house immigrants convicted of serious crimes and lesser crimes and those who have failed to appear for immigration hearings, it is important that others held on civil immigration issues not be co-mingled with the criminal population and that their treatment be substantially different. Altogether, the Commission found evidence to conclude that the Department of Homeland Security (DHS) in general and the Customs Border Protection in particular detained undocumented immigrants in a manner more akin to prison rather than civil detention, which is a violation of the Fifth Amendment.[19] Prior to this and since this time, other various levels of federal oversight, including federal district courts, have made similar decisions and left similar rulings as precedent.

Back to the Future: How Confusing Objectives Became Today's Quagmire

Perhaps, to make sense of what has become a confusing system with a number of unconstitutional outcomes and consequences, we should not just understand that criminal law and civil law are different. Rather, we must note that immigration proceedings and determinations are civil in nature due to historical etiology that can explain this development. As it turns out, the basis for these distinctions extends back to the late 1800s, when the Supreme Court held, in *Fong Yue Ting v. United States* (1893),[20] that deportation was a *civil* rather than a *criminal* sanction. In other words, deportation in and of itself is not punishment, per se, but is instead an administrative proceeding intended to simply return immigrants to their native countries of origin. At this time, the High Court reasoned that:

> The order of deportation is not a punishment for crime. It is not a banishment, in the sense in which that word is often applied to the expulsion of a citizen from his country by way of punishment. It is but a method of enforcing the return to his own country of an alien who has not complied with the conditions upon the performance of which the government of the nation . . . has determined that his continuing to reside here shall depend.[21]

The reasons for this ruling warrant that some context be given. During this time, Chinese laborers were immigrating into the United States in record numbers. In an effort to curtail the excessive numbers of immigrants, the Chinese Exclusion Act and the Geary Act restricted and/or delayed the immigration of additional Chinese into the United States. One of the key aspects of the Geary Act was that the burden of proof for demonstrating the right to be in the United States was placed upon the Chinese resident. During this time, Chinese immigrants were required to possess a "certificate of residence," which was proof of legal entry into the United States. Those without such a certificate, for whatever reason, were considered unlawfully in the United States and could be arrested, forced into hard labor for up to a year, and could be automatically deported thereafter.

Despite the fact that Chinese laborers could be given hard labor up to a year prior to deporta-tion, the Supreme Court continued to support the rationale that immigration proceedings were civil rather than criminal in nature. However, the true underlying reason for this has more to do with the fact that the court also maintained that immigration policy and the enforcement of that policy were issues of the legislative and executive branches of government. Along the way, the court upheld broad federal powers and, in recognizing that certain minimal levels of due process were required in immigra-tion and deportation proceedings, the court gave nearly unfettered power to Congress to define the standards, burdens of proof, and rules that applied. In the process, by making immigration proceedings civil in nature, a much lower burden of proof was required by the state (preponderance of the evidence rather than proof beyond a reasonable doubt), fewer protections were afforded the Chinese immigrants because the "loss of liberty" standard was irrelevant since they were being removed from the United States, and (at the same time) requiring additional measures (such as forced labor) was considered pay-ment for the cost of proceedings, not punishment for a wrong done.

Thus, by classifying deportation as a "civil" penalty, the court held that immigrants facing removal are not entitled to the same constitutional rights provided to defendants facing criminal punishment. It is for this reason that immigrants facing deportation today are not read their rights after being arrested, are not provided an attorney if they cannot afford one, and are not permitted to challenge an order of removal for being "cruel and unusual punishment." While undocumented immigrants are not required to do forced labor (this dropped out of usage several decades ago), the requirement to provide the protections afforded to someone charged in criminal court do not exist, yet at the same time, their experience while being detained may actually be similar to that of someone who has been charged with a criminal offense. Thus again, as in the late 1800s, it would seem that the blurring of these two legal systems allow the government to vacillate between one and/or the other so as to maximize deportation goals while also maintaining a covert punitive flavor, despite overt comments to the contrary. In short, it is a farce that allows the U.S. government to straddle both sides of the fence, to its advantage and in violation of what is constitutional.

Social Justice, Latin America, and the United States

The term social justice can have different meanings to different people, depending on who is asked, where they are asked, and when they are asked. For purposes of this chapter, the overall view of the United Nations will be considered. According to the Department of Economic and Social Affairs of the United Nations, "social justice is a relatively recent concept, born of the struggles surrounding the industrial revolution and the advent of socialist views on the organization of society."[22] Going further, social justice entails the idea that when people pursue economic goals, personal and professional growth, and/or the welfare of a community as a whole, inequality will be inescapable. Despite this, proponents of social justice believe that it is the duty of governments to ensure that these disparities be kept within tolerable limits of human dignity.

For advocates of social justice, the rise in worldwide economic inequality is seen as unjust and essentially criminal in intent. The Department of Economic and Social Affairs states that:

> In today's world, the enormous gap in the distribution of wealth, income and public benefits
> is growing ever wider, reflecting a general trend that is morally unfair, politically unwise and
> economically unsound. Injustices at the international level have produced a parallel increase
> in inequality between affluent and poor countries.[23]

While this commentary is leveled at economic growth, there are other incentives that are disparately available to individuals around the globe. For instance, there is disparity in access to opportunities among people in a region that are caused simply by an artificial border. Accordingly, there is the question as to whether some countries offer sufficient opportunities for people to engage in productive activities and to gain rewards that are commensurate with their talents and efforts. Indeed, the Department of Economic and Social Affairs (2006) notes that for many, this "represents justice or fairness in the broadest sense. It has traditionally been perceived as the basis for social justice in the United States of America, the economically dominant country today."[24]

Aside from the pursuit of economic wealth, which is the most visible yardstick of comparison in most capitalist countries, other concerns such as safety, humane treatment, access to education, health access, and so forth may not always fall within the spectrum of economics but are important for the overall well-being of the population. It is clear that access to these additional rewards to existence is not equal between the United States and its neighboring Latin countries. The question then becomes, does the United States have any responsibility to acknowledge this or even to help out their disadvantaged neighbors? Advocates for social justice would likely argue that yes, the United States does have such a responsibility, while staunchly conservative patriots might argue to the contrary.

For this chapter, the contention will be that, while the United States may be in need of examining its own response to immigrations, national status, and social justice, any responsibility begins and ends within the United States. The reason for this is simple—the very reasons that citizens are leaving Honduras, Guatemala, El Salvador, and Mexico are the same reasons that United States intervention within those countries will likely be moot; there is too much corruption at the governmental level. Indeed, most Central American nations experience problems with excessive economic corruption. It is because of this simple fact that the United States is largely powerless to provide stability, and there are resentments among many Latin nations against the United States for past military involvement into the affairs of these nations.[25] It is clear that, for better or worse, many leaders of Latin American countries have negative views of their northern neighbor.

Given this, it seems that the United States should take heed of what its neighbors are saying. This then means that Latin American nations will have to bail themselves out of the doldrums in which they find themselves. However, the nation of Bolivia has seen numerous gains by bringing people out of poverty, expanding its coverage for maternal health, boosting literacy, and investing in water and sanitation.[26] Indeed, President Evo Morales Ayma stated that "we live in sovereignty and dignity; no longer dominated by the North American empire . . . no longer being blackmailed by the International Monetary Fund."[27] This example shows both that these countries are capable of improving their condition and, just as important, that they tend to resent involvement by the United States. This is an important observation from a social justice point of view.

It would therefore appear that the official governments of these countries are not aligned with the United States and prefer, instead, to go it alone without U.S. help. While there is a possibility that these government leaders are themselves corrupt, this only serves to further restrict the United States in responding. Indeed, aside from some act of overt or covert warfare, there is little else that the U.S. can do to counter regimes of corruption, drug cartels that paralyze entire governments, and cultures that have developed around a "have" and "have not" mentality. Naturally, to engage in any form of armed intervention is both desperate and counterproductive, with the potential to further victimize and harm those persons whom the United States would be liberating so as to have better access to economic and social autonomy. Thus, the issue is complicated due to the perceptions touted by Latin American governments. This means that the argument for social justice becomes restricted to what lies within the borders of the United States.

America's Social Justice Responsibility?

The entire idea that nations should offer aid based on their identity as a nation-state and/or distinct culture falls in line with a book titled *Spheres of Justice*, by Michael Walzer.[28] In this book, Walzer writes from a "communitarian" perspective, arguing that the right of countries to exclude persons is, in some ways, constrained. As an example, Walzer contends that countries are similar to families, and that citizens of these countries often feel morally bound to specific groups of outsiders, such as groups who are ethnically similar or those who are in need of refuge due to threats to their existence or fundamental human rights.

Further, according to Walzer, the state is also constrained to not expel persons within the borders and confines of the country unless these individuals present an immediate threat to citizens of that nation. Likewise, the principle of mutual aid, or (in Walzer's words) the need to provide support to those least well off, is advocated by Walzer and is seen as important for relations with outsiders as it might be for individuals within the borders of that nation. Thus, Walzer provides a convincing moral case for protecting the status quo in immigration policy as it now stands, without adjustments by the current presidential administration.

Further, these points have been made and argued among our European neighbors, wherein Black[29] points toward previous experiences in Europe. He noted that in Europe, most West European nations were signatories to the Geneva Convention of 1951 on refugees and accept, at least in principle, the duty to provide asylum to individuals at severe risk of harm in their own nations of origin. Black also noted that most of these countries were also committed to the notion of "mutual aid," despite however lean such aid might be. He further states that "states' duties towards those with kinship ties to its own citizens are enshrined in policy."[30] He uses the examples of both German and Greek policy towards those of German or Greek ethnicity in the former Soviet Union, wherein both countries encourage the migration of their brethren into their respective nations of origin.

Given that there are many familial, cultural, and historical connections between Latino citizens of the United States and those from Mexico and Central America, it should come as no surprise that, according to Walzer's and Black's logic, there is a duty of the United States, based on kinship ties if nothing else, to extend aid and offer migration assistance. Further, given that the immigrant population within the United States is a reality and that the United States has only certain options in dealing with this population, it is not entirely clear what can be done now. Sending individuals back, en masse, seems to provoke danger for these individuals and also seems to go against the American philosophical grain. Indeed, it is the very spirit and essence of America to welcome immigrants, especially those who are tired, those who are poor, and the huddled masses seeking to live free. Thus, it is essentially an American characteristic to offer help. To send innocent individuals (especially youth) who simply seek to leave dangerous circumstances back to the very source of danger itself is simply un-American. While it may be unfortunate that the United States has absorbed the cost of providing humanitarian protection for these individuals, that cost is much more bearable than are other costs that would be incurred (i.e., human lives) were the U.S. to not offer aid to those fleeing bona fide dangerous locations. When deciding whether to provide assistance and welcome those who flee to our borders, we must ask ourselves the hypothetical question, "what would America do?"

Discussion Questions

1. From what you can tell, does the United States seem to follow its own standards and policies in how immigrants are processed?
2. Is it likely that immigrants who are permitted to stay in the United States are likely to find some sense of social justice?
3. Historically speaking, has the United States been altruistic or self-serving concerning its immigration policy? Explain your answer.
4. Concerning unaccompanied children who are immigrants from Central America, do you believe that they should be treated as refugees? Why or why not?
5. In your opinion, what is the author's primary point regarding the United States' response to immigrants currently in the United States. Do you agree or disagree?

Notes

1. *Padilla v. Kentucky*, 130 S. Ct. 1473, 1481 (U.S. 2010), p. 1486.
2. American Immigration Council. (2013). *Two systems of justice: How the immigration system fall short of American ideal of justice.* Washington, DC: Author.
3. Hanser, R. D. (2015). Using local law enforcement to enhance immigration law in the United States: A legal and social analysis. *Police Practice and Research: An International Journal, 16*(4), 303–315.
4. Barnes, R. (2012, June 25). Supreme Court rejects much of Arizona immigration law. *The Washington Post.*
5. *United States v. Brignoni-Ponce*, 422 U.S. 873 (1975).
6. *Ibid.*
7. American Immigration Council. (2017). *Challenging customs and border protection's unlawful practice of turning away asylum seekers.* Washington, DC: Author. Retrieved from www.americanimmigrationcouncil.org/litigation/challenging-customs-and-border-protections-unlawful-practice-turning-away-asylum-seekers
8. United Nations Convention of 1954 which, in Article 33(1), p. 117.
9. Dart, T. (2014, July 9). Child migrants at Texas border: An immigration crisis that's hardly new. *The Guardian, Houston.* Retrieved September 25, 2017, www.theguardian.com/world/2014/jul/09/us-immigration-undocumented-children-Texas
10. Park, H. (2014, October 21). Children at the border. *New York Times, New York.* Retrieved September 25, 2017, www.nytimes.com/interactive/2014/07/15/us/questions-about-the-border-kids.html?mcubz=1
11. *Trafficking Victims Protection Reauthorization Act of 2008*, PUB. L.110–457, 122 Stat. 5044.
12. Lanktree, G. (2017, September 21). Trump administration planning law to deport thousands of unaccompanied teens from Central America: Report. *Newsweek.* Retrieved September 25, 2017, www.newsweek.com/trump-administration-weighs-deporting-thousands-unaccompanied-child-migrants-668778
13. Greenberg, M. (2016). *Adequacy of the Department of Health and Human Services' efforts to protect unaccompanied alien children from human trafficking.* Washington, DC: U.S. Senate Committee on Homeland Security & Governmental Affairs.
14. Zong, J., & Batalova, J. (2017). *Frequently requested statistics on immigrants and immigration in the United States.* Washington, DC: Migration Policy Institute.
15. *Ibid.*
16. U.S. Commission on Civil Rights. (2015). *With liberty and justice for all: The state of civil rights at immigration detention facilities.* Washington, DC: United States Commission on Civil Rights.
17. *Ibid.*, p. 105.
18. *Ibid.*
19. *Ibid.*
20. *Fong Yue Ting v. United States*, 149 U.S. 698, 730 (1893).
21. *Ibid.*, p. 730.
22. Department of Economic and Social Affairs. (2006). *Social justice in an open world: The role of the United Nations.* Vienna, Austria: United Nations, p. 2.
23. *Ibid.*, p. 3.
24. *Ibid.*
25. UN News Centre. (2013). *Leaders of Latin American countries urge major push to promote social justice, end inequality.* Retrieved September 21, 2017, www.un.org/apps/news/story.asp?NewsID=46022#.WdKS0cahfIU
26. *Ibid.*
27. *Ibid.*, p. 1.
28. Walzer, M. (1983). *Spheres of justice: A defence of pluralism and equality.* Oxford: Blackwell Publishers.
29. Black, R. (1996). Immigration and social justice: Towards a progressive European immigration policy? *Institute of British Geographers, 21*(1), 64–75.
30. *Ibid.*, p. 69.

14

JUVENILES AND SOCIAL JUSTICE IN THE UNITED KINGDOM

Daniel Marshall

Introduction

Each generation views the behavior of its young people as worse than that experienced "20 years ago."[1] Youth[2] offending in England and Wales[3] has received much political attention and continues to be approached through criminal justice rather than wider policy initiatives, such as educational or welfare-based approaches. Criminal justice is delivered under the umbrella "criminal justice system," which indicates a system of closely linked parts working together efficiently with a clear input at one end and output at the other. The perceived linear and unified nature of this "system" masks the complex nature of youth offending and responses to this offending. System contact may in fact serve to further marginalize children and young people, particularly with access to education and employment, reducing the likelihood to desist from offending.[4] Young people have always tested the boundaries to the limit, and research has suggested that the wisest course may be to support young people as they grow out of crime.[5]

A new attitude toward law and order seemed to manifest in the early 1990s. Shadow Home Secretary Tony Blair proclaimed that we should be "tough on crime, tough on the causes of crime" (29 January 1993), and Prime Minister John Major declared that it was time to "condemn a little more and understand a little less" (21 February 1993). Commentators asserted that youth justice has since become "more vulnerable to shifts of public mood and political reaction," rather than based on knowledge and evidence.[6]

The Criminal Justice and Public Order Act 1994 introduced new powers, reversing the decarcerative provisions of youth justice law and policy that dated back to the Children Act 1908. This "punitive turn" appeared validated by the sharp increase in prison populations in England and Wales (and in most Western, industrialized societies) since the late 1990s.[7] The use of the term "punitive turn" as an explanatory concept, however, has been criticized for its exaggerated use and its suggestion of unidirectional punitive criminal justice approaches.[8]

Following outbreaks of public disorder in UK cities in August 2011, Prime Minister David Cameron reasserted the "tough on crime" message, stating, "no-one should doubt this government's determination to be tough on crime" (15 August 2011).[9] The reaction of the courts appeared to confirm the practical impact of high-profile political statements. The proportion of children prosecuted in relation to the public disorder (26%) and sentenced to custody (31%) was much higher than the previous year, and custodial sentences were an average of five months longer.[10]

At the center of contemporary youth justice is identifying, assessing, and managing young people "at risk" of offending. This "responsibilization" of young people[11] focuses on imposing change, surveillance, and control[12]—*what* they do—rather than addressing young people's own constructions of self, others, and the social world—*who* they are.[13] Criminal justice policies can exacerbate the widespread problems of social exclusion that other government policies aim to improve, making it harder for young people to lead crime-free lives.[14] Treating children and young people as "asocial" can prevent them from becoming active social participants.

Social Justice

Miller proposed four key tenets of "social justice": (1) equal citizenship—entitlement to an equal set of rights; (2) the social minimum—access to resources that adequately meet their essential needs; (3) equality of opportunity—life chances dependent only on motivation and aptitudes, not features such as gender, class, or ethnicity; and (4) fair distribution—resources can be distributed unequally, but this must reflect relevant factors such as personal desert or personal choice.[15] Equality, inclusion, and well-being of children and young people are critical for a social justice approach to youth offending, and appear to be reasonable and nondemanding principles for policy.

The extent to which these principles are promoted in the youth justice system in England and Wales is explored here, with the "system" taken to mean the interactions with and decision-making by the police, prosecution agencies, the judiciary, the prison service, the probation service, and children and youth services.

Minimum Age of Criminal Responsibility

Age has long been a factor in criminal justice, and children under the age of 18 years are dealt with separately from adults. Since the Children and Young Persons Act 1963 s.16, the minimum age of criminal responsibility (MACR) has been set at 10 years in England and Wales and is the lowest in Europe, a threshold shared with Northern Ireland and Switzerland. The Children Act 1989 legally defined under-18s as children, despite a long-standing practice of categorizing young people as aged 14–18 years and those below 14 as children. The Crime and Disorder Act 1998 s.34 effectively reduced the MACR by repealing the 700-year-old concept of *doli incapax* that stated that anyone between the ages of 10 to 14 who is prosecuted in the youth courts had to know what they were doing was wrong; removing this concept meant that all prosecuted children aged over 10 *did* know what they were doing.

This very low age could be construed as a denial of a child's right to not have their behavior criminalized at such an early age. Other countries have much higher ages of criminal responsibility: 13 in France, 15 in Scandinavian countries, and 18 in Belgium. The common MACR in Europe is 14 years.[16] The youth justice system in England and Wales can be viewed as trying to solve social and personal problems through a criminalization process with no due attention to the welfare or protection of the child.

In 2015, the four UK Children's Commissioners recommended that the MACR should be increased "as a matter of urgency," following repeated recommendations in 1995, 2002, and 2008.[17] In particular, "[t]he low age of MACR represents an infringement of Articles 37 and 40 UNCRC as it exposes children to a system that is inappropriate for their age and development."[18] The United Nations Committee on the Rights of the Child raised further concern with this low age in 2016, following multiple previous recommendations.[19] No government since enactment of the Children and Young Persons Act 1969 has given serious consideration to increasing the MACR, and none of the current political parties in the UK are willing to act on the commissioners' view. The recent exception in the UK was Scotland, which raised their MACR from 8 years to 12.[20] In 2016, Lord Faulks confirmed the UK government has no plans to raise the age of criminal responsibility in England and Wales, stating:

> The Government believe that children aged 10 and above are, for the most part, able to differentiate between bad behaviour and serious wrongdoing and should therefore be held accountable for their actions.[21]

Goldson advocates that "[a]dultifying children aged 10 years is a mutation of justice; a problem emanating from the law being in conflict with children as distinct from the converse."[22] The continuing politicization of youth justice and the system's failure to act on the evidence base was highlighted by a Conservative think tank, the Centre for Social Justice, which reported that "evidence indicates strongly that the current low MACR in England and Wales is unsafe, unjust and harmful to wider society",[23] recommending "it should be raised to 12";[24] however, "such a reform is implausible in the immediate term."[25] Highlighting the 1993 murder of 2-year-old James Bulger by two 10-year-old boys, the report claims that "[t]here appears to be little appetite for changing the law such that equivalent offenders would not be held criminally liable. To ignore this fact would be politically naive."[26]

Neurological science confirms the view that such a low age of criminal responsibility is unjust and harmful. The evidence strongly suggests "that the human brain is not fully developed in its capacity for cognitive functioning and emotional regulation well into the period of young adulthood."[27] Young teenagers have limited capacity for empathy toward others, which is known to act as a trigger for offending in older individuals.[28] Paradoxically, the criminal law deems all children aged 10 to be fully culpable for their actions and to know the difference between right and wrong. There is a fatal obstruction to the application of knowledge and evidence.[29]

As Bateman summarizes, the low MACR in England and Wales (1) is inconsistent with approaches to children in other areas of social policy, (2) tends to promote rather than prevent offending, (3) has long-term harmful repercussions for children drawn into the youth justice system at an early age, and (4) leads to increased levels of child incarceration.[30]

Key Aim of the Youth Justice System

The Crime and Disorder Act 1998 s.37 introduced, for the first time, a statutory requirement for the youth justice system to "prevent offending of children and young persons." To deliver this aim, youth offending teams (YOTs) were introduced, bringing together professionals from social work, probation, the police, education, and the health authority to pool their skills and draw upon their common experience to devise an appropriate response to youth offending. YOTs were to be overseen by a newly formed Youth Justice Board (YJB).

The Children and Young Persons Act 1933 s.44—still relevant today—states that criminal courts must always have regard for the welfare of the child in all decision-making. However, the Crime and Disorder Act made no reference to the welfare of children and young people. This appeared to be a missed opportunity to restate the welfare of the child as paramount to any decisions taken in the criminal justice process. In the context of the "punitive turn" or "popular punitivism" and the removal of *doli incapax*, this was another apparent politicized action, further obstructing the welfare of children and young people. Muncie has argued that "the causes of offending were side-stepped by the identification of 'risk conditions' (factors that correlate with known offending)" and broad philosophies of justice and welfare were ignored in favor of a "pragmatic strategy to prevent offending."[31] In addition, it appeared that youth offending teams have increasingly worked in silos, with other agencies withdrawing their support when a child offends and becomes involved with the youth offending team.[32] Taylor's 2016 review of the youth justice system in England and Wales advocated a more devolved system of youth justice with greater, appropriate powers for professionals in multi-agency youth offending teams to reduce the reoffending of the most challenging children and young people. In addition, he recommended enhancing the role of the court to allow magistrates more active roles in designing tailored plans for children and young people and holding the child, parents, and agencies to account.[33]

Policing and Regulating Antisocial Behavior

As the keepers of the Queen's peace, maintaining order on the streets and in public spaces, the police are the gatekeepers to children's formal entry into the youth justice system. Children and young people often gather socially with friends on the streets. This social gathering can sometimes be construed as antisocial, and the streets become a site of potential conflict between police and young people. Appropriate ways to deal with antisocial behavior has been subject to major political debate.

The Crime and Disorder Act 1998 s.1 introduced the Anti-Social Behaviour Order (ASBO). ASBOs were civil orders, but breach of this order was a criminal offense, resulting in the individual being summoned to the criminal courts rather than the civil courts. Breaches of ASBOs appeared to fast-track children into the youth justice system for behavior that was not necessarily even criminal. Rather than a diversionary order to keep children out of the formal system, it was having the "net widening" effect of drawing more children into the system.

Disproportionate targeting of children and young people by police officers due to policy aimed at increasing the number of offenses brought to justice (OBTJ) led to a 25% increase in the number of children cautioned or convicted between 2000/01 and 2006/07.[34] When OBTJs were replaced with targets to *reduce* the number of first-time entrants to the youth justice system by 20% within 12 years, the target was achieved within one year. This dramatic reversal highlighted the impact pursuing targets can have on the criminalization of children and young people. As Taylor highlighted:

> The substantial and continuing reductions in first-time entrants to the youth justice system since then also highlight just how many children were unnecessarily dragged into the system during this period.[35]

This "system" contact can have harmful impact on an individual's future employment prospects. Research has shown that police disclosure of criminal records to employers, including non-conviction information, can have a damaging impact on the individuals' employment prospects.[36]

Further harmful impact is evident in the application of ASBOs. In contrast to the youth courts, as the ASBO was made in the civil courts, anonymity requirements did not apply. Children, regardless of age, could be publicly named for antisocial behavior that could include non-criminal behavior, which was odd because they could have anonymity for criminal behavior. Some local authorities produced leaflets with names and photographs of children and the conditions imposed upon them; some of these appeared on the sides of buses.[37] Critics pointed out the damaging effect this publicity can have on young people's welfare, rights and well-being,[38] and in 2007, the United Nations found that the UK was not fully complying with the UN Convention on the Rights of Child, by not protecting children and young people from negative media representation and public "naming and shaming."[39] The coalition government of 2010 conducted a review and introduced the Anti-Social Behaviour, Crime and Policing Act 2014 which abolished the ASBO, replacing it with the Criminal Behaviour Order (CBO).

Section 13 of the ASBCP Act 2014 states that the reporting procedures of a CBO remain the same as the ASBO, and it is possible that children subject to a CBO could be publicized. Section 39 of the Children and Young Persons Act 1933 could be used to impose restrictions, but the guidance is not clear as to which criminal justice agency should apply for this.[40]

The Mosquito

The Mosquito Ultrasonic Teenage Youth Deterrent is used to exclude children and young people from public spaces. The device was introduced around 2005, and over 9,000 units are in use in the UK.[41] The device emits a pulsed tone of 17 KHz, which can only be heard by people aged under 25 years. The technology is similar to the invasive force of CCTV cameras, for which you do not need to be a criminal to be filmed. But with the Mosquito, it does not matter what you are doing, if you are under 25 it will affect you.[42]

Sections 30–36 of the Anti-Social Behaviour Act 2003 gave the police powers of dispersal of groups and removal of persons under 16 to their place of residence. As Little highlights:

> When applying the Mosquito to the above section from the Anti-Social Behaviour Act 2003, one can see how the device removes the rationality of these laws in favour of blanket discrimination to those under the age of 25.[43]

If such a device targeted any other social group, we might imagine a greater outcry. The Mosquito has received criticism for its discrimination against children, who are not necessarily misbehaving, yet does not affect adult law-breakers.

Campaign group Liberty[44] and the Parliamentary Assembly of the Council of Europe believe it contravenes Article 8 of the European Convention on Human Rights:

> The Assembly considers that the use of 'Mosquito'-type devices constitutes a disproportionate interference with Article 8 of the European Convention on Human Rights, which protects the right to respect for one's private life, including the right to respect for physical integrity.[45]

In addition, the Mosquito contravenes the Equality Act 2010[46] and use of the device may, paradoxically, be an act of antisocial behavior due to the physical and emotional harm it can induce. The Mosquito represents a disregard of children and young people's public and social rights, inclusion, and well-being.

At the Police Station

Children share the same two fundamental rights at the police station as adults: to have a solicitor and have someone informed of their whereabouts. The Police and Criminal Evidence Act (PACE) 1984 sections 56 and 58 provide this, and section 57 requires that the police take steps that are practicable to find out who is responsible for the welfare of the detained child. In addition, PACE Code of Practice C states that as a "vulnerable" group, children are entitled to have an "appropriate adult" with them during a police interview. An appropriate adult is a parent, guardian, social worker, or any responsible person over 18 who safeguards the welfare and rights and ensures the effective participation of children and vulnerable adults detained or interviewed by police.

The police have the right to take photographs of children (and adults), along with fingerprints and a DNA sample, if they have been arrested. They do not require the individuals' permission to do this. The Serious Organised Crime and Policing Act 2005 section 110 made every offense arrestable, regardless of severity. This contributed to an increase in the criminalization of children who committed minor offenses but became major contributors to various national databases. Examples of such minor offenses are a 12-year-old boy who was arrested and had his DNA sample taken following a "playground tiff"[47] or a 13-year-old girl who was held in police custody for four hours after hitting an off-duty police officer's car with a snowball.[48]

Children who are arrested are not necessarily charged, and estimates have suggested that the DNA of tens of thousands of innocent children is being stored on the national database every year.[49] In response to a legal challenge from an 11-year-old boy known as "S," the European Court of Human Rights ruled that indefinite DNA retention breached Article 8 (the right to privacy).[50] The Protection of Freedoms Act 2012 subsequently reformed legislation on the retention of DNA and fingerprints; a DNA sample must be destroyed within six months of being taken except where it is required for use as evidence in court. DNA samples are stored on the UK National DNA Database (NDNAD), and the UK holds over five million DNA profiles (including adults), making it the second largest per capita DNA database in the world.[51]

Strip Searches

Between April 2008 and December 2013, 4,638 children aged 10–16 were strip searched by the Metropolitan Police, with twice as many searched in 2013 compared to 2008.[52] No appropriate adult was present in 44% of these cases and half of children searched were released without charge.[53] Concerns were raised that police were not following relevant safeguards for children being "stripped for their own protection."[54]

In a case involving a 14-year-old girl, who had a history of mental illness and had been the victim of sexual abuse, the Court of Appeal ruled that children and vulnerable detainees being "stripped for their own protection" must have an "appropriate adult" present, except in exceptional circumstances. The girl had been arrested, handcuffed, and taken to the Wirral police station in 2010. She was subsequently forcibly stripped of her clothes for her own protection, by three female police officers, without her mother being informed. Police officers maintained that the relevant parts of PACE did not apply, as this was not a strip search. The appeal was dismissed, but the appeal court judges disagreed that PACE Code C safeguards should not apply in these cases.[55]

Where possible, children and young people should not be taken to police stations, as highlighted in Taylor's 2016 review of the youth justice system advocating that under-18s should be viewed by police as children first and offenders second.[56]

Courts and Sentencing

The original idea of the juvenile courts instituted in 1908 was to separate the child offender from the adult offender—in part to avoid "contamination." Juvenile courts became youth courts in 1992, and are under a duty to "have regard to the welfare of the child or young person" before them.[57] The youth court has always been closed to the public and restrictions have been placed on the reporting of proceedings to ensure that a child could not be identified. As part of the welfare duty, the idea was to allow children to grow out of crime and not be unnecessarily burdened by their youthful behavior in later life.

The UN Convention on the Rights of the Child upholds this principle in order that during youth justice proceedings every child is "treated in a manner consistent with the promotion of the child's sense of dignity and worth" reinforcing "the child's respect for the human rights and fundamental freedoms," "promoting the child's reintegration and the child's assuming a constructive role in society," and that the young persons "privacy [be] fully respected at all stages of the proceedings."[58]

Reporting restrictions may be lifted at the end of a case if it is considered to be in the public interest.[59]

> If a court is satisfied that it is in the public interest to do so, it may, in relation to a child or young person who has been convicted of an offence, by order dispense to any specified extent with the requirements of this section in relation to any proceedings before it.[60]

Defining "public interest" is problematic, and is distinct from matters that the "public are interested in." The seriousness of the crime may be taken into consideration, but it is difficult to avoid this "interest" being one of curiosity rather than its potential to "do good."

The case of 2-year-old James Bulger, who was killed by two 10-year-old children in Liverpool, was one high-profile example where reporting restrictions were lifted at the end of the case in the public interest, leading to extensive reporting. The *Daily Mirror* front page headline "Freaks of Nature" on 24 November 1993 with photographs of the two defendants was illustrative of the media's mood. The images fueled public aggression and support for a punitive response to the defendants.

Twelve months before Bulger, a similar case involving the manslaughter of an 18-month-old boy by an 11-year-old girl who was 12 at the time of her trial did not have reporting restrictions lifted.[61] In 2009, two boys aged 10 and 11 appeared in court for serious crimes of violence committed against two boys aged 9 and 11; neither was named and no photographic images were published. The fact that the defendants were brought up in public care of the local authority may have been reason for them to be identified in the "public interest."[62]

The European Court of Human Rights later criticized the whole procedure, declaring that UK Crown Courts sitting as Youth Courts were improperly organized and incompatible with Article 6 of the European Convention on Human Rights.[63] The UK government response at the time was to make the youth courts more friendly and better organized, but in 2004, another judgement in Europe declared the UK to still be defaulting on compliance with Article 6.[64] The situation appeared to have remained unchanged in 2016 when the Secretary of State for Justice described the UK Crown Courts sitting as Youth Courts as "like a circus."[65]

Youth Custody

Custody is the most severe punishment available to the youth court in England and Wales. Incarcerated children are detained in a secure estate comprising three types of establishment: (1) Young Offender Institutes (YOIs)—accommodating boys aged 15–17 years; (2) Secure Training Centres (STCs)—accommodating boys and girls aged 12–17 years; and (3) Secure Children's Homes (SCHs)—accommodating children from aged 10 years.

From 1993 to 2009, there was a significant increase in the number of children sentenced to prison,[66] but between 2010 and 2016, the youth custody population decreased by more than 60% (see Figure 14.1). This decrease has been attributed to an increase in diversionary measures in the youth justice system,[67] which also appear closely related to austerity.[68]

Despite the welcome decrease, child imprisonment remains costly and ineffective in reducing crime and the most damaging form of intervention.[70] More broadly, the youth justice system has been

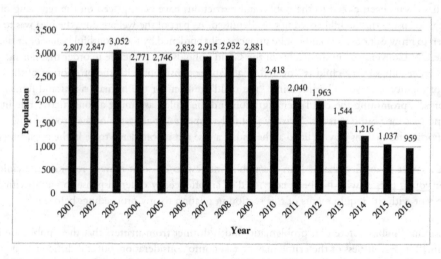

Figure 14.1 Average Population of the Secure Estate for Children and Young People, 2001–2016[69]

criticized for being insufficiently distinct from the adult system and contravening the United Nations Convention on the Rights of the Child.[71] Criminal legislation automatically applies to children unless they are explicitly excluded from its remit,[72] and it is apparent that levels of custody do not reflect levels of youth crime.[73]

In the *YJB Corporate Plan 2014–17 and Business Plan 2014/15*, the government stated their commitment to:

> promot[ing] the safety and welfare of children and young people in the criminal justice system . . . [and] to promoting equality, embracing diversity and working to ensure that the criminogenic risk factors of children and young people in the youth justice system are reduced.[74]

However, while overall youth custody numbers have more than halved between 2005–06 and 2014–15, the proportion of prisoners from Black, Asian, mixed race, or "other" ethnicity backgrounds (BME) increased to 40% in 2014–15 from 28% in 2005–06. This represents a proportionate rise of 75% for Asian prisoners, 67% for Black prisoners, 42% for mixed race prisoners, and almost a 15% decrease in White prisoners. The Young Review stated that there is now greater disproportionality in the number of Black people in prisons in the UK than in the United States.[75] This does not appear to promote equality and embrace diversity.

Safety and welfare in custody is of further concern. In March 2004, Gareth Myatt, aged 15, died in Rainsbrook STC from "positional asphyxia" after choking on his own vomit while being restrained by guards. Six months later Adam Rickwood, aged 14, was found hanging in his room shortly after being restrained by staff at Hassockfield STC. On the day of his death, staff had forcibly restrained Adam using a technique called "nose distraction"—placing upward pressure on the nose to cause pain. An inquest found that his restraint had been used outside Home Office rules, and subsequent changes to the rules were implemented.[76] These amended rules were found to breach Article 3 and 8 of the European Convention on Human Rights.[77]

A recent Ministry of Justice report highlighted persistence of restraint-related injuries to children across the youth custodial estate in 2015.[78] A 2015 HM Inspectorate of Prisons report[79] further found that a large minority of children in STCs had suffered abuse from other children or staff. Children in YOIs who reported feeling unsafe were more likely to (1) not understand spoken English; (2) consider shouting through windows to be a problem at their establishment; (3) have emotional or mental health problems on arrival; (4) not feel that they were treated with respect by staff; and (5) have more problems upon arrival at a YOI. In addition, effective resettlement plans were at the lowest point in 2014–15 compared to the previous five years.

The Prison Reform Trust reviewed deaths of children in prison between 2003 and 2010.[80] They highlighted the children's vulnerability and inadequate support and protection. Often these children ended up in prison due in part to failures by agencies working within and outside the criminal justice system to address their multiple and complex needs.

Prison can be seen to impose serious harm on children while not providing a means of reducing youth crime. Post-custodial reconviction rates for children remain high at 75% after one year of release[81] and 80% after two years.[82] Research and literature on the use of custodial sanctions as punishment further supports the view that they have a destructive effect and serve to increase recidivism rates.[83]

Summary

The persistent use of the criminal justice system to resolve social problems continues to marginalize children and young people, with little regard for their equality, rights, social inclusion, and well-being. The continued politicization of youth offending further blocks the application of knowledge and evidence throughout the youth justice process in favor of pragmatic risk strategies. The MACR set at 10 years remains damaging to children and young people, despite an increase of diversionary practice, a reduction in numbers of first-time entrants to the youth justice system, and a declining youth custodial population. The best diversionary strategy would be to raise the MACR,[84] which would require a new way of thinking about the misbehavior of children and young people. The principles of social justice would provide a good framework for thinking about this new way to treat youth misbehavior. Without a new approach, children and young people caught up in the youth justice system will continue to be failed.

Discussion Questions

1. No legal distinction is made between a child of 10 years and a child of 17 years. How might the differences in maturity and moral development play out here?
2. How might you feel if your youthful misbehavior had led to a criminal record and prevented you from following your chosen career?
3. Following arrest, the police may take photographs, DNA, and fingerprints of children and young people, even if no charges are made. How should the well-being and rights of the child be protected?
4. How should courts distinguish between "in the public interest" and matters that the "public are interested in," when considering the removal of reporting restrictions of young offenders?
5. To what extent should restraint of young prisoners be considered discipline and how does this protect the well-being and rights of the child?
6. How can we begin to address the disproportionate use of custody for children and young people from BME backgrounds?
7. What alternatives to custody could provide justice, crime prevention, and community safety, while protecting the equality, inclusion, rights, and well-being of children and young people?
8. Can social justice and criminal justice approaches to youth offending coexist?
9. What would a social justice approach to youth offending look like?

Notes

1. Pearson, G. (1983). *Hooligan: A history of respectable fears*. London: MacMillan.
2. A note on terminology: "Youth" and "youth justice" are used throughout this chapter to reflect the terms used in England and Wales.
3. The UK has three separate territorial jurisdictions, (1) England and Wales, (2) Northern Ireland, and (3) Scotland, and each jurisdiction has its own youth justice system. The focus of this chapter is on England and Wales, although it should be noted that this is not without its problems. Commentators have highlighted that processes of political devolution have seemingly undermined the notion of a unified jurisdiction, creating distinct youth justice approaches in the two countries. See Drakeford, M. (2010). Devolution and youth justice in Wales. *Criminology and Criminal Justice*, 10(2), 137–154.
4. McAra, L., & McVie, S. (2007). Youth justice? The impact of system contact on patterns of desistance from offending. *European Journal of Criminology*, 4(3), 315–345.
5. Rutherford, A. (1986). *Growing out of crime*. Harmondsworth: Penguin.
6. Garland, D. (2001). *The culture of control: Crime and social order in contemporary society*. Oxford: Oxford University Press, p. 172.
7. Muncie, J. (2015). *Youth and crime*, 4th ed. London: Sage.
8. Matthews, R. (2005). The myth of punitiveness. *Theoretical Criminology*, 9(2), 175–201.
9. Cameron, D. (2011). *"Prime Minister's speech on the fightback after the riots", 15 August*. London: Cabinet Office.
10. Ministry of Justice. (2011). *Statistical bulletin on the public disorder of 6–9 August 2011—October Update*. London: Ministry of Justice.
11. Phoenix, J., & Kelly, L. (2013). "You have to do it for yourself": Responsibilization in youth justice and young people's situated knowledge of youth justice practice. *British Journal of Criminology*, 53, 419–437.

12. Marshall, D., & Thomas, T. (forthcoming 2017). *Privacy and criminal justice.* London: Palgrave MacMillan.
13. Smith, R. (2011). *Doing justice to young people: Youth crime and social justice.* Oxon: Willan Publishing.
14. Barrow Cadbury Trust. (2005). *Lost in transition: A report of the Barrow Cadbury Commission on young adults and the criminal justice system.* London: Barrow Cadbury Trust.
15. Miller, D. (2005). What is social justice? In N. Pearce & W. Paxton (Eds.), *Social justice: Building a fairer Britain.* London: Politico's Publishing.
16. Dünkel, F. (2017). Juvenile justice and crime policy in Europe. In F. E. Zimring, M. Langer, & D. S. Tanenhaus (Eds.), *Juvenile justice in global perspective.* New York: New York University Press.
17. UK Children's Commissioners. (2015). *Report of the UK children's commissioners: UN Committee on the Rights of the Child: Examination of the fifth periodic report of the United Kingdom of Great Britain and Northern Ireland.* London: Children's Commissioner for Wales, NICCY, Children's Commissioner, SCCYP.
18. *Ibid.,* p. 42.
19. Sandberg, K., Kissack, P., & Mezmur, B. D. (2016). *Committee on the Rights of the Child reviews the report of the United Kingdom, Committee on the Rights of the Child, 24 May.* Geneva: United Nations Human Rights Office of the High Commissioner.
20. Scottish Government. (2016). *Minimum age of criminal responsibility: Analysis of consultation responses, and engagement with children and young people.* Edinburgh: Scottish Government.
21. House of Lords Debate 29 January 2016 c1574–5. Retrieved August 7, 2017, from www.publications. parliament.uk/pa/ld201516/ldhansrd/text/160129-0002.htm#16012936000265.
22. Goldson, B. (2013). "Unsafe, unjust and harmful to wider society": Grounds for raising the minimum age of criminal responsibility in England and Wales. *Youth Justice, 13*(2), 111–130.
23. Centre for Social Justice. (2012). *Rules of engagement: Changing the heart of youth justice.* London: Centre for Social Justice, p. 210.
24. *Ibid.,* p. 211.
25. *Ibid.,* p. 211.
26. *Ibid.,* p. 208.
27. Prior, D., Farrow, K., Hughes, N., Kelly, G., Manders, G., White, S., & Wilkinson, B. (2011). *Maturity, young adults and criminal justice: A literature review.* Birmingham: University of Birmingham.
28. Farmer, E. (2011). The age of criminal responsibility: Developmental science and human rights perspectives. *Journal of Children's Services, 6*(2).
29. Goldson, 2013.
30. Bateman, T. (2012). *Criminalising children for no good purpose: The age of criminal responsibility in England and Wales.* National Association for Youth Justice Campaign Paper. London: NAYJ.
31. Muncie, 2015, p. 292.
32. See for example, Marshall, D. J. (2012). *Practitioners in the youth justice system: A case study of the youth offending service* (Unpublished PhD thesis). University of Cambridge, Cambridge; Burnett, R., & Roberts, C. (2004). *What works in probation and youth justice: Developing evidence-based practice.* Cullompton: Willan; Souhami, A. (2007). *Transforming youth justice: Occupational identity and cultural change.* Cullompton: Willan.
33. Taylor, C. (2016). *Review of the youth justice system in England and Wales.* London: Ministry of Justice.
34. Ministry of Justice and Youth Justice Board. (2012). *Youth justice annual statistics: 2010 to 2011.* London: Ministry of Justice.
35. Taylor, 2016.
36. Marshall, D., & Thomas, T. (2015). The disclosure of police-held 'non-conviction information' to Employers. *International Journal of Police Science and Management, 17*(4), 237–245.
37. The Guardian. (2007). ASBO. *The Guardian,* 19 April.
38. Thomas, T. (2004). Anti-social behaviour orders: Publicity and young people. *Childright, 208,* July/August.
39. UN Committee on the Rights of the Child. (2008). *'Concluding observations: United Kingdom of Great Britain and Northern Ireland',* Forty-ninth session consideration of reports submitted by states parties under Article 44 of the Convention 20 October (ref. CRC/C/GBR/CO/4).
40. Home Office. (2015). *Anti-social behaviour, crime and policing Act 2014: Reform of anti-social behaviour powers: Statutory guidance for frontline professionals,* July, London.
41. Little, C. (2015). The "Mosquito" and the transformation of British public space. *Journal of Youth Studies, 18*(2), 167–182.
42. *Ibid.,* p. 167.
43. *Ibid.,* p. 173.
44. Liberty. (2017). *Buzz off.* Retrieved July 13, 2017, from www.liberty-human-rights.org.uk/buzz
45. Council of Europe. (2010). *Parliamentary assembly prohibiting the marketing and use of the 'Mosquito' youth dispersal device* (press release), 12 July.

46. Little, 2015.
47. Patrick, G. (2004, March 1). Cops DNA-test boy of 12, *The Sun*.
48. Hale, B., & Gill, C. (2005, February 4). Snow joke: Amy threw a snowball at an off-duty policeman's car. She was arrested, held for four hours, DNA tested and left with a criminal record, *Daily Mail*.
49. Dodd, V. (2013, May 20) Police retain DNA from thousands of children, *The Guardian*.
50. *S and Marper v. UK* [2008] ECHR 1581 4 December.
51. Home Office. (2015). *National DNA database strategy board annual report 2014/15*. London: Home Office.
52. Clarke, J. S. (2014, March 16). Metropolitan police strip searched more than 4,500 children in five years, *The Guardian*.
53. Children's Rights Alliance for England. (2014). *State of children's rights in England: Review of government action on United Nations' recommendations for strengthening children's rights in the UK*. London: CRAE.
54. See Marshall, D., & Thomas, T. (2017). *Privacy and criminal justice*. London: Palgrave.
55. *Davies v. Merseyside Police & Anor* [2015] EWCA Civ 114 (19 February 2015).
56. Taylor, 2016.
57. Children and Young Persons Act 1933 s.44.
58. UN 1989 Article 40.
59. see Children and Young Person's Act 1933 ss 39 and 49.
60. Children and Young Persons Act 1933 s49 (4A).
61. Pithers, M. (1992, April 30). Five years' custody for girl, 12, who killed baby. *The Guardian*.
62. See Wainwright, M. (2009, April 15). Brothers back in court over Doncaster quarry attack. *The Guardian*; Brooke, C., & Martin, A. (2010, January 23). Name the devil boys: We must not let them hide. *Daily Mail*.
63. *V and T v. United Kingdom* [1999] 30 EHRR 121.
64. *SC v. UK* [2004] 40 EHRR 10.
65. Taylor, 2016.
66. See Barnardo's (2008). *Locking up or giving up: Is custody for children always the right answer?* London: Barnardo's.
67. Bateman, T. (2012). Who pulled the plug? Towards an explanation of the fall in child imprisonment in England and Wales. *Youth Justice, 12*(1), 36–52.
68. Yates, J. (2012). What prospects youth justice? Children in trouble in the age of austerity. *Social Policy & Administration, 46*(4), 432–447.
69. Graph derived from Ministry of Justice. (2017). *Youth custody report: April 2017*. Retrieved June 22, 2017, from www.gov.uk/government/statistics/youth-custody-data
70. Goldson, B. (2010). The sleep of (criminological) reason: Knowledge-policy rupture and new labour's youth justice legacy. *Criminology & Criminal Justice, 10*(1), 155–178.
71. National Association for Youth Justice. (2015). *Manifesto 2015*. London: NAYJ.
72. Bateman, T. (2017). Youth justice. In J. Harding, P. Davies, & G. Mair (Eds.), *An introduction to criminal justice*. London: Sage.
73. Hagell, A. (2005). The use of custody for children and young people. In T. Bateman & J. Pitts (Eds.), *The RHP companion to youth justice* (pp. 151–157). Lyme Regis: Russell House Publishing.
74. Youth Justice Board. (2014). *YJB corporate plan 2014–17 and business plan 2014/15*. London: Youth Justice Board, p. 7.
75. The Young Review. (2014). *Improving outcomes for young black and/or Muslim men in the criminal justice system*. London: Clinks.
76. See the Secure Training Centre (Amendment) Rules 2007 no. 1709.
77. See *R (C) v. Secretary of State for Justice* [2008] EWCA Civ 882.
78. Alison, E., & Greierson, G. (2016, May 5). Restraint injuries persist at youth jail where boy died 12 years ago. *The Guardian*.
79. Redmond, A. (2015). *Children in custody 2014–15 2015: An analysis of 12–18-year-olds' perceptions of their experience in secure training centres and young offender institutions*. London: HM Inspectorate of Prisons.
80. Prison Reform Trust. (2012). *Fatally flawed: Has the state learned lessons from the deaths of children and young people in prison?* London: Prison Reform Trust.
81. Ministry of Justice. (2009). *Reoffending of juveniles: Results from the 2007 Cohort England and Wales*. Ministry of Justice Statistics Bulletin. London: Ministry of Justice.
82. House of Commons Committee of Public Accounts. (2004). *Youth offending: The delivery of community and custodial sentences*. Fortieth Report of Session 2003–04. London: The Stationery Office.
83. McGuire, J., & Priestley, P. (1995). Reviewing what works: Past, present and future. In J. McGuire (Ed.), *What works: Reducing reoffending*. Chichester: Wiley
84. Goldson, 2010.

15

LGBQ PEOPLE AND SOCIAL JUSTICE

Nicole L. Asquith, Vanessa R. Panfil, and Angela Dwyer

Introduction

Justice—whether social or criminal—is predicated on the inviolability and universality of human rights. Since the 1960s, the UN has operationalized the concept of social justice as the basic human right to "the fair and compassionate distribution of the fruits of economic growth."[1] While maldistribution of resources may influence how LGBQ[2] people experience social justice, as with any other of the rights afforded to all humans, social justice requires recognition.[3] For many people of diverse sexualities, recognition has been eschewed for much of the UN's history, and the recognition of LGBQ people in human rights discourses remains controversial and veiled in the language of "other status."[4] Even today, non-normative sexuality is barely mentioned in human rights instruments, is criminalized in some jurisdictions, and those who act on their attractions can be subject to extreme violence, including violence from criminal justice actors. Within these contexts, it is therefore timely to query and queer our understandings of social justice.

Since its original articulation in the late 1960s, the concept of social justice has developed beyond the narrow economic redistribution that framed the UN's initial definition. Charmaz suggests that inquiring into social justice requires us to "attend to inequities and equality, barriers and access, poverty and privilege, individual rights and the collective good, and their implication for suffering."[5] Here, social justice captures a wider range of attitudes, behaviors, and practices and extends the notion of social justice to include maldistribution of economic and noneconomic rewards, as well as the maldistribution of misrecognition and cultural silence.

From its very formation, to the signing of the Universal Declaration of Human Rights, through decades of reconceptualizing the harms caused by humans against humans, nonhuman animals, and their environment, the UN has sought to address social injustice. With each new injustice recognized, the UN has created declarations, treaties, memoranda of understanding, policies, practices, programs, and projects. Despite being identified as victims of the Third Reich, in the more than 70 years since the Holocaust, the specific rights of people of diverse sexualities have been silenced, ignored, and their concerns mothballed for another generation to address. While some declarations were passed by the UN in 2011 and 2014, and a "special expert" was appointed in 2016 for LGBQ people,[6] in all its major strategic plans linked to actioning social justice, LGBQ people are absent.[7] They are either not named at all, and when discussed, it is only in terms of "sexual orientation," and then most commonly in terms of refugee status, or violence and bullying. Further, as non-normative sexualities continue to be unacknowledged in UN human rights frameworks, the failure to recognize diverse sexualities trickles down to (a lack of) policies in criminal processing systems.[8]

To talk of "compassionate distribution" of wealth within this context appears to further silence and misrecognize the injustices experienced by sexual minorities, especially those living in the global South and in the intersectional margins of the global North, such as queer people of color, immigrants, and/or religious minorities. In this chapter, we query how justice is queered when we consider the experiences of lesbian, gay, bisexual, queer, or other sexually diverse people, and how the recognition of LGBQ people may in fact change what we mean by social justice. We focus on sexual minorities rather than gender minorities but acknowledge that gender-diverse people's experiences are important to understand and often intersect with those experienced by people of diverse sexualities.[9] We first outline what we mean by social justice, and then consider how the landscapes of social (in)justice change when we apply a southern gaze. Through the lenses of southern theory and queer criminology, we discuss the complex and at times contradictory intersections between social and criminal justice for LGBQ people by focusing on redistribution and recognition. We suggest that these two processes must work in tandem to achieve utopian ends, but often cannot due to structural and institutional constraints. From these critical positions, we then discuss how queer-blind social justice within criminal justice has negatively affected the lives of LGBQ people. We conclude by reflecting on dominant ethics and strategies for pursuing social justice.

Social Justice in Criminal Justice

Justice is a slippery concept that has occupied philosophers and social theorists since at least ancient Greece. However, what we know of justice, and how it has been operationalized in international declarations and treaties and in national laws and policies, is informed by Western individualism and chrononormativity.[10] Assumptions about who deserves justice—including how justice is meant to unfold—preclude a range of alternative experiences of justice that present as pragmatic ad hoc decisions, and are lived collectively rather than individually. Before considering how justice changes when we view it from the perspective of the global South, we first want to consider how the discourse of progress and the primacy of economic redistribution in concepts of social justice combine to obscure LGBQ experiences of injustice.

Justice remains a slippery concept to define because it is only through *in*justice that we can glimpse what human relations are when there is not a "fair and compassionate distribution of the fruits."[11] In criminal justice, the focus on the structural and economic coordinates of injustice is critical given the legitimated force over human life afforded to criminal justice actors. When the state kills on behalf of its citizenry—when it explicitly and deliberately chooses the targets of its "justice"—it shapes not only the distribution of justice in criminal processing systems but also the social justice meted out elsewhere.

As the final arbiter of criminal justice, the state models to its citizenry how other social justice resources ought to be distributed. For example, in the U.S. states of Alabama, Arizona, Delaware, Florida, Iowa, Kentucky, Mississippi, Nebraska, Nevada, Tennessee, Virginia, and Wyoming, those prosecuted for certain criminal offenses have their right to political participation (voting) automatically revoked; in some cases, for life.[12] Elsewhere in the U.S. and across the globe (including Lebanon, Kyrgyzstan, Australia, Luxembourg, the UK, Italy, China, and Taiwan), voting rights are revoked for the duration of imprisonment, parole, and/or probation.[13] Irrespective of the fact that a person may have "paid" for the injustice they caused—by years of degradation and isolation in prison, not to mention literal financial penalties—the state deepens that injustice by limiting the social justice available outside of criminal processing systems. Similarly, as the state models a particular set of social (in)justice principles, these principles are often mirrored in wider social relationships of exclusion, discrimination, intolerance, and illegitimate force.

During the 1990s and well into the 21st century, social theory—and theories of social justice, in particular—became the site of one of the most productive theoretical disputes over structure and agency.[14] Albeit overly structuralist in her initial account of social justice, Fraser's dual typology of maldistribution and misrecognition provides us with a tool to identify the specific structural and symbolic injustices experienced by LGBQ people.[15] It also provides us with a way to consider how injustice is woven into culture, and how maldistribution and misrecognition reinforce each other to create landscapes of destitution, exclusion, and prejudice.

In Fraser's typology, the injustices experienced by marginalized people can be understood in terms of the maldistribution of economic rewards and recognition.[16] Responses to injustice should therefore target the specific character of the injustice experienced. In her dual taxonomy, at one end of the distribution/recognition continuum is the experience of class-based injustice. Injustice as a result of the mode of production—slave labor and wage labor alike—is best addressed by changes to the economic system, such as welfare provisions and progressive taxation. At the other end of the continuum are injustices in recognition. Here, controversially, Fraser posits the experiences of "homosexuals,"[17] whose experiences of injustice are shaped by cultural and symbolic (mis)representation.[18] Unlike their working-class peers—ignoring for the moment that many queers are indeed working-class—Fraser suggests that while changes to the economic arrangements may assist some LGBQ people, they will not resolve the injustices of recognition per se.[19]

These accounts of (in)justice, while productive in framing our arguments, are problematic on several accounts. Fraser (and at times, Butler) frame their concepts of justice through the trope of progress; Western notions of progress at that. Cover et al. suggest that justice is too often framed in terms of inevitable, consistent progress.[20] Marked by this or that starting point,[21] a linear comparison is made between the unjust yesterday and the slightly more just today. Whether liberal-humanist or (neo-)Marxist, individualist or communitarian, progress through scientific innovation or class conflict is assumed to be good, automatic, and, like any utopic vision, an unfolding emancipatory process without a clear end.

But progress is rarely lived as such. For many LGBQ people, tiny incremental changes making their lives slightly less unjust is anything but utopian, especially when these glacial changes often do not address more immediate matters of life and death for LGBQ people already facing multiple forms of disadvantage. And, as Cover et al. caution, change does not necessarily favor the less powerful and loosen the grip of injustice they experience.[22] History is littered with examples of retrogression, retreat, and stagnation, especially when it comes to the social justice meted out to LGBQ people.

Criminal justice is but one variant or aspect of social justice. However, justice in crime processing is not an autonomous field. Justice elsewhere—in education, in citizenship, in the economy, in the family—shapes justice as it is experienced in and through criminal processing systems. In this respect, criminal justice represents a particular institutional form of social justice. However, when disconnected from institutions, it is clear that justice can only be achieved through both structural and cultural processes. Emphasizing one over the other, or considering each in isolation, ignores the intertwining of both structural and cultural processes in the creation of injustice. And conversely, when we label something as "merely cultural" or simply economic, we also limit our vision of what constitutes justice.

Queering Southern Criminal Justice

Just as we need to be cognizant of chrononormative, individualist, and structuralist biases of social justice research to date, we also need to be aware of the Western essence of these discussions about justice. Since her initial provocation in 2007, Connell has sparked a revolution in the social sciences and a regeneration of Southern theory.[23] In *Southern Theory*, she asks us to reflect on the production of social science knowledge, and the ways in which even radical theorists reinstantiate power inequalities through the reproduction of Western knowledge. More recently, Carrington, Hogg, and Sozzo have argued for the consideration of these ideas in criminological thought and research, given criminology has been a discipline grounded squarely in the global North.[24] When applied to criminal justice, Connell's perspective enables us to look beyond the experiences of those in the global North and consider the various other ways in which criminal justice is perceived and enacted.[25] Central to a critical analysis of crime is the understanding that crime is not absolute or universal; it varies across time and place.

Connell's critique applies equally when thinking about research on the nexus between sexuality and criminology. The coloniality of these forms of research is highlighted in sodomy laws imposed by colonial forces and even in the concept of "sexuality" as one that emerged from colonially imposed binaries and hierarchies.[26] Scholars are beginning to examine the experiences of LGBQ people in criminal processing systems worldwide, with the goal being increased recognition and more socially just outcomes for these communities.[27] In many cases, the damaging artifacts of colonization have included the imposition of retrograde Western norms about gender and sexuality, which created injustices still embedded in criminal processing systems today.

We need only refer to global sodomy laws to illustrate the colonizing path of sexuality and gender across the global South. Equally, the northwestern edges of marriage equality maps—or, alternatively, the skew of sexuality criminalization maps to the east and south—may give Western queers the idea that they are part of a more just future. However, they are not vanguard, nor are Western queers necessarily secure in their newfound rights, as illustrated by the rapid rollback of many rights afforded to LGBQ people in the United States since the 2016 presidential election, and the hard path to marriage equality in Australia. Carrington and Hogg argue that "peacetime criminology" has long glossed over "the criminogenic impact of colonialism on the diverse societies of the global south," and these colonialities have profoundly impacted global South nations the world over.[28] Placing Southern experiences on the agenda deepens our understanding of how crime (and justice) is constructed—and thus can be reconstructed—and the ways in which heteronormativity and heteronormative violence are differently resisted by Southern LGBQ people.[29]

Marriage equality has become a significant social justice issue for LGBQ people in developed nations around the world.[30] Yet, alongside this, LGBQ people in the global South continue to experience high levels of serious violence, including harassment, discrimination, "corrective" rape, and (extra-)judicial murder.[31] While a gay male couple in Sydney, Australia, may be concerned that until recently they could not marry, gay men in Uganda are being outed by journalists who print their names in the newspapers; this outing is then the motivation for arrest by police and incarceration in prisons, and sometimes leads to their murder.[32] The experiences of gay men in these examples diverge considerably and highlight the importance of examining issues as they are experienced by LGBQ people in the global South. Marriage equality is not high on the justice agenda of LGBQ people if their most basic human rights continue to be ignored.

We must, however, avoid homogenizing the experiences of LGBQ people in the global South—or, in fact, the experiences of marginalized queer people of color, immigrants, and/or religious minorities in the global North—nor should we offer global South experiences as salutary lessons in the need for Northern and Western activism (read: charity).[33] Before Western nations such as Australia even deigned to place the issue of marriage equality on the political agenda, nations in the global South had already granted LGBQ people the same rights as their heterosexual peers.[34] Argentina (2010), Brazil (2013), Colombia (2016), South Africa (2006), Uruguay (2013), and Taiwan (2017) represent the forerunners of LGBQ marriage rights in the global South, with Vietnam and Thailand are expected to enact laws soon (UNDP USAID, 2014).[35] Yulius, Tang, and Offord suggest that the impact of an increasingly global LGBQ identity is experienced variously in the global South, and that in some places, these discourses are strengthening those who seek to silence LGBQ people.[36] Similarly, human rights activities from LGBQ people in the global North can perpetuate the stigma around sexuality diversity in the global South by spectacularizing examples of "African [Arabic, Muslim, Asian] homophobia," for instance.[37] As such, Mhaoileon argues that how we achieve justice for LGBQ people in the global South is something that must be done in consultation with local LGBQ communities. This then reorients us to the potential difficulties in their everyday existence without reinforcing the global North "as a space for safety and progress."[38]

Justice as a concept also takes on a muddy character when thinking about the work of criminal processing systems with LGBQ people in the global South. Violent and discriminatory policing practices with LGBQ communities in the past[39] has seen Australian police organizations, for example, working hard to rebuild relationships with LGBQ communities. Many police organizations have established LGBTI police liaison programs to evidence their commitment to improvement.[40] As a result, policing encounters with LGBQ people in the global North generally do not end with death, and when police do use violence against LGBQ communities, community uproar is swift.[41]

These experiences directly contrast with the policing of LGBQ people in parts of the global South, where police are complicit in delivering violence upon LGBQ people and are often themselves directly involved in inflicting degradation, violence, and death upon LGBQ people.[42] LGBQ people in the global South might not champion the introduction of initiatives like LGBTI police liaison programs when they are yet to even feel safe in the presence of police. Further, programs like these seeking to make police more accountable and socially just may be experienced as further injustice in parts of the global South as they amplify, rather than ameliorate, existing structural inequalities.[43] As we discuss later, just adding LGBQ people to the mix of social justice in criminal justice often results in contradictory outcomes and further exclusion and violence. Queer(y)ing (querying and queering) justice is therefore an imperative for LGBQ people across the world.

Queer(y)ing Social Justice in Criminal Justice

We frame our querying of social justice with the assistance of the dual taxonomy advanced by Fraser: redistribution and recognition.[44] Fraser is concerned by the move from a focus on egalitarian redistribution to recognition, particularly in the context of growing global economic inequality.[45] She also argues that a focus on recognition, through identity politics, actually serves to reify particular cultural identities through an emphasis on "display[ing] an authentic, self-affirming and self-generated collective identity."[46] In her later reworking of the redistribution/recognition taxonomy, Fraser argues that a better way to achieve parity would be to advance "a politics aimed at overcoming subordination by establishing the misrecognized party as a full member of society, capable of participating on a par with the rest."[47] To this aim, we turn.

Recognition

Unlike redistribution that can be quantified, recognition is more abstract. Recognition refers more broadly to how people and groups create public identities in order to be recognized, and the process of recognition can result in formal modes of legal recognition, such as being counted in the census or being explicitly enumerated in laws as a protected group. The process of forming a collective group identity can include coming up with the group's preferred names, labels, and terminology of their choosing, which they can use among themselves or insist others utilize as well. One example would be the move to refer to same-sex-attracted people as gays or lesbians, as opposed to homosexuals, as the term "homosexual" has carried a clinical and dysfunctional connotation since its "invention" in the late 19th century.[48] Words to capture non-binary sexual identities, such as pansexual and queer, are also gaining traction. Recognition also includes valuing queer input into various matters of civic life and not just those related to sexuality, such as the push to have more candidates elected to public office who identify as LGBQ (as well as transgender, intersex, and gender nonconforming). This wider activism ensures LGBQ people can have political representation, but it also increases the diversity of voices creating policies that impact on justice for LGBQ people and other marginalized people.

Attempting to avoid misrecognition is also important. People with non-normative sexualities have long been maligned in legal statutes and crime reporting as depraved, deceptive, and with ill intentions. LGBQ people have been painted as child molesters, sexual predators, and disease spreaders, which have been used to justify statutes that control their sexual activities and to rationalize increased social control enacted upon them.[49] Instead of a positive portrayal of the victim, as many victims are represented, in news coverage of a gay murder victim, for example, the victim's "lifestyle" and sexual activities may be the focus.[50] And, we argue perhaps paradoxically that it *is* acceptable to portray LGBQ people as offenders, since that presupposes their capacity to participate in all forms of social life, even that which is negative.[51]

Formal recognition may entail a redistribution of resources. An ongoing issue related to the recognition of LGBQ people is the omission of sexuality and all gender categories in a country's accounting of itself. In Australia and the U.S.—two countries often presented as vanguards of LGBQ rights and recognition—sexuality has yet to be considered important enough to ask in the Census. It was proposed that these questions would be asked in the upcoming 2020 U.S. Census, but they have since been removed from the Census instruments.[52] The Australian Census and U.S. Census have never tried to count the number of LGBQ-identified people. Practically, many allocations for resources and strategies for implementing existing statutes are dependent on census data results, and thus LGBQ people will be denied services and protection. Symbolically, the unwillingness to count people represents an attempt to minimize, invalidate, or erase their existence, or at a minimum, exclude them from being considered valued citizens participating in civic life. In this case, the path to redistribution necessitates formal recognition.

In his critique of coming out—and of emancipatory discourses about coming out—Sanchez highlights not only the whiteness of this process, but also the Western tendency to privilege individual identity through state action (such as recognition in law).[53] Speaking from the perspective of a Latino gay man, he states, "when so much of queer visibility is grounded in white history, white bodies and white gatekeepers, we have to question who benefits from coming out." Drawing on Villicana, Delucio, and Biernat's research, Sanchez considers how coming out damages cultural and familial relationships in ways not represented by Western discourses of disclosure.[54] Villicana et al. found that as self-identification increased, White gay men are more likely than Latino men to verbally disclose their sexuality.[55] Latino men, in contrast, deployed a range of nonverbal cues to demonstrate their sexuality. In Western queer discourse, this veiled action and lack of a verbal declaration is read as "shame, self-hatred and repression" that can only be overcome by a courageous move out of the closet.[56]

In the ideal world of Western, White neoliberal individualism, recognition is simply a speech act; frightening at first, and at times when the social context is unclear or dangerous, but nonetheless just a few easy words—"I'm gay," "I'm queer," "I'm bisexual," "I'm lesbian," and so on. However, even in the safest, queerest of Western cities, these are words that parents continue to use to abuse their children, that communities use to shun individuals, that employers use to sack people (even when the law prohibits them from doing so), and that people use before they kill. Recognition, in Fraser's conceptualization, is therefore not just a matter of addressing the "*institutionalized* patterns of interpretation and evaluation that constitute one as comparatively unworthy of respect or esteem."[57] When the capacity to speak is forestalled, and when the speech act is turned from emancipation to punishment, how are we to change the patterns of interpretation and evaluation? Coming out is costly.

From the view of a culture where individualism and individual identity is shunned, and communitarian and familial ties are thought to be strengthened through sameness not difference, the act of coming out may be perceived negatively. Westernized, verbal acts of coming out may also be perceived negatively because they breach cultural norms—in Sanchez's case, the moral codes attached to *falta de respect*.[58] For Sanchez and the Latino gay men he knows, coming out in the Western sense of the term means losing the cultural artifacts that sustain life beyond libidinal desires. Sanchez does not want to lose the love of his father (and wider community) by declaring his sexual identity, but equally he does not want to lose the cultural meaning ascribed to his relationship with his partner. Insisting on breaking down the closet when the costs are borne too often by marginalized people—and when there is little to be embraced when coming out of that closet as a queer person of color[59]—is dangerous.

Redistribution

While Fraser was concerned about how the mode of production created maldistribution, we believe that this is a partial reading of how the (re)distributive forces of a society shape the experiences of LGBQ people.[60] Even within the productive sphere, LGBQ people experience high rates of unemployment and employment discrimination.[61] The International Gay and Lesbian Association found that at least 20% of European lesbians and gay men had experienced discrimination, and that 31–49% were closeted at work due to fear of discrimination.[62] Employment insecurity such as this can lead some people of diverse sexualities into the underground economies of illicit drug selling and street-based sex work, which in many jurisdictions remains criminalized.[63] These economies attract high police surveillance and intervention.[64]

Further elaboration of the maldistributive effects as they pertain to criminal justice is necessary. For most criminal justice agents—whether victim, offender, or practitioner—their access to social justice is conventionally framed by redistributive claims. Redistribution of resources could in fact refer to fairly direct redistribution of wealth, as advocated by socialist movements and even alluded to by the UN. However, redistribution takes on somewhat more intangible meaning in the crimino-legal world, especially for LGBQ people. Redistribution could refer to their unequal rights under the law (such as criminalizing same-sex activity and marriage equality), unequal access to safety (both in the general community and in criminal processing systems), unequal access to appropriate support services, and, if detained, unequal access to safe housing.

Unequal rights under the law is rightly the dominant issue faced by LGBQ people.[65] LGBQ people face laws that not only criminalize their behavior, but also withhold civil and human rights. In the last decade, much of the focus has been on the right to marriage equality, which has become a bellwether issue worldwide. Likewise, laws prohibiting same-sex sexual activity mark LGBQ people apart from the rest of the community, who are not punished for their sexuality. Given the considerable attention already afforded to these two issues, here we wish to focus on other forms of maldistribution impacting LGBQ people inequitably. In addition to their increased likelihood of encountering criminal processing systems by way of family exile and homelessness, LGBQ people are also subject to under- and over-policing.[66] Of the former, LGBQ people's experiences of hate crime and targeted violence has been ignored, minimized, or when acknowledged, criminal justice services are underresourced to adequately respond to the issues. In contrast, LGBQ people's use of public space—particularly, their queering of public space—is subjected to over-policing and the criminalization of simply being queer.[67] Criminal justice is also unequally distributed in terms of LGBQ people's rights to safety while in the care of criminal processing systems and access to support services for offenders seeking to desist from crime or victims seeking to resolve trauma.

The "wealth" available to be distributed within criminal processing systems is minimal. Culturally appropriate resources available to LGBQ offenders and victims are in most jurisdictions nonexistent. Even in relatively resource-rich jurisdictions such as those in the U.S. and Australia, critical victim services such as shelters, counseling, or support services for (gay) male victims of sexual and/or family violence do not exist, and only recently have phone counseling services been established in some places.[68] And even though ad hoc, short-term projects and trained mainstream services have existed for lesbians facing family violence, the same is not true for other sexually diverse victims.

For LGBQ offenders, the options are even more limited. LGBQ specific support or treatment programs may be necessary for just outcomes. However, for most LGBQ people internationally, these are luxuries afforded to those communities able to make claims from their state and criminal processing systems. Recognition is thus central to making claims and advocating for appropriate offender and victim services. However, in the space of imprisonment, between the time of being out and recognized as LGBQ, and making claims for appropriate support services and strategies (including safe housing), offenders may face increased violence from offenders and staff alike.[69] Even when offenders can safely identify as LGBQ in prison environments, they can face additional barriers to their survival and rehabilitation. For example, in juvenile facilities, Irvine found that young LGBQ offenders were required to participate in heteronormative sex education classes, and Curtin found that LGBQ-friendly publications (including nonfiction) were rarely made available.[70] Further, desistance programs based on family reunification and the social capital of loving, supporting families fail to acknowledge that family exile—leading to homelessness and survival crimes—is a key reason facilitating a young LGBQ person's incarceration.[71]

The issues of carceral arrangements and support services for queer offenders in the global North may appear frivolous when considered in light of global South experiences. For example, in their special focus on the UN's *2030 Agenda for Sustainable Development*, Prison Reform International (PRI) highlights that the right to safety and well-being while in the care of criminal processing agencies is widely divergent, with queer experiences of injustice in countries in the global South often exacerbated by wider issues related to the democratization of criminal justice.[72] PRI identified corruption at the heart of problems encountered by prisoners in Nigeria, Bulgaria, Mali, and Cambodia, where they are required to pay for even the basic necessities of life such as food or water.[73] Within the contexts of corruption and impoverishment, rights to sexual autonomy and self-identity are supplanted by the more immediate needs of survival.

When Criminal Justice Undermines Social Justice

From the perspective of these various journeys to social justice, it is clear that pragmatism—rather than utopian goals—drives much of the "progress" to date. Here, social justice in criminal justice is a competition of winners and losers, where rewards can be economic (redistributive) and seem to improve LGBQ people's lives, yet have no real impact on larger structural forces such as capitalism and systems of social control, or where rewards can be more sociocultural (recognition), yet still fundamentally tokenistic. Continuing with themes of recognition and redistribution, and informed by a queered Southern theory, we evaluate two in-depth examples that, respectively, provide insight into the ways that stagnation or "advancement" in criminal justice can similarly stymie social justice.

Criminalized and Victimized Activists

A key path to gaining recognition is to increase visibility. However, as discussed above, this poses a challenge for LGBQ people in the global South. This is affected significantly by the fact that many remaining (enforceable) sodomy laws are in countries in the global South. Not surprisingly, people fighting for the rights and dignity of LGBQ people are often perceived to be LGBQ or self-identify as LGBQ, meaning that their very existence or everyday activities put them at odds with the law. This also puts them at direct risk for prosecution, discriminatory treatment, and violence/victimization by community or state agents. And, in these particular contexts, those who commit violence against them may be regarded as justified and therefore no prosecution may occur. Victims may be seen as having brought upon their own victimization because they live outside the law, or if their complaints are taken seriously, victims may be maligned in court to hamper attempts to bring the offender to justice.

Several examples of the activities, deaths, and offender prosecution outcomes of several gay activists are illustrative. We present these details not to shock, but to illustrate the very real, sometimes life-and-death challenges related to recognition and redistribution. Eric Ohena Lembembe, a journalist and activist who contributed to Human Rights Watch's report on people prosecuted for homosexuality in Cameroon, was found dead in his home with broken feet and burns to his face, hands, and feet in 2013.[74] Part of his reporting included critiques of government officials who had ignored the torture or murder of other LGBQ people; indeed, over a year later, no meaningful action had been taken to find the perpetrators, and it appears that at the time of this writing, that remains the case.[75]

Brian Williamson was a prominent LGBT activist in Jamaica.[76] He was the co-founder of JFLAG (Jamaica Forum for Lesbians, All-Sexuals, and Gays), had run a gay club called Entourage, and wrote editorials using his own name to the national newspaper explicitly condemning murders of gays and lesbians there.[77] In 2004, in his own home, he was fatally stabbed multiple times in his head and neck, and his safe was stolen. An Amnesty International representative, who about a week earlier had warned the prime minister about anti-gay attacks, was slated to meet with Williamson the day of his death; upon arriving to his home, she found a crowd dancing, laughing, singing homophobic slurs, shouting his death was what he deserved for his sin, and otherwise celebrating the murder.[78] Although police arrested a man Williamson had employed and he was later convicted, the crime was investigated as a robbery with very little attention to heterosexist violence, perhaps because, as some news sources reported, the perpetrator was an allegedly closeted gay man.[79]

Xulhaz Mannan, an organizer of an annual "rainbow rally" and the co-founder of *Roopbaan*, Bangladesh's only magazine to promote acceptance of LGBT communities, was stabbed to death by a group of men posing as couriers so they could gain access to his apartment in 2016.[80] An LGBT activist blogging for Amnesty International under a pseudonym describes the chilling effect that violence against politically active people such as Mannan[81] has caused for other activists: they changed their phone numbers, moved numerous times, lived in safe houses, removed all traces of activism on the internet and social media, avoided organizing again, and even left the country. Their fear was magnified by the realities that police have made no sincere attempt to investigate the murder and instead harass LGBT people, and government officials speak about LGBT victims as though they brought it upon themselves.[82]

These are only three of the brutal murders of LGBQ people globally.[83] Regarding Lembembe's murder, a commentator from Human Rights Watch stated, "It's extremely ironic and really sad that Eric seems to have been killed by the same violence he was speaking out against."[84] However, under a criminalized state, we do not think it is ironic at all. People working for social justice and recognition can indeed become recognized, but within their country's own criminal justice contexts, they are seen as symbols that represent that country's disorder. They thus become scapegoats and targets. Our chapter's organizing conceptual framework tells us that this will be more likely to happen to people working for justice on behalf of LGBQ groups. This points to the fact that progress toward social justice, in forms such as overturning sodomy laws and gaining protections, may have to come from communities and allies rather than LGBQ-identified activists. People who are denied social, cultural, and/or economic capital cannot do the difficult work of redistribution on their own.

Hate Crimes Laws Versus Penal Abolition

To further complicate this issue, we present two pressing criminal justice and social justice issues—hate crimes statutes and penal abolition—that complicate our ideas about how LGBQ people can expect to achieve social justice through criminal justice. When we speak of protections, one perceived protection of LGBQ people is the existence of hate crimes laws. These laws specify separate crimes that people can be charged with, or enhanced penalties if a crime is motivated by animus based on certain protected statuses. In the United States, the Civil Rights Act of 1968 was the first piece of hate crimes legislation, but it did not contain provisions related to sexuality or gender. The Hate Crime Statistics Act of 1990 required the attorney general to collect data on crimes against someone because of their "sexual orientation." This statute allowed for hate crimes data to be collected through the Uniform Crime Reports (a major source of aggregate crime data), and also was the first federal statute to explicitly recognize LGB people.[85] This could be read as a step towards recognition, but in doing so, it expanded criminal justice–related administrative projects.[86]

Also in the U.S., the Matthew Shepard and James Byrd, Jr. Hate Crimes Prevention Act of 2009 was lauded as a major accomplishment in rights for LGBQ people. It dropped the prerequisite that the victim be engaged in a federally protected activity and added motivation based on a victim's actual or perceived gender, sexuality, or disability, which were not yet included at the federal level or in many states. The act was enacted over a decade after the murders of Shepard and Byrd, after 14 separate floor votes, and was only then signed by President Obama.[87] Thus, the act did not have consistent support across political coalitions or citizens. In fact, it was passed as part of a massive defense spending authorization bill, which also allocated money for a troop surge in Afghanistan.[88] Some queer critics of the legislation pointed out that it allowed Democrats—who had not backed past LGBQ equality measures or who actively blocked them (such as voting in favor of the anti-gay Defense of Marriage Act)—to appear both tough on crime and friendly to gay causes by voting for the bill.[89]

Interestingly and perhaps paradoxically, not all queer (or anti-violence) organizations favor hate crimes statutes because they increase the reach of the crimino-legal system.[90] Laws, police, and prisons have historically brutalized and punished LGBQ people, and the prison industrial complex continues to do so through unsafe prisons that funnel money from community services that could include LGBQ-specific health and empowerment programs, all the while having a questionable deterrent effect.[91] In Australia, where hate crime is approached differently in each of the eight jurisdictions, it is conventionally framed as an aggravating factor in sentencing, which is often bargained away in early phases of adjudication. In both the U.S. and Australia, hate crime provisions have done little to change either maldistributive or misrecognition artifacts of heterosexist violence. This has led abolitionists to question why LGBQ people would believe that criminal processing systems would now protect them. Legal scholar, abolitionist, and Sylvia Rivera Law Project co-founder Dean Spade asserts definitively: "Their laws will never make us safer."[92]

More generally, the push against criminal justice expansion is part of a larger social movement of penal abolition, which is critically concerned with issues such as:

- the devastating effects of mass incarceration, particularly on poor and minority communities;
- criminal processing system overreach (e.g., extended monitoring) that manifests myriad negative economic and social impacts;
- privatization and commodification of prisons and correctional labor; and
- physical and psychological harms committed against those incarcerated.

Specific to hate crimes laws, abolitionist and peacemaking groups point to how these statutes target individuals without addressing larger systems of heterosexism, do not help to heal victims nor perpetrators, and do not give more power to marginalized communities. Instead, these statutes allow the state to continue arresting and incarcerating people at disproportionate rates under the guise of protection.[93]

Thus, is it really "progress" for LGBQ people to exact more retribution and punishment against people acting in heterosexist ways? Why not—as penal abolitionists suggest and consistent with redistribution as discussed earlier—divest from prisons and instead reinvest in societal change that will target the heterosexism causing hate crime? Instead of retributive statutes, why not focus on justice reinvestment?[94] Why not illuminate how the state and its institutions fail to protect LGBQ people and then shift focus to building safer communities from the ground up? Indeed, these are key questions related to how we think about recognition and each can orient us towards a more just redistribution of social justice in criminal justice.

Conclusion

Misrecognition and cultural silencing of LGBQ people continue to be a problem with UN human rights frameworks, and these inform policies that shape how social justice is enacted at the local level. Too often, this silence means that justice—social or criminal—is not possible. Yet, recognition can be an incongruous and dangerous pursuit for LGBQ people. Moran and Skeggs point out that "recognition politics . . . assumes that groups can be made visible, want to be made visible, and that visibility can enable a claim to be made on the state."[95] Many LGBQ people are reticent about pursuing recognition precisely because increasing their visibility can lead to harassment and fatal violence from their communities, police, and the state, and public admonishment and outcry from conservative political groups. This raises the question of how we concurrently seek increased recognition and redistribution, when the latter requires the former, and when the former can be so dangerous to LGBQ bodies.

Social and criminal justice systems intersect for LGBQ people. Marginalization, economic deprivation, and discrimination in social systems lead LGBQ people to have contact with law enforcement officials and criminal processing systems. The more we continue to ignore social injustice, the more likely we are to see LGBQ people cycle in and out of criminal processing systems worldwide. Even if they do successfully transition out of criminal processing systems, we must address the deepening forms of marginalization, economic deprivation, and discrimination (particularly around employment) they will undoubtedly face upon reintegration with broader communities.

We must also question the ethics of deploying instruments of state violence we know all too well against those who would see us dead. Retribution and just deserts are incongruent to the experiences and lives of LGBQ people who have themselves been punished by way of retribution and just deserts. In achieving a modicum of power to shape the criminal and social justice meted out by the state to LGBQ people, are we then to use that same power over others, knowing full well the consequences of that surveillance and criminalization? And as in the case of U.S. hate crime provisions, was the bargain for our recognition worth the massive increase in military spending for a seemingly never-ending, colonizing war/occupation?

As we have highlighted throughout this chapter, awareness of, and seeking to address, issues for LGBQ people in the global South is of paramount importance. Developing the capacity for self-determination in the global South, and learning to consider the impact of how our global North claims to recognition and redistribution shape our peers in the South, are also critical. Of central concern must be those who lack the civic capacity to engage in ways that can produce justice outcomes on their terms. We also need to resist narratives that measure development around sexuality diversity against the "progress" and bellwether issues of the global North.[96] Drawing on the work of Binnie, Mhaoileon suggests that without this critical gaze, Western queer scholars will queer racism rather than query racism.[97]

As queer theorists writing from the luxury of our academic positions in the global North (albeit, two of us in the geographical South), we wanted to remain cognizant of how our contributions to this handbook could/have reinstantiated Western and global North perspectives. We raised, but did not foreground, the social injustice of marriage inequality; instead, we diverted your gaze to the everyday harassment, discrimination, and targeted violence experienced by LGBQ people worldwide. While we used the term occasionally and within context, we chose to frame the experiences documented in this chapter as those experienced by LGBQ people, not "queers"; to do otherwise would be to elide the harms caused by this nomenclature in the global South. While we talked of the contradictory nature of hate crime provisions—a luxury most commonly reserved for queers in the global

North—and penal abolitionism, we also discussed the individual and social costs in advocating for the human rights of LGBQ people in the global South.

Social justice, unlike criminal justice, is not tied to institution, place, or people. Social justice can be achieved in micro-encounters just as successfully as it can be achieved in macro-developments such as law making. Social justice is as much a product of our intersubjective moments of being human, and reaching out to others who share our humanity, as it is a product of policies, practices, projects, and programs. In this respect, social justice is not tethered in the way criminal justice is to jurisdictional laws, rules, regulations, and standard operating procedures. The rules of the game are not concretized in law, and, as such, in advocating for social justice we are offered more opportunities to change the experiences of LGBQ people, including their experiences of criminal injustice. Amending laws and getting safer prison cells—often in bargains we know are unjust—have yet to change the terms of our misrecognition and maldistribution. To this end, we suggest that in coalition with others who experience injustice, LGBQ people may better achieve criminal justice by addressing the social injustice too many encounter.

Acknowledgements

The authors thank Lori Sexton, Jennifer Sumner, Jace Valcore, Allyson Walker, and Aimee Wodda for their helpful comments on an earlier draft of this chapter.

Discussion Questions

1. What insights and interventions can Southern criminology provide for the ways we have typically conceptualized criminal justice and social justice?
2. How can we increase the recognition of LGBQ people without decreasing their safety once they are recognizable?
3. What resources are required to increase the social justice experienced by LGBQ people within the criminal processing system?
4. In what ways is the justice required by LGBQ people different from others' justice? What core social justice needs are shared by all people (including LGBQ people) who encounter the criminal processing system?
5. How do sexuality, class, race, and gender intersect in criminal justice encounters? What injustice do we prioritize?

Notes

1. United Nations. (1969). *Declaration on social progress and development.* (RES 2541 XXIV), 11 December 1969. Geneva: UN.
2. Lesbian, gay, bisexual, and queer/questioning. We use this acronym as a way to abbreviate our sentence structure rather than as boundary maintenance or a delimiter to our discussions. We acknowledge that non-normative human sexuality is varied and not reducible to these four categories. At times, in referring to other research, other forms of the rainbow acronym are used in this chapter when it is not possible to extrapolate only LGBQ results. Even the full acronym, LGBTIQA+ (lesbian, gay, bisexual, transgender, intersex, queer/questioning, asexual, and others) excludes some sexuality diverse and many gender variant people, including those who are gender nonconforming (GNC) and genderqueer (GQ). As this chapter only discusses sexuality and not gender (which is addressed by Walker et al. in this volume), we use the acronym LGBQ. The order in which each of the letters appears (and the absence or inclusion of some of these letters) says much about the development of the "queer community." In the early days of activism, it was all about the "gay and lesbian movement," which by the 1990s was expanded to include bisexual and transgender people. "Q" developed on the margins of the "community" around the same time that queer theory was percolating on college and university campuses after the publication of Butler's (1991) *Gender Trouble.* It wasn't until the

21st century that the "I" and "A" were to appear, sometimes, and with much political debate that continues to this day. To avoid the acronym becoming even longer, the UN has adopted sexual orientation and gender identity (SOGI), but social activists and scholars have adopted a range of other terms that do not limit sexuality to an orientation or gender to an identity. For example, sexuality and gender diversity (SGD or GSD) are used in Australia to mirror the policy language of cultural and linguistic diversity (CALD)..

3. Fraser, N. (1998). Heterosexism, misrecognition and capitalism: A response to Judith Butler. *New Left Review I*, *228*(March/April), 140–149.

4. Article 2 of the Universal Declaration of Human Rights outlines the characteristics that should not be used as a distinction between peoples. It states, in part, "Everyone is entitled to all the rights and freedoms set forth in this Declaration, without distinction of any kind, such as race, colour, sex, language, religion, political or other opinion, national or social origin, property, birth or *other status*" (UN, 1948; emphasis added). United Nations. (1948). *Universal declaration of human rights.* (RES 217 A), 10 December. Geneva: UN.

5. Charmaz, K. (2011). Grounded theory methods in social justice research. In N. K. Denzin & Y. S. Lincoln (Eds.), *The Sage handbook of qualitative research* (pp. 359–380). London, Thousand Oaks, & New Delhi: Sage, p. 359.

6. United Nations (Human Rights Council). (2014). *Human rights, sexual orientation and gender identity.* (A/HRC/RES/27/32). Geneva: UN; United Nations (Human Rights Council). (2011). *Human rights, sexual orientation and gender identity.* (A/HRC/RES/17/19). Geneva: UN; Muntarbhorn, V. (2016, November 30). *Press release: Opportunities for the human rights of all persons in a world of gender diversity.* Retrieved from bangkok.ohchr.org/news/press/VititFullStatement.aspx; United Nations (Human Rights Council). (2016). *Protection against violence and discrimination based on sexual orientation and gender identity.* (A/HRC/RES/32/2). Geneva: UN.

7. See, for example, United Nations. (2016). *Leaving no one behind: The imperative of inclusive development.* (ST/ESA/362). Geneva: UN; United Nations. (2015). *Transforming our work: The 2030 agenda for sustainable development.* (A/RES/70/1). Geneva: UN; United Nations. (2009). *Creating an inclusive society: Practical strategies to promote social integration.* Geneva: UN; United Nations. (1995). *Copenhagen declaration on social development (and program of action of the world summit for social development).* (A/CONF.166/9). Geneva: UN.

8. We use this term—criminal processing system—for two reasons: so as not to confuse the institution with the concept (criminal justice [system]), but also to reflect our more critical stance on justice in the field of crime and criminal offending and victimization. Some have argued that as there is no justice in the criminal justice system, we should stop calling it a criminal justice system (see, for example, Belknap [1996] and Scheingold's [1984] early discussion of the term). Instead, and to reflect the increasing bureaucratization of criminal justice, we use "criminal processing system" in this chapter. Belknap, J. (1996). *The invisible woman: Gender, crime, and justice.* Belmont, CA: Wadsworth; Scheingold, S. A. (1984). *The politics of law and order.* New York: Longman; Richards, K., & Dwyer, A. (2014). Unspeakably present: The (un)acknowledgement of diverse sexuality and gender human rights in Australian youth justice systems. *Australian Journal of Human Rights,* *20*(2), 63–79.

9. See, for example, Walker et al., this volume.

10. Chrononormative, first discussed in relation to queer temporalities by Elizabeth Freeman (2010), refers to normative developmental pathways expected of children and young people. Children and young people are measured against these largely heteronormative and gendered milestones, and despite having a queer temporality that differs significantly from the normative cisgender and heterosexual pathway, LGBTIQ young people are tested and found wanting, deficient, and requiring intervention. Freeman, E. (2010). *Time binds: Queer temporalities, queer histories.* Durham: Duke University Press.

11. UN, 1969.

12. The Sentencing Project. (2017). *Annual report 2016.* Washington, DC: The Sentencing Project.

13. Penal Reform International. (2016). *The rights of prisoners to vote: A global overview.* London: PRI.

14. See Swanson (2005) for discussion of this debate. Swanson, J. (2005). Recognition and redistribution: Rethinking culture and the economic. *Theory, Culture & Society,* *22*(4), 87–118.

15. Fraser, 1998; Fraser, N. (1995). From redistribution to recognition? Dilemmas of justice in a "post-socialist" age. New Left Review, 312(July/August), 68–93.

16. Fraser, 1995, 1998.

17. Fraser's awkward use of the term "homosexual" (in contrast to Butler's "queer") and the reduction of her arguments in most cases to the experiences of gay men, infers through action (if rejected in theory) an uneasiness with the language of LGBQ.

18. Fraser, 1995, 1998.

19. Fraser, 1995, 1998.

20. Cover, R., Rasmussen, M. L., Aggleton, P., & Marshall, D. (2017). Progress in question: The temporalities of politics, support and belonging in gender- and sexually-diverse pedagogies. *Continuum,* *31*(6), 767–779.

21. Progress is most commonly marked in terms of Western economic or political development, and thus linked to 16th-century mercantilism, the Glorious Revolution of 17th century, or the Industrial, French, or American revolutions of the 18th century.

22. Cover et al., 2017.

23. Connell, R. (2007). *Southern theory: The global dynamics of knowledge in social science.* Crows Nest, NSW: Allen and Unwin.

24. Carrington, K., Hogg, R., & Sozzo, M. (2016). Southern criminology. *British Journal of Criminology*, *57*(1), 1–20.

25. Connell, 2007.

26. Connell, 2007; Ball, M., & Dwyer, A. (2018, in press). Queer criminology and the global south: Setting queer and southern criminologies into dialogue (PP). In K. Carrington, R. Hogg, J. Scott, & M. Sozzo (Eds.), *Palgrave handbook of criminology and the global South.* Basingstoke: Palgrave Macmillan.

27. See, for example, Ball, M. (2016). *Criminology and queer theory: Dangerous bedfellows?* Basingstoke: Palgrave Macmillan; Dwyer, A., & Panfil, V. R. (2017). "We need to lead the charge"—"Talking only to each other is not enough": The Pulse Orlando mass shooting and the futures of queer Criminologies. *The Criminologist*, *42*(3), 1–7; Buist, C. L., & Lenning, E. (2016). *Queer criminology.* Oxon: Routledge; Panfil, V. R. (2017). *The gang's all queer: The lives of gay gang members.* New York: New York University Press.

28. Carrington, K., & Hogg, R. (2017). Deconstructing criminology's origin stories. *Asian Journal of Criminology*, *12*(3), 181–197.

29. Paredes, J. (2015). The neocolonial queer. In A. Tellis & S. Bala (Eds.), *The global trajectories of queerness* (pp. 229–240). Leiden: Brill.

30. Croome, R. (2015). *From this day forward: Marriage equality in Australia.* North Hobart: Walleah Press.

31. van Stapele, N. (2016). "We are not Kenyans": Extra-judicial killings, manhood and citizenship in Mathare, a Nairobi ghetto. *Conflict, Security & Development*, *16*(4), 301–325; Koraan, R., & Geduld, A. (2015). "Corrective rape" of lesbians in the era of transformative constitutionalism in South Africa. *PER: Potchefstroomse Elektroniese Regsblad*, *18*(5), 1931–1953.

32. Banning-Lover, R. (2017, March 1). Where are the most difficult places in the world to be gay or transgender? *The Guardian.* Retrieved from www.theguardian.com/global-development-professionals-network/2017/mar/01/where-are-the-most-difficult-places-in-the-world-to-be-gay-or-transgender-lgbt

33. Waites, M. (2017, July 8). Queer Asia 2017 conference review. *Sexuality Policy Watch.* Retrieved from http://sxpolitics.org/queer-asia-2017-conference-review/17134

34. Yulius, H., Tang, S., & Offord, B. (2018, in press). The globalization of LGBT identity and same-sex marriage as a catalyst of neoinstitutional values: Singapore and Indonesia in focus (PP). In B. Winter, M. Forest, & R. Sénac Réjane (Eds.), *Global perspectives on same-sex marriage: A neo-institutional approach.* London & New York: Palgrave MacMillan.

35. United Nations Development Programme & USAID. (2014). *Being LGBT in Asia: Indonesia country report.* Bangkok: UNDP.

36. Yulius, Tang and Offord, 2018.

37. Mhaoileon, N. N. (2017). The ironic gay spectator: The impacts of centring western subjects in international LGBT rights campaigns. *Sexualities.* Article first published online, doi: 10.1177/1363460717699778 (June 5).

38. *Ibid.*, p. 7.

39. Leonard, W., Mitchell, A., Patel, S., & Fox, C. (2008). *Coming forward: The underreporting of heterosexist violence and same sex partner abuse in Victoria.* Australian Centre for Sex, Health and Society Melbourne. Retrieved from www.glhv.org.au/sites/www.glhv.org.au/files/ComingForwardReport.pdf

40. Dwyer, A., & Ball, M. (2013). *GLBTI police liaison services: A critical analysis of existing literature.* Proceedings of the Australian and New Zealand Critical Criminology Conference, 12–13 July, 2012, University of Tasmania, Hobart, Australia, pp. 11–18.

41. Dwyer, A., & Tomsen, S. (2015). The past is the past? The impossibility of erasure of historical LGBTIQ policing. In A. Dwyer, M. Ball, & T. Crofts (Eds.), *Queering criminology* (pp. 36–53). London: Palgrave Macmillan. Importantly, a caveat exists; the safety of LGBQ people at the hands of police, in particular in the U.S., is layered by race and gender.

42. Crichlow, W. (2004). *Buller men and batty bwoys: Hidden men in Toronto and Halifax black communities.* Toronto: University of Toronto Press; J-FLAG, Women's Empowerment for Change (WE-Change), The Colour Pink Foundation, TransWave, Center for International Human Rights, Northwestern Pritzker School of Law of Northwestern University, Global Initiatives for Human Rights of Heartland Alliance for Human Needs & Human Rights (2016). *Human rights violations against Lesbian, Gay, Bisexual, and Transgender (LGBT) people in Jamaica: A shadow report.* Submitted for consideration at the 116th Session of the Human Rights Committee March 2016, Geneva.

43. Ball, & Dwyer, 2018.
44. Fraser, 1995, 1997a, 1997b, 1998.
45. Fraser, N. (2000). Rethinking recognition. *New Left Review, 3*(May/June), 107–120.
46. *Ibid.*, p. 112.
47. *Ibid.*, p. 113.
48. GLAAD. (2010). *Media reference guide*, 8th ed. New York: GLAAD; Foucault, M. (2008 [1976]). *The history of sexuality*, Vol. 1. London & New York: Penguin Press.
49. Mogul, J. L., Ritchie, A. J., & Whitlock, K. (2011). *Queer (in)justice: The criminalization of LGBT people in the United States*. Boston, MA: Beacon Press.
50. *Ibid.*
51. Panfil, V. R. (2014). Better left unsaid? The role of agency in queer criminological research. *Critical Criminology, 22*, 99–111.
52. Visser, N. (2017, March 29). The U.S. won't tally LGBT people in 2020 census. *Huffington Post*. Retrieved from www.huffingtonpost.com.au/entry/us-census-lgbt-americans_us_58db3894e4b0cb23e65c6cd9
53. Sanchez, A. A. (2017, July 7). The whiteness of "coming out": Culture and identify in the disclosure narrative. *Archer*. Retrieved from archermagazine.com.au/2017/07/culture-coming-out/
54. *Ibid.*; Villicana, A. J., Delucio, K., & Biernat, M. (2016). "Coming out" among gay Latino and gay White men: Implications of verbal disclosure for well-being. *Self and Identity, 15*(4), 468–487.
55. Villicana, Delucio, & Biernat, 2017.
56. Sanchez, 2017.
57. Fraser, 1998, p. 141; emphasis in original.
58. Sanchez, 2017.
59. Or queer person with disability, or queer refugee.
60. Fraser, 2000.
61. Asquith, N. L. (1999). Sexuality at work. *New Zealand Journal of Industrial Relations, 24*(1), 1–24; Willis, P. (2009). From exclusion to inclusion: Young queer workers' negotiations of sexually exclusive and inclusive spaces in Australian workplaces. *Journal of Youth Studies, 12*(6), 629–651.
62. International Lesbian, Gay, Bisexual, Trans & Intersex Association (ILGA)-Europe. (2016). *Annual review of the human rights situation of Lesbian, Gay, Bisexual, Trans and Intersex people in Europe*. Belgium: IGLA; James, S. E., Herman, J. L., Rankin, S., Keisling, M., Mottet, L., & Anafi, M. (2016). *The report of the 2015 U.S. transgender survey*. Washington, DC: National Center for Transgender Equality.
63. James et al., 2016.
64. Scott, S. (2013). "One is not born, but becomes a woman": A 14th amendment argument in support of housing male-to-female transgender inmates. *University of Pennsylvania Journal of Constitutional Law, 15*(4), 1259–1298; Sylvia Rivera Law Project. (2007). *"It's war in here": A report on the treatment of transgender and intersex people in New York State men's prisons*. New York: SRLP.
65. Center for American Progress and Movement Advancement Project. (2016). *Unjust: How the broken criminal justice system fails LGBT people*. Washington and Denver: CAP and MAP.
66. Rodgers, J., Asquith, N. L., & Dwyer, D. (2017). Cisnormativity, criminalisation, vulnerability: Transgender people in prisons. *TILES Briefing Paper* (No.12). Hobart: Tasmanian Institute of Law Enforcement Studies; Dwyer, A. (2015). Teaching young queers a lesson: How police teach lessons about non-heteronormativity in public spaces. *Sexuality and Culture, 19*(3), 493–512.
67. Dwyer, A. (2017). Embodying youthful vulnerabilities and policing public spaces. In N. L. Asquith, I. Bartkowiak-Théron, & K. Roberts (Eds.), *Policing encounters with vulnerability* (pp. 47–69). London: Palgrave MacMillan.
68. Seymour, K. (2017). (In)Visibility and recognition: Australia policy responses to "domestic violence". *Sexualities*. Article first published online, doi: 10.1177/1363460716681465 (February 17).
69. Scott, 2013; Dolovich, S. (2011). Strategic segregation in the modern prison. *American Criminal Law Review, 48*(1), 1–110.
70. Irvine, A. (2010). "We've had three of them": Addressing the invisibility of lesbian, gay, bisexual, and gender nonconforming youths in the juvenile justice system. *Columbia Journal of Gender and Law, 19*(3), 675–701; Curtin, M. (2002). Lesbian and bisexual girls in the juvenile justice system. *Child and Adolescent Social Work Journal, 19*(4), 285–301.
71. Rogers, Asquith, & Dwyer, 2017.
72. Penal Reform International, 2016.
73. *Ibid.*
74. Hirsch, A. (2013, July 18). Cameroon gay rights activist found tortured and killed. *The Guardian*. Retrieved from www.theguardian.com/world/2013/jul/18/cameroon-gay-rights-activist-killed

75. International Federation for Human Rights. (2014, July 11). *Cameroon: Assassination of Eric Ohena Lembembe, the investigation remains at a standstill*. Retrieved from www.fidh.org/en/region/Africa/cameroon/15738-cameroon-assassination-of-eric-ohena-lembembe-the-investigation-remains-at

76. At the time of writing, news of the death of Dexter Pottinger on September 2, 2017, had just been made public. Pottinger was also an important community organizer for the LGBT community in Jamaica.

77. Younge, G. (2006, April 26). Troubled island. *The Guardian*. Retrieved from www.theguardian.com/world/2006/apr/27/gayrights.comment

78. *Ibid.*

79. Stratton, J. (2004, June 24). Gay in Jamaica. *New Times*. Retrieved from www.browardpalmbeach.com/news/gay-in-jamaica-6318215

80. Hammadi, S., & Gani, A. (2016, April 25). Founder of Bangladesh's first and only LGBT magazine killed. *The Guardian*. Retrieved from www.theguardian.com/world/2016/apr/25/editor-bangladesh-first-lgbt-magazine-killed-reports-say-roopbaan

81. Mahbub Rabbi Tonoy was also killed in this attack.

82. Ta [pseudonym]. (2017, April 25). One year after the murders of Xulhaz Mannan and Mahbub Rabbi Tonoy. *Amnesty International*. Retrieved from www.amnesty.org/en/latest/news/2017/04/one-year-after-the-murders-of-xulhaz-mannan-and-mahbub-rabbi-tonoy/

83. This is not to say that murders of high-profile activists only happen in the global South—the assassination of openly gay elected official Harvey Milk and an ally in 1978 is a prominent example—but nearly 40 years have elapsed since this and some of our examples.

84. Hirsch, 2013.

85. Nolan, J. J., III, Akiyama, Y., & Berhanu, S. (2002). The *Hate Crime Statistics Act* of 1990: Developing a method for measuring the occurrence of hate violence. *American Behavioral Scientist, 46*(1), 136–153.

86. Whitlock, K. (2001). *In a time of broken bones: A call to dialogue on hate violence and the limitations of hate crimes legislation*. Philadelphia, PA: American Friends Service Committee.

87. Human Rights Campaign. (n.d.). *Hate crimes law: The Matthew Shepard and James Byrd, Jr. Hate Crimes Prevention Act*. Retrieved from www.hrc.org/resources/hate-crimes-law

88. Spade, D. (2013). Under the cover of gay rights. *NYU Review of Law & Social Change, 37*, 79–100.

89. Segura, L. (2012). Do hate crime laws do any good? In R. Conrad (Ed.), *Against equality: Prisons will not protect you* (pp. 23–34). Lewiston, ME: Against Equality Publishing Collective.

90. Sylvia Rivera Law Project. (2012, August 18). *SRLP on hate crime laws*. New York: SRLP.

91. Lamble, S. (2015). Transforming carceral logics: 10 reasons to dismantle the prison industrial complex using a queer/trans analysis. In E. A. Stanley & N. Smith (Eds.), *Captive genders: Trans embodiment and the Prison Industrial Complex* (2nd ed., pp. 269–299). Oakland, CA: AK Press.

92. Spade, D. (2013). Their laws will never make us safer. In R. Conrad (Ed.), *Against equality: Prisons will not protect you* (pp. 1–12). Lewiston, ME: Against Equality Publishing Collective, p. 1.

93. Lydon, J., for Black & Pink. (2012). A compilation of critiques on hate crime legislation. In R. Conrad (Ed.), *Against equality: Prisons will not protect you* (pp. 13–17). Lewiston, ME: Against Equality Publishing Collective.

94. Maruna, S. (2011). Lessons for justice reinvestment from restorative justice and the justice model experience: Some tips for an 8-year-old prodigy. *Criminology & Public Policy, 10*(3), 661–669.

95. Moran, L., & Skeggs, B. (2004). *Sexuality and the politics of violence and safety*. London & New York: Routledge, p. 5.

96. Mhaoileon, 2017.

97. *Ibid.*

Reference

Butler, J. (1991). *Gender Trouble: Feminism and the Subversion of Identity*. New York: Routledge.

16

AMERICAN INDIAN RIGHTS/JUSTICE

Larry French

Pre-Columbian Indigenous Cultures

The pre-Columbian indigenous groups in North and South America and the Caribbean represented a diversity of cultures and societies, from hunting-and-gathering tribes to horticultural groups and even sophisticated city-states such as those developed by the Aztec, Incan, and Mayan empires of Mexico and Central and South America. The population of pre-Columbian America is estimated to have been between 15 and 80 million at the time of White contact. The noted Smithsonian anthropologist and ethnographer James Mooney put the United States pre-Columbian aboriginal population at 1,152,950.[1] Others, including Douglas H. Ubelaker, felt that this was a low estimate and that Mooney most likely did not factor in deaths brought about by epidemics of European and African diseases such as smallpox, measles, and plague.[2] More recent research puts the pre-Columbian indigenous population in what is now the continental United States to be more than five million. By the end of the Revolutionary War, the American Indian population dwindled to a mere six hundred thousand. While the indigenous population was greatly reduced by disease, slaughter, slavery, wars, and cultural genocide (removal, concentration camps, militarized boarding schools, etc.), some 15 million African slaves were brought to the Americas between the 16th and 19th centuries, with nearly half of the Black slaves arriving during the 1700s.

Although numerous North American tribes had a long tradition of holding captured enemies as personal slaves, their practices paled in comparison with the practices their southern counterparts, the Aztec, who enslaved the Tlaxcalan Indian tribes. Thus, while Indian slavery already existed in the Americas prior to European conquests and the arrival of African slaves, the colonial powers expanded this practice considerably beyond the Aztec empire to north of central Mexico. Indian and African slaves played a significant role in both the colonial trade and the extermination of most of the southeastern tribes. The combination of disease, physical genocide, and slavery reduced the numerous southeastern tribes occupying what was then the 13 original colonies. The most notable of these tribes to survive were the Cherokee, Choctaw, Chickasaw, Creek, and Seminole, what became known as the Five Civilized Tribes. Enslaved Indians were often forced to fight against competing European colonial powers, notably the French and Spanish. Gary Nash wrote about this phenomenon in his book *Red, White, and Black*, in which he noted that the Indian slave trade was a feature of all British colonies and was especially crucial to the development of Charleston, South Carolina. He cites the 1708 Charleston census that listed a population of 5,300 Whites and 4,300 slaves, of which 1,400 were American Indians.[3]

The Indian slave trade involved all the horrors associated with the worst images of this institution, including beatings, killings, and tribal, clan, and family separation. The British were not alone in this practice. The Spanish had Indian slaves in their western American colonies where they were used to build and maintain the row of Catholic missions spread across California. Clearly, American Indian slavery was an integral part of the colonial economy. This practice also resulted in the emergence of "Black Indians"—a situation brought about by the miscegenation of Black and Indian slaves. Many of the escaped mixed-blood slaves sought refuge in the Spanish Florida everglades and came to comprise a significant portion of the Seminole Indian tribe. William Loren Katz wrote on the Black Indians, noting that a new race of mixed Indians and Blacks emerged during the colonial era among these escaped slaves. Katz attributes the emergence of the mixed-race slaves came about due to a shared worldview based on group cooperation, one that differed markedly from the Eurocentric concept of economic competition. Another aspect of Katz's thesis that the pre-Columbian indigenous population comprised 80 million American Indians with some 60 million succumbing to disease, genocide, and slavery is not given serious consideration, given that these figures do not appear feasible. Nonetheless, the remaining Indian tribes located within the United States consists of 556 federally recognized reservations (tribes, nations, bands, rancheros, and townships) collectively known as Indian Country. Off-reservation Indians receive some support through federally funded programs, mainly those located within urban Indian centers. The three largest American Indian groups in the United States are the Navajo, Cherokee, and Sioux. The Cherokee and Sioux comprise a number of separate tribes while both the Navajo (Dine) and Sioux have bands that transcend the U.S./Canada border.[4]

Contravening Worldviews: Harmony Ethos Versus the Protestant Ethic

Katz did address a significant sociocultural difference between North American aboriginal societies and that of the Euro-Americans who challenged them for this land and its natural resources. In addition to the obvious racial difference between American Indians and the intruding Caucasians, there existed major sociocultural differences between these two groups competing for America's land and resources. These differences also existed in each group's perception of justice. Western societies focus on individual rights and responsibilities relevant to legal matters, whereas aboriginal societies placed these responsibilities on the clan, making it the "collective individual." Even then, differences existed between various indigenous groups and their version of the Harmony Ethos, especially between those whose social organization was matrilineal, like the Cherokee and Navajo. Clearly, the essential difference between the Euro-American Protestant ethic and the aboriginal Harmony Ethos was the sense of personal responsibility, a major tenet of any justice model.

The Aboriginal Harmony Ethos

When looking at indigenous cultures at the time of White contact, it is important to realize that regardless of their complex clan organization and oral tradition, these groups did not have the wheel, horse, or steel implements for either tools or weapons. Consequently, many of these societies residing in what is now the United States and Canada stagnated in a semi-Stone Age existence. These above-mentioned items were brought by the colonists and greatly changed the aboriginal lifestyle of many tribes. Nonetheless, the basic values of the Harmony Ethos continued, especially among the tribal traditionalists. Conflict and competition existed within the Harmony Ethos much like it did (does) within other societies. Here, conflict and competition were an integral part of the cycle of maintaining both intra- and intergroup balance. Harmony meant collective balance with Mother Nature, Father Sky, and each other—clan member or outsider. The complexities of the Harmony Ethos is evident in the various linguistic groupings of pre-Columbian peoples, where some 350 different languages were spoken within the United States and Canada and another 1,500 languages spoken in

Mexico and Central and South America. Tribal groups usually formed larger allegiances based upon their linguistic affiliation, yet no tribal group is known to have had a written language or method for the mass dissemination of written literature during aboriginal times. The main vehicle for communicating history, culture, and current events was their rich oral tradition.

The clan provided the basic group structure from aboriginal times up to the time of White contact. Clan folkways provided the basic control mechanism and psychocultural identity for the group and its members, who shared a common language and geographical region. Unfortunately, European colonists generally viewed the tribe's aboriginal Stone Age existence and illiteracy as indicative of biological and racial inferiority. This view prevailed despite the fact that the great Aztec pyramid of Cholula in the Mexican state of Puebla is the largest ancient pyramid monument constructed in the world, being nearly a third larger than that of the Great Pyramid of Giza in Egypt, with these and numerous other pyramids within this region built with Stone Age tools.[5] However, tribes north of central Mexico, including those that extended into Canada and Alaska, were not as developed as their southern Mesoamerican counterparts. Many tribes relied on seasonal activities divided between horticulture, hunting and gathering, and fishing, with varying degrees of sophistication among clan and linguistic groups. Preston Holder described the aboriginal lifestyle of the Plains Indians in his book *The Hoe and the Horse on the Plains*. Holder describes the Plains as that region from North Dakota to the Gulf Coast of Texas, with the Rocky Mountains marking the western border and the Missouri and Mississippi Rivers denoting the eastern boundaries. The aboriginal Indian groups in this region lived a more primitive existence, surviving mainly as nomadic hunting-and-gathering groups with some marginal horticultural traits until European influence. This influence was also indicated by the eastern tribes being forced west by the impact of White settlers, notably British colonists. The French trappers also had an influence by introducing new technologies to the scattered tribes where they interacted. The introduction of the horse provided a new mode of mobility for indigenous groups. This allowed for the consolidation of these scattered, displaced Indian settlements, forging larger, more stable fortified villages for the purpose of mutual protection. The process of forced eviction began among the southeastern tribes in the 16th century and continued until the middle of the 18th century. Even then, certain groups remained nomadic, greatly expanding their hunting and raiding territory via the advent of the horse.[6]

Despite competition among clans within a linguistic group and conflict between tribes, a balance was maintained via the tenet of the Harmony Ethos, whose values derived from the natural relationship between Mother Earth, which provided sustenance for living creatures, and Father Sky, the creator who provided the cycles of life (seasons, rain, sun, day and night). Generally speaking, the Harmony Ethos consists of 12 basic tenets that regulate the individual's behaviors within his/her own clan and in inter-clan/-group interactions.

1. The avoidance of overt hostilities regarding interpersonal matters and an emphasis on nonaggression in intra-family/-clan/-tribe interactions.
2. The use of a neutral third person, or intermediary, for resolving personal altercations within the tribal community, e.g., the avoidance of direct confrontations.
3. A high value placed on independence and personal freedom to act as long as these actions conform to clan and tribal folkways and do not violate sacred taboos.
4. A resentment of authority: leaders command respect instead of demanding subordination by forced authority.
5. A general hesitancy to command others (corollary to item #4).
6. Caution in interactions with others, especially strangers.
7. A reluctance to refuse favors and an emphasis placed on generosity within the clan and tribe, including sharing events such as giveaways.
8. A reluctance to voice individual/personal opinions publicly. Matters of opinions rest with designated clan representatives and usually represent a collective consensus.

9. Avoidance of eye and body contact when interacting with others, especially with those outside the family/clan structure.
10. Emphasis placed on group cooperation and not on individual competition, except in circumstances where the individual is representing his/her clan, such as in stickball games and battlefield endeavors like counting coup.
11. Deference to elders: the aboriginal rule is "old equals good equals honor."
12. Challenging life in the raw; exploring life events firsthand as a test of their character vis-à-vis clan and tribal expectations.[7]

Aboriginal Justice—Blood Vengeance

Aboriginal justice occurred at the clan level with the ultimate goal of restoring balance or harmony to the tribe. Violations were seen as offenses against the clan and not individuals per se. In this sense, clans determined both the verdict and sentence relevant to intra-group violations of norms and mores. One of the best-documented examples of aboriginal justice is that of the Cherokee blood vengeance. The Cherokee was the largest tribal group in what is now the southeastern United States at the time of White contact. They had an elaborate network of townships and farms in what is now western North Carolina, north Georgia, east Tennessee, northeast Alabama, and portions of western South Carolina. The Cherokee were matrilineal and consisted of seven clans: Wolf, Deer, Bird, Paint, Long Hair or Blue, Wild Potato or Wild Savannah, and the Holly or Twisters clans. Each village/township had a Town House, a seven-sided structure where each clan was represented and all village decisions were made in a democratic process in which all adults, men and women, had a vote. The two sanctioned institutions governing the aboriginal Cherokee were the village council and the clan. Being a matrilineal society, men resided in their wife's village, a matrilocal arrangement in which single adults, men and women, sat with their respective clan section. The village council did not legislate or adjudicate; its role was to seek consensus and compromise in order to maintain harmony within the village. Each village council had a "white chief," who regulated domestic affairs during the agricultural season, and a "red chief" (priest warrior) who presided during the winter or war season. While these village officials were men, a female clan leader, "war woman," provided counsel to the chiefs. Each clan, in turn, had a designated Mother Clan village where ultimate decisions were made regarding restoring harmony through their unique method of restorative justice.

Blood vengeance was the traditional vehicle used in resolving serious transgressions, the most serious being the violation of marriage taboos and homicide. The clan played the major role in these matters, given that violation of taboos was a clan matter and not necessarily a village or personal matter. Hence, aboriginal Cherokee justice was based on clan blood vengeance. Sometimes the compromise included the death sentence. Here, the honorable method of dying was being killed in an intra-clan game of stickball. Otherwise, the condemned offender was hunted down by the avenging clan and killed. However, if the condemned offender could escape to a neutral village undetected until the beginning of the New Year, then he was allowed to live without any lasting stigma for his offense. Hence, the statute of limitations for all offenses within aboriginal Cherokee society did not exceed one year. Labels such as felon or murderer did not follow the person once the tribe celebrated its weeklong purification ritual at the end of the year. The New Year purification ritual represented an annual rebirth for the Cherokees, allowing them to focus anew on the upcoming spring planting and the rituals and ceremonies associated with their horticultural lifestyle.[8]

The Protestant Ethic and Personal Responsibility

While the Harmony Ethos provided the cooperative social foundation for aboriginal groups, the European colonists, notably the British, subscribed to the Protestant ethic and capitalist competition.

According to Max Weber, competitive capitalism arose from the Protestant concept of predestination. This worldview grew out of Calvinism, which endorsed the concept that certain individuals are predestined by God as being superior to other humans and that these individuals would be readily recognized by their possessions of certain virtues, including asceticism, high social status, and private wealth. Weber saw that the elements of social status and private wealth sowed the seeds for capitalism. Once the sacred element of asceticism was diminished, this paved the way for a secular mode of capitalism along with material wealth, social privilege, and conspicuous consumption. Fierce competition soon became the mantra of capitalism. This focus on individual competition and responsibility supported the adversarial justice system. In assessing American capitalism, Weber noted that it maintained a moral ethos that provided justification for exploitation and expansionism. Thus, this moral ethos, the proclaimed Covenant of Divine Providence, became the foundation of Manifest Destiny.[9]

The Early Republic and Its "Indian Problem"

One of the first actions of the new republic of the United States of America was to redefine what constituted an American Indian. Clearly, this was necessary if any legal protection was to be afforded the indigenous groups residing within the former 13 colonies. The United States chose to restrict the legal status of American Indians, much as it did for African slaves. Moreover, the basic legal/political category for American Indians was determined to be their tribal status, an artificially constructed entity that relied on Anglo documentation via "tribal rolls," which were established by the U.S. government. This process consolidated American Indians into political units that did not necessarily exist prior to U.S. independence, raising questions as to who was a federally recognized American Indian. It is these statutory definitions, subject to judicial review, that have regulated U.S. Indian police from the late 18th century to the present.

The Washington Doctrine

The *Reference Library of Native North America* notes that the acquisition of Indian lands during the colonial era was dictated by European international laws established in the 16th century. Here, it was felt that indigenous peoples in conquered lands were entitled to sovereignty and property rights. These rights applied to all Indian groups, including those who did not convert to Christianity. Under these rules, conflict with aboriginal groups was justified only when the local tribes refused Europeans the right to trade and to preach Christianity—Catholicism, Protestantism. An element of this Christian capitalist colonial pact was the "doctrine of discovery," which gave exclusive rights of negotiation with indigenous groups to the European nation that first claimed the territory. This not only established a superior/subordinate relationship between Whites and Natives, it provided the impetus for conflict among the European colonial powers themselves. The conflict between the King of England and the colonists soon evolved into challenges between the newly established U.S. federal government and those states coveting Indian lands protected by federal law.[10] President Washington set the stage for federal paternalism and exploitation of Indians by assigning them less-than-human status, equating them with wolves and other predatory animals. George Washington's policy statement on "Indian and Land Policy" is one of the first documents indicating the direction the United States would take toward American Indians. In referring to American Indians as simple-minded savages and expressing fear of continued bloodshed between Indians and White settlers, President Washington set the stage for the "trickery by treaty" Indian policy, one that dominated federal policy until the mid-20th century.[11]

The exclusive authority of the U.S. Congress to regulate Indian Country (federally recognized tribes), was formally established on October 15, 1783. Treaties, ordinances, and reports soon followed, including the "Treaty with the Six Nations" on October 22, 1784; the "Treaty of Fort McIntosh" on January 21, 1785; the "Treaty of Hopewell" with the Cherokees on November 28, 1785; the

"Ordinance for the Regulation of Indian Affairs" of August 7, 1786; and the "Northwest Ordinance" of July 13, 1787. From the outset, states questioned the role of Congress in dealing with Indian affairs. Loopholes were found to exist within the Articles of Confederation relevant to federal versus state authority regarding Indian matters. North Carolina and Georgia were guilty of violating federal protection of Indian Country that lay within the claimed boundaries of these two southern states. In trying to assert its exclusive jurisdictional authority over Indian affairs, the First Congress under the new Constitution established the War Department on August 7, 1789, making it responsible for Indian affairs until the establishment of the Interior Department in 1849. Under the new Constitution, Congress then legislated federal laws outlining U.S. relations within Indian Country. These became known as the Trade and Intercourse Acts, the first enacted in July 1790. This was also the year of the first U.S. federal census. The function of the census was to apportion seats in the U.S. House of Representatives and to assess federal taxes. It was at this time that distinctions were made according to social and political status in the United States: free White males aged 16 or older, free White males under age 16, free White women, number of slaves, and all other persons regardless of race or gender. Slaves counted as three-fifths of a human being for the purpose of apportioning seats in the U.S. House of Representatives, while American Indians were largely excluded by the clause "not taxed," which meant those not fully assimilated into the White Euro-American society. Ratification of the 14th Amendment to the U.S. Constitution in 1868 ended the fractional count of African Americans, but it was not until the 1940 census that American Indians were removed from the "not taxed/don't exist" status and counted as full members of U.S. society. American Indians were at a clear disadvantage in terms of legal status in the United States, unprotected by any judicial due process offered other citizens for over a century and a half. It was this disadvantage that fueled the blatant exploitation of tribes by both states and the federal government.[12]

Washington's push for strong congressional authority over Indian affairs was halted with Jefferson's presidency and the Louisiana Purchase on 1803. Jefferson sowed the seeds of tribal assimilation that led to the Five Civilized Tribes, those groups that changed their aboriginal communal cultures to mimic that of U.S. society. This change in policy also fostered false hopes among the major tribes of the southeast who were constantly harassed by their White neighbors. Jefferson's dilemma was accommodating the needs of White immigrants while dealing humanely with the indigenous Indian population. His assimilation plan was twofold: one, to reduce the size of traditional lands to make room for White settlers and, two, to have tribes adopt the Euro-American lifestyle. The five major tribes to subscribe to Jefferson's assimilation plan were the Cherokee, Choctaw, Chickasaw, Creek, and Seminole, collectively known as the Five Civilized Tribes. While these tribes made this transition to White America's civilization, including disenfranchising females and having Black slaves, this was a failed concept from the outset given that racial prejudice was pronounced within the Protestant ethic's tenet of Manifest Destiny and White supremacy. Moreover, American Indians did have equal rights under the United States legal system. President Jefferson saw the Louisiana Purchase as the solution to the U.S.'s "Indian problem" with the removal of tribes west of the Mississippi River into what would become Indian Territory, an area that doubled the size of the United States. Indian removal coupled with Manifest Destiny and the Monroe Doctrine became the new Indian policy for subsequent administrations. Bernard Sheehan, in his book *Seeds of Extinction: Jeffersonian Philanthropy and the American Indian*, noted that the Louisiana Purchase was obtained to provide a territory in which to dump the unwanted eastern tribes, hence Jefferson's solution to the Indian problem.[13]

Ethnic Cleansing: Removal of the Civilized Tribes

Chief Justice John Marshall, fourth chief justice of the U.S. Supreme Court, in *Johnson v. McIntosh* in 1823 reinforced the authority of the federal government as the major arbitrator regarding Indian affairs, overthrowing the purchase of tribal lands by private individuals. Here, Marshall noted the

European colonial tenet guaranteeing Indian tribes collective occupancy of their traditional lands even when the colonial ownership changed, hence establishing the concept of "aboriginal title" or "Indian title." This concept was challenged during the administration of Andrew Jackson (1829–1837), who strongly supported the Indian Removal Act of 1830.[14]

Jackson's anti-Indian sentiments were well known, fostering strong support for the forceful removal of the major southern tribes into Indian Territory, a tragedy known as the "Trail of Tears." The Indian Removal Act encouraged Georgia to lay claim to parts of the Cherokee Nation lying within its state boundaries. As soon as Jackson became president, Georgia attempted to extinguish Indian title, essentially invalidating the laws of the Cherokee Nation leading to two companion U.S. Supreme Court cases: the 1831 case, *Cherokee Nation v. the State of Georgia* and the 1832 case, *Worcester v. Georgia.* These two decisions constitute the foundation for the federal authority over Indian Country. Chief Justice Marshall, in *Cherokee v. Georgia,* established that Indian tribes were "domestic dependent nations," essentially protected wards of the federal government, hence providing the format for the structure and organization of Indian Country. In *Worcester v. Georgia,* the High Court decision articulated what constitutes Indian Country by noting that tribes constituted distinct political entities with territorial boundaries and land held in common.[15]

Unfortunately, the pressure for ethnic cleansing and U.S. expansionism resulted in a sorry history of Indian removal and wars extending into the 1890s. Part of this process involved the executive branch and Congress in certifying unwilling tribes as "savages" or "reneges" no longer entitled to federal protection as determined by the 1831 and 1832 Supreme Court decisions. Thus, if the U.S. government found it could not obtain Indian lands through treaties and trickery, it could do so merely by labeling uncooperative tribes as "enemies of the United States," thus justifying the use of force in subduing, manipulating, or eliminating them.

Contravening Indian Policies During the 19th and 20th Centuries

Clearly, race was a major factor relevant to discrimination against American Indians, but their lifestyle was equally important, playing a significant role in efforts to transform tribalism so that it conformed to Western-style societies. Enforcement of the dictates of capitalism and individual ownership of property was also a devious method of generating "surplus lands" for White settlement. To American Indians, these efforts clearly spelled cultural genocide and little else. This experience with "forced assimilation" was established in 1832 via church-run, government-funded, Indian boarding schools. Actually, attempts at resocialization via compulsory education extends back to the colonial era. In the emerging United States, the role of "civilizing" and Christianizing American Indians was assigned to church and educational groups with oversight provided by White federal Indian Agents, and later, the Bureau of Indian Affairs (BIA). The 1976 Indian Education Task Force noted that the sentiment concerning American Indians at the time of removal (1830s) was that the Indians need to be civilized or exterminated with no other alternatives.[16] Indian resocialization was conducted under the guise of federal paternalism (*parens patriae*), in which parents and students had no say or rights in the matter of the forceful removal of their children for educational purposes. Reluctant students were arrested and incarcerated in distant boarding schools where they were denied all aspects of their cultural traditions, including hair style, clothing, language, and rituals. Toward this end, Congress made abandoned military posts available for compulsory Indian resocialization schools. By the early 1800s, over a hundred Indian schools existed, including a dozen boarding schools. The latter included the Haskell Indian School in Lawrence, Kansas, and the Moravian Mission School in Bethel, Alaska. Clearly, cultural genocide was the primary goal of compulsory Indian education during this era that extended from the 1830s to the 1950s in both the United States and Canada. The clear intent was to stigmatize Indian youth and to denigrate their cultural heritage—to teach them "their inferior place" within American society.

Transforming Indian Country from Tribal Customs
to U.S. Federal Jurisdiction

Efforts to enforce laws within federal jurisdictions were first established by the Trade and Intercourse Acts beginning in 1790. In the 1834 version, following passage of the Removal Act of 1830, Congress tasked federal Indian agents and administrators with the arrest and adjudication of not only non-Indians in Indian Country, but also all Indians or non-Indians accused of committing any crime, offense, or misdemeanor within any state or territory who then fled to Indian Country to avoid apprehension. This was partly in response to the enactment of the Federal Crimes Act of 1825. The Federal Enclaves and Assimilation Crimes Acts were the norm in Indian Country following the Civil War and the ensuing Indian Wars (1862–1892) in the newly acquired western territories. In 1883, the Courts of Indian Offenses were established. Pro-Christian Indian judges were appointed by the White Indian agent with the intent of enforcing Anglo-style laws on the Indian populace. The U.S. Secretary of the Interior, Henry M. Teller, initiated the Courts of Indian Offenses to rid Indian Country of its "heathenish practices" such as the customs of purification rituals, vision quests, sun dances, and plural marriages.[17]

During this same time, attempts at maintaining traditional tribal customs were being played out in the U.S. courts in the Crow Dog incident. The Crow Dog case was sensational in that in 1881, a federally sponsored Sioux leader, Spotted Tail, was killed in an altercation with another Sioux leader, Crow Dog. Both were Brule Sioux from the Rosebud Reservation. The case was initially resolved using the Sioux's traditional form of restorative justice with consensus reached by their respective clans. The tribal resolution involved Crow Dog's clan compensating Spotted Tail's clan with a restitution of $600, eight horses, and a blanket. While this restored balance to the Sioux, it did not resonate well with the federal Indian agents and the U.S. Army, still smarting from Custer's 1876 defeat. Crow Dog was arrested and brought to Fort Niobrara in Nebraska for trial, convicted by an all-White jury and sentenced to be hanged. Crow Dog appealed his conviction, first to the Federal District Court of Dakota, where the same judge that sentenced him upheld his previous judgment. The case then went to the U.S. Supreme Court, which overturned Crow Dog's conviction in a case known as *Ex Parte Crow Dog*. The U.S. Congress responded to the U.S. Supreme Court's decision by enacting the Major Crimes Act of 1885, an action that significantly encroached on tribal authority and autonomy with lasting implications that continue to the present.[18]

An obvious problem with the Major Crimes Act was that American Indians did not have equal weight before the courts, especially when cases were being adjudicated by White judges and their fate decided by White juries. It would be another 39 years before American Indians were granted federal citizenships. Even then, citizenship did not guarantee equal status in local jurisdictions (some states continued to disenfranchise Indians until the 1970s following passage of the U.S. Civil Rights Acts). The Major Crimes Act, initially known as the "Seven Index Crimes," also set the stage for the FBI's involvement in Indian Country. In March 1893, following the conclusion of the 30-year U.S. Army Indian campaign, U.S. attorneys were given original jurisdiction regarding all legal matters within Indian Country, establishing the superior weight of U.S. and White interests over tribal interests in Indian Country. The imposition of White-dominated law enforcement in Indian Country set the stage for allotment and the end of Indian Territory.[19]

Allotment and the Era of Forced Acculturation

Allotment began during the Civil War when Congress passed an act protecting Indians desiring civilized life. Here, federal legal protection was promised to those tribal members in Indian Country, like the Five Civilized Tribes, who elected to adopt the ways of the dominant society.[20] However, the protective trust aspect of allotment failed and many allotted plots were taken over by unscrupulous

Whites in collusion with the White-run courts, resulting in a substantial number of non-Indians living within the tribal boundaries yet not subject to tribal authority. In the end, over 60% of Indian Country (86 million acres) was lost during the official allotment era, 1886–1934.[21] The Dawes Act was followed by a number of similar acts leading to the creation of the state of Oklahoma and the dissolving of Indian Territory initially created as a refuge for removed tribes. To better control displaced and disenchanted Indians, Congress, in July 1892, allowed the president to appoint Army officers to serve as Indian agents.

Indian Reorganization

A critical review of these blatant violations of treaty and congressional Indian rights was articulated in the 1928 Meriam Report leading to the 1934 Indian Reorganization Act (IRA or Wheeler-Howard Act). First and foremost, the IRA cancelled the further division of Indian Country through allotment. Essentially, the IRA provided the design for modern tribal government. The major premise of the IRA was that close supervision of tribes, organized as self-governing communities, was a better method for dealing with the outside influences and exploitation by non-Indians. During the two-year adoption period in which tribes could accept or reject the IRA standards, 258 tribes held elections, with 181 tribes accepting the act and 77 tribes rejecting it. Overall, by 1946, 161 constitutions and 131 corporate charters had been adopted. Nonetheless, the IRA model eventually became the standard for all tribal entities within Indian Country.[22]

Termination and Relocation

Ironically, certain elements of the IRA set the stage for the devastating programs established during the Eisenhower era that again were designed to dissolve Indian Country and federal responsibilities and treaty obligations.24 The IRA vehicle that fostered termination was the option given tribes to transfer communal lands to corporations with the provision to terminate federal supervision. The Eisenhower administration and its Republican Congress put forth their plans for termination in August 1953 with the passage of two complementary congressional acts: House Concurrent Resolution 108, ending federal responsibility among designated tribes, and Public Law 280, which replaced federal civil and criminal jurisdiction over Indian Country with that of the state in which the reservation was located. The initial designated Public Law 280 tribes were located in Alaska, California, Minnesota, Nebraska, Oregon, and Wisconsin, followed by Arizona, Florida, Idaho, Iowa, Montana, Nevada, North Dakota, South Dakota, Utah, and Washington. Altogether some 190 tribes were affected, including 1,362,155 acres in Indian Country already drastically shrunk by allotment, resulting in the further shrinkage of federal Indian trust lands by 3.2%. Common to these termination acts was the transformation of land ownership patterns from one of communally held tribal lands to a corporate or capitalist design. Here, tribal lands were appraised and sold by the U.S. government to a non-Indian bidder, often involving collusion, and the proceeds were then assigned to the tribe minus processing fees determined by the Secretary of the Interior. Tribes had no involvement in this process. Termination ended the trust responsibility, including federal expertise for land and resource management and federal protection from tax or other liens against Indian lands. Public Law 280 was designed for the transfer of federal jurisdiction to state and local authorities now placing the tribal members at the mercy of the White-dominated political and law enforcement apparatus, essentially ending tribal sovereignty[23]

The second component of the Eisenhower plan for eliminating Indian Country was relocation. Here, the federal government began resettlement programs in magnet cities like Denver, Salt Lake City, and Los Angles with the enticements of better education, training, and employment opportunities. By 1954, additional offices had been opened in San Francisco, Oakland, San Jose, St. Louis, Dallas,

Cleveland, Oklahoma City, and Tulsa. The 1977 Final Report of the American Indian Police Review Commission noted the dire failure of this program:

> The Federal Government not only failed to provide needed services to the Indians it relocated, but actually refused to provide those services. The Federal Relocation program was to be initiated by the BIA [Bureau of Indian Affairs] but was left to be implemented by local, State and county assistance programs, or churches or humanitarian organizations. The only thing that was shrugged off a reservation boundaries, it turned out, was Federal responsibility.[24]

Indian Civil Rights

One of President Lyndon Johnson's greatest contributions to U.S. society was his endeavor to get the Civil Rights Act passed. While the primary intent was the enfranchisement of Black Americans, he was the first to promote self-determination for American Indians. Toward this end, Congress passed the Civil Rights Act of 1968, in which Titles II–VII addressed American Indians. This was important legislation, given that while American Indians had been conferred federal citizenship in 1924, this legislation guaranteed them the right to vote in state and local elections. The Indian Civil Rights Act (ICRA) repealed termination, but let stand existing P.L. 280 provisions. It also provided more freedoms to individual members of tribes, as well as empowering tribes to accept or reject continued Public Law 280 influences. No tribe agreed to Public Law 280 conditions after given this opportunity, and most tribes that live under these imposed conditions would like the law rescinded. With the ICRA, tribal courts are now held to American laws and procedures, except for major crimes, where the U.S. Attorney and FBI still hold primary jurisdiction. Clearly, the 1968 ICRA served notice to Indian Country that only the U.S. style of civil and criminal justice will be tolerated and that tribal authority is to be greatly curtailed.[25]

A number of subsequent court cases have refined the strengths and limitations of tribal authority in the realm of criminal justice. In 1978, the U.S. Supreme Court, in *United States v. Wheeler*, ruled that tribes and tribal courts hold inherent criminal jurisdiction over only their enrolled members. That same year, the High Court, in *Oliphant v. Suquamish Indian Tribe*, ruled that tribal jurisdiction does not extend to non-Indians arrested in Indian Country. Later, in *Merrion v. Jicarilla Apache Tribe*, the federal courts recognized the tribes' power of exclusion for unwanted persons, including member Indians, nonmember Indians, and non-Indians, as long as these individuals do not hold federally conferring rights to be in Indian Country (e.g., federal officials including the FBI or U.S. military personnel). It was *Dura v. Reina* that led to statutory changes relating to tribal judicial authority over nontribal Indians. In 1990, the High Court stated that tribes do not hold criminal jurisdiction over nonmember Indians who commit crimes on the reservation. In 1991, the U.S. Congress exercised its authority as ultimate guardian in all matters within Indian Country passing Public Law 102–137, an act entitled "Criminal Jurisdiction over Indians," reinstating tribal judicial authority over all Indians in Indian Country, including nonmember Indians.28

Indian Country and the War on Terrorism

The War on Terrorism, stemming from the September 11, 2001 (9/11) attacks on New York City and the Pentagon and the ill-fated attempt on the U.S. Capitol, led to the creation of the Department of Homeland Security (DHS) in March 2003. Border security became a priority of DHS, with policies impacting Indian Country by challenging the historical cross-border rights of indigenous peoples that date back to the 1794 Jay Treaty (Treaty of London) that allowed for free intra-tribal movement across U.S. borders (U.S./Canada at this time). Actually, plans for increasing border security stem from

President Clinton's 1994 NAFTA (North American Free Trade Agreement) conditions, notably along the southern U.S. border with Mexico. Clinton's Southwest Border Strategy plan was designed to shore up the most porous section of the 1,933-mile-long U.S.-Mexico border, an area known as the Borderlands. These designated Borderland sites included cross-border tribes, notably the Tohono O'odham in Arizona and the Isleta Pueblo Indians in Texas, among others such as the Apache and Yaqui Indians.[26]

Both NAFTA and increased security efforts post-9/11 have their greatest impact on the indigenous populations of all three countries—Canada, Mexico, and the United States. These security measures, initiated by the United States, led to the militarization of the U.S. borders, with the greatest impact placed on its southern border with Mexico. A major outcome of these efforts is the travel restrictions spelled out under the Western Hemisphere Travel Initiative (WHTI), initiated in January 2009. Here, approved NAFTA groups have access to Free and Secure Trade Express (FAST) border passage while requiring official passports for all others, including North American Indians, many who do not possess a U.S.-approved birth certificate required for passport applications. U.S. border officials do not recognize tribal-issued identification cards, such as tribal membership/enrollment certificates, the only ID for some American Indians. Consequently, indigenous peoples, notably members of the 40 tribal groups whose traditional lands transcend either the Mexico-U.S. or Canada-U.S. borders, are among those most affected by this increased security.

Since 9/11 and the creation of DHS, the federal government has further intruded into the limited autonomy of tribal governance within Indian Country. The current situation allows for the U.S. military to again occupy tribal lands under the DHS's Tribal Consultation Policy, a measure not taken since Wounded Knee II in the 1970s. Under this imposed agreement, the U.S. government is free to intervene in Indian Country under any pretense that is authorized by DHS, including military interventions.[27]

Discussion Questions

1. Compare the relative status of White males, African slaves, and American Indians as defined by the first (1790) United States census.
2. Discuss President Washington's "trickery by treaty" solution to the "Indian problem" and how this departed from the European colonial mandate relevant to indigenous peoples.
3. Discuss how President Jefferson's Louisiana Purchase set the stage for forced "removal" of eastern Indian tribes and, subsequently, many other tribes.
4. How long after President Lincoln's Emancipation Proclamation did it take for American Indians to gain U.S. citizenship?
5. What congressional act eventually forced all states to enfranchise American Indians and Alaska Natives?
6. Discuss the U.S. policies in the late 19th and early 20th centuries that attempted to dissolve Indian Country and President Franklin D. Roosevelt's efforts to reinstate tribal autonomy with federal protection.
7. What role did the Eisenhower administration play in again attempting to end federal treaty rights and protection of American Indians and Alaska Natives?
8. How have post-9/11 security measures impacted American Indians, notably those tribes that transcend U.S.-Canada and U.S.-Mexico borders?

Notes

1. Mooney, J. (1928). The aboriginal population of America North of Mexico. In J. R. Swanton (Ed.), *Smithsonian miscellaneous collections* (Vol. 80, pp. 1–40). Washington, DC: Smithsonian Institute.
2. Ubelaker, D. H. (1976). Prehistoric new world population size: Historical review and current appraisal of North American estimates. *Journal of Physical Anthropology, 45*, 661–666.

3. Nash, G. (1974). *Red, White, and Black: The peoples of Early America.* Englewood Cliff, NJ: Prentice-Hall.

4. Dent, F. B. (2002, July 12). Federally recognized Indian tribes. *Federal Register, 67*(134), 46327–46333.

5. Mexico. (1990). *Hammond gold medallion world atlas.* Maplewood, NJ: Hammond Incorporated, pp. 150–152.

6. Holder, P. (1970). *The Hoe and the Horse on the plains.* Lincoln, NE: University of Nebraska Press, p. 28.

7. French, L. A. (1994). The aboriginal harmony ethos. In *The winds of injustice* (p. 5). New York: Garland.

8. Reid, J. P. (1970). *A law of blood.* New York: New York University Press.

9. Weber, M. (1930). *The protestant ethic and the spirit of capitalism* (T. Parsons, Trans.). New York: Charles Scribner's Sons; Stephanson, A. (1996). *Manifest destiny: American expansion and the empire of the right.* New York: Hill and Wang.

10. Champagne, D. (2001). Law and legislation (Ch. 5). In P. Kopper (Ed.), *Reference library of native North America* (Vol. 2, pp. 469–472). Farmington Hills, MI: Gale Group.

11. Fitzpatrick, J. C. (1784). To James Duane, September 7, 1783. In *The writings of George Washington, 1745–1799* (Vol. 27, pp. 133–140). Washington, DC: U.S. Government Printing Office.

12. Committee Report on the Southern Department. (1787, August 3). *Journals of the Continental Congress, 25,* 456–459; Congressional Apportionment—Historical Perspectives: Apportionment of the U.S. House of Representatives—1790 U.S. Federal Census. U.S. Census Bureau, Population Division. Pop@census.gov.

13. Sheehan, B. W. (1974). Removal (Cp. IX). In *Seeds of extinction: Jeffersonian philanthropy and the American Indian* (pp. 243–275). New York: W.W. Norton; Stephanson, A. (1995). *Manifest destiny: American expansionism and the empire of right.* New York: Hill and Wang.

14. *Johnson v. McIntosh,* 21 U.S. 543, 5 L. Ed. 681 (1823); *Indian Removal Act,* U.S. Statutes at Large, 4: 411–412, May 28, 1830.

15. *Cherokee Nation v. Georgia,* 30 U.S. 1, 5 Pet. 1, 8 L.Ed. 25 (1831); *Worcester v. Georgia,* 31 U.S. 515, 6 Pet. 8 L.Ed, 483 (1831).

16. Scheirbeck, H., et al. (1976). *Report on Indian education, task force five.* Washington, DC: U.S. Government Printing Office, p. 26.

17. Teller, H. M. (1883). Annual report of the secretary of the interior. *House Executive Document,* no.1, 48th Congress, 1st Session, serial 2190, pp. x–xii.

18. *Ex parte Crow Dog.* Supreme Court of the United States. 1883. 109 U.S. 556, 3 S.Ct. 396, 27 L.Ed. 1030; Harring, S. L. (1994). *Crow Dog's case: American Indian sovereignty, tribal law, and United States law in the 19th century.* New York: Cambridge University Press; *Major Crimes Act.* U.S. Statutes at Large, 23L: 385. 18 U.S.C.: 1153, 1885.

19. Section 175. United States Attorneys to Represent Indians (March 3, 1893). (1963). *United States code annotated, title 25—Indians.* St. Paul, MN: West Publishing Company, pp. 135–137.

20. Getches, D. H., Wilkinson, C. F., & Williams, R. A., Jr. Section 185. Protection of Indians Desiring Civilized Life. (1963). *United States code annotated, title 25—Indians.* St. Paul, MN: West Publishing Company, pp. 135–137.

21. Washburn, W. E. (1975). *The assault on Indian tribalism: The general allotment law (Dawes Act) of 1887.* Philadelphia, PA: J.B. Lippincott Company; *General Allotment Act (Dawes Act).* U.S. Statutes at Large, 24: 388–391. February 8, 1887.

22. *Indian Reorganization Act (Wheeler-Howard Act).* U.S. Statutes at Large, 48: 984–988. June 18, 1934.

23. Wilkinson, C. F., & Biggs, E. R. (1977). The evolution of the termination policy. *American Indian Law Review, 139,* 151–154.

24. Fixico, D. L. (1986). The relocation program and urbanization (Ch. 7). In *Termination and relocation: Federal Indian policy, 1945–1960* (pp. 134–157). Albuquerque, NM: University of New Mexico Press.

25. *Titles II–VII of the Civil Rights Act of 1968.* U.S. Statutes at Large, 82: 77–81.

26. French, L. A. (2016). *Policing American Indians: A unique chapter in American jurisprudence.* Boca Raton, FL: CRC/Taylor & Francis.

27. *Ibid.*

17

SOCIAL JUSTICE AND SECURITY CRISIS IN MEXICO

Elena Azaola

What Is Social Justice?

The United Nations General Assembly, during its 62nd session, approved February 20 to be "World Day of Social Justice." According to this resolution,

> social development and social justice are indispensable for the achievement and maintenance of peace and security within and among nations and that, in turn, social development and social justice cannot be attained in the absence of peace and security or in the absence of respect for all human rights and fundamental freedoms.[1]

Also, President Barack Obama stated in his final speech to the United Nations General Assembly in September 2016, "A world in which one percent of humanity controls as much wealth as the other 99 percent will never be stable."[2]

Social Justice in Mexico

Regarding the number of inhabitants, Mexico is 11th place in the world with a population of 126 million in 2016.[3] Even though Mexico has the 14th-largest economy in the world, it ranks in 71st position in the Human Development Index.[4]

More than half of its population, 54%, remains in a poverty situation despite Mexico having the second largest economy in Ibero-America. [A term that refers to those countries in America whose official language is Spanish.] Likewise, it is among the 25 countries with the highest levels of inequality.[5]

Most recent socioeconomic studies indicate that in recent decades, Mexico has experienced a growth in extreme inequality, while the economy has stagnated. Economic growth is meager, average wages do not grow, and poverty persists, but the fortunes of a few people continues to expand. In fact, while the GDP per capita grows at less than 1% annually, the fortune of the 16 wealthiest Mexicans has multiplied by five.[6]

In the Standardized World Income Inequality Database, with data between 2008 and 2012, Mexico has a Gini coefficient of 0.441,[7] while the world average is 0.373. Thus, it ranks 87th of 113 countries due to its inequality in income. In fact, Mexico is the country in the sample in which the wealthiest 1% has a higher percentage of the country's total income, 21%, while the average in other countries fluctuates around 10%.[8]

Productive employment and decent work are the key elements to achieve fair globalization and poverty reduction. Thus, they have become universal goals integrated in the most important declarations of human rights, among them are the 2011 Conference on Sustainable Development and the 2030 Agenda for Sustainable Development of the United Nations.[9]

"Decent work implies that all people have opportunities to perform a productive activity that provides a fair income, safety in the place of work and social protection for families; that offers better personal development perspectives and favors social integration."[10] However, in Mexico, the labor informality rate is 57.4%. This means that more than half of the working population works on their own or in unregistered small businesses, so they do not have social security. Regarding work hours, 28.4% of the occupied population works more than 48 hours a week, which is the maximum legal working time.[11]

Regarding income, it is important to point out that only 4.5% of working women and 7% of working men earn more than five times the minimum wage; that is, more than 20 dollars per day at the current exchange rate during the first semester of 2017.[12] It is also important to consider that almost half of these people who work, 47%, earn an income of less than 250 U.S. dollars per month (5,000 Mexican pesos). That is why, according to the Institute for Industrial Development and Economic Growth: "Job insecurity is a structural problem of the Mexican economy; probably, the most serious one."[13] This is shown in the fact that 62.5% of the working population does not have access to health institutions as part of their fringe benefits.[14]

Even though, according to *The Economist*, Mexico is one of the four countries with the lowest unemployment rate (4%), the creation of formal jobs continues to be insufficient; but, above all, the number of formally employed people with a pay higher than five times the minimum wage has systematically decreased since 2006. This means that only 5% of employed people earned, in the first quarter of 2017, more than five times the minimum wage, which is equivalent to 12 thousand pesos a month (about 632 U.S. dollars), while a decade before the percentage was twice as high.[15]

On the other hand, one of the aspects of inequality that is of great concern in Mexico and in other countries is the lack of opportunities for development faced by young people. The exclusion consists of a series of socioeconomic and political processes that are linked to full citizenship, in such a way that excluded groups do not enjoy their fundamental rights and freedoms. This is stated in a recent study titled *Save the Children*, which describes Mexican adolescents as an excluded group that is not benefiting from development progress, "and, on the contrary, the toxic combination of poverty and discrimination is taking them to make a series of decisions that negatively affect their present and future development opportunities, as well as their full exercise of their rights." This exclusion is preventing millions of teenagers from having access to health care, education, employment, and the protection they need (Save the Children 2016). For example, 65% of teenagers do not have social protection and 20% do not have access to healthcare services.[16]

Regarding education, according to the Mexicanos Primero organization, of every100 children that enroll in elementary school, 76 go to junior high school, 48 continue to senior high school, and 21 go to college, although only 13 of them will get a degree. Of the total number of adolescents in Mexico, only 54% are enrolled in the educational system, which accounts for the lowest average among the OECD countries (Organization for Economic Cooperation and Development).[17]

To this perspective, we should add that, according to the 2010 INEGI (Instituto Nacional de Estadística y Geografía)[18] *Encuesta sobre Juventud* (Survey on Youth), 25% of young people from 15 to 19 do not study or work, while the average in the OECD countries is 16%.[19] Additionally, we must consider that almost 3 million children and adolescents between ages 5 and 17 work, which accounts for 9% of the total population of that age.[20]

Another study carried out in several Mexican cities explains that young people lack incentives to continue studying, because they do not find opportunities for qualified employment. Job insecurity in the formal sector discourages people from seeking jobs there. Thus, the study states that young people decide to migrate or carry out informal or criminal activities. New generations do not focus their personal development anymore in obtaining a degree, getting a formal job, obtaining the benefits from social security, or forming a family.[21]

Furthermore, the Save the Children study published in 2016 in regard to the conditions faced by adolescents concludes that dropping out, unsuitable jobs, the lack and low quality of basic services, the lack of social protection, teenage pregnancy, and the reproduction of the cycle of poverty are only some of the impacts that affect adolescents throughout their lives and affect even more those who, because of their ethnic, gender, and/or exclusion characteristics, suffer more risks of falling in or perpetuating these conditions. It is clear, according to the same source, that these conditions are destructive and undermine trust, social cohesion, economic growth, and peace.[22]

Something similar was already stated years earlier in the *World Report on Violence*, where it was noted that there is a clear correlation between violence and inequality and not between violence and poverty. It also noted that the most egalitarian countries have lower violence rates.[23] In the same way, a report about Mexico from the United Nations Development Program stated that being poor in an evenly poor society is different from being poor in dual societies, where standards of living such as those of Geneva and Burundi coexist at the same time. The tension that is generated in the latter societies is very high and produces a feeling that there is no "fair play." This has an impact on the trust that people have in institutions. Great inequalities destroy social capital; they create distrust, cynicism, lack of interest in associativity, and apathy. In turn, the lack of trust undermines legitimacy and reduces democratic governability margins. Hence, this international organization recommended the creation of conditions for society to be convinced of living in a "fair play" framework.[24]

In the same sense, for the Inter-American Commission on Human Rights (IACHR), there is no doubt that socioeconomic factors have significantly influenced the high levels of violence that Mexico experiences today. The IACHR mentions the following factors, among others: "social exclusion and inequality, poverty, stigmatization and stereotypes, unemployment (especially among young people), low wages, discrimination, forced migration, low levels of education, poor housing conditions, insufficient health care services, easy access to weapons and impunity, among others."[25] In the following paragraphs, we will analyze the security crisis and the serious violations to human rights that Mexico faces today.

Security Crisis

As is well known, over the past decade (2008–2017) Mexico has been facing a serious security crisis. In this section, we will analyze some of the factors that have contributed to this escalation of crime and violence, and we will provide some data that will allow us to measure the severity of this crisis.

According to the *World Report on Violence*, no factor can explain why some individuals act violently towards others or why violence is more prevalent in some communities than in others. "Violence is the reciprocal and complex action of individual, related, social, cultural and environmental factors."[26]

One of the factors to consider in the security crisis and the high levels of violence is that Mexico shares a border with the United States, a country that spends around 130 billion U.S. dollars a year in illegal drug use. "With these resources, transnational organized crime has a huge capacity of spreading violence and corruption."[27]

In the opinion of Fernando Escalante, Mexico should review its commitment with the United States regarding the interdiction policy in drug production, traffic, and trade, above all, knowing that this policy has failed around the world and that Mexico should deem its high cost as unpayable. In the words of this specialist, "we have paid the 'good neighborliness' that no longer exists with the blood of 200 thousand Mexicans."[28]

Mexico is also a country of origin, transit, destination, and return of migrants. The migration corridor between Mexico and the United States has the highest flow in the world. Likewise, 70% of the weapons that illegally enter Mexico come from the United States.[29]

The *Armed Conflict Survey 2017* report, recently published by the Institute for Strategic Studies of the United Kingdom, stated that, after Syria, Mexico was the most violent country on the planet in 2016. It stated that the conflict in Mexico produced 23,000 violent deaths in 2016, a figure that was exceeded only by the 50,000 deaths produced by the conflict in Syria. One of the experts that wrote the report, Antonio Sampaio, explained that one of the main causes for this increase in violence is associated with the adoption of military tactics on behalf of some of the drug cartels. "On the one hand, we are seeing a militarization of the drug cartels' strategy, and on the other hand, many of the interventions of police and military forces end in shootings and violent clashes. We are before a very violent situation; before a high intensity conflict."[30]

In a similar way, the Institute for Economics and Peace points out that, of the 163 countries that were measured, Mexico ranks in the 140th position in the 2016 Global Peace Index. Among the factors that this index measures are internal and international conflicts, inequality, trust in authorities, corruption, gender equality, access to education and health care, number of refugees and displaced people due to violence, militarization, and police presence. In fact, Mexico fell back 47 positions since 2008, when it ranked in place 93. The total impact of violence in the country totaled almost 273 billion U.S. dollars, equivalent to 14% of the GDP.[31]

The security crisis experienced by Mexico has had, above all, a very high and deplorable cost with the loss, in round numbers, of a little more than 200,000 human lives.[32] Likewise, the crime rate and the proportion of people who have been victims of crime has increased. However, the percentage of crimes that are sanctioned has decreased. The trust index in authorities and law enforcement institutions has also decreased. Although it would be difficult to trace a cause/effect ratio, this increment in violence and insecurity took place in parallel with the decision of the Mexican government to launch a "war against drugs." Unfortunately, this war has not been able to deter the advancement of crime; instead, it has brought about another crisis that is also very severe—the increase of serious violations to human rights.[33]

Despite this coincidence between the increase of violence and the "war against drugs" policy, the four components of the security crisis we are referring to had been present for a long time. These components are (1) the existence of criminal groups with the capability of representing a threat to the state; (2) the fragility or incompetence of state institutions to contain them; (3) social decomposition that is evident in the growing number of people capable of committing crimes; and (4) the lack of efficient controls to stop abuse and violation of rights on behalf of state institutions. These components represent the existence of social, economic, political, and cultural processes that have been developing for decades with the deplorable results we now know. From this perspective, the war started by President Felipe Calderon's administration (2006–2012) against drug trafficking would have been only one of the triggering factors that brought about the emergence of a crisis, which had been brewing for a very long.[34]

Among the contributing factors to this crisis is not being able to overcome the historic weakness and incompetence of law enforcement institutions. That is, these institutions were not able to prevent, address, and sanction the different forms of violence that were ignored and tolerated, and since they were not being taken care of and did not receive the response required in the moment, today we must face their accumulated effects. These effects are evident in the spiral of violence, which is difficult to contain and whose repercussions we will suffer for many years. Behind the current levels of uncontrollable violence, we find longstanding social, economic, and political processes that incubated the seeds of violence in an imperceptible but sound way.

As Carlos Pascual, former U.S. ambassador to Mexico, said very well, "Security cannot be an end in itself, but rather, a condition to allow communities achieve normality and prosperity." Security programs should be made up of social and economic programs, and success should be measured with social indicators, besides the reduction of violence and crime.[35]

I agree with the approach of the former ambassador, although, unfortunately, the policy maintained by the Mexican government during the last decade has been that of favoring the use of force, especially military force, to confront organized crime, instead of bringing those responsible to justice. According to specialists in security topics, "the deployment of military troops and Federal Police continues being the core component of interventions in all the states that face severe challenges regarding security."[36]

However, other studies point out that the quality of good governance conditions in a country, regarding the legal framework and the policies that offer social protection, are a determining factor of levels of violence. Particularly, the degree to which society enforces existing laws on violence when detaining and charging criminals can work as a deterrent factor against violence.[37]

Meanwhile, Carlos Flores explains that the monopoly of violence on behalf of the state only becomes tolerable when it gives a clear sign of protecting at least one basic threshold of public interest. In his opinion, which I share, the violence that is seen in Mexico "is not but the most severe consequence of a deeper problem: the structural dysfunctionality of a State in which its essential functioning premises and mechanisms are deprived of basic contents of public interest."[38]

Regarding statistics related to homicides, the main indicator of violence, M. Molloy, from New Mexico State University, indicates that according to official figures between 2008 and 2016, there has been a total, in round numbers, of 200,000 homicides in Mexico. In his opinion, this high number of homicides is the result of the "war against drugs" ordered by President Calderón, even though during this period no U.S. agency has pointed out that the quantity of drugs available in the market has dropped or that their price had increased because of a lower flow of these substances. If these were the stated objectives of the "war against drugs," Molloy wonders, what has been the point of all these deaths?[39]

In Table 17.1, Molloy shows that homicides had a 63% increase between 2008 and 2016, which can largely be attributed to the "war against drugs."

Another researcher, Laura Atuesta, states, "the battle against organized crime is not feasible, nor produces positive results if it is not accompanied by a change in drug policies that reduces market profitability." The author maintains that militarization regarding public security, accompanied by the prohibition of illegal drugs, has produced unexpected results and has not met its proposed objectives. In fact, she says, "this combination generates the perfect situation for organized crime to grow, evolve and be very difficult to control."[40]

Even though there are no official figures, it is estimated (from information provided by press releases, for example) that approximately half of the homicides during 2008–2016 took place in the

Table 17.1 Homicides in Mexico, 2008–2016

Year	Number of homicides
2008	14,006
2009	19,803
2010	25,757
2011	27,213
2012	25,967
2013	23,063
2014	20,010
2015	20,525
2016	22,935
Total	199,279

(INEGI, Estadísticas de Mortalidad (Mortality Statistics) 2008–2016.

context of the so-called war against drug trafficking, whether because of the action of the authorities against supposed criminal groups or because of confrontations between alleged members of these groups.[41] Nevertheless, since force was used many times before investigating, it is difficult to say how many people among those who died were really involved in criminal activities and how many were victims of circumstance. Furthermore, most of the homicides have not been investigated and remain unpunished. According to the Mexico Peace Index, 90% of homicides committed in the country in recent years have remained unpunished.[42]

This is especially worrying, since impunity constitutes another factor that contributes to the escalation of violence, without ignoring, of course, the situation of hundreds of thousands of indirect victims who have seen their rights denied regarding truth, justice, and damage repair.[43]

Although considerable resources have been invested to increase the state of force and strengthen law enforcement agencies, this has not translated into more efficiency to contain the insecurity crisis and the violence that affect the country. An important factor has been the inability to deeply transform police institutions that suffer multiple deficiencies, among which we can highlight the limited autonomy of current authorities and their being more focused on serving the authorities instead of protecting citizens and their rights. Almost all the two thousand law enforcement institutions in the country have elements with very low levels of schooling and professionalization, low wages, little capability for controlling their officers, unclear or nonapplicable standards, and high levels of uncertainty, suffering abuse from their superiors and from corruption. Thus, it is not strange that police officers have very low levels of trust from citizens, since, as reported in different surveys, 90% of Mexicans consider police institutions to be corrupt.[44]

The first obstacle is that most of the crimes are not reported to authorities. According to the results of surveys on victimization, the percentage of crimes that are not reported have increased every year, representing 94% of committed crimes. That is, 9 out of every 10 crimes are not reported to the authorities, which, according to the National Survey on Victimization and Perception of Public Security, is mainly because victims see it as a waste of time and that they do not trust prosecuting attorneys.[45]

To place this percentage of not reporting within an international context, we would have to consider that, in 2013, according to official data of each country, 46% of the crimes in the United States were reported, in England, 41%, and in Chile, 44%, which allows us to put in perspective the data shown by surveys in Mexico, which is twice those figures.[46]

That said, of the crimes that are indeed reported, only a small percentage (6%) are investigated and another even smaller percentage (2%) are sanctioned.[47] We must add that the perception of insecurity of the 18-year-old or older population in 2016 was 72%. This means that, in average, 7 out of every 10 citizens do not feel safe in Mexico, regardless of the location they live in (INEGI 2016).

Other Mexico Peace Index data point out that crimes from organized crime groups (extortion, kidnapping, and drug-related crimes) increased 73% during the 2003–2013 period, while arms trafficking tripled, and 90% of extortions were not reported.[48]

Because of the insecurity described here, it follows that, at the end of President Calderón's administration, 55% of the population considered his security strategy to be a failure. At the beginning of his administration, 84% of the population thought that using the Army to fight against organized crime was adequate, but at the end, only 69% continued thinking this way; 54% thought that the war against drug trafficking was won by organized crime, and only 18% thought that the government had won.[49]

As we will see in the next section, the decision to employ the Army for public security, which is not part of their duties according to Mexico's Political Constitution, has had a strong impact on the increase and severity of violations to human rights during 2008–2016. In 2007, 45,000 members of the Army performed public security tasks, but in 2016, more than 100,000 military troops were deployed throughout the country to carry out these tasks.[50] We can add that between 2012 and 2015, the Army reported that they detained 17,000 people, even though this task is not part of their duties.[51]

Severe Violations to Human Rights

According to the Political Constitution of the United Mexican States, Mexico is a representative, democratic, and federal republic formed by 31 states and Mexico City. Since 2011, the Constitution raised all human rights norms contained in the treaties signed by the Mexican state to constitutional hierarchy. Likewise, Mexico has one of the most comprehensive public systems for the protection of human rights, formed by the National Commission on Human Rights, 31 state commissions, and one commission for Mexico City. Despite the broad coverage of this system, during the period of the so-called war against drugs the violations to human rights have increased significantly. This "war" has also had an important impact on international organizations, such as the Inter-American Commission of Human Rights, which has received more complaints from Mexico during the last decade than from any other country on the American continent.

Other international organizations have also made similar claims. So, for example, upon ending his visit to Mexico in October 2015, United Nations High Commissioner for Human Rights Zeid Ra'ad Al Hussein stated, "there is a wide national, regional and international consensus about the severity of the human rights situation in Mexico." He added that the case of the 43 missing students of the Rural Teachers' College of Ayotzinapa, "is a microcosm of chronic problems that lie beneath the relentless wave of violations to human rights that is happening throughout Mexico."[52]

Similarly, Special Rapporteur on extrajudicial, summary or arbitrary executions Christof Heyns, in the report about his visit to Mexico in 2013, pointed out, "the right to live is violated at intolerable degrees in Mexico and the change of government discourse in the current Administration in the sense of speaking less about violence, does not change this reality." He made an appeal for "public security tasks to be carried out by civil authorities that have clear guidelines about the use of force." He also recommended "to take all the necessary measures to prevent authorities from altering crime scenes and guarantee that the authorities who obstruct investigations be accountable for that."[53]

Also, the U.S. Department of State report of June 2015 warned, "in Mexico, critical problems continue in regard to human rights in which security officers are involved, including the police and the army." Among the most serious abuses highlighted were extrajudicial killings, torture, and forced disappearance. The report added, "impunity in violations on Human Rights continues being a problem throughout the country with extremely low or non-existent rates of indictments for all types of crimes."[54]

Some reports, such as the one issued by Open Society, have argued that extrajudicial killings, forced disappearances, and torture do not constitute isolated practices of law enforcement authorities in Mexico, but rather, they constitute an indiscriminate pattern of the use of force and, thus, can be categorized as crimes against humanity. When referring to this report, a *New York Times* article pointed out,

> They are killed at military checkpoints, vanished inside navy facilities or are tortured by federal police officers. Seldom are their cases investigated. A trial and conviction are even more rare. But are these cases just regrettable accidents during a decade-long government battle against drug violence? A new report by the Open Society Justice Initiative, *Undeniable Atrocities*, argues that they are not. Instead, the study says, they point to a pattern of indiscriminate force and impunity that is in an integral part of the state's policy. And, in the framework of international law, the study argues, the killings, forced disappearances and torture constitute crimes against humanity.[55]

Regarding the crime of torture, a frequent practice in Mexico, the report of the Inter-American Commission of Human Rights, titled *Situation of Human Rights in Mexico*, states that the General Attorney's Office (PGR, in Spanish) reported that in 2015, there were 2,420 investigations being processed for torture, while they only had 15 convictions for this same type of crime. The Commission adds that, even in an investigation so relevant and subjected to domestic and international public scrutiny, such as the case of the 43 missing students in Ayotzinapa, 77% of the people detained because of this crime said they had been tortured.[56] Likewise, there was no guilty verdict for the forced disappearance crime.[57]

Due to continuous finger pointing from both domestic and international organizations concerning the improper participation of the Army in public security tasks, the Armed Forces have exerted strong pressure for the constitutional framework to be modified and for them to be allowed to work with full legal support, which they have been doing *de facto* during recent years. However, in the opinion of the Belisario Dominguez Institute of the Mexican Senate,

> Increasing the attributions of Armed Forces to address security matters means give legal support to actions that, *de facto*, happen every day throughout national territory. But this option would maintain the problems that we now suffer, such as high levels of violence and impunity, lack of capability of Police force and civil authorities, little or no information for decision-making, and occurrence of serious damage to human rights.[58]

In the same sense, the nongovernmental organization WOLA (Washington Office on Latin America) commented in a report issued regarding the Bill on Homeland Security in Mexico.[59] In this report they stated that, according to the information provided by the Mexican Army in October 2016, soldiers were participating in operations to fight against crime in 23 of the 31 states of the Mexican Republic. They emphasized that the Bill on Homeland Security discussed in the Mexican Congress is looking to increase and standardize military presence, even though, after more than a decade, the military presence has not been able to reduce violence nor organized crime. In the opinion of WOLA, the discussion of this congressional act should consider the costs that the participation of the Army in public security activities has had in human rights. "Some crimes and violations to human rights committed by soldiers have been investigated and sanctioned; however, compared to the seriousness of the crimes and the results limited to criminal investigations, these steps forward are not enough," as shown in the Table 17.2.[60]

Based on the previous data, the WOLA report concluded, "the investigations of the PGR on crimes committed by soldiers are slow, bureaucratic and not very transparent." It also states, "The investigation and prosecution of crimes in Mexico is highly politicized" and "Mexico urgently needs a functional penal justice system, able to prosecute a soldier involved in crimes and violations on human rights."[61]

In the same way, both Special Rapporteur on extrajudicial, summary or arbitrary executions Christoph Heyns and High Commissioner for Human Rights Zeid Ra'ad Hussein have recommended to Mexico to change from a military-type security model to a citizen-type security model, through the gradual withdrawal of Armed Forces from tasks that are not part of their nature.[62]

Table 17.2 Violations to Human Rights Committed by Members of Armed Forces Between January 2012 and August 2016

Complaints before human rights organizations	Investigations	Ongoing trials	Results
Complaints due to violations to human rights recorded by the National Commission of Human Rights (CNDH, in Spanish)	Preliminary investigations started by the General Attorney's Office (PGR) due to violations to human rights	Criminal cases in federal courts	Final judgments
5,541	284	357	29

[*Source*: Washington Office on Latin America (WOLA), based on requests to access data to the National Commission on Human Rights and the General Attorney's Office (PGR, in Spanish).]

Another one of the most critical problems of violations to human rights during the period we have been referring to is the large number of people that have been reported as missing. As of March 1, 2017, there were 30,942 recorded cases of missing people.[63]

Just as critical and worrisome is the finding of many clandestine graves with bodies that have not been identified. According to the Special Report of the National Commission of Human Rights about Missing People and Clandestine Graves in Mexico, between 2007 and 2016, 855 illegal graves have been officially reported with a total of 1,548 bodies. However, according to the Commission, when comparing this information with what has been revealed by organizations of civil society, as well as by the mass media, a total of 1,143 graves with 3,230 bodies have been reported. Most human remains found have not been identified, while more than 30,000 people remain reported as missing.[64]

Another one of the most frequent violations is that of arbitrary detentions. According to the CNDH, during 2004–2014, they received a total of 58,381 complaints due to arbitrary detentions, of which 17,000 also included arguments about torture and mistreatments.[65]

Despite the panorama of critical violations to human rights mentioned, perhaps the most critical and frequent violations are the absence of law enforcement authorities and, when present, their lack of performing in an efficient, competent, and egalitarian way, respecting the laws and human rights. This is stated in a report that the General Attorney's Office recently sent to the Senate, in which it points out that it faces problems of corruption, backlog, and hiring personnel without following the established procedures: "Some of the most frequent irregular behaviors are, among others: extortions, foot-dragging, abuse of authority, illegal retentions and searches, lack of diligence and unduly integrations of preliminary investigations." The report states that, between 2015 and 2016, the institution received 3,165 complaints and reports against its public servants, due to alleged irregularities. Regarding efficiency levels, between 2014 and 2016, the institution opened more than 63,000 investigation files, of which 41,000 are pending determination. Also, according to the National Survey on Victimization and Perception of Political Security of 2016, 59% of the population said that it considered the PGR to be a corrupt institution.[66]

Since 2008, Mexico began the transformation of its criminal justice system, from the inquisitorial type to a new adversarial system. The transition from one system to the other should have been completed in 2016, but, to date, it is operating with many deficiencies. Among the deficiencies that a recent study considered to be the most important ones are (a) insufficient training for operators; (b) lack of a career civil service; (c) nonexistence of database and management models; (d) lack of assessments and measurements for system implementation; (e) use of an improvised IT system or without interconnectivity; (f) considerable backlog in the cases being processed or pending determination; (g) important deficiencies in public defender's offices; (h) deficit of 83% of legal advisors that are required; and (i) lack of performance follow-up and evaluation.[67]

Regarding the principle of equality before the law, there are also important deficiencies. One well-known specialist that has contributed to the reform of the criminal justice system, Ana Laura Magaloni, recently pointed out,

> One of the core elements for the lack of a rule of law in Mexico is the differentiated legal treatment based on the financial capacity and power of the people. The Law is not the same for all people; it compels and protects us in different ways, and that depends on who you are, who you know and how much money you have.

In real life, says the specialist, the Judiciary Council can influence the sentences given by judges.

> Thanks to this control, in some cases that have a significant economic value or that affect an *important* person, the meaning of the judgment can be agreed upon at the head of the Council. The judge follows these instructions, because his/her permanence or promotion in the Judicial Power depends on it.[68]

Another specialist, Ricardo Raphael, gave his opinion in the same sense,

> The Judicial Power in Mexico is subjected. The governors of each state appoint the judges and thus obtain unexpected loyalty from those who enforce the Law. The independence of this Power does not exist and politics is more relevant than the Law in Mexico. The control mechanism is easy. The governor appoints the president of the Superior Court of Justice and this person, in turn, appoints the judges through their respective Judiciary Council. If the judge shows insubordinate behavior, he/she will be removed as punishment for not obeying. The political control on judges continues operating thanks to the power of appointment: the person who appoints, rules.[69]

Other specialists have also stressed that the operators of the new penal justice system have not been duly trained, so they do not have the elements to allow them to meet the standards required by this system. In this sense, Alberto Olvera points out,

> In regard to the implementation of the criminal procedure reform, we note that the country experiments a legal and institutional simulation at great scale, that in practice, it has hindered the access to justice even more, instead of facilitating it. Both, the police departments, as well as public prosecutors prefer to prevent the investigation files of the new system to be opened, because they know that the technical demands of the reform exceed their actual capabilities, due to lack of training, equipment, personnel and moral leadership. . . . The Supreme Courts of Justice of the country largely lack the political autonomy and moral authority to comply with their roles.[70]

An additional problem for the judicial system to work properly is that the high level of corruption has not diminished and, in some cases, has increased. This is shown in the Corruption Perception Index published by Transparency International, which states that, during 2016, Mexico fell back 28 places from position 95 to 123, among a total of 176 countries.[71]

To conclude with this brief overview about the human rights situation in Mexico, we would like to do it by asking the questions that Jan Jarab, United Nations High Commissioner for Human Rights in Mexico recently asked: "Why does such a fascinating country, with so much cultural wealth and so much intellectual potential, fail so much regarding law enforcement? Why do tortured victims remain imprisoned and not the torturers? How can people live with an impunity rate so high?"[72] I would like to be able to offer some answers to these questions; unfortunately, I do not have them.

Conclusions

In this chapter, I have tried to show that the security crisis that Mexico faces today cannot be seen separately from the significant gaps that the country faces regarding social justice and that places it as one of the most unequal countries in the world. The data presented allow us to conclude that the high levels of violence suffered today in Mexico cannot be attributed solely to the activities of and confrontations among criminal groups; they are also the responsibility of the institutions and government policies that have tried to contain them without offering in-depth solutions to these long-term problems. At the same time, policies implemented to face crime have exceeded the limits imposed by legality, causing a severe crisis of human rights violations.

In summary, the balance between violence caused by crime and that caused by the policies that have unsuccessfully tried to contain violent crime, is critical, because of the number and type of harm and damages, most of the time irreparable, that the direct and indirect victims have suffered. The harm suffered by orphans, widows, and other relatives and close friends has only started to be made visible, while the answers that the victims have received from the state have been insufficient, inappropriate, and nonexistent or have caused them new harm. The consequences of this harm will be felt in society for many more years.

Discussion Questions

1. What aspects of inequality are of the greatest concern to Mexico?
2. What steps should the Mexican government take to reduce social inequities in Mexico?
3. What are problems attributed to Mexico's social inequalities?
4. What steps can the Mexican government take to increase crime reporting by its citizens?
5. What role does job insecurity play in creating an element of discouragement to Mexican citizens?

Notes

1. *World day of social justice: Resolution approved by the United Nations general assembly on November 26, 2007.* Retrieved February 14, 2017, from www.un.org/es/comun/docs/?symbol-A/RES/62/10
2. OXFAM. (2017). *Pobreza y desigualdad en México.* México: OXFAM. Retrieved from www.oxfammexico.org/wp-content/uploads/2017/01/bp-economy-for-99-percent-160117-es.pdf
3. Economic Commission for Latin America and Caribbean. (2016). *Statistical yearbook for Latin America and Caribbean 2016.* (LC/PUB.2017/2-P). Santiago Chile: United Nations ECLAC.
4. Acción Ciudadana Frente a la Pobreza. (2016). (Actions of citizens facing poverty) *Frente a la Pobreza y Desigualdad: Cohesión social. (Facing poverty and inequality: Social cohesion).* Retrieved February 16, 2017, from https://drive.google.com/file/d/0B5IhPrkcK1w9ZHBTSUpSNzIta00/view
5. TeleSur. (2016, August 1). *México: entre la pobreza y la desigualdad. (Mexico between poverty and inequality).* Retrieved February 14, 2017, from www.telesurtv.net/telesuragenda/Pobreza-en-Mexico-20160801-0040.html
6. Esquivel, G. (2015). *Desigualdad Extrema en México. Concentración del Poder Económico y Político*, p. 6. OXFAM. Retrieved from www.cambialasreglas.org/pdf/desigualdadextrema_informe.pdf.
7. The Gini coefficient is a measure of inequality of a distribution. It is defined as a ratio with values between 0 and 1. The numerator is the area between the Lorenz curve of the distribution and the uniform distribution line. The denominator is the area under the uniform distribution line.
8. Esquivel, 2015, pp. 12, 15.
9. Organización de las Naciones Unidas. *Objetivos del desarrollo sostenible.* (United Nations Organization). *Objectives of Sustainable Development.* Retrieved February 16, 2017, from www.un.org/sustainabledevelopment/es/objetivos-de-desarrollo-sostenible/
10. Instituto Nacional de Estadística, Geografía e Informática, INEGI. (2017a, febrero 17). *Estadísticas a propósito del Día Mundial de la Justicia Social. Boletín Informativo.* Ciudad de México: INEGI.
11. *Ibid.*, pp. 3–5.
12. *Ibid.*, p. 7.
13. Migueles, R. (2017, February 15). 24 millones de mexicanos, con salario menor a 5 mil pesos al mes. (Twenty four million Mexicans with wages under five thousand pesos a month). *El Universal*, B1.
14. Instituto Nacional de Estadística, Geografía e Informática, INEGI, 2017a, febrero 17, p. 8.
15. INEGI. (2017, Primer Trimestre). *Encuesta Nacional de Ocupación y Empleo.* (*National survey on occupation and employment*). Retrieved from www.beta.inegi.org.mx/proyectos/enchogares/regulares/enoe/; Migueles, R. (2017, May 17). Se achica cifra de trabajadores con salarios elevados. (Number of workers with high wages is getting smaller). *El Universal*, B1.
16. UNICEF—CONEVAL. (2016). *Análisis sobre pobreza y derechos sociales de niñas, niños y adolescentes en México.* Ciudad de México: UNICEF-CONEVAL.
17. Save the Children. (2016). *Las y los adolescentes que México ha olvidado.* Retrieved from www.savethechildren.mx/sites/savethechildren.mx/files/resources/Las%20y%20los%20%20adolescentes%20que%20Mexico%20ha%20olvidado_0.pdf
18. National Institute of Statistics and Geography (INEGI) by its name in Spanish, Instituto Nacional de Estadística y Geografía).
19. INEGI. (2011). *Encuesta Nacional de Juventud. (National youth survey).* Retrieved from www.imjuventud.gob.mx/imgs/uploads/Encuesta_Nacional_de_Juventud_2010_Resultados_Generales_18nov11.pdf

20. Instituto Nacional de Estadística, Geografía e Informática, INEGI. (2017b). *Encuesta Nacional de Ocupación y Empleo 2016*. Ciudad de México: INEGI.

21. CNPEVM. (2010). *Primeras conclusiones de los diagnósticos sobre las causas económicas, sociales y culturales de la violencia social y de género en seis ciudades mexicanas*. Ciudad de México: Comisión Nacional para Prevenir y Erradicar la Violencia Contra las Mujeres, pp. 9–10.

22. Sobre las condiciones que enfrenta la adolescencia en México, puede consultarse: Azaola, E. (2017). *Informe Especial. Adolescencia: Vulnerabilidad y Violencia*. Ciudad de México: Comisión Nacional de Derechos Humanos. (About the conditions that adolescents face in Mexico), you can consult: Azaola, E. (2017). *Special report: Adolescence: Vulnerability and violence*. Mexico City: National Commission of Human Rights. Retrieved February 16, 2017, from www.cndh.org.mx/search/file/informes%20especial%20adolescentes%20vulnerabilidad%20 y%20violencia

23. Organización Panamericana de la Salud, OPS. (2003). *Informe mundial sobre la violencia y la salud*. Washington, DC: OPS, p. 40.

24. PNUD. (2007). *Informe sobre derechos Humanos. México 2006–2007: Migración y desarrollo humano*. Ciudad de México: PNUD-México.

25. Comisión Interamericana de Derechos Humanos, CIDH. (2016). *Violencia, Inseguridad y Desapariciones en México. Situación de los Derechos Humanos en México*. Retrieved from www.oas.org/es/cidh/multimedia/2016/ mexico/mexico.html, p. 43.

26. Organización Panamericana de la Salud, OPS, 2003, p. 13.

27. Comisión Interamericana de Derechos Humanos, CIDH, 2016, p. 33.

28. Escalante, F. (2017, marzo). Apuntes para lidiar con Washington. *Revista Nexos*, *471*, 14–18.

29. Comisión Interamericana de Derechos Humanos, CIDH, 2016, pp. 45–46. Retrieved from www.oas.org/es/ cidh/multimedia/2016/mexico/mexico.html

30. Institute for Strategic Studies of the United Kingdom. (2017). *Armed Conflict Survey 2017* report. Retrieved May 9, 2017, from www.iiss.org/en/regions/latin-america-and-the-caribbean/mexico-murder-rate-9f41. Also: Bugarín, I. (2017, May 9). México, segundo más violento: Informe. (Mexico, second most violent: Report). *El Universal*, A14.

31. Institute for Economics and Peace, IEP. (2015). *Índice de Paz México 2015*. Ciudad de México: IEP.

32. INEGI. (2016). *Estadísticas de Mortalidad. (Mortality statistics)*. Retrieved January 31, 2016, from www.inegi. org.mx/lib/olap/consulta/general_ver4/MDXQueryDatos.asp?proy=mortgral_dh and Retrieved February 14, 2017, from www3.inegi.org.mx/sistemas/sisept/default.aspx?t=mvio20&s=est&c=22662

33. Azaola, E., & Newham, G. (2017). Violence and criminal justice in Mexico and South Africa. In D. Geldenhuys and H. González (Eds), *Global South powers in transition: A comparative analysis of Mexico and South Africa*. Johannesburg, SA: Unisa Press.

34. *Ibid.*

35. Pascual, C. (2010, noviembre 24). *México en una Encrucijada*. Conferencia impartida por el Embajador de Estados Unidos en México. El Colegio de México. Documento inédito, p. 10.

36. Guerrero, E. (2016, enero). La inseguridad 2013–2015. *Nexos*, 40–52, 50.

37. Organización Panamericana de la Salud, OPS, 2003, p. 41.

38. Flores, C. (2014, enero). Un asunto de impunidad: la colusión entre delincuencia organizada y la política y su efecto en la crisis de violencia en México. In *Gestión y Política Pública. Número Especial sobre Seguridad Pública* (pp. 43–82). Mexico City: CIDE.

39. Carrasco, J. (2017, de marzo 5). 2007–2016. La violencia cobró más de 208 mil vidas. *Proceso*, *2105*, 10–13.

40. Atuesta, L. (2017, marzo). Las cuentas de la militarización. *Revista Nexos*, *471*, 42–46, 46.

41. Las últimas estadísticas oficiales de la llamada Base de Datos de Fallecimientos Ocurridos por Presunta Rivalidad Delincuencial cerraron el 30 de septiembre de 2011 con un total de 47 mil 515 muertos. (The most recent official statistics of the so-called Data Base of Deaths Due to Alleged Criminal Rivalry closed on September 30, 2011 with a total of 47,515 deaths,) *Reforma*, August 15, 2013.

42. IEP, 2015.

43. *Si estimáramos, por ejemplo, que, por cada persona que ha muerto de manera violenta en el país en el periodo 2008–2016, hubiera, por lo menos, 10 personas entre sus familiares y allegados más cercanos que se hubieran visto afectados por dicha muerte, estaríamos hablando de un mínimo de dos millones de víctimas indirectas, 90% de las cuales no han tenido acceso a la justicia.* (If we estimate, for example, that for each person that died violently in the country between 2008 and 2016, there would be at least 10 people among his/her relatives and close friends who would have been affected for said death, we would be talking about a minimum of two million indirect victims, 90% of which have not had access to justice.)

44. IEP, 2015.

45. Instituto Nacional de Estadística, Geografía e Informática, INEGI. (2016). *Encuesta Nacional de Victimización y Percepción sobre Seguridad Pública*. Ciudad de México: INEGI.

46. Gerson, P. (2015, marzo). Impunidad: la desigualdad fundamental en México. *Este País*, *287*, 7–9, 8.

47. Datos reportados en el *Anexo Estadístico del Segundo Informe de Gobierno del Presidente Enrique Peña Nieto*, 2014. (Data reported in the *Statistical Appendix of the Second Presidential Address of President Enrique Peña Nieto*).

48. IEP, 2015.

49. Datos de la Onceava Encuesta Nacional sobre la Percepción de Seguridad Ciudadana, en: *Reforma*. (Data of the 11th National Survey on Security Citizen Perception, in *Reforma*.) (November 22, 2012). Narcotráfico: Fracaso del plan anticrimen. (Drug trafficking: Failure of the plan against crime).

50. Vela, D. S. (2016, December 25). En este sexenio se redujo en 93.6% las deserciones en el Ejército. *El Financiero*, *2*. (During this Administration, the percentage of Army desertion have decreased in 93.6%).

51. CIDH, 2016, p. 35.

52. Garduño, S., y Baptista, D. (2015, October 8). Encuentra intolerante la ONU al Gobierno. (The UN finds the government to be intolerant). *Reforma*, 7.

53. ONU. (2014). *Informe del Relator sobre Ejecuciones Extrajudiciales, Arbitrarias o Sumarias, Christof Heyns. (Report of the special rapporteour on extrajudicial, summary or arbitrary executions, Christof Heyns)*. Retrieved July 8, 2017, from http://hchr.org.mx/images/doc_pub/G1413997.pdf

54. Díaz Briseño, J. (2017, March 4). Exhibe Estados Unidos abusos a los derechos humanos en México (The United States). *Reforma*, *3*.

55. Malkin, E. (2016, June 6). Report accuses Mexico of crimes against humanity in drug war. *The New York Times*. Retrieved July 4, 2017, from www.opensocietyfoundations.org/sites/default/files/undeniable-atrocities-esp-20160602.pdf

56. CIDH, 2016, pp. 13–14.

57. *Ibid.*, p. 48.

58. Instituto Belisario Domínguez. (2017). *Seguridad Interior. Elementos para el Debate*. Boletín del Instituto Belisario Domínguez. Ciudad de México: Senado de la República; *Homeland security: Elements for debate*. Bulletin of the Belisario Domínguez Institute. Mexico City: Mexican Senate.

59. Suárez, X., y Meyer, M. (2017, febrero 8). *La Ley de Seguridad Interior de México: Pasando por Alto los Abusos Militares en Operaciones de Seguridad Pública*. Washington, DC: WOLA. Retrieved from www.wola.org/analysis/mexicos-law-internal-security-turning-blind-eye-military-abuses-public-security-operations/

60. *Ibid.*

61. *Ibid.*

62. Patrón, M. (2016, December 5). Debatir el Modelo de Seguridad. (Debate the security model). *El Universal*, 7.

63. Registro Nacional de Personas Extraviadas o Desaparecidas, RNPED. *(National Registry of Missing or Unidentified Persons). (RNDEP)*. Retrieved July 8, 2017, from http://secretariadoejecutivo.gob.mx/rnped/estadisticas-fuerocomun.php

64. National Human Rights Commission. (2017). *Special Report of the National Commission of Human Rights about Missing People and Clandestine Graves in Mexico*. Retrieved July 2, 2017, from www.cndh.org.mx/sites/all/doc/Informes/Especiales/InformeEspecial_20170406.pdf

65. CIDH, 2016, p. 141.

66. Guerrero, C., y López, M. (2017, February 17). Reconoce PGR malas prácticas. (PGR Recognizes Bad Practices). *El Universal*, 5.

67. Centro de Investigación para el Desarrollo A.C. (CIDAC). (2017). *Hallazgos 2016: Seguimiento y Evaluación de la Operación del Sistema de Justicia Penal en México*. Retrieved from http://cidac.org/wp-content/uploads/2017/06/DOCUMENTO-HALLAZGOS-2016_COMPLETO-digital.pdf

68. Magaloni, A. L. (2017, March 4). ¿Independencia judicial? (Judicial independence?) *Reforma*, 11.

69. Raphael, R. (2017, March 6). No más control sobre los jueces. (No more control over judges). *El Universal*, 12.

70. Olvera, A. (2016, diciembre 20). Palabras ante la XL Sesión Ordinaria del Consejo Nacional de Seguridad Pública, Palacio Nacional. *Documento inédito*, 1–2.

71. Transparency International. (2017). *Corruption perceptions index 2016*. Retrieved July 8, 2017, from www.transparency.org/news/feature/corruption_perceptions_index_2016

72. Jarab, J. (2017, June 13). Normalicemos los derechos, no las injusticias. (Let us normalize rights, not injustices). *El Universal*, A20.

18

PUNISHMENT AND SOCIAL JUSTICE IN SLOVENIA

Benjamin Flander, Gorazd Meško, and Matjaž Ambrož

Introduction

The issue of the social justice of punishment is a complex one. The most fundamental questions that may be posed about this intricate topic are as follows: Can punishment ever be just? Do the state and society hold a legitimate right to react against those violating their legal norms by encroaching upon their personal freedom, property, privacy, dignity, etc., thus causing them pain? Justifying punishment by referring to the need of a society to prevent crime is one thing, while its justification with respect to the punished person is a completely different matter. In fact, one may ask whether it is legitimate to impose the burden of punishment on an individual in order to safeguard social values and achieve the greater good. In general terms, the legitimacy of punishment is justified by claiming that we must accept the burdens imposed on us by society because we all reap the benefits of living in society (Hörnle, 2011). The fact that one holds and invokes certain rights also implies that one has the duty not to violate the rights of another. Therefore, any form of evil caused by an individual who violates fundamental social norms authorizes the community to respond, if they are found guilty, by inflicting evil upon them, without causing any injustice. However, this does not provide an answer as to which punishment is socially just in general and which punishment is considered just in a particular case.

If we rely on the basic (i.e., abolitionist) assumption that the death penalty and corporal punishment are inhumane and therefore unacceptable, we must also consider, at least at the general level, the problem of life imprisonment without parole, which was declared incompatible with the European Convention for the Protection of Human Rights and Fundamental Freedoms by the European Court of Human Rights (for more information, see Cvikl & Ambrož, 2017). About the social justice of punishment in individual cases, we ought to consider whether the penalties applied by society impose a fair and just burden on the individual concerned. The answer to this question is not metaphysical, but a matter of fickle social conventions, where the concepts of proportionality and equal treatment play a crucial role. In fact, punishment is considered socially just when it is proportionate to the committed offense and comparable with sanctions imposed by the courts in similar cases.

However, the issue of social justice with respect to punishment raises numerous other questions. Is it possible for any punishment to be just in an unjust society? Should the courts consider the fact that perpetrators come from socially underprivileged groups when determining the sentence? Is it socially just that the courts impose the same sentence for the same criminal offense regardless of the perpetrator's personal circumstances? How should one adequately evaluate the perpetrator's assets when determining the amount of a fine? Could the fact that most of prison population across the globe is composed of people from the lowest social classes be considered socially just?

In this chapter, we will reflect upon penal and prison policy in Slovenia by applying a common understanding of social justice in the punishment and sentencing of perpetrators of criminal acts. We will presume that a socially just policy is based on the principles of equality, equal treatment, and nondiscrimination, which apply in the imposition and enforcement of criminal sanctions. Penal and prison policies which are socially just should not resort to disproportionate and excessive punishment, mass incarceration, degrading prison conditions, and the abandonment of prisoner rehabilitation and reintegration programs. A state that strives to introduce or maintain a socially just punitive system should defy the current global trends aimed at transforming the imposition and enforcement of criminal sanctions into a punitive industry and converting a welfare state into a penal state (see Wacquant, 2009, 2011).

We believe that commitment to social justice in the penal system is best summed up in the old slogan "Good social policy is the best criminal policy." Welfarist social policies reduce social and welfare inequalities, create and strengthen social bonds, and enhance the development of social as well as economic capital. The stronger people's bonds or commitments to society, the weaker their propensity for deviant behavior and the need of the criminal justice system to punish them severely (Hirschi, 1969; Ambrož, Meško & Flander, 2017). Human Development Reports, which have been prepared by United Nations Development Program (UNDP) experts since 1990, emphasize that there is a strong correlation between increasing poverty and social exclusion on one hand and the growing number of prisoners on the other. Increasing social inequalities lead to social exclusion, which is reflected in ever harsher crime and penal policies. In a society characterized by disproportionate class distinctions, the agents of repression control individuals and groups from the lowest social classes by means that include threatening them with harsh penalties and distinguishing between honest and hardworking people on the one hand and dangerous delinquents on the other (Petrovec, 2000; Petrovec, Šugman & Tompa, 2007). As Lappi-Seppälä (2011: 309–310) put it, distance feeds exclusion and harshness, whereas equality and social bonds support inclusion and leniency. Factors such as small welfare differences, high levels of social and economic justice and security, and sustainable welfare policies (including social crime prevention policies) contribute to lower levels of punitiveness and repression.

We will open the chapter with a survey of the economic, social, and political developments that made the Slovenian penal regime, with its relatively mild and stable penal policy, low imprisonment rates, and good quality of prisoner treatment, to some degree exceptional when compared with the regimes of the vast majority of Eastern as well as a large number of Western European countries. We will then explore the developments that have sent penal and prison policy in Slovenia in a new, more punitive direction, making its penal system one that is apparently less devoted than before to the principles of social justice. We will try to find out what consequences and implications such tendencies towards a greater punitiveness have for a socially just operation of the Slovenian penal system. Finally, we will try to establish whether in Slovenia, despite declining welfarism and rising punitiveness, penal and prison policies that adhere to the principles of equality and social justice can survive.

Egalitarianism, Welfarism, and Social Justice: The Legacy of Slovene Penal Exceptionalism

The defenders of the so-called penal exceptionalism thesis claim that there is a clear link between penal leniency and a high degree of welfare state, as a society rooted in social cohesion, conformity, and egalitarianism, compared to a society with great social inequality, is less willing to impose heavy penalties upon its co-members (Flander & Meško, 2016). While increasing social inequality and lack of concern for the well-being of all members of society increase readiness for tougher actions, equality and cohesion have the opposite effect. Hence, in a welfare state, extensive social service networks are also supposed to function as effective crime prevention measures, sustaining less repressive policies by providing workable alternatives to imprisonment (see Lappi-Seppälä, 2007, 2008; Pratt, 2008; Pratt & Eriksson, 2012). In contrast, those scholars who are less enthusiastic about this thesis (see Barker, 2012) argue that welfarism and the welfare state are democratic in spirit but also retain a more exclusionary element. In the Nordic model of the welfare state, they claim, the structural barriers for those from the outside are high and hierarchical, particularly for those deemed "others." According to them, a deeper analysis of the issue reveals that the welfare state can be inaccessible and punitive for those individuals and social groups that are not fully incorporated in the social, economic, and political order (Barker, 2012; Flander & Meško, 2016). Thinking cautiously about the impact that the welfare state could have on the penal regime, we assume that in Slovenia relatively low levels of punitiveness and repression within the penal system and lenient penal and prison policies largely—albeit not exclusively—emerged from historical social conditions that provided for little class distinction and high levels of egalitarianism.

Kolarič, Kopač Mrak and Rakar (2011), for example, trace the roots of the Slovenian welfare model back to the late 19th and early 20th centuries, when Slovenia was part of the Austro-Hungarian Empire. The political and economic structures of the empire meant that the differences between the social classes in Slovenia were not as big as in its other parts. There were very small numbers of aristocrats and most of them were not Slovenes. This, together with practically no immigration and a strong religious (Catholic) homogeneity, ensured that there was a clear tendency towards egalitarianism and unity, despite political divisions and differences between the conservative rural and the liberal urban populations (Kolarič et al., 2011; Flander & Meško, 2016). After the empire's collapse and the establishment of the Kingdom of Serbs, Croats, and Slovenes in 1918, these political and social structures were maintained. While in this period of its history Slovenia experienced the emergence of a capitalist class, it was not a major force (Kolarič et al., 2011). During World War II, Slovenia not only went through the national liberation war against the Nazis, but also through a civil war, leading to the Communist revolution and the introduction of the socialist socioeconomic system.

In post-war socialist Slovenia, only the working class was formally recognized as an economic and social group. There was no nobility with political and economic privileges, no large estates, and no capitalist class. Hence, among many negative consequences of the socialist regime such as the violent nationalization of property and public ownership of the means of production, a high standard of egalitarianism in Slovene society was one of the more positive ones (Kolarič et al., 2011). Regardless of the authoritarian nature of the country's government, the state, local communities, companies, and organizations were committed to fulfilling the needs of society and thus provided high levels of social security (in principle, nobody would be excluded from the social security network). Obviously, Slovenia developed its welfare state in the specific political, economic, social, and institutional conditions of the former socialist system. Unsustainable in its essence, the welfare system endured due to credits and loans that were obtained by the Communist government from foreign countries and banks (Kolarič, 1992).

In most post-socialist countries, in their transition from socialism to capitalism, economic and welfare reforms have been carried out predominantly in the form of "shock therapy." Kolarič et al. (2011: 290) maintain that in Slovenia, in contrast to other ex-socialist countries, this transition was relatively smooth because the Slovene political elite decided to introduce gradual reforms in different social policy areas. The new-old political leaders and their parties opposed the neoliberal agenda, which appeared as the dominant economic paradigm immediately after the end of socialism when the country became an independent state. However, due to unfavorable economic and demographic trends, the Slovenian welfare system, in its current form, is not financially sustainable by itself. The system has been going through a process of significant reforms, which have been criticized by leftist experts and politicians for being directed by neoliberal economic policies with the aim of dismantling the welfare state (Stropnik, Stanovnik, Rebolj & Prevolnik-Rupel, 2003; Flander & Meško, 2016).

As asserted at the outset of this section, from a distant perspective at least, we may argue that in Slovenia the development of sound standards of cohesion, equality, social justice with small class divisions, and the welfare state has contributed to a non-excessive and non-stigmatizing system of punishment. When Slovenia was a part of the Austro-Hungarian Empire, the monarchy abolished corporal punishment, and several attempts were made to abolish the death penalty too. In 1849, the parliament adopted a decision on the abolition of the death penalty, which, however, was not confirmed by the emperor and never came into force (Studen, 2004). From 1918 until 1941, Slovenia was part of the Kingdom of Serbs, Croats, and Slovenes and the Kingdom of Yugoslavia. After the kingdom's parliament adopted its own penal laws, which replaced the old Austrian Penal Code, little is known about the imposition and enforcement of death sentences. According to Studen (2004), between 1923 and 1939 eight people were executed.

Undoubtedly, in terms of justice, the early years after World War II were the darkest period for the penal regime in Slovenia. Between 1945 and 1951, at a time of sharp political and penal repression, the Slovenian courts, controlled by the Communist Party, ordered the killing of more than two hundred people, of whom the great majority were political offenders (Šelih, 2012; Flander & Meško, 2016). However, in 1951 new penal legislation introduced considerably less severe penalties. In the decades before independence and democratization, the most severe ones issued by the Criminal Code of the socialist Slovenia included 20 years of imprisonment and capital punishment as an exceptional penalty. The latter was last carried out in 1957 (in contrast, the death penalty remained in use in the majority of other socialist countries). The formal abolition of capital punishment took place during the intense democratization process, two years before Slovenia gained its independence.[1]

The criminal justice system in Slovenia's socialist period underwent two distinct phases (Šelih, 2012; also see Flander & Meško, 2016). Before 1970, criminal justice institutions as well as crime, penal, and prison policy remained entirely under the influence of the Communist Party. During this period, penal institutions including prisons also seemed to be beyond the scope of public and academic supervision and discussion (Brinc, 1985). After 1970, reforms to the criminal justice system began paving the way towards a penal system founded on the ideals of social justice in the political and social climate of that time. Moving away from the early repressive authoritarian approach towards a more permissive one, Slovenia based its penal and prison policies on ideas of experiment, open prison, and prisoners' treatment and reintegration (Meško, 2009; see also Meško, Kanduč & Jere, 2012; Petrovec & Muršič, 2011).

This trend, together with a policy of crime prevention, continued in the 1980s, when Slovenia embarked on a path of intense social, political, and economic transformation. The end of the decade, known as the first wave of transition, led to far-reaching democratic reforms in the country's penal and criminal justice system, emphasizing human rights guarantees and further limiting penal repression. Driven by the influence of humanist criminologists, crime and penal policies remained reductionist and abolitionist (Meško et al., 2012; Flander & Meško, 2016).[2] Gaining international attention in penological literature (Dünkel, 2013), these policies contributed to relatively low levels of punitiveness within the Slovenian criminal justice system until the late 1990s.

Declining Welfarism, Rising Punitiveness

However, soon after obtaining independence and introducing a capitalist economy, Slovenia experienced a decline in levels of egalitarianism, social security, and solidarity. At the start of the 1990s, the advent of political pluralism and a free market economy brought with it greater social stratification and class differentiation, an increase in the numbers living in poverty, and lower levels of social justice. The situation was particularly unpromising for members of underprivileged social and ethnic minorities, such as the Roma people and "non-Slovenian" ex-Yugoslav citizens (Petrovec & Muršič, 2011). In that period, the labor market in Slovenia faced a crisis as the country's registered unemployment rate reached an average of 14%.

At the beginning of the new millennium, Slovenia experienced a period of economic prosperity, resulting in a decrease in the unemployment rate (in 2008 it fell to 6.7%). However, in 2011 the registered unemployment rate began to grow again and in 2012 reached 13%. This trend continued until 2016 when the rate started to decrease. The data on income inequality are even more alarming. Slovenia has one of the highest levels of disparity in the European Union. According to the statistical income and living conditions survey carried out by the Statistical Office of the Republic of Slovenia, 13.6% of the population was living below the poverty threshold in 2011 and 14.5% in 2013 (SURS, 2015a; Flander & Meško, 2016). Between 2009 and 2014, the at-risk-of-poverty rate increased by more than 3%. Similar developments could be observed with respect to the at-risk-of-social-exclusion rate, which grew by almost 2% in the same period. This means that 410,000 individuals were exposed to the risk of social exclusion in 2014 (SURS, 2015b).[3]

At the beginning of the transition period, hand in hand with these trends, Slovenia experienced a significant growth in crime which was observed everywhere in the Central and Eastern European region, regardless of the type of crime policy that individual countries pursued. A detailed overview of statistical data related to crimes recorded by the Slovenian police reveals that the increase in crime rates (from less than 45,000 to more than 90,000) lasted until 2005, when the country witnessed a stabilization of growth (Eurostat, 2013; Flander & Bučar Ručman, 2015).[4] Until the end of the 1990s, in the period also known as the so-called first wave of transition, new laws dealing with the criminal justice system were aimed primarily at preventing the escalation of crime, while at the same time guaranteeing the rule of law and limitation of state power. Crime policies in that period were focused on social crime prevention measures rather than the traditional means of prosecution, punishment, and repression (Meško et al., 2012).

The second wave of reforms, however, altered these trends significantly. The attitudes of the public and of politicians towards crime and punishment changed and led to demands for stricter criminal laws, wider powers for the formal social control agencies, and a more authoritarian concept of crime prevention (Flander & Bučar Ručman, 2015; Flander & Meško, 2016).

While the exceptionalist developments within the criminal justice system slowly began to lose momentum, changes in the country's legislation have resulted in a continuous sharpening of penal sanctions. In 1999, the maximum penalty in penal legislation was raised from 20 to 30 years. With the new Criminal Code of 2008 (CC-1), a penalty of life imprisonment was adopted for the most serious crimes.[5] Additionally, the CC-1 provided longer imprisonment for a number of different crimes.[6] This trend towards more punitive laws (and legislation giving "more effective" powers to law enforcement agencies) has been also reflected in amendments introduced to police and procedural criminal law, and to the various areas of law on minor offenses (Flander & Bučar Ručman, 2015; see also Flander & Meško, 2010).[7] In a quest for faster and more effective criminal procedures, and a more effective fight against economic crime in the light of the economic crisis, further changes in criminal law and legislation on minor offenses took place in late 2011. All in all, over the last 10 years, both ends of the political spectrum have carried out quite a number of reforms, either separately or together, continuing the trend of pushing the Slovenian criminal justice system towards greater punitiveness.

This trend is also reflected in a constant rise in prison rates. Here we should make it clear that unlike most of the Central and Eastern European post-socialist countries, Slovenia has traditionally had low levels of imprisonment (around 50 per 100,000 inhabitants in the 1960s and the beginning of the 1970s). Lately, however, these levels have been growing. The imprisonment rate increased from 57.3 in 2000 to 68.4 in 2014 (URSIKS, 2001, 2015; Tournier, 2001; Aebi & Delgrande, 2015), while the daily average number of prisoners held in penal institutions has increased by over 26% in the past

10 years. While in 2014 Slovenia recorded its highest-ever number of prisoners (1,511), the number has decreased by 6.2% to 1,376 in the last two years.

The total number of prisoners, the number of newly admitted prisoners, and the number of prisoners in premises with stricter regimes have increased over the last 10 years too. Slovenia has been warned on several occasions by both national and international monitoring bodies that its prisons are overcrowded[8] and most of them are old buildings that are not suitable for the enforcement of custodial sentences. Also problematic are the lack of privacy and inadequate facilities for work (which is not obligatory in Slovenian prisons) and free-time activities. Generally, the social climate in most Slovene penal institutions is rated as low by prisoners. Their dissatisfaction has led to an increasing number of complaints addressed to the internal and international monitoring mechanisms (such as the Slovene Human Rights Ombudsman and the European Court of Human Rights) as well as to suicidal behavior and hunger strikes.

From 2011 to 2013, the budget of the Prison Administration of the Republic of Slovenia was reduced by over 25%. There has been a 7% reduction in numbers of prison personnel since 2011 (in addition to a ban on employment), while from 2012 to 2013 daily costs for a prisoner were reduced from 69 to 64 euros (for a detailed survey see Meško et al., 2011; Flander & Meško, 2016). These negative facts and figures notwithstanding, Slovenia has succeeded in retaining one of the lowest incarceration rates in the world, like those in Scandinavian countries.[9]

Despite its relatively low incarceration rate, during the last decade and a half considerably harsher regimes have been established in Slovenia's penal institutions. Comparing prison climate in "experimentalist" small-size prisons on the one hand, and bigger institutions on the other, Petrovec and Muršič (2011) found that there were significant differences between them in the 1970s, 1980s, and even at the start of the 1990s. While the levels of staff support as perceived by prisoners, the involvement, interaction, and autonomy of prisoners was much higher in small-size institutions, the levels of staff control and recidivism was higher in bigger institutions.. In general, there were significant differences between smaller and bigger prisons in applying rehabilitative and socio-therapeutic approaches. In the late 1990s, however, changes were introduced that have resulted in the abandonment of the treatment ideology and a shift to a "law and order" orientation. The fact that the enthusiasm for the treatment model evaporated has had a far-reaching impact on the operation of the entire prison system in Slovenia (Petrovec & Muršič, 2011: 442).

Judicial Decision-Making and Social Justice

It has been indicated in the previous sections of the chapter that in its early days of democratization Slovenia, in contrast to most other post-socialist countries, succeeded in building and maintaining a penal system based on the ideals of social justice, with lenient penal laws, low levels of imprisonment, satisfactory prison conditions, and rehabilitation-oriented programs for prisoners. We argued that the fact that Slovenia has traditionally had high levels of egalitarianism and social security, embedded in the socialist-style welfare state with little class distinction, contributed importantly to its penal exceptionalism vis-à-vis the vast majority of other "old" and "new" democratic countries. In Slovenia, the development of sound standards of cohesion, equality, social justice with small class divisions, and the welfare state contributed to non-excessive and non-stigmatizing punishment. Further, we demonstrated that this picture changed considerably when the early period of democratization ended. As soon as Slovenia experienced a decline in levels of egalitarianism, social security, and solidarity, the public's and politicians' attitudes towards crime and punishment changed and led to demands for stricter criminal laws, harsher penalties, and wider powers for the formal social control agencies. While new legislation has introduced ever-harsher penal sanctions, Slovenia's trajectory towards a greater punitiveness is also reflected in a constant rise in prison rates, overcrowded penal institutions, tougher prison regimes, and weakened enthusiasm for the treatment model and, last but not least, prisoners' dissatisfaction. We concluded with a pessimistic view that these developments have turned penal and prison policy in a new, more punitive direction, making its penal system apparently less devoted to the principles of social justice.

In this section, the sensitive relation between punishment and social justice will be addressed in the light of judicial decision-making. We will examine whether the imposition of custodial sentences and other criminal sanctions in Slovenia is based on the principles of equal treatment and nondiscrimination, considered the fundamental elements of social justice.

First, we will summarize the system of penal sanctions in Slovenia. This system differentiates between three groups of sanctions for adult offenders. These include sentences, admonitory sanctions, and safety measures.[10] For the purposes of this chapter, we will mainly focus on custodial sentences and fines, as well as on conditional prison sentences and judicial admonitions, representing different types of admonitory sanctions. The Criminal Code stipulates that a prison sentence in Slovenia shall not be shorter than one month or longer than 30 years; however, as described above, certain heinous crimes may, under special conditions, carry a sentence of life imprisonment.[11] A court may impose admonitory sanctions on perpetrators who were found guilty of less serious criminal offenses, for which a shorter prison sentence or a fine is prescribed. A suspended sentence is the most frequently imposed admonitory sanction. When perpetrators receive shorter unconditional prison sentences, a court may decide to replace a convict's prison sentence with the so-called alternative criminal sanction (e.g., community sanctions).

The question of whether the imposition of a custodial sentence and other criminal sanctions in Slovenia could be considered socially just will be addressed on the basis of our evaluation of equal treatment, which we consider an important element of social justice. We are primarily interested in establishing whether individuals convicted by Slovenian courts are treated equally, regardless of their personal characteristics or circumstances, when it comes to imposing and determining their sentence. If not, this may represent grounds for discrimination.

Unfortunately, empirical research in the field has until now been relatively scarce. One of the very few targeted studies in this field was conducted by the Peace Institute and the Supreme Court of the Republic of Slovenia (see Kogovšek & Kmecl, 2005) over a decade ago. The research focused on criminal proceedings instituted for the purpose of prosecuting the criminal offense of larceny, as defined by Article 211 of the then Criminal Code,[12] which is the most frequently tried criminal offense in Slovenia, according to court statistics. Researchers obtained data from the local courts of Maribor and Novo Mesto, which are among the larger courts of first instance in Slovenia, and analyzed 365 cases that resulted in a final judgment in 2002, 2003, and 2004. The sample consisted of 226 defendants. Researchers examined the outcome of proceedings (whether these resulted in a conviction, an acquittal, or a dismissal of a charge) and the type of imposed sanctions (prison sentence, conditional prison sentence, or judicial admonition). They paid particular attention to personal characteristics that could represent grounds for discrimination and unjust treatment of defendants (i.e., gender, age, social status, and national and ethnic origin).

The sample comprised 14% female and 86% male defendants. The analysis showed that the gender representation among defendants contrasted significantly with the general gender structure in the population of Slovenia, in which women make up 52% of the total. Female defendants received unconditional prison sentences as the harshest sanction in 18% of all cases, while male defendants received the same sentence in 21% of all cases. A conditional prison sentence was imposed on female defendants in 54% of all cases, while male defendants received the same sentence in 49% of all cases. Conversely, 24% of all cases involving male defendants resulted in an acquittal, while the same result applied in only 11% of all cases involving a female defendant. The two courts were therefore more frequently imposing conditional sentences on women, while men were more likely to receive an unconditional prison sentence. However, cases involving female defendants were less likely to result in an acquittal. The analysis also pointed to the fact that first-time female offenders were more likely to receive an unconditional or conditional prison sentence than to be acquitted or fined (see Kogovšek & Kmecl, 2005).

The average number of women in Slovenian prisons increased continuously in the period from 1995 (40) to 2016 (97.8), despite occasional reductions. In 2016, the number of women serving a prison sentence amounted to 186 (7.3%), which represents the highest share of women thus far (URSIKS, 2017). Even though the analysis of punishment in relation to gender points to a potential deviation from the principles of equality and justice, it must be noted that the reliability of findings presented by the aforementioned research is relatively low due to the modest share of women in the sample of defendants.

The research also showed that the majority of completed criminal proceedings were instituted against persons aged between 25 and 29, while a slightly smaller share of proceedings involved defendants aged between 20 and 24. The number of proceedings against defendants aged 30 or more was lower, while the number of proceedings against persons aged between 40 and 44 was again slightly higher. The number of criminal proceedings involving defendants aged 45 or more decreased in proportion with their age.[13] Proceedings before the two courts had most frequently resulted in an acquittal in cases involving defendants younger than 25. The share of conditional prison sentences was relatively high in all age groups.[14] Unconditional prison sentences were imposed in 31% of all cases on defendants aged between 35 and 54, while only 17% of defendants younger than 35 and older than 55 received the same sentence (Kogovšek & Kmecl, 2005).

According to prison statistics, during the last decade and a half the majority of prisoners were middle-aged (URSIKS, 2001, 2013, 2015, 2017). Since a previous conviction serves as a ground for imposing harsher sanctions, one must—before potentially drawing a conclusion that defendants of a certain age group are subjected to unequal and socially unjust punishment—take into account that the share of previously convicted defendants aged between 35 and 54 (61%) is higher than the share of previously convicted defendants younger than 35 (51%) and those older than 55 (17%). Nevertheless, we could conclude that middle-aged defendants were slightly more likely to receive harsher sanctions in comparison to defendants belonging to other age groups.

The analysis of punishment in relation to social status focused on defendants' employment status, as this was the only parameter indicating their social status that could be obtained from the analyzed prosecution files (Kogovšek & Kmecl, 2005). The analysis showed that two out of three judicial admonitions (i.e., the most lenient among the sanctions studied) were issued to employed defendants. The proceedings involving both employed as well as unemployed defendants resulted in an acquittal in 22% of all cases. The share of imposed fines in both groups of defendants was also very similar (7% in unemployed and 11% in employed defendants); the same applied to conditional prison sentences (48% and 54% respectively). On the other hand, the unconditional prison sentence as the harshest sanction was imposed on unemployed defendants in 23% of all cases, while employed defendants received the same sentence in a mere 8% of all cases, which is approximately three times less frequently than for unemployed defendants. Notably, the two courts imposed conditional prison sentences on previously convicted employed and unemployed defendants in more or less equal shares (37% and 35% respectively). The two courts imposed the unconditional prison sentence as the most severe sanction on previously convicted unemployed defendants in 95% of all cases, while previously convicted employed defendants received the same sentence in all cases (100%). Therefore, one could conclude that in the studied period the likelihood of an unemployed defendant without previous convictions/sanctions receiving an unconditional prison sentence was higher in comparison to employed defendants (Kogovšek & Kmecl, 2005).

The analysis of punishment related to national and ethnic origin[15] included 126 (56%) Slovenian defendants, six Muslims, five Croatians, three Serbians, and one Bosnian defendant, while a whopping 85 (or 38% of all defendants) were of Roma origin.[16] The two courts most often imposed a conditional prison sentence on Slovenian defendants as well as on defendants of other national origins (Muslims, Croatians, Serbians, and Bosnians). However, the share of conditional prison sentences imposed on the Roma was much lower (38% of all cases) in comparison to Slovenian defendants (61% of all cases). Moreover, an unconditional prison sentence was imposed on the Roma defendants three times more frequently than on Slovenian defendants (almost every third defendant of Roma origin was sentenced to prison) and also much more frequently when compared to the members of other national communities (Roma defendants received a prison sentence in 30% of all cases, defendants of other national communities received the same sentence in 13% of all cases, while the defendants of the majority Slovenian community were given a prison sentence in a mere 10% of all cases). It is also worth noting that fines were imposed on Slovenian defendants in 8% of all cases, while defendants of other national origins[17] received the same sanction in 17% of all cases. Roma defendants, who were finally convicted by the two courts, received a prison sentence much more frequently than a fine, since the latter was only imposed in 6% of all cases. During the three-year period, the two analyzed courts issued a judicial admonition (the most lenient among sanctions) in only three cases, all of which involved defendants of Slovenian national origin (see Kogovšek & Kmecl, 2005).[18]

When drawing conclusions from the above data, one ought to be cautious. Statistical data show that proceedings involving Roma defendants result in the imposition of relatively harsher criminal sanctions. The above data refer to the type and length/severity of the sanction; however, details pertaining to the committed criminal offenses and certain other circumstances, which may affect the length/severity of the sanction, are not taken into account. Further multi-factor research studies would be necessary in order to obtain more reliable data regarding discriminatory and thus socially unjust treatment of the Roma population. Such research studies are difficult to carry out, and if they are to be of sufficient quality they require information to be obtained from individual prosecution files. Nevertheless, the statistical data presented above may provide a reason for concern and an indication that such research studies would indeed be necessary and relevant.

Concluding Remarks

Our main goal in this chapter was to explore what consequences and implications global punitive tendencies have for the Slovenian penal system, and ask whether they jeopardize its traditional allegiance to principles of social justice. We were interested in establishing whether and to what extent the imposition of custodial sentences and other criminal sanctions was based on the principles of equality and social justice. We established that despite rising punitiveness and declining social welfarism, Slovenia is rather successful in defying global trends aimed at transforming the criminal justice systems into a punitive industry. In our view, there are some good reasons to believe that soon the Slovenian penal system could remain, to a large extent, devoted to the principles of equality, nondiscrimination, and social justice.

In Slovenia, neoliberal social and criminal justice reforms that occurred during the so-called second wave of transition in the aftermath of the 1990s have not been as intense as in most other post-socialist countries. Slovenia, unlike most of the post-socialist countries, has not been facing an aggressive form of penal populism. The impact of punitive public attitudes and harsh political rhetoric on penal and prison policies has been milder than in some other post-socialist new democracies, so that crime and penal policy remain influenced by experts rather than driven by populist penal ideas. Moreover, punitive trends notwithstanding, Slovenia still jails fewer of its citizens than any other of the post-communist/socialist countries and fewer than most of the "old" democracies (Flander & Meško, 2016; see also Flander & Meško, 2010).

In the last three years, more prisoners were conditionally released, more alternative sanctions were imposed, and more prisoners served in open and semi-open regimes than in previous years. There have been no women among minors who have been serving in juvenile correctional facilities since 2013.

Also, in the last few years, there have been fewer prisoner complaints and fewer escapes from the open and semi-open departments than in the past. The average length of prison sentences (between one and two years) has been the shortest of all penal regimes in the Central and Eastern European region and no convict has yet been sentenced to life. Despite recent reductions, treatment-oriented programs for prisoners and prison authorities' commitment to provide prisoners with education and work while serving their sentences in Slovenia are still continuing, aiming to provide prisoners with social competencies and prepare them for living outside prison. Albeit primarily driven by utilitarian aims, these seem to be important indicators of a just operation of the Slovenian penal system.

One must not ignore, however, the fact that the research conducted by the Peace Institute and the Supreme Court of the Republic of Slovenia (Kogovšek & Kmecl, 2005) revealed certain deviations when it comes to the imposition of criminal sanctions in relation to defendants' gender, age, social structure, and national origin. Defendants from the Roma community are, even when one considers the corrective element of previous convictions, more likely to receive an unconditional prison sentence than are the defendants of Slovenian national origin.[19] In Slovenia, unemployed defendants, who had previously not been convicted of a crime, are much more likely to receive the unconditional prison sentence when compared to employed defendants. While middle-aged defendants are also slightly more likely to receive a harsher sanction than defendants of other age groups, similar deviations from the principle of equal and just imposition of criminal sanctions were also revealed by the analysis of punishment in relation to gender.

Due to the reasons discussed above, these findings must be primarily understood as indicators serving as a basis for making a rough assessment of the current state of affairs. At the same time, their significance should not be ignored or minimized. After all, they deserve serious consideration and an in-depth analysis, particularly in the light of examining the legitimacy and fairness of the penal system in the future.

Discussion Questions

1. Can you describe briefly the connection between criminal justice and social justice when it comes to punishment and sentencing?
2. Is there such a thing as socially just punishment? Can it be defined in abstract terms?
3. What are proportionate sentences? Are "proportionate" and "just" synonyms?
4. What exactly is meant by the slogan "Good social policy is the best criminal policy"?
5. What is the role of a welfare state when it comes to crime prevention?
6. Does the wealth distribution in a specific country shape its penal policy?
7. What is "penal populism"? What role does this phenomenon play in relation to social justice?
8. How did the transition process influence the penal policy in Slovenia?
9. Can you briefly summarize the findings of the Slovenian study on punishment and social justice in judicial decision-making?

Notes

1. Article 17 of the new Constitution (1991) of an autonomous and independent Slovenia stipulates that life is inviolable, and that capital punishment is prohibited.
2. Keresezi and Lévay (2008) maintain that in the early days of their transition to democratic rule, in the vast majority of post-communist/socialist countries, laws dealing with criminal justice were generally aimed at preventing the escalation of crime, while at the same time guaranteeing the rule of law and limitation of state power. While crime control issues were dominated by humanist criminologists and criminal justice experts and were not subject to intensive debate among politicians and the general public, the increase in crime rates had no significant influence on crime and penal policy (see also Šelih, 2012).
3. In 2014, pensioners accounted for the largest share of persons living below the poverty threshold, followed by the unemployed, children, and the active working population (SURS, 2015a).

4. When researching the connection between certain socioeconomic indicators and crime in Slovenia, Flander (2015) found that regions recording high rates of poverty and social exclusion were also characterized by a high number of persons convicted by a final judgment. Police administrations competent for these areas also dealt with a high number of criminal offenses. With respect to those regions where such a correlation could not be confirmed, the author of the research presumes that perpetrators originating from statistical regions characterized by unfavorable socioeconomic indicators did not commit criminal offenses in their local environment but in neighboring wealthier regions.

5. Before 2008, Spain, Portugal, and Slovenia were the only members of the European Union without a penalty of life imprisonment in their penal law.

6. An "anomaly" in a general trend towards more severe sentencing was in the area of juvenile crime (see Filipčič, 2009; Petrovec & Muršič, 2011).

7. Fines for traffic offenses have been increasing constantly from 1998 on, with most significant increases occurring in 2010 and 2012. A fine for exceeding the speed limit in built-up areas by 30 km/h, for example, in 1998 amounted to 200 euros. Over the years, a fine for this traffic offense has increased five-fold, up to 1,000 euros in 2012.

8. Prison overcrowding has been a problem in the country since 1996 (Meško et al., 2011). According to standards prescribed by the regulations on implementation of the prison sentence (2000) and guidelines of the Council of Europe's Committee for the Prevention of Torture, the capacity rate in all penal institutions was over 129%. In Ljubljana prison, the second largest institution in Slovenia, the capacity rate reached over 200% (URSIKS, 2013).

9. During the last decade, for example, the imprisonment rates in all other countries that formerly belonged to Yugoslavia doubled except in Slovenia (from 44.4 in 2000 to 102.8 in 2014 in Croatia; from 74.9 in 2005 to 140.0 in 2014 in Serbia; and from 69.0 in 2000 to 141.2 in 2014 in the FYR of Macedonia).

10. With respect to convicted juvenile offenders, a court may impose corrective measures or, exceptionally, principal sentences (prison sentences for juvenile offenders and fines), accessory sentences, and certain safety measures.

11. Since 2008, when the new Criminal Code introduced the sentence of life imprisonment, this criminal sanction has not been imposed on any convict in Slovenia.

12. The Criminal Code of the Republic of Slovenia of 1995, which was applicable at the time of the aforementioned research (and was replaced by a new Criminal Code in 2008), contained the following definition of (petty) larceny: "Whoever takes another's movable property with the intention of unlawfully appropriating it shall be sentenced to imprisonment for up to three years. If the stolen property is of low value and the perpetrator intended to appropriate this property, he shall be punished by a fine or sentenced to imprisonment for not more than one year."

13. One could draw a similar conclusion with respect to punishment and its relation to gender. The representation of certain age groups could point either to the fact that individuals aged between 25 and 29 are potentially discriminated against, since the majority of completed criminal proceedings was instituted against the members of this age group, or to the fact that individuals belonging to this age group are committing this particular criminal offense more frequently than others. The latter seems somewhat more likely.

14. This sentence was most frequently (in 85% of all cases) imposed on defendants older than 55; however, this finding cannot be considered statistically reliable due to the limited sample of persons belonging to this age group.

15. Results of the research showed that the analysis of correlation between defendants' citizenship, the courts' verdict, and the imposed sanction did not really make sense, since as much as 99% of all defendants held Slovenian citizenship. However, the differences proved to be much more significant when examining the element of national origin.

16. The vast majority of the Roma defendants (95%) were tried before the Novo Mesto Local Court. Even though this court is located in the southeast part of Slovenia, where a larger number of Roma actually live, the authors of the research emphasize that the representation of the Roma population before the Novo Mesto Local Court is highly disproportionate to the number of Roma living in this region. Apart from defendants originating from the Roma community, a higher share of defendants involved in proceedings before the Novo Mesto Local Court in the analyzed period also belonged to the Muslim, Croatian, Serbian, and Bosnian communities (10% in total), while the representation of other national communities before the Maribor Local Court was substantially lower. The share of Slovenians heard before the Novo Mesto Local Court was therefore much lower than the share of Slovenian defendants involved in proceedings before the Maribor Local Court (Kogovšek & Kmecl, 2005).

17. The sample of members of other national communities used in the research conducted by the Peace Institute and the Supreme Court of the Republic of Slovenia was rather limited (15 defendants, which accounts for a mere 7% of all defendants included in the sample), which is why one must be particularly careful when drawing conclusions or making assumptions regarding this group of defendants.

18. Researchers were also interested in establishing which types of sanctions were imposed by the two courts on previously convicted defendants (recidivists). After considering all imposed sanctions, they found that the share of previously convicted Slovenian defendants who received a conditional prison sentence was higher than the share of previously convicted members of the Roma community receiving the same sentence. Researchers concluded that a comparison between previously convicted Slovenian and Roma defendants showed that the latter were less likely to receive a conditional prison sentence or, in other words, that they were more likely to receive an unconditional prison sentence (or a fine).

19. Since the share of Roma defendants included in the analyzed sample was extremely high, one must pose at least the following two questions: First, are the members of the Roma community on average really committing criminal offenses more frequently than the members of other national communities are? (If the answer is affirmative, one ought to look into the reasons contributing to this state of affairs.) Second, what is the position of the Roma in procedures conducted by the police and prosecutors? (In this respect, a special research study ought to be conducted in order to establish whether the members of the Roma community involved in these procedures are treated equally and justly in comparison to the members of the majority community.)

References

Aebi, M. F., & Delgrande, N. (2015). *Council of Europe Annual Penal Statistics SPACEI: 2013 survey on prison populations*. Strasbourg: Council of Europe.

Ambrož, M., Meško, G., & Flander, B. (2017). Social crime prevention: Concepts, developments, and challenges. In J. Winterdyk (Ed.), *Crime prevention: International perspectives, issues, and trends* (pp. 209–230). Boca Raton, London, New York: CRC Press.

Barker, V. (2012). Nordic exceptionalism revisited: Explaining the paradox of a Janus-faced penal regime. *Theoretical Criminology, 17*(1), 5–25.

Brinc, F. (1985). Določitelji družbenega vzdušja v kazenskih zavodih v SR Sloveniji [Determinants of social climate in correctional institutions in the Socialist Republic of Slovenia]. *Revija za kriminalistiko in kriminologijo, 36*(1), 304–316.

Cvikl, L., & Ambrož, M. (2017). *Pravice v zaporu: pregled in ovrednotenje sodne prakse Evropskega sodišča za človekove pravice*. Ljubljana: Pravna fakulteta: Inštitut za kriminologijo pri Pravni fakulteti.

Dünkel, F. (2013). Slovenian exceptionalism? Die Entwicklung von Gefangenraten im internationalen Vergleich. In M. Ambrož, K. Filipčič, & A. Završnik (Eds.), *Zbornik za Alenko Šlih* (pp. 61–93). Ljubljana: Inštitut za kriminologijo pri Pravni fakulteti v Ljubljani.

Eurostat. (2013). *Crime and criminal justice*. Retrieved from http://epp.eurostat.ec.europa.eu/portal/page/portal/crime/data/database

Filipčič, K. (2009). La Slovénie [Slovenia]. *Deviance et societe, 33*, 367–382.

Flander, B., & Bučar Ručman, A. (2015). Lost in transition: Criminal justice reforms and the crises of legitimacy in Central and Eastern Europe. In G. Meško & J. Tankebe (Eds.), *Trust and legitimacy in criminal justice: European perspectives* (pp. 111–133). Cham, Heidelberg, New York, Dordrecht, London: Springer.

Flander, B., & Meško, G. (2010). "Punitiveness" and penal trends in Slovenia: On the "shady side of the Alps"? In H. Kury & E. Shea (Eds.), *Punitivity international developments* (pp. 227–249). Bochum: Universitätsverlag Brockmeyer.

Flander, B., & Meško, G. (2016). Penal and prison policy on the "sunny side of the Alps": The swansong of Slovenian exceptionalism. *European Journal on Criminal Policy and Research, 22*(4), 565–591.

Hirschi, T. (1969). *Causes of delinquency*. Berkeley, CA: University of California Press.

Hörnle, T. (2011). *Straftheorien*. Tübingen: Mohr Siebeck.

Keresezi, K., & Lévay, M. (2008). Criminology, crime and criminal justice in Hungary. *European Journal of Criminology, 5*(2), 239–260.

Kogovšek, N., & Kmecl, A. (2005). Vloga sodišč pri zagotavljanju spoštovanja načela enakega obravnavanja v kazenskih postopkih. In D. Zagorac (Ed.), *Enakost in diskriminacija: sodobni izzivi za pravosodje* (pp. 55–77). Ljubljana: Mirovni inštitut.

Kolarič, Z. (1992). From socialist to post-socialist social policy. In I. Svetlik (Ed.), *Social policy in Slovenia: Between tradition and innovation* (pp. 15–32). Aldershot: Avebury.

Kolarič, Z., Kopač Mrak, A., & Rakar, T. (2011). Welfare states in transition: The development of the welfare system in Slovenia. In M. Marija Stambolieva & S. Dehnert (Eds.), *Welfare states in transition: 20 years after the Yugoslav welfare model* (pp. 288–309). Sofia: Friedrich Ebert Foundation.

Lappi-Seppälä, T. (2007). *Trust, welfare and political economy: Cross-comparative perspectives in penal severity (Draft)*. Retrieved from www.rsf.uni-greifswald.de/fileadmin/mediapool/lehrstuehle/duenkel/LappiSeppala_Penal-Severity.pdf

Lappi-Seppälä, T. (2008). Trust, welfare, and political culture: Explaining differences in national penal policies. *Crime and Justice: A Review of Research, 37*, 313–387.

Lappi-Seppälä, T. (2011). Explaining imprisonment in Europe. *European Journal of Criminology, 8*(4), 303–328.

Meško, G. (2009). Transfer of crime control ideas: Introductory reflections. In G. Meško & H. Kury (Eds.), *Policy, crime control and crime prevention: Slovenian perspectives* (pp. 19–41). Ljubljana: Tipografija.

Meško, G., Fields, C., & Smole, T. (2011). A concise overview of penology and penal practice in Slovenia: The unchanged capacity, new standards, and prison overcrowding. *The Prison Journal, 4*(91), 398–424.

Meško, G., Kanduč, Z., & Jere, M. (2012). Social crime prevention in Slovenia—recent development. In P. Hebberecht & E. Baillergeau (Eds.), *Social crime prevention in late modern Europe: A comparative perspective* (pp. 303–319). Brussels: VUBPress.

Petrovec, D. (2000). Poverty and reaction to crime—freedom without responsibility. *European Journal of Crime, Criminal Law and Criminal Justice, 8*(4), 377–389.

Petrovec, D., & Muršič, M. (2011). Science fiction or reality: Opening prison institutions (The Slovenian penological heritage). *The Prison Journal, 4*(91), 425–447.

Petrovec, D., Šugman, K., & Tompa, G. (2007). Bogatvo, revščina in odziv na kriminaliteto—od leta 200 do 2007 [Wealth, poverty and reaction to crime—from 200 to 2007]. *Revija za kriminalistiko in kriminologijo, 58*(3), 246–253.

Pratt, J. (2008). Scandinavian exceptionalism in an era of penal excess. *British Journal of Criminology, 48*, 119–137.

Pratt, J., & Eriksson, A. (2012). In defense of Scandinavian exceptionalism. In T. Ugelvik & J. Dullum (Eds.), *Penal exceptionalism? Nordic prison policy and practice* (pp. 235–260). London: Routledge.

Šelih, A. (2012). Crime and crime control in transition countries. In A. Šelih & A. Završnik (Eds.), *Crime and transition in central and Eastern Europe* (pp. 3–34). New York: Springer.

Statistični Urad Republike Slovenije. (2015a). *Kazalniki dohodka in revščine, Slovenija, 2014.* Retrieved from www.stat.si/StatWeb/prikazi-novico?id=5426

Statistični Urad Republike Slovenije. (2015b). *Stopnja tveganja revščine glede na starost in spol, Slovenija, letno.* Retrieved from http://pxweb.stat.si/pxweb/Dialog/varval.asp?ma=0867636S&ti=&path=../Database/Dem_soc/08_zivljenjska_raven/08_silc_kazalniki_revsc/30_08676_kazaln_podp_strat_EU_2020/&lang=2015Stropnik, N., Stanovnik, T., Rebolj, M., & Prevolnik-Rupel, V. (2003). *Study on the social protection systems in the thirteen applicant countries—Slovenia country study.* Retrieved from http://europa.eu.int/comm/employment_social/soc-prot/social/slovenia_final.pdf

Studen, A. (2004). *Rabljev zamah: k zgodovini kriminala in kaznovanja na Slovenskem od 16. do začetka 21. stoletja.* Ljubljana: Slovenska matica.

Tournier, V. (2001). *Council of Europe Annual Penal Statistics SPACE I: 2000 enquiry on prison populations.* Strasbourg: Council of Europe.

Uprava za izvrševanje kazenskih sankcij. (2001). *Letno poročilo 2000.* Ljubljana: Ministrstvo za pravosodje, Uprava za izvrševanje kazenskih sankcij. Retrieved from www.mp.gov.si/fileadmin/mp.gov.si/pageuploads/UIKS/Letna_porocila/porocilo_uiks_2000.pdf

Uprava za izvrševanje kazenskih sankcij. (2013). *Letno poročilo 2012.* Ljubljana: Ministrstvo za pravosodje, Uprava za izvrševanje kazenskih sankcij. Retrieved from www.mp.gov.si/fileadmin/mp.gov.si/pageuploads/UIKS/Letna_porocila/LP_2012.pdf

Uprava za izvrševanje kazenskih sankcij. (2015). *Letno poročilo 2014.* Ljubljana: Ministrstvo za pravosodje, Uprava za izvrševanje kazenskih sankcij. Retrieved from www.mp.gov.si/fileadmin/mp.gov.si/pageuploads/UIKS/Letna_porocila/150519_Letno_porocilo_2014.pdf

Uprava za izvrševanje kazenskih sankcij. (2017). *Letno poročilo 2016.* Ljubljana: Ministrstvo za pravosodje, Uprava za izvrševanje kazenskih sankcij. Retrieved from www.mp.gov.si/fileadmin/mp.gov.si/pageuploads/UIKS/Letna_porocila/170503_Letno_porocilo_2016.pdf

Wacquant, L. (2009). *Punishing the poor: The neoliberal government of social insecurity.* Durham: Duke University Press.

Wacquant, L. (2011). The penalization of poverty and the rise of neo-liberalism. *European Journal on Criminal Policy and Research, 9*(4), 401–412.

PART IV

Criminal Justice and Social Status

19

EFFECTIVE ASSISTANCE OF COUNSEL

Melanie Worsley and Michelle Watson

Introduction

The Sixth Amendment to the United States Constitution guarantees every criminal defendant the right to assistance of counsel. The United States Supreme Court has interpreted this Sixth Amendment provision as requiring individuals to be informed of their right to counsel before a custodial interrogation and as protecting against ineffective assistance of counsel. The right to assistance of counsel also requires the government to provide defense counsel for indigent defendants in criminal cases.

States vary in their approaches to providing counsel for indigent criminal defendants. Some states have assigned counsel programs. In the assigned counsel model, courts appoint private attorneys to represent indigent defendants. Assigned counsel are paid on an hourly basis. Another model used by states is the contract attorney model. In the contract attorney program, the courts have a contract with private attorneys to provide indigent defense services. Contract attorney programs can involve either fixed-price contracts, under which private attorneys agree to accept an undesignated number of cases for a flat fee, or fixed-fee contracts, under which private attorneys agree to represent an undetermined number of indigent defendants at a predetermined fee per case. Other states use public defender programs. In the public defender model, there are full-time attorneys whose sole responsibility is to provide representation for indigent defendants.[1]

Despite the Sixth Amendment guarantee of assistance of counsel, jurisdictions across the United States are struggling to satisfy this constitutional mandate. From legal impediments to lack of funding for indigent defense programs, the right to assistance of counsel in the United States falls short of what is constitutionally guaranteed. This chapter will explore legal issues surrounding the right to effective assistance of counsel by examining the relevant constitutional amendments and case law. The chapter will then examine practical problems in the criminal justice system that undermine an individual's right to assistance of counsel and will end by exploring possible solutions to the criminal justice system's shortcomings in ensuring effective assistance of counsel.

Constitutional Protection

In recognition of the importance of legal representation for a person accused of committing a crime, specific provisions guaranteeing a criminal defendant's right to counsel are included in the United States Constitution's Bill of Rights. The Fifth Amendment provides that suspects must be informed of their right to an attorney before a custodial interrogation, while the Sixth Amendment guarantees criminal defendants the right to effective assistance of counsel after the beginning of criminal proceedings. The Sixth Amendment also protects individuals against ineffective assistance of counsel.

The Fifth Amendment

The Fifth Amendment to the United States Constitution provides in part that no person "shall be compelled in any criminal case to be a witness against himself."[2] To determine whether a defendant's incriminating statements are admissible at trial, courts focus on the voluntariness of the statements. In *Miranda v. Arizona*, the Supreme Court held that prior to a custodial interrogation, a suspect must be warned that he has "the right to remain silent, that any statement he does make may be used as evidence against him, and that he has a right to the presence of an attorney, either retained or appointed."[3] In reaching this conclusion, the Court emphasized the important role defense counsel plays in protecting an individual's right against self-incrimination. The Supreme Court noted that given the nature of custodial interrogations and

> the inherently compelling pressures which work to undermine the individual's will to resist and to compel him to speak . . . the accused must be adequately and effectively apprised of his rights and the exercise of those rights must be fully honored.[4]

If a law enforcement officer fails to *Mirandize* an individual prior to a custodial interrogation, any statements made during the interrogation are excluded at trial.

The Sixth Amendment

The Sixth Amendment states in pertinent part that the "accused shall enjoy the right to . . . have the assistance of counsel for his defense."[5] In the 1938 case of *Johnson v. Zerbst*, the United States Supreme Court examined the contours of this Sixth Amendment right to assistance of counsel. The Court held that absent a knowing and intelligent waiver, a conviction and sentence without assistance of counsel violates a defendant's Sixth Amendment rights.[6] At the time, the *Zerbst* holding only applied to federal court. It was not until *Gideon v. Wainwright* was issued in 1963 that the Sixth Amendment right to counsel was applied to the states.

In *Gideon v. Wainwright*, the defendant Gideon was charged with committing a felony in violation of Florida law. Gideon asked the trial court to appoint an attorney to represent him, but the court denied his request because Florida law at the time provided that defendants were only entitled to appointed counsel in capital cases. Gideon proceeded to represent himself at his jury trial and was subsequently convicted. After exhausting his remedies in state court, Gideon appealed to the United States Supreme Court, which held that the right to counsel is fundamental and essential to a fair trial so that the Sixth Amendment right to counsel applies to the states. In reaching this conclusion, the Supreme Court stressed that any criminal defendant "who is too poor to hire a lawyer . . . cannot be assured a fair trial unless counsel is provided for him."[7] Noting that the government devotes substantial resources in prosecuting defendants, the Court further stressed that assistance of counsel is a constitutional principle essential to ensuring a fair trial. Originally, the holding in *Gideon* was limited to defendants charged with felonies. In 1972, the Supreme Court extended the requirement that indigent criminal defendants be provided with counsel to misdemeanor cases where charges could result in incarceration.[8]

The language in *Gideon* emphasizing the importance of criminal defendants' right to counsel was strong and unambiguous. In order to appreciate the benefits and limitations of the *Gideon* holding, it is important to understand the practical implications of this decision. This includes examining when the right to an attorney attaches, at what proceedings a defendant is entitled to have counsel present, under what circumstances a defendant may waive the right to counsel, and what constitutes ineffective assistance of counsel.

The Sixth Amendment right to counsel attaches when "a prosecution is commenced." Accordingly, criminal defendants who cannot afford to hire an attorney have the right to have the government appoint counsel once the prosecution commences. According to the Supreme Court, a prosecution commences upon "the initiation of adversary judicial criminal proceedings whether by way of formal charge, preliminary hearing, indictment, information, or arraignment."[9] Once the right to counsel attaches, a defendant has the right to counsel at all "critical stages" of the prosecution of the case. A variety of judicial proceedings, including pretrial hearings, entry of guilty pleas, trials, and sentencing, have been found to be critical stages of the prosecution of a criminal case. The Supreme Court has also examined when events occurring outside of judicial proceedings are considered a critical stage of a criminal prosecution.

In *Massiah v. United States*, defendant Massiah was indicted on federal charges. He retained counsel and was granted pretrial release. Massiah's co-defendant, Colson, turned state's witness. At the request of federal agents, Colson contacted Massiah, and Massiah made incriminating statements to Colson. Federal agents recorded the conversation between Massiah and Colson, and Massiah challenged the admissibility of the recorded conversation. The United States Supreme Court held that the government's action of "deliberately eliciting" incriminating statements outside the presence of Massiah's attorney after the commencement of adversarial judicial criminal proceedings violated Massiah's Sixth Amendment right to counsel.[10] Thus, under *Massiah*, when the government acts to deliberately elicit incriminating information from a defendant after a defendant's right to counsel has attached, the defendant has the Sixth Amendment right to have counsel present. If, however, the informant is "merely a passive listener," then the defendant is not entitled to have counsel present.[11]

Other critical stages of the prosecution occurring outside of judicial proceedings include post-charge eyewitness identification. If the lineup occurs prior to the initiation of judicial criminal proceedings, however, then the right to counsel does not apply. The Supreme Court has also held that a post-charge interrogation is a critical stage. However, parole and probation revocation hearings are not considered critical stages of a prosecution for Sixth Amendment purposes.

Defendants may waive their Sixth Amendment right to counsel. A waiver of the right to counsel must be knowing and intelligent, and the waiver can be made outside of counsel's presence. The right to counsel is also "offense specific," meaning that law enforcement may question a defendant about nearly anything as long as the questions do not concern the actual offenses covered by the attorney-client relationship.

Right to Effective Counsel

Just as a criminal defendant has the constitutional right to counsel in critical stages of proceedings against him, a criminal defendant also has the right to reasonably *effective* counsel. As stated by the Seventh Circuit Court of Appeals, "While a criminal trial is not a game in which the participants are expected to enter the ring with a near match in skills, neither is it a sacrifice of unarmed prisoners to gladiators."[12] Criminal defendants are not left to fend for themselves; the right to effective counsel is more than the mere presence of a warm body with a Juris Doctor degree.[13] There are two main ways by which a defendant may be deprived of effective representation. First, the government violates the right to effective assistance if it impedes counsel's ability to make independent decisions about how to conduct the defense, such as a judge's requiring that the defendant be the first defense witness or barring defense counsel from consulting with his client during an overnight recess in the proceedings. Second, defense counsel can deprive a defendant of the right to effective assistance by failing to render adequate legal assistance.[14] The second means is the focus of this chapter.

Development of the Strickland *Test*

In the years preceding the late 20th century, questions arose concerning what considerations or factors would render counsel's performance ineffective. At both federal and state levels, courts were inconsistent with respect to their methods of determining whether counsel was ineffective or incompetent. Some courts applied the farce-and-mockery standard, which required the defendant to show that "the proceedings were a farce and mockery of justice," with exceptional circumstances, such that the case shocked the conscience of the reviewing court.[15] Other courts believed that counsel's representation could be ineffective even if counsel's conduct did not lead to a trial that was a sham, farce, or mockery and, thus, adopted the reasonably competent standard. This standard examined whether counsel's advice or services rendered fit within the range of competency as guided by the American Bar Association's standards relating to the administration of criminal justice.[16]

By the mid-1980s, all federal courts of appeal and most states had adopted some form of a reasonably effective assistance standard of assessing counsel's performance. For example, the Fifth Circuit Court of Appeals' interpretation of this standard espoused the idea that the right to effective counsel does not "mean . . . errorless counsel, and not counsel judged ineffective by hindsight, but counsel reasonably likely to render and rendering reasonably effective assistance."[17] Florida courts looked at whether counsel's performance reflected "any substantial and serious deficiency measurably below that of competent counsel that was likely to have affected the outcome of the . . . proceeding."[18] Prejudice to the defense became a major factor in considering ineffective assistance claims. Even though a majority of jurisdictions used a similar standard to examine the performance itself, courts nevertheless differed in their methods of determining whether a defendant was prejudiced by counsel's deficient performance.

These inconsistencies led to the United States Supreme Court's decision in *Strickland v. Washington*, where the Court established a bright-line rule for evaluating ineffective assistance of counsel claims. The two-prong *Strickland* test—still good law today—requires a defendant to show that (1) counsel's performance was deficient and (2) the deficiency prejudiced the defense. The first prong ties into the practice and expectations of the legal community, requiring counsel's performance to be reasonable under "prevailing professional norms."[19] The conduct in question must essentially amount to incompetence, which is different from a mere deviation from "best practices or most common custom."[20] The *Strickland* Court refused to give any specific checklist or rules of conduct, indicating that counsel has wide latitude in making tactical decisions and must not be hampered in making such choices. Moreover, specific rules of conduct could distract counsel from playing the essential role of vigorous advocate for the client. The Court further explained,

> [T]he purpose of the effective assistance guarantee of the Sixth Amendment is not to improve the quality of legal representation, although that is a goal of considerable importance to the legal system. The purpose is simply to ensure that criminal defendants receive a fair trial.[21]

Courts must examine the reasonableness of counsel's challenged conduct as of the time it was performed, in light of the facts and circumstances of the particular case. Courts presume that counsel's representation was adequate.

With regard to the second prejudice prong of the *Strickland* test, the defendant must show that, but for the constitutionally deficient representation, there is a reasonable probability that the result of the proceeding would have been different. A reasonable probability means there is a "probability sufficient to undermine confidence in the outcome."[22] The United States Supreme Court has cautioned that not every professionally unreasonable decision necessarily affects the outcome of a proceeding. In other words, the "likelihood of a different result must be substantial, not just conceivable."[23] The prejudice prong can be a difficult hurdle to overcome.

Effective Assistance: Various Phases of Criminal Proceedings

In discussing ineffective assistance of counsel, it is first helpful to know what does *not* constitute deficient performance. Strategic choices made after thorough investigation of relevant law and facts are virtually unchallengeable, as are reasonable decisions making investigation unnecessary and decisions selecting which issues to raise on appeal. Likewise, an attorney's inexperience with criminal proceedings, while a factor in evaluating counsel's performance, is generally not, by itself, sufficient to support a claim of ineffective assistance. Isolated poor strategy or bad trial tactics do not necessarily amount to ineffective assistance either.[24] When a defendant complains about the ineffectiveness of counsel's assistance, the defendant must show that counsel's representation fell below an objective standard of reasonableness. The right to effective counsel is not the right to perfect counsel. Even if counsel's representation is deficient, the defendant's claim will not prevail if prejudice is not shown, and in only rare instances will prejudice be presumed.[25]

Effective assistance of counsel is required in criminal cases at certain steps before trial, during trial, and during appeals. As previously stated, the United States Supreme Court has stated that critical stages of the criminal proceedings include arraignments, postindictment interrogations, postindictment lineups, and the entry of a guilty plea. Hence, a defendant has a right to effective assistance of counsel during such proceedings and during the plea process. Counsel has a duty to consult with the client before trial and to communicate the prosecution's formal plea offers that may be favorable. Ethical standards, while not benchmarks for effective assistance in and of themselves, can be important guides in examining specific instances of alleged deficient conduct. A court is generally not going to determine the adequacy of the representation solely on the amount of time counsel spent consulting with the client, but counsel cannot agree to represent a criminal defendant and then completely ignore him. A defendant has the right to be a part of his defense.[26]

Pretrial/Plea Bargaining Phase

Participating in one's own defense includes the opportunity to make well-informed decisions about formal plea offers. Counsel not only has a duty to present the defendant with favorable plea deals offered by the government but also must give advice that is not contrary to applicable law or an unreasonable interpretation of the law. In *Magana v. Hofbauer*, the Sixth Circuit Court of Appeals found the defendant was prejudiced where defense counsel advised the defendant to refuse the prosecution's plea deal because, according to counsel, the maximum possible sentence the defendant could receive for convictions at trial was the same as the sentence he would receive if he entered the plea. Unfortunately, this legal advice was incorrect. The defendant's criminal convictions at trial resulted in mandatory sentences that more than doubled the punishment he would have received had he accepted the government's offer.[27] This attorney's misunderstanding of and unreasonable interpretation of sentencing laws led to deficient representation that prejudiced the defendant.

Because the plea bargaining stage takes place before trial, the prejudice prong of the *Strickland* test—requiring the defendant to show that, but for counsel's deficiencies, the "result of the proceeding" would have been different—does not fit neatly into the analysis of an ineffective assistance claim. Consequently, in *Hill v. Lockhart*, the United States Supreme Court explained how to apply the prejudice prong to a plea bargain case. A defendant who asserts that counsel was ineffective for encouraging the defendant to plead guilty must prove that "there is a reasonable probability that, but for counsel's errors, he would not have pleaded guilty and would have insisted on going to trial."[28] The same type of analysis is applied to the flip side of this scenario. A defendant could argue that counsel was ineffective for encouraging the defendant to reject a plea bargain and go to trial.[29] The defendant would be required to show "a reasonable probability that he would have accepted the alleged proposed plea agreement absent defense counsel's advice."[30]

The same prejudice analysis applies even in plea bargain situations where a defendant has little to no defense to the criminal charges, if the defendant decides to accept a plea deal based on defense counsel's erroneous advice. In *Lee v. United States*, the United States Supreme Court addressed a situation in which the defendant pleaded guilty to possession of ecstasy with intent to distribute. Police officers discovered the drugs in the defendant's home, and the defendant admitted that the drugs were his and that he had given some to friends. The defendant, a non-citizen who had lived lawfully in the United States for years, was concerned about the possibility of deportation. He pleaded guilty to the drug possession charge, an aggravated felony, because defense counsel advised him that he would not be deported as a result of the plea and would receive a lighter sentence. However, under federal immigration laws the defendant was subject to mandatory deportation. Later, the defendant argued that, had he known of the consequences, he would have rejected any plea deal leading to deportation. The United States Supreme Court concluded that the defendant was prejudiced by following counsel's advice to enter a guilty plea, even though the defendant's chance of success at trial would have been slim to none.[31]

Other pretrial conduct that courts have deemed to be ineffective assistance includes defense counsel's failure to file a motion to dismiss an untimely indictment or counsel's failure to reasonably conduct a basic pretrial investigation, such as interview crucial eyewitnesses and explore alibi testimony and other mitigating evidence. As the defendant's representative, defense counsel plans a strategy that establishes a defense of criminal charges. Counsel's failure to timely notify the court of an alibi defense has been found to be ineffective, as has counsel's abandonment of potentially meritorious defenses.[32]

Trial Phase

As a case advances to jury selection, the right to effective counsel continues. In *Miller v. Webb*, the Sixth Circuit Court of Appeals addressed allegations of ineffective assistance during jury selection in an underlying murder trial. The deficient conduct included defense counsel's failure to challenge a prospective juror for cause after the juror had admitted that she would be "partial" to a key prosecution witness, whom she had met during Bible classes. The juror had stated during voir dire that she believed this particular witness was "the 'victim'" in the case.[33] Defense counsel took no steps to eject this prospective juror from the case, and she ultimately served on the jury that convicted the defendant of murder. The *Webb* court held that allowing a biased juror to serve on the jury violated the defendant's constitutional right to a fair trial with an impartial jury.

Although the government has the burden to prove its case beyond a reasonable doubt, defense counsel cannot take a hands-off approach to the case. Attorneys have a duty to be competent, which under the Model Rules of Professional Conduct requires the "legal knowledge, skill, thoroughness and preparation reasonably necessary for the representation."[34] Counsel must be attentive and alert during the trial, and obvious pitfalls, such as appearing in court while under the influence of alcohol or drugs or falling asleep in court, are red flags indicating that ineffective assistance allegations lie ahead.[35] Moreover, before and during trial, defense counsel, knowledgeable about the rules of evidence, must make choices and present arguments regarding the admissibility of evidence. In addition to the failure to investigate key evidence, counsel's failure to file a motion to suppress key evidence can also render counsel's representation ineffective. In *Northrop v. Trippett*, the Sixth Circuit Court of Appeals found trial counsel ineffective for failing to move to suppress drug evidence found in a duffle bag, where the drug evidence was the only basis for the defendant's drug possession conviction, and the discovery of the drugs flowed from an illegal seizure. The court stated that defense counsel should have known that such evidence was inadmissible under the fruit of the poisonous tree doctrine.[36] Along similar lines, in *Miller v. Anderson*, the Seventh Circuit Court of Appeals found defense counsel in an underlying murder trial was ineffective by presenting a witness who opened the door to the defendant's prior convictions, which included serious crimes against persons, such as kidnapping, rape, and sodomy.[37]

Sentencing Phase/Direct Appeal

The right to effective counsel continues through the sentencing phase and generally extends through the exhaustion of the direct appeal. With regard to sentencing proceedings, defense counsel's failure to uncover and present mitigating evidence, such as evidence pertaining to the defendant's mental health, family background, or military service, may be ineffective assistance.[38] Similarly, in the sentencing phase of a capital murder trial, defense counsel may be ineffective for failing to be prepared for the government's arguments regarding aggravating factors under state death penalty statutes. In *Rompilla v. Beard*, defense counsel failed to examine the defendant's files pertaining to prior convictions, where counsel knew the prosecution would seek the death penalty by showing the defendant had a significant history of felony convictions indicating the use or threat of violence, which was an aggravating factor under the applicable state death penalty statutes.[39] Equally, if not more, egregious is the situation where defense counsel argues *against* the defendant in the sentencing phase.[40]

After the district court imposes the sentence, the right to effective assistance of counsel carries through the defendant's first appeal of right. The United States Supreme Court applied the *Strickland* test to a claim of ineffective assistance of appellate counsel in *State v. Murray*, where appellate counsel made the decision to omit an evidentiary issue in the defendant's direct appeal. The court stated that an appellate attorney's process of "'winnowing out weaker arguments on appeal and focusing on' those more likely to prevail, far from being evidence of incompetence, is the hallmark of effective appellate advocacy."[41]

Post-Appeal

In general, a defendant does not have a constitutional right to counsel and, therefore, no right to effective counsel, in post-conviction proceedings, such as habeas corpus proceedings and discretionary petitions for review in state courts or the United States Supreme Court. Some states have held, however, that there is a state statutory right to counsel for collateral attacks under certain circumstances, and this right includes the right to effective assistance of counsel.[42]

Exceptions to the Prejudice Prong

Although the general rule requires courts to perform both prongs of the *Strickland* test, in *United States v. Cronic*, the United States Supreme Court pronounced narrow exceptions to *Strickland*'s second prong, holding that a defendant is not required to prove prejudice in three situations. Under these three rare categories of error, prejudice may be *presumed* where (1) there is a "complete denial of counsel" at a critical stage of the trial, such that counsel is either totally absent or prevented from assisting the accused; (2) counsel "entirely fails to subject the prosecution's case to meaningful adversarial testing"; or (3) under the "circumstances the likelihood that counsel could have performed as an effective adversary was so remote as to have made the trial inherently unfair."[43] The first *Cronic* category was present in *Mitchell v. Mason*, where the Sixth Circuit Court of Appeals held there was a complete denial of counsel in that the defendant's trial attorney spent approximately six minutes in the course of three separate meetings with the defendant in the courtroom bullpen before the start of trial.[44] The Tenth Circuit Court of Appeals found that the second *Cronic* category—failure to subject the government's case to meaningful adversarial testing—applied where defense counsel, who had filed a motion to withdraw, declined to comment at the defendant's competency hearing and mentioned that he possessed probative evidence but did not introduce it.[45] Deficient and incompetent closing argument alone may be per se ineffective assistance of counsel, particularly if defense counsel makes admissions of the defendant's guilt, such that counsel abandons an innocence-based defense against the client's wishes.[46] Circumstances falling into the third *Cronic* category include the appointment of counsel so close in time before trial that counsel fails to provide effective and substantial aid or a situation where counsel's loyalty is questioned by a conflict of interest.[47] As such, a breakdown in communication between a defendant and his attorney can be so severe to prevent "even the most able counsel from providing effective assistance."[48]

Criticisms and Possible Solutions

Despite the Sixth Amendment's guarantee of the right to effective assistance of counsel, denials of this constitutional right are still all too common. The law has created legal standards to address claims of ineffective assistance of counsel. Some scholars argue that these legal remedies are flawed and create undue procedural obstacles for defendants claiming ineffective assistance of counsel. For instance, defendants are guaranteed assistance of counsel solely for the first direct appeal, but some jurisdictions limit the subject matter of the appeal to evidence contained in the trial record. A claim of ineffective assistance of counsel often requires evidence outside the trial record, which means that a defendant faces an uphill battle to prove ineffective assistance of trial counsel during the direct appeal.[49]

Defendants can raise ineffective assistance of counsel claims through habeas corpus petitions. However, there are several drawbacks to this habeas corpus approach. First, there is no established constitutional requirement that defendants have access to counsel to provide assistance in filing habeas corpus actions. A lack of access to counsel places defendants at a severe disadvantage when arguing their case. Another drawback is the inevitable delay between the trial and when a defendant is able to file a habeas corpus action. Most jurisdictions require a defendant to wait to file a habeas corpus petition until the direct appeal is exhausted. During this delay, the risk of evidence being lost or otherwise compromised increases. Additionally, during this delay, defendants often serve their sentences and, upon being released, are no longer able to file a habeas corpus action.

An effective way to address these legal impediments is to require that defendants have limited assistance of counsel for habeas corpus petitions. Another solution to the procedural obstacles is to provide avenues for defendants to raise developed claims of ineffective assistance of counsel during their direct appeal. Both of these solutions, however, would require additional funding. In addition, such solutions are only reactive in nature. By the time the law permits defendants to raise concerns of ineffective assistance of counsel, defendants have already been negatively affected by ineffective assistance of counsel. These negative impacts include the entering of guilty pleas that might not otherwise have been entered, being found guilty of a crime, and being incarcerated. While reactive approaches to addressing ineffective assistance of counsel will remain necessary, reformers should also seek to develop proactive solutions that would, by their nature, prevent ineffective assistance of counsel in the first place.

There are also structural concerns that should be addressed to prevent ineffective assistance of counsel. In 1973, the National Advisory Commission on Criminal Justice Standards and Goals issued recommendations for improving the criminal justice system. Included in these recommendations were standards outlining the caseload for defense attorneys. According to the National Advisory Commission, each defense attorney should handle within the span of a year no more than 150 felony cases, 400 misdemeanor cases, 200 juvenile cases, 200 mental commitment cases, or 25 appeals. A Department of Justice's Bureau of Justice Statistics study, however, revealed, "almost three out of every four county-funded public defender offices have attorney caseloads that exceed nationally recognized maximum caseload standards."[50] For instance, in Florida, the annual caseload for a public defender averaged 500 felonies and 2,223 misdemeanors. In Tennessee, six public defenders covered approximately 10,000 misdemeanor cases, which is 1,667 cases per individual attorney.[51] These extreme caseloads hurt public defenders' ability to adequately represent their clients. Beyond presenting an ethical dilemma for public defenders weighed down by unmanageable caseloads, there is evidence to suggest that defendants who are represented by public defenders are less likely to be released on bail and are more likely to be convicted than defendants with retained counsel.[52]

Some suggest that the caseloads for public defenders could be lightened if local bars required members to do pro bono work and take on cases where they represent indigent defendants. Although requiring more pro bono work would be of benefit, it is unlikely to be able to fully address the overwhelming shortage of public defenders. Another way to ease the caseloads of public defenders is to hire more public defenders. It remains to be seen, however, if there is enough political motivation to further allocate public funds for hiring more public defenders. Another possible solution to a stressed public defense system is to decriminalize and even eliminate certain criminal violations. Experts estimate that eliminating or reclassifying nonviolent misdemeanors and other minor offenses could result in a savings of up to one billion dollars per year.[53]

Summary

The United States Constitution guarantees every criminal defendant the right to effective assistance of counsel. The ideal of every criminal defendant's having access to effective assistance of counsel, however, is not always the practical reality. Indigent defendants often have public defenders with little time to devote to their cases because of an increasingly unmanageable caseload, and legal impediments make it difficult for defendants to prove ineffective assistance of counsel claims. There are proposed legal and structural reforms that address these shortcomings, but these reforms require hard choices to be made, including providing additional funding. Because the right to effective assistance of counsel is part of the bedrock of the American criminal justice system, it is critical to continue to reform the current criminal justice system to ensure that every defendant has access to effective assistance of counsel.

Discussion Questions

1. What rights does the Sixth Amendment establish?
2. What are the three different types of indigent defense models? What are the benefits and drawbacks of each model?
3. When does an individual's Sixth Amendment right to counsel attach, and when does a defendant have the right to have counsel present?
4. Are there any concerns about allowing defendants to waive their right to assistance of counsel without first consulting with an attorney? Why or why not?
5. What is the two-part *Strickland* test? In what ways does the application of the second prong change when applied to a claim of ineffective assistance of counsel that occurred during the plea bargaining phase, as opposed to the trial?
6. Under *United States v. Cronic*, what are the three rare categories of error under which courts may presume that counsel's conduct prejudiced the defendant? What are some examples of conduct that a court might find presumptively prejudicial?
7. Courts examining the reasonableness of counsel's conduct must look at the challenged conduct *as of the time it was performed* and in light of the particular facts and circumstances. Why do you think this is required? What about the old maxim, "Hindsight is 20/20"?

Notes

1. Spangenberg, R. L., & Beeman, M. L. (1995). Indigent defense systems in the United States. *Law and Contemporary Problems, 58*(1), 32–37.
2. U.S. Const. amend. V.
3. *Miranda v. Arizona*, 384 U.S. 436, 444 (1966).
4. 384 U.S. at 467.
5. U.S. Const. amend. VI.

6. 304 U.S. 458 (1938).

7. 372 U.S. 335, 345 (1963).

8. *Argersinger v. Hamlin,* 407 U.S. 25 (1972).

9. *Kirby v. Illinois,* 406 U.S. 682, 689 (1972); see *Brewer v. Williams,* 430 U.S. 387, 398–399 (1977).

10. 377 U.S. 201 (1964).

11. *Kuhlman v. Wilson,* 447 U.S. 436, 459 (1986).

12. *United States ex rel. Williams v. Twomey,* 510 F.2d 634, 640 (7th Cir.); see *Woods v. Donald,* 135 S. Ct. 1372, 1376 (2015); *United States v. Cronic,* 466 U.S. 648, 656 (1984); *McMann v. Richardson,* 397 U.S. 759, 771 n.14 (1970).

13. See *Doe v. Mann,* 285 F. Supp. 2d 1229, 1240 (N.D. Cal. 2003).

14. *Strickland v. Washington,* 466 U.S. 668, 686 (1984); see *Geders v. United States,* 425 U.S. 80 (1976); *Brooks v. Tennessee,* 406 U.S. 605, 612–613 (1972).

15. *Diggs v. Welch,* 148 F.2d 667, 669 (D.C. Cir. 1945); see *Johnson v. United States,* 380 F.2d 810 (10th Cir. 1967); *Strong v. Huff,* 148 F.2d 692, 692–693 (D.C. Cir. 1945); Metze, P. S. (2012). Speaking truth to power: The obligation of the courts to enforce the right to counsel at trial. *Texas Tech Law Review, 45*(Winter), 228.

16. *Baxter v. Rose,* 523 S.W.2d 930, 936 (Tenn. 1975); see *United States v. DeCoster,* 487 F.2d 1197, 1202 (D.C. Cir. 1973).

17. *MacKenna v. Ellis,* 280 F.2d 592, 599 (5th Cir. 1960); see *Strickland,* 466 U.S. at 683.

18. *Strickland,* 466 U.S. at 677 (citing *Knight v. State,* 394 So. 2d 997 (Fla. 1981)).

19. 466 U.S. at 684–687.

20. *Harrington v. Richter,* 562 U.S. 86, 105 (2011).

21. *Strickland,* 466 U.S. at 689.

22. 466 U.S. at 694.

23. *Harrington,* 562 U.S. at 111; see *Strickland,* 466 U.S. at 691.

24. See, *e.g., Strickland,* 466 U.S. at 690–691; *United States v. Greer,* 643 F.2d 280, 283 n.9 (5th Cir. 1981); *Flynn v. State,* 136 P. 3d 909, 916–917 (Kan. 2006); *Taylor v. State,* 480 N.E.2d 924, 926 (Ind. 1985).

25. *United States v. Cronic,* 466 U.S. 648, 658–660 (1984); *Strickland,* 466 U.S. at 677–678.

26. See *Missouri v. Frye,* 566 U.S. 134, 140, 145–146 (2012); *Howard v. United States,* 743 F.3d 459, 468 (6th Cir. 2014); see also *White v. Ragen,* 324 U.S. 760 (1945); *State v. Carter,* 14 P. 3d 1138, 1143–1144 (Kan. 2000).

27. *Magana v. Hofbauer,* 263 F.3d 542, 545 (6th Cir. 2001).

28. *Hill v. Lockhart,* 474 U.S. 52, 58 (1985).

29. *Magana,* 263 F.3d at 547.

30. *Turner v. Tennessee,* 858 F.2d 1201, 1205 (6th Cir. 1988), *vacated on other grounds,* 492 U.S. 902 (1989), *reinstated on other grounds,* 940 F.2d 1000, 1002 (6th Cir.1991); see *United States v. Day,* 969 F.2d 39, 42 (3d Cir. 1992).

31. *Lee v. United States,* 137 S. Ct. 1958, 1963–1967 (2017).

32. *Wiggins v. Smith,* 539 U.S. 510 (2003); *Young v. Dretke,* 356 F.3d 616, 629–630 (5th Cir. 2004); see *Reynoso v. Giurbino,* 462 F.3d 1099 (9th Cir. 2006); *Clinkscale v. Carter,* 375 F.3d 430, 444–445 (6th Cir. 2004); *Riley v. Payne,* 352 F.3d 1313, 1325 (9th Cir. 2003); *Anderson v. Johnson,* 338 F.3d 382, 394 (5th Cir. 2003); *Rios v. Rocha,* 299 F.3d 796, 805–806 (9th Cir. 2002); *White v. Godinez,* 301 F.3d 796, 802 (7th Cir. 2002).

33. *Miller v. Webb,* 385 F.3d 666, 678 (6th Cir. 2004).

34. American Bar Association. (2017). *Model rules of professional conduct,* rule 1.1.

35. See *United States v. Ragin,* 820 F.3d 609 (4th Cir. 2016); *Haney v. State,* 603 So. 2d 368, 378 (Ala. Crim. App. 1991), *aff'd sub nom., Ex parte Haney,* 603 So. 2d 412 (Ala. 1992); Zimpleman, T. (2011). The ineffective assistance of counsel era. *South Carolina Law Review, 63*(Fall), 461.

36. *Northrop v. Trippett,* 265 F.3d 372, 378, 383 (6th Cir. 2001).

37. *Miller v. Anderson,* 255 F.3d 455, 459 (7th Cir.), *vacated on other grounds,* 268 F.3d 485 (7th Cir. 2001).

38. *Porter v. McCollum,* 558 U.S. 30 (2009); *Boyde v. Brown,* 404 F.3d 1159, 1176 (9th Cir.), *amended on reh'g,* 421 F.3d 1154 (9th Cir. 2005); *Lewis v. Dretke,* 355 F.3d 364, 366–367 (5th Cir. 2003).

39. *Rompilla v. Beard,* 545 U.S. 374 (2005).

40. *Horton v. Zant,* 941 F.2d 1449, 1462–1463 (11th Cir. 1991).

41. *Smith v. Murray,* 477 U.S. 527, 536 (1986); see *Pennsylvania v. Finley,* 481 U.S. 551, 555 (1987).

42. *Pennsylvania,* 481 U.S. at 555; *Wainwright v. Torna,* 455 U.S. 586, 587–588 (1982); *Ross v. Moffitt,* 417 U.S. 600 (1974); but see *Kargus v. State,* 162 P. 3d 818, 824 (Kan. 2007); *Brown v. State,* 101 P. 3d 1201, 1203–04 (Kan. 2004).

43. *United States v. Cronic,* 466 U.S. 648, 656, 650–661 (1984); see *Bell v. Cone,* 535 U.S. 685, 695–696 (2002).

44. *Mitchell v. Mason,* 325 F.3d 732, 741 (6th Cir. 2003).

45. *United States v. Collins,* 430 F.3d 1260 (10th Cir. 2005).

46. *State v. Carter,* 14 P. 3d 1138, 1148 (Kan. 2000); *State v. Harbison,* 337 S.E.2d 504, 507–508 (N.C. 1985).

47. *Cronic,* 466 U.S. at 660; *Frazer v. United States,* 18 F.3d 778, 787 (9th Cir. 1994).

48. *United States v. Soto Hernandez*, 849 F.2d 1325, 1328 (10th Cir. 1988).

49. Primus, E. B. (2009). Procedural obstacles to reviewing ineffective assistance of trial counsel claims in state and federal postconviction proceedings. *Criminal Justice, 24*(3), 7–11.

50. Benner, L. A. (2011). Eliminating excessive public defender workloads. *Criminal Justice, 26*(24), 25.

51. Primus, E. B. (2011). The illusory right to counsel. *Ohio Northern University Law Review, 37*(3), 604.

52. Williams, M. R. (2013). The effectiveness of public defenders in four Florida counties. *Journal of Criminal Justice, 41*, 205–212; see Joy, P. A. (2010). Ensuring the ethical representation of clients in the face of excessive caseloads. *Missouri Law Review, 75*(3), 771–792.

53. Boruchowitz, R. C. (2010). Diverting and reclassifying misdemeanors could save $1 billion per year: Reducing the need for and cost of appointed counsel. *American Constitution Society for Law and Public Policy*. Retrieved from http://lpdb.la.gov/Serving%20The%20Public/Reports/txtfiles/pdf/Boruchowitz%20Diverting%20and%20Reclassifying%20Misdemeanors.pdf

20

AGE AND SOCIAL JUSTICE

J. Harrison Watts

Introduction

What is social justice? It is a term frequently used in today's society. Social justice is debated on the news, on the internet, in courthouses, in legislative chambers, and on social media. There are entire college courses on social justice. In fact, one may earn a college degree with a major in social justice from Merrimack College and the University of Massachusetts, Amherst, among others. But what does social justice actually mean? According to the Heritage Foundation, the term originated with the Catholic Church and was first used around 1840 for a new kind of virtue (or habit) necessary for post-agrarian societies (Novak, 2009). What does social justice denote today? The answer can be found in five common uses of the term.

The first usage is found under the term distribution. This would include the distribution of advantages and disadvantages in society. When discussing advantages, one may think about income advantages. Consequently, wealth is a topic that falls under the label of social justice. Classic commitments to economic social justice, or an economic system in which the state limits corporate power, ensures a decent standard of living for all and encourages decent work (Rogers, 2017). What about our senior citizens who are no longer able to work? Are we as a society making sure that the elderly are adequately being financially taken care of? Is social security enough to have a distributed standard of living? Or are our seniors living below a distribution level that impacts their standard of living? The social justice of age may be able to explain and push solutions to these questions.

The second usage is equality. The expression of advantages and disadvantages supposes there is a norm of equality by which to measure both of these. According to Papageorgiou (1980), social justice implies, among other things, equality of the burdens, advantages, and opportunities of citizenship. Social justice is closely related to the concept of equality, and the violation of it is intimately related to the concept of inequality. Equality or the pursuit of it is seen directly in the Declaration of Independence as it proclaims that all men are created equal. We see equality as fairness, equity, or the equitable. However, what many see as equitable is often not to provide people the same portions, but rather to provide what is proportionate to the labors of each. So there is some debate as to what equality actually means. Perhaps it is equality of opportunity.

The United States is a very diverse place; however, with that diversity comes a bit of inequality. Should we as Americans promote equality or embrace genuine diversity? Is this a paradox that can never be reconciled or can we simply have it all?

Third, social justice is typically associated with notions of the common good. The common good suggests a benefit of the interests of all. Aristotle argued that injustice stands in the way of the common good (Smith, 1999). Most people speak of common good when they mean something noble and good. According to Wallis (2013), the common good has origins in the beginnings of Christianity. John Chrysostom, an early church leader, wrote,

> This is the rule of most perfect Christianity, its most exact definition, its highest point, namely, the seeking of the common good . . . for nothing can so make a person an imitator of Christ as caring for his neighbors.
>
> *(para. 2)*

In today's society, we strive for the common good among all of our neighbors (young and old included).

Finally, social justice is associated with a "progressive agenda." In this context, the progressive agenda is to "right" the perceived wrongs in our society. The progressive agenda can be defined as a set of goals that build upon the work of lawmakers, economists, and activists, with the aim of addressing inequality. The progressive agenda is about changing our national debate and, ultimately, changing policies that impact social justice (Ball, 2015). It is with these common uses that social justice is defined.

Age and Social Justice

Age is just a number, or so they say. But is age also a number that causes one to be discriminated against? In the majority of the states, 18 is the age of adulthood (with some exceptions) or what we call the legal age (knowing that among the 50 states there are 50 different definitions of the age of legality). What protections do those have who are not of legal age? In other words, what happens to little "Junior" when he is injured in an accident because of someone else? Can Junior legally file a lawsuit to seek damages? Federal and state laws generally don't permit minors to file lawsuits, as they do not possess capacity alone, and thus Junior needs assistance from someone who is deemed a representative. Moreover, many states, like Texas, recognize 18 as the "age of majority," at which time residents are legally considered adults (as opposed to "minors"). But Texas legal age laws also govern a minor's eligibility for more than having capacity to file a lawsuit. Areas such as emancipation and the legal capacity for signing a contract or consenting to medical treatment, all fall under the age of majority, which is restricted when someone is a minor.

Is Junior's being denied rights, which people over the age of 18 have, considered discrimination and a cause that social justice advocates should take up? The answer is yes and no. The law has developed separate rules for minors who have had their rights violated or who have been injured. In criminal matters, an entire portion of law relates to juvenile rights.

In this chapter, we will get into the details of age discrimination, the protections related to age and the workforce, as well as the applicable laws. The chapter includes many case examples that highlight laws protecting both young and old.

Discrimination Based on Age

Social media has become a normal part of everyday life for many Americans. One specific site, LinkedIn, allows professionals to connect with each other. Another feature of this social media site is targeted employment announcements. Recently, I received targeted announcements from the Federal Bureau of Investigation (FBI) through LinkedIn. Curiosity led me to look at the job requirements for a special agent position. Upon inspection, I noticed an age restriction. Candidates for employment must be younger than 37 at the time of appointment. Wait a minute, isn't this age discrimination? Yes it is. It is called legal age discrimination.

The Age Discrimination in Employment Act, which was passed in 1967, prohibits employment discrimination based on age, if the age is 40 years old or above. According to Kincel (2014), people 65 years and over living in the United States accounted for 40 million people or 13% of the total population. Those over 40 make up even more than that. This makes sense due to life expectancy increasing in the United States over the past 40 years. According to the National Center for Health Statistics (2016), between 1975 and 2015, life expectancy at birth increased from 72.6 to 78.8 years for the total U.S. population. Consequently, employees are working longer. Those employees who have had a longer tenure than new employees generally earn more in salary and cost a company or organization more in benefits. These issues may have an impact on a company's desire to continue employment of older workers. Moreover, older employees may retire from one career and decide to enter another career at an advanced age. Due to these issues, older workers need protections from discrimination. Ensuring these protections is an element of social justice.

Age Discrimination in Employment Act (ADEA)

The Age Discrimination in Employment Act (ADEA) is the federal law governing age prejudice. This act was passed in 1967 to encourage the employment of older workers based on their ability rather than on their age. In addition, the act was to prevent discrimination and resolve the issues that may result from an aging workforce. Many states also have laws prohibiting age discrimination and may have more restrictions than the ADEA. Congress' statement of findings and purpose of the ADEA according to Section 621 [section 2] are as follows:

(a) The Congress hereby finds and declares that—

    (1) in the face of rising productivity and affluence, older workers find themselves disadvantaged in their efforts to retain employment, and especially to regain employment when displaced from jobs;

    (2) the setting of arbitrary age limits regardless of potential for job performance has become a common practice, and certain otherwise desirable practices may work to the disadvantage of older persons;

    (3) the incidence of unemployment, especially long-term unemployment with resultant deterioration of skill, morale, and employer acceptability is, relative to the younger ages, high among older workers; their numbers are great and growing; and their employment problems grave;

    (4) the existence in industries affecting commerce, of arbitrary discrimination in employment because of age, burdens commerce and the free flow of goods in commerce.

(b) It is therefore the purpose of this chapter to promote employment of older persons based on their ability rather than age; to prohibit arbitrary age discrimination in employment; to help employers and workers find ways of meeting problems arising from the impact of age on employment.

The ADEA encompasses employers, including state and local governments, unions, and employment agencies in an industry affecting commerce, that have 20 or more employees. This act thus makes it illegal for an employer to fail, or refuse to hire, or to discharge any individual or otherwise discriminate against any individual with respect to his/her compensation, terms, conditions, or privileges of employment because of the individual's age. It further limits employers from segregating or classifying their employees in any way which would deprive, or tend to deprive, any individual of employment opportunities that would otherwise adversely affect his/her status as an employee, because of the individual's age. In addition, it limits employers from reducing the wages of any employee in order to comply with this act.

It is unlawful for an employment agency to fail, refuse, refer for employment, or otherwise discriminate against any individual because of the individual's age, or to classify or refer for employment any individual based on their age. However, the case of *Kimel v. Florida Board of Regents*, decided in January 2001, complicated this somewhat. Remember that the Age Discrimination in Employment Act of 1967 as amended makes it unlawful for an employer, including a state, to fail, refuse to hire, or discharge any individual or otherwise discriminate against any individual because of the individual's age. Although the ADEA does contain a clear statement of Congress' intent to repeal the states' immunity, that repeal exceeded Congress' authority under § 5 of the Fourteenth Amendment, and thus the Supreme Court held that the Eleventh Amendment provides state governments with immunity from suits, by private individuals, for damages under the ADEA. However, state governments are not immune to suits brought by the Equal Employment Opportunity Commission (EEOC), as opposed to private individuals who may not seek redress. Moreover, states are not immune from a federal suit seeking to compel the state to adhere to federal law. The EEOC may seek any remedy available under the law, including make whole remedies.

Bona Fide Occupational Qualification (BFOQ)

The Age Discrimination in Employment Act expands protections to cover age discrimination against persons over 40 years of age. There is, however, an exclusion: the BFOQ. Under certain conditions, an employer may discriminate if age, gender, or national origin can be shown to be a legitimate requirement to perform the job. The plaintiff must prove a *prima facie* case, as is required in Title VII cases; however, the ADEA does not include mixed-motive cases, as Title VII does. In order to establish a claim, the plaintiff must establish a *prima facie* case; if the employer offers a legitimate reason for the action, then the plaintiff must show the reason is being used as pretext for age discrimination. Two examples of age discrimination are as follows:

1. mandatory retirement of workers over age 55, while allowing workers under 55 to transfer to another plant or location; and
2. denial of promotion to a qualified worker who is over 50 years old.

Case Study 1

Western Air Lines Inc. v. Criswell, *472 U.S. 400 (1985)*

The Age Discrimination in Employment Act of 1967 (ADEA) generally prohibits mandatory retirement before age 70, but § 4(f)(1) of the Act provides an exception "where age is a bona fide occupational qualification [BFOQ] reasonably necessary to the normal operation of the particular business." Petitioner airline company requires that its flight engineers, who are members of the cockpit crews of petitioners' aircraft but do not operate flight controls unless both the pilot and the copilot become incapacitated, retire at age 60. A Federal Aviation

Administration regulation prohibits any person from serving as a pilot or copilot after reaching his 60th birthday. Certain of the respondents, who include flight engineers forced to retire at age 60 and pilots who, upon reaching 60, were denied reassignment as flight engineers, brought suit in Federal District Court against petitioner, contending that the age 60 retirement requirement for flight engineers violated the ADEA. Petitioner defended, in part, on the theory that the requirement is a BFOQ "reasonably necessary" to the safe operation of the airline. The physiological and psychological capabilities of persons over age 60, and the ability to detect disease or a precipitous decline in such capabilities on the basis of individual medical examinations, were the subject of conflicting expert testimony presented by the parties. The jury instructions included statements that the "BFOQ defense is available only if it is reasonably necessary to the normal operation or essence of [petitioner's] business"; "the essence of [petitioner's] business is the safe transportation of [its] passengers"; and petitioner could establish a BFOQ by proving both that "it was highly impractical for [petitioner] to deal with each [flight engineer] over age 60 on an individualized basis to determine his particular ability to perform his job safely" and that some flight engineers "over age 60 possess traits of a physiological, psychological or other nature which preclude safe and efficient job performance that cannot be ascertained by means other than knowing their age."

The District Court entered judgment based on the jury's verdict for the plaintiffs, and the Court of Appeals affirmed, rejecting petitioner's contention that the BFOQ instruction was insufficiently deferential to petitioner's legitimate concern for the safety of its passengers.

The Court's Holding

1. The ADEA's restrictive language, its legislative history, and the consistent interpretation of the administrative agencies charged with enforcing the statute establish that the BFOQ exception was meant to be an extremely narrow exception to the general prohibition of age discrimination contained in the ADEA.

2. The relevant considerations for resolving a BFOQ defense to an age-based qualification purportedly justified by safety interests are whether the job qualification is "reasonably necessary" to the overriding interest in public safety, and whether the employer is compelled to rely on age as a proxy for the safety-related job qualification validated in the first inquiry. The latter showing may be made by the employer's establishing either (a) that it had reasonable cause to believe that all or substantially all persons over the age qualification would be unable to perform safely the duties of the job, or (b) that it is highly impractical to deal with the older employees on an individualized basis.

3. The jury here was properly instructed on the elements of the BFOQ defense under the above standard, and the instructions were sufficiently protective of public safety.

   (a) Petitioner's contention that the jury should have been instructed to defer to petitioner's selection of job qualifications for flight engineers "that are reasonable in light of the safety risks" is at odds with Congress' decision, in adopting the ADEA, to subject such decisions to a test of objective justification in a court of law. The BFOQ standard adopted in the statute is one of "reasonable necessity," not reasonableness.

   The public interest in safety is adequately reflected in instructions that track the statute's language.

(b) The instructions were not defective for failing to inform the jury that an airline must conduct its operations "with the highest possible degree of safety." Viewing the record as a whole, the jury's attention was adequately focused on the importance of safety to the operation of petitioner's business.

(c) There is no merit to petitioner's contention that the jury should have been instructed under the standard that the ADEA only requires that the employer establish "a rational basis in fact" for believing that identification of those persons lacking suitable qualifications cannot be made on an individualized basis. Such standard conveys a meaning that is significantly different from that conveyed by the statutory phrase "reasonably necessary," and is inconsistent with the preference for individual evaluation expressed in the language and legislative history of the ADEA. Nor can such standard be justified on the ground that an employer must be allowed to resolve the controversy in a conservative manner when qualified experts disagree as to whether persons over a certain age can be dealt with on an individual basis. Such argument incorrectly assumes that all expert opinion is entitled to equal weight, and virtually ignores the function of the trier of fact in evaluating conflicting testimony.

709 F.2d 544, affirmed.

STEVENS, J., delivered the opinion of the Court, in which all other Members joined, except POWELL, J., who took no part in the decision of the case (Thomson, 2006).

Waivers of ADEA Rights

An employer may ask an employee to waive his/her rights or claims under the ADEA either in the settlement of an ADEA administrative or court claim or in connection with an exit incentive program or other employment termination program. The latter is very common, as organizations may offer early retirement to employees in an effort, through attrition, to save budget money. In order for an organization to do this, the ADEA sets out specific minimum standards which must be met in order for a waiver to be considered "knowing and voluntary" and, consequently, valid. Including other requirements, a valid ADEA waiver must include the following:

- The employee must be advised, in writing, to consult an attorney, and must be given at least 21 days before deciding whether to execute the waiver.
- The employee also must be allowed to revoke the waiver up to seven days after signing it.
- If the waiver is part of a termination incentive program, the employer must give the employee 45 days to consider the waiver.
- If the early retirement and waiver is offered to a class of employees, the employer must provide employees with the required information. The employer must also pay 80% of the cost for the employee to consult an attorney about the waiver.
- For any waiver involving a claim that is already before the EEOC or a court, employees must be given "reasonable time" to consider the waiver.
- In any suit involving a waiver of ADEA rights, the burden of proving the waiver complies with ADEA requirements is on the person asserting the waiver is valid.
- Any waiver doesn't affect an employee's right to contact the EEOC or the EEOC's right to pursue any claim.

Case Study 2

Oubre v. Entergy Operations, Inc., *522 U.S. 422 (1998)*

In consideration for receipt of severance pay under an employment termination agreement, petitioner Oubre signed a release of all claims against her employer, respondent Entergy Operations, Inc. In procuring the release, Entergy failed to comply in at least three respects with the requirements for a release under the Age Discrimination in Employment Act (ADEA), as set forth in the Older Workers Benefit Protection Act (OWBPA): It did not (1) give Oubre enough time to consider her options, (2) give her seven days to change her mind, or (3) make specific reference to ADEA claims. After receiving her last severance payment, Oubre sued Entergy, alleging constructive discharge on the basis of her age in violation of the ADEA and state law. Entergy moved for summary judgment, claiming Oubre had ratified the defective release by failing to return or offer to return the moneys she had received. The District Court agreed and entered summary judgment for Entergy. The Fifth Circuit affirmed.

Held: As the release did not comply with the OWBPA's requirements, it cannot bar Oubre's ADEA claim. The OWBPA provides: "An individual may not waive any [ADEA] claim . . . unless the waiver is knowing and voluntary. . . . [A] waiver may not be considered knowing and voluntary unless at a minimum" it satisfies certain enumerated requirements, including the three listed above. 29 U. S. C. § 626(f)(1). Thus, the OWBPA implements Congress' policy of protecting older workers' rights and benefits via a strict, unqualified statutory stricture on waivers, and this Court is bound to take Congress at its word. By imposing specific duties on employers seeking releases of ADEA claims and delineating these duties with precision and without exception or qualification, the statute makes its command clear: An employee "may not waive" an ADEA claim unless the waiver or release satisfies the OWBPA's requirements. Oubre's release does not do so. Nor did her mere retention of moneys amount to a ratification equivalent to a valid release of her ADEA claims, since the retention did not comply with the OWBPA any more than the original release did. Accordingly, even if Entergy has correctly stated the contract ratification and equitable estoppel principles on which it relies, its argument is unavailing because the authorities it cites do not consider the OWBPA's commands. Moreover, Entergy's proposed rule would frustrate the statute's practical operation as well as its formal command. A discharged employee often will have spent the moneys received and will lack the means to tender their return. These realities might tempt employers to risk noncompliance with the OWBPA's waiver provisions, knowing that it will be difficult to repay the moneys and relying on ratification. This Court ought not to open the door to an evasion of the statute by this device.

112 F.3d 787, reversed and remanded.

KENNEDY, J., delivered the opinion of the Court, in which STEVENS, O'CONNOR, SOUTER, GINSBURG, and BREYER, J., joined. BREYER, J., filed a concurring opinion, in which O'CONNOR, J., joined, post. SCALIA, J., filed a dissenting opinion, post. THOMAS, J., filed a dissenting opinion, in which REHNQUIST, C. J., joined, post.

The Equal Employment Opportunity Commission

The U.S. Equal Employment Opportunity Commission is responsible for enforcing federal laws that make it illegal to discriminate against a job applicant or an employee because of the person's race, color, religion, sex (including pregnancy, gender identity, and sexual orientation), national origin, age (40 or older), disability, or genetic information. It is also illegal to discriminate against a person because the person complained about discrimination, filed a charge of discrimination, or participated in an employment discrimination investigation or lawsuit. For example, the Equal Employment Opportunity Commission forbids a restaurant to seek "young" waiters, lest that discriminate against the elderly (Handlin & Handlin, 1995).

The EEOC has the authority to investigate charges of discrimination against employers who are covered by the law. Their role in an investigation is to fairly and accurately assess the allegations in the charge and then make a finding. If they find that discrimination has occurred, they will try to settle the charge. If they aren't successful, they have the authority to file a lawsuit to protect the rights of individuals and the interests of the public. They do not, however, file lawsuits in all cases where they find discrimination (EEOC, n.d.).

Most employers with at least 15 employees are covered by EEOC laws (20 employees in age discrimination cases). Most labor unions and employment agencies are also covered. Consequently, if someone alleges age discrimination, the EEOC is where an individual may start an investigation.

Social Justice and Minors

Minors in the Workforce

Minors (those typically we think of as under the age of 18, although this varies from state to state and subject to subject) have protections and limitations from discrimination in the workforce, education, and civil rights. Through a series of legislative acts and court cases, juvenile rights and protections have been established.

The federal child labor provisions of the Fair Labor Standards Act (FLSA), also known as the child labor laws, were enacted to ensure that when minors are employed, the working conditions are safe and do not jeopardize the health, well-being, or educational opportunities of the minor. These provisions also provide limited exemptions. In addition to the federal government, state governments have also established and enforce child labor laws to protect youth. The Fair Labor Standards Act was passed in 1938 and has regulated child labor at the federal level. It limits the number of hours and the type of work for 14- and 15-year-olds (Lee, 2007).

A surprisingly large proportion of American high school–aged youth works while in school. Nearly one-fifth of 14-year-olds, the youngest legal working age, works at least one week at any point while school is in session. The likelihood of working rises steadily with age: 29% of 15-year-olds; 60% of 16-year-olds; 71% of 17-year-olds (Lee, 2007). Due to so many minors working, there are rules that limit the types of jobs and number of hours they can work (there are agricultural work exceptions). In addition, states have laws that regulate the work of minors, and employers must follow both federal and state laws. If a minor is under 14 years of age, they are only allowed to work in the following fields:

- deliver newspapers to customers;
- babysit on a casual basis;
- work as an actor or performer in movies, TV, radio, or theater;
- work as a homeworker gathering evergreens and making evergreen wreaths; and
- work for a business owned entirely by their parents as long as it is not in mining, manufacturing, or one of 17 identified hazardous occupations.

Fourteen- and 15-year-olds are limited in what hours they can work and what jobs they can do. All work must be performed outside school hours and they may not work:

- more than 3 hours on a school day, including Friday;
- more than 18 hours per week when school is in session;

- more than 8 hours per day when school is not in session;
- more than 40 hours per week when school is not in session; and
- before 7 a.m. or after 7 p.m. on any day, except from June 1st through Labor Day, when night-time work hours are extended to 9 p.m.

Although there are no federal rules limiting the hours 16- and 17-year-olds may work, there are restrictions on the types of jobs they can do. At 16 years of age, these minors may work unlimited hours and are not restricted like that of a 15-year-old. They may perform any job that has not been declared hazardous by the Secretary of Labor. At 18-years-old, there are no restrictions.

Constitutional Protections for Minors

The First Amendment protects the people's right to practice religion, to speak freely, to assemble, to address the government, and of the free press. The *Tinker v. Des Moines Independent Community School District* (1969) is perhaps the most important case in history protecting the First Amendment rights of minors. This case is well known for Justice Fortas's statement: "it can hardly be argued that either students or teachers shed their constitutional rights to free speech at the schoolhouse gate." This occurred at a time when the Supreme Court was approaching a turnover in leadership and had undergone a much more conservative perspective regarding students' rights to free speech.

In *Tinker v. Des Moines Independent Community School District (1969)*, the United States Supreme Court had to address two main issues. The first issue inquired if First Amendment rights belonged to students in schools and not just adults in free society. Do students shed their First Amendment rights when they enter school grounds? In addressing this issue, the Supreme Court ruled in favor of the students with a 7–2 vote, stating that neither students nor teachers shed their First Amendment rights just because they enter onto school grounds.

The second issue questioned if wearing of a black armband as a symbolic protest was a form of "speech" protected by the First Amendment. The school had argued that schools were a place of learning and not a place for protest. However, the U.S. Supreme Court ruled primarily in favor of the students, stating that the wearing of the armband was a form of speech protected by the First Amendment. According to the Supreme Court, in wearing the armbands, the students "caused discussion outside of the classrooms, but no interference with work and no disorder." However, the court understood that there was a definite need to maintain order and safety in schools. As a result, the Supreme Court did not give students unlimited right to self-expression. The court actually restricted student free speech, stating it was allowed as long as it did not interfere or disrupt learning in the classroom or invade the rights of others.

In light of the school's right to maintain order, the envelope was pushed in the case of *Hazelwood School District v. Kuhlmeier* (1988). The United States Supreme Court ruled in favor of school districts, with a 5–3 vote, to allow the school administrator to censor school newspapers, restricting students from claiming their First Amendment right to freedom of speech. The court asserted that the school newspaper was a "supervised educational learning experience" and not an open public forum to voice opinions. The ruling allows schools to censor other school-related supervised learning activities such as yearbooks, theatrical productions, and graduation speeches.

The Fourth Amendment was tested in *New Jersey v. T.L.O.* (1985). T.L.O. was a 14-year-old freshman who was observed, by a teacher, smoking cigarettes with a friend in the high school restroom in Piscataway, New Jersey, in violation of school rules. Both of the students were taken to the principal's office, where they met with the assistant vice principal, Theodore Choplick, and were questioned. The friend admitted to smoking the cigarettes; however, T.L.O. denied smoking them. After T.L.O. denied smoking the cigarettes and claimed that she was not smoking at all, the assistant vice principal demanded to see T.L.O.'s purse. In searching inside the purse, he discovered several items, including a pack of cigarettes, cigarette rolling paper, a pipe, a small plastic bag that contained a grass-like substance, a wad of money, an index card with the names of several students that owed her money, and two letters that implicated her in dealing marijuana.

The assistant vice principal contacted the student's mother and the police, and he provided the officers with all of the contents that were found in T.L.O.'s purse to be used as evidence against her. The police contacted T.L.O.'s mother, and the mother brought her to the police department headquarters where she confessed to selling marijuana. The officers used the contents in the purse along with the confession and filed delinquency charges against her.

Before trial, T.L.O.'s attorney moved to suppress the evidence from the search and have the confession suppressed, arguing that T.L.O.'s Fourth Amendment right against unreasonable searches and seizures was violated. The court denied the motion to suppress the evidence. The Juvenile and Domestic Relations Court of New Jersey in Middlesex County adjudicated her as a delinquent and placed her on probation for one year. T.L.O.'s attorney appealed to the Superior Court of New Jersey, but the Superior Court affirmed the decision of the lower court. However, the New Jersey Supreme Court disagreed with the two lower courts, reversing the decision and ruling that the exclusionary rule applies to searches and seizures that are conducted by administrative officials in public schools.

The United States Supreme Court accepted the case and ruled in *New Jersey v. T.L.O.* (1985) with a 6–3 decision that the school's search of T.L.O.'s purse was constitutional, holding that school administrators can legally search a student's belongings if they have reasonable suspicion that a school rule has been broken or criminal activity is occurring. The court asserted that even though students have a "legitimate expectation of privacy," schools had a responsibility to maintain "an environment in which learning can take place." Based on the teacher's report that smoking had taken place, the initial search of T.L.O.'s purse was reasonable and the eventual discovery of the contents in her purse was justified. The ruling allows school administrators to search students' possessions with a lower burden of proof than police officers. School administrators are not required to reach the probable cause standard as required by police officers.

The Fifth Amendment protects people from being held for committing a crime unless they are properly indicted, being tried twice for the same crime, being forced to testify against yourself, and property being taken without just compensation. The leading case on self-incrimination is *Miranda v. Arizona* (1966). This landmark case held that both inculpatory and exculpatory statements made in response to interrogation by a defendant in police custody will be admissible at trial only if the prosecutor can show that the defendant was informed of the right to consult with an attorney before and during questioning and the right against self-incrimination.

In the case of *Fare v. Michael C.* (1979), Michael C. who, as a minor, was taken into custody on suspicion of murder, put the Fifth Amendment right not to self-incriminate to the test as a minor. Michael made some incriminating statements after asking for and being denied access to his probation officer (he had a long criminal history as a juvenile and thus was familiar with his probation officer) and attempted to have the statements suppressed, arguing that they had been obtained in violation of the Fifth Amendment right to remain silent. He argued that by asking for his probation officer he was invoking his right to remain silent, just as if he was seeking assistance from his legal counsel. The trial court denied the motion. On appeal, the Supreme Court of California reversed, holding that Michael's request for his probation officer was equivalent to asking for his attorney and automatically invoked his Fifth Amendment right against self-incrimination.

In a 5–4 decision, the United States Supreme Court ruled against Michael, stating that asking for a probation officer was not equivalent to asking for an attorney. The court ruled that a court must look at the "totality of the circumstance" in each case to determine whether a juvenile had waived his or her rights. In this case, Michael clearly waived his right to remain silent. In a dissenting opinion, Justice Thurgood Marshall argued that Miranda requires that police stop an interrogation any time that a juvenile request for an adult would represent his or her best interest.

When discussing the rights and protections of minors, one should know that there are federal and state laws that protect minors from dangerous and long working conditions. Priority is given to the advancement of minors through school, as these regulations take the minor's education into high consideration. When discussing minors' constitutional rights, the courts have leaned in the other direction. Minors do not have the same rights as adults (18 and over, generally) and for the protection of the educational process, the courts have leaned towards the school and a safe place for education over the rights of minors.

Summary

Social justice may take many names and/or many forms. Social justice is said to be extracted through distribution, equality, the common good, and the progressive movement. Social justice applies to people of all ages and especially the country's most vulnerable, such as minors and the elderly. Legislative bodies have pushed social justice through acts and/or laws that protect certain classes of people: namely the young and the old. These acts include the Age Discrimination in Employment Act and the Fair Labor Standards Act, which protect workers both young and old.

In addition, case law has established a separate body of rules that protect these two groups. Although both groups (young and old) are protected, it has been established that the young (minors) lack some of the same constitutional protections that adults have. Landmark cases such as *Tinker v. Des Moines Independent Community School District* (1969); *Hazelwood School District v. Kuhlmeier* (1988); *New Jersey v. T.L.O.* (1985); and *Fare v. Michael C.* (1979) impact the rights of minors.

Discussion Questions

1. What is social justice?
2. What protections are embodied in the Age Discrimination in Employment Act?
3. What are the regulations for employing minors?
4. What restrictions are placed on minors' freedom of speech while in an educational setting?
5. What is the legality of school administrators searching and seizing minor's property while at school?

References

Age Discrimination in Employment Act (ADEA), 29 U.S. Code § 621 [section 2] 1967.
Ball, M. (2015). The Equalizer. *The Atlantic Monthly*, *316*, 52–56, 58, 60–61.
Equal Employment Opportunity Commission. (n.d.). *Overview*. Retrieved from www.eeoc.gov/eeoc/index.cfm
Fare v. Michael C. 439 U.S. 1310 (1979).
Handlin, L., & Handlin, O. (1995). America and its discontents. *American Scholar*, *64*(1), 15.
Hazelwood School District v. Kuhlmeier, 484 U.S. 260 (1988).
Kimel v. Florida Board of Regents, 528 U.S. 62 (2000).
Kincel, B. (2014). *The centenarian population: 2007–2011: American community survey briefs*. U.S. Department of Commerce. Retrieved from www.census.gov/prod/2014pubs/acsbr12-18.pdf
Lee, C. (2007). *Three essays on child labor, schooling outcomes and health* (Order No. 3274904). Available from Business Premium Collection. (304852377). Retrieved from https://search.proquest.com/docview/304852377?accountid=39522
Miranda v. Arizona, 384 U.S. 436 (1966).
National Center for Health Statistics. (2016). *Health, United States: With chartbook on long-term trends in health*. Hyattsville, MD: National Center for Health Statistics. Retrieved from www.cdc.gov/nchs/data/hus/hus16.pdf
New Jersey v. T.L.O., 469 U.S. 325 (1985).
Novak, M. (2009). *Social justice: Not what you think it is*. The Heritage Foundation. Retrieved from www.heritage.org/poverty-and-inequality/report/social-justice-not-what-you-think-it
Oubre v. Entergy Operations, Inc., 522 U.S. 422 (1998).

Papageorgiou, G. J. (1980). Social values and social justice. *Economic Geography, 56*(2), 110–119.

Rogers, B. (2017). Basic income in a just society. *Boston Review, 42*(1), 11–29.

Smith, T. (1999). Aristotle on the conditions for and limits of the common good. *The American Political Science Review, 93*(3), 625–636.

Tinker v. Des Moines Independent Community School District, 393 U.S. 503 (1969).

Thomson, N. F. (2006). Is this a bona fide occupational qualification? *Journal of the International Academy for Case Studies, 12*(4), 17–21.

Wallis, J. (2013). Whatever happened to the common good? *Time.* Retrieved from http://ideas.time.com/2013/04/04/whatever-happened-to-the-common-good/

Western Air Lines Inc. v. Criswell, 472 U.S. 400 (1985).

21

TRANSITIONING TO SOCIAL JUSTICE

Transgender and Non-Binary Individuals

*Allyson Walker, Lori Sexton, Jace L. Valcore, Jennifer Sumner,
and Aimee Wodda*

Introduction

On July 26, 2017, the following message was issued from the Twitter account @realDonaldTrump:

> After consultation with my Generals and military experts, please be advised that the United
> States Government will not accept or allow . . . Transgender individuals to serve in any capac-
> ity in the U.S. Military. Our military must be focused on decisive and overwhelming . . .
> victory and cannot be burdened with the tremendous medical costs and disruption that
> transgender [sic][1] in the military would entail. Thank you

While this announcement was made under the guise of cost to the United States government, the
stronger purpose served by the message was to make it clear that, despite many small steps toward
social justice, the transgender and non-binary population is still vulnerable to attack—to being scape-
goated, vilified, and denied their rights—when it is politically convenient. Indeed, it has since been
countered that the annual medical costs run up by transgender individuals in the military amount to,
for example, one-fifth of the annual costs of military spending on Viagra alone.[2] A strong backlash
ensued after these tweets were issued, with leaders along the political continuum speaking out against
potential policy banning transgender people from the military. Despite this backlash and obvious economic counterpoints, however, there exist few policies within the United States, and indeed, within
the global North, granting legal protections to transgender individuals.

Throughout most of the global North, lesbians, gay men, and bisexual individuals have in recent
years been afforded increasing access to social justice in many forms, while being largely ignored by
the criminal justice system. Perhaps ironically, the opposite could be argued for transgender and non-
binary individuals.[3] Transgender and non-binary people are at an economic disadvantage as compared to the general population and are frequently the targets of violence. At the same time, they are
also targeted by the criminal system, through legislation that criminalizes their day-to-day existence,
and by police who make assumptions about the offending status of this population. This chapter
examines these issues and also explores the needs of transgender and non-binary offenders, which
often vary greatly from the needs of offenders in the general population. Finally, the chapter explores
issues related to transgender criminal justice practitioners, who have been regularly overlooked by
researchers as well as the systems in which they work. In order to advance social justice more

generally, it is crucial to understand the issues facing those among us who are most marginalized—including, but not limited to, the myriad ways in which their lives intersect with the criminal justice system.

Economic Disadvantage Faced by Transgender and Non-Binary Individuals

Before considering other social justice issues faced by transgender individuals, economic issues must be discussed. In conceptualizing social justice as fair and equal distribution of wealth and resources, transgender and non-binary individuals come up short. Research completed over the past 10 years has begun to show that transgender people are at an economic disadvantage when compared to the wider population: a 2012 survey by the National Center for Transgender Equality[4] showed that 15% of respondents (as compared to only 4% of the general population of the United States) made a yearly income of under $10,000. Other research[5] has shown that transgender individuals earn lower incomes than the general population on average. While this is unfortunate, it is hardly surprising. There are no federal laws against employment discrimination regarding gender identity. According to the Movement Advancement Project,[6] only twenty states, as well as the District of Columbia, have employment nondiscrimination laws covering gender identity, some of which also protect gender presentation or expression. Several other states have executive rulings protecting state employees from gender identity-related employment discrimination, but no protections for individuals who do not work for the state.

Even in states where it is against the law for employers to discriminate regarding gender identity, employment discrimination continues to exist. Lambda Legal[7] notes that a common experience among transgender and gender nonconforming individuals is receiving a job interview and being told, when the employer meets the interviewee, that the position has already been filled. A 2010 study by Make the Road[8] used two matched pairs of job searchers, with one transgender and one cisgender (i.e., not transgender) individual in each pair. Both job searchers in each pair were matched on ethnicity, gender, age, and educational experience. The pairs applied in person for retail jobs within New York City, which has laws against gender identity-based employment discrimination. The study found a 42% rate of discrimination among employers: in 11 of the 24 employers tested, a cisgender control applicant was offered a job while the transgender applicant was not; in only one of the 24 was the transgender applicant offered a job while the cisgender control applicant was not.

The employment and income disparities between cisgender individuals and transgender/non-binary individuals are even more prevalent among transgender women and trans people of color. Both people of color and women are already at an economic disadvantage when compared to white individuals and men.[9] Importantly, in the Make the Road study described above, the only transgender job applicant to have been given a job offer was white and male; the other transgender job applicant was an Asian trans woman, and she was offered no jobs. Additionally, a research study[10] exploring the effect of medically transitioning (transition using hormone replacement therapy and/or surgery) on income showed that individuals who transitioned from female to male experienced a slight increase in income when compared to their wage before their transition, while those who transitioned from male to female experienced a decrease.

Transgender and non-binary individuals experience further threats to their economic well-being that may contribute to, or exacerbate, the circumstances surrounding their employment and income. In a 2009 study by GLSEN,[11] transgender youth reported experiencing high rates of gender-related verbal and physical harassment, as well as physical assault, in school settings. Over one-third of transgender youth also reported hearing school staff members making sexist comments and negative remarks about gender expression, and few students said that school staff commonly intervened when hearing negative remarks about gender identity. Transgender students were more likely to miss school due to concerns about their personal safety than cisgender students, and transgender students had lower GPAs than cisgender students. Transgender students who faced high levels of harassment were also less likely to report plans to go to college. In a study of Wisconsin high school students, transgender and gender-nonconforming youth additionally reported gender-related discrimination from school staff, resulting in lowered GPAs and increased suspensions and expulsions.[12]

Transgender and non-binary individuals are also at a high risk of housing instability: a study[13] of trans and non-binary individuals in San Francisco showed that 32% had experienced housing discrimination, while 19% of survey participants did not have stable housing at the time they were surveyed. In a national survey[14] of transgender individuals, 8% of respondents who had come out to their families had been kicked out of their homes due to being transgender. Thirty percent of participants reported experiencing homelessness at some point over their lives, while 12% reported experiencing homelessness in the past year. Among those who were homeless in the past year, over one-quarter avoided staying in a shelter due to safety concerns related to their gender identity.

As transgender and non-binary individuals face reduced access to economic benefits compared to the general population, they may be at a higher risk for involvement in some types of crime. Given denial of opportunity for participation in legal economies, populations that experience economic disadvantage may be more likely to participate in underground economies. Additionally, economically disadvantaged individuals are more likely to be unfairly targeted by law enforcement, for the reasons discussed below.

Criminalization of Transgender and Non-Binary Individuals

Criminalization is a process that marks an activity as a criminal offense and an individual as a criminal. Often, the subjects of criminalization are punished for engaging in activities in which other groups engage without concern for criminal justice involvement (e.g., people who are homeless might be criminalized for "loitering," while law enforcement might ignore a non-homeless person who might be regarded as just "hanging out"). This section considers the criminalization of transgender and non-binary persons as a social justice issue.[15] Transgender and non-binary populations experience criminalization in a number of arenas—those most deeply and frequently impacted by criminalization are trans youth of color, trans women of color, and trans (im)migrants.[16] This criminalization is a social justice concern due to the structural nature of transphobia, which contributes to the continuing marginalization of transgender and non-binary populations, where trans women of color are most deeply impacted.[17]

Because cultural norms in most countries demand adherence to the gender binary, trans individuals who do not "pass" often experience abuse, bias, discrimination, harassment, and criminalization. Unlike individuals who conform to the gender binary, trans and non-binary people are often placed at risk for merely existing.[18] Additional hazards arise when others perceive trans individuals to be improperly inhabiting a space (e.g., a bathroom) and/or when they are trying to protect themselves (e.g., holding condoms). Economic inequality remains a factor in the criminalization of trans people,[19] as transgender and non-binary individuals who sell sex, especially transgender and non-binary people of color, may be either more visible (e.g., selling on the street) and/or more likely to be profiled by law enforcement officers. Income inequality is a major issue for transgender and non-binary people of color. Because bias and discrimination may leave transgender and non-binary individuals unemployed or underemployed, some persons look to the street economy in order to supplement meager or absent paychecks.

The criminalization of transgender and non-binary people operates in different but often interconnected arenas. For example, recent legal maneuvers in the United States known as "bathroom bills" demonize this population by portraying them as perverts and rapists.[20] At the same time, these bills put transgender and non-binary people at risk. In the United States, a number of municipalities have proposed so-called "bathroom bills," which aim to limit admittance to toilet facilities to persons whose assigned birth sex matches the bathroom's gender icon. Many of these bills were authored in response to broad human rights legislation that allowed transgender and non-binary individuals to use toilet facilities that matched their gender identity. "Bathroom bills" push back against broad human rights legislation that is inclusive of transgender and non-binary rights.

Supporters of "bathroom bills" argue that allowing transgender and non-binary individuals to use toilet facilities that match their gender identity is dangerous. They believe that trans individuals are mentally ill, perverse, dangerous, and harmful.[21] Additionally, although there is no evidence that transgender and non-binary populations are harmful to cisgender populations in public restrooms, there is ample evidence of harm towards trans populations from cisgender assailants.[22] Although trans youth are impacted by debates about bathroom use, other pressing social justice issues may be of more immediate concern.[23] For example, trans youth of color in the United States are disproportionately represented in the juvenile justice system and are increasingly at risk of becoming homeless.[24] This is the direct result of rejection by families and communities and victimization in school settings.[25]

Transgender women become the target of arrests in places where police regard the possession of condoms as evidence of prostitution.[26] HIV criminalization laws in the United States disproportionately affect trans people, who are at the highest risk of contracting HIV.[27] Globally, trans women are more at risk of acquiring HIV; an estimated 19% of trans women, worldwide, live with HIV.[28] Human Rights Watch estimates that, globally, transgender people are 50 times more likely to acquire HIV than the population as a whole. Contributing factors include stigma and difficulty accessing medical care.

The conflation of the criminal justice and immigration enforcement systems is a continuing concern for social justice practitioners. Trans and non-binary immigrants are particularly vulnerable to profiling, anti-immigrant bias, and criminalization; transgender and non-binary immigrants of color are most at risk of criminalization during this process.[29] Finally, in some countries (e.g., Malaysia, Kuwait, Nigeria), transgender existence itself is criminalized—laws characterize transgender and non-binary individuals as "males posing as women" and "females posing as men."[30] The social justice implications of the criminalization of transgender and non-binary individuals are far reaching. Sanctioning the criminalization of transgender and non-binary populations leads directly to victimization of those who refuse or fail to conform to gendered social norms.

Victimization of Transgender and Non-Binary Individuals

Feminist theorist Judith Butler wrote: "gender is a performance with clearly punitive consequences . . . those who fail to do their gender right are regularly punished."[31] For the majority of transgender and non-binary individuals, the policing of gender and corresponding punishments for nonconformity are a constant source of anxiety and fear, because they are victimized at disproportionate rates and with disparate levels of violence.[32] Self-report surveys and agency reports consistently show that transgender and non-binary people are targeted for various forms of violence, ranging from bullying and verbal abuse to sexual assault and homicide, because of their gender identity and perceived gender nonconformity.[33] Research shows that the majority of transgender and non-binary people will experience violent victimization during their lifetime at higher rates than the general population, and that their risk for such treatment begins at an early age.[34]

Transgender individuals are highly overrepresented among hate crime victims: the FBI reported that gender identity bias was the cause of 2% of the hate crime incidents in 2015, yet estimates from The Williams Institute suggest that only about 0.6% of the United States population is transgender.[35] The full extent of transgender victimization, however, cannot currently be determined. Official sources cannot be relied upon because, for instance, the federal government does not collect crime data based upon gender identity and only 15 states include gender identity in their hate crime statutes. The most valid information about transgender victimization is obtained from nongovernment sources, but sampling issues, inconsistent measures, and differing definitions of transgender mean that reliable and comparable data about the scope and prevalence of anti-transgender violence and abuse do not exist.[36] This absence of thorough, consistent, and official documentation ensures the number of known hate crime incidents presents a marked undercounting.

Crimes against transgender and non-binary individuals are not only undercounted by formal agencies, but also are severely underreported by those who experience them because they fear discrimination, stigma, violence, and indifference from both police and service providers.[37] Fear and distrust of law enforcement is pervasive in the transgender community.[38] Nearly half (46%) of the respondents who completed the National Transgender Discrimination Survey indicated that they were uncomfortable seeking assistance from the police,[39] and this was echoed in the 2015 U.S. Transgender Survey where 57% reported that they would be uncomfortable asking the police for help.[40] Even more troubling is that 58% of respondents had been mistreated *by police* in the past year, including verbal harassment, physical and/or sexual assault, being intentionally misgendered, and being asked to engage in sex acts to avoid arrest. Transgender women of color face the most harassment and abuse from police and report being stopped or arrested for "walking while trans"; 33% of Black trans women and 30% of multiracial trans women reported interacting with officers who assumed they were sex workers.

It is not simply transphobia, or fear of/prejudice towards transgender and non-binary individuals, that influences their victimization, but also misogyny, classism, and racism.[41] The high rate at which transgender women of color, in particular, are targeted and killed, is troubling. Of the 24 hate-motivated homicides reported by the 2015 NCAVP *Report on Hate Violence Against Lesbian, Gay, Bisexual, Transgender, Queer and HIV-Affected Communities*, 16 involved transgender or gender nonconforming victims, 13 of whom were trans women of color.

Victim blaming is unfortunately common and represents another reason transgender individuals decline to report victimization. Offenders of anti-transgender violence are typically males motivated by transphobia or transmisogyny and are often relative strangers to the victim.[42] A common explanation given by offenders is referred to as the "trans panic" defense; an offender learns that his sexual partner is transgender and reacts with such horror or disgust that he lashes out violently against the victim, sometimes resulting in homicide.[43] News media analysis by Schilt and Westbrook (2009) indicates that females do not react to such revelations with violence, perhaps because their femininity cannot be reclaimed in such a manner. But such violent reactions are often excusable in the mind of the offender and some members of the general public because transgender individuals are assumed to be deceptive, untrustworthy, and a threat to the masculinity of cisgender heterosexual males.[44]

Existing scholarship frequently mentions visibility and the inability to "pass" as cisgender as risk factors for transgender and non-binary victimization.[45] Transgender and non-binary individuals may fail to readily conform to social expectations regarding gender presentation and expression, putting them at risk for verbal harassment and/or physical assault. Those who fail to pass and those who are currently undergoing a process of gender transition or reassignment are most at risk for victimization.[46] Violence is a constant risk for transgender women in particular, especially in public places like streets, schools, and rest rooms.[47] Transgender women report a consistent fear of violent assault and struggle to find places where they can feel safe and cease the hypervigilance they must otherwise maintain. As previously noted, one of the primary locations of this harassment and abuse is public restrooms that are designated for a single sex. The 2015 U.S. Trans Survey found that 12% of respondents had been verbally harassed, physically assaulted, or sexually harassed in a public restroom in the previous year, 24% had their presence in a restroom challenged or questioned, 9% had been denied access, and 59% reported avoiding public restrooms for fear of negative confrontations.

Prevailing stereotypical expectations about gender presentation and expression, and the constant social and legal monitoring of gender-based norms and policies, place transgender and non-binary people at disproportionately high risk of verbal, physical, and sexual abuse. Their victimization is often connected to their overcriminalization, as the policing of public bathrooms shows, and can lead to arrests and convictions that place them in jails or prisons where they face unique challenges and continued victimization.

Needs of Transgender and Non-Binary Offenders

As a result of the economic marginalization, criminalization, and various forms of social injustice described above, many transgender and non-binary individuals find themselves entangled in the criminal justice system. Transgender and non-binary offenders are precariously positioned within the criminal justice system that operate on a strict gender binary with little to no comprehension of the differences between sex, gender, and even sexuality.[48] Within this context, the unique needs of transgender and non-binary individuals remain unaddressed, and are often exacerbated during the entirety of their criminal justice system involvement. These needs, how systems fail to meet them, and the consequences for transgender and non-binary offenders are presented below in terms of three broad categories: dignity, safety, and health. As the majority of empirical research and policy analysis of issues affecting transgender and non-binary offenders has been conducted in the United States and Australia, generalizations based on the information presented below should be made with extreme caution. A small but burgeoning literature on trans and non-binary offenders in Sri Lanka is instructive in this regard; it suggests that much of our largely U.S.- and Australia-based understanding of transgender and non-binary offenders' needs can be applied more broadly, even as findings demonstrate that the nuances of sex, gender, and sexuality are immeasurably intricate and culturally specific.[49]

While the maintenance of dignity for all offenders entangled within the criminal justice system warrants increased attention, transgender and non-binary individuals are uniquely at risk of degradation. When transgender and non-binary offenders first come into contact with the police, they are often misgendered (either intentionally or unintentionally) by officers.[50] This initial misgendering is often the catalyst for a chain of events that further degrades the dignity of transgender and non-binary offenders—including the use of incorrect names and inappropriately gendered pronouns and the denial of gender-affirming clothing—that persists throughout their time in the system, from policing to courts to corrections.[51] This misgendering also has physical consequences: body searches both in the field and in custody are usually conducted by officers of another gender who fail to treat transgender and non-binary offenders' bodies with dignity, particularly in the absence of agency policy providing related directives. Once detained—whether in police custody, pretrial confinement, or serving time on a sentence—the misgendering of transgender and non-binary offenders continues to have grave consequences for dignity: transgender and non-binary offenders are often housed according to assessments made on the basis of their genitalia, rather than their gender.[52]

Beyond the affront to dignity, placement in inappropriately gendered housing puts transgender and non-binary offenders—trans women in particular—at risk for verbal harassment, physical victimization, and sexual assault while in custody. The sexual victimization statistics are most revealing. According to research conducted by the Bureau of Justice Statistics, more than one-third of transgender prisoners in the U.S. have been sexually assaulted in the past year, as compared to 4% of the larger prisoner population.[53] These findings are in line with conclusions from California, where trans women in prisons for men are 13 times more vulnerable to sexual assault than men in the same prisons,[54] as well as findings from outside the U.S.[55] In Australia, in-depth interviews with Australian trans women and Indigenous Australian "sister-girls" who were current or former prisoners revealed daily experiences of sexual victimization, although difficulties identifying this population made it impossible to determine prevalence.[56] This increased vulnerability is often managed through the use of "protective custody" by way of segregation or isolation of transgender prisoners.[57] While such housing placements are ostensibly not intended as punishment, their effects are undeniably punitive, as they decrease transgender prisoners' access to already limited resources and sometimes result in solitary confinement.[58] Even in group settings, such as protective custody housing units where transgender prisoners are relatively protected from victimization by other prisoners, they report increased levels of harassment and assault by correctional staff.[59]

In addition to medical needs—both physical and mental—brought about by victimization, transgender offenders also have gender-related medical needs that often go unacknowledged by the criminal justice system, with significant consequences. The most basic of these medical needs are hormones and gender-affirming surgery. Despite the consensus among medical experts that such treatments are safe, effective, and can be medically necessary, transgender prisoners are frequently denied gender-related care.[60] Furthermore, access to this care is often contingent upon a diagnosis of "gender dysphoria"—a mental illness codified in the *Diagnostic and Statistical Manual* of the American Psychiatric Association—ensuring that transgender and non-binary offenders must pathologize themselves in order to receive medical care.[61] Inadequate medical care puts transgender prisoners at risk of myriad physical and mental health consequences, including depression, anxiety, and physical withdrawal from previously stable hormone therapy. State departments of corrections have increasingly acknowledged transgender prisoners' rights to hormone therapy over the past decade, but access is still not necessarily guaranteed and the administration of hormones can be sporadic.[62] Recently, however, a landmark legal victory for transgender prisoners was achieved: the California Department of Corrections and Rehabilitation was ordered to provide gender confirmation surgery to Shiloh Quine, a trans woman housed in one of the state's prisons for men.[63]

Thus, the assault to dignity that begins with inaccurate pronouns can have disastrous consequences for transgender and non-binary offenders. The criminal justice system is ill-equipped to handle, or even properly understand, the gender-related needs of transgender offenders. Far less is known about the criminal justice system's treatment of non-binary offenders, since the system's strictly binary, sex-based classification renders them invisible. This outmoded binary understanding of gender, concomitant with the persistent conflation of sex, gender, and sexuality by criminal justice practitioners and policymakers, affronts transgender and non-binary offenders' dignity, jeopardizes their safety, and denies them adequate medical care. As costly, high-profile lawsuits are brought against criminal justice agencies and as transgender offenders' unique needs continue to receive media attention, police departments and correctional agencies are increasingly forced to reckon with their inadequate treatment of this group. As a result, this policy domain is rapidly evolving, with a trend toward agencies developing gender-responsive policy regarding treatment, custody, and medical care for transgender offenders.[64]

Transgender and Non-Binary Criminal Justice Practitioners

Within the context of economic discrimination described above, transgender and non-binary criminal justice practitioners also face considerable challenges in their employment. While scholars have begun to develop research that examines the experiences of lesbian, gay, and bisexual police officers,[65] transgender and non-binary criminal justice practitioners remain almost entirely absent from this work. Thus, much of what is known about transgender and non-binary employees in criminal justice is merely gleaned from research on employment of transgender individuals more generally. As noted earlier, this research reveals that transgender individuals, particularly trans people of color and trans women, are more likely to be unemployed and to face discrimination and harassment when they are employed, compared to those who are cisgender.[66] Challenges experienced in other workplace settings may be further enhanced within criminal justice agencies—characteristically gendered organizations, in which policies and practices are structured according to gendered meanings and hierarchies.[67] Historically, criminal justice agencies in the United States, particularly police departments, have been predominantly "white, working-class male enclaves" with female employees regularly relegated to "peripheral" tasks, and men of color regularly excluded.[68] These agencies routinely operate according to a pseudo-military structure, including rigid hierarchical chains of command and a culture characterized by hegemonic hypermasculinity and heteronormativity, group loyalty, and strict codes of silence, especially within the United States.[69] Agency policies and practices structured upon sex segregation further rely upon specific and highly limited binary definitions and assumptions of sex and gender.

Within this organizational context, transgender employees in the criminal justice system are both highly visible, by virtue of their small numbers and the negative attention they receive, and highly *in*visible within an organization designed to exclude them. There is considerable, and regularly unwanted, media attention on transgender employees that focuses on the experiences of "firsts"—the presumed first transgender employee in a particular agency—often neglecting the discriminatory experiences of others or the extent to which many transgender employees are not "out" at work, particularly in the field of criminal justice.[70] Yet transgender employee policies in criminal justice agencies are still not ubiquitous, and there remains a dearth of social science research that systematically documents the experiences of this group.

The most extensive documentation of the experiences of transgender criminal justice employees in the United States is presented as part of an analysis of discrimination based on sexual orientation and gender identity in public employment more broadly, conducted by the Williams Institute.[71] The study revealed extensive experiences of discrimination among those working in law enforcement and corrections. In their analysis of nearly 400 examples of discrimination, the research indicates that more than 40% were from these fields.[72] Drawing upon data provided by the Transgender Community of Police and Sheriffs (TCOPS),[73] the authors report that out of the 60 TCOPS "members who were contacted about their experiences related to transitioning on the job, '56 [93%] reported negative experiences with their departments,'" including completed and threatened termination, verbal harassment, and threats and acts of violence.[74] Over half (53%) of those reporting negative experiences indicated that they "felt that their safety was jeopardized due to isolation by peers."[75] This heightened threat to safety is particular to working in the field of criminal justice, wherein one relies upon the support of coworkers when at risk on the job. Another work-related barrier to inclusion that transgender police and correctional officers face pertains to searches, which commonly include same-sex requirements, and have been presented as a justification for exclusion.[76]

Challenges that transgender criminal justice practitioners face include both informal and formal barriers to inclusion: transgender employees commonly experience hostility and abuse from coworkers and supervisors, exclusions from workplace activities, and barriers to both job retention and promotion. In this context of negative experiences, including transition-specific mistreatment such as inaccurate name and pronoun use and denied access to restrooms, many transgender employees keep their gender identities hidden while at work. Still, not all transgender law enforcement officers report negative experiences. Some report positive, and even improved, experiences transitioning on the job.[77] Positive experiences with transition may be enhanced to the extent that transgender employees may retain their jobs, have supervisor support, maintain consistent job responsibilities, have access to gender-appropriate restrooms and uniforms, are not harassed, and have coworkers that use appropriate pronouns and names.[78] Overall, model employment policies include guidelines that affirm one's gender identity and use of gender-neutral work requirements, such as uniforms.[79] Increasing the adoption of inclusive policies and practices for transgender and non-binary criminal justice practitioners will not only increase their safety and well-being, but will increase diversity in these settings.

Conclusion

Transgender and non-binary individuals' precarious position in the criminal justice system is largely an extension of their position within society as a whole. Denied justice at almost every turn, transgender and non-binary people face economic disadvantage, criminalization, and victimization—factors which contribute to their entanglement with the criminal justice system as offenders and complicate their roles as criminal justice practitioners. It should come as no surprise that transgender and non-binary people experience injustice in a system that is rooted in a false binary and routinely conflates sex and gender, while collapsing the contours of the two into a single dimension with two discrete categories: female and male. Even when systems attempt to accommodate transgender people who transition from one socially constructed category to the next (e.g., male to female), these same attempts simply serve to reinforce the very binary that was problematic in the first place.

Thus, while the system is uniquely challenging for transgender individuals who traverse commonly understood gender categories, it is a particularly poor fit for non-binary individuals who defy conventional gender categorization altogether. Logically, much of what we know about the transgender community—including their societal marginalization and unique needs—can reasonably be extended to the non-binary community as well. If society as a whole, and our criminal justice system in particular, are ill-equipped to handle individuals whose gender complicates conventional lay understandings, then it stands to reason that people whose gender eschews these categories altogether would be similarly misunderstood and mistreated. Beyond this initial misunderstanding and misgendering, however, non-binary people face many unique challenges that simply have not been adequately examined. Much of the research presented above is based on transgender samples that may or may not include non-binary individuals; seldom does the literature even acknowledge these differences, let alone orient to these two groups as empirically and analytically distinct. Thus, our current understandings of how non-binary individuals are situated with regard to justice is primarily a matter of extrapolation from transgender samples.

Beyond the limitations of both criminal justice systems and the scholarly literature related to transgender and non-binary individuals, there is also the crucial matter of attending to the source of this research and the population on which it is focused. The vast majority of the research presented above is from the global West and North. Despite the shortcomings in the literature from the U.S., for instance, there exists an increasing amount of information on transgender (and, to a lesser degree, non-binary) people's experiences of injustice in that country. A small but robust literature from Australia and nascent body of research from Sri Lanka notwithstanding, however, our scholarly understandings remain U.S.-centric. As our colleagues in this volume discuss in their chapter titled "LGBQ People and Social Justice," this domination of research and theory by Western nations "reinstantiate[s] power inequalities through the reproduction of Western knowledge."[80] Given the lopsided nature of the literature, it would be misguided to assume that the conclusions presented above apply evenly and neatly across the globe. Not only are criminal justice systems different across geographic location (even across jurisdictions within a single country), but so too is gender. The nuances and intricacies of the contours of gender are culturally, geographically, and temporally informed. Even within the U.S., we know far less about the experiences of, for instance, transgender and non-binary people of color, or transgender and non-binary people with disabilities. As the body of research on transgender and non-binary people continues to grow, scholars would do well to keep these current limitations in mind and get to work remedying them.

Acknowledgements

The authors would like to thank Nicole Asquith, Angela Dwyer, and Vanessa Panfil for the helpful feedback they provided on an earlier version of this chapter.

Discussion Questions

1. This chapter discusses multiple ways in which transgender and non-binary individuals face economic disadvantage. What policies could be enacted in order to alleviate some of this

disadvantage, and how might such policies affect offending behaviors among transgender and gender-nonconforming people?

2. In a 2009 study, GLSEN reported that transgender students were less likely than cisgender students to report plans to go to college. Why might this be the case? What can high schools and colleges do to better encourage transgender students to go to college?

3. So-called "bathroom bills" are intended to limit access to toilet facilities to a narrowly defined population. For example, the language in these bills criminalizes transgender women and girls for accessing restroom facilities supposedly reserved for cisgender girls and women. There is no evidence that a trans woman or girl has caused harm in a restroom, and someone who is regarded as occupying the "wrong" space can be at risk. How can transgender and non-binary persons protect themselves in the face of criminalizing legislation like this?

4. Human Rights Watch estimates that, globally, transgender women are more at risk of acquiring HIV. In some jurisdictions, transgender women have been arrested for carrying condoms, as this practice is regarded as evidence of prostitution. What are some of the social justice issues inherent in this issue—particularly given that people who do not use condoms in order to practice safer sex may be subject to state laws criminalizing HIV?

5. What are some of the implications of the criminal justice system's conflation of sex, gender, and sexuality for transgender and non-binary offenders' lived experiences as well as for policymakers and practitioners?

6. As evidenced in this chapter, the majority of the empirical research on transgender and non-binary offenders is focused specifically on transgender women. What steps can we take to better understand and treat transgender men and non-binary individuals in the criminal justice system? In what ways is our knowledge of transgender women useful for understanding the larger transgender and non-binary population, and in what ways is it limiting?

7. Transgender and non-binary individuals often fail to report their victimization experiences because they fear contact with law enforcement and the criminal legal system. What can law enforcement agencies do to address this?

8. Transgender and non-binary individuals face high rates of harassment and abuse simply because they do not fit into stereotypical expectations about gender. What can you do in your personal and/or professional life to try to change this?

9. Why do you think there remains so little research conducted on the issues facing trans and non-binary practitioners working in the criminal justice system? What is the value of conducting more research on these experiences?

10. In what ways could a more inclusive work environment for trans and non-binary criminal justice practitioners affect the relationship between criminal justice agencies and the broader community?

Notes

1. The authors of this chapter find it important to note that the usage "transgender in the military" is incorrect in this context: "transgender" here is a descriptor; therefore, the tweet should have read "transgender individuals."

2. Ingraham, C. (2017, July 26). The military spends five times as much on Viagra as it would on transgender troops' medical care. *The Washington Post*. Retrieved from www.washingtonpost.com/news/wonk/wp/2017/07/26/the-military-spends-five-times-as-much-on-viagra-as-it-would-on-transgender-troops-medical-care/

3. While the authors recognize that there are many varied and distinct labels for those who fall under the trans umbrella, including transgender, genderqueer, non-binary, and intersex people, we use the phrase "transgender and non-binary individuals" to refer to all of these categories. However, when specific research studies are discussed, we note the populations referred to in those studies. Notably, little research included intersex or non-binary individuals in their samples. See the GLAAD Media Guide for more on terminology: Creager, C., Tillman, D., & Bass, A. (2010). *GLAAD media reference guide*. Los Angeles: GLAAD.

4. Grant, J. M., Mottet, L. A., Tanis, J., Harrison, J., Herman, J. L., & Keisling, M. (2012). *National transgender discrimination survey*. Washington, DC: National Center for Transgender Equality.

5. Conron, K. J., Scott, G., Stowell, G. S., & Landers, S. J. (2012). Transgender health in Massachusetts: Results from a household probability sample of adults. *American Journal of Public Health, 102*(1), 118–122; Rosser, B. R. S., Oakes, J. M., Bockting, W. O., & Miner, M. (2007). Capturing the social demographics of hidden sexual minorities: An internet study of the transgender population in the United States. *Sexuality Research and Social Policy, 4*(2), 50–64.

6. Movement Advancement Project. (2016). *State employment non-discrimination laws*. R. Denver, CO: Author.

7. Lambda Legal. (n.d.). *FAQ: Answers to common questions about transgender workplace rights*. Retrieved from www.lambdalegal.org/know-your-rights/article/trans-workplace-faq

8. Make the Road New York. (2010). *Transgender need not apply: A report on gender identity job discrimination*. New York: Author.

9. Pew Research Center. (2013). *10 Findings about women in the workplace*. Washington, DC: Author. Retrieved from www.pewsocialtrends.org/2013/12/11/10-findings-about-women-in-the-workplace/; Sullivan, L., Meschede, T., Dietrich, L., & Shapiro, T. (2015). *The racial wealth gap*. Waltham, MA: Institute for Assets and Social Policy, Brandeis University.

10. Schilt, K., & Wiswall, M. (2008). Before and after: Gender transitions, human capital, and workplace experiences. *The BE Journal of Economic Analysis & Policy, 8*(1), 1–28.

11. Greytak, E. A., Kosciw, J. G., & Diaz, E. M. (2009). *Harsh realities: The experiences of transgender youth in our nation's schools*. New York: Gay, Lesbian and Straight Education Network (GLSEN).

12. McKinnon, S. L., & Gattis, M. N. (2015). *School experiences of transgender and gender non-conforming students in Wisconsin*. Madison, WI: GSafe.

13. Minter, S., & Daley, C. (2003). *Trans realities: A legal needs assessment of San Francisco's transgender communities*. San Francisco, CA: National Center for Lesbian Rights.

14. James, S. E., Herman, J. L., Rankin, S., Keisling, M., Mottet, L., & Anafi, M. (2016). *The report of the 2015 U.S. transgender survey*. Washington, DC: National Center for Transgender Equality.

15. Mogul, J. L., Ritchie, A. J., & Whitlock, K. (2011). *Queer (in) justice: The criminalization of LGBT people in the United States*, Vol. 5. Boston, MA: Beacon Press.

16. Johnson, J. R. (2013). Cisgender privilege, intersectionality, and the criminalization of CeCe McDonald: Why intercultural communication needs transgender studies. *Journal of International and Intercultural Communication, 6*(2), 135–144.

17. Bettcher, T. M. (2007). Evil deceivers and make-believers: On transphobic violence and the politics of illusion. *Hypatia, 22*(3), 43–65.

18. Human Rights Watch. (2011). Retrieved from www.hrw.org/world-report/2016/rights-in-transition

19. Spade, D. (2008). Compliance is gendered: Struggling for gender self-determination in a hostile economy. In P. Currah, R. Juang, & S. Minter (Eds.), *Transgender rights*, 2006. Retrieved from SSRN: https://ssrn.com/abstract=1209984

20. Valcore, J. (2017, February 5). The real victims of the senate's bathroom bill. *TribTalk*. Retrieved from www.tribtalk.org/2017/02/15/the-real-victims-of-the-senates-bathroom-bill/

21. Esseks, J. (2016, April 19). Anti-trans bathroom bills have nothing to do with privacy and everything to do with fear and hatred. *American Civil Liberties Union (ACLU) Blog*. Retrieved from www.aclu.org/blog/speak-freely/anti-trans-bathroom-bills-have-nothing-do-privacy-and-everything-do-fear-and?page=3

22. Trotta, D. (2016, December 7). U.S. transgender people harassed in public restrooms: Landmark survey. *Reuters*. Retrieved from www.reuters.com/article/us-usa-lgbt-survey-idUSKBN13X0BK See also: The National Center for Transgender Equality (NCTE). (2016). *The U.S. Transgender Survey (USTS) preliminary findings*. Retrieved from https://static1.squarespace.com/static/54f76238e4b03766696d8f4c/t/5782a8d919 7aeaa57b589608/1468180715744/USTS-Preliminary-Findings-July-2016-2.pdf

23. Alessi, K. (2017, March 10). Why justice for queer and trans youth goes beyond bathrooms. *Rewire*. Retrieved from https://rewire.news/article/2017/03/10/justice-queer-trans-youth-goes-beyond-bathrooms/

24. Durso, L. E., & Gates, G. J. (2012). *Serving our youth: Findings from a national survey of service providers working with lesbian, gay, bisexual, and transgender youth who are homeless or at risk of becoming homeless*. Los Angeles: The Williams Institute with True Colors Fund and the Palette Fund.

25. Hunt, J., & Moodie-Mills, A. C. (2012). The unfair criminalization of gay and transgender youth: An overview of the experiences of LGBT youth in the juvenile justice system. *Center for American Progress, 29*, 1–12.

26. Wurth, M. H., Schleifer, R., McLemore, M., Todrys, K. W., & Amon, J. J. (2013). Condoms as evidence of prostitution in the United States and the criminalization of sex work. *Journal of the International AIDS Society, 16*(1), 1–3. See also: Irvine, A. (2014). You can't run from the police: Developing a feminist criminology that incorporates Black transgender women. *Southwestern Law Review, 44*, 553–561.

27. Grant, J. M., Mottet, L. A., Tanis, J., Harrison, J., Herman, J. L., & Keisling, J. (2011). *Injustice at every turn: A report of the national transgender discrimination survey.* Washington: National Center for Transgender Equality and National Gay and Lesbian Task Force. See also: Kaplan, R. L. et al. (2016). *Journal of the International AIDS Society, 19*(Suppl. 2), 20787. Retrieved from www.jiasociety.org/index.php/jias/article/view/20787 | http://dx.doi.org/10.7448/IAS.19.3.20787

28. Baral, S. D., Poteat, T., Stro¨mdahl, S., Wirtz, A. L., Guadamuz, T. E., & Beyrer, C. (2013). Worldwide burden of HIV in transgender women: A systematic review and meta-analysis. *Lancet Infect Dis., 13,* 214–222. See also: UNAIDS (2016). Retrieved from www.unaids.org/sites/default/files/media_asset/global-AIDS-update-2016_en.pdf

29. Gehi, P. (2012). Gendered (in) security: Migration and criminalization in the security state. *Harvard Journal of Law & Gender, 35,* 357–398. Retrieved from http://harvardjlg.com/wp-content/uploads/2012/01/Gehi.pdf

30. Human Rights Watch. (2017). Retrieved from www.hrw.org/sites/default/files/world_report_download/wr2017-web.pdf

31. Butler, J. (1988). Performative acts and gender constitution: An essay in phenomenology and feminist theory. *Theatre Journal, 40*(4), 519–531. (reference on page 522)

32. Ellis, S. J., Bailey, L., & McNeil, J. (2016). Transphobic victimization and perceptions of future risk: A large-scale study of the experiences of trans people in the UK. *Psychology & Sexuality, 7*(3), 211–224.

33. Stotzer, R. L. (2009). Violence against transgender people: A review of United States data. *Aggression & Violent Behavior, 14,* 170–179.

34. Ellis, Bailey, & McNeil, 2016; Stotzer, 2009.

35. Flores, A. R., Herman, J. L., Gates, G. J., & Brown, T. N. T. (2016). *How many adults identify as transgender in the United States?* Los Angeles, CA: The Williams Institute; June 2016; Federal Bureau of Investigation. (2015). *2015 hate crime statistics.* Retrieved from https://ucr.fbi.gov/hate-crime/2015/topic-pages/incidentsandoffenses_final

36. Stotzer, R. L. (2014). Bias crimes based on sexual orientation and gender identity: Global prevalence, impacts, and causes. In D. Peterson & V. R. Panfil (Eds.), *Handbook of LGBT communities, crime, and justice* (pp. 45–64). New York: Springer.

37. Papazian, N., & Ball, M. (2016). Intimate-partner violence within the Queensland transgender community: Barriers to accessing services and seeking help. In A. Dwyer, M. Ball, & T. Crofts (Eds.), *Queering criminology* (pp. 229–247). New York: Palgrave Macmillan.

38. Buist, C. L., & Stone, C. (2014). Transgender victims and offenders: Failures of the United States criminal justice system and the necessity of queer criminology. *Critical Criminology, 22,* 35–47.

39. Grant, J. M., Mottet, L. A., Tanis, J., Harrison, J., Herman, J. L., & Keisling, M. (2011). *Injustice at every turn: A report of the national transgender discrimination survey.* Washington: National Center for Transgender Equality and National Gay and Lesbian Task Force.

40. James, S. E., Herman, J. L., Rankin, S., Keisling, M., Mottet, L., & Anafi, M. (2016). *The report of the 2015 U.S. transgender survey.* Washington, DC: National Center for Transgender Equality.

41. Meyer, D. (2015). *Violence against queer people: Race, class, gender, and the persistence of anti-LGBT discrimination.* New Brunswick, NJ: Rutgers University Press.

42. Schilt, K., & Westbrook, L. (2009). Doing gender, doing heteronormativity: "Gender normals," transgender people, and the social maintenance of heterosexuality. *Gender & Society, 23*(4), 440–464.

43. Tomsen, S. (2002). *Hatred, murder and male honour: Anti-homosexual killings in New South Wales* (Research and Public Policy Series 43). Canberra: Australian Institute of Criminology;
Wodda, A., & Panfil, V. R. (2015). "Don't talk to me about deception": The necessary erosion of the transgender and non-binary panic defense. *Albany Law Review, 78*(3), 927–971.

44. Schilt, & Westbrook, 2009.

45. Bettcher, T. M. (2007). Evil deceivers and make-believers: On transphobic violence and the politics of illusion. *Hypatia, 22*(3), 43–65; Shelley, C. A. (2009). Trans people and social justice. *The Journal of Individual Psychology, 65*(4), 386–396.

46. Ellis, Bailey, & McNeil, 2016; Shelley, 2009.

47. Perry, B., & Dyck, D. R. (2014). "I don't know where it is safe": Trans women's experiences of violence. *Critical Criminology, 22,* 49–63.

48. Sumner, J., & Sexton, L. (2016). Same difference: The "dilemma of difference" in the custody and care of transgender prisoners. *Law & Social Inquiry, 41*(3), 616–642.

49. Miller, J. (2002). Violence and coercion in Sri Lanka's commercial sex industry: Intersections of gender, sexuality, culture, and the law. *Violence against Women, 8*(9), 1044–1073; Miller, J., & Carbone-Lopez, K. (2013). Gendered carceral regimes in Sri Lanka: Colonial laws, postcolonial practices, and the social control of sex

workers. *Signs: Journal of Women in Culture and Society, 39*(1), 79–103; Nichols, A. (2010). Dance ponnaya, dance! police abuses against transgender sex workers in Sri Lanka. *Feminist Criminology, 5*(2), 195–222.

50. Stotzer, R. L. (2014). Law enforcement and criminal justice personnel interactions with transgender people in the United States: A literature review. *Aggression and Violent Behavior, 14*, 263–277.
51. Grant, Mottet, Tanis, Harrison, Herman, & Keisling, 2011.
52. Mann, R. (2006). The treatment of transgender prisoners, not just an American problem: A comparative analysis of American, Australian and Canadian prison policies regarding the treatment of transgender prisoners and a "universal" recommendation to improve treatment. *Law & Sexuality, 15*, 92–133; Newcomen, N. (2017). *Learning lessons bulletin: Transgender prisoners.* London: Prisons and Probation Ombudsman. Retrieved from www.ppo.gov.uk/app/uploads/2017/01/PPO-Learning-Lessons-Bulletin_Transgender-prisoners_Final_WEB_Jan-17.pdf; Sumner, J., & Jenness, V. (2014). Gender integration in sex-segregated U.S. prisons: The paradox of transgender correctional policy. In D. Peterson & V. R. Panfil (Eds.), *Handbook of LGBT communities, crime, and justice.* New York: Springer.
53. U.S. Department of Justice. (2011). *Sexual victimization in prisons and jails reported by inmates, 2011–12.* Washington, DC: Office of Justice Programs, Bureau of Justice Statistics.
54. Jenness, V., Maxson, C., Matsuda, K., & Sumner, J. (2007). *Violence in California correctional facilities: An empirical examination of sexual assault.* Report submitted to the California Department of Corrections and Rehabilitation. Sacramento, CA; Jenness, V., Sexton, L., & Sumner, J. (2011). *Transgender inmates in California prisons: An empirical study of a vulnerable population.* Report submitted to the California Department of Corrections and Rehabilitation. Sacramento, CA.
55. Blight, J. (2000). *Transgender inmates: Trends & issues in Crime and Criminal Justice.* Canberra: Australian Institute of Criminology.
56. Wilson, M., Simpson, P. L., Butler, T. G., Richters, J., Yap, L., & Donovan, B. (2017). "You're a woman, a convenience, a cat, a poof, a thing, an idiot": Transgender women negotiating sexual experiences in men's prisons in Australia. *Sexualities, 20*(3), 380–402.
57. Dolovich, S. (2011). Strategic segregation in the modern prison. *American Criminal Law Review, 48*(1), 1–110.
58. Sumner, & Sexton, 2016.
59. Sylvia Rivera Law Project. (2007). *"It's war in here": A report on the treatment of transgender and intersex people in New York State men's prisons.* Retrieved from http://archive.srlp.org/resources/pubs/warinhere
60. Brown, G. R., & McDuffie, E. (2009). Health care policies addressing transgender inmates in prison systems in the United States. *Journal of Correctional Health Care, 15*(4), 280–291.
61. Rodgers, J., Asquith, N., & Dwyer, A. (2017). *Cisnormativity, criminalisation, vulnerability: Transgender people in prisons.* Hobart, Tasmania: Tasmanian Institute of Law Enforcement Studies.
62. Sylvia Rivera Law Project, 2007.
63. Acevedo, B. (2017). The constitutionality and future of sex reassignment surgery in United States Prisons. *Hastings Women's Law Journal, 28*(1), 81–96.
64. Routh, D., Abess, G., Makin, D., Stohr, M. K., Hemmens, C., & Yoo, J. (2017). Transgender inmates in prisons: A review of applicable statutes and policies. *International Journal of Offender Therapy and Comparative Criminology, 61*(6), 645–666.
65. Belkin, A., & McNichol, L. (2002). Pink and blue: Outcomes associated with the integration of open gay and lesbian personnel in the San Diego police department. *Police Quarterly, 5*(1), 63–95; Jones, M., & Williams, M. L. (2015). Twenty years on: Lesbian, gay and bisexual police officers' experiences of workplace discrimination in England and Wales. *Police and Society: An International Journal of Research and Policy, 25*(2), 188–211; Miller, S. L., Forest, K. B., & Jurik, N. C. (2003). Diversity in blue: Lesbian and gay police officers in a masculine occupation. *Men and Masculinities, 5*, 355–385.
66. Grant, Mottet, Tanis, Harrison, Herman, & Keisling, 2012; Hartzell, E., Frazer, M. S., Wertz, K., & Davis, M. (2009). *The state of transgender California: Results from the 2008 California transgender economic health survey.* San Francisco, CA: Transgender Law Center; Schilt, K. (2010). *Just one of the guys? Transgender men and the persistence of gender inequality.* Chicago, IL: The University of Chicago Press.
67. Acker, J. (1990). Hierarchies, jobs, bodies: A theory of gendered organizations. *Gender & Society, 4*(2), 139–158; Britton, D. M. (2003). *At work in the iron cage: The prison as gendered organization.* New York: New York University Press; Miller, Forest, & Jurik, 2003.
68. Martin, S. E., & Jurik, N. C. (1996). *Doing justice, doing gender: Women in criminal justice occupations.* Thousand Oaks, CA: Sage; Miller, Forest, & Jurik, 2003, p. 358.
69. Nolan, T. (2009). Behind the blue wall of silence. *Men and Masculinities, 12*(2), 250–257.
70. Grant, Mottet, Tanis, Harrison, Herman, & Keisling, 2012.
71. Mallory, C., Hasenbush, A., & Sears, B. (2013). *Discrimination against law enforcement officers on the basis of sexual orientation and gender identity: 2000 to 2013.* Los Angeles, CA: The Williams Institute.

72. *Ibid.*, n.p.
73. TCOPS is a nonprofit organization based in the United States that provides peer support to transgender and non-binary law enforcement officers throughout the world. Transgender Community of Police and Sheriffs. (2017). Retrieved from www.tcops-international.org/
74. Mallory, Hasenbush, & Sears, 2013, n.p.
75. *Ibid.*
76. Little, C., Stephens, P., & Whittle, S. (2002). The praxis and politics of policing: Problems facing transgender people. *Queensland University of Technology Law and Justice Journal, 2*(2), 226–243.
77. Bender-Baird, K. (2011). *Transgender employment experiences: Gendered perceptions and the law.* Albany, NY: SUNY Press; Grant, Mottet, Tanis, Harrison, Herman, & Keisling, 2012; Schilt, 2010.
78. Schilt, 2010.
79. Transgender Law Center. (n.d.). *Model transgender employment policy: Negotiating for inclusive workplaces.* Oakland, CA: Author.
80. Asquith, Panfil, and Dwyer, this volume.

22

MIGRANT WORKERS IN CROP AGRICULTURE AND MEATPACKING INDUSTRY

Andrea Gómez Cervantes and Daniel Ryan Alvord

Introduction

In this chapter, we explore the development of low-wage migration systems in the United States and its proximity to immigration laws and their enforcement. We argue that the confluence of global capitalism and immigration policies have historically created a system of low-waged, highly exploitative migrant labor. And in recent decades, the neoliberalization of this system has led to the criminalization of migrant workers, making them susceptible to worker exploitation and denying them protections or rights. Specifically, under the "threat of deportation," migrant workers become a disposable labor force profiting corporations and governmental agencies. Mass deportation has become a tool to ensure profits for capitalistic enterprises, while the criminalization of migrant workers, particularly of Latino men, maintains their exploitation in the shadows.

We use two main examples to demonstrate these exploitative mechanisms. First, we detail the case of Latino/a migrant workers in crop agriculture. This sector of the economy has one of the longest histories with migrant labor. Second, we investigate the more recent expansion of the meatpacking industry and its growing Latina/o immigrant workforce. According to the Department of Agriculture,[1] crops and livestock, the two main components of agriculture, together are valued at over $350 billion. The overwhelming majority of workers in this industry are migrant laborers of Latin American origins and often with precarious legal statuses. According to the Department of Labor's 2013–14 National Agricultural Workers Survey (NAWS), 68% of farmworkers interviewed for the survey were born in Mexico, 27% were born in the United States, and 4% were born in Central America.[2] Of those born in the United States, 27% were Hispanic.[3] Additionally, of those interviewed, 53% had some form of work authorization in the United States. Similar demographic trends are found among those in the meatpacking industry. According to census estimates from 2010, approximately 33% of meat-processing labor is foreign-born.[4] Additionaly, the Pew Hispanic Center estimates that 27% of undocumented immigrants in the U.S. work in some capacity of the meatpacking industry .[5]

In the first section of this chapter, we briefly describe the development of migrant labor systems, utilizing Marxist and Latin American scholarship. Second, we outline the immigration policies in the U.S. that have led to the criminalization and expansion of a reserve migrant labor force. In the third section, we use the first example, crop agriculture migrant farmworkers, to depict the ties between immigration policies, the migrant labor system of the U.S., and its consequences for farmworkers and

their families. Following that, we use the case of the meatpacking industry to demonstrate the consequences of immigration enforcement on this growing migrant worker population. We conclude with
a brief discussion on the possibilities for social justice for migrant workers.

Migrant Labor Systems

Marxist and Latin American scholars have explored the complex aspects of international labor migration. Labor migration reflects and contributes to systems of global capitalism, rooted in complex relationships between and within low-income countries (also known as periphery and/or semi-periphery
by world-systems theorists) and high-income nations (also known as core or center nations).[6] As
Sassen[7] argues, international migrations involve multilayered processes and actors, including multina-
tional corporations that internationalize production processes and establish links between the sending
and receiving countries involved; governments that reproduce military conflicts displacing people; the
supranational organizations such as the International Monetary Fund (IMF) or World Bank, which
through their development efforts widen inequalities and create mobile unemployed populations;
and free-trade agreements that promote cross-border flow of capital and information, but not always
workers. The globalization of capitalism, exacerbated in recent decades by the ascendance of neoliberal ideologies, have endorsed a growing interdependence of political and economic institutions,
while creating the conditions for a vulnerable and mobile population in need of work.[8]

In its capitalistic development, the U.S. has employed various groups of immigrant workers for
arduous labor at different time periods. Starting in the late 1800s through to World War II, Mexican, Chinese, Japanese, and Filipino male workers were recruited to build railroads and work in the
agriculture and textile sectors.[9] During these earlier periods, the U.S. experienced great expansion
through its colonization of land, turning land into public property while encountering shortages of
labor supply.[10] At the same time, the country's rapid development of industrialization produced high
demand for workers, and economic growth in Europe slowed Western European migration.[11] Thus,
laws attempted to recruit workers from other countries. For example, in the 1860s, Congress passed
a law that authorized employers to pay for migrant workers' travel and signed a treaty with China
to import labor.[12] And the first federal immigration law, titled An Act to Encourage Immigration
of 1864, was "in response to industrialists' complaints of reductions in the labor supply during the
Civil War."[13] But by 1882 the Chinese Exclusion Act was signed, barring Chinese labor migration.
Immigrant labor along with immigration policies were used as a temporary solution to employment
shortages in particular sectors.

With the expansion of capitalism into a global system, migrant workers grew to be part of productive processes of society, becoming a permanent component of the global economic structure.[14]
Immigrant labor fulfills three major aspects of the capitalist global system that remain in place today.
First, it develops a source of labor force in the host country; second, it provides the necessary means
for survival of the workers and their families (many of whom remain in their home country); and
third, it externalizes the costs of the renewal of labor to the home country.[15] Thus, migrant labor
functions as a regulator of capitalism.[16] Migrant labor systems are sustained and enforced through
legal mechanisms (i.e., immigration laws and their enforcement) that leave migrants without rights
or citizenship.

Arguably, in recent years there has been a move towards the criminalization of migrant worker
populations through political and ideological movements around the securitization of nations and
borders.[17] In the U.S., immigration laws and their enforcement in the past few decades contributed to
the criminalization of migrant workers, particularly those who are hired for low-skilled and low-wage
labor, by enlisting a system of mass deportation and mass incarceration.[18]

Immigration Laws and Deportability

Immigration laws and policies in the U.S. have historically been crafted to contain at least two primary elements.[19] On the one hand, immigration policy has been crafted with consideration towards reinforcing and legitimating global capitalism. In this sense, immigrants are constructed primarily as laborers. As Lowe[20] explains, the state attempts to "produce and regulate" immigrant workers "as means of 'resolving' economic exigencies." The state utilizes immigration policies with "deserving" and "undeserving" frames resulting in the "inclusion" and "exclusion" of certain groups while reinforcing racialized and gendered labor bodies and their exploitation. As a result, migrant workers remain at the margins lacking full citizen rights, making them disposable and replaceable.[21] For example, when an industry needs more workers, policies are enacted to encourage migration of certain sectors of workers. Yet, if the same industry is facing a recession, then migrant workers are easily laid off.[22]

On the other hand, immigration policy has also been crafted with consideration towards nativist and restrictionist sentiments. Here, immigrants are construed as cultural or political threats to the nation. Throughout U.S. history, various immigrant groups have been perceived to be threats. For instance, Chavez[23] notes there has been a German language threat, a Catholic threat, an Irish threat, a Chinese threat, and more recently a Latino threat. While the group may change, threat narratives all tend to reflect a deep and persistent dichotomy between "deserving" and "undeserving" immigrants.[24] That is, threat narratives construct immigrant groups as a destructive force rather than a constructive force.[25]

These two elements of U.S. immigration policy—economic laborers and cultural threats—work together to reinforce the exploitative nature of migrant labor. This is particularly clear when it comes to border enforcement and the Border Patrol. Prior to 1924, the United States paid very little attention to border security. Indeed, only 60 Bureau of Immigration agents were stationed along the entire U.S.-Mexico border before 1924.[26] And even when the U.S. government established the Border Patrol in an attempt to enforce new immigration policies, Border Patrol agents "were mostly concerned with stopping Asians and Europeans from entering without inspection" and "only selectively applied immigration laws to Mexican migrants."[27] This selectivity was driven by the economic needs of employers in the Southwest who relied heavily upon Mexican laborers who crossed the border to work during the agricultural season and returned south after the harvest.

As de Genova notes, for the first 15 years of its existence, the Border Patrol was actually housed and operated under the Department of Labor.[28] According to Hernandez,[29] Mexican immigrants at the time were framed as "at least temporary if not contained, and their transitory presence in the fields of the Southwest would benefit agribusiness without having any major or long-term impact upon American society." National borders contribute to the international division of labor in the global economy and accumulation of capital.[30] Border enforcement fulfills the demands of nativist and restrictionist ideology by its presumption to "protect native workers" and citizen interests. However, as border enforcement is selective, this often reinforces capital interests that are fulfilled by migrant labor.[31] Simultaneously, border enforcement places criminal statuses on certain migrant workers (i.e., those who enter without proper authorization). And undocumented migrant workers become a working class without rights or protections from the state.

The Immigration Reform and Control Act (IRCA) of 1986 imposed sanctions on employers, making it illegal to knowingly hire an undocumented worker. However, many employers simply skirt these requirements anyway through different processes such as using subcontractors. Moreover, enforcement of these requirements involve raids on businesses. Yet, inspectors often give employers three days' notice of planned raids. The result is that, prior to a raid, employers fire or discharge undocumented workers in order to avoid the fine.[32] However, IRCA also drastically increased the number of crimes that could trigger deportation for immigrants themselves. Since IRCA, nearly every immigration law and decision has increased immigrant deportability. The Illegal Immigration Reform and Immigrant Responsibility Act of 1996 (IIRIRA), for instance, dramatically expanded the number of crimes considered felonies. IIRIRA also barred undocumented immigrants from receiving a type of Social Security benefit as well as federal student financial aid.[33] Another such example is a 2009 U.S. Supreme Court ruling that using false documents constituted "aggravated identity theft," which carries a mandatory two-year prison sentence. This statue has been used to charge immigrant workers who use someone else's documents to obtain work with identity theft, as was the case in the Postville, Iowa, raids.[34] What was previously only a civil violation of using someone else's documents was elevated to a felony, a crime that not only triggers deportation but also bars lawful reentry.[35]

Additionally, through these laws, immigration enforcement has moved to the interior of the country. Section 287(g) of IIRIRA encouraged local criminal justice agencies to participate in immigration enforcement through monetary incentives. This was later solidified through the Secure Communities Program in 2008, where through a memorandum of agreement, local agencies actively participate in the apprehension and detention of potential undocumented immigrants.[36] As a result, immigrants who work, live, pray, go to school, and have most likely settled into their communities become targets for deportation.

The dramatic increase in enforcement practices, however, has failed to achieve their stated goals. What they have achieved, instead, is helping to create a disposable workforce. This is demonstrated by the fact that the vast majority of immigration enforcement focuses on apprehending undocumented workers rather than prosecuting employers.

The construction of immigrant "illegality" and the threat of deportation serve to create and sustain a vulnerable—and cheap—workforce.[37] Deportability refers to the "the possibility of being removed from the space of the nation-state."[38] The possibility of deportation, or the "deportation threat," is produced, legitimated, and justified by the mass removal of immigrants, mostly Latino men. Between 2003 and 2016, 4,001,882 immigrants were deported, with the most deportations in 2012 when 407,821 immigrants were forcefully removed. Over 90% of those deported were men of mostly Mexican and Central American backgrounds.[39] The majority of these deportations were made through apprehensions in the interior of the country, not the border. Interior enforcement has increased as immigration laws such as the Secure Communities Program made it possible for local criminal justice agencies to enforce immigration law. The main cause for deportation in this period was entry without inspection (EWI), or crossing the border without proper authorization, technically a civil and not a criminal offense.[40] Yet, under the criminalization of immigration law, immigrant offenses are treated as criminal ones and punished as such.[41]

The deportability of undocumented immigrants makes their labor economically and politically profitable.[42] As Burawoy[43] argues, "the reproduction of a system of migrant labor hinges on the inability of migrants either as groups or individuals, to influence institutions that subordinate them." Leaving undocumented immigrants at the margins of society, with limited rights or protections, their deportability makes them vulnerable to exploitation. As de Genova explains, the deportability of undocumented migrants makes them a "disposable commodity."[44]

Migrant Farmworkers in the Fields

Starting in 1879, ethnic and racially marginalized groups have filled the low-waged, strenuous, temporary positions of crop agriculture. Immigrants from China, Japan, India, Pakistan, and Mexico worked in agricultural fields, until the 1940s, when the Bracero Program was enacted.[45] Since then and to this day, Mexican and most recently Central American laborers are the largest worker population of this sector. Together, Mexicans and Central Americans made up 72% of crop agricultural workers in 2014, and the overwhelming majority were men.[46]

The Bracero Program, a binational agreement between the U.S. and Mexico, allowed millions of Mexican laborers to work under short-term labor contracts in the U.S. and then return to Mexico.[47] The Bracero Program was a circular migration policy to help growers in California, Texas, and Arizona hire the labor they needed during the labor shortage caused by the Second World War. The Bracero Program was described at the time as a grower's "dream of heaven" because of the mass of cheap and temporary labor.[48]

However, by the early 1950s, increases in migrant workers lead to a backlash with nativist commentators who decried the "magnitude of the wetback traffic."[49] The U.S. then moved to impose sanctions on anyone found "harboring" undocumented immigrants. However, due to pressure from growers, employment was excluded from the definition of harboring. This program, known as PL-78, or the Mexican Farm Labor Program, essentially expanded the Bracero Program. Although the Bracero Program initially stipulated working conditions for Mexican nationals, including work hours, wages, housing, food, and healthcare, these were largely ignored. This program ultimately changed the face of big agriculture, first by making Mexican workers the bodies of agricultural labor, and second by reshaping the structure and organization of farm work. Growers became dependent on contractual, temporary laborers who would do the harshest and most physically demanding jobs for the lowest pay.[50]

The Bracero Program lasted until 1964. The following year saw one of the most significant immigration policy changes with the passage of the Immigration and Nationality Act in 1965. This policy cancelled many of the guest worker programs with Mexico and also implemented numerical limits on immigration from the Western Hemisphere.[51] Massey, Durand, and Pren note,

> by the late 1970s Mexico was placed under a quota of just 20,000 legal resident visas per year and no temporary work visas at all, as compared with 50,000 permanent resident entries and 450,000 temporary work entries in the late 1950s.[52]

However, agricultural growers' reliance on migrant labor had not changed in just one year. The result was that this migration flow continued, only now it continued as undocumented migration. As Kitty Calavita explains, the "guest workers of one era became the illegal immigrants of the next."[53]

By 1986's IRCA, the U.S. Congress revived the H-2 guest worker program. The H-2 visa program was split into H-2A and H-2B visas. H-2A was established specifically for agricultural workers, while H-2B was set up for nonagricultural workers. These visas are generally granted for a year or less, and H-2 visa holders are barred from seeking permanent residence or citizenship.[54] Additionally, employers seeking to hire workers with H-2 visas must demonstrate that they first tried to hire a U.S. employee. If they could hire a worker domestically, then they are not eligible for the H-2 program.[55] However, even when an employer hires an H-2 worker, the employer will often "recoup" the fees associated with filing the immigration forms, thus immediately indebting the worker to the employer.[56] In addition, the Special Agricultural Worker (SAW) program was also created under IRCA. SAW provided a path to legalization of unauthorized farmworkers. Approximately 1.3 million immigrants applied for SAW status and by 1992 nearly all gained legal status.[57] A major goal of both H2 and SAW programs was to create a stable agricultural workforce. However, after gaining legal status and given the poor working conditions and low wages, many of the legalized workers left the agricultural sector for other jobs.[58] And although newly implemented immigration policies aimed to deter new undocumented migration, these did not fully deter employers from hiring new arrivals. As a result, a new wave of immigrant workers, mostly undocumented and from Mexico, filled the jobs.

Agricultural labor involves strenuous, demanding jobs that pay little and have direct consequences to workers, both physically and emotionally. As demonstrated by the ethnographic work of Holmes,[59] immigrant farmworkers must face a series of violent conditions where immigration and work laws, agribusiness industries, and local work organizations lead to the structured violation of their bodies. Working at an agricultural migrant labor camp with Mexican laborers, Holmes finds that immigrants face myriad worker violations, exploitation, discrimination, abuse, and violence in their everyday work life. Starting with living conditions, farmworkers often must live in worker camps, where individuals and families are cramped together in small spaces, lacking privacy or hygiene. In Holmes's ethnography, the workdays often last between 12 to 18 hours, seven days a week. And workers are not always paid by the hour, but rather per pound of fruit harvested or per unit of fruit. In his study, Holmes's participants averaged 14 cents per pound. In a normal workday, this means that workers would have to pick 51 pounds every hour to make $7.16 per hour (the state minimum wage at the time of the study). In the most recent report by the National Agricultural Workers Survey (NAWS), workers average 44 hours per week and make on average $9.71 if paid by the hour and $11.57 on average if paid by the piece.[60] According to the Bureau of Labor Statistics, farmworkers make on average $22,540 per year.[61] In addition to low wages, pre- and post-harvest times make work hours and pay unstable; as a result, many families live below poverty thresholds.

Agricultural labor has significant health hazards. Working 12 hours crouched down on the knees, moving fast from one side to the other, often leads to long-term injury of the knees, back, shoulders, hands, or neck. Thus, long-term musculoskeletal diseases are common.[62] Additionally, working with pesticides has left many workers with respiratory diseases and skin conditions.[63] Yet, regardless of the backbreaking and dangerous labor, farmworkers are denied access to healthcare or worker protections. According to the NAWS, only 35% of farmworkers have some form of health insurance.[64]

Working the Line in Meatpacking Plants

Similar to crop agriculture, the meatpacking industry (processing cattle, chicken, and pork) has relied heavily on an immigrant labor force. For instance, in 1911, the U.S. Immigration Commission estimated that 60% of the labor force in meatpacking industry was foreign-born.[65] Meatpacking plants in the early 20th century in major cities like Chicago and New York relied heavily on eastern European immigrant groups for their labor supply.[66] However, by the start of the 21st century, the meatpacking industry had undergone several major changes. Notably, meatpacking has moved out of major metropolitan areas and into rural areas. This shift can mostly be attributed to what is referred to as the IBP revolution. This is named after the Iowa Beef Packers (IBP) plant established in 1960, which changed the location of meatpacking industries from near railroad centers to near the agricultural producing areas.[67] Before IBP, the majority of meatpacking plants were located in metropolitan areas, mostly Chicago, up to the 1980s. However by the early 2000s, 60% of meatpacking plants were located in rural areas.[68] And many of these plants now process more animals than ever before. For instance, just in Tyson meat-processing plants alone, 35 million chickens, 125,000 head of cattle, and 415,000 pigs are killed per week.[69]

Moving to rural areas benefitted the meatpacking industry greatly, as they were able to cut transportation costs by moving closer to the animal production, and being away from cities also decreased union formation and lowered environmental restrictions.[70] The restructuring of the meatpacking industry was accompanied by the active recruitment of Latino/a and minority workers for meatpacking jobs beginning in the late 1980s/early 1990s.[71] As meat processing became more industrialized, this increased the need for easily replaceable, low-cost labor.[72] For example, recruiters were often sent to U.S.-Mexico border towns as well as locations of low employment to find potential new hires.[73] Those who were able to bring new hires were incentivized with bonuses.[74] Additionally, the meatpacking industry has lobbied for a three-year visa for meatpacking labor.[75] Finally, refugee resettlement programs have brought Asian and African immigrant groups to Midwestern rural communities. And given that meatpacking work is year-round as opposed to crop agriculture, many see working these line jobs as a form of social mobility.

As Olivos and Sandoval[76] explain, following neoliberalization and the opening of global markets, the new organization of the meatpacking industry led to the de-unionizing, growing global meat markets and new structuring of labor involving mostly Latino/a workers. While crop agriculture has been shrinking, meatpacking has grown substantially. Today the U.S. is the first exporter and producer of meat. In 2016, for instance, the U.S. exported 1,187,050 metric tons of beef and 2,311,277 metric tons of pork around the world.[77] The export of meat is valued in the billions (in 2016, beef exports were valued at $6.3 billion and pork was valued at $5.9 billion). However, according to the Bureau of Labor Statistics, the mean annual wage for workers in meat processing is $27,140.[78]

The demands of meatpacking labor, including physical exhaustion, dangerous work conditions, low wages, and limited worker protections, along with recruitment practices have led to the racialization of this job and the industry's the reliance on an immigrant Latino/a labor force.[79] For the industry, this maximizes their profits. As explained by Olivos and Sandoval,[80] hiring undocumented workers

> solves potential labor crises (i.e., potential unionization, demands for safe work environments and living wages, realistic output quotas, etc.) also addresses likely profit-cutting ones as well (i.e., labor shortages, increased federal regulations, health scares, input expenses such as feed and equipment, etc.).

This is particularly true when the industry can rely on deportability and illegality as strategies of social control of their workers. Additionally, in comparison to other jobs with comparable wages, working the line in a slaughterhouse is often unattractive to native-born workers.[81]

In her ethnography about working the line of a hog processing plant in North Carolina, Ribas[82] sheds light on the grueling and exploitative conditions of the meatpacking industry. Ribas finds that many of the migrant female workers at the meatpacking plant had previous experience in agricultural jobs either in their home countries or in the United States. Latino/a immigrants made up the majority of workers on the kill floor and knife jobs in Ribas's hog plant, whereas African Americans worked mostly in processing departments. Ribas described working conditions as "difficult and uncomfortable in certain departments and insecure if the department was working less than forty hours a week, to brutal and despairing in other departments, and unbearable if the department was working seventy-five hours a week."[83] Working the line requires making the same movement for hours at a time and at a fast pace, with surveillance by coworkers and managers and limited breaks.

While working conditions in meatpacking plants are often dangerous, rates of injuries and illness have declined in recent years.[84] Yet, they still remain higher than any other manufacturing jobs. Furthermore, injuries often go unreported, so there is a question of the full impact this type of work has on health.[85] The types of injuries that workers can experience in meatpacking plants range from burns to their eyes caused by chemicals or steam, concussions, hearing loss, respiratory irritation or asphyxiation, bruises and fractures, strains, and other musculoskeletal disorders.[86] In addition to physical harms caused by the work, there are emotional and psychological harms done by management practices in these plants. For instance, the increased speed of production to maximize profits leads to physical and emotional distress.[87] Among the most heinous is the denial of bathroom breaks, leading some workers to face the indignity of having to wear diapers while they work.[88]

By the mid-1990s, approximately 25% of meatpacking workers in the Midwest were unauthorized immigrants.[89] This was followed by stringent sanctions against the hiring of undocumented workers, enacted by the IRCA of 1986 and reinforced by the IIRIRA of 1996. In 1998–99, the Immigration Naturalization Services (INS, which now is operated by Immigration Customs Enforcement [ICE], Border Patrol, and U.S. Citizenship and Immigration Services) launched operation Vanguard, sending raids in search of undocumented migrants in meatpacking plants, where workers were apprehended, detained, deported, and pushed to quit.[90] Although this was countered by an allied force of the meatpacking industry, agribusiness, and Latinx organizations fighting for the end to raids,[91] by 2006 the use of raids by ICE in meatpacking plants increased. Six plants owned by Swift were raided on December 12, 2006, apprehending almost 20% of the day workers at their plants.[92] Similarly, after a raid in a poultry processor in Georgia, three-fourths of 900 workers were apprehended.[93] Perhaps the most documented case was the raid conducted on May 12, 2008, in Postville, IL. This was also the largest immigration raid conducted in the United States. That Monday morning, 900 ICE agents uniformed, armed, and assisted by an UH-60 helicopter apprehended 390 workers during their morning shift at a meatpacking plant in small-town Postville.[94] From those apprehended, 306 were held for prosecution. Migrant workers were then placed in the Cattle Congress as the "detention center" in the same place they were processed in groups by built-up federal courts lacking immigration attorneys or proper interpreters.[95] While many of these immigrants had their lives totally disrupted and their livelihoods taken from them, the plant itself survived. After being sold to new owners, the state's economic development team gave the plant $600,000 in grants and forgivable loans. And two of the managers who pled guilty and served jail time related to charges of harboring undocumented immigrants were immediately hired back at the plant after their release. The new owners described them as "super managers" who deserve second chances.[96]

Conclusions

The continuance of migrant labor systems, particularly in the two major sectors of agriculture, crop agriculture and the meatpacking industry, is accompanied by complex, multifaceted relationships among individuals, globalization, and capitalism. As Ribas[97] explains, "capital satisfies as well as creates the demand for super-exploitable workers in a shifting sociopolitical environment," yet conditions are constantly changing and so are the relationships among workers, their employers, and the larger social context. The criminal justice system acts as an important component in capitalist economic production. By expanding the range of criminal offenses, the criminal justice system (broadly defined) helps to create and perpetuate a precarious labor force from which industries can draw. Crop agriculture and the meatpacking industry, in particular, have benefited from this arrangement. Historically, both of these industries have relied heavily upon immigrant workers. Because of the heavy reliance upon immigrant labor, these industries are susceptible to changes in immigration laws. For instance, laws can become too exclusionary for the agricultural industry. It is tricky to strike the right balance between laws that are too hostile for businesses, but still exclusionary enough to create a vulnerable workforce. This tension can be seen in the agricultural industry response to the extremely exclusionary laws passed in Arizona and Alabama. In both cases, the agriculture and business communities helped overturn these laws because of the toll it was taking on their profits. For instance, in Alabama, after the passage of HB56, farmers complained that there was no one left to pick tomatoes.[98] And the ways in which immigration enforcement and the legal context has changed can be seen in the changing conditions of this type of work, which has grown even more precarious and dangerous, and human rights violations continue.

It would be wrong, however, to deny migrant workers their agency in these situations. Many scholars assume that the presence of undocumented migrants makes unionization efforts more difficult. Indeed, some scholars argue that the presence of undocumented migrants actually deter unionization efforts in certain industries because they are seen as fearful of confrontation with authorities and, thus, docile.[99] However, this stereotype turns out to be untrue. Not only have researchers found a high degree of interest in unionization among immigrant workers,[100] but also there are cases where migrant workers did successfully unionize.[101] Such was the case with one of the most well-known and successful social mobilizations among farmworkers in the United States, guided by Cesar Chavez and Dolores Huerta in the 1960s–1970s, leading to the farmworker coalition that is now known as The United Farm Workers of America (UFW). The UFW committed to years of organizing, protesting, boycotting, walk-outs, and political action, even in the shadow of large corporations and immigration enforcement, and fought to protect the rights of farmworkers for years. Perhaps the most pronounced moment was the Delano grape strike in 1965.[102] After a 300-mile march, farmworkers' rights became aligned with other racial and poverty justice issues, merging their plight to the rest of the civil rights movements of the time and becoming symbolic to public eyes.[103]

Mobilizations among migrant workers and their communities continue to this day in search of worker rights and protections from exploitation. On the morning of February 16, 2017, a meatpacking plant in rural Kansas and restaurants and shops in California and Washington, DC, were found closed with signs stating "A Day Without an Immigrant." As the Univision news website posted, "February 16, a day to show the world what 'a day without an immigrant' would look like."[104] Immigrants and advocates across the country have joined forces demonstrating that immigrants, although faced with daunting obstacles and restraining and oppressive conditions, are able to resist and fight back. Social support and organizing continues throughout social media with hashtags such as #NoWallNoBan or #HereToStay, as immigrants claim space and advocates demonstrate support against the amplification of the immigration enforcement.

Summary

Agriculture and meatpacking industries have historically relied on immigrant labor. However, immigrant labor in these industries has grown more precarious as the legal context of immigration has changed. Immigration policy used to accommodate capital's demand for cheap and disposable labor by establishing temporary working programs like the Bracero Program. Increasingly, however, the disposability of immigrant labor is being determined by exclusionary policies, workplace raids by immigration authorities, and threats of deportation. The hostile legal context has largely contributed to the agricultural and meatpacking industries remaining two of the most dangerous sectors of work, as vulnerable workers no longer feel safe voicing complaints. This is not to say that immigrants are passive. Motivated by collective action campaigns, such as 2017's "A Day Without an Immigrant," immigrants organize and make their voices and presence known as the fight for social justice continues.

Discussion Questions

1. Can you think of other industries where migrant labor systems have developed? How are they similar to or different from crop agriculture and/or meatpacking?
2. How have immigration policies benefited big industries and failed migrant workers?
3. How do immigration policies and their enforcement contribute to making migrant labor "deportable"? And what does that mean?
4. How does immigrant precarity contribute to dangerous working conditions?
5. How do unionization efforts overlook the needs of immigrant workers?
6. In what other ways does the legal system create and maintain unequal power relations between workers and business owners?

Notes

1. Crops account for the largest share of the value of U.S. agricultural production. (2016). Washington, DC: United States Department of Agriculture. Retrieved from www.ers.usda.gov/data-products/chart-gallery/gallery/chart-detail/?chartId=58328
2. Hernandez, T., Gabbard, S., & Carroll, D. (2016). *Findings from the National Agricultural Workers Survey (NAWS) 2013–2014*. Washington, DC: U.S. Department of Labor Employment and Training Administration Office of Policy Development and Research. Retrieved from www.doleta.gov/agworker/pdf/NAWS_Research_Report_12_Final_508_Compliant.pdf
3. *Ibid.*

4. Artz, G. M. (2012). Immigration and meatpacking in the midwest. *Choices*. Retrieved from www.choicesmagazine.org/choices-magazine/theme-articles/immigration-and-agriculture/immigration-and-meatpacking-in-the-midwest

5. Passel, J. S. (2006). *The size and characteristics of the unauthorized migrant population in the U.S.* Washington, DC: Pew Hispanic Center.

6. Portes, A., & Walton, J. (1981). *Labor, class, and the international system.* New York: Academic Press.

7. Sassen, S. Regulating immigration in a global age: A new policy landscape. (2000). *The ANNALS of the American Academy of Political and Social Science, 570,* 35–45.

8. De Genova, N. (2002). Migrant "illegality" and deportability in everyday life. *Annual Review of Anthropology, 31*(1), 419–447; Golash-Boza, T. M. (2015). *Deported: Immigrant policing, disposable labor, and global capitalism.* New York: New York University Press.

9. Lowe, L. (1996). *Immigrant acts: On Asian American cultural politics.* Durham, NC: Duke University Press.

10. *Ibid.*; Sassen-Koob, S. (1981). Towards a conceptualizaton of immigrant labor. *Social Problems, 29*(1), 65–85.

11. Sassen-Koob, 1981.

12. *Ibid.*

13. Calavita, K. (2010). *Inside the state: The Bracero program, immigration, and the I.N.S.* New York: Routledge, p. 4.

14. Castles, S. (1989). *Migrant workers and the transformation of western societies.* Cornell: Center for International Studies, Cornell University.

15. Burawoy, M. (1976). The functions and reproduction of migrant labor: Comparative material from Southern Africa and the United States. *American Journal of Sociology, 81*(5), 1050–1087.

16. *Ibid.*; Castles, 1989.

17. Menjívar, C. (2014). Immigration law beyond borders: Externalizing and internalizing border controls in an era of securitization. *Annual Review of Law and Social Science, 10,* 353–369.

18. De Genova, N. (2005). *Working the boundaries: Race, space, and "illegality" in Mexican Chicago.* Durham, NC: Duke University Press; Golash-Boza, T. (2016). The parallels between mass incarceration and mass deportation: An intersectional analysis of state repression. *Journal of World-Systems Research, 22*(2), 484–509; Kubrin, C. E., Zatz, M. E., & Martínez, Jr., R. (2012). *Punishing immigrants: Policy, politics, and injustice.* New York: New York University Press; Menjívar, C., & Kanstroom, D. (2014). *Constructing immigrant "illegality": Critiques, experiences, and responses, eBook.* New York: Cambridge University Press.

19. Zolberg, A. R. (2006). *A nation by design.* New York: Russell Sage Foundation.

20. Lowe, 1996, p. 10.

21. Castles, 1989, p. 18; De Genova, 2002; Golash-Boza, 2015.

22. Burawoy, 1976, p. 1065.

23. Chavez, L. R. (2013). *Latino threat: Constructing immigrants, citizens, and the nation,* 2nd ed. Stanford, CA: Stanford University Press.

24. Newton, L. (2005). It is not a question of being anti-immigration: Categories of deservedness in immigration policy making. In *Deserving and entitled: Social constructions and public policy* (pp. 139–172). Albany, NY: State University of New York Press.

25. Chavez, 2013.

26. Lee, E., & Yung, J. (2010). *Angel Island: Immigrant gateway to America.* New York: Oxford University Press.

27. *Ibid.*, p. 251.

28. De Genova, 2002, p. 422.

29. Hernandez, K. L. (2010). *Migra! A history of the U.S. border patrol.* Berkeley, CA: University of California Press.

30. Sassen-Koob, 1981.

31. *Ibid.*

32. De Genova, N. (2013). Immigration "reform" and the production of "illegality". In C. Menjívar & D. Kanstroom (Eds.), *Constructing immigrant "illegality": Critiques, experiences, and responses* (pp. 37–62). New York: Cambridge University Press.

33. *Ibid.*

34. Camayd-Freixas, E. (2009). *Postville: La Criminalización de Los Migrantes. Guatemala.* Guatemala City: F&G Editores.

35. Enchautegui, M., & Menjívar, C. (2015). Paradoxes of family immigration policy: Separation, reorganization, and reunification of families under current immigration laws. *Law & Policy, 37*(1–2), 32–60.

36. Menjívar, & Kanstroom, 2014.

37. De Genova, 2005.

38. *Ibid.*, p. 439.

39. Golash-Boza, 2016; Golash-Boza, T., & Hondagneu-Sotelo, P. (2013). Latino immigrant men and the deportation crisis: A gendered racial removal program. *Latino Studies, 11*(3), 271–292.

40. Tracking immigration and customs enforcement removals. (2016). TRAC Immigration. Retrieved from http://trac.syr.edu/phptools/immigration/remove/
41. Kubrin, Zatz, & Martínez, Jr., 2012.
42. De Genova, N. (2007). The production of culprits: From deportability to detainability in the aftermath of "homeland security". *Citizenship Studies, 11*(5), 421–448.
43. Burawoy, "The Functions and Reproduction of Migrant Labor: Comparative Material from Southern Africa and the United States."
44. De Genova, 2005.
45. Wells, B. (2013). *Daughters and granddaughters of farmworkers: Emerging from the long shadow of farm labor.* New Brunswick, NJ: Rutgers University Press.
46. Hernandez, Gabbard, & Carroll, 2016..
47. Calavita, 2010.
48. *Ibid.*, p. 21.
49. *Ibid.*, p. 47.
50. Wells, 2013.
51. Massey, D. S., Durand, J., & Pren, K. A. (2016). Why border enforcement backfired. *American Sociological Journal, 121*(5), 1557–1600.
52. *Ibid.*, p. 1559.
53. Calavita, 2010, p. 289.
54. Griffith, D. (2009). U.S. migrant worker law: The interstices of immigration law and labor and employment law. *Comparative Labor Law & Policy Journal, 31*(1), 125–162.
55. *Ibid.*
56. *Ibid.*
57. Wells, 2013.
58. *Ibid.*
59. Holmes, S. (2013). *Fresh fruit: Migrant farmworkers in the United States.* Berkeley, CA: University of California Press.
60. Hernandez, Gabbard, & Carroll, 2016.
61. Quick facts: Agricultural workers. (2016). Washington, DC: Bureau of Labor Statistics. Retrieved from www.bls.gov/ooh/farming-fishing-and-forestry/agricultural-workers.htm
62. Holmes, 2013.
63. *Ibid.*
64. Hernandez, Gabbard, & Carroll, 2016.
65. Broadway, M. (2007). Meatpacking and the transformation of rural communities: A comparison of brooks, Alberta and Garden City, Kansas. *Rural Sociology, 72*(4), 560–582; Purcell, T. D. (1953). *The worker speaks his mind on company and union.* Cambridge, MA: Harvard University Press.
66. Barret, J. (1990). *Work and community in the jungle.* Champaign, IL: University of Illinois Press.
67. Broadway, 2007.
68. Artz, G., Jackson, R., & Orazem, P. F. (2010). Is it a jungle out there? Meat packing, immigrants, and rural communities. *Journal of Agricultural and Resource Economics, 35*(2), 299–315.
69. Investor relations. (2016). *Tyson fact book.* Retrieved from http://ir.tyson.com/investor-relations/investor-overview/tyson-factbook/default.aspx
70. Kandel, W., & Parrado, E. (2005). Restructuring of the US meat processing industry and new Hispanic migrant destinations. *Population and Development Review, 31*(3), 447–471; Martin, P. (2013). Migration and US agricultural competitiveness. *Migration Letters, 10*(2), 159–179; Olivos, E. M., & Sandoval, G. F. (2015). Latina/O identities, the racialization of work, and the global reserve army of labor: Becoming Latino in Postville, Iowa. *Ethnicities, 15*(2), 190–210.
71. Griffith, D. (2012). Labor recruitment and immigration in the Eastern North Carolina Food Industry. *International Journal of Sociology of Agriculture and Food, 19*(1), 102–118; Miraftab, F. (2016). *Global heartland: Displaced labor, transnational lives, and local placemaking.* Bloomington, IN: Indiana University Press.
72. Champlin, D., & Hake, E. (2006). Immigration as industrial strategy in American meatpacking. *Review of Political Economy, 18*(1), 49–69.
73. Miraftab, 2016.
74. *Ibid.*
75. Staff, R. (2013). US meat industry seeks 3-year worker visa in immigration reform. *Reuters News Agency.* Retrieved from www.reuters.com/article/usa-immigration-agriculture-idUSL1N0BQDWD20130227
76. Olivos, & Sandoval, 2015.
77. Export statistics. (2017). Denver, CO: U.S. Meat Export Federation. Retrieved from www.usmef.org/news-statistics/statistics/

78. Occupational employment and wages, slaughters and meat packers. (2016). Washington, DC: Bureau of Labor Statistics. Retrieved from www.bls.gov/oes/current/oes513023.htm

79. Olivos, & Sandoval, 2015.

80. *Ibid.*, p. 200.

81. Kandel, & Parrado, 2005.

82. Ribas, V. *On the line: Slaughterhouse lives and the making of the New South.* (2016). Oakland, CA: University of California Press.

83. *Ibid.*, p. 47.

84. Workplace safety and health: Additional data needed to address continued hazards in the meat and poultry industry. (2016). Washington, DC: Government Accountability Office. Retrieved from www.gao.gov/assets/680/676796.pdf

85. *Ibid.*

86. *Ibid.*

87. The speed kills you: The voice of Nebraska's meatpacking workers. (2009). *Nebraska Appleseed.* Retrieved from https://neappleseed.org/wp-content/uploads/downloads/2013/01/the_speed_kills_you_100410.pdf

88. No relief: Denial of bathroom breaks in the poultry industry. (2016). Oxfam. Retrieved from www.oxfamamerica.org/static/media/files/No_Relief.pdf

89. Artz, Jackson, & Orazem, 2010; Martin, 2013.

90. Warren, W. J. (2007). *Tied to the great packing machine: The midwest and meatpacking.* Iowa city: University of Iowa Press.

91. Martin, 2013.

92. *Ibid.*

93. *Ibid.*

94. Rigg, R. R. (2011). The Postville raid: A postmortem. *Rutgers Race and Law Review, 12*(2), 271–300.

95. *Ibid.*

96. Leys, T. (2010, April 14). Convicted agriprocessors managers out of jail and back at work. *The Des Moines Register.*

97. 2016, p. 62.

98. Pilkington, E. (2011, October 14). Alabama immigration: Crops rot as workers vanish to avoid crackdown. *The Guardian.* Retrieved from www.theguardian.com/world/2011/oct/14/alabama-immigration-law-workers

99. Milkman, R. (2002). New workers, new labor, and new Los Angeles. In *Unions in a globalized environment: Changing orders, organizational boundaries, and oscial roles.* Armonk, NY: M.E. Sharpe.

100. Gabriel, J. (2006). Organizing the jungle: Industrial restructuring and immigrant unionization in the American meatpacking industry. *Journal of Labor and Society, 9*(3), 337–359.

101. Milkman, R., & Wong, K. (2001). Organizing immigrant workers: Case studies from Southern California. In *Rekindling the movement: Labor's quest for relevance in the twenty-first century.* Ithaca, NY: Cornell University Press.

102. Shaw, R. (2008). *Beyond the fields: Cesar Chavez, the UFW, and the struggle for justice in the 21st century.* Berkeley, CA: University of California Press.

103. Bratt, P. (2017). *Dolores.* Documentary. PBS Distribution. www.doloresthemovie.com

104. Santiago, P. V. (2017, February 16). Un Día Sin inmigrantes: La protesta ontra Trump cierra comercios Y restaurantes en Varias ciudades de EEUU. *Univision Noticias,* sec. Inmigracion. Retrieved from www.univision.com/noticias/inmigracion/un-dia-sin-inmigrantes-la-protesta-con-la-que-rechazan-las-medidas-migratorias-de-trump

23

NATIONAL AND INTERNATIONAL ORGANIZATIONS THAT PROMOTE AND PROTECT SOCIAL JUSTICE

Kathryn Elvey and Danielle Marie Carkin

Introduction

Social justice is defined in a variety of ways, but ultimately, those who engage in social justice reform seek to address the inequality of resources and opportunities. The inequality can be very diverse in nature, ranging from citizenship to access to education to the ability to run for or be represented in politics. Given the vast array of areas that social justice interests intersect, there are numerous organizations that represent social justice issues. Social justice organizations are broken into three types of groups: nongovernmental organizations, governmental organizations, and a third overlapping group of intergovernmental organizations. The following discussion touches on nongovernmental, governmental, and intergovernmental organizations in the United States and across the globe, which seek to promote and protect social justice in varying and diverse ways.

Before discussing the extensive and diverse organizations that promote and protect social justice, it is important to define certain concepts that help lay the groundwork for understanding how these operations are funded and structured. All of the organizations discussed throughout this chapter differ in the scope of their work and ability to promote social justice based on their funding, mission, qualifications, and capacity. Therefore, it is important to understand the type of organization being discussed and where their funding, mission, and qualifications come from. From example, a nongovernmental organization (NGO) is a nonprofit entity that is separate or independent from governmental or intergovernmental organizations. They are often funded by donations and grants.[1] In contrast, a governmental organization is just that—a program fully funded by a state's government operating on state funds, rules, and regulations. Finally, a third category of structure and funding for programs that promote social justice are intergovernmental organizations, also known as international organizations (IGOs). These IGOs are composed of member states, which voluntarily choose to participate in the organization and its cause or causes. Intergovernmental organizations each differ in their structure, function, membership, and mission.

As stated above, numerous organizations promote social justice—it is impossible to list, discuss, and qualify these organizations, both in the United States and internationally. This chapter takes just a quick glance at some of the more commonly recognized and regarded social justice promoters and protectors. Furthermore, many of the organizations discussed may have innumerable social justice initiatives, which they are currently trying to protect or promote. Beyond that, many have overlapping goals and interests—some work together and some work independently, depending on their structure. However, the importance of these organizations and their work in promoting and protecting social justice cannot be overstated. This chapter begins with a discussion of nongovernmental social justice organizations in the United States, followed by a discussion of international NGOs that promote and protect social justice. Next, the chapter will examine U.S. governmental organizations that promote and protect social justice, then discuss intergovernmental, international social justice organizations. Finally, a summary and discussion of the complexity, breadth, and depth of these organizations will be provided.

Nongovernmental Social Justice Organizations

Across the globe, there are many nongovernmental social justice organizations seeking to accomplish a variety of goals pertinent to equality of resources and opportunities. The number of social justice organizations is extensive and range quite widely in funding, size, operation, and initiatives. These nongovernmental organizations are nonprofit organizations that are funded in various ways, ranging from donations to grants, with many volunteer organizations operating across the globe as well; this allows them to operate in a manner that is deemed best fit for their social justice activities.

Some of the more commonly known social justice groups are nationally and internationally recognized, such as the American Civil Liberties Union and Amnesty International. These organizations aim to generate action toward ensuring human rights and justice through conducting research, advocating in the courtroom, disseminating information to the public in the United States, and promoting humanistic policies. While they all operate in their own independent ways, they share similar objectives.

Throughout the states, many independent social justice organizations operate for their local jurisdictions. To provide an exhaustive list of them would be daunting, but their efforts are not unrecognized. Thus, we have highlighted a number of well-known organizations, but applaud and appreciate those not mentioned.

Advocates for Human Rights

Since 1983, The Advocates for Human Rights have engaged in social justice activities at various capacities to "investigate and expose human rights violations, represent immigrants and refugees seeking asylum, train and assist groups that protect human rights, engage the public, policy-makers, and children; and push for legal reform and advocates for sound policy."[2] While based in the United States, they operate on a global scale, seeking to promote international social justice.

The Advocates for Human Rights is a nonprofit organization that relies heavily on the participation of volunteers and community partners to continue their progression toward social justice.

American Civil Liberties Union (ACLU)

The ACLU is a proactive nonprofit organization that operates with the intent to ensure all rights, as described in the U.S. Constitution and laws, are protected.[3] The ACLU engages in a variety of undertakings, including advocating, lobbying, and litigating for the promotion and protection of human rights. The ACLU considers themselves a grassroots volunteer resistance movement. They work diligently to ensure that individuals are not only able to defend their rights, but also to ensure that they have an understanding of their rights.

Individual branches of the ACLU can be found within each state, where they focus primarily on the issues at hand within the boundary lines of their state; however, the ACLU frequently appears before the Supreme Court to tackle federal cases. In addition to appearing in court, the ACLU engages in lobbying to encourage Congress to pass bills pertinent to social justice.

Amnesty International

Amnesty International operates globally within many countries to ensure the rights of individuals throughout the world. The organization seeks to ensure that individuals' rights are being met according to the appropriate law of the land, including international law. Their activities in promoting social justice include publishing and distributing information, lobbying and campaigning, and many more.

Amnesty International was initially developed and operated out of London, but has now opened offices in over 70 countries across the globe. Regional offices enable them to seek justice regardless of where it is happening to ensure continued movement toward social justice.

Center for Constitutional Rights (CCR)

The Center for Constitutional Rights aims to ensure the rights of the underprivileged and those with minimal protections through legal action. They seek to right the wrongs of injustices of immigration, human rights, discriminatory policing, LGBTQI, profiling, incarceration, racism, and many other important civil rights issues.[4] The Center for Constitutional Rights empowers individuals through litigation, education, and advocacy.

In 1966, a group of lawyers active during the civil rights movements in the U.S. banded together to found the CCR with the intent to utilize law as a means of promoting social justice.[5] The CCR is a nonprofit organization, currently operated out of New York, which has established many legal precedents from their successful court cases.

Human Rights Watch

Human Rights Watch is a nonprofit organization that operates on a global level and seeks to ensure the basic human rights of all individuals. Human Rights Watch conducts research regarding injustices that have occurred and develops reports to disseminate to the public. They publish over 100 reports and briefings each year; these reports cover international human rights conditions and often lead to more awareness, enabling them to meet with respective governments to generate change within the legal and political realms.[6]

International Justice Mission

The International Justice Mission is housed in the United States and has offices across the globe. The organization advocates on behalf of individual rights and is known for its stance on anti-slavery, sex trafficking, and offenses against children. The International Justice Mission is a nonprofit organization made up of over "750 lawyers, investigators, social workers, community activists, and other professionals."[7] While housed in Washington, DC, the IJM has 17 filed offices across the globe, allowing them to stay on top of issues regardless of where they occur.

Southern Poverty Law Center

Founded in 1971, the Southern Poverty Law Center advocates for individuals on the basis of civil rights, particularly for individuals of vulnerable populations. The SPLC predominantly focuses on legal cases against extremist groups based on hate and racism.[8] They work on cases pertinent to discrimination, segregation, unconstitutionality, and mistreatment.

Along with legal cases, the Southern Poverty Law Center operates two projects: the Intelligence Project and the Teaching Tolerance Program. The Intelligence Project monitors and exposes hate groups and extremists throughout the United States and shares the information they have with the media and law enforcement agencies.[9] The Teaching Tolerance Program aims to promote education about prejudice and equality in the classroom; they provide resources to the classroom, including "documentaries, lesson plans and curricula, *Teaching Tolerance* magazine," and other materials.[10]

Summation of Nongovernmental Social Justice Organizations

As stated previously, given the extensive number of nongovernmental organizations, it is difficult to capture even a fraction of the total in operation.

Throughout the United States, there are also topic-specific social justice groups, such as the Anti-Defamation League, Children's Defense Fund, Innocence Project, International Organization for Migration, National Action Network, National Urban League, Native American Rights Fund, Planned Parenthood, WITNESS, and many others. Each of these groups operates to improve the quality of life for individuals living within the United States.

It is also important to note that the United States is not the only country with social justice organizations operating within its borders. Just a few of the many other great organizations outside of the United States include the Social Justice Coalition of South Africa (www.sjc.org.za), members of SOLIDAR in Europe (www.solidar.org), Aotearora of New Zealand (www.peace.net.nz/links/peace-organisations-aotearoa-new-zealand), and the Social Platform of Belgium (www.socialplatform.org).

U.S. Governmental Social Justice Organizations

Unlike nongovernmental social justice organizations, governmental organizations that promote and protect social justice receive their funding, mission, and initiatives directly from the state for which they work. As with the NGOs discussed above, varying governmental organizations seek to promote social justice in different ways. Several large and important sectors of the U.S. federal government oversee the promotion and protection of social justice issues within the U.S.[11] The federal government has specific branches and divisions that handle various issues based on their stated mission.[12] It is important to note that each major executive agency (e.g., Department of Agriculture, Department of State, Department of Homeland Security, etc.) within the federal government has its own civil rights division that addresses the inequality of resources and opportunities for individuals working with that office and ensures that each executive agency is upholding the federal law in regards to equality and opportunity. While this chapter cannot cover each executive agency or every governmental board, commission, and committee, it is important to point out that these offices do exist. Below is a discussion of the different branches, structure, and mission of some of the divisions that promote social justice, as well as varying examples of how these agencies promote and protect social justice.

United State Department of Justice: Civil Rights Division

The United States Department of Justice (DOJ) oversees many different functions and departments.[13] The mission of the DOJ is:

> To enforce the law and defend the interests of the United States according to the law; to ensure public safety against threats foreign and domestic; to provide federal leadership in preventing and controlling crime; to seek just punishment for those guilty of unlawful behavior; and to ensure fair and impartial administration of justice for all Americans.[14]

Most importantly—with concerns to the promotion and protection of social justice—the DOJ oversees the Civil Rights Division. The Civil Rights Division of the Department of Justice was created through the enactment of the Civil Rights Act of 1957. The Civil Rights Act aims to uphold and promote civil and constitutional rights, particularly for the most vulnerable members of society.[15] For example, the Civil Rights Division "enforces federal statutes prohibiting discrimination on the basis of race, color, sex, disability, religion, familial status and national origin."[16]

The Civil Rights Division's work is carried out by 11 separate sections, some of which heavily promote and protect the social justice interests of individuals in the U.S.; these sections are:

- Appellate Section
- Criminal Section
- Disability Rights Section
- Educational Opportunities Section
- Employment Litigation Section
- Federal Coordination and Compliance
- Housing and Civil Enforcement Section
- Immigrant and Employee Rights Section
- Policy and Strategy Section
- Special Litigation Section
- Voting Section[17]

These sections focus deliberately on their specific issues and cases to make sure that individuals' rights are not being denied; specifically, in regards to issues in equality and opportunity. For example, the Housing and Civil Enforcement Section "works to protect some of the most fundamental rights of individuals, including the right to access housing free from discrimination."[18] This section follows and enforces the rules put forth in the Fair Housing Act,[19] the Equal Credit Opportunity Act,[20] Title II of the Civil Rights Act of 1964,[21] Religious Land Use and Institutionalized Persons Act,[22] and the Servicemembers Civil Relief Act.[23] Like the Housing and Civil Enforcement Section, each of the sections has a mission and laws that they aim to uphold—again directed at addressing the inequality of resources and opportunities, particularly for the most vulnerable members of society within the U.S.

It is also important to note that the DOJ and the sections of the Civil Rights Division do not always act independently of other governmental agencies and branches. For example, the U.S. Department of Housing and Urban Development (HUD) has an Office of Fair Housing and Equal Opportunity. Both the DOJ and HUD are jointly responsible for enforcing the federal Fair Housing Act.[24] The Fair Housing Act prohibits providers of housing from discriminatory practices based on race, religion, sex, national origin, familial status, or disability of the tenants or potential tenants in an effort to promote equality of opportunity in housing.[25]

Another example of the promotion and protection of social justice issues that the Civil Rights Division of the DOJ carries out comes from the Immigrant and Employee Rights Section. (IER). The IER enforces the antidiscrimination provision of the Immigration and Nationality Act (INA),[26] which prohibits:

- Citizenship status discrimination in hiring, firing, or recruitment or referral for a fee
- National origin discrimination in hiring, firing, or recruitment or referral for a fee
- Unfair documentary practices during the employment eligibility verification, Form I-9 and E-Verify
- Retaliation or intimidation against those who file charges with the IER[27]

In order to protect and promote social justice, ensuring that individuals are not discriminated against, the IER offers many different services. For example, the IER has hotlines that employees who feel they have been discriminated against can call for advice or to seek assistance on immigrant-related issues.[28]

The Housing and Civil Enforcement Section, HUD, and the IER are just a few examples of the many ways the U.S. government—through the Department of Justice—tries to promote and protect social justice within the country. Only a small number of laws and initiatives were touched upon above; however, these specific examples should help illustrate ways in which the government seeks to promote and protect social justice.

United State Department of Education: Office for Civil Rights

Like the Department of Justice, the Department of Education (DOE) has its own Office for Civil Rights (OCR).[29] However, this office does not have different sections and instead focuses on the singular issue of fairness in education. The mission of the Office of Civil Rights in the Department of Education "is to ensure equal access to education and to promote educational excellence through vigorous enforcement of civil rights in our nation's schools."[30] The Office of Civil Rights in the Department of Education has the duty to enforce regulations set forth by the U.S. government. For example, the OCR for the DOE oversees the compliance and enforcement of disability discrimination,[31] discrimination based on sex,[32] and discrimination based on race and national origin.[33]

U.S. Equal Employment Opportunity Commission

The U.S. Equal Opportunity Commission (EEOC) is not a major executive agency, but rather a commission designed to protect job applicants and employees from being discriminated against based on their race, religion, sex, national origin, disability, or genetic information. The EEOC also protects individuals from being retaliated against should they file a complaint against their employer because of perceived or actual discriminatory practices.[34] Moreover, the EEOC also promotes social justice and stopping discrimination before it happens through education, outreach, and technical assistance programs.[35]

The EEOC is just one example of the numerous U.S. federal government commissions created to protect and promote social justice. In this case, the EEOCs mission is to protect individuals from discrimination in hiring, while other commissions deal with other social justice initiatives.[36] Oftentimes, the EEOC has to work closely with the IER to determine if the complaint against the employer violates the mandates of the INA, which the IER would cover, or if the complaint is an issue that the EEOC is responsible for. This is just one of the multitude of examples of the complexity and overlap between the various governmental organizations that promote social justice within the United States.

Intergovernmental Organizations

IGOs are composed of member states, which voluntarily choose to participate in the organization and their cause or causes. Intergovernmental organizations each differ in their structure, function, membership, and mission based. Several very well-known and well-supported IGOs have made the promotion of social justice one of their core issues. Below is a discussion of the efforts of several of these IGOs and their initiatives regarding social justice. As with the NGOs and governmental organizations, there are far too many IGOs to discuss; therefore, two of the most well-recognized IGOs are discussed and their social justice practices highlighted below.[37]

United Nations

The United Nations (UN) is a multifaceted, multipurpose international organization. It is hard to qualify the goals of the UN in a few simple sentences, given its immense reach and numerous programs and initiatives. The UN is self-described as confronting and acting on issues such as "peace and security, climate change, sustainable development, human rights, disarmament, terrorism, humanitarian and health emergencies, gender equality, governance, food production, and more."[38] Its powers come from—or are vested through—the Charter of the United Nations ("The Charter"). The Charter was signed on 26 June 1945 in San Francisco and came into force on 24 October 1945.[39] When The Charter was originally signed, there were 51 member states; currently there are 193 member states.[40] The UN has innumerable social justice initiatives, only a few of which are highlighted below.[41] It is important to note that all member states participate in the General Assembly, which is one of the six principal organs of the UN. The general assembly meets annually to discuss issues concerning policymaking, and its member states help to set the agenda.[42]

While the UN has a long history of social justice initiatives, it was not until 2006 that the UN defined and categorized its initiatives and activities concerning social justice.[43] The UN divided and defined three critical domains of equality and equity: equality of rights, equality of opportunities, and equity in living conditions.[44] The UN went on to establish some of the more concrete elements of social justice that they could begin to tackle, broken into six categories:

- Inequalities in the distribution of income
- Inequalities in the distribution of assets
- Inequalities in the distribution of opportunities for work and remunerated employment
- Inequalities in the distribution of access to knowledge
- Inequalities in the distribution of health services, social security and the provision of a safe environment
- Inequalities in the distribution of opportunities for civic and political participation[45]

Using these three domains and six categories, the UN has reflected on the need for promotion, policy, and understanding of social justice across the globe. In 2007, the UN General Assembly went on to declare February 20 as the World Day of Social Justice.[46] On this day, the UN invites its member states to "devote the day to promoting national activities in accordance with the objectives and goals of the World Summit for Social Development."[47] Another specific example of the way the UN has advocated for social justice is by creating the Office of the High Commissioner for Human Rights (OHCHR), which promotes and protects human rights across the globe. The OHCHR works with governments to train, educate, and reform practices in different countries to promote and protect social justice.[48]

The World Bank

The World Bank is composed of 189 member states and provides financial and technical assistance to developing countries, with a goal to end extreme poverty and promote sustainable growth. Currently, The World Bank's two main goals are specifically:

- End extreme poverty by decreasing the percentage of people living on less than $1.90 a day to no more than 3%
- Promote shared prosperity by fostering the income growth of the bottom 40% for every country[49]

The World Bank aims to reach their two goals by 2030. However, it has come under fire for some of its practices, with critics asserting that the World Bank may do more harm than good in its ability to protect and promote social justice.[50] Despite these criticisms, the World Bank has long history of helping to promote social justice worldwide.[51]

Summation of Governmental and Intergovernmental Social Justice Organizations

As with the NGOs, both nationally and internationally, there are just far too many governmental and intergovernmental organizations to identify, examine, and discuss. The above examination of the U.S. government, the UN, and the World Bank are only a small fragment of the numerous and commendable organizations that exist to promote and protect social justice across the globe.

Summary

As stated repeatedly above, there is an extensive network of social justice organizations across the U.S. and around the globe. These organizations work tirelessly to protect and promote social justice for different individuals and groups in an attempt to make the world a more equitable place. With such an abundance of organizations that have different missions, goals, and initiatives, readers should be encouraged to research organizations that may appeal to their own social justice interests, as they no doubt exist.

Furthermore, given the vast and varying nature of such organizations, it is also important to highlight the complex issues that arise when studying these organizations. For example, as illustrated above, the U.S. government may have multiple offices that overlap in their mission and that have to work together to solve social justice issues. Another example comes from the UN, which works with governments and other intergovernmental organizations that promote social justice, creating a web of support that can sometimes be difficult to navigate.

Despite the complexity of examining and studying these organizations, it is crucial to note that the work they do is paramount in protecting and promoting social justice in the U.S. and around the globe. Without these diverse and wide-ranging organizations and their efforts, inequality of resources and opportunities would no doubt abound. Therefore, the work that nongovernmental organizations, governmental organizations, and intergovernmental organizations do to promote and protect social justice should be celebrated and supported.

Discussion Questions

1. Do you think that the United States should be involved in promoting social justice or that the responsibility of social justice promotion is better left to NGOs?
2. What role do intergovernmental organizations actually play in promoting and enforcing social justice?
3. Do you think social justice is something that can be enforced, or is it only something that can be promoted? Why or why not?
4. Given the innumerable social justice organizations nationally and internationally, do you think that it would be more sensible to have a few larger organizations for ease of access and promotion, rather than thousands of smaller organizations? Why or why not?
5. What issues in social justice are you interested in? Which organizations promote and protect those issues?

Notes

1. The World Bank. (1990). *How the World Bank works with non-governmental organizations*, pp. 13–16.
2. The Advocates for Human Rights. (n.d.). *About us*. Retrieved from www.theadvocatesforhumanrights.org/about_us
3. ACLU. (n.d.). *About*. Retrieved from www.aclu.org/about-aclu
4. Center for Constitutional Rights. (n.d.). *Who we are, mission and history*. Retrieved from https://ccrjustice.org/home/who-we-are/mission-and-history

5. *Ibid.*

6. Human Rights Watch. (n.d.). *About.* Retrieved from www.hrw.org/about

7. International Justice Mission. (n.d.). *Who we are.* Retrieved from www.ijm.org/who-we-are

8. Southern Poverty Law Center. (n.d.). *About us.* Retrieved from www.splcenter.org/about

9. Southern Poverty Law Center. *Hate and extremism.* Retrieved from www.splcenter.org/issues/hate-and-extremism

10. Southern Poverty Law Center. *Teaching tolerance.* Retrieved from www.splcenter.org/teaching-tolerance

11. It is important to note that the U.S. participates in the promotion of social justice both within and outside the U.S. in varying capacities. This section discusses those within the U.S., and the section titled "Intergovernmental Organizations" discusses the promotion of social justice through intergovernmental cooperation outside the U.S.

12. For an overview of the U.S. government federal structure, please see Library of Congress. (2017). *Official US executive branch websites.* Retrieved from www.loc.gov/rr/news/fedgov.html. This roadmap may help readers understand the complexity and varying organizations within the U.S. federal government.

13. U.S. Department of Justice [USDOJ]. (2015). *Organizational chart.* Retrieved from www.justice.gov/sites/default/files/doj/pages/attachments/2015/04/27/doj_june_2015_2.pdf

14. USDOJ. (n.d.). *About.* Retrieved from www.justice.gov/about

15. USDOJ. (n.d.). *About the division.* Retrieved from www.justice.gov/crt/about-division

16. *Ibid.*

17. *Ibid.* Please visit USDOJ, *About the division*, to learn more about each section of the Office of Civil Rights and what laws each section upholds. The breadth and depth of the initiatives of these each sections in their mission for equality and opportunities is far too wide to cover here.

18. USDOJ. (n.d.). *Housing and civil enforcement section.* Retrieved from www.justice.gov/crt/housing-and-civil-enforcement-section

19. The Fair Housing Act, 42 U.S.C. 3601 et seq.

20. Equal Credit Opportunity Act, 15 U.S.C. § 1691 et seq.

21. The Civil Rights Act of 1964, Title II, 42 U.S.C. §2000a.

22. Religious Land Use and Institutionalized Persons Act, 42 U.S.C. § 2000cc et seq.

23. Servicemembers Civil Relief Act, 50 U.S.C. §§ 3901–4043.

24. U.S. Department of Housing and Urban Development, & Office of Fair Housing and Equal Opportunity. (2004). *Reasonable accommodations under the Fair Housing Act.* Retrieved from www.justice.gov/crt/us-department-housing-and-urban-development

25. *Ibid.*

26. Immigration and Nationality Act (INA). 8 U.S.C. § 1324b.

27. *Ibid.*

28. USDOJ. (2017). *Frequently asked questions.* Retrieved from www.justice.gov/crt/frequently-asked-questions-faqs

29. Again, each department has its own Civil Rights Office (names vary based on the department) and not all of them will or can be discussed. The DOE and the DOJ are just two examples that help highlight some of the ways the U.S. protects and promotes social justice.

30. Department of Education [DOE]. (2017). *Office for civil rights.* Retrieved from www2.ed.gov/about/offices/list/ocr/index.html

31. The Americans with Disabilities Act of 1990, Title II, 42 U.S.C. § 12101.

32. Education Amendments of 1972, Title IX, 20 U.S.C. §§ 1681–1688.

33. Civil Rights Act of 1964, Title VI, 42 U.S.C. 2000d et seq.

34. US Equal Opportunity Commission. (n.d.). *Overview.* Retrieved from www.eeoc.gov/eeoc/index.cfm

35. *Ibid.*

36. A list of the different agencies and commissions can be found at *Official US executive branch websites.* (2017).

37. The United Nations provides a list of several different IGOs with which it works. UN. (2017). *Intergovernmental organizations.* Retrieved from www.un.org/en/sections/member-states/intergovernmental-organizations/

38. United Nations [UN]. (2017). *Overview.* Retrieved from www.un.org/en/sections/about-un/overview/index.html

39. *Ibid.*

40. UN. (2013). *The world today. Map No. 4136 Rev., 11.* Retrieved from www.un.org/Depts/Cartographic/map/profile/world00.pdf; UN. (2017). *Member states.* Retrieved from www.un.org/en/member-states/index.html; UN. (2017). *History.* www.un.org/en/sections/history/history-united-nations/

41. In 2006, the UN highlighted its role in promoting and enacting social justice changes globally, see The International Forum for Social Development. (2006). *Social justice in an open world the role of the United Nations.* New York: United Nations.

42. UN. (2017). *About the general assembly*. Retrieved from www.un.org/en/ga/about/

43. The International Forum for Social Development, 2006.

44. *Ibid.*, pp. 15–17.

45. *Ibid.*, pp. 17–19.

46. UN. (2017). *World day of social justice*. Retrieved from www.un.org/en/events/socialjusticeday/background. shtml

47. *Ibid.*

48. For specific examples of the work the OHCHR does, see Flinterman, C., & Zwamborn, M. (2003). *Global review of the OHCHR Technical cooperation programme: Synthesis report*. United Nations. Retrieved from www. ohchr.org/Documents/Countries/global-reviewsynthesis.pdf

49. The World Bank. (2017). *What we do*. Retrieved from www.worldbank.org/en/about/what-we-do

50. Goldman, M. (2006). *Imperial nature: The World Bank and struggles for social justice in the age of globalization*. New Haven, CT: Yale University Press.

51. The World Bank. (2017). *History*. Retrieved from www.worldbank.org/en/about/history

24

SYSTEMIC EFFECTS OF PRIVATIZATION ON HUMAN SERVICE AGENCIES

Maren B. Trochmann

The History of Human Service Delivery in the United States

The scope and breadth of current human service agencies, and the reach of local, state, and federal government into these functions, is vast. Human services include, but are not limited to, welfare and social security, mental health services, Medicaid, Medicare, homeless services and shelters, community development and low-income housing, foster care, food assistance, veterans' services, workforce training, and drug and alcohol rehabilitation. The government's role in providing these services might involve direct service delivery, providing subsidies or grants to service providers, contracting out services, and/or oversight and regulation of those service providers. Service providers may be federal, state, or local government, sub-government agencies, nonprofit organizations, or for-profit businesses or groups.

While the government's role in human services is far-reaching, this was not always the case. Prior to the New Deal in the 1930s, nongovernmental agencies, both secular and religious, performed the traditional work of human service agencies—housing the poor, caring for the indigent, and fostering children. The state's role was more limited until changes in the 1930s with the New Deal expanded the role of government into human services. This first section outlines early human service models, the government's nascent and growing involvement in the delivery of human services through the 20th century, and increased privatization of service delivery from the 1980s onward.

Settlement Houses and Pre-New Deal Human Services

Voluntary, primarily female-led organizations known as settlement houses arose in the late 19th century to address the needs of impoverished neighborhoods and inner cities. The most famous of these was known as Hull House in Chicago, founded in 1889 by Jane Addams and Ellen Gates Star after their visit to Toynbee Hall in London. Jane Addams is considered the "mother of social work," and the Hull House hosted a thousand people each week, providing educational, recreational, and civic engagement opportunities that were lacking in the industrial, working poor neighborhood.

Jane Addams's settlement house movement provided a human- and community-centered approach to service delivery, viewing city as "home" rather than city as "business."[1] This was a notable contrast to another type of public service philosophy arising with the New York Bureau of Municipal Research (NYBMR)—founded in 1912—that sought local government service delivery to match efficiency standards of private business.[2] While both movements pursued progressive solutions to ameliorate problems unaddressed by governments, their methods and philosophies differed. The NYBMR was founded to push for transparency in New York City government to improve the lives of the poor through increased efficiency in its service delivery, while the settlement houses sought a human-centered approach that valued community and "home" over efficiency and principals of scientific (i.e., efficient, business-based) management. The two distinct approaches to public service delivery and the competing values and tensions inherent within them are a recurring theme throughout the debate of public service privatization.

Despite the altruistic and civic-minded aims of the settlement houses, their scope was limited. These homes served poor migrants of European descent in northern cities, so a parallel movement, founded by middle-class African American women and supported by religious organizations and churches, expanded into the rural South and the growing African American urban ghettos.[3] These southern settlement houses were a precursor to the civil rights and social justice movement decades later through creating a place for empowerment, activism, and shared conscious.[4] Whether secular or religious, settlement houses provided a foundation for human services agencies that was rooted in social justice, activism, and concepts of community.

From the New Deal to the Great Society

Settlement houses provided key services to needy populations, but during the Great Depression that need grew to a point of crisis. The government became a major provider of human services during the New Deal of the 1930s. Programs established in the 20th century, from the New Deal to President Lyndon Johnson's Great Society, established the government as a major provider of human services and guarantor of the social safety net.

President Franklin D. Roosevelt's administration sought to address unemployment, hunger, poverty, and homelessness, which impacted large swaths of the American population during the Great Depression era, through direct government intervention. Through programs established under the New Deal, the government provided direct employment on initiatives deemed important, such as conservation, infrastructure, civil service, and public works (Civilian Conservation Corps [1933], Civil Works Administration [1933], Tennessee Valley Authority [1933], and Works Progress Administration [1935]). It provided job training (National Youth Administration [1935]) and unemployment assistance (Federal Emergency Relief Administration [1933]), and established social security as a key pillar in the social safety net (Social Security Administration [1935]). The United States Housing Act was passed in 1937 to establish subsidies for low-income housing to local Public Housing Authorities.[5] These programs ushered in a new era of government involvement and changed the understanding of the federal government's role for decades to come.

The U.S. involvement in World War II and a subsequent economic boom followed the New Deal era, but poverty and divides—along class, racial, and economic lines—persisted. By the 1960s, anti-war protesters, civil rights activists, and feminists were pushing for changes. President Lyndon Johnson in 1965 proposed to wage a war on poverty and set out to implement his vision for a Great Society to address poverty and racial injustice.

The Great Society built upon and expanded New Deal programs, established new human services roles for the government, and addressed discrimination. Legislation passed under President Johnson established the Economic Opportunity Act creating a job corps and vocational training, the Head Start program to provide preschool to disadvantaged and low-income youth, Medicare and Medicaid to provide health services for the elderly and low-income Americans, respectively, and Volunteers in Service to America (VISTA) to assist impoverished regions in America through a domestic program modeled after the Peace Corps. In conjunction with these programs to provide social services, legislation to promote social justice and guarantee equal treatment under the law was also passed: the Civil Rights Act to prohibit racial and ethnic discrimination, the Voting Rights Act to ban literacy tests and other methods to effectively deny the vote to African Americans, the Fair Housing Act to outlaw discrimination in housing, and the Immigration Act to end discriminatory ethnic-origin quotas.[6] Thus, the promotion and expansion of human service agencies occurred concurrently with the expansion of civil rights and protections against discrimination.

Federalism and the Birth of Privatization

A parallel and competing vision for American government arose during President Johnson's tenure. This vision evoked a distrust of a strong, central government to solve the ills of society, whether through human service agencies and programs or regulations and antidiscrimination laws. The mechanism of block grants and grant-in-aid programs proliferated; grant-in-aid programs, such as Social Security Disability (SSI) or Aid to Families with Dependent Children (AFDC, commonly known as traditional welfare), provided funding to states or local governmental agencies to administer programs in line with federal guidelines. The goal of the decentralization of these programs was to enhance the administrative capacity of an expanding government mandate while allowing for state flexibility in meeting place-based demands.[7] These programs and the federalist arrangement created an increasingly complex landscape of intergovernmental management.[8]

The complexity of social programs coupled with disappointment in the failures of the war on poverty to effectively eradicate social and economic divides led to a willingness to mandate a new approach. President Ronald Reagan was elected and outlined a new course in his inaugural address:

> In this present crisis, government is not the solution to our problem; government is the problem . . . It is time to check and reverse the growth of government, which shows signs of having grown beyond the consent of the governed.[9]

With this promise, a new era of privatization of human services, deregulation, and federalism began.

Reinventing Government, New Public Management, and the Hollow State

The 1980s under President Reagan saw an increased reliance on business models as a solution for the growth of government. However, the executive branch still had an obligation to implement those social service programs enacted in previous decades. With vast constituencies relying on these benefits, coupled with a constitutional duty to execute and implement the will of the legislature, the Reagan Administration had to maintain these programs and services. A disdain for government bureaucracy, which was viewed as bloated and inefficient, and a faith in the free market led to a new solution: contracting out of these services to the private sector.

The Reagan administration sought to shrink the bureaucracy, improve cost efficiency of services, and implement a market- and business-based model in government.[10] The administration expanded contracting out to private sector organizations by increasing the use of Circular A-76, which required cost comparisons of government services with private sector organizations. In 1987, the Congressional Budget Office (CBO) estimated competitively bid contracts could replace approximately 1.4 million federal workers.[11] State and local governments followed suit. All levels of government contracted out services such as social welfare programs, education, transportation, and corrections.

This paradigm shift was known as New Public Management (NPM) and it focused on results, efficiency, and cost savings using a customer-service business model. Under this paradigm, the citizen was a customer, seeking the lowest-cost and most efficient delivery of services given the choices the private market might offer. Osborne and Gaebler's landmark book *Reinventing Government* synthesizes this shift as changing incentives for public sector institutions to be more market-based.[12] Osborne and Gaebler believed that bureaucracies and government monopolies providing human services stifled innovation and entrepreneurship. They emphasized effectiveness, innovation, and accountability, which they argued might be achieved by adapting private-sector business principles in government.

The "hollow state" is another name for this shift towards privatization. The term is adopted from the private sector term "the hollow corporation," which refers to new organizational forms replacing traditional management of internal production with coordination of a network of subcontractors. The hollow state relies on the public sector and nonprofit agencies to deliver services funded by taxpayer dollars.[13] While the size of government, in terms of employees directly hired and paid by federal, state, or local agencies, has shrunk, a "hollow" government of contractors has grown to fill in those roles to provide human services for programs created decades earlier.

Another feature of this shift towards NPM has been an increased emphasis on performance measurement, on outputs and efficiency; this shift has impacted both contractors and government service providers. In 1993, President Bill Clinton signed the Government Performance and Review Act (GPRA), introducing extensive performance reporting requirements for federal agencies and departments, reflecting the intense focus on outputs, including efficiency and service delivery. These reforms continued as the George W. Bush Administration expanded on GPRA, implementing the Program Assessment Rating Tool (PART) to assess performance of over a thousand government programs. In 2010, reforms to GPRA were passed and signed into law by President Barack Obama, who continued a performance-based budgeting (PBB) model and emphasis on program evaluation and transparent management.[14] Thus, remnants of NPM continue to be powerful tools within human service delivery, regardless of political orientation or administration.

What Is Public Versus Private?

The distinction between direct government service delivery by the public sector and contracting out may seem obvious. However, the definition of public versus private organizations is not straightforward, and the lines blur between public, private, and nonprofit organizations. This section explores the typologies and classifications that scholars have utilized to clarify and define dimensions of "publicness" in organizations. While there is not overall agreement on the topic, this distinction is an essential precursor to articulate the pros and cons of privatization of human services agencies.

Classic economic foundations and assumptions of market failure underlie some theories for the usefulness of public or nonprofit service delivery. The market failure explanation asserts it is inefficient for some public goods to be provided on the free market, due to free riders, transaction costs, and exclusion costs.[15] In a capitalist economy, certain activities are not profitable for private industry to perform, such as serving high-cost elderly clientele in the regular medical insurance market; thus, the state steps in to provide these services where the free market cannot or will not do so efficiently.

In 1953, political scientists Robert Dahl and Charles Lindblom proposed that all organizations fall on a spectrum between government agencies at one end and privately owned enterprises on the other. They argue economic markets (i.e., private enterprises) address products and choices and incentivize profit gains, whereas governmental authority—which they define as "polyarchy" or complex political hierarchy—addresses social activities where there is a market failure to provide a public good.[16] Public goods are those goods and services provided by the government for which exclusion is impossible; for instance, national defense is a purely public good because all will benefit from it jointly and it is not divisible.[17]

Decades later, this distinction was expanded by defining "publicness" based on two criteria: (1) public or private *ownership* and *operation* of an organization, and (2) public or private sources of the organization's *financial resources*.[18] This expansion distinguished between four discrete categories of organizations:

1. Publicly owned organizations with public funding received through government appropriations (e.g., federal agencies such as the DOD, state agencies, police departments).
2. Publicly owned organizations with funding from private sources (e.g., state-owned enterprises, common in some nations).
3. Privately owned organizations with large portions of their funding from public resources such as grants or subsidies or sales to, or contracts with, the government.
4. Privately owned organizations with most or all of their financial resources from private sources such as sales or donations (e.g., business firms).

While these distinctions are useful, they are overly simplistic and do not capture the complex environment in which many organizations, government agencies, and enterprises operate.

Perhaps the dominant theory of publicness is that of Barry Bozeman. Bozeman describes organizations on two spectrums of political authority and economic authority. Rather than grouping organizations into four major categories, he described how organizations fell along a continuum and noted that the distinctions were not dichotomous. Economic authority is the degree to which an organization may transfer ownership interests, while political authority relates to the legitimacy of an organization to exist, whether flowing from the consent of the governed or legal and constitutional foundations. The greater an organization is constrained by political authority, the more public it is. Conversely, the more economic authority rules an organization, the more private it is. Bozeman notes that since all organizations operate with some degree of political authority—whether via direct public mandate, public funding, regulations governing essential organizational processes, or laws allowing organizations to operate and exist—Bozeman argues that all organizations are public.[19]

Recent scholarship articulates three dimensions of publicness: (1) ownership, (2) funding, and (3) control.[20] Moreover, determining the extent to which an organization focuses on public values can capture dimensions of publicness. Moulton articulates two components of a publicness framework:

> (1) realized publicness, or the realization of public values demonstrated by organizational behavior or outcomes; and (2) institutionalized public values as influences on publicness (public value institutions), including regulations, associations, and cultures in an organizations' environment . . . that embody public values and thus influence the organization toward realized public outcomes.[21]

Organizations may be more (or less) public based on whether their mission and goals focus on producing and providing for public goods and services. An organization may also be more (or less) public based on the value inputs that inform its work (e.g., taking public feedback, allowing for participative democracy, being responsive to legislation and constitutional directives).

These frameworks demonstrate how distinctions between public and private organizations can be overly simplistic, creating dichotomies when relationships between public and private organizations are less distinct and more intertwined. Moreover, much government work in human services and service delivery now takes place in vertical governance networks, utilizing public agencies to oversee third-party service providers such as state or local government providers, nonprofit agencies, and private sector organizations.[22] These networked structures further complicate empirical comparisons between public and private sector service delivery. This complex environment informs the subsequent section, which explores the pros and cons of privatization.

Benefits and Challenges of Privatization

One reason that this debate lingers is that those who deliver services have vast discretion over service delivery. While performing their jobs in human service fields, situations are bound to arise that have not been spelled out by management in policy or regulation. Any person tasked with human service delivery, whether a public servant or a contractor, has a multitude of opportunities to respond to and interact with citizens and clients. These responses have a broad impact on policy implementation and how citizens view and understand the government and human services they receive.[23] Thus, the professionalism of the individual, along with the stated purposes, goals, and mission (i.e., the publicness) of the organization, matters immensely. This section outlines the arguments of proponents of human service privatizations as well as some potential pitfalls of privatization.

The Touted Benefits of Privatization

The arguments for privatization are focused on several values: first, privatization might inject human service delivery with marketplace values of efficiency and innovation. Second, private organizations may have more capacity than traditional bureaucracies and government agencies, which face expanded missions and demands along with shrinking budgets. Third, private-sector contracts necessitate a focus on performance and outcome measuring, increasing transparency. Finally, privatization may allow for more place-based and local flexibility than direct administration by one central government agency.

Proponents of privatization and contracting out of services argue that the private market operates more efficiently and innovatively than traditional forms of bureaucracy. The top-down model of traditional bureaucracy can be a restraint and brake on quick responsiveness and action. The federal bureaucracy, for instance, has a mission that has expanded over time and is constrained by Congress, the President, and the courts, which may make it inflexible, slow to act, and inefficient.[24] Private industry, on the other hand, is driven by free-market forces to continue to innovate, offering the best product or service, at the most competitive price and efficient delivery. Thus, utilizing business-based models, human service delivery might overcome the slow nature of bureaucracy, injecting an entrepreneurial spirit into government work rather than bureaucratic stagnation and gridlock.[25]

As demands on the bureaucracy grew over the 20th century and budgets shrunk, privatization also offered a solution to address the lack of capacity. Osborne and Gaebler describe this as "steering, not rowing."[26] Bureaucrats might be able to focus more on leadership through contracting out, rather than focusing on management of direct service delivery themselves. As budgets shrink, governments must find ways to do more with less. Utilizing the private market and relying on other organizations to provide human services is one way to narrow the scope of agency's responsibilities.

Focus on performance outcomes and transparency is another touted benefit of the NPM movement and the shift towards contracting out and privatization. When nongovernmental organizations compete for contracts, they seek out the most efficient, competitive, and attainable methods of service delivery. These contractors are then expected to produce measurable outcomes and key deliverables within a certain timeframe. They are motivated to deliver on their promises or face the threat of losing their contract and financial resources. Contract oversight and grants management, thus, might ensure that results are measurable and transparent.

Finally, proponents argue that contracting out and privatization allow for more flexible program oversight, rather than one strong, central service provider. Privatization, like federalism, is one tool to decentralize decision-making and allow for local governance and discretion. Rather than a strong, central government managing service delivery in a one-size-fits-all model, privatization and contracting may allow for place-based flexibility given local contexts and environments.

The Challenges and Potential Pitfalls of Privatization

Despite the trumpeted benefits of privatization, there are numerous valid concerns about potential pitfalls and challenges related to privatizing public services. A primary concern relates to the constitutional role public servants play to safeguard regime values and public ethics in a government work. Another concern relates to the nature of human services, which are coproduced with clients or citizens and inherently difficult to quantify success, making a business model an incongruent fit. Finally, a single-minded focus on efficiency and cost savings might present a tradeoff for other values of public service, such as equity and fairness.

Public servants take an oath of office to serve the public in line with laws and the Constitution, but private citizens and companies have no such constraints. Laws and regulations spell out only those actions that are specifically *prohibited* to the private sector; thus, those operating as private businesses or citizens may do *anything* except that which is explicitly disallowed. Conversely, the law guides bureaucratic agencies' actions and directs public agencies to implement only that which Congress and the courts explicitly *allow*. Thus, constitutional norms and separations of powers are paramount concepts guiding public service work.

Normative arguments for the importance of regime values and constitutional principles demonstrate one key concern related to privatization. Companies have external motivations, such as the maximization of profits, whereas public service motivation, congressional and judicial directives, and political influence of elected officials guide government agencies. Regime values are a helpful term in understanding this distinction. Political scientist John Rohr describes regime values as the fundamental constitutional principles of a polity that guide administrative behavior, including public law.[27] These values are historically grounded, consist of dialectic opinions (i.e., these values are complex and multifaceted), are concrete and based on real experiences, and are pertinent and nontrivial.[28] This argument underlines a key point: American public administration is a constitutional institution.[29] Thus, those who have an orientation towards safeguarding regime values and the Constitution are best equipped to implement key governmental initiatives, including delivery of human services.

To underline this point from a different paradigm, public administration reflects the constitutional separation of powers model in its three primary responsibilities: managerial, political, and legal.[30] The managerial responsibilities orient the public servant towards implementation and efficiency, much like the business model and aligned with the executive branch. The political aspects of the public servant's role relate to being representative of the American people, responsive to Congress, and accountable to political leadership, much like the legislative branch. The legal responsibilities of the administrator focus the public servant towards administrative law, impartiality, due process, equity, and independence, like the judicial branch. Public administration scholar David Rosenbloom calls this the three-legged stool of public administration.[31] However, managerial concerns of efficiency have often eclipsed the key legal foundations of public administration.[32] When key aspects of human service delivery are outsourced to private companies, the legal and political approaches to administration are inherently lost.

A key benefit of privatization outlined above related to increased efficiency, improved outcomes, and transparency. However, these benefits are tempered by the nature of the problems and the complexity of the solutions in human service delivery. Difficulties addressed by human services agencies—such as child abuse, addiction, poverty, and homelessness—are often called wicked problems. Wicked problems are those social issues that are ill-defined, with inherently political and often unachievable solutions, and with grave and serious consequences.[33] The problem may be ill-defined or hard to quantify because it is often hidden or hard to measure, such as addiction or homelessness. The solutions are political since these problems are highly charged social issues, which could be addressed from an activist standpoint or an individualist, family-values frame. Moreover, success to ever fully address these problems is often elusive, as poverty, homelessness, and crime will always persist in some form or to some extent. Finally, the problems, though difficult to address, do have serious consequences for those impacted.

To exam outcome metrics and transparency from a "wicked problems" lens raises significant questions. For instance, contracting out a service relies upon a measure of success, but how could a service provider be able to ensure there are zero cases of addiction, child abuse, or homeless families? If a goal of zero cases *cannot* be achieved, what does success look like? In other words, how many addicted persons, harmed children, or homeless families are few enough? Conversely, what incentive does a private company have to achieve zero cases, if its contract and funding is based on the problem persisting? These questions and many others make social problems faced by human service agencies particularly "wicked."

Moreover, any form of success in human services relies on a degree of coproduction, or the citizens' actions in support of achieving a goal with the public servant.[34] For instance, a police officer may be able to arrest and detain unlawful citizens, but they also rely on crime prevention hotlines, community engagement, and reporting of crimes or unlawful behavior. Coproduction of outcomes relies on citizens' actions, not just the actions of the bureaucrat, private sector employee, or nonprofit agent. Thus, measuring outcomes is increasingly difficult.

Contracts work well with quantifiable, easily defined, and achievable outcomes that can be precisely monitored. The difficulty with this is that in human service delivery, outputs are not simply driven by profit or numerical figures. Both the human service provider and the recipient play a key role in driving outputs; moreover, success is difficult to achieve and define. Translating a business profit-based model onto human services creates issues in measurement and performance monitoring that may not be accounted for in any purported efficiency or transparency gains.

Finally, a focus on efficiency as a key value presents a tradeoff with other values and norms. These norms include responsiveness and democratic participation. Interaction with human service providers informs citizens' opinions about their government, their willingness to participate in civic engagement, and their understanding of their role in a democracy. Customers may desire efficiency, but citizens may desire equitable and fair treatment. Metrics of efficiency do not readily capture values of due process, fairness, and equity. Moreover, while a large bureaucracy and government-run services may be inherently slow and inflexible, some values associated with these characteristics, such as stability over time, are lost. The executive branch and the bureaucracy serves in a constitutional democracy as a key break on the whims of any one party or branch of government. Stability, equity, and responsiveness should be weighed carefully against the import of efficiency.

Current Trends and Future Trends

Regardless of arguments for and against privatization, those concerned with social justice and human service delivery must understand and operate within the current, complex landscape. As the government's role in service delivery has grown, there have always been waves of reform, swinging towards and away from different service delivery methods and all focusing to some degree on performance management and measurement of outcomes.[35] These reforms, restructures, and new promises will continue for years and administrations to come. Moreover, the reforms and reinventions of the past have created a diverse environment in which performance measurement and management of human service delivery often also involves managing a diverse set of actors within a complex and comprehensive network. In this context, government agencies, private sector and nonprofit contractors, and subgrantees all operate, intersect, and overlap in human service delivery. Finally, while the push towards empirical metrics, efficiency, and public sector or business solutions continues, there is an alternate pull towards serving, rather than steering, for public administrators.[36]

Summary

This chapter has outlined the evolution of human service delivery, from its social justice roots in the settlement house movement to its expansion into government-run services. It has explored competing visions of human services, from federalism to NPM to contracting out. The chapter outlined the continuum on which private and public organizations operate, based on their funding, ownership, control, and values. Finally, some systemic effects of privatization were outlined in the closing section. Proponents of privatization argue for efficiency and innovation, capacity and cost savings, and transparent outcome measurement, while critics warn that constitutional safeguards and regime values may be lost in such a transition. Privatization of human services poses its own challenges in the "wicked problems" and coproduction context in which these providers or contractors must operate.

Since the earliest days, providers of human services have espoused competing values and visions for those they serve. Do they deserve efficiency and transparency and view their city as "business"? Or do they deserve humane and community-centered service delivery, viewing their city as "home"?[37] These values are not mutually exclusive, of course, but this tension, in one form or another, has informed the evolution of human service delivery and colors the current debate.

Discussion Questions

1. What were the origins of human service agencies in the United States? How did those origins impact future social movements and an understanding of social justice?
2. In what context did privatization of human service agencies arise? In what context did it evolve? How do you think historical movements and events influenced this evolution?
3. Define a public versus a private organization. How might this definition and distinction matter?
4. What were the touted benefits of privatization when it grew in popularity in the United States?
5. What are some potential downsides of privatization?
6. How do you think that privatization may impact specific sectors of human service agencies? Pick one example and describe some pros and cons of privatization.

Notes

1. Stivers, C. (2000). *Bureau men, settlement women: Constructing public administration in the progressive era.* Lawrence, KS: University Press of Kansas.
2. Hopkins, G. (1912). The New York bureau of municipal research. *The Annals of the American Academy of Political and Social Science, 41,* 235–244.
3. Lasch-Quinn, E. (1993). *Black neighbors: Race and the limits of reform in the American settlement house movement, 1890–1945.* Chapel Hill, NC: University of North Carolina Press.
4. Hounmenou, C. (2012). Black settlement houses and oppositional consciousness. *Journal of Black Studies, 43*(6), 646–666.
5. Conkin, P. K. (1992). *The new deal.* Berkeley, CA: Wiley-Blackwell.
6. Lowe, S. (2014). *A transformative era: Lyndon Baines Johnson and the development of the American administrative state.* Washington, DC: American University Press.
7. Derthick, M. (1987). American federalism: Madison's middle ground in the 1980s. *Public Administration Review, 47*(1), 66–74.
8. Pressman, J. L., & Wildavsky, A. B. (1973). *Implementation: How great expectations in Washington are dashed in Oakland.* Berkeley, CA: University of California Press.
9. Reagan, R. (1981). *Inaugural address.* Retrieved August 24, 2017, from https://reaganlibrary.archives.gov/archives/speeches/1981/12081a.htm
10. Estes, C. L. (1991). The Reagan legacy: Privatization, the welfare state, and aging in the 1990s. In J. Myles & J. Quadagno (Eds.), *States, labor markets, and the future of old age policy* (pp. 59–83). Philadelphia, PA: Temple University Press.
11. Kearns, P. (1996). Privatization of human services: Problems with contracting out theory. *Journal of Health and Human Services Administration, 19*(1), 61–78.

12. Osborne, D., & Gaebler, T. (1993). *Reinventing government: How the entrepreneurial spirit is transforming the public sector.* New York: Penguin Books, p. 308.
13. Milward, H. B., & Provan, K. G. (2000). Governing the hollow state. *Journal of Public Administration Research and Theory, 10*(2), 359–379, 362.
14. Joyce, P. G. (2012). The Obama administration and PBB: Building on the legacy of federal performance informed budgeting? *Public Administration Review,* 356–367.
15. Samuelson, P. A. (1966). *The collected scientific papers of Paul A. Samuelson,* Vol. 2. Cambridge, MA: MIT press.
16. Dahl, R. A., & Lindblom, C. E. (1953). *Politics, economics, and welfare.* New York: Harper Collins.
17. Ostrom, V., & Ostrom, E. (1971). Public choice: A different approach to the study of public administration. *Public Administration Review, 31*(2), 203–216.
18. Wamsley, G. L., & Zald, M. N. (1973). *The political economy of public organizations.* Lexington, MA: Heath.
19. Bozeman, B. (1987). *All organizations are public.* San Francisco: Jossey-Bass Publishers.
20. Andrews, R., Boyne, G. A., & Walker, R. M. (2011). Dimensions of publicness and organizational performance: A review of the evidence. *Journal of Public Administration Research and Theory, 21*(suppl 3), i301–i319.
21. Moulton, S. (2009). Putting together the publicness puzzle: A framework for realized publicness. *Public Administration Review, 69*(5), 889–900, 891.
22. Frederickson, D. G., & Frederickson, H. G. (2006). *Measuring the performance of the hollow state.* Washington, DC: Georgetown University Press.
23. Lipsky, M. (1980). *Street-level bureaucracy: Dilemmas of the individual in public services.* New York: Russell Sage Foundation.
24. Wilson, J. Q. (1991). *Bureaucracy: What government agencies do and why they do It.* New York: Basic Books.
25. *Ibid.,* p. 20.
26. *Ibid.*
27. Rohr, J. A. (1976). The study of ethics in public administration curriculum. *Public Administration Review, 36*(4), 398–406.
28. Rohr, J. A. (1989). *Ethics for bureaucrats: An essay on law and values,* 2nd ed. New York: Marcel Dekker.
29. Bertelli, A. M., & Lynn, Jr., L. E. (2006). *Madison's managers: Public administration and the constitution.* Baltimore, MD: Johns Hopkins University Press.
30. Rosenbloom, D. H. (1983). Public administrative theory and the separation of powers. *Public Administration Review, 43*(3), 219–227.
31. *Ibid.*
32. Moynihan, D. P. (2009). "Our usable past": A historical contextual approach to administrative values. *Public Administration Review, 69*(5), 813–822.
33. Rittel, H. W., & Webber, M. M. (1973). Dilemmas in a general theory of planning. *Policy Sciences, 4,* 155–169.
34. Parks, R. B., Baker, P. C., Kiser, L., Oakerson, R., Ostrom, E., Ostrom, V., & Wilson, R. (1981). Consumers as coproducers of public services: Some economic and institutional considerations. *Policy Studies Journal, 9*(7), 1001–1011.
35. Light, P. (2006). The tides of reform revisited: Patterns in making government work, 1945–2002. *Public Administration Review, 66*(1), 6–19.
36. Denhardt, J. V., & Denhardt, R. B. (2011). *The new public service: Serving, not steering.* Armonk, NY: M. E. Sharpe, Inc.
37. *Ibid.,* p. 1.

PART V

Government and Social Justice

25

10 KEY ELEMENTS TO ENHANCE PROCEDURAL JUSTICE IN THE CRIMINAL JUSTICE SYSTEM

Matthew O'Deane

Procedural Justice History and Definition of Terms

I would like to start off the chapter with a brief overview of the history of the concept commonly known as "procedural justice." In 1975, John Thibaut (social psychologist) and Laurens Walker (law professor) published *Procedural Justice: A Psychological Analysis* (Thibaut & Walker, 1975). The researchers found that disputants in a process were often just as concerned with the fairness of a process as with the outcome itself, so they coined the term "procedural justice." Additionally, research found that if disputants do not see procedures as fair, they will not accord legitimacy to the police or the criminal justice system. Tom Tyler at Yale University Law School conducted a study in Chicago in which he and his team interviewed Chicago residents who had interactions with police and the court system. The study revealed that perceptions of fairness and treatment were the strongest determinants of outcome satisfaction. Those who perceived the procedure as fair remained positive about the authorities even when the outcome was unfavorable. The study concluded that people who come in contact with the criminal justice system and see it as fair will accord system legitimacy and accept or comply with decision.

The purpose of the Criminal Justice System is to deliver justice for all, by protecting the innocent, convicting and punishing the guilty, and helping them to stop offending. The criminal justice system is composed of numerous agencies and processes established by governments to control crime and impose penalties on those who violate laws. External procedural justice is concerned with the processes involved in operating the justice system. When people have contacts with the criminal justice system, such as the police, the fairness with which system is perceived to act affects citizen's trust and confidence in the system and their sense that the laws and law enforcement officers deserve to be obeyed—that is, the procedural justice that citizens subjectively experience affects the legitimacy of the police.

External procedural justice focuses on the ways officers and other legal authorities interact with the public and how the characteristics of those interactions shape the public's trust of the police. It is important to understand that a key component of external procedural justice, the practice of fair and impartial policing, is built on understanding and acknowledging human biases, both explicit and implicit. Internal procedural justice tells us that officers who feel respected by their supervisors and peers are more likely to accept departmental policies, understand decisions, and comply with them voluntarily. It follows that officers who feel respected by their organizations are more likely to bring this respect into their interactions with the people they serve.

Procedural justice operates in two phases: (1) an evidence of "process" phase (procedural justice) and (2) a "decision" phase (legitimacy). If we break down the name procedural justice, we have two distinct terms that need to be defined—procedural and justice.

Procedural Defined

Criminal procedure is the adjudication process of criminal law. Procedural law provides the process that a case will go through (whether or not it goes to trial). Procedural fairness is concerned with the procedures used by a decision maker, rather than the actual outcome reached (Kunard, 2011). It requires a fair and proper procedure to be used when making a decision. A decision maker who follows a fair procedure is more likely to reach a fair and correct decision. Procedural law determines how a proceeding concerning the enforcement of substantive law will occur. Substantive law defines how the facts in the case will be handled, as well as how the crime is to be charged. For example, the procedures or steps in the federal criminal process include the investigation, charging, initial hearing/ arraignment, discovery, plea bargaining, preliminary hearing, pretrial motions, and trial.

While criminal procedure differs dramatically by jurisdiction, the process generally begins with a formal criminal charge and results in the conviction or acquittal of the defendant. Procedural law or adjective law comprises the rules by which a court hears and determines what happens in a civil lawsuit or in criminal or administrative proceedings. Consider, for example, some of the crucial milestones in a criminal case flowing to trial. First, based on a crime report, the police investigate particular neighborhoods and persons of interest and ultimately arrest a suspect. Second, the prosecutor decides to charge the suspect with a particular crime. Third, the judge makes decisions about bail and pretrial detention. Fourth, the defendant decides whether to accept a plea bargain after consulting with the defense attorney, often a public defender or court-appointed private counsel. Fifth, if the case goes to trial, the judge manages the proceedings while the jury decides whether the defendant is guilty. Finally, if convicted, the defendant must be sentenced. At each of these stages, implicit biases can have an important impact.

Justice Defined

Justice can be defined as the quality of being just; righteousness, equitableness, or moral rightness; to uphold the justice of a cause; rightfulness or lawfulness, as of a claim or title; the maintenance or administration of what is just by law, as by judicial or other proceedings; judgment of persons or causes by judicial process; or to administer justice in a community. The criminal justice process is like a funnel, wide at the top and narrow at the bottom. Early in the criminal justice process, there are many cases, but the number of cases dwindles as decision makers remove cases from the process. Some cases are dismissed, while others are referred for treatment or counseling. It is often during the funneling down of cases that procedural justice is the most critical. Procedural justice also requires all components of the criminal justice system, including the (1) legislative branch (create laws); (2) adjudication (courts); and (3) corrections (jails, prisons, probation, and parole), to work together towards the same goal of fairness in all procedural decisions. Other aspects of procedural justice can also be found in social psychology and sociology issues and organizational psychology. In law, substantive justice is the opposite of procedural justice. A clear definition for substantive justice is that it is a just behavior or treatment that is fair and reasonable.

External Procedural Justice

Research around the globe has shown repeatedly that when people believe that police are legitimate, they are more likely to accept police decisions and comply with police requests and directives, more likely to cooperate with the police, and more likely even to abide by the law. Procedural justice is the "vehicle" that produces the "legitimacy" sought by police and citizens alike. Procedural justice is not a practice but a philosophy and a movement that promotes police legitimacy in the community (COPS Office, 2013). The large body of empirical research tells us procedural justice comes down to the manner in which a person is treated, from initial contact to the journey through the entire justice system. It is a matter of treating people with dignity and respect, giving them an opportunity to explain their situation, and listening to what they have to say (Fischer, 2014). In reviewing the research, we get a clear picture of how and why people view the police the way they do and how and why they may or may not comply with the law or the directives and decision of police officers. This is not a theory; the research backs up a way of policing that has been used by many officers throughout history (COPS Office, 2013; Tyler, 2014).

Procedural justice (sometimes called procedural fairness) describes the idea that how individuals regard the justice system is tied more to the perceived fairness of the *process* and how they were treated rather than to the perceived fairness of the *outcome*. In other words, even someone who receives a traffic ticket or "loses" his/her case in court will rate the system favorably if he/she feels that the outcome is arrived at fairly (MacCoun, 2005).

Theory: How procedural justice produces benefits

(What police do) + (How a citizen feels) = (How a citizen behaves)

Internal Procedural Justice

Procedural Justice: Internal Application

Adopting procedural justice as the guiding principle for internal and external policies and practices can be the underpinning of a change in culture and should contribute to building trust and confidence in the community. Organizational culture created through employee interaction with management can be linked to officers' interactions with citizens. When an agency creates an environment that promotes internal procedural justice, it encourages its officers to demonstrate external procedural justice. And just as employees are more likely to take direction from management when they believe management's authority is legitimate, citizens are more likely to cooperate with the police when they believe the officers' authority is legitimate. Internal procedural justice begins with the clear articulation of organizational core values and the transparent creation and fair application of an organization's policies, protocols, and decision-making processes.

Furthermore, there is a growing recognition of the need for police executives to treat their employees with the same sense of legitimacy and procedural justice that applies to members of the public. This is sometimes referred to as "internal legitimacy" or "internal procedural justice." When the leaders of a police department treat their officers with dignity, respect, and fairness—for example, by creating meaningful and transparent paths for career advancement, ensuring that disciplinary systems are fair, and soliciting officers' views about major issues of policy—and because the effectiveness of police operations often depends at least in part on the public's willingness to provide information to and otherwise help the police.

The concept of perception of fairness is an imperative concept for employees because it affects their attitudes and behaviors, which in turn lead to positive or negative employee satisfaction and performance. An unfair perception leads to dissatisfaction with outcomes or rewards; an employee will exert less effort on the job and will ultimately part with the organization. Employees who have a sense of equality and feel that they are rewarded fairly for their genuine contributions to the organization are satisfied. The reward may include multiple benefits and perks other than financial gains. Employees with high job satisfaction tend to exert higher levels of performance, productivity, and commitment and have higher rates of retention. Therefore, organizational justice must prevail.

Like the public, police officers sometimes complain that their supervisors do not listen, do not explain their policies, and are not concerned about the issues that matter to officers (Kates, 2014a). Consequently, studies indicate that officers who feel unappreciated are less likely to follow department rules for behavior on the street and less willing to voluntarily cooperate with their supervisors in the department's efforts to manage social order. Employees of law enforcement agencies—both sworn and civilian—are more likely to view their organizations as legitimate and to comply with workplace policies and procedures when the agency exhibits a culture where transparency, impartiality, fairness, and voice are embraced and modeled through internal decision-making, policy, and overall treatment of personnel. Police executives and supervisors must become more effective in fostering an environment where procedural justice principles become a standard practice within their agency (Tyler, 2014).

When procedural justice is embedded into the very fabric of the policing culture, beginning with the chief and continuing down through the ranks of sworn and civilian personnel, it will ultimately have an impact on the way frontline officers and civilian personnel interact with individual community members. In order for the community to view the law enforcement agency and its personnel as legitimate, the principles of procedural justice must be a part of the agency's organizational culture. How an officer responds to a situation will impact the community's perception and level of trust in the agency (Tyler, 1990). As officers and civilian employees of law enforcement agencies experience a culture of fairness, transparency, impartiality, and voice, their behavior will ultimately shift, reflecting in the ways that they treat one another as well as members of the public. Adopting procedural justice principles from the top of the agency on down and also modeling fair behavior are both important to transforming the culture of an agency (Hollander & Tyler, 2008).

Establish Legitimacy

Legitimacy is the very foundation of police authority. A legitimate police force demonstrates to citizens why its access to and exercise of power is rightful, and why those subject to its power have a corresponding duty to obey (Tyler, 2014). Legitimacy is linked to the ability of the police to prevent crime and keep neighborhoods safe. If the public's trust and confidence in the police is undermined, the ability of the police to prevent crime will be weakened by lawsuits, declining willingness to obey the law, and withdrawal from existing partnerships. The political fallout from illegitimate police actions can seriously impede the ability of police departments to engage innovative crime control tactics. While residents in neighborhoods suffering from high levels of crime often demand higher levels of enforcement, they still want the police to be respectful and lawful in their crime control efforts (Meares & Skogan, 2004; Tyler, 2014). Residents don't want family members, friends, and neighbors to be targeted unfairly by enforcement efforts or treated poorly by what they perceive to be overaggressive police officers (Tyler & Jackson, 2014).

The common definitions of legitimacy define it as being lawful, or acting in accordance with established rules, principles, or standards, or to show or declare to be legitimate or proper. Legitimacy is based on several key judgments. The first is public trust and confidence in the police (Kane, 2005). Such confidence involves the belief that the police are honest, that they try to do their jobs well, and that they are trying to protect the community against crime and violence. Second, legitimacy reflects the willingness of residents to defer to the law and to police authority, i.e., their sense of obligation and responsibility to accept police authority (Mentel, 2012). Finally, legitimacy involves the belief that police actions are morally justified and appropriate to the circumstances (POST, 2016).

Trust and legitimacy require hiring only the best people to be police officers. According to Plato, "Only those with the most impeccable character should be chosen to bear the responsibility of protecting the democracy." I think we would all agree with Plato that we must select the highest quality people to be police officers. We have seen what happens when standards are reduced, applicants are not properly screened, psychological red flags are missed, and past unethical conduct is tolerated. One approach to accomplish this goal of hiring only procedurally just police officers is to not wait for young people to grow up and decide to join our profession; we need to go get them via active recruiting methods. It is imperative to recruit and hire individuals who have a service orientation and the character necessary to uphold high standards of integrity, as well as the ability to withstand the temptation to deviate from these standards.

Initiatives like the San Diego Sheriff's Explorer Program motivate young people to consider law enforcement as a career and take steps to ensure they will meet the high standards of the profession when they reach the age to apply. By encouraging positive citizenship, ethical conduct, sound morals, patriotism, and a respect for law and order, we will build the next generation of police officers. Explorers and cadets also serve as mentors for other youth; they assist with community events, and by being everyday goodwill ambassadors and role models for their peers they can help dispel the view that the police are "the enemy," as some of our youth are taught (Murphy, 2013). We also need to aggressively seek out a diverse mix of officers; we want our police forces to mirror the cultural and ethnic makeup of our communities, supporting race, gender, language, and different cultural backgrounds, which further builds trust and legitimacy.

Build Trust

The common definitions of trust define it as a firm belief in the reliability, truth, ability, or strength of someone or something, or the obligation or responsibility imposed on a person in whom confidence or authority is placed. Scientific research supports the premise that people are more likely to obey the law when they trust that those enforcing the law have the legitimate authority to do so, and that it is done in a fair and impartial manner. Building trust is difficult but not impossible. We do this by collectively engaging with local communities. The key word is here is *collectively*—without community involvement, it is impossible to truly achieve trust (Kochel, 2011). The building and maintenance of trust takes a great deal of continuous effort from the police and community alike. Trust and legitimacy grow from positive interactions based on more than just enforcement interactions (Horowitz, 2007). Law enforcement agencies build trust one contact at a time. They achieve trust and legitimacy by establishing a positive presence at community activities and events, participating in proactive problem solving, and ensuring that communities have a voice and seat at the table working with officers (COPS Office, 2013).

Suggestions on HOW TO BUILD TRUST

Maintain personal integrity. It is the foundation of trust in any organization and for any individual. Integrity must begin at the top (the Chief) and then move down through the ranks. This means, among other things, always telling the truth, no matter how difficult it might be. If its people have integrity, an organization can be trusted.

Do what's right, regardless of personal risk. We all know intuitively what's "right" in nearly every situation. Following this instinctive sense and ignoring any personal consequences, will nearly always create respect from those around us. From this respect will come trust.

Do what you say you will do. If you say one thing and do another, you will not be worthy of trust. Be reliable, dependable, and work to be trustworthy.

Communicate your vision and values. What do you believe, what do you value, what is your vision of the future? Communication is critical, since it provides the avenue for an exchange of information which is essential to building trust.

Focus on shared, rather than personal goals. When people feel everyone is pulling together to accomplish a shared vision, rather than a series of personal agendas, trust results. This is the essence of teamwork. When a team really works, the players trust one another.

Research demonstrates that when the principles of procedural justice are followed, they can contribute to positive relationships between authorities and the community and can increase community trust and confidence in the police, seeing them as honest, unbiased, benevolent, and lawful; the community feels obligated to follow the law and the dictates of legal authorities; and the community feels that it shares a common set of interests and values with the police (Goodman-Delahunty, 2010; Tyler & Huo, 2002; Tyler & Murphy, 2011).

Develop Community Partnerships and Outreach

Our police officers are not the only ones who need to take responsibility for building trust and maintaining positive relationships—communities and their leaders also need to take active steps to engage with the police in positive ways. It starts with the willingness of community leaders to want to develop the relationship; if they do not, they are doing a tremendous disservice to the community they claim to represent. Many of our agencies have ride-along programs, internships for youth, and student worker or volunteer programs that allow youth to see police work in real life. Others have established citizen academies, which offer a behind-the-scenes look at the criminal justice/government systems. According to the National Citizens Police Academy Association, the objective is not to train an individual to be a police officer but to produce informed citizens. The citizens and officers meet each other face to face in a neutral, friendly setting and each becomes a person to the other. Programs like the District Attorney and Carlsbad Police Citizen Academies, and other programs such as the Sheriff Senior Volunteer Patrol and the San Diego Police recruiting events are local examples of how our region engages with the community and encourages community members to join law enforcement, becoming part of the solution, not the problem.

Trust and legitimacy require community outreach, education, and givebacks. Outreach is the way we provide awareness, education, and information to the community about public safety issues. Our law enforcement officers engage in education programs on a daily basis, from educating kids about the dangers of drugs (DARE) and gangs (GREAT) to providing driver safety education, coordinating neighborhood watch association meetings, speaking to businesses, schools, and a variety of community groups about crime issues, and always striving to create a friendly environment for our communities (Hough, Jackson, Bradford, Myhill & Quinton, 2010).

San Diego law enforcement officers are some of the most charitable people we have in our region. Our agencies, police unions, police foundations, and a variety of organizations conduct over 100 events each year in which the proceeds directly benefit local charities, and all of the hours involved are volunteered by the officers. I think we need to keep advertising the good we do—if we don't it is probable the media will not. Many of our officers are coaches for youth sports programs, volunteer with their churches and schools, and act as role models and teachers. By giving their personal time and energy to the community, by getting to know at-risk youth and providing positive role models, we build trust one relationship at a time (Hinds, 2007). With events such as Shop with a Cop and the San Diego Regional Teddy Bear Drive, we are making a difference in the lives of others and enhancing public trust and legitimacy. Most importantly, these are events that the officers truly enjoy doing.

San Diego law enforcement agencies will continue to work to achieve trust and legitimacy by establishing a positive presence in our communities, participating in proactive problem solving, and ensuring that communities have a voice and a seat at the table working with officers, not against them. All community members are encouraged to contact their police agency and see what programs they have to address these issues and support their efforts.

Show Respect and Dignity

Treating people with dignity and respect is a mandate for all departments. We must practice the Golden Rule, treating every person, no matter their status in life, with the same basic level of respect and dignity, and failing to do so will undermine our legitimacy and authority. The notion that fair procedures are the best guarantee for fair outcomes is a popular one. Procedural justice is concerned with making and implementing decisions according to fair processes. People feel affirmed if the procedures that are adopted treat them with respect and dignity, making it easier to even accept outcomes they do not like. The unfortunate reality is that involvement with the criminal justice system, such as being arrested and booked in jail and subsequent court proceedings, can be confounding and dehumanizing experiences for many (Wemmers, 2013). Courtroom participants do not deliberately attempt to cause confusion or undermine confidence in the system; however, trying to communicate complex, technical information as quickly as possible sometimes causes confusion and undermines legitimacy and tends to show a lack of respect for those working through the criminal justice process (Watson & Angell, 2012). There are numerous real-world obstacles, including overwhelming caseloads and increasing cultural and linguistic diversity among court participants. Similar challenges exist during routine traffic stops, probation intake sessions, parole board hearings—the list goes on and on (COPS Office, 2013).

In courts, among other things, this takes the form of rethinking how courtroom rules are posted, explained, and enforced, or how court clerk or court officers provide information while court is in session. Criminal justice facilities—like many government buildings—can be difficult to navigate for those unfamiliar with their halls. As an exercise, try to examine your facility with fresh eyes from the perspective of a new user. In high-traffic areas, ensure that building rules and instructions for getting assistance are clearly posted, easy to read, and provided in commonly spoken languages other than English, if necessary. Law enforcement professionals are typically the first point of contact for people processed through the justice system. Procedural justice strategies can help shape an individual's perception of the system and improve compliance.

Practice Fairness and Neutrality

Procedural fairness requires a fair and proper procedure be used when making a decision. A decision maker who follows a fair procedure is more likely to reach a fair and correct decision. Studies of personal encounters with the police consistently document that post-experience feelings are determined by the fairness with which the problem was handled (Tyler, 2001). The Committee to Review Research on Police Policy and Practices identifies four dimensions of fairness in police–citizen interactions (Skogan & Frydl, 2004). First, citizens need to have meaningful participation in interactions. Importantly, citizens must have the ability to explain situations and communicate with the police. Appearing approachable and accessible is a key component of procedural justice. When interviewing suspects or witnesses, make eye contact and use body language to convey respect. Thank citizens for their cooperation with the process as a means of yielding increased cooperation in the future. Those directly affected by the decisions should have a voice and representation in the process. Having representation affirms the status of group members and inspires trust in the decision-making system. This is especially important for weaker parties whose voices often go unheard.

Second, citizens need to feel that the police officers are neutral in their assessments of situations by using objective indicators to make decisions rather than personal views. *Neutrality* includes the perception that the decision-making process is unbiased and trustworthy, and *respect* includes the perception that system players treat you with dignity and respect. Those carrying out the procedures must be impartial and neutral. Unbiased decision makers must carry out the procedures to reach a fair and accurate conclusion. Those involved should believe that the intentions of third-party authorities are benevolent, that they want to treat people fairly and take the viewpoint and needs of interested parties into account. If people trust the third party, they are more likely to view the decision-making process as fair.

Third, citizens must feel that they are being treated with respect and dignity by the police during interactions. Fourth, police officers need to inspire trust in the citizenry. If people believe authorities care about their well-being and are considerate of their needs and concerns, they view procedures as fairer. Police can encourage the public to view them as trustworthy by explaining their decisions and accounting for their conduct. Finally, the processes that are implemented should be transparent. Decisions should be reached through open procedures, without secrecy or deception. Procedurally just policing emphasizes values that police and communities share, shared values based upon a common conception of what social order is and how it should be maintained, and encourages the collaborative, voluntary maintenance of a law-abiding community (Jackson, Huq, Bradford & Tyler, 2013).

But what makes procedures fair? First, there is an emphasis on consistency. Fair procedures should guarantee that like cases are treated alike. Any distinctions "should reflect genuine aspects of personal identity rather than extraneous features of the differentiating mechanism itself." Fair procedures tend to inspire feelings of loyalty to one's group, legitimize the authority of leaders, and help to ensure voluntary compliance with the rules. This is true in a variety of settings, from the workplace to political organizations to legal contexts. Issues of procedural justice thus arise in the making of many different types of decisions. In the context of legal proceedings, procedural justice has to do with ensuring that a fair trial takes place. The application of law is supposed to ensure impartiality, consistency, and transparency. In order to ensure that retributive justice is served and that offenders receive fair punishments, judges and juries must be unbiased and evenhanded in their sentencings. Drug sentencing laws in the U.S. have, for instance, been challenged as being procedurally unjust. In particular, federal sentencing structures hand out tougher sentences for crack cocaine than for powder cocaine, a substance more popular with White, wealthier users. The outcome of the wide disparity has been a racial imbalance in federal prisons, which are overcrowded with poor African American offenders. Powder cocaine offenders, meanwhile, are thought to "get off easy," despite scientific evidence that neither substance is more addictive than the other.

The Fair Sentencing Act (FSA), a law passed by Congress in 2010, aimed to correct unfair sentencing procedures by reducing the sentencing disparity between crack and powder cocaine from a 100:1 to an 18:1 weight ratio. Nonetheless, many activists are calling for further reforms, including applying the FSA retroactively, which would correct past injustices, and eliminating the disparity entirely.

Give Voice and Communication

Giving individuals a "voice" during encounters includes listening to what people have to say. By giving a person their voice (or the perception that their side of the story has been heard), we improve communication and increase listening opportunities to enhance procedural justice. Giving people an opportunity to speak and have their concerns heard can add a few extra minutes to the average interaction, but it is time well spent in the context of police community relations and engagement. Research shows that having your voice heard increases perceptions of fairness, even when the person is told that his/her views will not influence the ultimate decision or outcome. Officers should always be considering how they can maximize the citizens' voice in contexts where it may be limited, such as traffic and street stops or walk-in inquiries (Rosenfeld & Fornango, 2014).

It is also important to explain what you're doing and why you're doing it. For many individuals, a routine traffic stop or other interaction with law enforcement can be a traumatic event. The legal jargon and procedures (familiar to practitioners in the field) can be confusing and intimidating to the average person. Whenever possible, use simple terms to explain your actions, the legal and/or practical reasons for doing so, and any consequences they may have for the person. For example, when issuing a summons, clearly explain the process for appearing in court to resolve the matter—including providing directions to the courthouse, if and how a lawyer will be provided, and whether there are options to resolve the matter by mail or online. These strategies can help promote compliance. We all want to be valued, we all want to be heard, and we all want to be respected.

Communication is complex for several reasons. It is interactive because many processes are involved. It is symbolic because symbols are open to interpretation. It is personal and cultural because a person's culture can add a new or different meaning to a phrase or gesture. It is irreversible because once a message is sent, it cannot be taken back. It is circular because it involves both original messages and feedback, which is necessary to confirm communication. It is purposeful because there is always a reason behind a message and it helps meet our needs. It is impossible to duplicate because each interaction is unique.

First, citizens need to have meaningful participation in interactions with the police. Importantly, citizens must have the ability to explain situations and communicate with the police. This requires the police to be approachable and accessible; this is a key component of procedural justice. For example, when interviewing suspects or witnesses, officers should make eye contact and use body language to convey respect. Ethical communication means that a communicator follows the morals and codes of conduct within a society. It is how a person behaves and how they treat others. They are informed and are able to support what they say with facts and examples that are true. They are logical with developed reasoning skills and the ability to draw conclusions and reach decisions. They are accountable, taking responsibility for their information, decisions, and actions. They are reliable, which means they can be trusted to keep their word even if a decision may not benefit them.

The importance of procedurally just "dialogue" during frontline police–citizen encounters cultivates perceptions of legitimacy (Belvedere, Worrall & Tibetts, 2005). The consequences of ongoing claims to legitimacy from the power holders (i.e., frontline police) and iterative responses from citizens mean that legitimacy needs to be perceived as always dialogic and relational in character.

Procedural Justice Communication

Sir, please step over here and explain what happened.
Let me tell you what is going to happen now.
I understand your frustration. Let's work through this together.

Procedural Injustice Communication

Shut up and wait your turn!
I'll ask the questions. You give me the answers!

So why does communication matter, what are the benefits of this? From a police point of view, I believe it is fair to say officer safety will increase—people are often willing to accept and defer to appropriate use of police authority. It also has the ability to reduce officer and community stress, result in fewer complaints against the officer or the department, and often results in greater cooperation from citizens (Myhill & Quinton, 2011). It can also have an impact on crime reduction—if people evaluate police practices as fair, they view the police as legitimate and accept their decisions, and they may also be more willing to report crimes and get involved.

To take one example, quality-of-life issues sometimes are most important to community members, even in districts with high levels of crime. Police chiefs often speak of arriving at community meetings ready to discuss the details of violent crime patterns and police countermeasures—only to be surprised when residents do not seem interested in discussing crime in their neighborhood. Instead, they seem more interested in talking about issues like abandoned cars, vandalism, speeding by motorists and other traffic violations on their streets, and other matters that the police may see as a less important issue. Issues of legitimacy and procedural justice are important in such a situation. By listening carefully to residents about the issues that concern them and responding to those concerns, police can build trust in the community and increase residents' respect for police authority. (That is not to say that police should ignore the issues that the police think are important; those can be discussed as well.) Furthermore, police can increase their level of perceived legitimacy by explaining their actions to the people who are directly involved in those actions (Reisig & Lloyd, 2009).

For example, in the situation described above where residents say they are worried about motorists speeding through their streets, the police may respond with targeted traffic enforcement. That will presumably please the residents who complained about the speeding, but motorists who are stopped may wonder why police are spending resources on traffic enforcement instead of focusing the available workforce on violent crime. In this example, officers making the traffic stops can provide a brief explanation that the reason for the stop is that residents of the neighborhood have expressed concerns about pedestrians being hurt by speeding motorists (Ward, 2011). When such initiatives address a real public safety problem, and if police make it their business to provide a brief explanation of that problem every time they make a stop, the same traffic enforcement strategy can result in an *increased* sense that the police are acting legitimately, rather than in damage to the police department's reputation.

Complaint Procedures

All agencies should have a clearly delineated procedure to investigate complaints, and that procedure should be publicly available on their website. The term "complaining citizen" is used as a shorthand way of describing a person who has filed a complaint of misconduct against a police officer or department. It also includes those individuals who are not citizens. The state of California and many other states have a standard form for filing a complaint against a peace officer or law enforcement agency. California's statutes and regulations provide that a governmental authority, agent, or person acting on behalf of a governmental authority is prohibited from engaging in a pattern or practice of conduct by law enforcement officers that deprives any person of rights, privileges, or immunities secured or protected by state or federal law.

Maintain Transparency

Transparency involves conveying trustworthy motives and explaining your actions, including *understanding* and comprehension of the criminal justice process and how decisions are made; including the level of *helpfulness* or the perception that system players are interested in your personal situation to the extent that the law allows.

San Diego agencies collect data on all police–citizen interactions, and we share our policing data (e.g., officer-involved shootings, uses of force, traffic and pedestrian stops, arrest data, etc.) with the community. The most significant issue related to transparency on a national and local level has been where an officer has been involved in a shooting incident. The San Diego District Attorney's Office recently released the regional policy that governs the sharing of officer-involved shooting videos. This policy strikes a balance between the public's desire to know and the due process rights of those involved.

The policy states videos will be released whenever possible, as soon as it's appropriate to do so, but there are some caveats. Footage will not be released until the district attorney (DA) has reviewed the shooting and presented its findings to the agency involved, and it won't be released if criminal charges are filed, as this may undermine the integrity of the criminal case. We have all seen incidents when video is presented out of context—it can lead to false and inflammatory narratives about shootings. With context, video evidence can aid the public in understanding why and how it occurred. When the decision to release a video has been made, it is done so at a press conference at which the video plays along with a description of the facts presented by the DA. Proactively engaging the local media can be an effective way to influence community perception of a police department or even a specific incident. Whether or not a department has a specifically designated public information officer, all of our agencies have spokespeople who use their contacts to conduct proactive outreach, disseminating information, good or bad, from an officer-involved shooting to highlighting successful programs within the department.

Transparency and legitimacy must be a part of all of our agencies' culture, meaning that leaders at all levels of the organization must understand their role in promoting transparency and accountability, which results in legitimacy. Building trust and nurturing legitimacy on both sides of the police–citizen divide is the foundational principle underlying the nature of police community relations. People tend to mistrust things they do not understand; therefore, trust is a two-way street and is not given but earned. Public trust in law enforcement may be fleeting if police executives do not continually reinforce sound, ethical policies and procedures to agency personnel and to the public. Law enforcement executives, therefore, bear the responsibility for demonstrating proper behavior, informing the community about their department's role in maintaining honor and integrity within the organization, and building and sustaining a trusting working relationship between the public and the police.

Enforce Accountability and Oversight

Trust and Legitimacy Require Accountability and Oversight

We have 20 California Peace Officer Standards of Training (POST) law enforcement agencies in San Diego County with more than 6,000 officers and a couple thousand more when we add in the probation department and our federal partners. Unfortunately, the ethical work of these thousands of local law enforcement officers is easily undone by the actions of one unethical officer, discrediting the officer, the agency, and often the broader law enforcement community; this is true everywhere in America. As such, it is all of our responsibility to identify and address problematic behavior as quickly and efficiently as possible and to hold ourselves and our officers accountable for their actions. When our communities know our policies and procedures, and that we follow them, this creates trust. To build community trust, it is incumbent upon the chiefs of police and managing supervisors to foster a culture and environment within their departments in which ethical behavior is expected and each individual is responsible for meeting those expectations. Every member of a police department represents the entire agency, personal conduct is his or her own responsibility, and he or she will be held accountable for all conduct, whether positive or negative.

The common definitions of oversight define it as the supervision or watchful care of an agency; oversight is conducted both internally and externally in San Diego.

Accountability is sometimes referred to as internal oversight.

All San Diego agencies have Internal Affairs Units to maintain the integrity and professionalism of our agencies. There are many ways to ensure compliance with a policy; the most effective is having active and engaged first-line supervisors. Many of the misconduct cases that have occurred in San Diego over the past decade have demonstrated a lack of adequate first-line supervision. In these instances, supervisors were not engaged with the behaviors and actions of their subordinates, and one could argue in many of the cases that had there been internal oversight in the field, these supervisors may have been able to intervene before these behaviors escalated to misconduct. Another issue with first-line supervision, if not monitored, can be the inconsistent application of policy and procedures within a department on a squad-by-squad basis. This undermines the trust officers have in their leaders, their department, and their agency policies.

External oversight is from outside our agencies. The appropriate form and structure of civilian oversight varies to meet the needs of each community and agency. There is no one-size-fits-all form of community oversight, so all agencies should assess this idea to determine what will work best for them.

External oversight can be from any entity that is not part of the agency involved in the incident. A citizen's review board is a municipal body composed of citizen representatives charged with the investigation of complaints, by members of the public, concerning misconduct by police officers. Such bodies may be independent agencies or part of a law enforcement agency. Generally, the power of a civilian review board is restricted to reviewing an already completed internal police investigation, and commenting on it to the chief of police or sheriff. In San Diego County, seven cities with municipal police departments, including Carlsbad, Chula Vista, Coronado, El Cajon, Escondido, La Mesa, and Oceanside, do not currently have external citizen oversight—they investigate citizen complaints internally.

All of our agencies should evaluate and assess the need and desire for new or additional civilian oversight, and this evaluation should include input from our police officers because the people to be overseen should be part of the process that will oversee them. This guarantees that the principles of procedural justice are in place to benefit both the police and the communities we serve. There are important arguments for having civilian oversight, even though we lack strong empirical research and evidence that it works. Therefore, I can see the need for further research, based on the guiding principle of procedural justice, to find evidence-based practices to implement successful civilian oversight mechanisms in the future.

These are not, or should not be, difficult things for officers to do. It is important to emphasize to officers that procedural justice is a very positive thing; it is beneficial in all aspects of the job.

Implement Education and Training Programs

California Penal Code Section 13519.4 mandates that all California police officers attend refresher training in the area of racial and cultural diversity and racial profiling. The courses are designed to explore the evolving role of law enforcement in a rapidly changing, increasingly diverse society. Not a day goes by without a story about communities and law enforcement agencies struggling with the issue of race in America, in particular complaints of racial profiling. But what is racial profiling? What is it not? What are the ethical issues involved for both police and communities? The Museum of Tolerance (MOT) offers courses on racial profiling that delve into the legal, moral, and ethical boundaries surrounding this controversial issue. All investigators and police officers in my region, San Diego, California, are required by law to attend a POST-mandated racial profiling training class every five years.

Most officers in southern California attend the course offered at the Museum of Tolerance. The MOT course provides officers with an updated and enhanced understanding of racial profiling. Using the prior POST training as a template, this course utilizes videos and interactive activities to further explore the issue, including defining racial profiling, legal considerations, the history of civil rights, community considerations, and ethical considerations. The Museum of Tolerance (MOT) was established in 1993 as the educational arm of the Simon Wiesenthal Center, an internationally renowned human rights organization. Through interactive exhibits, special events, and customized programs, the museum engages visitors' hearts and minds, while challenging them to assume personal responsibility for positive change. The MOT has been a key provider of California POST-certified training for southern California law enforcement professionals since 1996. The classes are designed to equip law enforcement professionals with the tools they need to deliver an effective level of service to their communities. The MOT engages participants in an in-depth exploration of the process of dehumanization during the Holocaust and other genocides and an examination of historical and contemporary examples of intolerance, including hate vs. free speech, the civil rights movement, exploitation of women and children, and the plight of refugees by utilizing a variety of learning methods including interactive technology, personal testimonies, and group discussion. It provides an educational experience that engages students on many levels. The program is inclusive and geared toward sworn and non-sworn civilian personnel at every level (e.g., from recruits to the chief). Participants examine the process of building trust and respect and enhance their critical thinking skills in the areas of diversity, ethics, and values.

One of the exhibits at the MOT is the Point of View Diner, a recreation of a 1950's diner, red booths and all, that "serves" a menu of controversial topics on video jukeboxes. It uses cutting edge technology to relay the overall message of personal responsibility. Scenarios focus on bullying, drunk driving and hate speech; this interactive exhibit allows visitors to input their opinions on what they have seen and question relevant characters. The results are then instantly tabulated for the participants to see and evaluate.

POST programs and services have historically included training in community-based policing, racial and cultural diversity, racial profiling and discrimination, persons with developmental disabilities or mental illness, and a full spectrum of other training designed to help law enforcement build cooperative relationships with the communities they serve, while at the same time decreasing the emergence of racial animosities. Taking measures to enhance procedural justice within law enforcement agencies is becoming increasingly possible. The Museum of Tolerance and others have created training for line officers and command staff that teaches them how to apply powerful procedural justice principles to their routine contacts with the public. Indeed, there are many good reasons to cultivate a respectful relationship between police and communities, but the most important is that communities in which police are considered legitimate are safer and more law-abiding.

Police academies need to include training that addresses the "how" and "why" aspects of the police profession. Officers are policing people and communities that may not have the same experiences as the officers. Community culture and the history of policing may influence how a person perceives an action by a police officer. Basic academy training has traditionally focused on "what" a police officer needs to be able to do in order for the officer to perform his or her job—the knowledge of the law and how to apply it, police officer authority under the law, and the skills (like defensive tactics and use of force) that may be necessary to perform their job tasks. The "how" includes efforts to establish the police as legitimate within society, so the people believe the police ought to be able to do their jobs, keep people safe, and maintain order through the proper exercise of police authority. The "how" relates to the process officers use rather than the outcome. Establishing this legitimacy requires the police understand and apply the principles of procedural justice. For the police to legitimately exercise their authority, they also need to understand the "why" of policing—that the police exist to assist in providing for a safe community where people are not victims of crime, and where the people and the police feel safe. Police officers need to understand the underlying tension that has influenced the relationship between government, including the police, and the people since before this country declared its independence—the balance between governmental authority and individual rights—because it plays out every day for police officers on the street.

Training needs to continue beyond the basic police academy. We need to ensure that police officers receive ongoing training to reduce the cynicism that can build and to keep their perishable skills fresh. In addition to the training of police officers in basic academy courses, we need to train field training officers, police supervisors, managers, and administrators to meet the standards of work in 21st-century police agencies. We cannot neglect the need for ongoing training for police officers. Officers need to keep their skills current in all areas. It is easy for police officers to become cynical and lose motivation when they are dealing with the same problems day after day; one of the antidotes for this is regular training to expose them to new ideas and concepts that challenge their thinking. We need field training officers who understand what will be required to police in the 21st century and their role in training officers to fill that role. Change is not going to happen overnight, but it will not happen unless there are people and forces pushing for change. Policing culture will take some time to change, but one of the best places to start that change is with the training provided in basic police academies.

Create Proper Procedures and Policy

A policy is a course or line of action adopted and pursued by an agency that provides guidance on the department's philosophy and governs how officers are to behave and conduct business. A procedure is a detailed description of how a policy is to be accomplished, describing the steps to be taken and the persons responsible for completing the tasks. Procedures are specific guidelines for officers to follow, and they proscribe specific behavior that will result in employees being disciplined for failing to follow the guidelines provided.

Policymakers must remember that when developing policies and procedures, they should be comprehensive, clearly written, and easy to use. Having a policy is only half of the battle; the other half is making sure the policy is enforced. A policy is meaningless if not understood and enforced, and this situation is often more problematic than not having a policy at all, as it potentially increases a department's exposure to civil liability. Policies and procedures should also be consistent with the organizational philosophy, legal requirements, and standards of each agency. In addition, officers must receive adequate training about the policies and the reasons for their existence.

It is recommended that all policies articulate the department's core values, mission statement, and vision statement; these documents should not be something you just memorize before a promotional exam. A policy and procedures manual can encourage the desired behaviors we want to see in our officers, and it will encourage a strong and consistent culture and value system throughout the department. When properly developed and implemented, a policy-procedure manual provides officers with the information to act decisively, consistently, and legally. All policies should be considered living documents, as they will need to be reviewed and adapted to the times, reflecting state and national best practices. Policies must also be kept up to date—industry standards suggest reviewing them at a minimum on an annual basis, if not more often, to ensure they are in compliance with current case law and legal standards. They should be ongoing products of changing case law, practices, and procedures that provide guidance and direction to every member of your agency. Employees suggesting any corrections or amendments should notify their immediate supervisors.

Organizations call their policy and procedures manual different names—policy and procedures, operations manual, standard operating procedures. Regardless of the name, the document provides staff with the guidance necessary to perform department operations. Every policy manual should consider the following items and define the terms used.

Standard—Guidelines or performance requirements that establish benchmarks for agencies to use in developing the organizational structure and measuring its service delivery system.

Policy—A course or line of action adopted and pursued by an agency that provides guidance on the department's philosophy on identified issues.

Procedure—A detailed description of how a policy is to be accomplished. It describes the steps to be taken, the frequency of the task, and the persons responsible for completing the tasks.

General Orders—Written directives related to policy, procedures, rules, and regulations involving more than one organizational unit. General orders typically have a broad statement of policy as well as the procedures for implementing the policy.

Special Orders—Directives regulating one segment of the department or a statement of policy and procedure regarding a specific circumstance or event that is temporary in nature.

Personnel Orders—Announcements of changes in status of personnel such as transfers or promotions.

Rules and Regulations—Procedures that apply each and every time a situation occurs with specific guidelines for staff to follow. Rules and regulations usually proscribe specific behavior that will result in employees being disciplined for failing to follow the guidelines provided.

Employee Handbook—Manual provided by the governing authority that introduces employees to the organization, its benefits/compensation package, and an abbreviated listing of policies.

Developing a policy manual is a critical undertaking. One of the first tasks to be completed is the selection of a policy project coordinator. The selection of the proper person for this position is critical to the success of the development and implementation of the operations manual. In most agencies, this appointment is not a full-time assignment. Instead, the person must complete these responsibilities in addition to their current duties. As the leader, the policy project coordinator must have the authority, knowledge, and motivation to make assignments, draft policies, coordinate meetings, and complete the process. In addition, the coordinator must have sufficient administrative or clerical support to expedite the development process.

Mutual aid agreements, emergency operation plans, and previously agreed upon protocols (e.g., child abuse/molestation investigations) often outline binding procedures for officers to follow while working with other agencies. Because these documents are often updated on a schedule different from the review of the manual, it is good to place the latest copy of the agreements in the appendices and refer to them in the body of the policy. Since police operations are similar throughout the United States, there is no need to reinvent the wheel.

Policies from other departments are an excellent resource for expediting the development process.

Officers must be given sufficient opportunity to read the policy, officers must be trained on the manual and fully understand its requirements before it can be implemented. This training should cover administrative and operational topics, with particular emphasis being placed on high-liability issues. In addition to introductory training, time should be designated during every in-service training class to review the department's operational procedures relating to the topic of instruction and the department's performance standards. This is a convenient way to ensure training is relevant and staff remains current on the department's standards of conduct. Some departments issue the policies to officers as they are developed and approved. This incremental approach has the advantage of allowing staff more time to digest requirements of the policy. At the same time, tracking and maintaining records of distribution are more cumbersome.

When the training is complete, documentation should be maintained that officers have been issued their manuals, were trained on the content, and understand its requirements. Once the new manual has been implemented, only half of the work is completed. Department officials must ensure the policies are being followed. If the work is not done in accordance with the policy, the manual is meaningless because the custom is the policy. This situation is more problematic than not having a policy.

Informal customs attack the credibility of the department's operational procedures and administration. It also increases the department's exposure to potential liability. What gets inspected is what gets done. There are several ways to ensure compliance with the manual. One way is to form a check sheet that lists various inspections that are to be conducted, by which staff, and how frequently. It is a simple process of checking off when the inspection is complete. In some cases, policy may require internal and external inspections. In the event officers are not in compliance with the department policy, a decision must be made as to the appropriate corrective action, ranging from remedial training to counseling to punishment. In some cases, a change in policy may be required. Finally, the entire manual should be reviewed on at least an annual basis. This review helps to ensure the manual is in compliance with current management, operational, and legal standards.

Bias and Natural Justice

In English law, "natural justice" is technical terminology for the rule against bias (*nemo iudex in causa sua*) and the right to a fair hearing (*audi alteram partem*). While the term natural justice is often retained as a general concept, it has largely been replaced and extended by the general "duty to act fairly."

The principles of natural justice concern procedural fairness and ensure a fair decision is reached by an objective decision maker. Maintaining procedural fairness protects the rights of individuals and enhances public confidence in the process.

In their book *Blindspot: Hidden Biases of Good People*, Banaji and Greenwald (2013) describe biases as bits of knowledge about social groups. Once lodged in our minds, hidden biases can influence our behavior toward members of particular social groups, but we remain oblivious to their influence. Most people find it unbelievable that their behavior can be guided by mental content of which they are unaware; however, the phenomenon has been proven true in significant empirical research. Explicit biases are attitudes and stereotypes that are consciously accessible through introspection *and* endorsed as appropriate. If no social norm against these biases exists within a given context, a person will freely broadcast them to others. But if such a norm exists, then explicit biases can be concealed to manage the impressions that others have of us. By contrast, implicit biases are attitudes and stereotypes that are not consciously accessible through introspection. If we find out that we have them, we may indeed reject them as inappropriate.

Malcolm Gladwell discusses implicit bias in his bestseller, *Blink*, this way: all of us have implicit biases to some degree. This does not necessarily mean we will act in an inappropriate or discriminatory manner, only that our first "blink" sends us certain information. Acknowledging and understanding this implicit response and its value and role is critical to informed decision-making and is particularly critical to those whose decisions must embody fairness and justice. In the epilogue of *Blink: The Power of Thinking Without Thinking*, Gladwell (2005) explains how the audition by the son of an administrator for the Munich Philharmonic Orchestra in 1980 led to a unique change in the way auditions were conducted. To avoid a biased response from judges, who may recognize the administrator's son, screens were used to conceal the identity of the performers. At this time in history, prejudices largely prevented women and minorities from being hired with the same pay as male musicians. This practice, which ensured merit would prevail over prejudicial factors, led to the diversification of orchestras. In other words, using screens to take the focus away from one's gender and race led administrators to hire talented musicians based on their abilities rather than their demographic characteristics (Gladwell, 2005). The underlying message from this lesson is that by taking control of our environment, we are capable of making positive changes in our decision-making behaviors. Gladwell's book is filled with numerous scenarios that explain how the brain allows us to think without thinking. Gladwell draws on the fields of neuroscience and psychology to explicate why we tend to make the decisions that we do.

Because thinking through biases with respect to human beings evokes so much potential emotional resistance, sometimes it is easier to apply them to something less fraught than gender, race, religion, and the like. So, consider a vegetarian's biases against meat. He has a negative attitude (that is, prejudice) toward meat. He also believes that eating meat is bad for his health (a stereotype). He is aware of this attitude and stereotype. He also endorses them as appropriate. That is, he feels that it is okay to have a negative reaction to meat. He also believes it accurate enough to believe that meat is generally bad for human health and that there is no reason to avoid behaving in accordance with this belief. These are *explicit* biases. Now, if this vegetarian is running for political office and campaigning in a region famous for barbecue, he or she will probably keep his views to themselves. They could, for example, avoid showing disgust on their face or making critical comments when a plate of ribs is placed in front of them. Indeed, they might even take a bite and compliment the cook. This is an example of *concealed* bias (explicit bias that is hidden to manage impressions).

For the legal profession, understanding implicit bias and ways to debias one's approach to law-related issues and decisions is critical to a fair and representative perception and reality of access to justice and equity. The problem of implicit bias has been described by one researcher as follows: we naturally assign people into various social categories divided by salient and chronically accessible traits, such as age, gender, race, and role. And just as we might have implicit cognitions that help us walk and drive, we have implicit social cognitions that guide our thinking about social categories.

Where do these schemas come from? They come from our experiences with other people, some of them direct (i.e., real-world encounters) but most of them vicarious (i.e., relayed to us through stories, books, movies, media, and culture). If we unpack these schemas further, we see that some of the underlying cognitions include stereotypes, which are simply traits that we associate with a category. For instance, if we think that a particular category of human beings is frail—such as the elderly—we will not raise our guard. If we think that another category is foreign—such as Asians—we will be surprised by their fluent English. These cognitions also include attitudes, which are overall evaluative feelings that are positive or negative. For instance, if we identify someone as having graduated from our beloved alma mater, we will feel more at ease. The following are some key terms used when discussing bias:

The term "implicit bias" includes both implicit stereotypes and implicit attitudes. Though our shorthand schemas of people may be helpful in some situations, they also can lead to discriminatory behaviors if we are not careful. Given the critical importance of exercising fairness and equality in the court system, lawyers, judges, jurors, and staff should be particularly concerned about identifying such possibilities.

Stereotype: An exaggerated belief, image, or distorted truth about a person or group. A generalization that allows for little or no individual differences or social variation. Stereotypes are based on images in mass media or reputations passed on by parents, peers, and other members of society. Stereotypes can be positive or negative. Stereotypes are the belief that most members of a group have some characteristic. Some examples of stereotypes are the belief that women are nurturing or the belief that police officers like donuts. An explicit stereotype is the kind that you deliberately think about and report. An implicit stereotype is one that occurs outside of conscious awareness and control. Even if you say that men and women are equally good at math, it is possible that you associate math with men without knowing it. In this case, we would say that you have an implicit math-men stereotype.

Prejudice: An opinion, prejudgment, or attitude about a group or its individual members. Prejudices are often accompanied by ignorance, fear, or hatred and are formed by a complex psychological process that begins with attachment to a close circle of acquaintances or an "in-group" such as a family. Prejudice is often aimed at "out-groups."

Discrimination: Behavior that treats people unequally because of their group memberships. Discriminatory behavior, ranging from slights to hate crimes, often begins with negative stereotypes and prejudices.

Types of bias: Nationality bias is defined as a preformed negative opinion or attitude toward a group of persons based on their national origin. Gender bias is defined as a preformed negative opinion or attitude toward a group of persons based on their gender. Age bias is defined as a preformed negative opinion or attitude toward a group of persons based on their age. Religion bias is defined as a preformed negative opinion or attitude toward a group of persons based on religious beliefs regarding the origin and purpose of the universe and the existence or nonexistence of a supreme being. Examples are Catholics, Jews, Protestants, or Atheists. Gender identity or expression bias is defined as a preformed negative opinion or attitude toward a group of persons based on how that group chooses to identify or express their gender preference. Sexual orientation bias is defined as a preformed negative opinion or attitude toward a group of persons based on sexual preferences and/or attractions toward and responsiveness to members of their own or opposite sexes. Mental disability bias is defined as a preformed negative opinion or attitude toward a group of persons based on mental impediments/challenges, whether such disabilities are congenital or acquired by heredity, accident, injury, advanced age, or illness. Physical disability bias is defined as a preformed negative opinion or attitude toward a group of persons based on physical impediments/challenges, whether such disabilities are congenital or acquired by heredity, accident, injury, advanced age, or illness.

Explicit Bias

What is explicit bias? It is the attitudes and beliefs we have about a person or group on a *conscious level*. Much of the time, these biases and their expression arise as the direct result of a perceived threat.

Regardless of the specific approach employed or tactics engaged, policing will generate an increased amount of police–citizen contacts in very small areas. Police behavior in these areas will greatly influence the amount of support and involvement from the affected community members. To maximize their ability to manage crime problems in these places, police managers should strive to ensure fair police–citizen interactions and the development of strong partnerships with community members (Kates, 2014b). While the work is difficult, long-term community engagement efforts can pay large dividends in improving the quality of police–community relationships and collaborative crime prevention efforts. The concentration of crime at specific hot spot locations within neighborhoods provides an important opportunity for police to make connections with those citizens who are most vulnerable to victimization and experience fear and diminished quality of life.

Regrettably, these community members are often the same people who view the police with suspicion and question the legitimacy of police efforts to control crime in their neighborhoods. In this sense, residents and business owners in high-activity crime places represent "hot spots" of community dissatisfaction with and mistrust of the police. If police departments are concerned with improving their relationships with community members, these residents and business owners seem like a logical place to start. Like crime, poor police–community relationships are not evenly spread throughout city environments. If the police can win the hearts and minds of long-suffering community members in hot spot areas, it seems likely this will produce larger impacts on the overall legitimacy of police departments in the city than developing stronger relationships with community members in more stable neighborhoods, who are more likely to already have generally positive perceptions of police services (Braga & Weisburd, 2010).

Implicit Bias

What is implicit bias? They are the attitudes or stereotypes that affect our understanding, actions, and decisions in an *unconscious manner*.

An attitude is an overall feeling, positive or negative, associated with an individual or group; the tendency to like or dislike, or to act favorably or disfavorably, toward something or someone. An attitude is your evaluation of some concept (person, place, thing, or idea). An explicit attitude is the kind of attitude that you deliberately think about and report. For example, you could tell someone whether or not you like math. That is your explicit attitude. Implicit attitudes are positive and negative evaluations that occur outside of our conscious awareness and control. Even if you say that you like math (your explicit attitude), it is possible that you associate math with negativity without knowing it. In this case, we would say that your implicit attitude toward math is negative.

An *attitude* is an association between some concept (in this case a social group) and an evaluative valence, either positive or negative. A *stereotype* is an association between a concept (again, in this case a social group) and a trait. Although interconnected, attitudes and stereotypes should be distinguished, because a positive attitude does not foreclose negative stereotypes and vice versa. For instance, one might have a positive overall attitude toward African Americans and yet still associate them with weapons. Or, one might have a positive stereotype of Asian Americans as mathematically able but still have an overall negative attitude towards them. The conventional wisdom has been that these social cognitions—attitudes and stereotypes about social groups—are explicit, in the sense that they are both consciously accessible through introspection *and* endorsed as appropriate by the person who possesses them. Indeed, this understanding has shaped much of current antidiscrimination law. The conventional wisdom is also that the social cognitions that individuals hold are relatively stable, in the sense that they operate in the same way over time and across different situations.

Intrapersonal communication is communication that occurs in your own mind. It is "self-talk," which is the inner speech or mental conversations that we carry on with ourselves. It is the basis of your feelings, biases, prejudices, and beliefs.

- Examples are when you make any kind of decision, e.g., what to eat or wear, and when you think about something, e.g., what you want to do on the weekend or when you think about another person.
- You can also communicate with yourself when you dream at night.

All human beings have biases or prejudices as a result of their experiences, and these biases influence how they might react when dealing with unfamiliar people or situations. An explicit bias is a conscious bias about certain populations based upon race, gender, socioeconomic status, sexual orientation, or other attributes. Common sense shows that explicit bias is incredibly damaging to police–community relations, and there is a growing body of research evidence that shows that implicit bias—the biases people are not even aware they have—is harmful as well.

According to the Department of Justice's National Initiative for Building Community Trust and Justice Implicit Bias Resources, implicit bias describes the automatic association people make between groups of people and stereotypes about those groups. Under certain conditions, those automatic associations can influence behavior—making people respond in biased ways even when they are not explicitly prejudiced. More than 30 years of research in neurology and social and cognitive psychology has shown that people hold implicit biases even in the absence of heartfelt bigotry, simply by paying attention to the social world around them. Implicit racial bias has given rise to a phenomenon known as "racism without racists," which can cause institutions or individuals to act on racial prejudices, even in spite of good intentions and nondiscriminatory policies or standards. In the context of criminal justice and community safety, implicit bias has been shown to have significant influence in the outcomes of interactions between police and citizens. While conscious, "traditional" racism has declined significantly in recent decades, research suggests that "implicit attitudes may be better at predicting and/or influencing behavior than self-reported explicit attitudes."

The Impact of Implicit Racial Bias on the Exercise of Prosecutorial Discretion

But scholars have yet to conduct an in-depth examination of how implicit bias might affect one of the most noteworthy parts of the criminal justice system—prosecutorial discretion, and no empirical projects focused on implicit bias have gained access to prosecutors as study participants (Smith & Levinson, 2012). From the arrest of a suspect to the sentencing of a defendant, consider the range of discretion-based decisions that prosecutors must make on a daily basis: Should an arrested citizen be charged with a crime? At what level should bail be recommended? Should bail be opposed? What crime or crimes will be charged? Should charges be dropped? Should a plea bargain be offered or negotiated? Which prosecuting attorney will prosecute which alleged crime? What will the trial strategy be? Will minority jurors be challenged for cause or with peremptory challenges?

This range of discretion offers a starting point from which to investigate how implicit bias might infect the prosecutorial process. Following a long line of scholarship examining the causes of racial disparities in the criminal justice system, implicit racial bias describes the cognitive processes whereby, despite even the best intentions, people automatically classify information in racially biased ways. Since the late 1990s, a vast amount of research on implicit bias has demonstrated that a majority of Americans, for example, harbor negative implicit attitudes toward Blacks and other socially disadvantaged groups, associate women with family and men with the workplace, associate Asian Americans with foreigners, and more (Vickrey, Denton & Jefferson, 2013).

Implicit Association Test (IAT)

The Implicit Association Test (IAT) measures attitudes and beliefs that people may be unwilling or unable to report. The IAT may be especially interesting if it shows that you have an implicit attitude that you did not know about. For example, you may believe that women and men should be equally associated with science, but your automatic associations could show that you (like many others) associate men with science more than you associate women with science.

People don't always say what's on their minds. One reason is that they are unwilling. For example, someone might report smoking a pack of cigarettes per day because they are embarrassed to admit that they smoke two. Another reason is that they are unable. A smoker might truly believe that she smokes a pack a day, or she might not keep track at all. The difference between being unwilling and unable is the difference between purposely hiding something from someone and unknowingly hiding something from yourself.

When doing an IAT, you are asked to quickly sort words into categories that are on the left and right hand side of the computer screen by pressing the "e" key if the word belongs to the category on the left and the "i" key if the word belongs to the category on the right. The IAT has five main parts. In the first part of the IAT, you sort words relating to the concepts (e.g., fat people, thin people) into categories. So if the category "Fat People" was on the left, and a picture of a heavy person appeared on the screen, you would press the "e" key.

In the second part of the IAT, you sort words relating to the evaluation (e.g., good, bad). So if the category "good" was on the left, and a pleasant word appeared on the screen, you would press the "e" key. In the third part of the test, the categories are combined and you are asked to sort both concept and evaluation words. So the categories on the left side would be Fat People/Good and the categories on the right hand side would be Thin People/Bad. It is important to note that the order in which the blocks are presented varies across participants, so some people will do the Fat People/Good, Thin People/Bad part first, and other people will do the Fat People/Bad, Thin People/Good part first.

In the fourth part of the IAT, the placement of the concepts switches. If the category "Fat People" were previously on the left, now it would be on the right. Importantly, the number of trials in this part of the test is increased in order to minimize the effects of practice. In the final part of the IAT, the categories are combined in a way that is opposite what they were before. If the category on the left were previously Fat People/Good, it would now be Fat People/Bad.

The IAT score is based on how long it takes a person, on average, to sort the words in the third part of the test versus the fifth part of the test. We would say that one has an implicit preference for thin people relative to fat people if they are faster to categorize words when Thin People and Good share a response key and Fat People and Bad share a response key, relative to the reverse. Social psychologists use the word prejudice to describe people who report and approve negative attitudes toward outgroups. Most people who show an implicit preference for one group (e.g., White people) over another (e.g., Black people) are not prejudiced by this definition. The IAT shows biases that are not endorsed and that may even be contradictory to what one consciously believes. So, no, we would not say that such people are prejudiced. It is important to know, however, that implicit biases can predict behavior. When we relax our active efforts to be egalitarian, our implicit biases can lead to discriminatory behavior, so it is critical to be mindful of this possibility if we want to avoid prejudice and discrimination.

Implicit preferences for majority groups (e.g., White people) are common because of strong negative associations with Black people in American society. Black people are often portrayed negatively in culture and mass media, and there is a long history of racial discrimination in the United States (Peffley & Hurwitz, 2010). However, even if our attitudes come from our culture, they are still in our own minds and can influence our behavior if we are not vigilant to not let them.

Implicit Association Test
https://implicit.harvard.edu/implicit/takeatest.html

It is well established that implicit preferences can affect behavior, but there is not yet enough research to say for sure that implicit biases can be reduced, let alone eliminated. Therefore, we encourage people not to focus on strategies for reducing bias, but to focus instead on strategies that deny implicit biases the chance to operate. One such strategy is ensuring that implicit biases don't leak out in the first place. To do that, you can "blind" yourself from learning a person's gender, race, etc. when you're making a decision about them (e.g., having their name removed from the top of a resume). If you only evaluate a person on the things that matter for a decision, then you can't be swayed by demographic factors. Another strategy is to try to compensate for your implicit preferences. For example, if you have an implicit preference for young people, you can try to be friendlier toward elderly people. Although it has not been well studied, based on what we know about how biases form we also recommend that people consider what gets into their minds in the first place. This might mean avoiding television programs and movies that portray women and minority group members in negative or stereotypical ways. Research suggests that biased associations can be gradually unlearned and replaced with nonbiased ones. Perhaps even more encouragingly, one can reduce the influence of implicit bias simply by changing the context in which an interaction takes place. Consequently, through policy and training, it is possible to mend the harm that racial stereotypes do to our minds and our public safety. Consequently, through policy and training, it is possible to mend the harm that racial stereotypes do to our minds and our public safety. The following are a few simple suggestions that we can all do to reduce our potential for bias.

- Put yourself in the shoes of others and understand their perspectives.
- Be motivated and be mindful to change.
- Increase positive contact with groups with whom you hold stereotypical views.
- Increase the diversity of individuals in your social and professional circles.
- Think and make good decisions.

In his book *Thinking, Fast and Slow*, Daniel Kahneman (2011) endeavors to identify the two systems that drive how we think and arrive at decisions. The first system is fast, intuitive, and emotionally charged, while the second is slower, deliberate, and logical. This work exposes the flaws and biases associated with fast thinking, because intuitive impressions are pervasively influential on our thinking processes and actions. As such, Kahneman delineates the significance of appropriately assessing risk, acknowledging the effects of cognitive biases on how we view others, how both fear and optimism assume dual roles that can be productive or counterproductive, and the ephemeral nature of our memory given our experience. It is only by attempting to understand and grasp how these two cognitive systems work together that we are better able to tailor our judgments and decisions. By harnessing our slow thinking capabilities, we are able to utilize more enlightened and thoughtful insights to guide our actions.

Discussion Questions

1. What are the key components of procedural justice?
2. Explain the Implicit Association Test.
3. What is the difference between implicit and explicit bias?
4. What factors is the IAT score is based on?
5. What steps should be taken to avoid prejudice and discrimination?

References

Banaji, M. R., & Greenwald, A. G. (2013). *Blindspot: Hidden biases of good people.* New York: Delacorte Press.

Belvedere, K., Worrall, J. L., & Tibbetts, S. G. (2005). Explaining suspect resistance in police-citizen encounters. *Criminal Justice Review, 30*(1), 30–44.

Braga, A. A., & Weisburd, D. L. (2010). *Policing problem places: Crime hot spots and effective prevention.* New York: Oxford University Press.

COPS Office. (2013). *Comprehensive law enforcement review: Procedural justice and legitimacy.* Retrieved February 2, 2017, from www.cops.usdoj.gov/pdf/taskforce/Procedural-Justice-and-Legitimacy-LE-Review-Summary.pdf

Denton, D. G. *Justice in focus: The strategic plan for California Judicial Branch, 2006–2012* (2006). San Francisco, CA: Judicial Council of California.

Fischer, C. (2014). Legitimacy and procedural justice: A new element of police leadership. A Report by the Police Executive Research Forum (PERF). U.S. Department of Justice, Bureau of Justice Assistance. Washington, DC: Government Printing Office.

Gladwell, M. (2005). *Blink: The power of thinking without thinking.* New York: Little, Brown and Company.

Goodman-Delahunty, J. (2010). Four ingredients: New recipes for procedural justice in Australian policing. *Policing: A Journal of Policing and Practice, 4*, 403–410.

Hinds, L. (2007). Building police-youth relationships: The importance of procedural justice. *Youth Justice, 7*(3), 195–209.

Hollander, R., & Tyler, T. R. (2008). Procedural Justice in Negotiation: Procedural Fairness, Outcome Acceptance, and Integrative Potential. *Journal of the American Bar Association, 33*(2), 473–500.

Horowitz, J. (2007). Making every encounter count: Building trust and confidence in the police. *National Institute of Justice Journal, 256*, 8–11.

Hough, M., Jackson, J., Bradford, B., Myhill, A., & Quinton, P. (2010). Procedural justice, trust, and institutional legitimacy. *Policing, 4*(3), 203–210.

Jackson, J., Huq, A. Z., Bradford, B., & Tyler, T. R. (2013). Monopolizing force? Police legitimacy and public attitudes toward the acceptability of violence. *Psychology, Public Policy and Law, 19*(4), 479–497.

Judicial Council of California. (2011). *Procedural fairness in California: Initiatives, challenges, and recommendations.* San Francisco, CA: Center for Court Innovation.

Kahneman, D. (2011). *Thinking, fast and slow.* New York: Farrar, Straus and Giroux.

Kane, R. J. (2005). Compromised police legitimacy as a predictor of violent crime in structurally disadvantages communities. *Criminology, 43*(2), 469–498.

Kates, G. (2014a). Melekian: Give beat cops a voice in community policing. *The crime report.* New York: John Jay University. Retrieved from https://thecrimereport.org/2014/09/05/2014-09-melekian-give-beat-cops-a-voice-in-community-policin/

Kates, G. (2014b). The crisis of confidence in police-community relations. *The crime report.*

Kochel, T. R. (2011). Can police legitimacy promote collective efficacy? *Justice Quarterly, 29*(3), 384–419. doi: 10.1080/07418825.2011.561805

Kunard, L. (2011). Procedural Justice for Law Enforcement Agencies. Center for Public Safety and Justice. Institute of Government and Public Affairs. Champaign, Il: University of Illinois. Retrieved from https://cops.usdoj.gov/pdf/conference/2011/ProceduralJustice-Kunard.pdf

MacCoun, R. J. (2005). Voice, control, and belonging: The double-edged sword of procedural fairness. *Annual Review of Law and Social Science, 1*, 171–201.

Mazerolle, L., Bennett, S., Davis, J., Sargeant, E., & Manning, M. (2013). Procedural justice and police legitimacy: A systematic review of the research evidence. *Journal of Experimental Criminology, 9*(3), 245–274.

Meares, T. & Skogan, W. (2004). Lawful policing. *Faculty Scholarship Series,* 521. Retrieved from http://digital commons.law.yale.edu/fss_papers/521

Mentel, Z. (2012). *Racial reconciliation, truth telling and police legitimacy.* Community Oriented Policing Services, US Department of Justice. Washington DC. Retrieved from https://ric-zai-inc.com/Publications/cops-p241-pub.pdf

Murphy, K. (2013). Does procedural justice matter to youth? *Policing and Society, 25*(1), 53–73.

Myhill, A., & Bradford, B. (2012). Can police enhance confidence in improving quality of service? *Policing and Society, 22*(4), 397–425.

Myhill, A., & Quinton, P. (2011). *It's a fair cop? Police legitimacy, public cooperation and crime reduction.* London, UK: National Policing Improvement Agency.

Peffley, M., & Hurwitz, J. (2010). *Justice in America: The separate realities of Blacks and Whites.* New York: Cambridge University Press.

POST. (2016). California Peace Officers Standards of Training. Retrieved from https://post.ca.gov/procedural-justice-and-police-legitimacy.aspx

Reisig, M. D., & Lloyd, C. (2009). Procedural justice, police legitimacy, and helping the police fight crime. *Police Quarterly, 12*(1), 42–62.

Rosenfeld, R., & Fornango, R. (2014). The impact of police stops on precinct robbery and burglary rates in New York city, 2003–2010. *Justice Quarterly, 31*, 132–158.

Rottman, D. B. (2005). *Trust and confidence in the California courts.* Sacramento, CA: Judicial Council of California.

Skogan, W., & Frydl, K. (Eds.). (2004). *Fairness and effectiveness in policing: The evidence.* Committee to Review Research on Police Policy and Practices, Committee on Law and Justice, Division of Behavioral and Social Sciences and Education. Washington, DC: The National Academies Press.

Smith, R. J., & Levinson, J. D. (2012). The impact of implicit racial bias on the exercise of prosecutorial discretion. *Seattle University Law Review*, *35*(795), 2012.

Tyler, T. R. (1990). *Why people obey the law*. New Haven, CT: Yale University Press. *See also* Frazer, M. S. (2006). *The impact of the community court model on defendant perceptions of fairness: A case study at the Red Hook Community Justice Center*. New York: Center for Court Innovation.

Tyler, T. R. (2001). A psychological perspective on the legitimacy of institutions and authorities. In J. Jost & B. Major (Eds.), *The psychology of legitimacy* (pp. 416–436). Cambridge: Cambridge University Press.

Tyler, T. R. (2014, March). *Legitimacy and procedural justice: A new element of police leadership*. Washington, DC: Police Executive Research Forum.

Tyler, T. R., & Huo, Y. J. (2002). *Trust in the Law: Encouraging Public Cooperation With the Police and the Courts*. New York: Russell Sage Foundation.

Tyler, T. R., & Jackson, J. (2014). Popular legitimacy and the exercise of legal authority: Motivating compliance, cooperation and engagement. *Psychology, Public Policy and Law*, *20*, 78–95.

Tyler, T. R., & Murphy, K. (2011). Procedural justice, police legitimacy and cooperation with the police: A new paradigm for policing. *CEPS Briefing Paper Series*. Retrieved from http://www.ceps.edu.au/?q=CEPS-Briefing-Paper-Series.

Vickrey, W. C., Denton, D. G., & Jefferson, W. B. (2013). *Opinions as the voice of the court: How state Supreme Courts can communicate effectively and promote procedural fairness*. Harvard: Kennedy School.

Ward, J. T. (2011). Caught in their own speed trap: The intersection of speed enforcement policy, police legitimacy, and decision acceptance. *Police Quarterly*, *14*, 251–276.

Watson, A. C., & Angell, B. (2012). The role of stigma and uncertainty in moderating the effect of procedural justice on cooperation and resistance in police encounters with persons with mental illnesses. *Psychology, Public Policy and Law*, *19*(1), 30–39.

Wemmers, J. M. (2013). Victims' experiences in the criminal justice system and their recovery from crime. *International Review of Victimology*, *19*, 221–233.

26

DATA PROTECTION AND RIGHTS TO PRIVACY INVOLVED IN GATHERING AND INTERNATIONAL INTELLIGENCE EXCHANGE

David Lowe

Concerns Over the Surveillance Society: The Snowden Revelations

Granting intelligence and policing agencies wider surveillance powers in relation to electronic communications generates fears of a surveillance society where data protection and rights to privacy are abused by those agencies. In 2013, those fears were confirmed following the revelations by the former employee of the U.S. National Security Agency (NSA), Edward Snowden, on the practices of the NSA and the UK's General Communications Headquarters (GCHQ) in relation to Operation PRISM.[1] In June 2013, the UK newspaper *The Guardian* and the U.S. newspaper *The Washington Post* broke with the news story regarding the NSA and the PRISM program that gave U.S. federal agencies direct access to servers in the biggest web firms, including Google, Microsoft, Facebook, Yahoo, Skype, and Apple.[2] Snowden released top secret documents to a *Guardian* journalist, Glenn Greenwald, who, in the first of a number of reports, revealed the NSA was collecting telephone records of millions of U.S. customers under a top secret order issued in April 2013, saying, "the communication records of millions of US citizens are being collected indiscriminately and in bulk regardless of whether they are suspected of any wrongdoing."[3] Adding that the NSA's mission had transformed from being exclusively devoted to foreign intelligence gathering, Greenwald said it now focused on domestic communications. As the revelations from the documents Snowden passed on regarding the NSA's activities increased, *The Guardian* reported that GCHQ also gained access to the network of cables carrying the world's phone calls and internet traffic and processed vast streams of sensitive personal information, sharing this with the NSA.[4] This followed on from earlier reports that GCHQ accessed the NSA's PRISM program to secretly gather intelligence, where between May 2012 and April 2013, 197 PRISM intelligence reports were passed onto the UK's security agencies, MI5, MI6, and Special Branch's Counter-Terrorism Unit.[5]

The shock waves of the NSA's actions reverberated around the world, more so when it was revealed that politicians in EU member states were also spied on by the NSA, in particular German Chancellor Angela Merkel.[6] For Greenwald, what is more remarkable are the revelations that the NSA was spying on millions of European citizens, saying, "in addition to foreign leaders the United States . . . also spied extensively on international organisations such as the United Nations to gain a diplomatic advantage."[7]

During this dialogue, the difference in legal culture between the EU and the U.S. raised its head regarding individuals' rights, where the EU's focus centers on the dignity of citizens. In protecting fundamental human rights under the aegis of the rule of law, the EU requires a system of protection of an individual citizen's data privacy.[8] There is no such explicit protection to a general right to privacy under the U.S. Bill of Rights—it is inferred in the First, Fourth, Fifth, and Ninth Amendments.[9] This is important, as Snowden's revelations had the potential to damage not only diplomatic relations between the U.S. and EU member states, but also affect the terrorism and organized crime–related intelligence sharing between European counterterrorism agencies via the EU's policing agency, Europol, and U.S. federal agencies.

EU Data Protection and Right to Privacy Laws

Many states have some form of legislative protection of citizens' personal data and rights to privacy. This varies widely as to how stringent they are in protecting those rights and prohibiting state agencies from interfering with them. As covered later in this chapter, the U.S. has little legislative protection of those rights, and the EU has the most stringent. As EU law has to be followed by its current 28 member states, one could argue that globally its legislation provides the most protection that strictly controls the circumstances when state agencies can legally interfere with those rights. It is not just within the member states that EU law applies; another country (referred to as a third country) that wishes to conduct business with EU member states or to cooperate in terrorism and criminal investigations must have cognizance of EU law. This section will provide an overview of the EU's legislation that is followed by two recent important cases from the Court of Justice of the European Union (CJEU), where its decisions had far-reaching consequences in relation to international relations with third countries.

EU Primary Legislation Covering Data Protection

In relation to data protection, Article 16 of the Treaty on the Functioning of the EU (TFEU) states everyone has the right to the protection of personal data concerning them. Under Article 16, the European Parliament and Council must act in accordance with ordinary legislative procedure, laying down rules protecting the processing of personal data by EU institutions, bodies, offices, and agencies when carrying out activities that fall within the scope of EU law. This legal obligation is also present in Article 39 in the Treaty of Union. Underpinning these articles' provisions is the EU's Charter of Fundamental Rights and Freedoms (CFRF). Since the Treaty of Lisbon 2009 came into force, the CFRF has become a legally binding document ensuring all EU institutions and member states apply the Charter's principles when implementing EU law. Article 8 CFRF states that everyone has the right to the protection of personal data concerning them. When EU institutions or member states access the data, it "must be processed fairly for specified purposes on the basis of consent of the person concerned or some other legitimate basis laid down by law."[10] This is in addition to the respect they must have for a person's right to their private and family life, home, and communication.[11]

The 1995 Data Protection Directive[12] states personal data can only be collected for specified, explicit, and legitimate purpose and must not be processed in a way incompatible with these purposes.[13] Member states can only derogate from the 1995 Directive where it is necessary to safeguard national security, defense, public security, and the prevention, investigation, detection, or prosecution of criminal offenses.[14] The Directive on the protection of personal data processed for the purposes of preventing, investigating, detecting, or prosecuting criminal matters[15] came into force on May 5, 2016, for member states to transpose into their national law by May 6, 2018.[16] In the preamble it is recognized that rapid technological developments and globalization has brought new challenges for the protection of personal data where the scale of collecting and sharing this data has increased significantly, and this directly applies to agencies involved in the prevention, investigation, or detection of criminal offenses.[17] The Directive states that in the processing of personal data, these agencies can only collect it for specific, explicit, and legitimate purposes,[18] and to be lawful, the processing of personal data has to be necessary in the prevention, investigation, or detection of criminal offenses.[19] The Directive is also very clear that when processing personal data, fundamental rights and freedoms must be protected, especially the right of the protection of personal data.[20] This requirement follows the CJEU decision in *Google Spain SL, Google Inc. v. Agencia Espanola de Protección de Datos (APED)*,[21] which held that data retention without any link to risk or suspicion is not proportionate. Important in protecting personal data are the safeguards present in any legislative provision. In the 2016 Directive, this includes:

1. Member states and the EU itself shall create a "controller"[22] who has a number of obligations under the Directive to oversee the processing and exchange of personal data. This includes ensuring the requests by relevant agencies for personal data are proportionate to the purposes of processing the data,[23] and integrating the necessary safeguards in to the processing of the data;[24]
2. Member states shall provide a data protection officer[25] whose roles include advising the controller and employees from agencies carrying out the processing of personal data and monitoring compliance with the Directive;[26]
3. Where the data subject conspires their personal protection rights have been infringed, member states must ensure data subjects have the right to an effective judicial remedy (which in practice will be through a judicial review process).[27]

The transfer of personal data to a third country having to meet the requirements of being necessary and proportionate for the purposes of preventing, investigating, or detecting criminal offenses,[28] it is of paramount importance that the third country with whom the data is transferred has an adequate level of protection of personal data.[29] If there is an absence of adequacy or protection in a third country, transfer of personal data under the 2016 Directive can only occur where such conditions are implemented under a negotiated legally binding instrument.[30] With the 2016 Directive having to be introduced by EU member states by May 2018, it is questionable if the UK will introduce it into its domestic legislation. It will be unfortunate if it does not, as by doing so it will help to guarantee that intelligence generated by UK agencies has sufficient safeguards in relation to personal data protection. This would ease intelligence exchange with EU member states post-Brexit, as the EU would be satisfied there is an adequate provision for data protection in the UK that would satisfy the statutory provisions contained within EU law. Be it EU member states or third countries, which the UK will be post-Brexit, in matters of police cooperation ensuring the CJEU will examine the adequacy of data protection in states' legislation related to surveillance, especially surveillance of electronic communications and intelligence gathering.

Court of Justice of the European Union's Scrutiny on Data Protection and Rights to Privacy

It is important to ensure that the state and its intelligence and policing agencies are accountable. This includes, as far as is possible without compromising national security, that their actions are transparent, and this is a key role of the judiciary when interpreting primary law. This section examines some of the challenges to state agencies' surveillance practices that have come before the EU's Court of Justice of the European Union.

CJEU's Decision in Digital Rights *Case*

If one wants to measure the EU's adherence to its laws and its legal legitimacy in relation to data protection and rights to privacy, it can be done by examining the CJEU's judicial interpretation of decisions that demonstrates how those rights are deeply embedded in EU law. How CJEU decisions impact on EU and member states' law was seen in *Digital Rights Ireland*,[31] where the court ruled that an EU Directive was invalid.[32] The case centered mainly on Directive 2006/24/EC that laid down an obligation on publicly available electronic communications services or public communications networks to retain certain data generated or processed by them. As collaboration between EU member states was seen as critical, the Directive was introduced following the Al Qaeda attack in London 2005, with the intention to facilitate the exchange of personal data in order to enhance the prevention capabilities regarding acts of terrorism and crime.[33] The 2006 Directive was also introduced to shift data protection rights from national to EU level, thereby ensuring the police and the judiciary in one member state respect the data protection rights in another member state.[34] As the Directive allowed EU member states' intelligence and policing agencies to collect bulk data, the CJEU examined the acceptable limits of mass surveillance and the function of data protection[35] in relation to compatibility with Articles 7 and 8 CFRF.[36] In doing so, the CJEU assessed:

1. The nature of the right at issue;
2. The nature of the interference with the right;
3. How serious was the interference with the right; and
4. What the object of the interference was.[37]

Regarding data protection, the CJEU found the 2006 Directive to be invalid. Key to this decision was Article 4 of the Directive allowing member states to adopt into its national law measures ensuring that data retention is provided only to the competent national authorities in specific cases.

There were two key legal issues the CJEU saw as important to ensure personal data is protected:

1. EU legislation must lay down *clear* and *precise* rules governing the scope and application of the measure in question;
2. Minimum safeguards are imposed to provide sufficient guarantees, effectively protecting personal data against the risk of abuse and against unlawful access and use.[38]

(Emphasis added)

Analyzing the inadequacies of Article 4 in the 2006 Directive, the CJEU held it did not expressly provide that access to the use of the data was strictly restricted for the purpose of preventing and detecting precisely defined serious offenses or of conducting criminal prosecutions relating to such crimes; the only conditions for member states to retain data specified in Article 4 was when it was necessary and proportionate to do so.[39] The CJEU also held the 2006 Directive did not have in place a high enough level of protection of personal data, nor did it ensure there was an irreversible destruction of the data at the end of the data retention period.[40] In declaring the Directive to be invalid, the reason the CJEU came to this decision was due to the Directive's retention measures being too vague, as the principles of necessity cannot justify imposing limitations on citizens' rights.[41] The CJEU did acknowledge that data retention is an important strand in terrorism and serious crime investigations to ensure public safety, and it is in these specific grounds there could be a justification.[42] Terrorism is certainly a legitimate aim that meets the required justification and objectives of general interest recognized by the EU when balancing the needs of national security with protection of rights and freedoms, in particular balancing the right to life with data protection.

In his analysis of *Digital Rights*, Ojanen states the more systemic and wide the collection, retention, and analysis of bulk data becomes,

> the closer it can be seen as moving towards the core area of privacy and data protection with the outcome that at least the most massive, systematic forms of collection and analysis of [bulk data] can be regarded as constituting an intrusion into the inviolable core of privacy and data protection.[43]

The CJEU decision in *Digital Rights* is not a "total knockout" to mandatory retention.[44] In drawing up legislation that specifically gives the legitimate aim for the retention such as to support investigations into acts of terrorism or serious organized crime, specifying realistic periods of data retention and sufficient safeguards into protecting rights of privacy and data protection would be sufficient. This decision imposes on the EU legislator a new level of responsibility to protect fundamental rights; it composes substantive instructions for lawmakers at EU and national levels to guarantee the protection of data protection and, importantly, provides a strict judicial scrutiny test.[45]

The impact of a strict judicial scrutiny test laid down in *Digital Rights* is seen in the UK's High Court decision in *R (on the application of Davis and ors) v. Secretary of State for the Home Department*[46] regarding the provisions in the Data Retention and Investigatory Powers Act 2014 (DRIPA).[47] Introduced by the UK government in response to the *Digital Rights* decision, DRIPA requires communications operators to retain data[48] up to a period not exceeding 12 months.[49] It also allows for authorization of interception warrants to UK intelligence and policing agencies to access the communications data when necessary in the interests of national security.[50] The High Court agreed with the CJEU's findings that in the 2006 Directive, the EU legislator had exceeded the limits imposed by compliance with the principle of proportionality and held that it must follow on from that any domestic statute containing identical terms would have the same failings.[51] The court added that failing to provide sufficient safeguards against unlawful access to and use of retained data by public authorities will infringe the principle of proportionality.[52] Lord Justice Bean made it clear that in protecting fundamental rights in relation to personal data, derogations and limitations to that right must only occur when it is strictly necessary, and this can only be achieved if legislation lays down clear and precise rules governing the scope of that derogation and limitation.[53] He also added that sufficient safeguards should be imposed in order to give sufficient protection against the risk of abuse or unlawful access to that data. In saying this, he stressed the point that legislation permitting a general retention of personal data must expressly be restricted to the purpose of preventing, detecting, or conducting prosecutions for serious offenses.[54] On the topic of safeguards, Lord Justice Bean saw judicial approval as important to ensure surveillance authorities are not abused, and he did not see the implication of this process being "particularly cumbersome," adding that EU law requires independent approval and such a procedure, "must be put in place."[55] As Section 1 DRIPA did not lay down clear and precise rules providing access to and the use of communications data, and with there not being any prior review by a court to assess if the access is necessary to attain the objectives pursued, the High Court held this statutory provision was inconsistent with EU law.[56] As DRIPA contained a sunset clause for it to expire on the December 31, 2016, the High Court did not suspend the act because the UK replaced DRIPA with the Investigatory Powers Act 2016, and the court were in no doubt the UK government will ensure the new statute will be compliant with EU law.[57]

The *Digital Rights* decision has not just affected UK legislation. In March 2015, a national Dutch court in The Hague followed the CJEU and found Holland's surveillance and data retention law fell under the EU law and the CFRF. As the Dutch law failed to conform adequately to Articles 7 and 8 of the CFRF, along with the court also finding insufficient safeguards, the court suspended the Dutch law.[58] Similar legal issues were found in the respective domestic statutory provisions regarding surveillance of communications post-*Digital Rights* by the respective judiciaries in Sweden, Romania, and Belgium, where their respective courts have held their legislation to be in breach of EU law.[59] All of the member state domestic court findings centered on two key legal points raised in *Digital Rights*, which are vague provisions to access and retain communications data and the lack of sufficient safeguards protecting potential abuse in the use of that data. From these court decisions, it is clear that to achieve sufficient safeguards of data protection, the responsibility must be taken from politicians and placed with the judiciary or totally independent bodies.

The Schrems *Decision and Ending of the U.S.-EU Safe Harbor Agreement*

The CJEU's decision in *Schrems v. Data Protestation Commissioner*[60] was delivered on October 6, 2015. This case centers on the transfer of personal data from the EU and its member states to the U.S. under the Safe Harbor agreement. This agreement was introduced to enable a freer flow of personal data for trade and industry purposes. However, following the revelations of the U.S. National Security Agency's use of bulk data collection that included accessing the personal data of EU citizens, an Austrian citizen brought his case before the CJEU claiming the NSA would have probably accessed his data held by the social media company Facebook. This section examines what legal factors led to the CJEU making the decision that resulted in the ending of the Safe Harbor agreement and why it is important that third countries with whom the EU has agreements have in place adequate legal provisions regarding data protection.

The Safe Harbor Agreement

To protect EU citizens' personal data, the EU-U.S. Safe Harbor agreement was signed in 2000 under Decision 2000/520/EC in order to provide a streamlined process for U.S. companies to comply with the EU's Data Protection Directive.[61] Among the privacy principles in the agreement, it states that organizations must take reasonable precautions to protect personal information from loss, misuse, and unauthorized access, disclosure, alteration, and destruction.[62] If U.S. organizations flout EU privacy law, the EU Commission can reverse the decision to grant the Safe Harbor arrangement.[63] The agreement was mainly aimed at the private sector's access to personal data for business purposes, but in November 2013 the European Commission expressed concerns over the large-scale access by U.S. intelligence agencies to data transferred by Safe Harbor certified companies.[64] This concern came from the disclosure and revelations by former NSA employee Edward Snowden that the NSA was involved in bulk data collection, as covered above.[65] This led to the European Commission stressing the importance of the national security exception in the Safe-Harbor Decision should only be used when it is, "strictly necessary or proportionate."[66]

How Schrems *Ended the Safe Harbor Agreement*

Since 2008, Maximillian Schrems, an Austrian citizen, used the social media network Facebook. Although his contract was registered within the EU at the time of his registration with Facebook Ireland, this is a subsidiary of Facebook Incorporated established in the U.S., where Facebook Ireland users' personal data is then transferred to. Schrems contended that the law and practice in the U.S. did not ensure sufficient protection of his personal data and in referring to the Snowden revelations of NSA practices, he claimed his personal data could have been subject to retention by the NSA and other U.S. federal agencies.[67] Perceiving Schrems's complaint as unsustainable in law and bound to fail because he saw it as vexatious, the Irish Data Protection Commissioner did not see himself as being required to investigate the complaint, as there was no specific evidence that Schrems's personal data had been accessed by the NSA.[68] In Schrems's judicial review of the Irish Commissioner's decision,[69] the Irish High Court held that once personal data has been transferred to the U.S., it is capable of being accessed by the NSA and other U.S. federal agencies in the course of indiscriminate surveillance and interception of communications.[70] Justice Hogan said if this matter was to be measured solely by Irish law and Irish constitutional standards, a serious issue would arise which the commissioner would have been required to investigate whether U.S. law and practice in relation to privacy, interception, and surveillance matched those standards.[71] Acknowledging the Snowden revelations had exposed "gaping holes" in contemporary U.S. data protection practice,[72] Justice Hogan did not see Schrems's complaints as "frivolous or vexatious"[73] and refereed it to the CJEU.

In the opinion of the advocate general, Advocate General Bot held that as intervention of independent supervisory authorities is at the heart of the EU's system of personal data protection, there must be a similar system of protection in the third country to which the data flows from the EU.[74] In this case under the U.S.'s surveillance act, Foreign Intelligence Surveillance Act 1978, the NSA accessed personal data inputted in Austria that was held by Facebook at a server in the United States. Advocate General Bot held that the Foreign Intelligence Surveillance Court does not offer an effective judicial remedy to EU citizens whose personal data has been transferred to the U.S.[75] He proposed that when the case went to the CJEU, it should answer the question if the agreement is invalid.[76] The CJEU did answer this question and declared Decision 2000/520 invalid,[77] and consequently brought to an end the Safe Harbor agreement. Crucial to the court reaching this decision were the requirements of Article 25 of the 95/46 Directive on data protection. Where communications data is transferred from outside the EU to a third country, the EU is responsible for ensuring the third country has an adequate level of data protection. In doing so, consideration is given to the nature of the data, the purpose, and the duration of the processing operation of the data, the country of origin and final country of destination, the law in operation related to data protection in the third country, and the professional rules and security measures deployed regarding the data in the third country.[78]

The most pertinent part of Article 25 related to the issue in *Schrems* is it being the Commission's responsibility to find that the third country ensures an adequate level of protection of basic freedoms and rights of individuals.[79] Should the Commission find the third country does not provide an adequate level of protection, member states are to take measures to prevent the transfer of data to that third country.[80] Crucial to determining this is what is meant by the term "adequate." The third country is not required to ensure there is a level of data protection identical to that guaranteed in EU law.[81] Advocate General Bot said that the protection implemented by the third country may differ from EU law, but it must provide adequate protection that is equivalent to that afforded by the 95/46 Directive.[82] Adopting the linguistic viewpoint of the word "adequate," which means satisfactory or sufficient, Advocate General Bot said the obligation of the Commission is to ensure the third country has a sufficiently high level of protection of fundamental rights.[83] The obligation to ensure the adequacy of data protection is not a one-off obligation made at the time of agreement. The obligation for the third country is an ongoing obligation to ensure that no changes in circumstances arise that can call into question the initial assessment,[84] and it is expected the Commission will regularly review the third country's level of protection.[85] It was on this legal point that Schrems was successful, as the CJEU found the 2000 decision did not cover the situation to limit interference by U.S. state bodies authorized under legitimate objectives, such as national security, in U.S. law to interfere with personal data transferred from the EU.[86] The court added that legislation permitting public authorities access to the content of electronic communications on a *generalized basis* must be regarded as compromising the essence of the fundamental right to privacy under the CFRF.[87] This echoes the CJEU's decision in *Digital Rights*,[88] where an authority for a state agency to access communications data must be specific with a legitimate aim along with sufficient safeguards protecting potential abuse by a state agency's use of that data. On the latter point, in *Schrems* the CJEU found there to be no effective remedy for an individual to ensure the data was used in compliance with legal provisions similar to those found in the EU.[89]

The main surprise from cases like *Schrems* is not in finding that the Safe Harbor agreement was ruled invalid, it is that this agreement lasted for 15 years. Supporting this point, there is no single authority dedicated to overseeing data protection law in the U.S.; as Sotto and Simpson observe, the U.S. legislative framework designed to protect personal data resembles a "patchwork quilt."[90] As the U.S. favors commercial enterprises, personal data is largely regulated by trade associations.[91] Although the U.S. Federal Trade Commission (FTC) oversees the provisions of the agreement regarding consumer privacy issues, including the collection and use of personal information, with an authority to do so under Section 5 FTC Act,[92] it is only in relation to unfair acts or practices affecting commerce. The Safe Harbor agreement only required U.S. companies to develop their own self-regulatory privacy policies to conform with the EU's data protection principles to qualify them for Safe Harbor[93] rather than adherence to a federal law providing greater safeguards. The problem with self-certification is it lends personal data open to potential abuse. These are the gaping holes Judge Hogan referred to when *Schrems* was at the Irish High Court. Potential abuse was found by the EU in their first two reviews of Safe Harbor that raised significant concerns. The 2002 review found that a substantial number of organizations that signed up to self-certified adherence were not observing the expected degree of transparency regarding the contents of their privacy policies, and in the 2004 review it was found that less than half of the organizations signed up to the agreement reflected observance of all seven Safe Harbor principles.[94] As this agreement was set up to facilitate a freer movement of data in relation to international trade, it could explain why some of these points were overlooked. While there is an argument for self-regulation due to its lower burden on business and trade,[95] the weakness of Safe Harbor is that EU citizens' personal data was transferred to a jurisdiction with fewer privacy protections, leaving that data vulnerable to access and abuse by U.S. federal agencies like the NSA. Following the Snowden revelations, the U.S. and the EU negotiated an update to Safe Harbor since 2013, with the EU looking to limit the circumstances U.S. federal agencies could access the transferred data. Even though the U.S. has agreed to this, there is the concern that U.S. politicians may retaliate against the *Schrems* decision at a future date by refusing to grant the privilege.[96] However, transnational business and trade needs may overcome politicians' petulance and a new agreement, the EU-U.S. Privacy Shield, was made in 2016 that was adopted on July 12, 2016. The agreement includes stronger protection obligations on companies receiving personal data from the EU, improved safeguards on the U.S. government to access the data, and effective protection and redress for individuals.[97] This is to ensure that there is adequate protection that is more in line with the 95/46 Directive.

It may come as a surprise that the United States has no legislation that deeply embeds data protection within its legal system. Other Western states that have agreements with the EU

appear to apply similar legal principles that provide adequate protection of personal data. For example, the U.S.'s northern neighbor, Canada, has the Privacy Act 1985 as well as the Personal Information Protection and Electronic Documents Act 2000, the latter being concerned solely with the use of electronically stored personal data. Both acts are clear that personal information cannot be used unless it meets strict criteria[98] similar to the provisions in the 95/46 Directive, and both acts also have sufficient safeguards where individuals can make complaints to the Privacy Commissioner[99] and the Canadian courts.[100] Likewise, Australia's Privacy Act 1988 contains similar provisions as the Canadian legislation, with Section 7 promoting the privacy of an individual's personal data with the safeguards including complaints to the Australian Privacy Commissioner[101] or to an Australian Court.[102] As both Canada and Australia have agreements with the EU regarding the processing and transfer of passenger name record data held by air carriers,[103] the two respective states' legislation clearly offers a level of protection equivalent to that afforded by the 95/46 Directive.

The CJEU's decision in *Schrems* that ended the Safe-Harbor agreement between the EU and the U.S. was a courageous move by the court on two counts. First, the CJEU knew the implications that ending the agreement would have in relation to business and financial institutions effectiveness to operate on both sides of the Atlantic Ocean. Second, through the CJEU, the EU was not deterred in aggravating one of the most politically and economically powerful states, the United States, as the *Schrems* decision is a strong condemnation of U.S. data protection law, or, as was found, its lack of data protection law. *Schrems* is not the EU seeking revenge on the U.S. following the revelations of the NSA's abuse in the collection and use of communications data related to EU citizens, this decision was made to ensure future agreements operate under the rule of law, reassuring citizens the activities of intelligence and policing agencies operate on a sound legal footing. As we now live in the age of transnational companies and financial institutions having operating centers and district headquarters in various states throughout the world, the transfer of personal data is one of the crucial components in oiling the wheels of industry. It is vital that any third county where personal data is transferred from an EU member state has adequate legal protection and safeguards in relation to personal data, especially where it can be accessed by that third country's state agencies. The decisions in *Digital Rights* and *Schrems* demonstrate how EU law views the importance in protecting personal data and why it is best placed as an international actor to encourage those third countries it has agreements with to adopt similar measures in relation to data protection.

U.S. Court Decisions on State Agencies' Surveillance Practices Related to Terrorism Investigations

This section examines how U.S. domestic courts have examined areas of law related to electronic surveillance practices used by the security services and police in terrorism investigations. This section summarizes how the U.S. courts' decisions related to this activity were reached before and after the Snowden revelations.

U.S. Surveillance Laws: Court Decisions Pre-Snowden

A balancing of the provisions of state surveillance and individuals' liberty under the Fourth Amendment was established by the U.S. Supreme Court in *Katz v. United States*[104] who held the test for privacy is only dependent where one would have a reasonable expectation of privacy. Harlan J stated that society is prepared to expect an intrusion into their privacy by state agencies only when it is reasonable for those agencies to do so. Harlan J did emphasize the point that the situation changes when a citizen exposes their activities with others then privacy is not protected by the Fourth Amendment.[105] In *Katz* the court emphasized the Fourth Amendment was introduced to protect people not places.[106]

In balancing the rights of citizens to protecting national security Pious comments there should be the best combination of guarantees within the due process of law that protects citizens' privacy that can run alongside:

> '. . . strong government action that protects national security and our personal security as
> we travel on buses, trains, and airplanes.'[107]

The rationale for adhering to due process of law is that it not only protects the accused, but it also helps guard against the prosecutorial zeal that sends false signals about who is a terrorist and what terrorists might be doing.[108] An example of the U.S. protecting individuals' safety by focusing on liberty rather than the dignity of the individual is seen in the surveillance powers granted to U.S. federal agencies where the Patriot Act 2001 amended the FISA provisions by changing the wording regarding the aim of intelligence gathering under the original FISA from a "primary" purpose to a "significant" purpose.[109] This allowed intelligence to be obtained from a wider range of potential sources,[110] as these amendments bypass the U.S. Constitution's Fourth Amendment regarding citizens' right to be secure in their persons, houses, paper and effects against unreasonable actions by government and police actions.

The United States Foreign Intelligence Surveillance Court of Review considered the implications of this subtle change *In Re Sealed Case* N.02–0001.[111] The Court held the shift from "primary" to "significant" purpose is a relaxation of the requirement of government to show its primary purpose was other than criminal prosecution saying:

> '. . . In many cases, surveillance will have two key goals—the gathering of foreign intelligence, and the gathering of evidence for a criminal prosecution. Determining which purpose is the 'primary' purpose of the investigation can be difficult, and will only become more so as we coordinate our intelligence and law enforcement efforts in the war against terror. Rather than forcing law enforcement to decide which purpose is primary—law enforcement or foreign intelligence gathering, this bill strikes a new balance. It will now require that a 'significant' purpose of the investigation must be foreign intelligence gathering to proceed with surveillance under FISA. The effect of this provision will be to make it easier for law enforcement to obtain FISA search or surveillance warrant for these cases where the subject of the surveillance is both a potential source of valuable intelligence and the potential target of a criminal prosecution.'[112]

As a result of the Court's decision, the FBI can now help local law enforcement agencies bypass the Fourth Amendment requirements in gathering evidence in matters related to foreign intelligence even where it might not be for wholly related ordinary crimes.[113]

Another example of how national security can override individual's liberty provisions in U.S. anti-terrorism law is seen in *Clapper (Director of National Intelligence et al.) v. Amnesty International.*[114] The U.S. Supreme Court was asked to examine the Foreign Intelligence Surveillance Amendment Act 2008 amendments to section 702 Foreign Intelligence Surveillance Act 1978 (FISA) and the warrant-less wiretapping power. The respondents (who were lawyers and human rights and media organizations) claimed that in bypassing their Fourth Amendment rights, the surveillance powers contained in the amendment was unconstitutional. The foundation of their claim was they were regularly engaging in sensitive international communications with individuals likely to be targets of surveillance, and being U.S. citizens they stated their Fourth Amendment rights were breached by the surveillance orders. By a 5–4 majority, the U.S. Supreme Court dismissed the respondents' claim as purely speculative. In delivering the judgement, Justice Alito said, "respondents have no actual knowledge of the Government's targeting practices. Instead, respondents *merely speculate and make assumptions* about whether their communications with their foreign contacts will be acquired under s.702."[115]

(Emphasis added)

This decision was subject to much criticism from U.S. human rights and lawyer groups. The American Bar Association argued that the U.S. president does have a constitutional obligation to authorize all surveillance.[116] Opinions are summed up by legal advocates, claiming the *Clapper* decision handed the U.S. government a "get out of jail free" card for national security statutes.[117] With no judicial supervision on the wiretapping powers and, even if it was a speculative assumption, the fact is that there was the opportunity for the state to interfere. If this had gone before a European court, it is likely that the court would have found for the respondents. This is supported by the four dissenting judges, where Justice Breyer said the U.S. Constitution does not require concrete proof, only something where there is a "reasonable probability" or a "high probability."[118]

U.S. Court Decisions Post-Snowden

In December 2013, two significant cases were heard in which, following the Snowden revelations, the applicants claimed their Fourth Amendment rights had been violated by the NSA and the federal government. In *Klayman et al. v. Obama et al.,*[119] the U.S. District Court for the District of Columbia heard a judicial review challenging the authorization of intelligence gathering relating to the whole-sale collection of phone record metadata of all U.S. citizens. An authority was granted by the Foreign

Intelligence Surveillance Court in April 2013 concerning the applicants, where in his judgment Judge Leon held the applicants have sufficient legal standing to challenge the constitutionality of the federal government's bulk collection of phone record metadata under their Fourth Amendment claim. In his deliberations, Judge Leon said that while Congress has great latitude to create statutory schemes like FISA, "it may not hang a cloak of secrecy over the [U.S.] Constitution."[120] Distinguishing the applicants' claim in *Klayman* from the U.S. Supreme Court's finding in *Clapper*, Judge Leon said in *Clapper* the applicants could only speculate as to whether they were "surveilled," whereas in *Klayman* there was strong evidence their telephony metadata had been collected.[121] Underlying Judge Leon's judgement was his skepticism relating to the impact such wide surveillance practices have on identifying terrorists and thereby preventing terrorist attacks. He said:

> I am not convinced at this point in the litigation that the NSA's database has ever truly served the purpose of rapidly identifying terrorists in time-sensitive investigations, and so I am *certainly* not convinced that the removal of two individuals from the database will "degrade" the program in any meaningful sense.[122]

> *(Emphasis in original)*

Again concerning the NSA's collection of phone record metadata, 11 days after the *Klayman* decision, Justice Pauley III from the U.S. District Court for the Southern District of New York took an opposite view in his judgement in *American Civil Liberties Union et al. v. James R. Clapper et al.*[123] After commencing his judgement with the pre-9/11 example of the hijacker Khalid al-Mihdhar (who had seven telephone calls intercepted by the NSA, but they could not capture the telephone number identifier. If they could, they would have been able to pass onto the FBI that he was calling a Yemeni safe house from inside the U.S.),[124] Justice Pauley III cites a number of NSA investigations where he justifies the effectiveness of NSA's surveillance through bulk telephony metadata.[125] Acknowledging that if left unchecked, this investigative tool can imperil citizens' liberty along with the fact that Snowden's "unauthorized disclosure" of Foreign Intelligence Surveillance Court orders has provoked a public debate, he held these orders were lawful.[126] In his summation, Justice Pauley III found there to be no evidence that the U.S. government had used any of the bulk telephony data for any other purpose than investigating and "disrupting" terrorist attacks,[127] saying, "The choice between liberty and security is a false one, as nothing is more apt to imperil civil liberties than the success of a terrorist attack."[128]

This is important, as the interests of national security and protecting individual liberties are not exclusive, they are inclusive. This is where the legal principle of proportionality plays an important part in judicial decision-making. Utilitarian in nature, proportionality balances the interests of wider society with the interests of the individual.

In 2015, *American Civil Liberties Union (ACLU) and others v. Clapper and others*[129] went before the United States Court of Appeals for the Second Circuit. The court followed the approach taken by U.S. District Court for the District of Columbia in *Klayman et al. v. Obama et al.*,[130] where the District Court stayed the applicants' injunction and ordered the NSA to terminate its bulk data collection. In *ACLU v. Clapper*, the ACLU's claim was the NSA's metadata collection program exceeded the authority granted to them by the Foreign Intelligence Surveillance Courts (FISC). The Court of Appeals held that as the applicants had shown there was a degree of certainty that their telephone use was under a FISA authority and that this was illegal, the applicants were deprived of their constitutional rights.[131] At the time of making their decision, the court did recognize that Section 215 FISA was scheduled to expire and that Congress was to debate the Patriot Act's sunset clause.[132] In reaching their decision, the court said:

> This case serves as an example of the increasing complexity of balancing the paramount interest in protecting the security of our nation—a job in which, as the President has stated,

"actions are second guessed, success in unreported, and failure can be catastrophic." . . . Reconciling the clash of these values [national security and rights to privacy] requires productive contribution from all three branches of government, each of which is uniquely suited to the task in its own way.[133]

Impact of U.S. Court Decisions on Legislation: The Freedom Act 2015

On June 2, 2015, Congress passed the Freedom Act 2015. This act amends FISA, effectively replacing the amendment provisions to FISA by the Patriot Act 2001, mainly affecting section 215 FISA. The act also covers the retention of communications data by U.S. federal agencies, in particular the NSA. The act was introduced following U.S. President Barak Obama's promise to change FISA following the Snowden revelations. Among the key changes the Freedom Act 2015 makes to FISA includes a prohibition of bulk data collection; the collection now has to be targeted to a "specific section term." A "specific selection term" is defined as that which "specifically identifies a person, account, address, or personal device or any other specific identifier."[134] The act makes it clear that a specific identifier does not include an identifier that has no limit to the scope of information sought and cannot be a method of surveillance gathering unless the provider is the subject of an authorized investigation for which the specific selection term is used as the basis for the use.

Regarding unlawfully obtained information, a court can order a correction of a deficiency, but no information or evidence so derived and certified by the court as being deficient concerning a U.S. citizen can be received as evidence in any trial, hearing, or other court proceeding except with the approval of the attorney general, where that information indicates a threat of death or serious bodily harm to a person.[135] Decisions, opinions, and surveillance authorities granted under FISA are delivered by one of the four Federal Intelligence Surveillance Courts (FISC) in the U.S. (two of which ae located in Washington, DC). The act also guarantees greater transparency of the decision-making of the FISC, whose hearings have been *in camera*. The act requests declassification of the FISC's decisions, orders, and opinions are carried out to make publicly available to the "greatest extent" practicable,[136] but where necessary they can be released in a redacted form.[137]

Responses to the act have been mixed. Acknowledging the Freedom Act is a historic step forward, Neemah Guiliani, the ACLU legislative counsel, said the act is not as strong as they wanted and would like to see the following reforms:

1. Urge the U.S. president and Congress to rein in surveillance orders used to collect information about millions of U.S. citizens absent from any judicial process;
2. Add a reform to FISA that allows the government to collect the content of Americans' communications with individuals abroad; and
3. Reject efforts to expand surveillance through cybersecurity information-sharing legislation.[138]

The senator for Minnesota, Al Franken, described the Freedom Act as a measured compromise legislation that is the result of lengthy negotiations that bring much needed reform to the issuing of authorities, saying in relation to the declassification of FISC decisions,

[The act] strikes a balance that we need, but of course the public can't know if we are succeeding in striking that balance if they don't have access to even the most basic information about the surveillance process.[139]

Not all senators see the Freedom Act as striking a balance between the needs of national security and the protection of privacy. For the Kentucky senator, Mitch McConnell, the act undermines national security. During the act's passage through Congress, he said, "To dismantle our counterterrorism tools [the president has] not only been inflexible [but also] extremely ill-timed," adding that Snowden handed a "playbook" to the Islamic State and Al Qaeda the scope of NSA surveillance programs, saying:

> Our nation has a regrettable history of drawing our forces and capabilities only to find ourselves ill prepared for the next great struggle. . . . [The Freedom Act] is ending the tools created by the previous administration to wage the war on terror.[140]

What the amendments in Freedom Act 2015 reveal is that court decisions do have an impact on state legislators to amend legislation, and that the act has in effect made Congress introduce increased safeguards in relation to citizens' personal data.

Summary

There appears to be a conflict between those who advocate the importance of protecting the interests of national security with those who see the need to protect personal data and privacy rights being the primary concern. Yet these two positions are not exclusive; they are inclusive. As the judiciary have commented in the case decisions covered in this chapter, even where those decisions found legislation violated statutory rights provisions, the need to ensure that national security is protected in cases of terrorism and to support agencies investigating organized criminal activity, there is a need for the respective agencies to carry out surveillance of electronic communications. Here is the nub of the issue— surveillance must be balanced with respect for ensuring that personal data protection and privacy rights provisions are met. If agencies want access to personal data, the need must be necessary and proportionate, related to a specific investigation. In such cases, the needs of national security are paramount and will supersede some citizens' rights. There is no justification, however, for agencies to simply gather data where it is not necessary, and this is what the courts have been assessing in their decisions in their role of ensuring the state and its agencies act within the law and in protecting citizens' rights.

Discussion Questions

1. Discuss why states feel the requirement to expand their intelligence and policing agencies' international intelligence exchange capabilities.
2. Why are safeguards related to personal data important related to international intelligence exchange?
3. Critically assess if there is a true balance between protecting the interests of national security and individual rights in relation to international intelligence exchange.
4. Critically determine the key legal issues the courts consider when balancing the needs of national security and protection of citizens' rights.
5. Discuss whether the courts have had an impact in bringing about changes to legislation related to data protection and rights to privacy.

Notes

1. Greenwald, G. (2014). *No place to hide: Edward Snowden, the NSA and the US surveillance state*. New York: Metropolitan Books, pp. 33–42.
2. BBC News. (2013, 7 June). *Web privacy: Outsourced to the U.S. and China?* Retrieved September 1, 2016, from www.bbc.co.uk/news/technology-22811002

3. Greenwald, G. (2013, June 6). NSA collecting phone records of millions of Verizon customers daily. *The Guardian*. Retrieved September 1, 2016, from www.theguardian.com/world/2013/jun/06/nsa-phone-records-verizon-court-order

4. MacAskell, E., Borger, J., Hopkins, N., Davies, N., & Ball, J. (2013, June 21). GCHQ taps fibre-optic cables for secret access to world's communications. *The Guardian*. Retrieved September 1, 2016, from www.theguardian.com/uk/2013/jun/21/gchq-cables-secret-world-communications-nsa

5. Hopkins, N. (2013, June 7). UK gathering secret intelligence via covert NSA operation. *The Guardian*. Retrieved September 1, 2013, from www.theguardian.com/technology/2013/jun/07/uk-gathering-secret-intelligence-nsa-prism

6. Greenwald, G. (2014). *No place to hide: Edward Snowden, the NSA and the US surveillance state.* New York: Metropolitan Books, p. 141.

7. *Ibid.*, p. 142.

8. Murphy, C. (2012). *EU counter-terrorism law: Pre-emption and the rule of law.* Oxford: Hart Publishing, p. 149.

9. Whitman, J. (2004). The two western cultures of privacy: Dignity versus liberty. *Yale Law Journal, 113,* 1151–1221, 1155.

10. Article 8(2) CFRF.

11. Article 7 CFRF.

12. European Parliament and Council Directive 95/46/EC.

13. *Ibid.*, Article 6(1)(b).

14. *Ibid.*, Article 13(1).

15. Directive 2016/680.

16. European Commission. (2016). *Reform of EU data protection rules.* Retrieved September 26, 2016, from http://ec.europa.eu/justice/data-protection/reform/index_en.htm

17. Directive 2016/680, paragraph 2.

18. *Ibid.*, paragraph 29.

19. *Ibid.*, paragraph 35.

20. *Ibid.*, Article 1(2).

21. (2014) Case C-131/12.

22. Directive 2016/680, Article 3(8).

23. *Ibid.*, Article 19.

24. *Ibid.*, Article 20.

25. *Ibid.*, Article 32.

26. *Ibid.*, Article 34.

27. *Ibid.*, Article 54.

28. *Ibid.*, Article 35.

29. *Ibid.*, Article 36(1).

30. *Ibid.*, Article 37.

31. [2014] EUECJ C-293/12, [2014] 3 WLR 1607.

32. *Ibid.*, paragraph 71.

33. Bignami, F. (2007). Privacy and law enforcement in the European Union: The data retention directive. *Chicago Journal of International Law, 8*(1), 233, p. 237.

34. *Ibid.*, pp. 234–236.

35. Roberts, A. (2015). Privacy, data retention and domination: Digital Rights Ireland Ltd v. Minister for Communications. *Modern Law Review, 78*(3), 535–548, 538.

36. *Ibid.*

37. *Ibid.*, p. 540.

38. *Digital Rights Ireland* [2014] EUECJ C-293/12, paragraph 54.

39. *Ibid.*, paragraph 61.

40. *Ibid.*, paragraph 67.

41. *Ibid.*, paragraph 66.

42. *Ibid.*, paragraph 51.

43. Ojanen, T. (2014). Privacy is more than just a seven-letter word: The court of justice of the European Union sets constitutional limits on mass surveillance. *European Constitutional Law Review, 10*(3), 528–541, 537.

44. *Ibid.*, p. 539.

45. Granger, M.-P., & Irion, K. (2014). The court of justice and the data retention directive in Digital Rights Ireland: Telling off the EU legislator and teaching a lesson in privacy and data protection. *European Law Review, 39*(6), 835–850, 849.

46. [2015] EWHC 2092 (Admin).

47. Now repealed by the Investigatory Powers Act 2016.
48. Data Retention and Investigatory Powers Act 2014, s.1(2).
49. *Ibid.*, s.1(5).
50. *Ibid.*, s.3(2).
51. *R (on the application of Davis and ors) v. Secretary of State for the Home Department*[2015] EWHC 2092 (Admin), paragraph 83.
52. *Ibid.*, paragraph 88.
53. *Ibid.*, paragraph 91a.
54. *Ibid.*, paragraph 91b.
55. *Ibid.*, paragraph 98.
56. *Ibid.*, paragraph 114.
57. *Ibid.*, paragraph 121.
58. Meyer, D. (2015, March 11). *Dutch court suspends metadata surveillance law over privacy*. Retrieved August 20, 2016, from http://tech.eu/news/dutch-court-suspends-data-retention-law/
59. *Digital Rights*, paragraph 111.
60. [2015] EUECJ C-362/14.
61. Actually termed the European Parliament and Council Directive 95/46/EC.
62. Annex I, paragraph 12 Dec 2000/520, Export.gov, US-EU Safe Harbor Overview. Retrieved September 23, 2016, from www.export.gov/safeharbor/eu/eg_main_018476.asp
63. Art 3(4) Dec 2000/520; European Commission (2012, September 10). *How will "safe harbor" arrangement for personal data transfer to the US work?* Retrieved September 23, 2016, from http://ec.europa.eu/justice/policies/privacy/thridcountries/adequacy-faq1_en.htm
64. European Commission. (2013). Communication on the functioning of the Safe-Harbour from the perspectives of EU citizens and companies established in the US. *COM*, 847 Final, p. 18.
65. Greenwald, G. (2014). *No place to hide: Edward Snowden, the NSA and the US surveillance state*. New York: Metropolitan Books, p. 92.
66. Dec 2000/520, p. 19.
67. *Ibid.*, paragraphs 26–30.
68. *Maximillian Schrems v. Data Protection Commissioner* Case C-362/14 (Advocate General Opinion—delivered 23rd September 2015), paragraph 30.
69. *Maximillian Schrems v. Data Protection Commissioner* [2014] IEHC 310.
70. *Ibid.*, paragraph 14.
71. *Ibid.*, paragraph 79.
72. *Ibid.*, paragraph 69.
73. *Ibid.*, paragraph 74.
74. *Maximillian Schrems v. Data Protection Commissioner* Case C-362/14 (Advocate General Opinion—delivered 23rd September 2015), paragraph 210.
75. *Ibid.*, paragraphs 210–211.
76. *Ibid.*, paragraph 237.
77. *Digital Rights*, paragraph 107.
78. Article 25(2) Directive 95/46/EC.
79. *Ibid.*, Article 25(6).
80. *Ibid.*, Article 25(4).
81. [2015] EUECJ C-362/14, paragraph 7.
82. *Maximillian Schrems v. Data Protection Commissioner* Case C-362/14 (Advocate General Opinion—delivered 23rd September 2015), paragraph 141.
83. *Ibid.*, paragraph 142.
84. *Ibid.*, paragraph 147.
85. *Ibid.*, paragraph 137.
86. [2015] EUECJ C-362/14, paragraph 88.
87. *Ibid.*, paragraph 94.
88. [2014] EUECJ C-293/12, [2014] 3 WLR 1607.
89. *Schrems*, paragraph 95.
90. Sotto, L. J., & Simpson, A. P. (2014). United States. In R. P. Jay (Ed.), *Data protection & privacy in 26 jurisdictions worldwide 2014* (p. 191). London: Law Business Research.
91. Muir, A., & Oppenheim, C. (2002). National information policy developments worldwide IV: Copyright, freedom of Information and data protection. *Journal of Information Science*, (28), 467–488, 478.
92. Annex V Dec2000/520.

93. *Ibid.*, Annex I, paragraph 3.

94. Connelly, C. (2008). *The U.S. Safe Harbor: Fact or fiction?* Sydney, Australia: Galexia Pty Ltd, paragraph 2.

95. Haynes, D. (2015, October 12). End of Safe Harbour isn't the end of the world: Let's hope its successor is better. *The Conversation.* Retrieved October 13, 2016, from http://theconversation.com/end-of-safe-harbour-isnt-the-end-of-the-world-lets-hope-its-successor-is-better-48841

96. Kelion, L. (2015, October 6). Facebook data transfers threatened by Safe Harbour ruling. *BBC News.* Retrieved October 6, 2015, from www.bbc.co.uk/news/technology-34442618

97. European Commission. (2016). The EU-U.S. privacy shield. Retrieved July 8, 2017, from http://ec.europa.eu/justice/data-protection/international-transfers/eu-us-privacy-shield/index_en.htm

98. Section 7 Privacy Act (1985 (Canada), s.4 Personal Information Protection and Electronic Documents Act 2000 (Canada).

99. *Ibid.*, Section 29, Section11.

100. *Ibid.*, Section 29, Section11.

101. Section 34 Privacy Act 1988 (Australia).

102. *Ibid.*, Section 46.

103. *Ibid.*, Section 46.

104. 389 U.S. 347 (1967).

105. *Ibid.*, paragraph 361.

106. Donohue, 2008, p. 221.

107. Pious, R. M. (2006). *The war in terrorism and the rule of law.* Los Angeles, CA: Roxbury Publishing Company, p. 13.

108. *Ibid.*, p. 16.

109. *Ibid.*, p. 34.

110. Gearty, C. (2013). *Liberty & security.* Cambridge: Polity Press, p. 78.

111. 310 F.3d 717 (2002).

112. *Ibid.*, p. 723.

113. Pious, 2006, p. 48; Gearty, 2013; Donohue, 2008, p. 234.

114. (2013) 568 US No. 11–1025.

115. *Ibid.*, paragraph IIIA.

116. International Commission of Jurists. (2009). *Report of the eminent jurists panel on terrorism, counter-terrorism and human rights,* p. 70. Retrieved November 20, 2016, from www.icj.org/wp-content/uploads/2012/04/Report-on-Terrorism-Counter-terrorism-and-Human-Rights-Eminent-Jurists-Panel-on-Terrorism-series-2009.pdf

117. Sledge, M. (2013, February 27). Supreme court's Clapper v Amnesty International Decision Could Affect indefinite detention lawsuit. *Huffington Post.* Retrieved September 5, 2016, from www.huffingtonpost.com/2013/02/27/clapper-v-amnesty-international_n_2769294.html

118. (2013) 568 US No. 11–1025 at 20 paragraph 4.

119. (2013) Civil Action Number 13–0881 (RJL).

120. *Ibid.*, p. 34.

121. *Ibid.*, p. 36.

122. *Ibid.*, p. 66.

123. (2013) 13 Civ 3994 (WHP).

124. *Ibid.*, paragraphs 1–2.

125. *Ibid.*, paragraphs 48–49.

126. *Ibid.*, paragraph 2.

127. *Ibid.*, paragraph 2.

128. *Ibid.*, paragraph 52.

129. (2015) Case 14–42.

130. (2013) Civil Action Number 13–0881 (RJL).

131. *Ibid.*, p. 94.

132. *Ibid.*, p. 96.

133. *Ibid.*, pp. 96–97.

134. Freedom Act 2015 Section 201(b).

135. *Ibid.*, Section 301.

136. *Ibid.*, Section 602(a).

137. *Ibid.*, Section 602(b).

138. Guiliani, N. (2015). What's next for surveillance reform after the USA Freedom Act. Retrieved June 3, 2017, from www.aclu.org/blog/washington-markup/whats-next-surveillance-reform-after-usa-freedom-act

139. Yuhas, A. (2015, June 2). NSA reform: USA Freedom Act passes first surveillance reform in decade. *The Guardian.* Retrieved June 3, 2017, from www.theguardian.com/us-news/live/2015/jun/02/senate-nsa-surveillance-usa-freedom-act-congress-live
140. *Ibid.*

References

Bignami, F. (2007). Privacy and law enforcement in the European Union: The data retention directive. *Chicago Journal of International Law, 8*(1), 233.

Gearty, C. (2013). *Liberty & security.* Cambridge: Polity Press.

Greenwald, G. (2014). *No place to hide: Edward Snowden, the NSA and the US surveillance state.* New York: Metropolitan Books.

Muir, A., & Oppenheim, C. (2002). National information policy developments worldwide IV: Copyright, freedom of information and data protection. *Journal of Information Science,* (28), 467–488.

Murphy, C. (2012). *EU counter-terrorism law: Pre-emption and the rule of law.* Oxford: Hart Publishing.

Pious, R. M. (2006). *The war in terrorism and the rule of law.* Los Angeles, CA: Roxbury Publishing Company.

Roberts, A. (2015). Privacy, data retention and domination: Digital rights Ireland Ltd v Minister for communications'. *Modern Law Review, 78*(3), 535–548.

27

SOCIAL JUSTICE CONTEXTUALIZED

Jason Jolicoeur and Erin Grant

Introduction

Social justice and associated terminology have been buzzwords used in the changing political climate of the United States. Many groups suggest that the provision of social justice in the United States is diminishing. While the term social justice has become increasingly fashionable today, it is not a new phenomenon. Rather, references to the concept have been made for some time in relation to the definitive need for respect and empathy for all persons and groups. For example, the term social justice has been used in the counseling field for some time. Social justice influences the relationship between a practitioner and client in four ways. First, the practitioner considers the way in which diversity creates complexities within relationships. Second, a counselor must remain mindful that any semblance of oppression may negatively influence their client's well-being. Third, clients must be understood in the lens of their own social environment, rather than that of the professional. Finally, the previous three principles must be integrated into all interactions between clients and practitioners.[1]

This example sheds some light onto how social justice manifests itself in the realm of criminal justice. The focus of this chapter is to examine the relationship between social justice, economic and environmental structures in contemporary American society, and how these factors interact with the criminal justice system. The chapter will begin with a breakdown of the ways in which economic structure can be understood and observed. Towards this end, the stratification, opportunity hoarding, and Marxist approaches will each be presented. Community stability and state-sanctioned violence will then be discussed at some length. Community stability will be presented in such a manner that the way in which individuals can provide protection for one another through social platforms can be better understood. A definition and brief history of American state-sanctioned violence will then be discussed. Finally, the concepts of social and criminal justice or injustice will be outlined before the chapter concludes with a focused evaluation of the relationship between economics, environment, and the formal provision of justice in contemporary society.

Background

Numerous variables affect social justice and influence the manner in which the criminal justice system treats the individuals who rely upon its services. Prior to exploring this relationship, some key variables will need to be outlined and operationalized in order to facilitate broader forthcoming discussions. This chapter begins with a brief overview of the economic and environmental structures that are commonly believed to influence inequality in this country. A brief breakdown of both social and criminal justice concepts is also provided before a discussion pertaining to how each of these variables affect one another is undertaken. This chapter is intended to provide not only a review of individually significant factors, but perhaps more importantly, some elaboration regarding how these various factors are thought to have a greater collective influence on the provision of social justice principles.

Economic Structure and Inequality

Several approaches can be taken when outlining economic structure; three of these will be presented. The stratification approach may be the most intuitive. People naturally cluster around attributes affecting their access to employment (e.g., education, resources, and social connections), thus the source of the strata: under, lower, middle, and upper classes. Note, it is not one of these attributes alone, but their interconnection, that determines class per this approach.[2] The middle class is made up of individuals with the resources and education needed to find gainful employment and thus operate successfully in society. The upper-class echelon possesses the resources and social connections necessary to live separate from all other classes. Lower-class individuals have the resources available to live above the poverty line, though without the security or ability to cultivate the meaningful social relationships that might improve their status through upward social and economic mobility. The most marginalized group is the underclass, who are relegated to a lower status in society; these individuals lack the education, skills, and support needed to secure stable and meaningful employment.

Employment is a critical aspect to this and other approaches to economic structure; it provides individuals with specific opportunities to acquire the wealth that ultimately places them in their respective income strata. Those unable to gain employment when they also possess no other resources tend to find limited opportunities outside of the underclass. Individuals with the credentials to become a dentist, accountant, or some other needed profession will find themselves with opportunities to enter the middle-class strata. The settings in which one has been raised greatly determines educational opportunities. If, during the developmental years, an individual has little access to a high-quality primary and secondary education, no meaningful access to higher education, and little familial support for educational achievement, access to a well-paying job is greatly diminished. The United States educational system is structured in such a manner that poor families tend to have inferior access to education when compared to those of the middle and upper classes. This lack of access to quality educational opportunities, especially when intermingled with an absence of support services for lower- and underclass families, sets children up for economic failure. The effects of this deprivation are exacerbated by the deindustrialization of the American economy and lack of job-training programs for those left unemployed by industrial changes. People at the lower end of the class spectrum are left with little opportunity to raise their status.[3]

A Weberian approach to economic structure focuses specifically on opportunities for employment, rather than evaluating these opportunities in reference to additional resources or social connections. Per this perspective, middle-class jobs are kept out of reach of the lower end of the working-class spectrum by restricting the supply of people eligible for desirable employment. This phenomenon is termed opportunity hoarding.[4] Certain professional opportunities such as an attorney, teacher, or plumber require specialized training that many do not have equal access to. The procedures and high costs associated with attaining this education prevents those with fewer economic resources from changing their economic status. Well-educated people remain in low supply and are compensated accordingly. It may be argued that if everyone had access to higher education, everyone would have the same opportunity for gainful employment. It is more likely, however, that such changes would only lead to those with more financial resources continuing their education and thus remaining at an advantage in the job market. The United States was the first country to undertake a program of massive expansion of its higher education system.[5] Ultimately, this meant that those with few resources could attend college at a reasonable cost. The multitiered system of higher education (e.g., community colleges to private universities) made it possible for a broader segment of the population to acquire credentials and middle-class employment. This system also helped create middle-class jobs that required educated or trained individuals. Historically, this process was accompanied by job creation that did not always require an advanced education.

Weber's approach places the population into one of three categories: capitalists, middle class, and working class. Capitalists own the means of production, providing employment for the working class to fill. The middle class is comprised of individuals who can compete for better-paying jobs due to their higher education, but who do not have enough resources to create new positions or industry of their own. It should be noted that, contrary to popular rhetoric, there is no agreement as to whether the U.S. was ever an overwhelmingly middle-class society.[6] Most jobs have not offered advantages solely based on exclusionary credentials. Additionally, there has been a recent erosion of processes and structures resulting in greater middle-class exclusion. The labor market itself has seen a correction since the 1970s, with many positions no longer secured by historically valued credentials. Thus, while it is still certainly the case that higher education and, increasingly, advanced academic degrees play a central role in providing access to many of the best jobs in the American economy, it is unclear what, if any, prospects remain for a broad established middle class.

The Weberian approach focuses on market advantage without evaluating the various relationships that exist between groups in society. The social aspect of broader economic structure is the focus of a Marxist approach. The exploitation and domination of workers becomes particularly relevant within this lens, especially concerning the economic system in capitalist societies. This perspective provides that educated professionals and technical workers maintain autonomy from domination in the workplace due to their valuable knowledge, skills, and vocational knowledge but gives little more than a nod to the idea of the middle class. These approaches can provide insight into the economic structure of the United States. Each has value and there is no reason to view them as being mutually exclusive. What each has in common, at its very core, is a breakdown of people into different groups in relation to their ability to thrive and prosper. The result is that the economic structure of our country is of the most polarizing of all developed capitalist countries.[7]

Environmental Concepts

Community Stability

The overwhelming consensus in social science literature is that the stability of a community is related to economics, poverty, crime, familial structure (single parenthood, etc.), and other significant quality-of-life variables. A community that lacks stability is one in which there is a relative flux in the population; this is often accompanied by the inability to create or a disruption of social networks and a lack of cohesion between residents. There is also a reduction in communal commitment to norms, resulting in an increase in the propensity for criminal behavior. Community stability, on the other hand, promotes social control, an increased commitment to communal norms, and lower crime rates.[8] With community stability comes social capital, which is the ability of a community to act together for the broader social good or mutual benefit. In this type of environment, residents are able to create networks based on trust and mutually agreed upon standards of behavior. Social capital provides that individuals share resources to help one another thrive within the community. As resources are more equitably shared, increasingly stable communities are created that are characterized by educational attainment and effective civic institutions.[9]

Strong ties between individuals within society are not necessarily indicated when there is social control. Trust and willingness to look out for one another are key to shard expectations within a community. This is termed a collective efficacy or an ability to maintain social order through shared expectations and engagement and a common sense of commitment.[10] The diversity of a community can undermine the emergence of social capital. This may be in part due to difficulties in communication between more diverse community constituents or a sense of cultural isolation, which tends to breed distrust and suspicion. Without the trust that emerges when individuals can communicate with one another, people may remain in flux, preventing them from communal engagement, which might otherwise stabilize the community. Without shared norms, social disorganization occurs and non-stable communities follow. Those communities that lack stability can quickly become a breeding ground for drug use and crime, the response to which will be discussed next.[11]

State-Sanctioned Violence

The term state-sanctioned violence evokes images of the many totalitarian regimes of the past, such as those associated with Stalin and Hitler, during which violence was used to terrorize the masses into complying with their demands. This oppressive behavior can be seen in the colonial eras, during which violence aided in the maintenance of territories. It has since been seen, during the Cold War in Latin America, to prevent opposition movements. The purpose of state-sanctioned violence is to coerce citizens into complying with the wishes of social and political elites. This violence works as a deterrent to dissent, instilling fear into those not directly subject to the actual acts of violence. In this way, they are forced to consider altering their views and behaviors in a manner desired by the actor demonstrating a willingness to use violence.[12] Violence is typically thought of as being physical, such as assaults or murders. These are indeed ways in which some states attempt to alter behavior within their citizens; however, there are other types of violence employed as well. It is useful to examine instances of violence beyond those just embodied in injury to provide a more multifaceted analysis. This perspective would permit individuals to consider connections between structural factors and interpersonal violence within the broad social structure.

By its very nature, the state is the only entity that has formal legitimacy to use violence. Weber observed that violence, whether it is practiced or threatened, is the essence of the state.[13] In the United States, violence and control occur at a number of levels beyond those practices in most comparable Western countries. While claiming the title of freest country in the world, the United States currently incarcerates more than two million of its residents. On a global scale, approximately one-quarter of all prisoners are incarcerated in American prisons; the largest percentage of those imprisoned being Black males. The United States government, in addition to locking up offenders as a broader deterrent, uses direct measures to prevent dissent. The National Security Agency (NSA) taps wires and records e-mail communication ostensibly as a means of preventing terrorism. Foreign nationals are deported when they have violated an ever-fluctuating set of immigration statutes, often leading to their separation from family members. A final example of the threat of state violence are the ongoing wars against drugs and crime. Note that the name of these prevention programs alone is enough to evoke a perception of violence among some.[14]

Due to these "wars," the police have taken on increasingly aggressive enforcement tactics and a more militarized character. There has been an increased reliance on the use of special weapons and tactics (SWAT) teams, which are essentially tactical units initially designed for high-risk entries and arrests. Municipal police have been able to acquire war-related equipment, such as surplus weaponry, military gear (bulletproof vests, etc.), and armored vehicles through the United States Department of Defense. The future appears to provide greater opportunities through which citizens can be exposed to state violence. In his campaign, President Donald Trump promised more aggressive forms of social control and mass deportations.[15] Ultimately, many believe that the state establishes self-serving rules to benefit its own interests at the expense of a more localized practice of power. State interests often align with those of the wealthy and powerful who compose the elite or capitalist class in American society. This relationship between economics, environment, and state-sanctioned crime will be discussed later in the chapter. However, before this discussion is undertaken, it is important to examine a number of justice-related concepts. This is because it is difficult at best to understand injustice without first developing a clear understanding of what justice is.

Justice-Related Concepts

Social Justice

At its core, social justice is a concept that is fundamentally based upon the underlying ideals of equity in treatment and fairness in opportunity. Social justice has been said to represent a process for determining how both good and bad aspects of society are dispersed across populations.[16] Others have argued that social justice refers to a two-step process involving the identification of what is meant by the term justice and a subsequent decision regarding whether justice, as we have defined it, is made available to all.[17] Still others have noted that social justice refers primarily to decisions, at least insofar as those decisions contribute to final determinations regarding the societal distribution of benefits.[18] The equitable distribution concept that is an inherent part of these and many other definitions of social justice can refer to a variety of disparate social, economic, and political commodities. While many tend to associate social justice largely with the equitable distribution of fiscal resources, such as income inequality, this alone does not adequately describe the full breadth and depth of the larger concept. Meaningful equity in the provision of educational, political, residential, and familial commodities is also an important part of the broader social justice concept. In practice, this means that no one group should experience greater societal benefits or preferential treatment at the expense of other groups. This is especially significant in relation to the total distribution of the many benefits offered to those participating in contemporary society. Rather, societal benefits should be equally and justly distributed across society, hence the advent of the related term, distributive justice.

The concept of social justice is based at least in part on the assumption that both individuals and institutions within society are assigned roles and have duties to both each other and to the larger community. Individuals have a duty to actively seek methods through which they can advance the cause of a more just and fair society through their actions and behaviors. Further, individuals must attempt to treat others in a manner that is conducive with broader social justice principles. For example, equity is a concept that is commonly associated with social justice; as a result, individuals should endeavor to treat others equitably during the course of their interactions. Social justice holds that organizations and institutions within society, both public and private, have a fundamental duty to work towards improving the general welfare. Government agencies in particular play an important role in relation to the provision of social justice in contemporary society. These organizations are expected to carry out larger social justice mandates for all those in society through the provision and continuation of basic rights, privileges, services, and protections. Oftentimes, the provision of these items is accomplished through the creation of specific government agencies. For instance, basic access to education is provided through the creation of public universities and local public school districts. While the provision of basic rights, services, and protections of this nature is important, it is not necessarily enough to ensure social justice. This is because the provision of a service or right alone doesn't guarantee equality in these rights and services. As a result, the provision of basic services is oftentimes accompanied by legislation or policy standards that attempt to ensure equity across service provision. Legislation aimed at improving underperforming public schools provides an example of how legislation and provision can work collectively to achieve social justice.

313

Critics argue that there are a number of limitations that undermine the value of the social justice concept from both a pragmatic and theoretical standpoint. From a theoretical standpoint, a number of limitations are thought to arise from the vague and somewhat abstract nature of the structural terminology that helps to operationalize the social justice concept. For instance, social justice is based on the assumption that the benefits of society should be equitably distributed across all members of the population. Critics argue that it is difficult to operationalize both of these terms in a satisfactory manner, because there is no universal consensus regarding what a societal benefit is or what amounts to an equitable distribution of such a benefit. If we are unable to adequately represent the foundational concepts upon which the social justice concept is built, it becomes more difficult to determine how to operationalize this concept. From a pragmatic standpoint, it is also challenging to establish the procedural means by which social justice might be implemented. Despite criticisms of this nature, social justice continues to be a critical consideration in many areas of contemporary life. This is especially true concerning calls for equity and fairness in relation to the treatment that individuals receive within the contemporary criminal justice and legal systems.

Criminal Justice and Injustice

Public perceptions regarding the criminal justice system vary greatly and are at least partially dependent on the context surrounding the definition and the perspective of the individual or group making the assessment. To most, the term represents the broader institutionalized system that has been put in place to formally respond to issues of crime and disorder within contemporary society. From this standpoint, the criminal justice system includes not only those individuals and agencies that are assigned responsibility for dealing with criminal offending, but also the systemic and procedural structures and elements that are associated with the processing of individuals thought to be responsible for these offenses. The system itself represents society's attempts to protect the public from the harm done by those operating outside of the standards and values associated with the broader collective social conscience. Protective efforts of this nature entail both proactive and reactive strategies, as the system works to prevent crime when possible and to respond to instances of criminal offending when preventative efforts are not successful. For many, the general connotation associated with the criminal justice system is a positive one; however, this is not always the case, as both the direction and intensity of opinions vary. What represents protection and safety to some can come to characterize uncertainty and oppression to others. Systemic connotations are thought to represent broader individual experiences with the criminal justice system, the vicarious conceptualizations of the system that are relayed to individuals by others around them, subcultural attitudes and beliefs about the system and its representatives, descriptive media portrayals of the system, and a variety of other factors.

The criminal justice system is a particularly important societal institution given the significance of the various tasks that it is responsible for undertaking (crime prevention, criminal investigation, apprehension of offenders, etc.) and the substantive influence that systemic processing can have on individuals. In transitioning from more informal to more formal methods of social control, society has increasingly come to rely upon the criminal justice system to control and regulate human behavior and the nature of relations between individuals. The system provides protection from the harm posed by criminal offending through both prevention and apprehension efforts, and it maintains societal integrity by ensuring compliance with existing and evolving social norms and standards. Crime victims are especially reliant on the system to provide the services they need and the sense of physical and emotional security required to bring a sense of cessation to the trauma associated with their victimization experience. The families of victims are also reliant on the system to provide a form of retributive justice that is otherwise prohibited to them by contemporary legal and societal prohibitions. While many associate the influence of the system solely with crime victims, in reality it extends to offenders who are systemically engaged and processed. Individuals processed through the criminal justice system can experience financial costs, familial disruption, loss of freedom, and significant social stigmatization. These factors can have a major influence on both those facing systemic processing and those who care about or are reliant upon them. Effects of this nature are thought to be especially significant for the children of those being processed, given the lack of emotional involvement and financial support.[19] Ultimately, the criminal justice system can have pervasive and far-reaching impacts that transcend social boundaries in influencing all aspects and individuals within contemporary society.

Given the importance of the role played by the criminal justice system in contemporary society, the systemic outcomes associated with the system have been a cause of great societal consideration and concern. If the system itself, and the actions of those employed within the system, are to provide social justice, the benefits of the system must be evenly distributed among all members of society. In practice, this means that the protections associated with the system should be evenly dispersed throughout all communities regardless of the individual characteristics and demographics that differentiate those communities. This also means that there should be equity in the quality of services provided by the individuals employed within the various branches of the system (policing, courts, corrections, etc.), regardless of the individual characteristics of those receiving their services. Perhaps more importantly, social justice dictates that the burdens associated with the system should be minimized to the greatest extent possible and any remaining burdens uniformly disseminated across society, rather than being concentrated in certain communities. When the burdens associated with any socially constructed institution, including the criminal justice system, are disproportionately distributed without sufficient justification, public faith in that institution and in social justice principles more generally can be undermined. The adverse impact that disproportionate minority confinement has had on communities of color provides an example of what is oftentimes thought to represent the unequal distribution of systemic burdens.[20] While the issue of social justice is often viewed at a systemic level in relation to the criminal justice institutions, it is important to remember that the system itself is composed of individual workers, and the behaviors and actions of these workers can have a significant influence on the provision of social justice.

Criminal justice practitioners typically have a great deal of discretion in relation to how they carry out their assigned duties. This discretion can translate into differential treatment or contribute to questionable decision-making, both of which can help undermine social justice. If criminal justice practitioners do not treat individuals in a professional manner, engage in unethical conduct that causes harm to others, purposefully target only some populations for criminal enforcement, or contribute to miscarriages of justice, equitable distribution is undermined, and it is likely that certain individuals or groups will benefit at the expense of others. Social justice is also undermined when practitioners refuse to provide equal enforcement of the law during the course of their professional duties. Disparate treatment of this nature can be manifest in favoritism towards certain types of victims, or conversely, hostility towards other types of victims. For instance, an officer who disproportionately arrests offenders who target victims of a certain race or ethnicity may be demonstrating either favoritism towards those victims or distaste for victims of other races or ethnicities. If social justice is to be fully realized, criminal justice practitioners must undertake their duties in an impartial manner towards both the victims of crime and the perpetrators of criminal offenses that they encounter during the course of their work.

The criminal justice system is an especially important concern from a social justice perspective because of the substantive aggregate disadvantages that can accumulate across the course of systemic involvement. This process, often referred to as cumulative disadvantage, refers to how individual acts or instances of disadvantage accumulate with prolonged and repeated exposure to the criminal justice system.[21] In other words, an individual offender who experiences disparities in treatment at the point of investigation, arrest, prosecution, sentencing, and post-correctional release will experience significantly more disadvantage than would have been the case had they experienced a disparity at only one point in during their processing. However, the nature of the criminal justice system is such that cumulative disadvantage is a reality for many individuals, especially those individuals who lack social power and influence. While each individual act that undermines social justice is significant, collectively the multiple individual acts of this nature are even more significant, as they become more destructive and difficult to overcome when examined from an aggregate perspective. Ultimately, the collective influence of multiple individual acts of this nature can contribute to broader systemic disparities, which can come to characterize the system as a whole, rather than just the individual acts themselves.

While public perceptions regarding the ability of the criminal justice system to provide social justice are significant in their own right, these attitudes may also have a more pragmatic influence on broader systemic efficacy. In order for the criminal justice system to accomplish its objectives, it must have the support and respect of the public. If not, the public becomes less likely to view the system itself, the systemic outcomes it undertakes, or even its employees as having any substantive legitimacy. As a result, the public willingness to assist representatives of the various branches of the criminal justice system declines and systemic efficacy suffers. If the public is unwilling to report criminal offenses or to provide information to investigators, the ability of the police to identify offenders is undermined. If community members do not trust the official representatives of the legal system (judges, prosecutors, etc.), they may become less willing to convict offenders during criminal court proceedings. The efficacy of the system is largely dependent on a number of factors that are both independent but interrelated. If the system is not viewed as providing social justice in the form of distributive justice, it may be viewed as abusive and public support in at least some communities may wane. At the same time, if the system does not have public support, it may become unable to achieve its stated purposes; it then loses legitimacy in the eyes of the public and can do little to support broader social justice principles. In order to be truly effective, the system must be viewed as being both competent in its mission and equitable in its application.

Economics, Environment, and Criminal and Social Justice

One of the primary underlying assumptions pertaining to social justice is that individuals will be treated in an equitable manner, will have equal opportunities to achieve their goals and objectives, and will be capable of accessing their fair share of societal capital.[22] This equality in treatment and opportunity applies to a wide variety of human rights, social phenomena, civil liberties, and governmental services. While the application of the social justice topic is quite broad, a number of primary factors are thought to be commonly related to its application in contemporary society. Two of these key factors are economics and criminal justice. These factors are thought to be of particular importance, given that full social justice is likely a practical impossibility without equity in the two related spheres of economics and criminal justice. The relationship between these two concepts is complicated by the fact that many believe it is a symbiotic one, so that one concept cannot be fully understood or properly evaluated without considering interactions with the other. Evaluations of this relationship have taken a number of different forms, but have tended to focus primarily on disparities in behaviors, treatments, and outcomes pertaining to both criminal offenders and crime victims.[23]

Research related to economic factors and criminal victimization has focused largely on environmental risk factors and differential systemic outcomes. While these two avenues of research differ, they have ultimately centered on the evaluation of a similar outcome in the form of how income inequality is related to the equitable distribution of justice in contemporary society. Environmental analyses have indicated that as income increases, individuals tend to have more options that minimize their victimization risk and enhance their personal safety and the safety of the surrounding community. In contrast, poorer individuals tend to be constrained by an environmental structure that enhances their victimization risk. Those living in poverty tend to be more likely to reside, work, and shop in higher crime areas, which contributes to an enhanced risk of victimization. At the same time, a lack of financial resources can limit opportunities to avoid victimization risks through physical relocation to lower-crime neighborhoods that are frequently substantively more expensive. Limited relocation opportunities are further complicated by the inability of the poor to purchase equipment intended to construct a safer physical environment in their current home, such as security systems and sturdy entry doors. Finally, income deprivation enhances victimization risk by limiting the legitimate hobbies that are available to poorer individuals in society or by driving them towards deviant diversions (drinking, drugs, etc.) that are more easily available. Legitimate leisure activities might provide individuals with a chance to temporarily escape the environmental conditions that would otherwise enhance their victimization risk, while deviant ones might actually increase their risk of victimization.[24]

Research has indicated that substantive differences in systemic outcomes exist in relation to the individual characteristics of crime victims. Research of this nature has evaluated the significance of the age, race, gender, and ethnicity of the victim in relation to criminal justice outcomes.[25] While all of the information that has been gained from research of this nature is important, studies focusing on victim income have produced some of the more significant, but also most complicated, results related to differences in systemic outcomes.[26] The complicated nature of these findings is at least partially a result of victimization outcomes being correlated with a variety of factors in addition to income. It is difficult to determine the relative importance of each of these individual factors because unraveling their interconnectedness to each other in order to examine their individual specific contribution is a challenging undertaking. In spite of the complicated nature of this process, research supports the contention that there are a number of important criminal justice outcomes associated with disparities in victim income. Research has indicated that, in general, poorer individuals are more likely than wealthier individuals to become victims of criminal offenses. Research highlighting differences of this nature in relation to property crimes has existed for some time.[27] More recent data underscore that this is also true of violent crimes in contemporary society, with the poor at a significantly higher risk of victimization than the wealthy across all categories of nonfatal violent criminal offenses.[28]

While each of the individual victimization factors that have been discussed are significant in their own right, collectively they take on even greater importance. Poverty can influence a number of environmental factors, which appear to enhance the risk of individual and collective criminal victimization. However, this finding alone provides an incomplete understanding of the rather complex nature of the relationship between income and victimization. In order to fully understand this relationship, information regarding systemic contributions must also be considered. Prior research has underscored a number of substantive and procedural characteristics of the criminal justice system that appear to work to the disadvantage of the poor. Systemic aspects of the legislative process are thought to contribute to the creation of criminal laws that penalize the crimes of the poor, while either legalizing or largely decriminalizing the deviant acts of the wealthy.[29] Even in instances when punishment is disseminated across members of different economic groups, penalties for the wealthy are more likely to involve fiscal sanctions, while those for the poor are more reliant on incarceration. Some believe that broader institutionalized racism is an endemic characteristic of the system and that this systemic bias works to the disadvantage of the poor. While race itself is not a direct correlate of socioeconomic status, data do indicate that racial and ethnic minorities tend to be disproportionately more likely to live in poverty than do Whites.[30] As a result, information about systemic racial disparities is often considered when evaluating criminal justice inequities thought to be related to income.

A number of procedural aspects of the criminal justice system are also thought to work toward the disadvantage and marginalization of the poor. The systemic practice of assigning court-appointed counsel to indigent defendants has been found to contribute to an increased likelihood of negative criminal court outcomes.[31] Additionally, the disproportionate inability of the poor to gain access to bail as a pretrial release mechanism has been associated with a greater probability of deleterious legal consequences, such as an increased likelihood of being found guilty and a higher possibility of receiving a longer prison sentence once found guilty.[32,33] Collectively, the various structural elements of the criminal justice system that have been examined are thought to enhance and reinforce the economic and environmental factors that are already believed to place the poor at a disadvantage in regard to equitable treatment before the law and within the criminal justice system. While equitable treatment within the justice system is not necessarily synonymous with the broader provision of social justice, it is an important barometer for the degree to which society values social justice principles and is able to secure these provisions across all segments of contemporary society.

Conclusion

Social justice is a critical concept in contemporary society, given changing societal expectations and ongoing developments in public attitudes towards the role and purpose of the relationship between the individual and the state. Fluctuations of this nature have resulted in growing calls for expanded civil liberties and additional protections from what many believe amounts to the excessive exercise and application of governmental power. Recent public concerns of this nature have been particularly salient concerning the criminal justice system. Protests and criticisms related to the actions and behaviors of law enforcement officers and the purpose of the police function are particularly illustrative of public concerns of this nature. Demonstrations driven by these concerns have captured public attention and contributed to a growing political and social divide in public opinion regarding the fundamental role of the criminal justice system in contemporary society. Controversies of this nature are especially problematic when they involve individuals facing economic disadvantage and an environmental context that precludes fair and equitable treatment before the law.

Many believe that there is a synergistic relationship between economic disadvantage and the broader provision or deprivation of social justice. Indeed, without the equitable distribution of economic resources and equal access to the means of fiscal advancement, it is hard to comprehend how social justice can become a pragmatic reality for all individuals across contemporary society. This disparity is important in its own right, but it becomes even more significant when viewed through a broader holistic perspective. This is because the relationship that is thought to exist between economic deprivation and social injustice is also believed to contribute to related inequalities in civil and legal protections within the criminal justice and legal systems. Perhaps more importantly, inequities in each of these individual areas often combine to create an even more substantive collective context of concentrated disadvantage for some groups. Given the interrelated nature of these different factors, it is clear that any effort to provide equity in one area will necessitate a broader effort to provide equality in the others. Without such concerted efforts, meaningful social justice will inevitably remain an ever-elusive concept for those living in contemporary society.

Discussion Questions

1. What are three approaches by which one might look at the economic structure in the United States?
2. Describe what is meant by the term "cumulative disadvantage" and how this concept relates to the provision of social justice.
3. What can be said about the changing nature of the middle class?
4. Which procedural aspects of the criminal justice system are thought to work toward the disadvantage and marginalization of the poor?
5. How do economics and environment relate to one another?
6. How does community stability lead to a greater sharing of resources?

7. Is a discussion pertaining to the equitable distribution of fiscal resources sufficient to fully and completely describe social justice? Why or why not?

8. How might the economic structure of the U.S. relate to community stability?

9. According to critics, what are the factors that undermine the value of the social justice concept?

10. Is an evaluation of crime victims sufficient to explain the role of social justice in the criminal justice system? Why or why not?

Notes

1. Ratts, M. J., Singh, A. A., Nassar-McMillan, S., Butler, S. K., & McCullough, J. R. (2016). Multicultural and social justice counseling competencies: Guidelines for the counseling profession. *Multicultural Counseling and Development, 44*, 28–48.

2. Wright, E. O. (2009). Understanding class: Towards and integrated approach. *New Left Review, 60*, 101–116.

3. *Ibid.*

4. *Ibid.*

5. *Ibid.*

6. *Ibid.*

7. *Ibid.*

8. Sampson, R. J., & Graif, C. (2009). Neighborhood social capital as differential social organization: Residential and leadership dimensions. *American Behavioral Scientist, 52*(11), 1579–1605.

9. Lochner, K. A., Kawachi, I., Brennan, R. T., & Buka, S. L. (2003). Social capital and neighborhood mortality rates in Chicago. *Social Science and Medicine, 56*(8), 1797–1805.

10. Sampson, & Graif, 2009.

11. Petersilia, J. (2001). Prisoner reentry: Public safety and reintegration challenges. *The Prison Journal, 81*, 360–375.

12. Mitchell, C., Stohl, M., Carleton, D., & Lopez, G. A. (1986). State terrorism: Issues of concept and measurement. In M. Stohl & G. A. Lopez (Eds.), *Government violence and oppression: An agenda for research* (pp. 1–26). Westport, CT: Greenwood Press.

13. Alimahomed-Wilson, J., & Williams, D. (2016). State violence, social control, and resistance. *Journal of Social Justice, 6*, 1–15.

14. Mitchell, Stohl, Carleton, & Lopez, 1986; Alimahomed-Wilson, & Williams, 2016.

15. Alimahomed-Wilson, & Williams, 2016.

16. Miller, D. (1999). *Principles of social justice*. Cambridge, MA: Cambridge University Press.

17. Capeheart, L., & Milovanovic, D. (2007). *Social justice: Theories, issues, and movements*. New Brunswick, NJ: Rutgers University Press.

18. Clayton, M., & Williams, A. (2004). Introduction. In M. Clayton & A. Williams (Eds.), *Social justice* (pp. 1–18). Malden, MA: Blackwell Publishing.

19. Wildeman, C., Wakefield, S., & Lee, H. (2016). Tough on crime, tough on families? Criminal justice and family life in America. *The Annals of the American Academy of Political and Social Science, 665*(1), 8–21.

20. Alexander, M. (2010). *The new Jim Crow: Mass incarceration in the age of color blindness*. New York: The New Press.

21. Kutateladze, B. L., Andiloro, N. R., Johnson, B. D., & Spohn, C. (2014). Cumulative disadvantage: Examining racial and ethnic disparity in prosecution and sentencing. *Criminology, 52*(3), 514–551.

22. Caravelis, C., & Robinson, M. (2016). *Social justice, criminal justice: The role of American law in effecting and preventing social change*. New York: Routledge.

23. Hagan, J., & Peterson, R. D. (1995). Introduction. In J. Hagan & R. D. Peterson (Eds.), *Crime and inequality* (pp. 1–13). Stanford, CA: Stanford University Press.

24. Meier, R. F., & Meithe, T. D. (1997). Understanding theories of criminal victimization. In M. McShane & F. P. Williams (Eds.), *Victims of crime and the victimization process* (pp. 225–266). New York: Garland Publishing.

25. Daigle, L. E. (2018). *Victimology: The essentials*, 2nd ed. Thousand Oaks, CA: Sage.

26. Sharkey, P., Besbris, M., & Friedson, M. (2016). Poverty and crime. In D. Brady & L. M. Burton (Eds.), *The Oxford handbook of the social science of poverty* (pp. 623–636). New York: Oxford University Press.

27. Laub, J. H. (1990). Patterns of criminal victimization in the United States. In A. J. Lurigio, W. G. Skogan, & R. C. Davis (Eds.), *Victims of crime: Problems, policies, and programs*. Newbury Park, CA: Sage.

28. Harrell, E., Langton, L., Berzofsky, M., Couzens, L., & Smiley-McDonald, H. (2014). *Household poverty and nonfatal violent victimization, 2008–2012*. Washington, DC: United States Department of Justice, Office of Justice Programs.

29. Hudson, B. (2000). Punishing the poor: Dilemmas of justice and difference. In W. C. Hefferman & J. Kleinig (Eds.), *From social justice to criminal justice: Poverty and the administration of criminal law* (pp. 189–216). New York: Oxford University Press.

30. Macartney, S., Bishaw, A., & Fontenot, K. (2013). *Poverty rates for selected detailed race and Hispanic groups by state and place: 2007–2011.* Washington, DC: United State Census Bureau.

31. Karmen, A. (2000). Poverty, crime, and criminal justice. In W. C. Hefferman & J. Kleinig (Eds.), *From social justice to criminal justice: Poverty and the administration of criminal law* (pp. 25–46). New York: Oxford University Press.

32. Oleson, J. C., Lowenkamp, C. T., Cadigan, T. P., VanNorstrand, M., & Wooldredge, J. (2014). The effect of pretrial detention on sentencing in two federal districts. *Justice Quarterly, 33*(6), 1103–1122.

33. Kalhous, C., & Meringolo, J. (2012). Bail pending trial: Changing interpretations of the bail reform act and the importance of bail from defense attorneys perspectives. *Pace Law Review, 32*(3), 800–855.

28

WAIVING JUVENILES
TO CRIMINAL COURT

Jordan Papp

Introduction

Waiving a juvenile to criminal court is the process by which a juvenile court transfers jurisdiction of a case to adult court. This is done to deny the youth the protection that juvenile jurisdiction provides. Most often, the intent is for harsher and more-restrictive sentences to be imposed upon the youth in adult court than they otherwise would have received in juvenile court.[1] This process is reserved for juveniles who have been deemed to have lost their "youthfulness" and are no longer seen as fit for the juvenile system. Some readers may have heard the expression, "commit an adult crime, do adult time." This adage is often used as a quick rationale for waiving youth to adult courts.[2] However, while this expression is catchy and may seem immediately appealing, a much more in-depth discussion about the implications of waiving youth to adult court is needed to fully understand the impact that it can have on youth.

The use of waivers to adult court has been hotly debated by supporters and dissenters of waiver policies. Two of the main sources of critique are as follows. First, many have criticized these policies for being overly harsh on youth who are not fully cognitively developed.[3] Those who take this position would argue that because youth are not fully cognitively developed, they are not fully culpable for their actions and should not be dealt with as adults. Along this same line of inquiry, one could argue that because of the increased plasticity of the adolescent brain relative to adults, they are more susceptible to change through rehabilitation.[4] Second, waiver policies have also been criticized for being discriminatory toward minority youth.[5] Those who weigh this critique argue that waiver decisions are largely left up to the discretion of judges and prosecutors, and for this reason, individual biases can creep into the decision-making process. Some have also argued that crimes that legislators make eligible for waiver can be done in a way that targets certain groups of youth. This argument will be discussed in more depth later in this chapter.

Conversely, supporters of waiver policies have argued that transferring youth to adult court creates safer communities by incapacitating the most dangerous youth for longer periods and in more-restrictive forms of housing.[6] Those who support this claim would suggest that some youth are simply too dangerous to be dealt with by the juvenile justice system and need to be dealt with as adults. Additionally, supporters of waiver policies claim that having youth who are very dangerous and highly resistant to change impedes the rehabilitative goals of the juvenile justice system.[7]

All arguments for and against waiving youth to adult court are worth considering and will be examined in this chapter. However, the purpose of this chapter will not be to try to sway opinion one way or the other on the efficacy of waiver policies. That is beyond the scope of this chapter and can be done independently by a careful review of the relevant research that compares the benefits and drawbacks of waiver policies.[8] Rather, the purpose of this chapter will be to review how waivers may be used disproportionately for certain groups of youth (e.g., racial minorities).

Most importantly, and most relevant to this handbook on social justice, this chapter will review whether waiver policies are applied in a socially just manner. Equality is a common thread that runs through many writings on justice. This is true even in writings about justice that are centuries old. For instance, writings from as far back as Aristotle stressed the importance of equality in societies under various forms of government.[9] Modern writings also stress the importance of equality in justice but do so in a manner that is more applicable to modern societies.[10],[11] Based on the principles of justice put forth in these writings, this chapter will review whether waiver policies are applied equally to all groups of people, regardless of their individual characteristics that are not relevant to law (e.g., race and gender). These discussions are necessary, as they can be used to inform future changes that may be needed for policies on waivers or training of those who have the authority to waive youth to adult court.

This chapter will proceed by first examining the purpose of juvenile courts and their historical background. In this section, the goals of both the adult and juvenile justice systems will be discussed, so each can be compared and contrasted. Next, the criteria necessary for transferring youth to adult court will be considered. This section will discuss the criteria that judges and other court officials use to make their decisions about which youth should be transferred. This section will also discuss why these criteria are used. Following this, various methods for waiving youth to adult court will be reviewed and discussed. Next, research on disparities in the use of waivers for certain groups of youth will be reviewed. This section will review recent research that has found evidence that certain groups of youth (e.g., racial minorities) are waived to adult court at higher rates than other groups of youth. Additionally, research that has not found said disparities will be reviewed, and a discussion will be had as to why this conflicting research may exist. Finally, a method for reducing disparities in the use of waivers for certain groups of youth will be reviewed and considered.

Juvenile Versus Adult Court

For centuries, it has been recognized that delinquent youth should receive deferential treatment compared to their adult counterparts.[12] One reason for this is that the behavior of youth is more malleable than that of adults, and thus youth are more susceptible to the benefits of treatment. Another reason is that juveniles are not deemed as culpable for their actions because they are unable to control their behaviors like adults. Much of the research on this topic concludes that this is because of a lack of cognitive development.[13] This research shows that youth are less apt to make clear and thoughtful decisions than adults are, which supports the claim that youth are less culpable for their actions.[14] For these reasons, juveniles and adults are separated by the judicial system.

While it has been recognized for centuries that delinquents should be treated differently than criminal adults, it was not until the late 19th century that a coherent juvenile justice system was formed in the United States. The formation of a separate justice system for youth was in large part due the child savers movement. Child savers were a group who advocated for the reformation of youth rather than punishment. This movement was based around the idea that youth could be rehabilitated and that punishment was an impediment to the rehabilitation process. For this reason, child savers advocated for a greater focus on treatment and movement away from punishment.

Until today, the goals of the juvenile justice system are more focused on rehabilitation as compared to the goals of the adult system, which are more focused on punishment and retribution.[15] Even with a shift toward rehabilitation in the adult system in the last few decades, the juvenile system is still oriented much more toward reforming youth than the adult system is in reforming adults. This difference in goals between the two systems is why waivers are used to put some youth in the adult system. It is believed that the youth waived to the adult system are no longer fit for the juvenile system and are deserving of the harshness of the adult system. The behavior of some youth seems so solidified and abhorrent that attempting to change their behavior would be an exercise in futility, which is why some believe that these youth would be best dealt with in the adult system. These opinions are held even though behavior intervention strategies have shown that many behaviors can be changed with enough effort.[16] But still, the judicial system deems some youth too risky to stay in the juvenile system and waives them to the adult system. The criteria for choosing who is waived to the adult system is discussed in the next section.

Criteria for Transferring Juveniles

Two criteria dictate which youth should be waived to the adult system: dangerousness and amenability to treatment. The dangerousness criteria suggests that youth who pose a significant threat to the public should be waived to adult court. This could include, for instance, a youth who has a known history of delinquency and who has committed a particularly violent act, such as attempted murder or assault with a deadly weapon. Because the youth has showed a disposition for violence, and has done so on a continual basis, this youth would be considered particularly dangerous and a significant threat to the community. Another example would be a first-time sex offender who committed a particularly heinous act. Even though this was only the offender's first offense and he may be unlikely to offend again, some judges would be inclined to transfer the youth to the adult system because of the severity of their crime and the significant harm that it would cause if they committed another similar act.

The amenability to treatment criteria would suggest that youth who are deemed "untreatable" should also be waived to adult court. This may include, for example, a youth who has come into contact with the juvenile justice system multiple times in the past, has been given treatment on each of those occasions, and still returned for a new offense each time after being treated. For this youth, he has been given multiple opportunities to change and has been given help, but still has not changed. For this reason, this youth may be considered untreatable.

Meeting these two criteria is sufficient for transferring a youth to adult court. The decision of whether a youth is particularly dangerous and untreatable is left up to the professional discretion of the judge. While this is a significant decision, a judge often is provided assistance from other professionals. For instance, in many cases, a probation officer writes a report that provides a judge with more information to base their decision on. In other cases, judges may even call upon other professionals, such as a licensed psychologist, to examine the mental health of a youth. These other sources of information allow judges to make more-informed decisions about which youth to transfer. However, in the end, the judge still has to use a certain amount of discretion to decide which youth to transfer. Additionally, there are alternative methods for transferring a youth to adult court other than just via the decision of a judge. These alternative methods will be discussed in the following section.

Types of Waivers

Three avenues exist for transferring youth to adult court. One involves a formal hearing in which a judge decides whether a case should be waived to adult court. In this instance, the above-mentioned criteria for waiver are considered by the judge, and the judge makes a determination of whether, in the judge's professional opinion, the youth meets the criteria necessary to be waived to adult court. This type of waiver is referred to as a "judicial waiver."

Second, some jurisdictions grant the prosecutor the discretionary power to decide where she wants to file a case. This allows the prosecutor to decide whether to file a case in juvenile or adult court. Filing the case in adult court would ultimately lead to a waiver of the youth to adult court. This is referred to as a "prosecutorial waiver."

Finally, many legislatures have created laws that make certain crimes automatically eligible for a waiver. For instance, in many jurisdictions, youth charged with homicide are eligible for automatic wavier to adult court regardless of whether they seem treatable. In these instances, the dangerousness criteria mentioned above overrides the amenability to change criteria because a murderer, no matter how likely they are to murder again, pose a significant threat to the safety of the community. These waivers are referred to as "statutory waivers."

Besides statutory waivers,[17] it should be easy to recognize that a significant amount of discretion is given to judges and prosecutors when deciding which youth should be transferred to adult court. This allows personal biases to creep into the decision-making process, which is cause for concern when considering Albonetti's (1991) theory of judicial discretion, referred to as attribution theory.[18] Albonetti (1991) suggests that "judges attempt to manage uncertainty by developing 'patterned responses' that are the product of an attribution process involving assessments of an offender's likelihood of committing future crime" (p. 247).[19] What Albonetti means is that some judges use their own conceptions of what may constitute dangerousness in order to manage the uncertainty that they might have about a decision. Albonetti goes on to explain that personal biases, including racial biases, may be used to fill in gaps when uncertainty exists.[20] For example, as it relates to judicial waivers, if a judge (even implicitly) believes that minority youth are more dangerous than White youth, they may be more likely to waive minority youth to adult court. Or, if a judge feels as though urban youth are less likely to be changed through treatment because they are more likely to live in an area with a street culture that promotes antisocial behavior, the judge may perceive these youth to be less amenable to change. These racial biases, and any other conceivable bias, may influence the decision-making process of judges and prosecutors, thus warranting concern about the potential for disparate use of waivers for certain groups of youth. Keep attribution theory in mind when reading the following section that reviews the research on disparities in waiver decisions, as it may provide context for the findings that will be discussed.

Disparities in Waivers

Before reviewing the research on the use of waivers, it is important to discuss when inequalities in the use of waivers would be considered "unjust." In his famous theory of social justice, Rawls (2009) posits a theory of "justice as fairness."[21] Rawls points out that in a democratic society such as ours, equal treatment of citizens is regarded as sacrosanct.[22] As Robinson (2013) sums up,

> whether something is just or unjust depends on whether it promotes or hinders equality of access to civil liberties, human rights, opportunities for healthy and fulfilling lives, as well as whether it allocates a fair share of benefits to the least advantaged members of society.[23]

This quote nicely sums up the many instances that would indicate that there is an unequal application of justice in a society. Criteria for determining whether inequalities in society are justifiable, as not all inequalities are necessarily unjustified, is laid out by Miller (1999).[24] These criteria allow for a simple determination of whether an inequality is justifiable. The following paragraph lays out these criteria and shows how disparities in the use of waivers to adult courts based on determinants outside of the law are not justifiable.

In his theory of social justice, Miller (1999) points out that not all inequalities in society are considered unjust.[25] For instance, Miller claims that economic inequalities that can motive people are not always unjust.[26] For instance, if all citizens in a society are allotted enough money so that their basic needs are met, inequalities in incomes can be justified. However, if some citizens in a society are exorbitantly wealthy while other do not have enough money to meet their basic needs while working a full-time job, these inequalities are unjustified. Miller also claims that inequalities are justifiable when based on differences in merit.[27] For example, it would be justifiable to pay two employees (who perform identical job functions) differently if one outperforms the other. This is justified, as the higher-performing employee provides greater benefits for the company than does the underperforming employee. However, Miller also states that these inequalities should be within reason, so that the basic needs of both employees are being met and that extra rewards only go beyond the pay needed to meet basic needs.[28] What is important to realize from Miller's theory is that any inequalities in the use of waivers are not justifiable under Miller's criteria for justifiable inequalities.[29] For this reason, no inequalities should exist in the use of waivers that cannot be justified under the law.

As with much research in criminal justice, research on waivers to adult court have shown disparities for minorities and other groups of youth (e.g., males). Specifically, research has shown that minority youth are more likely to be waived to adult court than to are White youth.[30],[31],[32],[33] Research has also shown that older youth are more likely to be transferred than younger youth.[34] Finally, research suggests that male youth are more likely to be transferred than females.[35] It is important to note that all of these disparities are true after holding other factors constant, such as the type of crime that a youth committed and their criminal history.

Also concerning, survey research on the public's perception of waivers has shown that citizens are also more willing to transfer minority youth to adult courts than White youth.[36] In a survey of a random sample of citizens of the New Orleans Metropolitan area, Feiler and Sheley (1999) asked respondents various questions about their opinions of waiving youth to adult court.[37] While they found that the demographic characteristics of the respondent were unrelated to their opinions held about waivers of youth, these researchers did find that the race of the youth was related to the respondents' perception about waiving that youth to adult court. Interestingly, the characteristics of the victim did not matter either, only the race of the offender. Other information about an incident taken into consideration by citizens was the presence of a weapon (gun or knife) during the commission of a crime and whether the victim was assaulted while a weapon was present during the commission of the assault.

Additionally, research has also been conducted to determine whether there are disparities in sentencing in adult courts for youth who have been transferred to adult court. Put another way, this research examines if youth transferred to adult court actually receive harsher sentences than youth who are not transferred. This is important for understanding the later effects that result from a youth being transferred. Research on this topic has shown that Black and Hispanic youth receive harsher sentences in adult courts than do White youth.[38] Thus, there are not only disparities in the use of waivers, but there are also more disparities later in adult court after a youth has been transferred.

The previously mentioned findings are a serious problem, because even after controlling for factors such as age, gender, criminal history, mitigating circumstances, and many other variables, minority youth are still more likely to be transferred to adult court. Thus, minority youth are being waved at higher rates than their White counterparts, regardless of other factors. These findings support Albonetti's (1991) attribution theory that judges and other actors of the criminal justice system turn to their own notions of what predicts dangerousness.[39] As it applies to this situation, this would suggest that all else being equal, judges perceive minority youth as more dangerous and less amenable to change than White youth. Put simply, this is not justice.

It is also important to point out that some research shows that racial disparities do not exist in the use of waivers.[40],[41] In other words, this research shows that all youth, regardless of race, are transferred to adult court at equal rates. However, the purpose of research is to take the weight of evidence into consideration when making conclusions. Thus, as there is evidence to support both sides, it is safe to conclude that at the very least, race and other demographic factors are playing some role in the decision-making process in some jurisdictions. However, because there is conflicting evidence, more research is needed to make more confident conclusion about how race and other demographic characteristics influence the use of waivers.

A Method to Reduce Disparities in Waivers

One potential method to reduce disparities in the use of waivers is the use of actuarial risk assessment. Actuarial mathematics have been used for nearly 300 years as a procedure to predict the likelihood that an event will occur. For example, these methods can be used to predict the likelihood that an individual will default on their mortgage or that an offender will commit another crime.[42] Traditionally, actuarial science has been used primarily in the financial sector to set insurance premiums and to identify low-risk investment opportunities. For example, when setting health insurance premiums, an insurer will ask its clients if they have a history of heart attack in the family, if they are a smoker, if they have diabetes, and so on. Then, the health insurance company uses this information to set the client's health insurance premium. The health insurer asks its clients all of these questions because it uses that information to predict the risk that the client poses for having a health problem requiring a doctor, which would ultimately cost the health insurance company money. In this instance, the health insurance company is using all of the known correlates of bad health to determine the risk that their client poses for costing them money. A similar process is now being used in the criminal justice field to predict a host of different outcomes.

Risk assessment is used in the criminal justice system most commonly by the corrections system. The corrections system uses risk assessment to determine which delinquents pose the greatest risk for recidivating. This information can then be used to determine the level of supervision that an offender needs to be under and to inform the amount of treatment that an offender might need.[43] To be more specific, research shows that offenders who pose a higher risk for reoffending need a larger dose of treatment than do offenders who pose little risk of recidivating.[44]

Risk assessment tools used in the corrections field use only known correlates of offending to determine the likelihood that an offender will recidivate.[45] These correlates include factors such as criminal history, personality, peer associations, substance abuse problems, etc. Using only empirically validated correlates of offending creates tools that can accurately predict the likelihood that an offender will recidivate. Additionally, using only empirically validated correlates of offending objectifies the decision-making process by making other factors, such as race, absent from the decision-making process.[46] Research has shown that because risk assessment objectifies the decision-making process, disparities in decision-making by criminal justice actors can be reduced.[47] For example, Maloney and Miller (2015) found that in some jurisdictions, the implementation of a risk assessment tool in a court significantly reduced the influence that race had on sentencing decisions.[48] For this reason, risk assessment also has the potential for reducing racial disparities in waiving juveniles to adult court by allowing judges to base their decisions on empirically validated correlates of dangerousness to the community and amenability to change.

Most research on risk assessment equivocally shows that it is an effective means of predicting the likelihood that an offender will reoffend.[49] It is likely that risk assessment tools could also be created to determine the dangerousness a youth poses to the community and their amenability to treatment, as these outcomes are similar to those that criminal justice researchers have already been successful in predicting with risk assessment tools. For this reason, it is worth considering the creation and validation of risk assessment tools that will assess youth to determine those who are best suited to be transferred to adult court. However, it is important to point out that this is under the assumption that waivers are here to stay. It is reasonable to assume that advocating for changing the policy surrounding waivers to adult court would be a nearly insurmountable task. This is why it is being suggested here that risk assessment would be the next best option. If waiver policies are here to stay, a valid method for assessing the most dangerous and least persuadable youth is needed, and risk assessment can serve this purpose.

It is important to point out that risk assessment has its critics. The critiques of risk assessment largely surround the fact that risk assessments classify some youth as high risk who never recidivate and some youth as low risk who recidivate. Since of course it is impossible to predict human behavior perfectly, the question becomes, "is risk assessment better than what we do now, namely, allowing judges and prosecutors to use their discretion?" The answer to this question is quite simple, yes. Nearly all research on actuarial risk assessment concludes that it is far better than human judgement at predicting outcomes in the criminal justice setting.[50] Others also criticize risk assessment for measuring factors that are proxies for certain characteristics of an individual, such as his or her race. For instance, some argue that measuring the risk of the neighborhood in which an offender resides can sometimes be a proxy for race. However, these problems can be easily avoided by not including measures on a risk assessment tool that might be associated with a certain group of people. Thus, while risk assessment has its limitations, if these limitations are recognized and addressed, it could likely greatly improve the decisions made by court officials as to which youth should be waived to adult court, thereby creating a more just system.

Summary

For the most part, research shows that certain groups of youth are waived to adult court at a higher rate than other groups of youth. The most concerning example of this is minority youth being transferred to adult court at a higher rate than their White counterparts. This should be of particular concern for policymakers who seek equality in the application of the law to all youth, regardless of their individual demographic characteristics. For these reasons, certain actions can and should be taken to reduce the disparities seen in the use of waivers. One method reviewed in this chapter, risk assessment, should be considered for reducing said disparities. Follow-up research could tell us whether this method works at reducing disparities in the use of waivers. This evidence could then be used to determine whether disparities are actually being reduced and whether the use of risk assessment should be continued. Additionally, risk assessment could also improve the decision-making process of judges and prosecutors in determining which youth are the most dangerous and least amenable to change. Using evidence-based criteria to inform decision-making in the juvenile court would generally be a good next step in ensuring the best for our youth and the safety of our communities.

Discussion Questions

1. Do you think that risk assessment is a good method for determining which youth are the most dangerous and the least amenable for change? If not, can you think of an alternative method? Why do you think that this alternative could reduce disparities in the use of waivers?
2. What do you think some of the harmful effects of transferring youth to adult court could be on the youth? Do you think that these harmful effects may be particularly acute for some groups of youth more than others?
3. Do you think that juvenile courts should have the option of transferring youth to adult court? Why or why not? Explain the potential benefits and drawbacks of your opinion.
4. Should there be a minimum age cutoff for transferring youth to adult court or should it be dependent on the maturity level of the youth? In other words, is age a good cutoff for determining when youth should be eligible for transfer or is it arbitrary because of individual differences in maturity between youth?
5. Do you think that the disparities seen in the use of waivers are a product of overt bias of court officials or more implicit forms of bias? If you think that it may be a result of implicit biases, do you think that these biases can be controlled or changed? Do you think that risk assessment could restrict the harm done by implicit biases?
6. What do you think might be some of the factors that could be used to predict the dangerousness of a youth and the threat that they pose to public safety by committing another crime?
7. Similar to question 6, what do you think might be some of the factors that could be used to predict a youth's amenability to change?

Notes

1. Guttman, C. R. (1995). Listen to the children: The decision to transfer juveniles to adult court. *Harvard Civil Rights–Civil Liberties Law Review, 30*(2), 507–542.
2. Klein, E. K. (1997). Dennis the Menace or Billy the Kid: An analysis of the role of transfer to criminal court in juvenile justice. *American Criminal Law Review, 35*(2), 371–410.
3. Fontaine, R. G. (2008). Social information processing, subtypes of violence, and a progressive construction of culpability and punishment in juvenile justice. *International Journal of Law and Psychiatry, 31*(2), 136–149.
4. Duffau, H. (2006). Brain plasticity: From pathophysiological mechanisms to therapeutic applications. *Journal of Clinical Neuroscience, 13*(9), 885–897.
5. Fagan, J., & Deschenes, E. P. (1990). Determinants of judicial waiver decisions for violent juvenile offenders. *The Journal of Criminal Law and Criminology, 81*(2), 314–347.
6. Guttman, 1995.
7. *Ibid.*
8. McGowan, A., Hahn, R., Liberman, A., Crosby, A., Fullilove, M., Johnson, R., Moscicki, E., Price, L., Snyder, S., Tuma, F., Lowy, J., Briss, P., Cory, S., & Stone, G. (2007). Effects on violence of laws and policies facilitating the transfer of juveniles from the juvenile justice system to the adult justice system: A systematic review. *American Journal of Preventive Medicine, 32*(4), 7–28.
9. Gaus, G. F. (2000). *Political concepts and political theories.* Boulder, CO: Westview Press.
10. Miller, D. (1999). *Principles of social justice.* Cambridge, MA: Harvard University Press.
11. Rawls, J. (2009). *A theory of justice.* Cambridge, MA: Harvard University Press.
12. Platt, A. M. (1977). *The child savers: The invention of delinquency.* Chicago, IL: University of Chicago Press.
13. Steinberg, L. (2005). Cognitive and affective development in adolescence. *Trends in Cognitive Sciences, 9*(2), 69–74.
14. Fontaine, 2008.
15. Cullen, F. T., & Gilbert, K. E. (2012). *Reaffirming rehabilitation.* New York: Routledge.
16. Spiegler, M. D., & Guevremont, D. C. (1993). *Contemporary behavior therapy.* Pacific Grove, CA: Brooks.
17. However, some may even argue that statutory waivers could be manipulated by lawmakers to be discriminatory for certain groups of youth, by making crimes that are committed at higher rates by those groups eligible for waiver so as to target that specific group.
18. Albonetti, C. A. (1991). An integration of theories to explain judicial discretion. *Social Problems, 38*(2), 247–266.
19. *Ibid.*
20. *Ibid.*
21. Rawls, 2009.
22. *Ibid.*
23. Robison, M. (2013). *What is social justice?* Retrieved from https://gjs.appstate.edu/social-justice-and-human-rights/what-social-justice
24. Miller, 1999.
25. *Ibid.*
26. *Ibid.*
27. *Ibid.*
28. *Ibid.*
29. *Ibid.*
30. Barnes, C. W., & Franz, R. S. (1989). Questionably adult: Determinants and effects of the juvenile waiver decision. *Justice Quarterly, 6*(1), 117–135.
31. Fagan, & Deschenes, 1990.
32. Males, M., & Macallair, D. (2000). *The color of justice: An analysis of Juvenile Adult Court transfers in California.* Report prepared for the Center on Juvenile and Criminal Justice. Washington, DC.
33. Schiraldi, V., & Ziedenberg, J. (1999). *The Florida experiment: An analysis of the impact of granting prosecutors discretion to try juveniles as adults.* Report prepared by the Justice Policy Institute. Washington, DC.
34. Fagan, & Deschenes, 1990.
35. Schiraldi, & Ziedenberg, 1999.
36. Feiler, S., & Sheley, J. (1999). Legal and racial elements of public willingness to transfer juvenile offenders to adult court. *Journal of Criminal Justice, 27*(1), 55–64.
37. Feiler, & Sheley, 1999.
38. Jordan, K. L., & Freiburger, T. L. (2010). Examining the impact of race and ethnicity on the sentencing of juveniles in the adult court. *Criminal Justice Policy Review, 21*(2), 185–201.

39. Albonetti, 1991.
40. Podkopacz, M. R., & Feld, B. C. (1996). The end of the line: An empirical study of judicial waiver. *The Journal of Criminal Law and Criminology, 86*(2), 449–492.
41. Sridharan, S., Greenfield, L., & Blakley, B. (2004). A study of prosecutor certification practice in Virginia. *Criminology & Public Policy, 3*(4), 605–632.
42. Lewin, C. (2001). The creation of actuarial science. *Zentralblatt für Didaktik der Mathematik, 33*(2), 61–66.
43. Andrews, D. A., & Bonta, J. (2010). *The psychology of criminal conduct.* New York: Routledge.
44. Makarios, M., Sperber, K. G., & Latessa, E. J. (2014). Treatment dosage and the risk principle: A refinement and extension. *Journal of Offender Rehabilitation, 53*(5), 334–350.
45. Latessa, E. J., Listwan, S. J., & Koetzle, D. (2013). *What works (and doesn't) in reducing recidivism.* New York: Routledge.
46. Bonta, J. (2007). Offender risk assessment and sentencing. *Canadian Journal of Criminology and Criminal Justice, 49*(4), 519–529.
47. Maloney, C., & Miller, J. (2015). The impact of a risk assessment instrument on juvenile detention decision-making: A check on "perceptual shorthand" and "going rates"? *Justice Quarterly, 32*(5), 900–927.
48. *Ibid.*
49. Andrews, & Bonta, 2010.
50. *Ibid.*

29

MASS INCARCERATION

Ross Kleinstuber

Introduction

Mass incarceration represents one of the most poignant examples of the disjunction between legality and justice. Despite evidence indicating that mass incarceration disproportionately targets minorities while doing little to reduce crime, the United States continues to incarcerate a greater number and proportion of its inhabitants than any other nation on Earth, housing 21.4% of the world's prisoners despite containing just 4.4% of the world's population.[1] This phenomenon cannot be explained by American crime rates, which are comparable to those in other advanced democracies.[2] Rather, the high incarceration rate in the U.S. is better explained as the consequence of political decisions.[3] These decisions were neither necessary nor inevitable, but they did have profoundly detrimental consequences. Because mass incarceration is both ineffective and disproportionate to the harm caused by crime, it exacerbates rather than alleviates human suffering, and since American criminal laws tend to target the behaviors of minorities, mass incarceration has helped to maintain and even strengthen existing racial hierarchies. So, mass incarceration may be legal, but it is far from just. There are other options for dealing with socially harmful behaviors that cause less suffering, are more effective, and are less discriminatory.

Mass Incarceration in Perspective

Mass incarceration is a uniquely American response to crime that is primarily the result of political decisions made since the late 1960s. Despite having crime rates that are similar to those in Europe and Canada,[4] the U.S. ended up with an incarceration rate that far outpaces that of any other industrialized nation.[5] From 1960 to 1990, the U.S. experienced a quadrupling of its incarceration rate, while Germany saw its rate remain flat and Finland experienced a 60% decline in its imprisonment rate.[6] Today, 670 out of every 100,000 Americans and 870 out of every 100,000 American adults are in prison or jail.[7] In neighboring Canada, the adult incarceration rate is only 139 per 100,000 adults,[8] and in Europe, the overall incarceration rate is 192 per 100,000 persons.[9] The European nation with the highest incarceration rate is Russia at 445 per 100,000 persons.[10]

The reason for these disparities is that the U.S. punishes far more punitively than other nations by sending a greater proportion of offenders to prison and for longer periods of time. From 1995 to 2000, the U.S. sentenced nearly 70% of convicted adults to prison; in Canada, that number was less than 34%, and in England and Wales, Finland, and Germany, it was under 10%.[11] The average sentence length in the U.S. in 2006 was 63 months, compared to 36 months in Australia, 13 months in England and Wales, 6–12 months in Germany, 10 months in Finland, and 4 months in Canada.[12] Even comparing offenders convicted of the same crime, the U.S. sentences far more punitively than do other advanced democracies.[13] For example, U.S. federal law mandates a 10-year minimum sentence for selling one kilogram of heroin, compared to six months in England.[14] The average sentence for drug *possession* in the U.S. is four *years*.[15] On top of that, the U.S. relies on life sentences more than any other country. Life without parole (LWOP) sentences are banned in Europe,[16] and several European and Latin American nations have even abolished life with parole.[17] Yet, in the U.S., one in every nine prisoners—nearly 162,000 people—is serving a life sentence, and nearly a third of those (53,290 people) are serving LWOP. There are also an additional 44,000 prisoners serving sentences of 50 years or more.[18] The U.S. even utilizes life sentences for first-time, nonviolent offenders, and it is the only nation in the world that sentences children to LWOP.[19]

It has not always been like this. In fact, for most of American history, incarceration rates were relatively low, hovering around 100 sentenced inmates per 100,000 persons for the first three-quarters of the 20th century.[20] Yet, in the 1970s, the U.S. declared a war on crime and drugs, which led to an explosion in incarceration rates.[21] In 1972, there were 95 sentenced inmates in federal and state prison for every 100,000 persons. That number would increase five-fold over the next four decades, peaking at 506 per 100,000 in 2008 before beginning a slow decline to 458 in 2015.[22] The primary reason for this surge was a change in sentencing policies. The average sentence length of federal inmates in the U.S. more than doubled from 1988 to 2012.[23] At the state level, average sentence lengths increased by nearly one-third from 1993 to 2013 while the likelihood of being admitted to prison following an arrest also increased.[24]

This punishment strategy is incredibly expensive, and it has created an enormous amount of needless suffering. Correctional spending in the U.S. has been growing at three times the rate of educational spending since 1979, and in 2012, it surpassed $70 billion.[25] This money is being spent to lock people in cages, many of whom either pose little public safety risk or would be better served in other environments. For example, 12 out of every 13 federal inmates and nearly half of all state prisoners are serving time for nonviolent offenses,[26] while more than half of those in prison and nearly two-thirds of those in jail are mentally ill.[27] Prison usually exacerbates rather than alleviates mental illness, yet there are 10 times more mentally ill persons in prisons and jails than there are in state psychiatric hospitals.[28] Furthermore, by causing prison overcrowding, mass incarceration contributes to inhumane conditions of confinement that serve to increase the amount of unnecessary suffering.[29] Overcrowding has been linked to increases in prison violence, sexual assault, suicide, and prisoner abuse.[30] It also contributes to a decline in basic services like medical care, mental health counseling, and rehabilitative programs for inmates.[31]

Effectiveness of Mass Incarceration

Now, this crime-fighting strategy might nevertheless still be justified if there was some evidence that it reduced crime or made society safer, but as the National Research Council reported, "Nearly every leading survey of the deterrence literature" since 1978 has concluded that higher rates of imprisonment and lengthy prison sentences do not reduce crime.[32] Similarly, "the great majority of studies" on recidivism indicate that the prison experience has either no effect or potentially a criminogenic effect on future offending.[33] By the 1990s, even conservative scholars such as James Q. Wilson, whose 1975 book *Thinking About Crime* provided the theoretical underpinnings for the use of harsher punishments, admitted, "It would be foolhardy to explain this drop in crime by the rise in imprisonment rates."[34]

On the contrary, many scholars have suggested that mass incarceration may actually make the crime problem worse. First, spending money on prison diverts resources from other programs, such as education, drug treatment, job training, and public assistance that have been shown to reduce crime.[35] Second, by sending people to prison, society marginalizes and stigmatizes them, making it harder for them to acquire employment, housing, or public assistance, all of which increases their propensity to commit future offenses.[36] Third, mass incarceration reduces opportunities for prisoners to access rehabilitative programs that reduce future offending by providing them with the education, skills, and treatment needed to live crime-free lifestyles.[37] Fourth, by depriving inmates of contact with non-criminal peers and forcing them to associate with other offenders, prisons tend to socialize inmates into a criminal lifestyle.[38]

Finally, and perhaps most significantly, the impact of mass incarceration extends far beyond the individuals who experience the inside of a prison. It decimates entire communities. By weakening community and family structures, sapping entire communities of human and social capital, increasing social disorganization, eroding economic strength, and reducing the amount of informal social control, mass incarceration creates conditions that are conducive to crime.[39] As Donald Braman's ethnographic work has revealed, the lost income, social isolation, and distortion of family structures caused by mass incarceration has in many ways harmed society more than criminal offenders have.[40] It is well documented that children with incarcerated parents suffer from the experience and are thus more likely to experience depression,[41] have difficulty in school,[42] and turn to crime themselves.[43] The stigma of criminality also impedes job opportunities and encourages employers to relocate, which hinders economic mobility and makes crime more appealing.[44] Thus, entire communities are harmed by mass incarceration.

Mass incarceration also fails to serve victims. Trials and punishment tend to marginalize and disempower victims,[45] and rather than producing closure or satisfaction, vengeance has been shown to increase aggression by causing the victim to fixate on the offender.[46] The needs of victims are actually best met through dialogue, which creates a feeling of empowerment and allows victims to seek restitution rather than retribution.[47] It has been repeatedly shown that victims who participate in victim-offender dialogue have more satisfaction with the justice system and lower levels of fear.[48] Forgiveness, rather than vengeance, has been shown to have beneficial effects for victims, and victims who receive an apology or restitution are better able to forgive and report lower levels of fear and anger.[49]

Mass Incarceration and Discrimination

The inhumanity and injustice of mass incarceration becomes even more glaring when one considers its racial dynamics. In fact, these racial dynamics may explain why it took root and blossomed despite the stunning lack of evidence that it reduces crime and the very real possibility that it makes crime worse. The history and impact of mass incarceration suggest that it was never intended to reduce crime in the first place. Rather, as Loïc Wacquant has pointed out, it was designed to contain and control a "supernumerary" and "dangerous" Black population in the wake of the successes of the civil rights movement.[50] Mass incarceration may be disguised in race-neutral language like "law and order" or "tough on crime," but in reality it has served as a form of racial control. Mass incarceration may not look like Jim Crow or slavery, but it performs the same role of maintaining White supremacy as those earlier institutions did.[51] As such, it is *the* civil rights issue of the early 21st century.

It is no coincidence that the explosion in the use of incarceration described above began shortly after the successes of the civil rights movement in the 1960s or that it has disproportionately targeted people of color. This was a deliberate public policy choice made by Republicans in an effort to win over disaffected White southern Democrats following the passage of the Civil Rights Act through the use of coded racial messaging. During the civil rights movement, segregationists equated the protestors with the crime and disorder of the era. In this way, crime came to be racially defined. Therefore, Republicans were able to appeal to the racist sentiments of southern Whites by referring to "crime" and "law and order."[52] As President Nixon's domestic policy chief, John Ehrlichman, explained in a 1994 interview:

> We knew we couldn't make it illegal to be either against the war or black, but by getting the public to associate the hippies with marijuana and blacks with heroin, and then criminalizing both heavily, we could disrupt those communities. We could arrest their leaders, raid their homes, break up their meetings, and vilify them night after night on the evening news. Did we know we were lying about the drugs? Of course we did.[53]

This same strategy was successfully employed by Republicans for a generation before Bill Clinton wrestled the issue of "law and order" away from Republicans in 1992 by adopting the same racialized rhetoric and tough-on-crime policies.[54] The result of all this was less a crime-fighting strategy than "a violent assault on racial progress made during the civil rights era."[55] A slew of laws and policies targeting the behavior of poor minorities—such as the 1986 Anti-Drug Abuse Act, which penalized possession of crack cocaine (a drug common among poor minorities) at 100 times the rate of powder cocaine (which is more common among affluent Whites), even though both forms of the drug have the same pharmacological effects[56]—have been enacted since the 1970s. On top of this, policing and sentencing practices have also disproportionately targeted minorities.[57] Studies consistently find that police are more likely to stop and search Black motorists and pedestrians even though they are less likely to have contraband.[58] Despite similar usage rates, African Americans are 3.73 times more likely to be arrested for marijuana possession than Whites are,[59] and although surveys consistently indicate that all racial groups use illicit drugs at roughly the same rate, Black men are incarcerated in state prisons on drug charges at 13 times the rate of White men.[60] Currently, 78% of those serving time for drug offenses in federal prison and 59% of state inmates serving time for drug offenses are Black or Hispanic,[61] even though these two groups combine to account for less than 31% of the U.S. population.[62] When it comes to sentencing, research at both the federal and state level has consistently found that non-Whites are more likely to be sent to prison and receive longer sentences than similarly situated White offenders.[63]

Predictably, these practices have had a tragic effect on Black and Brown communities. Black adults are incarcerated at 5.6 times the rate of White adults, and Hispanic adults are incarcerated at 2.6 times the White adult rate.[64] The U.S. now imprisons a larger percentage of its minority population than any other nation in the world; even at the heart of apartheid, South Africa imprisoned a smaller percentage of its Black population than the U.S. does today.[65] There are currently more African Americans under correctional supervision than there were enslaved in 1850.[66] In 2003, the Bureau of Justice Statistics (BJS) estimated that under then-current trends, one out of every three Black males born in 2001 would go to prison during his lifetime, compared to one out of every six Hispanic males and one out of every 17 white males.[67] (It is worth noting that the Black male incarceration rate declined by 26% from 2001 to 2015, and the BJS has not issued a revised estimate since 2003.) These disparities grow even more when looking at prisoners sentenced to life: non-Whites represent more than two-thirds of the lifer population and nearly five-sixths of those serving LWOP for nonviolent crimes in the U.S.[68]

As such, the devastating impact that mass incarceration has on entire communities is even more acutely felt in poor communities of color. In many cities, more than 75% of young Black males will serve time in prison,[69] and due primarily to early death and mass incarceration, many communities of color experience dramatic gender imbalances that contribute to out-of-wedlock births, single motherhood, domestic violence, family disruption, and a lack of human capital.[70] Whereas there are 99 White males for every 100 White females aged 25–54 in free society, there are only 83 Black men for every 100 Black women in the same age group, and the ratio is worse many cities. The majority of Blacks live in locations with significantly fewer men than women, while the majority of Whites live in areas with near gender parity.[71] This also means that Black children are far more likely to experience the incarceration of a parent and all of the negative consequences that come along with that: 1 in 28 American children overall have an incarcerated parent, while 1 in 9 African American children do.[72] In this regard, mass incarceration has served as an impediment to social mobility and a contributor to crime and violence within African American communities, which has helped to sustain racial inequality.

Summary

In this chapter, it has been shown that the U.S. relies on incarceration far more than any other nation, and that this approach is demonstrably ineffective as a crime-fighting strategy, contributes to the inhumane treatment of convicted offenders, and functions to maintain White supremacy. Given this evidence, mass incarceration can be described as nothing less than "a crime of the state, the significance of which is far greater than the petty crimes committed by many of today's offenders."[73] However, there is a path forward. There are methods of dealing with crime that are both more effective and more humane. First, preventing crime by alleviating poverty, inequality, unemployment, and other social conditions conducive to crime is more cost-effective than punishing crime after the fact, so investing in education, welfare programs, job training, and community-based drug treatment programs would do more to reduce crime—and be more humane—than harsh prison sentences.[74] Second, fewer lawbreakers should be incarcerated and for shorter periods of time. As documented above, this is the norm in other Western democracies, and they have not experienced higher crime rates because of it. Many nonviolent and drug offenders who are currently sentenced to prison pose little public safety risk and could safely be given community supervision. Those with mental illnesses would be better served with mental health services than prison,[75] and since certainty of punishment is a more important deterrent than severity,[76] the length of sentences should be shortened (which would also reduce the number of erroneous guilty pleas). Even for violent crime, restorative justice approaches that focus on making amends to the victim would benefit many victims and offenders more than retributive punishment. In Australia, victims reported higher satisfaction with restorative justice conferences than with traditional court procedures, and both victims and offenders perceived these conferences to be fairer.[77]

Finally, for those who are sent to prison, the conditions of confinement should be more humane and better prepare them to re-enter society. In Norway, for example, the conditions inside prison are designed to be as similar to the conditions outside prison as possible.[78] There are no bars, and inmates are given their own room with a shower, toilet, refrigerator, desk, and flat-screen TV.[79] They are allowed to wear their own clothes, prepare their own meals, and participate in numerous leisure, educational, and work activities.[80] The prisons are designed to minimize the psychological stress of incarceration and reduce conflict. Most prisons house fewer than 50 people, and the staff try to prevent violence through mediation sessions.[81] In an effort to maintain social bonds, the prisoners are housed close their families and given access to private visiting rooms, and families are allowed to stay overnight in a house located in the prison.[82] Thirty percent of Norway's prisons even allow prisoners to keep their outside jobs and commute to work daily while serving time.[83] The correctional officers are also more like social workers than enforcers, existing to help inmates get the services they need. They socialize and engage with inmates, sharing meals, playing cards, making music, and participating in athletic activities together. They treat inmates with respect and attempt to build relationships in order to help prepare inmates for life after they are released.[84] As the governor of Norway's Bastoy Prison put it, "It's really very simple: Treat people like dirt and they will be dirt. Treat them like human beings and they will act like human beings."[85]

Although measurement differences make it difficult to make cross-national comparisons of recidivism rates, the evidence from the U.S. suggests that when inmates are given drug treatment, job training, and education; able to maintain strong family and community ties; and able to obtain stable employment upon release, they are less likely to recidivate.[86] The data on the few American jails that have attempted to minimize the feeling of institutionalization through designs similar to the Norwegian model show that they have less violence and lower recidivism rates.[87] Recently, the head of North Dakota's prison system decided to implement changes to the system inspired by a tour of Norway's prisons, and the result has been less violence within the prisons.[88]

Therefore, we have a choice. We can either double down a failed, inhumane, and racially biased approach to combatting crime or demonstrate a commitment to social justice by reimagining the purpose and function of criminal sanctions. Bipartisan opposition to mass incarceration and support for criminal justice reform has emerged in recent years,[89] but the election of Donald Trump, who used coded racist rhetoric while voicing support for tougher criminal justice policies during the 2016 presidential campaign, threatens those reform efforts.[90] Therefore, it is imperative that activists from both sides of the aisle continue to agitate for a more fiscally responsible, effective, humane, and racially neutral justice system. We cannot continue to rip people from their communities, traumatize them, deprive them of human capital, return them to their communities, and then expect them to succeed.

Discussion Questions

1. Why do you think prison is so ineffective at reducing crime?
2. Why do you think the U.S. chose the path of mass incarceration?
3. What role do you think race played in the decision to get "tough on crime"? Can you imagine anything remotely similar to mass incarceration happening to White men?
4. In what ways has mass incarceration helped to sustain or even exacerbate racial inequality? Do minority groups *benefit* in any way from mass incarceration?
5. What are the benefits and weaknesses of mass incarceration compared to the responses to crime utilized in other advanced democracies?
6. Should prisoners be afforded the luxuries they are given in nations like Norway? Why or why not?
7. What crime-fighting strategies should the U.S. adopt going forward? Is there a better way to reduce crime, and can the U.S. undo some of the harms caused by mass incarceration?

Notes

1. Walmsley, R. (2016). *World prison population list*, 11th ed. Retrieved from World Prison Brief Website www.prisonstudies.org/sites/default/files/resources/downloads/world_prison_population_list_11th_edition_0.pdf. Technically, Seychelles has a higher incarceration rate, but because the population of Seychelles is so small (92,000), a small change in the number of people incarcerated leads to a large change in the incarceration rate.
2. Beckett, K., & Sasson, T. (2004). *The politics of injustice: Crime and punishment in America*, 2nd ed. Thousand Oaks, CA: Sage; Donziger, S. R. (Ed.). (1996). *The real war on crime: The report of the National Criminal Justice Commission*. New York: Harper Perennial; van Dijk, J., van Kesteren, J., & Smit, P. (2008). *Criminal victimisation in international perspective: Key findings from the 2004–2005 ICVS and EU ICS*. Retrieved from http://wp.unil.ch/icvs/files/2012/11/ICVS2004_051.pdf
3. Beckett, & Sasson, 2004.
4. *Ibid.*; Donziger, 1996; van Dijk, van Kesteren, & Smit, 2008.
5. Walmsley, 2016.
6. Alexander, M. (2012). *The new Jim Crow: Mass incarceration in the age of color blindness*, revised ed. New York: The New Press, p. 7.
7. Kaebble, D., & Glaze, L. (2016). *Correctional populations in the United States, 2015* (Report No. NCJ 250374). Retrieved from Bureau of Justice Statistics Website www.bjs.gov/content/pub/pdf/cpus15.pdf
8. Reitano, J. (2017, March 1). *Adult correctional statistics in Canada 2015/2016*. Retrieved from www.statcan.gc.ca/pub/85-002-x/2017001/article/14700-eng.htm
9. Walmsley, 2016.
10. *Ibid.*

11. Justice Policy Institute. (2011). *Finding direction: Expanding criminal justice options by considering policies of other nations*. Retrieved from www.justicepolicy.org/uploads/justicepolicy/documents/sentencing.pdf
12. *Ibid.*
13. *Ibid.*
14. Alexander, 2012.
15. Bonczar, T. P., Hughes, T. A., Wilson, D. J., & Ditton, P. M. (2011). *National corrections reporting program: Sentence length of state prisoners, by offense, admission type, sex, and race*. Retrieved from www.bjs.gov/index.cfm?ty=pbdetail&iid=2056
16. *Case of Vinter and Others v. the United Kingdom*, 66069/09, 130/10, and 3896/10 (European Court of Human Rights July 9, 2013).
17. Henry, J. S. (2012). Death-in-prison sentences: Overutilized and underscrutinized. In C. J. Ogletree & A. Sarat (Eds.), *Life without parole: America's new death penalty?* (pp. 66–95). New York: NYU Press.
18. Nellis, A. (2017). *Still life: America's increasing use of life and long-term sentences*. Retrieved from The Sentencing Project Website www.sentencingproject.org/publications/still-life-americas-increasing-use-life-long-term-sentences/
19. Henry, 2012; Nellis, 2017.
20. Cahalan, M. W. (1986). *Historical corrections statistics in the United States, 1850–1984* (Report No. NCJ 102529). Retrieved from Bureau of Justice Statistics Website www.bjs.gov/content/pub/pdf/hcsus5084.pdf
21. Alexander, 2012; Beckett, & Sasson, 2004.
22. Carson, E. A., & Anderson, E. (2016). *Prisoners in 2015* (Report No. NCJ 250229). Retrieved from Bureau of Justice Statistics Website www.bjs.gov/content/pub/pdf/p15.pdf
23. Pew Charitable Trusts. (2015). *Prison time surges for federal inmates*. Retrieved from www.pewtrusts.org/~/media/assets/2015/11/prison_time_surges_for_federal_inmates.pdf
24. Carson, E. A., & Sabol, W. J. (2016). *Aging of the state prison population, 1993–2013* (Report No. NCJ 248766), pp. 19–22. Retrieved from Bureau of Justice Statistics Website www.bjs.gov/content/pub/pdf/aspp9313.pdf
25. Stullich, S., Morgan, I., & Schak, O. (2016). *State and local expenditures on corrections and education*. Retrieved from US Department of Education Website www2.ed.gov/rschstat/eval/other/expenditures-corrections-education/brief.pdf
26. Carson, & Anderson, 2016.
27. James, D. J., & Glaze, L. E. (2006). *Mental health problems of prison and jail inmates* (Report No. NCJ 213600). Retrieved from Bureau of Justice Statistics Website www.bjs.gov/content/pub/pdf/mhppji.pdf
28. Torrey, E. F., Zdanowicz, M. T., Kennard, A. D., Lamb, H. R., Eslinger, D. F., Biasotti, M. C., & Fuller, D. A. (2014). *The treatment of persons with mental illness in prisons and jails: A state survey*. Retrieved from Treatment Advocacy Center Website www.treatmentadvocacycenter.org/storage/documents/treatment-behind-bars/treatment-behind-bars.pdf
29. Simon, J. (2014). *Mass incarceration on trial: A remarkable court decision and the future of prisons in America*. New York: New Press.
30. Government Accountability Office. (2012). *Growing inmate crowding negatively affects inmates, staff, and infrastructure* (Report No. GAO-12-743). Retrieved from www.gao.gov/assets/650/648123.pdf; Kupers, T. A. (1996). Trauma and its sequelae in male prisoners: Effects of confinement, overcrowding, and diminished services. *American Journal of Orthopsychiatry, 66*(2), 189–196; Lahm, K. F. (2008). Inmate-on-inmate assault: A multilevel examination of prison violence. *Criminal Justice and Behavior, 35*(1), 120–137; Simon, 2014.
31. *Brown v. Plata*, 563 U.S. 492 (2011); Kupers, 1996; Simon, 2014.
32. Travis, J., Western, B., & Redbum, S. (2014). *The growth of incarceration in the United States: Exploring causes and consequences*. Washington, DC: National Academies Press, pp. 90, 155–156.
33. Nagin, D. S., Cullen, F. T., & Jonson, C. L. (2009). Imprisonment and reoffending. *Crime and Justice, 38*(1), 115–200, 178.
34. Wilson, J. Q. (1994, September). What to do about crime. *Commentary*. Retrieved from www.commentary-magazine.com/articles/what-to-do-about-crime/
35. Beckett, & Sasson, 2004; Donziger, 1996.
36. Alexander, 2012; Shannon, S., & Uggen, C. (2013, February 19). *Visualizing punishment*. Retrieved from https://thesocietypages.org/papers/visualizing-punishment/
37. Government Accountability Office, 2012; Kupers, 1996; Kupers, T. (2016). How to create madness in prison. In J. Casella, J. Ridgeway, & S. Shourd (Eds.), *Hell is a very small place: Voices from solitary confinement* (pp. 163–178). New York: New Press.
38. Cullen, F. T., Johnson, C. L., & Nagin, D. S. (2011). Prisons do not reduce recidivism: The high cost of ignoring science. *The Prison Journal, 91*(3), 48S–65S; Neminski, M. (2014). The professionalization of crime: How prisons create more criminals. *The Core Journal, 23*, 81–92.

39. Clear, T. R. (2007). *Imprisoning communities: How mass incarceration makes communities worse.* New York: Oxford University Press; Rose, D. R., & Clear, T. R. (1998). Incarceration, social capital, and crime: Implications for social disorganization theory. *Criminology, 36*(3), 441–480.

40. Braman, D. (2004). *Doing time on the outside: Incarceration and family life in urban America.* Ann Arbor, MI: University of Michigan Press.

41. Turney, K. (2014). Stress proliferation across generations? Examining the relationship between parental incarceration and childhood health. *Journal of Health and Social Behavior, 55*(3), 302–319.

42. Johnson, R. C. (2009). Ever-increasing levels of parental incarceration and the consequences for children. In S. Raphael & M. Stoll (Eds.), *Do prisons make us safer? The benefits and costs of the prison boom* (pp. 177–206). New York: Russell Sage Foundation.

43. Aaron, L., & Dallaire, D. (2010). Parental incarceration and multiple risk experiences: Effects on family dynamics and children's delinquency. *Journal of Youth & Adolescence, 39*(12), 1471–1484; Murray, J., Bijleveld, C. C. J. H., Farrington, D. P., & Loeber, R. (2014). *Effects of parental incarceration on children: Cross-national comparative studies.* Washington, DC: American Psychological Association; Pew Charitable Trusts. (2010). *Collateral costs: Incarceration's effect on economic mobility.* Retrieved from www.pewtrusts.org/~/media/legacy/uploadedfiles/pcs_assets/2010/collateralcosts1pdf.pdf

44. Pew Charitable Trusts, 2010.

45. Dreisinger, B. (2016). *Incarceration nations: A journey to justice in prisons around the world.* New York: Other Press, p. 82.

46. Wilson, K. M., Wilson, T. D., & Gilbert, D. T. (2008). The paradoxical consequences of revenge. *Journal of Personality and Social Psychology, 95*(6), 1316–1324.

47. Dreisinger, 2016, p. 82.

48. *Ibid.*, p. 82.

49. *Ibid.*, p. 83.

50. Wacquant, L. (2000). The new 'peculiar institution': On the prison as surrogate ghetto. *Theoretical Criminology, 4*(3), 377–389.

51. Alexander, 2012.

52. *Ibid.*; Beckett, & Sasson, 2004.

53. Baum, D. (2016, April). Legalize it all: How to win the war on drugs. *Harper's.* Retrieved from https://harpers.org/archive/2016/04/legalize-it-all/

54. Alexander, 2012; Beckett, & Sasson, 2004.

55. Dreisinger, 2016, p. 15.

56. Donziger, 1996.

57. Alexander, 2012.

58. *Ibid.*; New York Civil Liberties Union. (2014). *Stop-and-frisk during the Bloomberg Administration.* Retrieved from www.nyclu.org/files/publications/08182014_Stop-and-Frisk_Briefer_2002-2013_final.pdf

59. Edwards, E., Bunting, W., & Garcia, L. (2013). *The war on marijuana in black and white: Billions of dollars wasted on racially biased arrests.* Retrieved from American Civil Liberties Union Website www.aclu.org/sites/default/files/field_document/1114413-mj-report-rfs-rel1.pdf

60. Alexander, 2012; Substance Abuse and Mental Health Services Administration. (2014). *Results from the 2013 National Survey on Drug Use and Health: Summary of National Findings* (NSDUH Series H-48, HHS Publication No. (SMA) 14-4863). Retrieved from www.samhsa.gov/data/sites/default/files/NSDUHresultsPDF-WHTML2013/Web/NSDUHresults2013.pdf

61. Carson, & Anderson, 2016.

62. Quick Facts. (n.d.). Retrieved June 14, 2017, from www.census.gov/quickfacts/

63. American Civil Liberties Union. (2014). *Written submission of the American Civil Liberties Union on racial disparities in sentencing.* Retrieved from www.aclu.org/sites/default/files/assets/141027_iachr_racial_disparities_aclu_submission_0.pdf; Franklin, T. W. (2015). Race and ethnicity effects in federal sentencing: A propensity score analysis. *Justice Quarterly, 32*(4), 653–679; Kansal, T. (2005). *Racial disparity in sentencing: A review of the literature.* Washington, DC: The Sentencing Project; Saris, P. B., Carr, Jr., W. B., Jackson, K. B., Hinojosa, R. C., Howell, B. A., Friedrich, D. L., . . . Wroblewski, J. J. (2012). *Report on the continuing impact of United States v. Booker on federal sentencing.* Retrieved from United States Sentencing Commission Website www.ussc.gov/sites/default/files/pdf/news/congressional-testimony-and-reports/booker-reports/2012-booker/Part_A.pdf; Ulmer, J. T. (2012). Recent developments and new directions in sentencing research. *Justice Quarterly, 29*(1), 1–40.

64. Carson, & Anderson, 2016.

65. Alexander, 2012.

66. Dreisinger, 2016, p. 8.

67. Bonczar, T. P. (2003). *Prevalence of imprisonment in the U.S. population, 1974–2001* (Report No. NCJ 197976). Retrieved from Bureau of Justice Statistics Website www.bjs.gov/content/pub/pdf/piusp01.pdf

68. American Civil Liberties Union, 2014; Nellis, 2017, pp. 14–15.
69. Braman, 2004.
70. Wolfers, J., Leonhardt, D., & Qualy, K. (2015, April 20). 1.5 million missing black men. *New York Times.* Retrieved from www.nytimes.com
71. *Ibid.*
72. Pew Charitable Trusts, 2010.
73. Beckett, & Sasson, 2004, p. 190.
74. *Ibid.*; Donziger, 1996.
75. Torrey, Zdanowicz, Kennard, Lamb, Eslinger, Biasotti, & Fuller, 2014.
76. Nagin, D. S. (2013). Deterrence in the twenty-first century: A review of the evidence. In M. Tonry (Ed.), *Crime and justice: A review of research* (Vol. 42, pp. 199–263). Chicago, IL: University of Chicago Press.
77. Beckett, & Sasson, 2004.
78. Benforado, A. (2015). *Unfair: The new science of criminal injustice.* New York: Crown, p. 233; Dreisinger, 2016, p. 273; Gentleman, A. (2012, May 18). Inside Halden, the most humane prison in the world. *The Guardian.* Retrieved from www.theguardian.com
79. Benforado, 2015; Benko, J. (2015, March 26). The radical humaneness of Norway's Halden Prison. *New York Times.* Retrieved from www.nytimes.com; Dreisinger, 2016; Gentleman, 2012.
80. Benforado, 2015, p. 232; Gentleman, 2012.
81. Benko, 2015; Dreisinger, 2016, p. 273.
82. Benforado, 2015, pp. 232–234; Dreisinger, 2016, pp. 273–288; Gentleman, 2012.
83. Dreisigner, 2015, p. 276.
84. Benforado, 2015; Benko, 2015; Dreisinger, 2015; Gentleman, 2012.
85. Quoted in Dreisinger, 2016, p. 277.
86. Beckett, & Sasson, 2004; Benforado, 2015; Berg, M. T., & Huebner, B. M. (2011). Reentry and the ties that bind: An examination of social ties, employment, and recidivism. *Justice Quarterly, 28*(2), 382–410; Dreisinger, 2016, p. 283.
87. Benko, 2015.
88. Slater, D. (2017, July/August). North Dakota's Norway experiment. *Mother Jones.* Retrieved from www.motherjones.com/crime-justice/2017/07/north-dakota-norway-prisons-experiment/
89. Dagan, D., & Teles, S. (2016). *Prison break: Why conservatives turned against mass incarceration.* New York: Oxford University Press; Ford, M. (2015, February 25). Can bipartisanship end mass incarceration? A major shift in criminal justice is coming, but will it be enough? *The Atlantic.* Retrieved from www.theatlantic.com/politics/archive/2015/02/can-bipartisanship-end-mass-incarceration/386012/; Green, D. A. (2015). US penal-reform catalysts, drivers, and prospects. *Punishment & Society, 17*(3), 271–298.
90. For example, see ABC News. (2016, July 22). *Full Text: Donald Trump's 2016 republican national convention speech.* Retrieved from http://abcnews.go.com/Politics/full-text-donald-trumps-2016-republican-national-convention/story?id=40786529; Jacobs, B. (2016, August 22). Trump: Inner cities run by Democrats are more dangerous than war zones. *The Guardian.* Retrieved from www.theguardian.com

30

SOCIAL SECURITY FRAUD VERSUS WHITE-COLLAR CRIME

Petter Gottschalk and Lars Gunnesdal

Introduction

The police have limited resources to investigate economic crime. The police have to prioritize their resources by dropping a large portion of cases (Brooks & Button, 2011). The question we ask here is, should law enforcement primarily dismiss social security fraud cases or white-collar crime cases?

The two types of cases are in many ways two extremes on the scale of economic criminals. While social security fraud is committed by people who basically need financial help from the community to live decent lives, white-collar crime is committed by individuals in the upper echelon of society, who abuse their positions to enrich themselves or organizations they are associated with (Gottschalk, 2016).

In this chapter, we apply social conflict theory to discuss the issue of priorities in law enforcement. First, two cases are presented, one social security fraudster and one white-collar criminal in Norway. Next, white-collar crime and chief executive officers are described. Then, social conflict theory and white-collar crime are presented. Finally, social conflict theory is discussed in terms of social security fraud versus white-collar crime.

A Social Security Fraudster

She was 73 years old and sentenced to prison for one year and six months by the Agder court of appeals in Norway in 2015. She had been paid a disability pension of just under 1 million kroner over five and a half years, without disclosing that she once had revenues from fortunetelling totaling 1.7 million Norwegian kroner (US$212.00). Her income as a fortuneteller was not reported to the authorities.

She worked as a fortuneteller in a business that provided fortune telling by telephone. The fortune telling was marketed in newspapers and magazines. Each fortuneteller had a unique artist name and a dedicated phone number. Callers were charged by elapsed time and paid in most cases over the phone bill. The per-minute price was 7 kroner (88 cents).

When she started to work as a fortuneteller, she contacted her local social security office and asked what she was allowed to earn in addition to her disability pension. She was told that she could make no more than 5,000 kroner ($625) per month. She followed instructions received from Nav (the Norwegian social security authority), and she was awarded 5,000 kroner per month for about 10 months per year from startup until she went over on retirement after six year. The compensation of 5,000 kroner was awarded to her regardless of how much she actually made as a fortuneteller. She did not work very much, partly because she had to care for her mother for a long time. After retirement, she worked legally and had earnings by the hour. Her salary was taxed in the normal way. She denied that she received any funds beyond the specified amount of 5,000 kroner per month.

The Agder (2015) court of appeals, however, found it proven beyond any reasonable and sensible doubt that she received remuneration at her fortune-telling business beyond the 5,000 crowns that were reported to tax authorities and Nav. The court of appeals disregarded the possibility that other persons may have used the same phone number, or that there had been confusion of different fortunetellers.

The appellate court found it proven that for many years she conducted fortune telling that was paid for in cash from the business, which is why it was not registered in bank transfers or bank deposits.

She told the court that she lived very soberly, had only one holiday trip in 23 years, and owned an older car bought with borrowed money. She said she borrowed money from the bank for renovation and repairs of residential property, that she had an open and straightforward relationship with the bank, and that she communicated with Nav on the topic of income for work in addition to disability pension.

Larvik district court also sentenced her to imprisonment for one year and six months. The judge wrote in the verdict:

> As a general rule, the sentencing court emphasizes the need for deterrent mechanisms regarding social security fraud and tax evasion. On social security fraud, which is the most serious offence by the defendant, the Supreme Court has emphasized that such cases involve abuse of key welfare benefits that largely is based on confidence that recipients provide an honest and correct description of their economic and social situation. For many, the barrier against committing this kind of crime is low, since it is society at large and not individuals who is a victim of the crime. It is therefore essential that this type of violation is met with a tactile reaction. This is particularly true in the case of fraud in the magnitude that we are facing here.

The court of appeals endorsed the district court's standpoint. The court referred to a number of previous convictions for social security fraud, in which offenders were sentenced to 10 months imprisonment for fraud of 650,000 kroner; one year of imprisonment for fraud of 1.1 million; one year and four months for fraud of one million; and one year and six months for fraud of two million.

The appellate court wrote, "even if the defendant has experienced many dramatic and sad events in her immediate surroundings over the years, the court does not find any grounds to argue that there are mitigating circumstances in this case."

A claim of 993,994 kroner was submitted by Nav for payment of compensation. Nav upheld, and she was sentenced to pay the amount to Nav.

A White-Collar Criminal

He was 63 years old and was sentenced to prison for one year and four months by the Gulating court of appeals in Norway in 2016. He established a company in Scotland and owned two million shares in the company. Six million new shares were issued to new shareholders. All shares were transferred to a new company in Cyprus. He then created a company in the Isle of Man and was the sole shareholder in the company. He transferred all his shares from Cyprus to the Isle of Man.

The same year, he transferred ownership of an apartment building in Bergen in Norway from one company to another, whereupon he entered into a lease agreement for the building with the company in Scotland.

The Supreme Court dismissed his appeal, and the sentence for tax evasion became final. He was convicted of having evaded 29 million Norwegian kroner (US$3.6 million) in income and 200 million ($25 million) in assets from taxation. Evaded income and assets were related to shareholdings in foreign companies registered in Scotland, Cyprus, and the Isle of Man.

The appellate court of Gulating (2016) found that he had deliberately withheld relevant income and assets from taxation in Norway, and that he had been entirely absent in relation to Norwegian tax authorities when it came to documentation relating to income and assets abroad.

As far as sentencing is concerned, the court found that general deterrence considerations indicate a strict sanction, and that the appropriate punishment was basically jail for three years. Due to long processing in the criminal justice system, however, the penalty was reduced by one year, and eight months were suspended.

He was a civil engineer with a master's degree from the University of Trondheim in Norway and active in the oil industry all his professional life. He was the CEO of several drilling companies. He also established and operated oil-related companies in Norway.

White-Collar Crime

White-collar crime is committed for financial gain in an organizational setting by deviant behavior. The motive for crime is profit that can help avoid threats or help reach desired goals. The location for crime is the organization to which the offender belongs or is associated. The behavior for crime deviates from normal behavior (Sutherland, 1949).

The typical profile of a white-collar criminal includes the following attributes (Benson & Simpson, 2015):

- The person has a high social status and considerable influence, enjoys respect and trust, and belongs to the elite.
- The elite generally have more knowledge, money, and prestige and occupy higher positions than do others in the population.
- Privileges and authority by the elite are often not visible or transparent, but nevertheless known to everybody.
- The elite can be found in business, public administration, politics, congregations, and many other sectors in society.
- The elite are a minority that behave as an authority towards others.
- The person is often wealthy and does not really need income from crime to live a good life.
- The person is typically well educated and connects to important networks of partners and friends.
- The person exploits his or her position to commit financial crime.
- The person does not look at himself or herself as a criminal, but rather as a community builder who applies personal rules to their own behavior.
- The person may be in a position that makes the police reluctant to initiate a crime investigation.

Gottschalk (2017) introduces convenience theory to understand white-collar crime. Convenience orientation is conceptualized as the value that individuals and organizations place on actions with inherent characteristics of saving time and effort. Convenience orientation can be considered a value-like construct that influences behavior and decision-making. Mai and Olsen (2016) measured convenience orientation in terms of a desire to spend as little time as possible on the task, in terms of an attitude that the less effort needed the better, as well as in terms of a consideration that it is a waste of time to spend a long time on the task. Convenience orientation toward illegal actions increases as negative attitudes towards legal actions increase. The basic elements in convenience orientation are the executive attitudes toward the saving of time, effort, and discomfort in the planning, action, and achievement of goals. Generally, convenience orientation is the degree to which an executive is inclined to save time and effort to reach goals. Convenience orientation refers to a person's general preference for convenient maneuvers. A convenience-oriented person is one who seeks to accomplish a task in the shortest time with the least expenditure of human energy.

It is the organizational opportunity that distinguishes white-collar crime from financial crime generally. Opportunity is a distinct characteristic of white-collar crime and varies depending on the kinds of criminals involved (Michel, 2008). An opportunity is attractive as a means of responding to desires (Bucy, Formby, Raspanti & Rooney, 2008). It is the organizational dimension that provides the white-collar criminal an opportunity to commit financial crime and conceal it in legal organizational activities. While opportunity in the economic dimension of convenience theory is concerned with goals (such as sales and bonuses), opportunity in the organizational dimension is concerned with crime (such as corruption and embezzlement).

Aguilera and Vadera (2008: 434) describe a criminal opportunity as "the presence of a favorable combination of circumstances that renders a possible course of action relevant." Opportunity arises when individuals or groups can engage in illegal and unethical behavior and expect, with reasonable confidence, to avoid detection and punishment. Opportunity to commit crime may include macro- and micro-level factors. Macro-level factors encompass the characteristics of the industries in which the business finds itself embedded, such as market structure and business assets of an industry, that is, companies whose actions are visible to one another and variations in the regulatory environment.

Benson and Simpson (2015) argue that many white-collar offenses manifest the following opportunity properties: (1) the offender has legitimate access to the location in which the crime is committed, (2) the offender is spatially separate from the victim, and (3) the offender's actions have a superficial appearance of legitimacy. Opportunity occurs in terms of those three properties that are typically the case for executives and other individuals in the elite. In terms of convenience, these three properties may be attractive and convenient when considering white-collar crime to solve a financial problem. It is convenient for the offender to conceal the crime and give it an appearance of outward respectability.

Chief Executive Officers

Many convicted white-collar criminals were chief executive officers, as exemplified by the Norwegian offender. The chief executive officer (CEO) is the only executive at level 1 in the hierarchy of an organization (Carpenter & Wade, 2002). All other executives in the organization are at lower levels. At level 2, we find senior executives who report to the CEO. Level 3 includes the next tier of executives if the organization is of substantial size in terms of the number of employees.

CEOs typically enjoy substantial individual freedom in their professions with little or no control. The CEO is the only person at that hierarchical level in the organization. Below the CEO, there are a number of executives at the same hierarchical level. Above the CEO, there are a number of board members at the same hierarchical level. But the CEO is alone at his or her level. The CEO is supposed to be controlled by the board, but boards of directors in most countries only meet once in a while to discuss business cases. Executives below the CEO are typically appointed by the CEO and tend to be loyal to the CEO. Therefore, power, influence, and freedom are characteristics of CEO positions.

CEO power and influence can be illustrated by what is labeled CEO fraud in law enforcement. CEO fraud is not fraud by CEOs. Rather, CEO fraud is fraud committed by someone claiming to be the CEO. If someone claims to be the CEO, most people in the organization will do what they are told. As long as they believe that the message stems from the real CEO, they are completely obedient and do as they are told by the fake CEO. The U.S. Federal Bureau of Investigation (FBI) warned in

2016 about a dramatic increase in CEO fraud, e-mail scams in which the attacker spoofs a message from the boss and tricks someone at the organization into wiring funds to the fraudsters. The FBI estimates that these scams cost organizations in the United States more than one billion dollars per year. Organizations that are victimized by CEO fraud can be characterized by a combination of CEO power and obedience culture.

As suggested in agency theory, CEOs have a tendency to become opportunistic agents (Shen, 2002). Based on their charisma, external stakeholders and board members lose control over CEO activities (Fanelli & Misangyi, 2006). Narcissistic organizational identification is one of several perspectives on CEO criminal behavior (Galvin, Lange & Ashforth, 2015: 163):

> It is not uncommon to learn of individuals in positions of power and responsibility, especially CEOs, who exploit and undermine their organizations for personal gain. A circumstance not well explained in the literature, however, is that some of those individuals may highly identify with their organization, meaning that they see little difference between their identity and the organization's identity—between their interests and the organization's interest. This presents a paradox, because organizational identification typically is not noted for its adverse consequences on the organization.

Power is here emphasized by Galvin et al. (2015) as an explanation for criminal behavior. Similarly, Bendahan, Zehnder, Pralong and Antonakis (2015) found that power can cause CEO crime. If the CEO is in a position to make decisions regarding many employees, or enjoys tremendous freedom and can make decisions on his or her own with significant consequences for others, then the temptation to abuse the power for personal or organizational gain is strong.

An example of CEO criminal behavior is involvement in transnational corporate bribery (Lord, 2016). CEOs sometimes find themselves in situations where they are to establish subsidiaries, get licenses, or close deals in corrupt countries.

A distinction can be made between mundane offenders and serious predators among criminal CEOs. Mundane offenders commit mainly minor offenses of ambiguous criminality, that is to say, the criminal status of the act is contested (e.g., occasional use of bribes) or the act is petty and widespread among ordinary people. Unlike serious predators, mundane offenders are sensitive to moral considerations and are not unabashedly devoted to a criminal lifestyle. Most of the time, it is important to them to be normal law-abiding executives who have some stake in social conformity. Their offenses tend to be committed intermittently, and they tend to be committed in situations that lack clear moral markers of their wrongfulness (Ceccato & Benson, 2016).

Social Conflict Theory

Social conflict theory suggests that the powerful and wealthy in the upper class of society define what is right and what is wrong. The rich and mighty people can behave like "robber barons" because they make the laws. Therefore, the ruling class does not consider a white-collar offense a regular crime, and certainly not similar to street crime. Why would the powerful punish their own?

Social conflict theory views financial crime as a function of the conflict that exists in society (Siegel, 2011). The theory suggests that class conflict causes crime in any society, and that those in power create laws to protect their rights and interests. For example, embezzlement by employees is a violation of law to protect the interests of the employer. However, it might be argued that employers must and should protect their own assets. Bank fraud is a crime to protect the powerful banking sector. However, in the perspective of conflict theory, one might argue that a bank should have systems making bank fraud impossible and suffer if they do not. If an employee has no opportunity to commit embezzlement, and if a fraudster has no opportunity to commit bank fraud, then these kinds of financial crime would never occur, and there would be no need to have laws against such offenses. Law enforcement protects powerful companies against counterfeit products, although they should be able to protect themselves by reducing opportunities for the production of such products.

Social conflict theory holds that laws and law enforcement are used by dominant groups in society to minimize threats to their interests posed by those whom they perceive as dangerous and greedy (Petrocelli, Piquero & Smith, 2003). Crime is defined by legal codes and sanctioned by institutions of criminal justice to secure order in society. The ruling class secures order in the ruled class by means of laws and law enforcement. Conflicts and clashes between interest groups are restrained and stabilized by law enforcement (Schwendinger & Schwendinger, 2014).

According to social conflict theory, the justice system is biased and designed to protect the wealthy and powerful. The wealthy and powerful can take substantial assets out of their own companies at their own discretion whenever they like, although employed workers in the companies were the ones who created the values. The superrich can exploit their own wealth that they created as owners of corporations as long as they do not hurt other shareholders. Employees have no right to object. It is no crime to take out values from own enterprises and build private mansions with the money. Even when the owners just inherited the wealth created by earlier generations, they can dispose freely of it for private consumption. Similarly, top executives who are on each other's corporate boards grant each other salaries that are 10 or 20 times higher than regular employee salaries. As Haines (2014: 21) puts it, "financial practices that threaten corporate interests, such as embezzlement, are clearly identified as criminal even as obscenely high salaries remain relatively untouched by regulatory controls." Furthermore, sharp practices such as insider trading that threaten confidence in equities markets have enjoyed vigorous prosecution, since the powerful see them as opaque transactions that give an unfair advantage to those who are not members of the market institutions.

Karl Marx, who analyzed capitalism and suggested the transition to socialism and ultimately to communism, created the basis for social conflict theory. Capitalism is an economic system in which persons privately own firms, shops, and means of production and operate these enterprises for profit. Socialism is an economic system characterized by cooperative enterprises, common ownership, and state ownership. Communism is a socioeconomic system structured upon the common ownership of the means of production and characterized by the absence of social classes.

Marxist criminology views the competitive nature of the capitalist system as a major cause of financial crime (Siegel, 2011). It focuses on what creates stability and continuity in society, and it adopts a predefined political philosophy. Marxist criminology focuses on why things change by identifying the disruptive forces in capitalist societies and describing how power, wealth, prestige, and perceptions of the world divide every society. The economic struggle is the central venue for the Marxists. Marx divided society into two unequal classes and demonstrated the inequality in the historical transition from patrician and slave to capitalist and wage worker. It is the rulers versus the ruled. Marx also underlined that all societies have a certain hierarchy wherein the higher class has more privileges than the lower one. In a capitalist society where economic resources equate to power, it is in the interest of the ascendant class to maintain economic stratification in order to dictate the legal order (Petrocelli et al., 2003).

Discussion

McKeever (2012) suggests that those who are socially, economically, and politically vulnerable are those who typically benefit from the social security system. Social security fraud can vary from sophisticated, organized, and large-scale offenses to minor, low-level frauds committed by individual claimants. While the money defrauded through a minor fraud is relatively little, the cumulative amount lost to low-level frauds constitutes a significant sum (Ceccato & Benson, 2016).

When studying relatively minor social security frauds committed by individual claimants, McKeever (2012) found that the legal response to these frauds in both the UK and Australia are quite harsh. She suggests that a new policy framework is required, within which low-level fraud is decriminalized. She argues that, at present, minor fraud is so broadly defined that it encompasses as a norm behavior that does not uniformly meet proper standards of criminal culpability, pulling into its path claimants who have not intentionally and dishonestly committed fraud.

In contrast to this view, social conflict theory explains why the ruling class never will allow a decriminalization of social security fraud. They will never accept the view that minor fraud prosecution represents a kind of overcriminalization targeted at the losers in society.

An illustration of the class perspective is the extent to which the police start investigating reported cases of social security fraud cases compared to white-collar crime cases, such as bankruptcy cases. The police in Oslo start investigations of 85% of all cases reported by Nav, but only 10% of all cases reported by bankruptcy lawyers (Solem, 2016).

Evasion of social security contributions can set disincentives for people to return to the official labor markets. Instead, benefit abusers become engaged in the shadow economy (Petersen, Thiessen & Wohlleben, 2010).

Estimating the magnitude of white-collar crime is a greater challenge than estimating social security fraud or tax evasion, as illustrated in Figure 30.1.

The only known size for the scope is the total of convicted white-collar criminals. As illustrated in the figure, this is a small circle within the larger circle of total white-collar crime. When estimating social security fraud or tax evasion, there are two known sizes, not only one: there is the detected fraud as well as the total payments in social security, and there is the detected evasion as well as the total tax revenues in tax collection.

In estimating probabilities, there is a need for both psychology and statistics to guide expert elicitation. When experts are asked about the magnitude of three different kinds of economic crime as illustrated in the figure, psychological biases may, for example, cause left-wing respondents to claim a large fraction of undetected white-collar crime, while right-wing respondents may claim a large

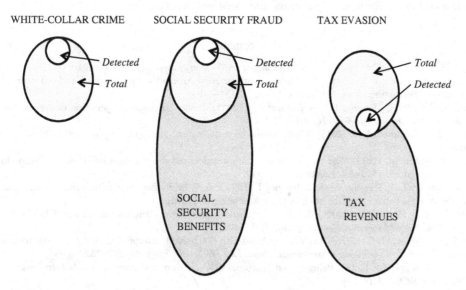

Figure 30.1   Estimation of the Magnitude of Different Forms of Financial Crime

fraction of undetected social security fraud, simply because they disagree on priorities in law enforcement. Kynn (2008) argues that humans make probability judgments through a series of heuristics that lead to systematic and predictable bias. She suggests that researchers should be equally concerned with what they ask experts to assess and how they ask it. Probability elicitation is influenced by a number of factors, such as the tendency to judge the frequency of an event by the ease of remembering specific examples. Furthermore, anchoring and adjustment are the tendency to anchor probability estimates at an initial estimate and to adjust it outwards. Insufficient adjustment results in biases of overestimation or underestimation when judging.

Conclusion

Social conflict theory suggests that laws and regulations are implemented by the elite to control others in society. However, to stay in charge, the elite does sometimes have to punish their own. An example of a convicted white-collar criminal in Norway was presented in this chapter. When compared to another example in this chapter—a convicted social security fraudster—it seems that the sentencing varies depending on class. The social security fraudster was sentenced to slightly longer imprisonment, while the white-collar criminal had committed a more serious crime in terms of the amount of money involved in his offense.

Discussion Questions

1. What do you think is most harmful to society, white-collar crime or social security fraud? Why?
2. What do you think has the highest priority in law enforcement: white-collar crime or social security fraud? Why?
3. What kind of knowledge is needed to investigate white-collar crime compared to knowledge to investigate social security fraud?
4. Do you see any difference among political parties in their criminal justice priorities of combatting white-collar crime versus social security fraud?
5. How do motives for white-collar crime and social security fraud differ?

References

Agder. (2015). Case LA-2015–195071, *Agder lagmannsrett (Agder court of appeals)*, September 30.

Aguilera, R. V., & Vadera, A. K. (2008). The dark side of authority: Antecedents, mechanisms, and outcomes of organizational corruption. *Journal of Business Ethics*, 77, 431–449.

Bendahan, S., Zehnder, C., Pralong, F. P., & Antonakis, J. (2015). Leader corruption depends on power and testosterone. *The Leadership Quarterly*, 26, 101–122.

Benson, M. L., & Simpson, S. S. (2015). *Understanding white-collar crime: An opportunity perspective*. New York: Routledge.

Brooks, G., & Button, M. (2011). The police and fraud investigation and the case for a nationalized solution in the United Kingdom. *The Police Journal*, 84, 305–319.

Bucy, P. H., Formby, E. P., Raspanti, M. S., & Rooney, K. E. (2008). Why do they do it?: The motives, mores, and character of white collar criminals. *St. John's Law Review*, 82, 401–571.

Carpenter, M. A., & Wade, J. B. (2002). Microlevel opportunity structures as determinants of non-CEO executive pay. *Academy of Management Journal*, 45(6), 1085–1103.

Ceccato, V., & Benson, M. L. (2016). Tax evasion in Sweden 2002–2013: Interpreting changes in the rot/rut deduction system and predicting future trends. *Crime, Law and Social Change*, 66, 217–232.

Fanelli, A., & Misangyi, V. F. (2006). Bringing out charisma: CEO charisma and external stakeholders. *Academy of Management Review*, 31(4), 1049–1061.

Galvin, B. M., Lange, D., & Ashforth, B. E. (2015). Narcissistic organizational identification: Seeing oneself as central to the organization's identity. *Academy of Management Review*, 40(2), 163–181.

Gottschalk, P. (2016). Private policing of financial crime: Fraud examiners in white-collar crime investigations. *International Journal of Police Science & Management, 18*(3), 173–183.

Gottschalk, P. (2017). *Understanding white-collar crime: A convenience perspective.* Boca Raton, FL: CRC Press, Taylor & Francis Publishing.

Gulating. (2016). Case 16–025863AST-GULA/AVD2, *Gulating lagmannsrett (Gulating court of appeals)*, June 27.

Haines, F. (2014). Corporate fraud as misplaced confidence? Exploring ambiguity in the accuracy of accounts and the materiality of money. *Theoretical Criminology, 18*(1), 20–37.

Kynn, M. (2008). The 'heuristics and biases' bias in expert elicitation. *Journal of the Royal Statistical Society, 171,* 239–264.

Lord, N. (2016). Establishing enforcement legitimacy in the pursuit of rule-breaking "global elites": The case of transnational corporate bribery. *Theoretical Criminology, 20*(3), 376–399.

Mai, H. T. X., & Olsen, S. O. (2016). Consumer participation in self-production: The role of control mechanisms, convenience orientation, and moral obligation. *Journal of Marketing Theory and Practice, 24*(2), 209–223.

McKeever, G. (2012). Social citizenship and social security fraud in the UK and Australia. *Social Policy & Administration, 46*(4), 465–482.

Michel, P. (2008). Financial crimes: The constant challenge of seeking effective prevention solutions. *Journal of Financial Crime, 15*(4), 383–397.

Petersen, H. G., Thiessen, U., & Wohlleben, P. (2010). Shadow economy, tax evasion, and transfer fraud: Definition, measurement, and data problems. *International Economic Journal, 24*(4), 421–441.

Petrocelli, M., Piquero, A. R., & Smith, M. R. (2003). Conflict theory and racial profiling: An empirical analysis of police traffic stop data. *Journal of Criminal Justice, 31,* 1–11.

Schwendinger, H., & Schwendinger, J. (2014). Defenders of order or guardians of human rights? *Social Justice, 40*(1/2), 87–117.

Shen, W., & Cannella, A. A. (2002). Power dynamics within top management and their impacts on CEO dismissal followed by inside succession. *Academy of Management Journal, 45*(6), 1195–1206.

Siegel, L. J. (2011). *Criminology,* 11th ed. Belmont, CA: Wadsworth Publishing.

Solem, L. K. (2016). Kan slippe med 10 måneder i fengsel (Can get away with 10 months in prison), daily Norwegian business newspaper. *Dagens Næringsliv,* Friday, September 25, 12–13.

Sutherland, E. H. (1949). *White-collar crime.* New York: Holt, Rinehart and Winston Publishing.

31

NO HOPE

Life Without the Possibility of Parole

Patricia Dahl

Introduction

Sentencing policies and practices in the United States have undergone dramatic changes over the past 40 years. With over two million people passing through American prisons, it is not surprising to find that the federal prison system alone saw an increase of 700% more inmates since the 1970s.[1] The number of life sentences in state and federal prisons quadrupled over the past 30 years, with nearly 49,000 of those prisoners serving a life sentence without the possibility of parole (LWOP). Over 10,000 of the life sentences were for crimes occurring before the offender turned 18, with one in four of these juveniles receiving an LWOP sentence.[2]

Prior to the 1980s, LWOP sentences in the U.S. were infrequent. The LWOP sentences gained momentum in the United States as use of the death penalty declined, as the American parole system diminished, as policymakers opted for a "get tough on crime" approach, and as harsher mandatory-minimum sentences were integrated into federal and state determinate sentencing practices. Today, proposed changes to some federal and state crime legislation to revise earlier, harsher sentencing laws are underway. Some recent declines in the American prison population are a positive sign.

LWOP sentencing practices in the U.S.—unprecedented in the history of the world[3]—challenge us to consider the goals of sentencing and the expectations for basic human rights. Requiring someone to spend the rest of their natural life living in a prison with no possibility of release raises important legal, social, psychological, moral, religious, economic, and human dignity questions. This chapter examines the nature of LWOP sentences and reviews some of the common arguments in support of and against this controversial sentencing practice.

Overview

Incarcerating individuals as punishment for criminal behavior began as a more humane alternative to the physical punishments typically used in the early American correctional system. Incapacitation through incarceration is based on the concept that crimes can be prevented by taking offenders out of society and eliminating further opportunities for them to commit crimes. It assumes that if the offender were free, more criminal activity would occur by that individual.[4] Today, anyone who is convicted of a capital offense and does not receive the death penalty will most likely die in prison through a life-without-the-possibility-of-parole sentence.[5]

A formal definition of LWOP can be found in the United Nations Convention on the Rights of the Child as life imprisonment without the possibility of release.[6] Life without the possibility of release or parole means individuals will spend the rest of their natural life as incarcerated prisoners and will die as such. No matter how it is defined, receiving a whole-life sentence is typically considered the harshest punishment an individual can receive outside of the death penalty. It removes any hope of being released from prison and rejoining society.

The LWOP Population

A 2013 report indicates that despite the FBI statistics showing a drop in violent crime over the past decade, the number of life sentences in state and federal prisons has quadrupled since the mid-1980s to over 159,000, with approximately 49,000 LWOP cases.[7] These life-sentence statistics also represent over 10,000 convictions for violent and nonviolent crimes that occurred when the offender was under the age of 18, resulting from increased transfers from the juvenile to the adult criminal court system.

At the time of this writing, approximately one in nine prisoners in the United States is serving life sentences, with a third of those inmates ineligible for parole.[8] The number of women serving whole-life sentences has also seen an increase of approximately 14% over the past 10 years, with 300 of these being LWOP cases and with the majority having experienced sexual abuse during childhood.[9] As is the case in other areas within the criminal justice system, disproportionate rates exist in life sentences: nearly half of the whole-life prisoners are African American and Latino, with 60% of LWOP prisoners being African American.[10] LWOP prisoners tend to be overrepresented in the five states of California, Florida, Pennsylvania, Louisiana, and Michigan; the LWOP prisoners in these five states reportedly make up more than half of all LWOP prisoners in the U.S.[11]

Changes in policy, rather than crime rates, have caused America's federal prisons to house 700% more inmates over the past 40 years. The Sentencing Project, a national organization dedicated to investigatory research, advocacy, and studies of public policy, reports that the growth in America's prison population is the result of a drastic increase in federal drug convictions, the widespread use of mandatory sentencing policies, the abandonment of the U.S. parole system, and sentencing guidelines that go beyond what is necessary "to achieve the United States Sentencing Commission's goals of just punishment, deterrence, incapacitation, and rehabilitation."[12]

Life without parole sentences became more popular in the United States when the landmark case *Furman v. Georgia*[13] ruled that the death penalty would be abolished and an alternative sentence scheme would be needed. Following the *Furman* case, LWOP found increasingly greater support when the U.S. Supreme Court confirmed the acceptability of LWOP in *Schick v. Reed*[14] and paved the way for widespread use of LWOP laws in the United States.[15]

LWOP statutes were created with two philosophical purposes in mind: first, as a means of administering an alternative (to the death penalty) retributive "just desserts" sentence and, second, as an avenue for addressing habitual, "revolving door" offenders. Most of the U.S. states offering the death penalty sentence also offer an LWOP sentence for individuals who did not receive the death penalty for a capital offense or first-degree murder. Currently, all U.S. states (except for Alaska) provide LWOP sentences.[16]

Violent and Nonviolent Crimes

The common perception is that LWOP sentences are reserved for the most heinous crimes and violent offenders. Currently, approximately 3,000 prisoners have received LWOP sentences for committing nonviolent offenses, with 80% of these for drug-related convictions.[17] The inclusion of nonviolent offenses for such a severe sanction is the result of dramatic changes in U.S. sentencing policies for drug-related offenses during the 1980s–1990s and the decline in using parole as a federal community-based supervision option.

Most of the prisoners serving LWOP for nonviolent crimes received their sentences under the collection of mandatory sentencing, habitual offender, or firearms laws that appeared in the 1980s and

1990s and in states that eliminated their parole system.[18] These included sentencing law changes called the "three strikes" laws that require a life sentence without any chance of receiving parole when there is a third felony—even if the third felony is less serious or nonviolent.[19]

To begin with, an increasing number of states extended LWOP sentences to offenses related to drug trafficking and large-scale drug possession. The 1986 Anti-Drug Abuse Act introduced a range of mandatory-minimum sanctions for drug and gun convictions, most notably illustrated in the infamous crack versus powder cocaine sentences that resulted in widespread sentencing disparities (later revised through the 2010 Fair Sentencing Act). In retrospect, the U.S. Sentencing Commission found that the intent to target major drug traffickers through earlier mandatory-minimum penalties was unsuccessful: the broad application of the laws worked against the goal of targeting serious drug traffickers. The result was a rapid growth of mandatory-minimum laws across the U.S. that, while unintentional, increased the number of nonviolent offenders receiving life and LWOP sentences.[20]

In the 1991 case of *Harmelin v. Michigan*, the U.S. Supreme Court decided that LWOP was not constitutionally disproportionate as a mandatory sentence for a first-time offense involving possession of large amounts of drugs.[21] The 1994 Violent Crime Control and Law Enforcement Act targeted both violent crimes and drug trafficking offenses as grounds for a mandatory life sentence for offenders with three or more felony convictions. Additionally, Congress allowed for the possession of some firearm convictions associated with drug trafficking crimes to receive LWOP sentences if the crime was a second or third offense. As a result, the American Civil Liberties Union (ACLU) reported that more than 80% of federal prisoners serving LWOP sentences in the late 1990s to the mid-2000s were the result of nonviolent firearm convictions.[22]

Recent proposed changes to some federal crime legislation are revising the earlier, more rigid sentencing LWOP laws. The Smarter Sentencing Act would reduce the number of years of LWOP sentences for drug offenses, while making the Fair Sentencing Act retroactive and giving judges the ability to deviate from mandatory-minimum sentences. And the Safe Justice Act would support community corrections programs, enhance the services for indigent defendants, and pave the way for earlier release of elderly inmates—in addition to reducing the mandatory-minimum life sentences for second drug offenses involving serious bodily injury or death.[23] President Barack Obama highlighted the need to differentiate between violent and nonviolent crimes for LWOP when he granted clemency to 141 prisoners who were sentenced to LWOP for nonviolent drug offenses.[24] At the state level, legislation has also seen some changes to the mandatory-minimum laws as states revise approaches to nonviolent crimes and incorporate more attempts at diversion and rehabilitation.[25] At the time of this writing, the "three strikes" laws are undergoing review and thousands of federal prisoners serving LWOP sentences may become eligible for resentencing opportunities.

Juveniles

Juveniles tried and sentenced as adults can and do receive life sentences—including LWOP—for crimes they committed while under the age of 18. Research showing that the brains of juveniles are not fully developed until later in their 20s has helped change views on juvenile decision-making, risk management, and self-control.[26] At the time of this writing, over 7,000 prisoners are serving life sentences for juvenile-aged crimes, and more than 2,000 of these individuals were sentenced to LWOP, even though the crimes were committed when they were juveniles.[27]

In 2011, the U.S. Supreme Court reviewed *Graham v. Florida* and ruled that offenses not involving a homicide and occurring before the offender turned 18 could not be given an LWOP sentence because it constituted cruel and unusual punishment.[28]*Graham* also noted how LWOP sentences are very similar to death sentences: "the sentence alters the offender's life by a forfeiture that is irrevocable. It deprives the convict of the most basic liberties without giving hope of restoration."[29] The 2012 U.S. Supreme Court case of *Miller v. Alabama* determined that mandatory life sentences and statues requiring LWOP for juvenile offenders were unconstitutional because it violated the Eighth Amendment.[30] The *Miller* case also raised questions about whether the decision could be applied retroactively to the more than 2,000 prisoners serving LWOP sentences for crimes committed when they were under the age of 18. In 2016, *Montgomery v. Louisiana* helped to answer that question and ruled LWOP sentences should not apply to persons who committed murder as juveniles and the ruling should be applied retroactively to allow individuals serving life sentences for crimes committed as juveniles a chance to have their cases reviewed.[31]

Parole, Appeal, and Clemency

For the most part, "life" sentences used to include the possibility of an eventual release from prison—typically through the mechanism of the American parole system. The federal correctional system once allowed parole reviews after serving 15 years.[32] The congressional elimination of the federal parole system through the 1984 Sentencing Reform Act resulted in offenders being required to serve 85% of their sentence before becoming eligible for release.[33] Currently, the federal criminal code does not allow for the possibility of parole for offenses after 1987 even though the parole system still operates to serve inmates with pre-1987 offenses.[34] The abandoning of parole also meant that prisoners serving life sentences must remain incarcerated for life. According to the American Civil Liberties Union (ACLU), no offender serving an LWOP sentence has ever been released on parole.[35]

The LWOP sentences are also limited in the appeal process: offenders are afforded one appeal opportunity, which typically must occur within two years of sentencing.[36] As U.S. Supreme Court Justice Antonin Scalia once noted, "The reality is that any innocent defendant is infinitely better off appealing a death sentence than a sentence of life imprisonment."[37] The only other possible option for release under an LWOP sentence—beyond an unexpected exoneration—is through the power of executive clemency—an act of mercy by the executive branch of government where the punishment is reduced. Clemency can be granted by either a governor, a board of advisors, or the president of the United States (for federal cases).[38] However, governors nationwide have repeatedly denied clemency requests, suggesting that clemency decisions may rely more on politics than a prisoner's readiness to be released.[39]

Reasons for and Against LWOP

The decline in use of the death penalty in recent years has given way to greater reliance on life and LWOP sentences. As one law professor notes, death row has been replaced by life row.[40]

The death penalty and LWOP, as the two severest sentences in America, are often the basis for comparison as policymakers grapple with what type of punishment is most appropriate, effective, and economical for dangerous criminals. Most Americans reportedly favor LWOP over the death penalty as America's harshest sanction.[41] Arguments for or against LWOP are often for moral, social, legal, economic, or psychological reasons. The following section reviews some of the common propositions in support of or in opposition to LWOP sentencing practices.

Public Safety/Deterrence

One of the primary arguments for LWOP is the belief that it helps protect society by deterring and preventing further criminal acts by some dangerous offenders through the guarantee that these individuals will be imprisoned for the remainder of their natural lives. The inability of past parole boards to predict the future criminal behavior of the more violent offenders further makes the LWOP sentence appealing to the public and policymakers.[42] The sheer cruelty of forcing someone to spend the rest of their life incarcerated in a prison is believed by some to deter certain types of criminal behavior before occurring. However, there is not enough evidence to support the idea that harsh sentences directly influence the thinking of potential criminal offenders and effectively deter future crime.[43]

Questions of public safety also arise when a prisoner is no longer a known threat to self and others. Extensive criminal justice research has long supported the idea that offenders, after a certain age, are far less likely to commit another violent offense.[44] Similarly, the ACLU predicts that by 2030, a third of the prison population will be over the age of 55. Older prisoners who have committed the most serious crimes and are serving the longest sentences are among the least likely to commit new crimes if released.[45] It is not clear how public policies will address the aging prison populations relative to the criminal justice system's goal of protecting public safety. Currently, LWOP sentences appear to ignore the fact that recidivism rates drop as prisoners age. As Smith (2016) notes, LWOP sentences define prisoners by their worst behavior without any chance for redemption.[46]

Justice/Retribution

For some victims/survivors of murder, an LWOP sentence is believed to be an avenue for moving forward with their lives more quickly than if they had to face years of wading through court hearings while the judicial system processes numerous appeals for death penalty sentences. It could be argued, too, that waiting for completion of an LWOP sentence—which amounts to waiting for the LWOP prisoner to die in prison—can also extend the pain and suffering of victims/survivors and reduce the feeling that justice is served.

Some supporters of LWOP feel that justice is served to the victims when the offenders are forced to suffer the pains of imprisonment for the rest of their lives because of the heinous crimes they committed. Using an LWOP sentence as retribution is an argument often made when the death penalty is not available as a sanction. The next harshest punishment would be LWOP through its death-by-incarceration. LWOP, as a brand of justice in place of the death penalty, can be appealing to not only the victim, but also the courts, the policymakers, and even some supporters of capital punishment.[47] The results of earlier research show support for the death penalty declining if LWOP can be offered as an alternative. Others feel that an LWOP sentence is just as severe and harsh as the death penalty: the LWOP prisoner is sentenced to die in prison.[48]

Economic/Costs

One of the common arguments in support of LWOP is the perceived costs: some supporters believe that it is cheaper to sentence someone to death than it is to finance a whole-life prison term. Nearly all studies reviewing the death penalty have found that the costs of LWOP are far less than the costs of sentencing an offender to death.[49] The ACLU reports that it is usually three times more expensive to execute someone than it is to pay for the costs of whole-life sentences.[50] As one example, the state of California, with the highest number of prisoners and life sentences, has spent approximately $90,000 more per inmate, per year to house a death penalty prisoner than a general population inmate, including LWOP prisoners.[51]

Spending vast amounts of money to house LWOP prisoners can also be viewed as a questionable use of funds and resources in corrections.[52] Estimates for what it costs to have an inmate on parole range from $1,250 to over $4,000 annually.[53] When parole costs are compared to life-in-prison costs, the differences are staggering.

Finality/Certainty

The 1963 works of legal scholar Paul Bator proposed that "finality" is often viewed in the criminal justice system as a "virtue." He noted how continuous court processes can squander precious resources, defeat the goals of deterrence and rehabilitation, and leave judges frustrated with making decisions that may not lead to final conclusions.[54] Those opposing LWOP and supporting the death penalty may do so because of the finality implied in a death sentence—even though death row inmates may die of natural causes amid the long appeal process.[55] On the other hand, one could also argue, as sentencing expert Douglas Berman notes, that judicial officials and policymakers should be less concerned with the finality of a sentence and more focused on whether the length of a sentence is fair and appropriate based on what research tells us and what any new case information might reveal.[56]

Yet, the certainty associated with a whole-life sentence can provide some supporters with a sense of finality. One of the earliest reasons for public support of LWOP was because of the belief that criminal offenders given life sentences did not truly spend their entire lives behind bars. This public sentiment was also expressed through the creation of truth-in-sentencing laws. Mechanisms such as the parole system offered early release options, which also played a role in the public's concern with too many early releases from prison. The LWOP sentence seems to satisfy a need to see that a life-behind-bars sentence is truly a life spent behind bars.[57]

"Finality" can also come in the form of rehabilitation, serving a sentence, reintegrating back into society, ending the legal proceedings, and closing a case.[58] An LWOP sentence seems to imply that "no possible piece of information that could be learned between sentencing and death" could have any bearing on the punishment the LWOP prisoner received—no new evidence, no rehabilitative factors, no changing views of the victims' families, and no public forgiveness will make a difference.[59] An LWOP is meant to be unconditionally final—perhaps even more so than the death penalty where the opportunity for numerous legal appeals and access to defense attorneys are possible beyond what is afforded to LWOP prisoners. It is this finality and certainty that makes LWOP attractive to some and abhorred by others.

Human Rights/Human Dignity

In 1958, sociologist Gresham Sykes conducted a study at a New Jersey prison and found that long-term incarceration produced a level of psychological stress on an inmate's psyche that is comparable to the pain of physical punishment on the body experienced by incarcerated individuals. Sykes noted that the harsh psychological effects of long-term confinement were caused from being deprived in five areas: liberty, goods and services, heterosexual relationships, autonomy, and safety/security. The severe effects of deprivation on long-term inmates became known as the pains of imprisonment.[60]

The pains of imprisonment—which can also be compounded by monotony, the permanent separation from family, and the increased chances for a mental breakdown—may be more strongly felt by LWOP inmates simply because they know the deprivations are "a punishment in perpetual motion" that continues until the prisoner has died during incarceration.[61] Most LWOP prisoners are said to lead "miserable lives"[62] if for no other reason than the punishment occurs for such a long period of time. Given the age of many LWOP prisoners when entering prison and the general life expectancy of Americans, the typical LWOP sentence can last nearly 40 years—more so if the prisoner is incarcerated at a younger age.[63]

Since the chances of being released from prison do not really exist for LWOP prisoners, these inmates face "death by incarceration"[64] and must learn to cope with the fact that they will never be released from prison no matter what they do. Their ability to adapt to serving a whole-life sentence may be more complicated than the general population of prisoners.[65] A study published in 2015 found that LWOP prisoners experience the Kubler-Ross stages of grief (denial, anger, bargaining, depression, and acceptance) as the inmates struggle to find ways of dealing with their loss of self resulting from a life of confinement and permanent separation from society.[66] LWOP inmates may also have less privileges and access to programs than other prisoners do since they are typically confined to maximum security facilities that may be far in distance from their families, with more surveillance and fewer opportunities for privacy. In short, LWOP prisoners are seemingly denied the ability to be rehabilitated. The sheer length of a whole-life sentence sends the message that LWOP prisoners cannot change and are not redeemable enough to live in society ever again.[67]

Justice Kennedy wrote (in *Graham v. Florida)* that the "concept of rehabilitation is imprecise."[68] As one law professor noted, rehabilitation, then, can be interpreted narrowly (making an inmate "fit" for citizenship again) or broadly (making an inmate "fit" as a human being).[69] When an LWOP prisoner is denied the possibility of rehabilitation using either of these interpretations, it strips the individual of human dignity and extinguishes a basic human right.

Summary

This chapter explored a common and controversial sentencing practice used in the United States: the judicial decision that an individual must spend the rest of their natural life incarcerated in a prison without any real chance for release. This sentence is commonly referred to as life without the possibility of parole (LWOP). At the time of this writing, nearly one in nine prisoners in the United States is serving a life sentence, with a third of these inmates serving an LWOP sentence.[70]

The LWOP sentences gained popularity in the United States as the use of the death penalty declined, as the U.S. parole system dissolved, as policymakers promoted a "get tough on crime" approach, as harsher mandatory-minimum sentences were implemented nationwide, and as the fear of violent crime and drug-related offenses increased among citizens. The drive to seek retribution for violent crimes and to stop the habitual offender led to greater support and use of LWOP sentences over the past 30 years. Many nonviolent offenders were caught in the net intended for the more serious and dangerous criminals. This has resulted in nearly 49,000 prisoners serving LWOP sentences.

While incarceration was intended to be a more humane alternative to the physical punishments of yesteryear, the concept of confining someone to a prison for what could be 40 years or more challenges the definition of humane sanctions. A sentence of life without the possibility of parole seems to deny the individual access to one of the primary goals of the American correctional system: rehabilitation.

Discussion Questions

1. Do you support or oppose the use of LWOP sentencing practices? Why?
2. What does the use of LWOP sentences suggest about parole systems? Is there a case for bringing back the parole in the U.S.? Why or why not?
3. Should the use of LWOP in the U.S. be influenced by what other countries think or do? Why or why not?
4. Should the use of executive clemency be increased in the U.S.? Why or why not? What effect might this have on LWOP sentences?
5. How much consideration, if any, should be given to the effect of an LWOP sentence on the offender's family? On the victim/survivor's family? Why?
6. If you were an offender and forced to choose between an LWOP sentence and the death penalty, which would you choose? Why?

Notes

1. Letter from Marc Mauer, Executive Director, the Sentencing Project to the Honorable William H. Pryor, Jr., Acting Chair, United States Sentencing Commission; July 27, 2017.
2. The Sentencing Project. (2013). Life goes on: The historic rise in life sentences in America.
3. Berry, W. W., III. (2015). Life-with-hope sentencing: The argument for replacing life-without-parole sentences with presumptive life sentences. *Ohio State Law Journal, 76*(5), 1051–1085.

4. Sarma, B. J., & Cull, S. (2015). The emerging eighth amendment consensus against life without parole sentences for nonviolent offenses. *Case Western Reserve Law Review, 2*(66), 526–580.

5. Radelet, M. L. (2016). The incremental retributive impact of a death sentence over life without parole. *University of Michigan Journal of Law Reform, 49*(4), 795–815.

6. 1989, Article 37(a).

7. Bishop, J. (2016). A victim's family member on juvenile life without parole sentences: "Brutal finality" and unfinished souls. *DePaul Journal for Social Science, 9*(1), 84–92; Willis, A. K., & Zaitzow, B. H. (2015). Doing "life": A glimpse into the long-term incarceration experience. *Laws, 4*, 559–578.

8. The Sentencing Project, 2013.

9. *Ibid.*

10. Sarma, & Cull, 2015.

11. The Sentencing Project, 2013.

12. Letter from Marc Mauer, Executive Director, the Sentencing Project to the Honorable William H. Pryor, Jr., Acting Chair, United States Sentencing Commission; July 27, 2017.

13. *Furman v. Georgia*, 408 U.S. 238 (1972).

14. *Schick v. Reed*, 419 U.S. 256 (1974).

15. Wright, J. H. (1990). Life-without-parole: An alternative to death or not much of a life at all? *Vanderbilt Law Review, 43*, 529–568.

16. Death Penalty Center, 2013.

17. Sarma, & Cull, 2015; www.democracynow.org/2013/11/15/jailed_for_life_for_stealing_a

18. Sarma, & Cull, 2015.

19. Appleton, C., & Grover, B. (2007). The pros and cons of life without parole. *British Journal of Criminology, 47*, 597–615.

20. Sarma, & Cull, 2015.

21. Appleton, & Grover, 2007; Van Zyl Smit, 2001, p. 299.

22. Sarma, & Cull, 2015.

23. *Ibid.*

24. www.washingtonpost.com/world/national-security/obama-commutes-the-sentences-of-102-more-federal-drug-offenders/2016/10/06/e66578d6–8bff–11e6-bf8a-3d26847eeed4_story.html?utm_term=.e4cf36c624f1

25. Horwitz, & Sarie, 2016; Washington Post.

26. Smith, C. (2016, February 8). The meaning of life without parole. *The New Yorker.*

27. Willis, A. K., & Zaitzow, B. H. (2015). Doing "life": A glimpse into the long-term incarceration experience. *Laws, 4*, 559–578.

28. *Graham v. Florida.* 130 S.Ct. 2011 (2010).

29. Sarma, & Cull, 2015.

30. Willis, & Zaitzow, 2015.

31. Smith, 2016, February 8.

32. The Sentencing Project, 2013.

33. Berry, 2015.

34. The Economist, 2013.

35. www.aclunc.org/article/truth-about-life-without-parole-condemned-die-prison

36. www.aclunc.org/article/truth-about-life-without-parole-condemned-die-prison

37. Garrett, Brandon L. (2017, October 26). The moral problem of life-without-parole sentences. *Time.* Retrieved from https://supreme.justia.com/cases/federal/us/576/14-7955/#annotation

38. https://deathpenaltyinfo.org/clemency

39. The Sentencing Project, 2013.

40. Garrett, 2017; http://time.com/4998858/death-penalty-life-without-parole/

41. Public Religion Research Institute, 2015; www.prri.org/research/survey-anxiety-nostalgia-and-mistrust-findings-from-the-2015-american-values-survey/#.VlR1qN-rR7N

42. Appleton, & Grover, 2007.

43. *Ibid.*

44. Smith, 2016, February 8; Prison Legal News, 2015.

45. Prison Legal News, 2015.

46. Smith, 2016, February 8.

47. Appleton, & Grover, 2007.

48. *Ibid.*

49. Radelet, 2016.

50. ACLU. (2008). Retrieved from https://deathpenaltyinfo.org/costs-death-penalty
51. www.aclunc.org/article/truth-about-life-without-parole-condemned-die-prison; Nellis, A. (2010). Throwing away the key: The expansion of life without parole sentences in the United States. *Federal Sentencing Reporter, 23*(2010), 27–32.
52. Willis, & Zaitzow, 2015.
53. McFarland, T. (2016). The death penalty vs. life incarceration: A financial analysis. *Susquehanna University Political Review, 7*(4), 46–87.
54. Bator, P. M. (1963). Finality in criminal law and federal habeas corpus for state. *Harvard Law Review, 76*, 441; Bishop, 2016.
55. Bishop, J. (2016). A victims' family member on juvenile life without parole sentences: "Brutal Finality" and unfinished souls, 9 DePaul J. for Soc. Just. Retrieved from www.aclunc.org/article/truth-about-life-without-parole-condemned-die-prison
56. Bishop, 2016.
57. Appleton, & Grover, 2007.
58. Bishop, 2016.
59. Lackey, 2016—The NY Times.
60. Sykes, G. (1958). *The society of captives: A study of a maximum-security prison.* Princeton, NJ: Princeton University Press.
61. Palusch, J. (2004). *A life for a life: Life imprisonment: America's other death penalty.* Los Angeles: Roxbury Publishing Co.
62. Johnson, R., & McGunnigall-Smith, S. (2008). Life without parole, America's other death penalty. *The Prison Journal,* (88), 332–336.
63. Radelet, 2016.
64. Johnson, & McGunigall-Smith, 2008, p. 328.
65. Willis, & Zaitzow, 2015.
66. Silva, S. M. (2015). On the meaning of life: A qualitative interpretive meta synthesis of the lived experience of life without parole. *Journal of Social Work, 15*(5), 498–515.
67. Appleton, & Grover, 2007.
68. www.law.cornell.edu/supct/html/08-7412.ZO.html
69. Lerner, C. S. (2013). *Life without parole as a conflicted punishment.* Economics Research Paper Series (13–50), Vol. 48. George Mason University School of Law.
70. The Sentencing Project, 2013.

CONTRIBUTORS

Brittany Acquaviva is currently a master's student and graduate research assistant at Illinois State University. She plans to further her education by obtaining a PhD. Her research interests include sexual assault and sexual offenders. She is currently in the process of her thesis research, titled *Perceptions of Sexual Assault Regarding Illinois State University Students*. Brittany was a part of a panel presentation for the Zonta International Conference (District 6), where she presented statistics about sexual assault on college campuses and stalking tendencies between intimate partners. She presented her research on Agnew's General Strain Theory in relation to the television show *Gotham* at Illinois State University's Research Symposium, and will also present at a panel at the Midwestern Criminal Justice Association, on the use of comics in the classroom as a teaching aid. She plans to publish research that she performed alongside Dr. Clevenger on violence in comics and the criminal justice system.

Daniel Ryan Alvord is a PhD candidate in sociology and a research assistant for the Center for Migration Research at the University of Kansas. His research focuses broadly on the catalysts and responses to institutional, legal, and political changes in areas such as fiscal policy and immigration.

Matjaž Ambrož, PhD, is Professor of Criminal Law at the Faculty of Law, University of Ljubljana, and a researcher at the Ljubljana Institute of Criminology. He has been a visiting research fellow at the Max Planck Institute for Foreign and International Criminal Law (Freiburg, Germany) in 2003, 2007, 2015, and 2017. His current research interests include substantive criminal law, sociology of criminal law, and theories on justifying legal punishment.

Nicole L. Asquith is Associate Professor of Policing and Criminal Justice at Western Sydney University, a research associate with the Translational Health Research Institute, and a university associate with the Tasmanian Institute of Law Enforcement Studies. Nicole's transdisciplinary work focuses on the intersections between vulnerability and policing, with a focus on how disability, and sexuality and gender diversity, shape experiences of the criminal justice system. Her current research investigates how propinquity shapes small-town policing and the critical social relationships underpinning policing in remote communities. She is the co-editor of *Policing Vulnerability* (Federation Press, 2014), lead editor of *Policing Encounters With Vulnerability* (Palgrave, 2017), and author of the forthcoming book *Critical Policing Studies* (Palgrave, 2018).

Elena Azaola is Emeritus Professor at the Center for Advanced Studies and Research in Social Anthropology located in Mexico City. She received a PhD in anthropology from the same center and did postgraduate study at Columbia University on deviant behavior. She is also a psychoanalyst. Elena is presently one of five Mexican citizens who are members of the National Security Agency. The National Security Agency advises the president and state governors in Mexico on matters involving criminal justice. In addition, she was an advisor with the National Commission of Human Rights and a Council Member at the Federal District Commission of Human Rights. She coordinated the European Commission project for street children in Mexico (1997–1999). She has published more than 125 journal articles and numerous books on human behavior, crime, and human rights. Her research on the commercial sexual exploitation of children was sponsored by the United Nations Children Fund. She co-coordinated a National Report on Violence sponsored by the World Health Organization. She was the board chair of the Institute for Security and Democracy, which created the first center for police accreditation in Mexico and won the MacArthur Foundation Award for Creative and Effective Institutions.

Danielle Marie Carkin is Assistant Professor at Stonehill College. Her research interests include criminal careers, factors that pertain to desistance and persistence, juvenile delinquency and justice, mental illness and substance abuse of offenders, and evidence-based practices.

Andrea Gómez Cervantes is a PhD candidate in the Department of Sociology at the University of Kansas. She is a Ford Fellow and an American Sociological Association MFP Fellow. Her research, which explores the effects of immigration policy on indigenous and non-indigenous Latinxs' social integration in the U.S., has received generous funding from the National Science Foundation. In other projects, she investigates the privatization of immigrant detention, the criminalization of immigrants, skin color inequality, and Latinxs in higher education.

Shelly Clevenger is Assistant Professor at Illinois State University. Her research interests include sexual assault, intimate partner abuse, and cyber victimization. She has authored peer-reviewed publications on these topics appearing in such journals as *Feminist Criminology*, *Sexual Abuse*, *The Security Journal*, *The Journal of Criminal Justice Education*, *Journal of School Violence*, and *Contemporary Rural Social Work*, with further upcoming journal publications. Shelly has also served as an editor, as well as contributor, for the edited volume, *The Virtual Enemy: The Intersection Between Intimate Partner Abuse, Technology, and Cybercrime*. She presented her research on survivors of sexual assault and intimate partner violence and the connection to cybervictimizations at a special research panel at the United Nations Women conference in December. She has also done speaking engagements throughout the state of Illinois on her work and activism. Currently, she is continuing her qualitative research with survivors, with a focus on LGBTQ survivors, as well as a special project interviewing mothers who have had children conceived during rape and then went on to raise that child. Shelly has a forthcoming *Victimology* textbook to be published by Taylor and Francis, a teaching theory book to be published by Cognella in 2018, and *Gendering Criminology; Crime and Justice Today*, a book focusing on gender, to be published in 2019 by University of California Press. She has also been recognized for her teaching in these areas by Illinois State University with college and university faculty teacher of the year awards and the American Society of Criminology, Division of Victimology, Outstanding Teaching Award.

Amanda K. Cox is a lecturer in the Department of Sociology at Ohio University where she teaches a range of criminology courses, including The Death Penalty in the United States, Criminology, Introduction to Sociology, Media and Crime, and Ethics in Criminal Justice. She has taught for nine years at colleges and universities in Pennsylvania, Minnesota, and Ohio. Her research focuses primarily on death penalty attitudes and has appeared in journals including the *Journal of Criminal Justice*

Education, International Journal of Police Science and Management, and *Violence Against Women*. She also has contributed to a variety of reference books including *The Encyclopedia of Criminology and Criminal Justice*, *The Social History of Crime and Punishment in America*, and *The Encyclopedia of Race and Crime*.

Patricia Dahl earned her master's degree in criminal justice and a PhD in public affairs with a criminal justice emphasis from the University of Colorado in Denver. She has been teaching criminal justice classes for the past 18 years in both Colorado and Kansas. Patricia has worked in the criminal justice field in a variety of capacities. Her background includes work at the Colorado State Patrol, the Colorado Judicial Branch, the Colorado Bureau of Investigation, the FBI, a county probation department, and as a victim advocate at crime scenes.

Angela Dwyer is a sociologist and Associate Professor in Police Studies and Emergency Management at the School of Social Sciences, College of Arts, Law, and Education at the University of Tasmania. She is also Adjunct Professor with the Crime and Justice Research Centre at the Queensland University of Technology and a senior researcher with the Tasmanian Institute of Law Enforcement Studies. Angela is a leading international scholar on the policing experiences of lesbian, gay, bisexual, transgender, and intersex (LGBTI) people; how sexuality, gender, and sex diversity influence criminal justice experiences; and how young people from vulnerable groups experience policing. She is the lead editor of *Queering Criminology* (co-edited with Matthew Ball and Thomas Crofts, Palgrave).

Kathryn Elvey is Assistant Professor of Criminal Justice at Plymouth State University. Her research interests include victimology, social justice issues, and crime prevention. She earned a PhD in criminal justice from the University of Cincinnati. She has published in *Catholic University Law Review* and *Human Rights Quarterly*.

John A. Eterno, PhD is Professor, Associate Dean, and Director of Graduate Studies in Criminal Justice at Molloy College in Rockville Centre, New York. John is a retired captain in the New York City Police Department, and former managing editor and now on the Board of Editors for Police Practice and Research. He is a representative to the United Nations for the NGO the International Police Executive Symposium. He serves on the board of the American Academy of Law Enforcement Professionals–Long Island. John was recognized by the federal courts as an expert witness on police, is regularly quoted in various media outlets, and speaks internationally on his areas of expertise: police performance management, police behavior, law and policing, terrorism, corruption, and other police related topics. He is widely published and examples of his works can be seen in *Justice Quarterly*, *Public Administration Review*, *The International Journal of Police Science and Management*, *The Criminal Law Bulletin*, and many others. His recent books include *The Crime Numbers Game: Management by Manipulation* (with Eli B. Silverman), *The Detective's Handbook* (with Cliff Roberson), and *The New York City Police Department: The Impact of Its Policies and Practices*.

Benjamin Flander, PhD, is Associate Professor of Law at the Faculty of Criminal Justice and Security, University of Maribor, Slovenia. His areas of specialization are constitutional law and human rights in criminal justice systems. He is the author of two books and co-author of chapters in *Trust and Legitimacy in Criminal Justice* (edited by Gorazd Meško and Justice Tankebe) and *Crime Prevention: International Perspectives, Issues, and Trends* (edited by John A. Winterdyk). His research interests include new critical legal studies and critical criminology. He has been active as an evaluator at the Group of States Against Corruption (GRECO). E-mail: benjamin.flander@fvv.uni-mb.si

Larry French: Larry grew up in a French-Canadian parish in New Hampshire, which was also home to many Metis families (French/Indian mix). Following his enlistment in the USMC and education under the GI Bill, he applied his sociological and cultural psychology training with many American Indian groups. Here, he was fortunate to further his involvement in Indian Country, first with the Eastern Band of Cherokee Indians followed by engagement with the Siouan groups in Nebraska and the Dakotas as well as the Lincoln Indian Center. Next, he worked closely with the southwestern tribes (Pueblo tribes, Apache, Navajo, etc.). He served as faculty advisor to the Native American Student Organizations respectively at Western Carolina University and Western New Mexico University. He also had the opportunity to interact with both Mexican Indians and Mestizos as well as Canadian and northeastern U.S. tribes. He now resides in his home state of New Hampshire, where he is an affiliate professor of justice studies at the University of New Hampshire. French is the author of many articles, chapters, and book on the American Indian. He can be reached at frogwnmu@yahoo.com.

Petter Gottschalk is Professor in the Department of Leadership and Organizational Behavior at BI Norwegian Business School in Oslo, Norway. He has been the CEO of several companies. Petter has published extensively on fraud examinations, police investigations, knowledge management, financial crime, white-collar crime, and organized crime.

Erin Grant is Assistant Professor of Criminal Justice at Washburn University. She teaches courses in communication, research, and the role of gender in the criminal justice system. Erin also serves as faculty mentor for the criminal justice clubs on campus. Prior to her time at Washburn, she worked as a research specialist for Travis Country Criminal Justice Planning, engaging in program evaluation and program creation and focusing on reentry efforts. Her interest in reentry and program evaluation, as well as in environmental causes of crime and experiential learning in higher education internships, continue as part of her research at Washburn.

Lars Gunnesdal is an economist at the think tank Manifest Center for Social Analysis in Oslo, Norway. He has written several reports on international tax policy, financial secrecy, tax evasion, welfare and pension reform, income and wealth inequality, and financial crisis. His current research is focused on estimating the total magnitude of white-collar crime compared to the magnitude of social security fraud.

Robert D. Hanser is Coordinator of the Department of Criminal Justice at the University of Louisiana at Monroe. He is a past administrator of North Delta Regional Training Academy (NDTRA), where he provided oversight for police officer and jailer training throughout northeast Louisiana. Robert currently serves as a governor-appointed member of the Louisiana Reentry Advisory Council and is also the director of Offender Programming for LaSalle Corrections, where he is responsible for overseeing inmate reception, drug rehabilitation, sex offender treatment, and inmate reentry. In addition, he is the board president for Freedmen, Inc., a nonprofit organization that operates group homes and provides services for ex-offenders in the community. Robert is a past president on the Board of Directors for the Louisiana Coalition Against Domestic Violence (LCADV) and is the director of the 4th Judicial District's Batterer Intervention Program (BIP). Lastly, he has written seven textbooks as sole author or lead author, and has been a co-author of five more textbooks and/or anthologies. He has written numerous peer-reviewed journal articles as well as book chapters and reference works. He has conducted extensive research in his areas of interest that has been funded at the federal, state, and local levels.

Ralph E. Ioimo is currently Chair of the Department of Justice and Public Safety at Auburn University, Montgomery, Alabama. He has over 40 years of law enforcement and public management experience. He is a nationally recognized expert in criminal justice information systems, specifically in the areas of police mobile computing, computer-aided dispatch, record management, and crime-analysis and support systems. Ralph has extensive experience in grant and project management, financial management, system planning, development, implementation, and operation of public safety programs in local cities. He also has nine years of direct law enforcement experience as a sworn police officer, attaining the rank of deputy chief of police in a city with a population of 150,000.

Jason Jolicoeur is Assistant Professor of Criminal Justice in the Criminal Justice and Legal Studies Department at Washburn University. He earned his PhD in education from the University of Missouri-St. Louis and his MA and BS in criminal justice from Wichita State University. He has previously published in a variety of professional journals, and his current research interests focus on the relationship between personal religious orientation and human behavior, criminal justice training and education practices, and the scholarship of teaching and learning in criminal justice higher education programs. Jason can be contacted at 785-670-2057 or by e-mail at jason.jolicoeur@washburn.edu.

Ross Kleinstuber is Associate Professor of Justice Administration and Criminology at the University of Pittsburgh at Johnstown. His research interests include law and society, capital punishment, victim impact evidence, inequality, mass incarceration, and human rights abuses. His publications have mostly focused on the role America's culture of individualism plays in capital sentencing, but he has also written about the role of racial inequality in the justice system, the impact of "judicial override" statutes that allow judges to override a jury's sentencing decision in capital cases, the problems with life without parole sentences, the influence of victim impact evidence in capital trials, and genocide. His work has been cited by the Delaware Supreme Court in its decision to declare that state's capital sentencing law unconstitutional. He is currently studying victim impact evidence in Delaware and the role of racial threat in explaining mass incarceration and support for punitive sentencing policies.

David Lowe is a former police officer who carried out a variety of uniform and detective roles during his service. On retiring from the police, David became a principal lecturer at the School of Law at Liverpool John Moores University, where he managed the law degree programs. On leaving university in 2017, David set up his own terrorism and security consultancy business. He gives legal advice in the areas of terrorism and security, criminal law, and policing and provides expert witness services; he is currently assisting the Metropolitan Police's counterterrorism unit, SO15 in terrorists' use of tradecraft (counter-surveillance techniques). He is still active in writing up his research in terrorism and security as well as policing. He has many publications in these areas in books, book chapters, and peer reviewed and online journals. His latest book, titled *Terrorism: Law and Policy*, was published by Routledge in November 2017. Due to his expertise, David is consistently consulted by the media (television, radio, and print media) and frequently used by the BBC, Sky News, Australian Broadcasting Company, CNN, Al Jazeera, and Al Arabiya, among others. David's website can be accessed at drdavidlowe.co.uk.

Daniel Marshall is Senior Lecturer in Criminal Justice at Liverpool John Moores University and Visiting Scholar at the Institute of Criminology, University of Cambridge. Daniel's research interests explore children's rights, youth crime and justice, privacy, colonialism, and innovative justice and enterprise. He is currently involved with multiple international projects focusing on these issues. His recent work has focused on privacy and the criminal justice process. His book, *Privacy and Criminal Justice* (co-authored with Terry Thomas), was published in 2017.

Gorazd Meško, PhD, is Professor of Criminology at the Faculty of Criminal Justice and Security, University of Maribor, Slovenia. He has recently completed a research project on the legitimacy of policing, criminal justice, and execution of penal sanctions (2013–2016). He has coedited a book titled *Trust and Legitimacy in Criminal Justice: European Perspectives* (Gorazd Meško and Justice Tankebe,

2015). He is currently a lead researcher in a national research project on safety and security in local communities (2015–2018), which also includes research into social responses to crime, including social justice. E-mail: gorazd.mesko@fvv.uni-mb.si

Jordana N. Navarro is Assistant Professor of Criminal Justice in the Department of Criminal Justice at The Citadel. Her two main research areas are cybervictimization and domestic violence. Her most recent work focuses on the prevalence and underreporting of sexual violence on college campuses and particularly among male survivors. She has authored several articles on a wide array of topics concerning cybervictimization and domestic violence as well as served as the lead editor on a text exploring the intersection of cybercrime and domestic abuse. She currently lives in Charleston, South Carolina, with her husband and two children.

Matthew O'Deane has been with the San Diego County District Attorney's Office Bureau of Investigation since May of 2002. He is currently the Commander overseeing the Gang Prosecution, Cold Case Homicide, and Narcotics units. Prior to joining the DA's office, Matthew was a National City Police Officer from 1992 to 2002. He worked as a patrol sergeant, narcotics detective at the Operation Alliance Task Force, and patrol officer. Matthew has a PhD in public policy and administration, a master's degree in public administration, and a bachelor's degree in criminal justice. He is also a subject matter expert (SME) for the Peace Officers Standards of Training and has taught in the witness protection course and extraditions course since 2005. In 2015, Matthew drafted the initial proposal to create the San Diego County Regional Leadership Institute (SDCRLI) and co-designed the three-week institute for SD County Law Enforcement Leaders.

Vanessa R. Panfil is an ethnographer, sociologist, criminologist, and advocate. She is the author of *The Gang's All Queer: The Lives of Gay Gang Members* (NYU Press, 2017) and the co-editor of the *Handbook of LGBT Communities, Crime, and Justice* (Springer, 2014). Centrally involved in developing the emergent field of queer criminology, her research explores how intersections of gender and sexuality shape individuals' experiences with gangs, crime, victimization, and the criminal and juvenile justice systems. Much of her work focuses specifically on urban LGBTQ young people of color. She is currently Assistant Professor in the Department of Sociology and Criminal Justice at Old Dominion University in Norfolk, Virginia.

Jordan Papp is a doctoral student in the Department of Criminal Justice at the University of Cincinnati. He received both his master's (2015) and bachelor's (2013) degrees from Wayne State University. Jordan's current research interest focuses on the use of risk assessment in corrections. He has also been involved in research and publishing on topics in policing, which include citizen willingness to cooperate with the police and media reporting on police-involved shootings. His research has recently been published in *Corrections*, *Child and Youth Services Review*, and *Policing and Society*.

Dwayne Roberson, EdD, is an educator in the Houston Independent School District. His area of interest includes disadvantaged students and students who drop out of the education system prior to graduation. He served in the U.S. Army, attended college at the University of Houston, and received his EdD from Lamar University.

Lori Sexton is Assistant Professor of Criminal Justice and Criminology at the University of Missouri, Kansas City. She has a PhD in criminology, law, and society from the University of California, Irvine, and an MA in criminology from the University of Pennsylvania. Lori's interests lie at the intersection of criminology and sociolegal studies, with a specific focus on prisons, punishment, and the lived experience of penal sanctions among transgender prisoners. Her research has been funded by the

National Science Foundation, the National Institute of Justice, and the Fletcher Jones Foundation and has been published in *Law & Social Inquiry*, *Punishment & Society*, *Justice Quarterly*, *Critical Criminology*, and *Criminology & Public Policy*, as well as numerous edited volumes.

Eli B. Silverman, PhD, is Professor Emeritus at John Jay College of Criminal Justice and the Graduate Center of City University of New York. He has previously served with the U.S. Department of Justice and the National Academy of Public Administration in Washington, DC, and was Visiting Exchange Professor at the Police Staff College in Bramshill, England. He has lectured, consulted with, and trained numerous police agencies in the U.S., UK, Canada, Mexico, Europe, Asia, and Australia. His areas of interest include police performance management, community policing, policy analysis, training, integrity control, policy analysis, Compstat, and crime mapping. His recent publications include *The Crime Numbers Game: Management by Manipulation*, with John Eterno, 2012, Taylor and Francis; "NYPD's Compstat: Compare Statistics or Compose Statistics?" with John A. Eterno, *International Journal of Police Science and Management*, 2010, Vol. 12, No. 3; *NYPD Battles Crime: Innovative Strategies in Policing*, Northeastern University Press, 2001; "The Compstat Innovation" in David Weisburd and Anthony Braga (eds.), *Police Innovation: Contrasting Perspectives*, Cambridge: Cambridge University Press; and "Forcible Stops: Police and Citizens Speak Out," with John Eterno and Christine Barrow, *Public Administration Review*, Vol. XX, 2016.

Jennifer Sumner is Assistant Professor of Criminal Justice Administration in the Department of Public Administration at California State University, Dominguez Hills. She completed her doctorate in criminology, law, and society at the University of California, Irvine. Her research examines correctional policy, practice, and culture and the relationship between gender, sexuality, and the criminal justice system. She has obtained research funding from the National Science Foundation to examine correctional policy in international settings. Her research has been published in journals such as *Critical Criminology*, *Deviant Behavior*, *Journal of Crime and Justice*, *Justice Quarterly*, and *Law & Social Inquiry* as well as in several edited volumes. She is also co-author of two reports to the California Department of Corrections and Rehabilitation on studies of violence and victimization in California prisons.

Melissa Thorne is a graduate student at the University of Louisiana at Monroe. Melissa provides psycho-educational classes to offenders at Richwood Correctional Center in Louisiana. In addition, Melissa is an ancillary author for Sage Publications. She has conducted research with the offender population and has worked in the field of intelligence testing. Melissa has expertise and interest in all facets of law and psychology, as well the field of corrections. Melissa has presented at numerous conferences on topics ranging from gender differences in rating culpability and punishment for crime to the effects on long-term incarceration of juveniles.

Maren B. Trochmann, ABD, is a doctoral student at the University of Colorado Denver in the School of Public Affairs. Maren holds a BS from Georgetown University in international culture and politics. Her research interests include social equity, bureaucratic discretion, federal government rulemaking, place-based social policy, and intersections of race, class, and gender. Her dissertation work investigates how federal agencies promote procedural and substantive equity gains through rulemaking. Maren has worked for the federal government in the low-income housing sector for almost a decade and strives to bring practitioner insights and experience into scholarly work.

Jace L. Valcore is an Assistant Professor of Criminal Justice at the University of Houston Downtown. Their research interests and focus are on issues of LGBTQ equality and equity in both criminal and social justice. They have published work on hate crime laws and gender in policing, and are currently completing projects on the measurement of gender in criminological research and on the experiences of LGBTQ police officers. They provide workshops and trainings on gender/sexual diversity competency for students, educators, professionals, and community members, including specific trainings for UHD faculty as part of their 2017–18 Faculty Teaching Fellowship.

Allyson Walker is a Postdoctoral Research Associate at the Utah Criminal Justice Center in The University of Utah College of Social Work. They earned their PhD at John Jay College and the Graduate Center at the City University of New York. Their work explores the relationships between stigma, system involvement, criminal activity, and mental health. Their current research agenda examines resilience, as it relates to emotional health and offending, among minor-attracted individuals. Their research has been published in *The Journal of Marriage and Family*, *The Journal of Interpersonal Violence*, and *Critical Criminology*.

Michelle Watson is an attorney and assistant professor in the Criminal Justice and Legal Studies Department at Washburn University. She has a Bachelor of Arts degree (1993), with a major in English and minor in mathematics from the University of Alabama in Huntsville and a Juris Doctor degree (1998) from Washburn University School of Law. Before starting as full-time faculty at Washburn University in August 2016, Michelle worked for the Kansas Appellate Courts, chiefly the Kansas Supreme Court, for almost 20 years, serving as the chambers attorney for several judges and justices, including Honorable Marla J. Luckert and Honorable Fred N. Six. She also served as the Kansas Supreme Court Motions Attorney.

J. Harrison Watts, PhD, is Professor of Criminology and Criminal Justice at Our Lady of the Lake University. He is a former police practitioner with 15 years of progressive law enforcement experience, 10 of which were at the administrative level with assignments in patrol, internal affairs, criminal investigations, and training. He also served two terms as an elected city commissioner in Vernon, Texas. His research interests surround police policy and management, and he is the author of numerous book chapters, journal articles, and textbooks.

Nicole Wilkes is a doctoral student in the School of Criminal Justice at the University of Cincinnati. Prior to starting the PhD program, she worked at the Crime Victims' Institute at Sam Houston State University. Nicole started her career as a victim service advocate in Minnesota for individuals and families experiencing domestic violence, sexual assault, child abuse, and homelessness. Her research interests include violence against women, crime victims' rights, victim services, and victims' interactions within the criminal justice system.

Tamara L. Wilkins is Associate Professor and former Director of the Law Enforcement Program at Minnesota State University, Mankato, Minnesota. She earned her bachelor's degree in criminal justice and master's degree in sociology at Texas A & M, Commerce, Texas (formerly East Texas State University). She received her PhD from Florida State University, Tallahassee, Florida. She is currently completing her final semester towards a master's degree in experiential education from the Department of Education Leadership at Minnesota State University, Mankato. Her primary teaching and research interests include police response to victims/survivors and the educational training of future peace officers. She is a national executive council member and chapter advisor of Alpha Phi Sigma, the Criminal Justice Honor Society. She also serves as a faculty advisor for Phi Delta Theta Fraternity. Virtually every year she leads a study abroad tour to Europe over winter break for students interested in comparative criminal justice systems. She is dedicated to giving her students the opportunity to travel abroad to learn about new cultures, and she is a committed lifelong learner of people and places. Her hobbies include traveling, reading, gardening, and watching baseball.

Aimee Wodda is a PhD candidate (ABD) in the Department of Criminology, Law, and Justice at the University of Illinois at Chicago. Her teaching interests include gender, sexuality, and the law, social injustice, and juvenile (in)justice. Her research interests include queer criminology, transgender legal theory, ethnography, narrative research, and visual sociology.

Kevin Wong is Associate Director of the Policy Evaluation and Research Unit (PERU) at Manchester Metropolitan University. He has over 20 years' experience in criminal justice policy and practice as a researcher, practitioner, and policy advisor. He has researched and written extensively on justice reinvestment, including articles in international journals and a book co-authored with PERU colleagues Chris Fox and Kevin Albertson. Prior to joining PERU, he was Acting Director of the Hallam Centre for Community Justice (HCCJ) at Sheffield Hallam University, where he managed high-profile, complex multi-site research projects, commissioned by the UK Ministry of Justice (MoJ), National Offender Management Service (NOMS), and Home Office. This included two payments by results pilots, the Local Justice Reinvestment Pilot and Youth Justice Reinvestment Custody Pathfinder. His other research interests include integrated offender management, resettlement, alternatives to custody, and hate crime. Kevin was previously an assistant director at Nacro, the principal crime reduction charity in the UK, where he had extensive experience of working with local criminal justice agencies, VCS, and statutory agencies to develop support services for victims and offenders.

Melanie Worsley is Assistant Professor in the Criminal Justice and Legal Studies Department at Washburn University and is the program coordinator for the undergraduate criminal justice degree. Melanie is a graduate of the Washburn University School of Law and a licensed attorney and court-approved mediator in Kansas. Her legal experience includes working for the Kansas Supreme Court, the Kansas Court of Appeals, and the U.S. District Court for the District of Kansas.

INDEX

Note: Italicized page numbers indicate a figure on the corresponding page. Page numbers in bold indicate a table on the corresponding page.